The Scaremongers

A. J. A. Morris

The Scaremongers

The Advocacy of
War and Rearmament
1896–1914

ROUTLEDGE & KEGAN PAUL
London, Boston, Melbourne and Henley

First published in 1984
by Routledge & Kegan Paul plc

14 Leicester Square, London WC2H 7PH, England

9 Park Street, Boston, Mass. 02108, USA

464 St Kilda Road, Melbourne,
Victoria 3004, Australia and

Broadway House, Newtown Road,
Henley-on-Thames, Oxon RG9 1EN, England

Set in Linotron Ehrhardt
by Input Typesetting Ltd, London
and printed in Great Britain
by Hartnell Print
Bodmin, Cornwall

Library of Congress Cataloging in Publication Data

Morris, A. J. Anthony.

The scaremongers: the advocacy of war and rearmament
1896–1914.
Bibliography: p.
Includes index.
1. Germany—Foreign opinion, British. 2. Public
opinion—Great Britain—History—20th century. 3. Press
and propaganda—Great Britain. I. Title.
DA47.2.M67   1984   943   84-4930

British Library CIP data also available

ISBN 0–7102–0162–1

Hunc dono meritae tibi libellum

Quae conviva comesque amica conjunx

Eras caecilia es precorque semper

Sis conviva comesque amica conjunx

Contents

Contents

Preface

Although very different in design and conception, this work is intended to complement a book I published in 1972, *Radicalism Against War*, which examined the case and the advocates of a policy of peace and retrenchment in armament expenditure for Britain before 1914. This present book is neither a study of the growth of Anglo-German antagonism, nor yet another attempt to consider the causes that led to the outbreak of the Great War. I have had to deal with these large and important themes but my major concern has been with those British journalists and journals scathingly referred to by their contemporary critics as Teutophobe, yellow, patriotic, jingo or scaremonger. I have set out, as far as the sources allow, the scaremongers' perception of events and personalities and to explain in their own terms why they wrote as they did and what purposes they supposed they were serving. In the Epilogue are my conclusions about certain questions that can be asked of the evidence provided by the narrative chapters that form the greater part of the book.

Did the scaremongers deserve their title? Were there good or sufficient reasons for the way in which they presented Germany to their readers and interpreted that Power's intentions? Did they deliberately exaggerate or falsify? Were they genuinely seeking to serve a national interest, as they so frequently insisted, or were they inspired by the thought of personal gain and sectarian advantage as their critics claimed? What restraints were placed upon their activities and to what extent did their actions inspire or hinder the policy makers? Were they more often manipulators or manipulated? Do they stand properly condemned of the charges brought against them by their Radical contemporaries, that they deliberately set out to poison Anglo-German relations and to create by their scaremongering such a climate of public opinion that war between the two Great Powers became inevitable? How much influence did the scaremongers have with the general public? Did politicians listen or ever act at their behest? Newspaper barons, like Northcliffe, certainly liked to think so. He and his friends never doubted that their newspapers were an active and influential force in shaping public ideas, manners and dispositions. More importantly, their detractors shared this view.

Clearly there is an important difference between formulating and exaggerating opinion, between guiding and stampeding the public. Is it possible to distinguish between a genuine expression of apprehension for Germany's supposed hostile intentions and deliberate scaremongering? No one would deny the difference is considerable and significant. However, it has always to

be remembered that the distinction may be determined as much by the prejudice and expectation of the reader as by the intention of the writer. As Stephen
Koss has observed in his recent study *The Rise and Fall of the Political Press in
Britain*, Northcliffe was incapable of understanding that one man's patriotism
is another's political prejudice. The same may be said of Northcliffe's Radical
critics. As frequently as he, they ignored uncomfortable facts and inconvenient
distinctions where they clashed with their preconceived estimate of Anglo-
German relations and the proper function of the journalist.

The particular emphases, the simple explanations designed to serve the
immediate purpose of a journalist anxious to meet an unremitting deadline,
score off an adversary or satisfy the dictates of an owner or editor, often
obscure the complexity and intimacy of connections between apparently
disparate subjects. Domestic themes and international concerns were threads
forming a single fabric. An obvious example is the question of expenditure on
armaments. The advocacy of retrenchment cannot be separated from the
Liberal desire to finance an ambitious and costly programme of domestic social
improvement, a dilemma that was crudely exploited by the *Daily Mail* in its
headline, 'Pensions or Dreadnoughts?' On the other side of the political divide,
in the context of the internecine strife between free trade and protectionist
Tories, the tariff reformers argued that their policy was a specific to ward off
the evils of socialism, the guarantee of a regenerated British economy, the only
means to forge imperial unity. But as important an argument for protection
was fear of Germany. Domestic and foreign policies never operated in hermet-
ically sealed isolation. They interacted one with the other. Similarly, political
parties were almost as often as opposed to their nominal allies as their foes.
Between Radical Liberal and Liberal Imperialist, free trade Unionist and
tariff reformer, German and Briton, there was enmity, collusion, self-delusion,
confusion and deceit.

The story of the scaremongers is part of the fabric of late Victorian and
Edwardian politics. A complex tale, it has been made more so by the myths
surrounding it. It concerns men of every rank and degree, but always at its
centre – arguing, persuading, cajoling, wheedling, hiding, warning, censuring,
advertising – are the owners, editors and correspondents who, for different
reasons at different times, insisted that Germany and Britain were set upon a
collision course and whose doom-laden prophecies became dreadful reality on
4 August 1914.

It is a pleasure to acknowledge how much I owe to those who helped me in
various ways to sustain and complete this task. The Research Committee of
the Ulster Polytechnic granted me a sabbatical year and funded part of my
research, while the encouragement of my colleagues at the Polytechnic, particularly members of the School of Philosophy, Politics and History, was very
important. I am greatly indebted to the Nuffield Foundation for the award of
a Research Fellowship for the academic year 1981–2, during which time I was
able to complete most of the first draft of this book. I am also pleased to
acknowledge the generosity of the British Academy for an award that made it
possible to work on archival material in the United States of America.

Various long-suffering friends and colleagues were kind enough to read and comment in detail upon various sections of my typescript: Chris Andrew, James Cornford, Alistair Elliot, Robert Gavin, John Grigg, Michael Howard, Andrew Jones, Paul Kennedy, Ruddock Mackay, Bruce Murray, Zara Steiner and Andrew Wheatcroft. My gratitude to them is immense for their comments greatly improved the quality of the final text.

From the staff of all the archives I visited I received nothing but unfailing courtesy and assistance. My particular thanks are owed to Nicholas Cox, Eileen Dunlap, Patricia Gill, Timothy Hollins, Helen Langley, Gordon Phillips, Anne Piggott and Charles Potts.

By the warmth and generosity of their hospitality, many goods friends made my researches much easier, providing me with a temporary home on my frequent visits across the Irish Sea. I am very grateful to Jean and Roy Douglas, Barbara and Alistair Elliot, Sarah and David Green, Barbara and John Griffith, Alison and Ruddock Mackay, Marcia Massie, Chris and Si Mathews, Margaret and Brian Sawyer and Rowena Wilson.

For the patience, good humour and skill with which she deciphered my work to produce the final typescript I owe much to Sharon Inch.

The greatest debt I owe to those nearest and dearest to me for bearing without complaint the burden of my writing this book. Fiona helped me with translations from German and French sources while Anthony, by his detailed and careful reading of the typescript, saved me from many errors of judgment and fact. They will best understand when I say I owe most to their mother who has supported and encouraged me throughout this task as with all my work. I dedicate this book to Cis with all my love.

A.J.A.M.

Acknowledgments

I gratefully acknowledge permission to quote from material the copyright in which belongs to the following: the Controller of Her Majesty's Stationery Office, the Clerk of the Records of the House of Lords, the trustees of the British Library, the National Library of Scotland, the Scottish Record Office, the Library of Congress, the Imperial War Museum, the National Maritime Museum, the Liddell Hart Centre for Military Archives, the Bedford Estate, the Bodleian Library, the Cambridge University Library, the National Peace Society, Times Newspapers Ltd, the University of Birmingham, the London School of Economics and Political Science, the Humanities Center at the University of Texas, Austin, the Librarian of the *Spectator*, the County Archivist of the West Sussex Record Office, the Master and Fellows of Churchill College, the Beaverbrook Foundation and the Warden and Fellows of New College.

I also wish to thank the following for their help as well as giving permission for me to quote from copyright material: Lady Arthur, Correlli Barnett, Mrs Belinda Bell, William Bell, B. S. Benedickz, John Boland, P. M. Cadell, Mark Bonham Carter, Dr Pauline Dower, M. P. G. Draper, Lord Esher, John Grigg, Ian Crum Hamilton, Lord Hardinge of Penshurst, Julian Hardinge, Sir Ian Hogg, J. H. Hutson, Mrs D. M. Maxse, David McKenna, Patricia Methven, Sir Hector Monro, R. A. Morriss, John L. Nevinson, A. E. B. Owen, Mrs Mary Z. Pain, Charles Seaton, Lord Selborne, Mrs Ursula Slaghek, Roderick Suddaby, the Marquess of Tavistock, Alan Taylor and Lady Willmer.

Every effort has been made to trace and to secure permission from holders of copyright. I apologise to anyone whose right I might inadvertently have infringed.

Scaremongering: the charge rehearsed, accepted and enhanced

Your claim to be the true prophet of war does not call for dispute. It has always been your part to prophesy war and cultivate hate. . . . You have done these things because they were the short cut to success – that success which is the only thing you reverence amidst all the mysteries and sanctities of life.

A. G. Gardiner to Northcliffe

I do not in the least mind personal attacks, nor do I care what the public think about me. The fact that my newspapers are almost the only ones that are not shrinking rapidly at the present moment shows that my readers have faith in them. If the readers attacked me, I should begin to think that I am the wicked man the little tradesmen of Fleet Street believe me to be.

Northcliffe to Lovat Fraser

At eleven o'clock on 4 August 1914, Britain's ultimatum to Germany expired. The two nations were at war. That late summer evening London's streets were filled with cheering, flag-waving crowds. The ferment of patriotism worked among all ages and social classes.

The mood of those gathered outside the German Embassy in Carlton House Terrace was less happy. When hisses and groans were not enough, stones were thrown. To the sound of smashing glass a force of police, mounted and on foot, hurried from Cannon Row police station. Only with difficulty was order eventually restored and the patriotic stone throwers dispersed.

The news that Britain was at war with Germany spread like wildfire. Along Pall Mall, the members leaned not a little drunkenly from the balconies of their clubs and noisily encouraged the tumult passing below. In Trafalgar Square, while there was yet room to move, the crowd sang, danced and wound in solemn procession about Nelson's column. Through Admiralty Arch the crowd surged down The Mall, united in roaring defiance of Germany, asserting with one raucous voice loyalty to king and country, advertising a willingness to fight the despicable Hun.

In Fleet Street, new editions of the newspapers were being rushed from the presses. The banner headlines pronounced 'War', 'Hands off Belgium', 'Britain United', 'The German Menace', 'The Navy is Ready'. But even these were not enough to please one newspaper boy eagerly touting his wares.

'Great naval battle off Margate,' he howled as he sped down St Martin's Lane.

'Why Margate?' asked a middle class girl of her middle class boy. 'Why do they want to fight off Margate? Why, that's where we go for our holidays.'

Her escort bought a paper. Of course, there was no such news.[1]

At Buckingham Palace the good-humoured, high-spirited, banner-waving, jostling, singing crowd pressed hard against the railings. The more intrepid spirits who had climbed the Victoria Memorial were the first to see the king and queen appear on the balcony to acknowledge and be acknowledged by their cheering subjects. In ecstatic harmony voices were raised to sing the national anthem. No one present could have doubted that the universal mood was to fight the good fight, to come to grips with the Germans, to teach the Hun the lesson he had so long deserved. Britain's despatch of the ultimatum was a technical nicety: it was Germany that was actually responsible for sundering the peace. This was what the Kaiser had long planned. Germany's ally Austria had tried to humiliate Serbia. Now Germany was threatening brave little neutral Belgium. Europe's bully deserved to be punished. A journalist, Hamilton Fyfe, later wrote of his feelings as the strokes of Big Ben in Parliament Square told Londoners that the long peace was ended.

> I pictured France and Russia as the victims of aggression. . . . I felt the Jingo spirit rising within me. I symphathised with the Frenchman who muttered, 'Nous en avons assez.' We all had had enough of it. If they asked for it, they should have it. Let the wager of battle decide.[2]

The mood of the crowd that evening was not one of reluctant acquiescence; rather it suggested the willing consummation of a long-held desire to be at war with Germany. In the days immediately following the declaration of war there was virtually no public dissent from that decision, no protest that was noticed, no strikes, no 'war against war'. Those socialists and pacifists who only days earlier had advertised their determination and ability to maintain peace were now obliged to admit, in Keir Hardie's words, that their demonstrations, speeches, resolutions had all alike been futile. 'We simply do not count.'[3] The weekly *Nation*, the persistent voice of the Radical conscience, admitted defeat. 'We have no criticism to offer.'[4] With the self-righteousness and the malignity of the late convert proved right in its apostasy, the socialist weekly, *New Age*, asked its readers:

> Who in the future will pay attention to the *Daily News, Nation,* the *Manchester Guardian* and other journals of the same stamp? These idealists . . . who refused to look reality in the face and preferred to be deceived and to deceive their followers. . . . Who will heed when the Courtneys, the Wedgwoods, the Trevelyans presume to air their baby views on so complicated a subject as foreign politics and our duties towards our friends and allies? I venture to say after what has happened, no one.[5]

Like a number of other journals, *New Age* was now only too anxious to claim it had long foreseen that war with Germany was inevitable. At Carmelite House, the offices of the *Daily Mail*, a recent recruit to the editorial staff, Twells Brex, was commanded by the newspaper's owner, Lord Northcliffe, to collect an anthology that would confirm the *Mail*'s daily boast that it had 'persistently forewarned the public about the war'. The task was soon completed and in late November 1914 a substantial booklet was published, paper bound, priced sixpence and boldly titled in black and red, *Scaremongerings from the Daily Mail 1896–1914: the paper that foretold the war*. This collection of snippets culled from the files of the *Mail* implied that from its foundation it had shown not only an amazing perspicacity about Germany's hostile intent towards Britain, but also had made 'unremitting effort, in the face of intense opposition, to urge that the British Navy and Army should be kept in a condition to meet the present crisis'. In sad contradistinction, the booklet concluded with a substantial section headed by a legend borrowed from the Radical *Daily News*: 'There will be no war with Germany.' Here, the pacific injunctions of the *Daily Mail*'s contemporaries were quoted and the *Manchester Guardian, Daily Graphic, Nation* and *Daily News* designated as 'the pro-German Press'.

From August 1914 until November 1918, Britain was engaged in the most intense, cataclysmic and savage war it had ever known. Only with peace came the time and opportunity for many of the survivors to ask themselves how and why such a dreadful fate had overtaken them and their world. Voices that had gone unheeded in August 1914, swamped in the passion of patriotism, dismissed at Westminster as 'the dregs and lees of debate',[6] pilloried and abused during the war as 'defeatist', 'cowardly', 'pro-Hun',[7] at last found auditors prepared to listen. Politicians, diplomats, admirals, generals, armament manufacturers – all were allotted some greater or lesser share of responsibility for promoting the carnage. One further claim was made: before the war the nation's wits had been stolen, its nerves enfeebled, a 'national neurasthania' induced. Arraigned as the culprit to answer this charge was the so-called patriotic press. It was claimed that for two decades before 1914, the lies and half-truths of irresponsible journalists had encouraged militarism and promoted an unreasoning hatred of Germany. What made this deceit even more contemptible was that the long, despicable campaign had been inspired not by any genuine apprehension about German hostility but by a sordid, irresponsible pursuit of private profit. Germany had been only the excuse 'to exploit the degenerate mind of the public for the sake of inordinate gain'. The claim of patriotism had concealed 'the mean and ruthless exploitation of a nationalist craze'. A 'partial, passionate and brutal tone' was deliberately adopted in order 'to feed public alarm with unverifiable rumour'. The continual 'dropping of hints of terror into the public ear' had the intended effect of 'representing Germany as an enemy state with which, sooner or later [Britain was] bound to be at war. By such a process of national self-suggestion war ultimately developed from imagination into actuality.'[8] Those who in 1914 had boasted the accolade of 'scaremonger', had competed to be acclaimed as the best fitted to wear that title, now found themselves charged with being a cause of the war that had embraced and destroyed old Europe and decimated a generation.

Long before 1914 there had been journalists, politicians and scholars who were convinced that the angry words and sentiments exchanged across the North Sea by the patriotic editors of Germany and Britain permanently injured Anglo-German relations. They were particularly concerned about the 'Teutophobia' so often manifest in the Unionist press, more particularly in the new, popular, half-penny dailies like the *Mail* and *Express*. These jingo rags they considered much the worst product of the new style of journalism – newspapers that seemed to delight in publishing irresponsible, ridiculous, scaremongering stories about spies, saboteurs and invading armies as though Germany, at the first opportune moment, was anxious to leap at England's throat. Eight years before the outbreak of war, the socialist and pacifist H. S. Perris confidently instructed his readers that 'press polemics are the greatest single danger to good international relations'.[9] As long after the war as 1930, so level-headed and unsensational a commentator as J. A. Spender could write, 'There has been much talk since the War of the evils of secret diplomacy, but the dangers of a rash and inexpert handling of publicity are written just as large in the records.'[10]

Among the leaders of the Unionist press it was inevitable, if only because of the size of his newspaper empire and his ownership of *The Times*, that Alfred Harmsworth, raised to the peerage as Northcliffe, should become the personification of the Teutophobe, scaremongering element within the Tory party and its press. Those who were antipathetic to the least manifestation of jingoism derided his commercial success, despised his methods and scorned his newspapers for their meagre moral and intellectual force. But they also feared Northcliffe as a thoroughly dangerous and evil influence. The ubiquity of that influence was reflected in a parody of the Creed.

Whosoever will exist, before all things it is essential that he do swallow the Northcliffe Creed.

Which Creed, unless swallowed whole and retained, must result in terrestrial damnation.

The Northcliffe Creed is this: that we believe in three papers as one paper and one paper as three papers.

We must not confound the papers nor confuse the issues.

For there is one *Times*, of the *Daily Mail* and of the *Evening News* is all one; and the variety great and the colour yellow.

Such as the *Times* is, so is the *Daily Mail* and so is the *Evening News*.

The *Times* is insurpassable, the *Daily Mail* is insurpassable and the *Evening News* is insurpassable.

The *Times* manhunts, the *Daily Mail* manhunts and the *Evening News* manhunts.

And yet, there are not three manhunts but one manhunt.

As the *Times* is Northcliffe, the *Daily Mail* is Northcliffe and the *Evening News* is Northcliffe.

And yet, there are not three Northcliffes but one Northcliffe.[11]

It was concern about the influence he supposed Northcliffe commanded over general opinion that had prompted A. G. Gardiner, editor of the *Daily News*, to take the press baron to task for his *Scaremongerings* anthology. 'The student of your career', he wrote in a public letter, 'will have no difficulty in pointing to the wars you have fomented, the hatreds you have cultivated, the causes you have deserted, the sensations you have spread broadcast.'[12] Northcliffe rejected the advice that he should answer Gardiner claiming that the buoyant sales of his newspapers confirmed the soundness of his opinions. They were the best possible rejoinder to any critic.[13]

J. A. Spender had long before concluded that Northcliffe 'more naturally judged good journalism by reference to the circulation books'.[14] Max Pemberton, a close associate of Northcliffe's early years, wrote, 'Alfred took the business side of his newspapers as a much more serious matter than the politics.'[15] When he launched the *Daily Mail* in 1896, Alfred Harmsworth's name was synonymous with shallow commercial schemes and cheap publicity stunts. His newspapers were supposed to epitomise the 'new journalism' – simple-minded, vulgar trash. The then Prime Minister, Lord Salisbury, dismissed the rising newspaper tycoon as the begetter of newspapers that were 'written by office boys for office boys'. Measuring by the ledger of profit and loss, none could deny Northcliffe's success. But what he sought was much more than the material riches he had already accrued in plenty. He wanted to be a voice of consequence in the councils of the nation's political leaders. 'How am I to get influence?' he had eagerly inquired of Spender.

In 1895 Northcliffe had stood as a Unionist parliamentary candidate for Portsmouth. The Tories triumphed in the country but Northcliffe, despite prodigious expenditure of money and effort, came a poor third to his two Liberal opponents. His immediate bravura response was to insist that his place was in the House of Lords where he would not again have to face the indignity of fighting an election. Though later to deny it, he had not then altogether abandoned his hopes of a parliamentary career.[16] Slowly he discovered an obvious truth about himself. His gifts were not those that could best be displayed at Westminster; his was not the temperament to be confined by the traditional limits of party loyalty and precept; his vocation was journalism. Being the man he was, he made a virtue of necessity. Twenty years later he told a journalist who was considering accepting a parliamentary candidature, 'It is best to choose one's own battle ground in fighting Governments. . . . The pages of my newspapers form far better entrenchments from which to deliver one's attack than the floor of either House. . . . From Printing House Square or Carmelite House I am able to bombard every day with good result.'[17]

The *Daily Mail* always retained a special place in Northcliffe's affections. His friend J. L. Garvin, though well aware of this, bluntly informed Northcliffe that the newspaper's comments on public questions were 'meagre and inconspicuous, detached, spasmodic and incalculable'. As a *vehicle of opinion* it would never be taken seriously 'because it does not take itself seriously'. In saying this Garvin knew exactly what Northcliffe wanted and offered it to him – a prize so glittering that it would have tempted any newspaper proprietor: a prize that seemed realisable at a time when the press enjoyed an almost unchallenged monopoly of mass communication. Garvin promised Northcliffe that he could give him a consistent, influential, public voice. 'You can do through your papers, if you like, what no man could through any medium . . . make a Nation and its Government. . . . Nothing LESS!'[18]

It was not until 1908 that Northcliffe secured the outstanding journalistic abilities of Garvin as editor, not of the *Daily Mail* but of the *Observer*. Significant as this was to prove, the immediate apprehensions of those who despised and feared Northcliffe were roused much more by his capture that same year of *The Times*. If Northcliffe 'aspired to participate in the government of the world . . . by sway of language and reason over the minds of men', he now possessed the engine best suited to consummate that purpose; for, as 'those of a philosophic bent traced events to what they call "public opinion", with almost the same meaning practical men simply spoke of *The Times*'.[19]

One of the least well-kept secrets of Fleet Street was that when Northcliffe purchased *The Times* he promised that he would not interfere with editorial policy *unless* the editor failed to warn his readers of the German peril. He was supposed to have said, 'I insist upon that duty being discharged.' Why did he impose this single imperative? If we examine Northcliffe's ideas about foreign affairs we see that they embraced a generous patriotism which he expressed in a mixture of jingo polemic and vague platitudes about the need for national efficiency. Men are what matter, he asserted, men before ideas and certainly before party. Foreign affairs were a national concern. As such, their satisfactory conduct required not party but national policies. Such ideas were congenial to him as they justified his own independence. He was not a profound political thinker but he did possess what he was pleased to call his 'sixth sense'. It was this that first prompted him to link the future of the British Empire with what was then no more than a vague concern about the exact intentions of Germany's Kaiser. A letter he wrote in 1898 to Rosebery, then recently retired as Liberal Prime Minister, catches his mood. He wanted Rosebery to persuade the Prince of Wales to visit the United States of America and Canada so that Edward might 'reduce the German Emperor's trip to a mere side-show'.

> I urge you as one Imperialist to another, as one who plays his little part
> in the stage management of the new world drama. . . . You yawn: all
> this is so horribly antique and Daily Mailesque – I write the more
> boresomely and vehemently perhaps because I am one of the many
> whose nerves are suffering from a little too much of the Emperor and his
> world movements.[20]

Northcliffe's apprehensions concerning the Kaiser were the nervous complement of his naive ideas about Britain's world role and imperial destiny. Like many others in Britain he was impressed by German energy, discipline and ambition, qualities that the British seemed in danger of losing.

Despite the *Pax Britannica*, the Unionist press frequently and loudly asserted that international relations were about conflict and competition. Victory invariably went to the strongest armed Power. The truth of Karl von Clausewitz's dictum – 'War is the continuation of politics by other means' – was never questioned. Successful nations accumulated an ever-larger share of the world's finite resources. The implication for a nation that already claimed to possess an empire upon which the sun never set was intended to be as obvious as its converse. It was politic to guard against covetous rivals. These views were particularly offensive to the latter-day disciples of Richard Cobden in the Liberal party. They were convinced that the world might grow ever richer provided it accepted the doctrine of free trade. Peace and harmony among nations were assured so long as nations were wise enough to disarm and settle their disputes not by armed conflict but by international arbitration. While they emphasised the world's increasing trade, productivity and prosperity, the Unionist press drew attention to Britain's relative economic decline warning that she was inexorably losing her place at the head of the league table of industrial and commercial nations. The coupling of this pessimism with envy created a particular focus of discontent and concern – Wilhelmine Germany.

Under Prussia's tutelage, a German empire had been created and established as the dominant military force in continental Europe. Now, inspired by a youthful, restless monarch, William II, Germany was pursuing a new policy, a new course, *Weltmachtpolitik*. She sought an overseas empire and the status of a first-class naval Power. Was it possible to suppose that all Germany's ambitions were sated when her military, naval and economic strength continued to grow so rapidly and relentlessly? The Germans were an inventive, energetic, disciplined people. The fact that the political ambitions of their volatile monarch were, as yet, not fully articulated, made them the more threatening. The Prussians were notorious for getting what they wanted by a combination of iron will, diplomatic intrigue and overwhelming military might. 'The main fact which should impress itself upon Englishmen when considering the actual international outlook', Leo Maxse, editor of the *National Review*, wrote in November 1901, 'is the extraordinary growth of Germany.' Britain was then engaged in fighting with the Boers, a war in which she had forfeited both the friendship and respect of almost all her neighbours. The threat that a strong, ambitious, militant Germany posed to an exhausted, inefficient, complacent Britain seemed so obvious to Maxse and those who thought like him that they supposed only the purblind and prejudiced could choose to ignore it.

The most ardent, earnest advocates of British imperialism were those most concerned about the empire's decline. The lessons of history, the immutable rules of political economy, the inherent psychological disposition of man, ideas culled with greater certainty than accuracy from Darwin's great thesis and the emerging science of eugenics, all coalesced in their minds to produce one pessimistic conclusion. In the near future, at best Britain would be hard pressed to maintain her empire; at worst, her place would be usurped by another Power better fitted to assume the imperial mantle. Those who warned that Germany aspired to that part also insisted that the Germans had chosen it for themselves. Of their own volition they had chosen to pursue *Weltpolitik*. A controlled press, directly instigated by Germany's leaders, published a stream of insults and calumnies designed to poison Anglo-German relations. The Kaiser had undoubtedly 'tried it on' with his Kruger telegram after the Jameson Raid and subsequently had made life both difficult and dangerous with his speeches and interviews, his crusades and appearances in 'shining armour' designed to discomfort and bully Britain's diplomatic friends and partners. Though he tried to conceal his real intentions behind a cloud of dissimulation and false avowals of friendship, Prince Bülow as Germany's Chancellor had directed policy against England's interests. But above all else, the decision to build a huge fleet of battleships could have been designed only to challenge Britain's position as mistress of the seas. The imperial fleet in the North Sea – or the German Ocean as the Kaiser preferred it to be known – was a constant, growing threat to British security. Whatever else, that could never be ignored. Such was the evidence adduced that confirmed and sharpened British apprehension that Germany's intentions towards England were very far from friendly.

Radical critics insisted that jingo publicists relentlessly and consistently in the pre-war years misrepresented and pilloried Germany in the press. The caricature of Teutophobia, however, hid a significant ambivalence of attitude towards Germany. J. L. Garvin, for example, banned by Lord Burnham from writing on Germany in the *Daily Telegraph* because he was considered hopelessly prejudiced against that nation, could admit in a private letter written in August 1909, like Northcliffe, he admired many 'qualities of the German character'.

> I owe everything to German culture and their spirit is what appeals to me.
> It is just because they are so great that the danger is great: they have
> every qualification for taking our place and are bound to aspire to it more
> and more ardently as time goes on and their trade and wealth and fleet
> expand together.... But there I know we are in peculiar agreement.[21]

Northcliffe's attitude towards Germany was complex and at different times dictated by different imperatives. One of his biographers has pertinently observed that before 1914, 'if at one moment an exhibition of arrogance on the part of the Kaiser would cause Northcliffe resentment, inevitably followed the saving wishful thought that, after all it was the Twentieth Century and no Great Power would be so mad when it came to the point as to loose a world war.'[22] One factor, however, was constant in Northcliffe's thinking. He never considered that the profit of any of his enterprises should be ignored or treated other than very seriously. Northcliffe commissioned Fred Wile, the *Daily Mail's* Berlin correspondent, to write a study of *Our German Cousins* 'that gives a fair picture of Germany as she is today'. He instructed Wile in January 1909 to 'desist from Kaiser baiting' and it was 'in line with that policy' that a year later the Berlin correspondent maintained that he had 'sought out stories particularly friendly to the Kaiser and Germany'. As late as October 1912 Wile was reminding Herr Goldschmidt, advertisement manager of the continental edition of the *Daily Mail*, that the hostility of the newspaper to Germany was 'simply and purely a fiction.... How many know that the "Daily Mail" has published in the past, and still publishes, countless articles revealing Germany and Germans in the most favourable light?'[23]

It must never be forgotten that the measure of Northcliffe's genius and in large part the reason for his phenomenal commercial success was that he shared the prejudices of his readers. Though he rode in a Rolls Royce motor car he retained an uncanny ability to know exactly what the passengers on a Clapham omnibus were thinking and saying to each other. His popular newspapers were like megaphones that broadcast widely and loudly the changing thoughts and fancies of the man in the street. 'We don't direct the ordinary man's opinion,' he told one of his employees, 'we reflect it.'[24] In 1916, however, when he published *The Rise of the Daily Mail*, Northcliffe wished to emphasise the consistency of his warnings and opposition to Germany, his single-mindedness and independence of government influence. From the founding of the *Mail* in 1896, he had warned of Germany's nefarious designs; that 'unlike ambassadors, naval and military attachés and the Secret Service [he had] always visualised what was coming'. Had he not frequently told Blumenfeld, the editor of the *Daily Express*, that the Germans were 'being led definitely and irrevocably to make war on the rest of Europe and we will have to take part in it'?[25]

No one was better than Northcliffe, the great salesman, at creating and sustaining myths about himself and his newspapers. His prescience about the intentions of the 'wicked Hun' was much less certain than he chose to remember, but it certainly smacked better to a nation locked in seemingly interminable conflict with the Germans than the carping of his critics who before 1914 had spoken incessantly of Anglo-German friendship while censuring him as an irresponsible scaremonger and Teutophobe. The irony was that the pre-war criticisms of his Radical press enemies became the buttress of Northcliffe's subsequent pose as the one, supreme prophet of Armageddon.

Fifteen years before Twells Brex compiled his anthology of *Scaremongerings from the Daily Mail*, Bülow, accompanying the Kaiser on a visit to England, prepared a confidential memorandum for Prince Chlodwig zu Hohenlohe-Schillingsfürst. 'There is no doubt', Bülow concluded, 'that feeling in England generally is far less anti-German than German feeling is anti-British. Therefore the most dangerous Englishmen for us are those who, like Chirol and Saunders, know from personal observation how sharp and deep is the German dislike of England.'[26] Bülow's perceptive and detailed memorandum mentioned neither Northcliffe nor the *Daily Mail*.

•••••••••• **PART 1** ••••••••••

Making friends and choosing enemies: the diplomats

The Kaiser sends a telegram and Chirol is aggrieved

The one failing of every German whether he is an exalted personage, a diplomat or of the lower classes is that he lies and lies without blushing.
Col L. V. Swaine in a Memorandum to the Foreign Office

I was so incensed at the idea of your orders having been disobeyed and thereby Peace and the security also of my fellow countrymen endangered, that I thought it necessary to show that publicly. It has, I am sorry to say, been totally misunderstood by the British Press. I was standing up for law, order and obedience to a Sovereign whom I revere and admire.
William II to Victoria

You know how influential Chirol of The Times is. A few years ago, when correspondent here, he went so far as to write an article against his own government, and the yielding of the government was probably at least partially brought about by this article. After the Kruger telegram Chirol and I naturally drifted apart, as each of us defended his government.
Holstein to Hatzfeldt

The Queen's Speech to Parliament in 1896 did not include the customary reference to continuing good relations with other nations. Thus Britain publicly acknowledged that she stood alone in the world. Some called this diplomatic isolation 'splendid', an inappropriate adjective for something that was more a matter of unavoidable circumstance than choice. The *Morning Post*'s observation was more accurate: 'We have no friends and nobody loves us.'[1] Though Lord Salisbury, Britain's venerable Prime Minister and Foreign Secretary, did not seem particularly concerned, few shared his monumental composure. There were those bold enough to ask (though not too loudly) whether the marquis still maintained his former sound grip upon affairs.

Salisbury was a realist. To thwart Russian ambitions in Persia and Afghanistan he had worked closely with Germany. Reassuming responsibility for Britain's foreign policy after the fall of Lord Rosebery's short-lived Liberal ministry in June 1895, Salisbury recognised there would have to be changes made, but he was not inclined to hurry or be hurried. 'We know that we shall maintain against all comers that which we possess, and we know, in spite of the jargon about isolation, that we are amply competent to do so.'[2]

The 1890s was a decade of change and uncertainty in British fortunes abroad, at the Foreign Office, and also at Printing House Square, home of *The Times*. When Arthur Fraser Walter succeeded his father as chief proprietor of that newspaper in 1894, he determined to increase its circulation, restore its finances, repair its tarnished image and resuscitate its influence both at home and abroad. George Buckle, editor of *The Times* since 1884, shared Walter's concern about the recent decline of the paper, but was not without hope for the immediate future. Walter had issued a diktat that *The Times* should be less politically partisan. Buckle replied:

> In quiet times, such as we trust we are entering on now, the 'critical' or
> 'umpire' attitude of the Paper . . . is certainly the right one. When a
> great national question comes up, the Paper has to take a strong line, and
> if possible, make its view prevail. . . . If I have any bias beyond a bias
> in favour of the great principles to which the Paper is committed you may
> be sure I shall do my best to shake it off.[3]

The exchange between Buckle and Walter had been prompted by domestic political issues, but both men's minds were as much exercised by the newspaper's recent comparatively poor coverage and comment on foreign affairs. In large part they attached the blame for this upon *The Times*'s Paris correspondent, the unique, flamboyant, irrepressible, Henri Stefan Opper de Blowitz.

Since his appointment in 1875 as Paris correspondent, de Blowitz had been such a dominant influence that he had largely determined the approach of *The Times* to foreign news. Fluent, dogmatic and opinionated, de Blowitz was convinced that the key to journalistic success was sentiment and sensationalism. Sadly, over the years, his 'curiosity had outstripped his sense of accuracy, and his personal vanity his sense of discretion'.[4] German diplomats, used to their own rigorously controlled press, had been much upset by 'the unspeakable diatribes of the Paris correspondent regarded in Germany as the expression of British public opinion'. Their exasperation was shared 'by the younger, more advanced members of the British Cabinet', who had promised, according to Herbert Bismarck, that they would 'do their utmost to induce "The Times" to cease opening its columns in future to its correspondents uncontrolled'.[5] Ministerial and diplomatic displeasure had achieved nothing. Arthur Walter was not only determined to stifle de Blowitz, he had the power to do something about it.

Although *The Times*'s foreign service was still highly regarded in most of Europe, Walter knew that 'the *Standard, Morning Post* and *Daily Telegraph* were often equal and sometimes superior in news and comment'. With his manager, C. F. Moberly Bell, he was determined to replan *The Times*'s foreign news service. Buckle would still retain overall editorial control, but Bell, his authority enhanced by the new regime instituted by Walter, would become a very important influence in deciding the paper's stance on questions of foreign policy. Manager and proprietor created a new department for foreign news and appointed as its head the most experienced and distinguished correspondent available, Donald MacKenzie Wallace.

Wallace was not a big man physically, but he cut a formidable figure. By disposition more a scholar than journalist, in everything he did he was thorough, imperturbable, tactful and discreet. There could not have been a greater distinction of character, style and temperament than between him and de Blowitz. Wallace was never inclined to be subservient to governments, but he was anxious to work whenever possible in accord with the Foreign Office. He both liked and admired Salisbury, supported and trusted him. Cautious and conservative, Wallace could be counted upon to act as a brake on the restless triumvirate of Buckle, Bell and Chirol. That was the opinion of the Permanent Under Secretary at the Foreign Office, Thomas Sanderson, who thought the three men regarded the British Empire as 'a sort of elephant to rush about trumpeting and knocking down everything that comes in its way'.[6]

Though initially reluctant, Bell had given in to Wallace's insistence that Valentine Chirol should be appointed as the new Berlin correspondent of *The Times*. Chirol was then aged 40, ten years Wallace's junior. He had joined the Foreign Office as a clerk in 1872 but had resigned four years later and never given any reason for this decision.[7] For the next sixteen years he travelled extensively, supporting himself by his writing. He had very few close friends, but numbered among them were Sir Frank Lascelles, appointed British Ambassador to Berlin in 1895, and Lascelles's son-in-law, Cecil Spring Rice, appointed Secretary to the Berlin embassy that same year. A life-long bachelor, Chirol's appearance was invariably if over-fussily neat, his demeanour earnest, and he pursued his duties with what can only be described as an extraordinary conscientiousness. He had little sense of humour and would take affront at the least supposed slight to his considerable dignity. So secretive was he in conversation that he would peep about him constantly as though he supposed his every word might be overheard. No one ever trifled with him in an argument for he defended his views with a stubbornness that was born as much of a perverse nature as intellectual commitment.

When Chirol took up his appointment in Berlin, the German Chancellor was Count Caprivi who supported closer relations with Britain rather than Russia. He was also opposed to Germany pursuing a policy of unlimited colonial expansion. Caprivi was supported by all the leading representatives of the British press in Berlin, most notably, William Maxwell of the *Standard*, George Saunders of the *Morning Post*, and Chirol. When Caprivi was dismissed from office in 1894, they were more than a little suspicious of his successor, Hohenlohe, and openly hostile to those political groups that had engineered the Chancellor's fall.

German policy now inclined towards Russia and away from England, and this was made abundantly apparent during the Sino-Japanese war. British diplomatic initiatives were summarily rejected while a Russian initiative was responded to with alacrity by the Germans. These actions prompted the British press to express concern and doubt. A leader in the *Standard* asked whether Germany's new attitude was dictated 'by a perverse desire to do the opposite of whatever Britain favoured', or was it 'no more than the sudden impulse of the German Ruler'?[8] Despite these vagaries of German policy and a sharpening of the belligerence and invective of the German 'kept' press against England, Spring Rice informed a friend that Chirol remained 'an ardent advocate of a good understanding with Germany [and] a great admirer of several members of the present administration'.[9]

The unhappy press relations between Germany and England were suddenly made much worse by two egregiously patronising editorials in the *Standard* written by its chief leader writer, the Poet Laureate, Alfred Austin. These effusions, written to mark a visit by Kaiser William to Cowes and intended to heal the rift between Germany and England, had the opposite effect. William, his *amour propre* already dented by a supposed snub from Salisbury, was hurt beyond measure. The German press erupted with hysterical condemnation of Britain and everything British. Because Austin was Salisbury's friend, they supposed the Prime Minister was responsible for the editorials.

What had particularly incensed the Kaiser was Austin's gauche implication that Germany had secured her colonies by an act of British charity. The Germans had hoped that Salisbury would have been easier to work with than Rosebery, but their hints of a closer alignment had been summarily rejected. Now, presumably at the Prime Minister's request, insult had been added to injury. The Kaiser assumed the explanation was that Salisbury must be working covertly to strike a bargain with Russia. Assumption became conviction in William's mind because of the attitude adopted by the British press during the Armenian crisis. The Kaiser, who chose to ignore the frothings and fulminations against Britain of German newspapers and journals, eagerly fastened upon every grubby morsel spewed out from Fleet Street. He insisted that 'the purposeless scandal of the Armenian question is due entirely to the British press and its influence upon public opinion'.[10] Despite frequent assurances to the contrary, the Germans were utterly convinced that the British government controlled much that was said by the press on foreign policy. English newspapers were eagerly and regularly scanned by the Kaiser, his Ambassador in London, Count Hatzfeldt, and by high officials in the German foreign office, the Wilhelmstrasse. If the *Morning Post* was belligerent towards Germany, then Hatzfeldt in London and the Kaiser in Berlin naturally supposed the offending articles were written by the command of Salisbury. They were not. The actual source of the newspaper's anti-German comment was its Berlin correspondent, George Saunders.[11]

With the Armenian problem still unsettled, another crisis, this time in South Africa, rocked Anglo-German relations. The fabulous wealth of the Witwatersrand gold reef in the Transvaal excited the greed of all European Powers and the political destiny of that infant republic was a subject of consuming interest. Celebrating the Kaiser's birthday in Pretoria, President Paul Kruger alluded to Germany as the 'grown-up Power that would stop England from kicking his child Republic'. Relations between Pretoria and Berlin were sedulously cultivated. Accorded special favours by Kruger, the Germans were only too eager to provide the Transvaal with capital and technical expertise to counter British influence there. German money and technicians contributed substantially to the building of a railway linking Pretoria with Delagoa Bay that gave the Transvaal independent access to the Indian Ocean. The British, unofficially but busily intent upon 'absorbing' the Transvaal, were angered by the help the Germans were giving Kruger. Their frustration was nowhere more evident than in Sir Edward Malet's behaviour when quitting his post as Ambassador in Berlin. He bluntly warned Marschall, the German Foreign Secretary, that any further encouragement of Kruger might well lead to 'serious consequences'. When told of Malet's outburst, the Kaiser immediately bearded the British military attaché. 'Sir Edward', William shouted at Colonel Swaine, 'went so far as to mention the astounding word "war". For a few square miles full of niggers and palm trees, England has threatened her one true friend.' The Kaiser concluded his extraordinary monologue to, by now, a thoroughly alarmed Swaine, with a warning: 'England can only escape from her present complete isolation into which her policy of selfishness and bullying has plunged her by a frank and outspoken attitude either for or against the Triple Alliance.'[12]

When told of the Kaiser's diatribe, Salisbury simply disavowed Malet's words. In a spirit of sweet reasonableness he asked the German Ambassador how could the Transvaal ever be the cause of bad relations between their two countries when both Germany and Britain wanted to maintain the *status quo?* Either Salisbury's question was purposely ingenuous or it reflected his profound ignorance and unconcern about what Chamberlain was plotting and planning at the Colonial Office. The Prime Minister was to show a similar imperturbability when he was told of the Jameson Raid, an enterprise intended to afford armed aid to an Uitlander uprising against the Boers which ended in fiasco.

The excitement triggered among all classes in England by the raid left Salisbury quite unmoved. 'No great harm seems to have been done in the Transvaal,' he wrote to Chamberlain. 'If filibustering fails it is always disreputable.'[13] Queen Victoria seemed to consider the Boers' capture of 'the excellent and able' Jameson almost a personal humiliation. Her subjects who, for the most part, shared her sentiments, were determined to view what was an ill-conceived and hopelessly bungled act of brigandage as a noble attempt to bring succour to a deserving group denied their legitimate constitutional rights. In the British press, Jameson was described as a knight errant – a false picture that was particularly encouraged by *The Times*. An editorial did admit that Jameson's act was 'technically incorrect' but argued it had been inspired by the morally worthy desire 'to protect the lives of British women and children'. Presumably, this shameless untruth was intended to hide some very red faces at Printing House Square where Moberly Bell and Buckle had known of Jameson's plan from the beginning.[14]

The British sided with Jameson and his company, but the Germans as vehemently supported the Boers. When Jameson was captured at Doornkop, German jubilation exactly matched British bitterness and humiliation. From Berlin, Chirol sent a chilling message to Wallace: 'As far as Germany is concerned the issue of this question may determine her whole policy towards England.'[15] Next day, 4 January 1896, the publication of the text of a telegram the Kaiser had sent to Kruger, significantly altered the whole picture. The Kaiser had telegraphed:

I express my sincere congratulations that, supported by your people, without appealing for the help of friendly Powers, you have succeeded by your own energetic actions against armed bands which invaded your country as disturbers of the peace, and have thus been enabled to restore peace and safeguard the independence of the country against attacks from outside.[16]

At *The Times*, Wallace's initial reaction was to treat the telegram as nothing more than another personal effusion by the notoriously self-willed and indiscreet Kaiser. This charitable interpretation could not be sustained when a despatch from Chirol clearly fixed the telegram's official character. Consequently *The Times* now censured the telegram as 'an act of diplomatic chauvinism' and reasserted British determination to retain their rights in the Transvaal. The tone of the editorial had been restrained for, as Wallace told Chirol, he 'could not consider it as an "insult". . . . At the same time it is just as well that HM should know how his *démarche* is regarded in England.' Chirol was not inclined to show the same restraint as Wallace.

> In this question I can see nothing but a desire not only to thwart our so-called pretensions in South Africa but to make political capital out of existing complications at our expense and to humiliate us.
>   The conviction has grown upon me that the German Government is . . . distinctly malevolent. I can put no other structure upon the Emperor's telegram to Kruger. . . .[17]

Within a few days there was a noticeable drop in the temperature of reports in British newspapers. The German Ambassador was convinced this was because he had advised Salisbury to recommend to the British press that they should refrain from making any more personal attacks on the Kaiser, and Salisbury had 'promised heartily' to comply.[18] The Prime Minister seemed unusually keen to smooth over any possible misunderstanding with the Germans. *The Times*, however, if anything, became even more strident in its censures of Germany and William. If this was dictated by reason rather than emotion then the explanation is probably the further letter Chirol wrote to Wallace which showed that the Kaiser's telegram had been not a momentary rush of blood to the imperial head but 'prepared *de longue main*'.

Chirol had already spoken to Marschall, the German Foreign Secretary, but now he was summoned to talk with Holstein, a man who exercised an enormous influence upon the conduct of Germany's relations with other powers. Holstein began by appealing to the friendly and confidential personal relations that he and Chirol had enjoyed for a number of years. He wanted Chirol 'for [his] country's sake' to do what he could to impress upon his friends at the British Foreign Office how dangerously placed England was. Holstein also spoke of 'teaching England a lesson in the Transvaal' and suggested the Kaiser had the agreement of the Portuguese to land German troops at Delagoa Bay to guarantee the Transvaal's integrity. Chirol passed on Holstein's messages to Lascelles who, in his turn, telegraphed Salisbury.

In a letter to Lascelles later that month, Chirol, recalling the incident, concluded that he had been made use of by the German Foreign Office to further a policy of empty intimidation to which it hesitated to give official expression. He had been Holstein's unwitting pawn. When the Germans later complained to the British embassy about the virulent anti-German tone of Chirol's telegrams to *The Times*, the Berlin correspondent responded, 'They have only themselves to thank for it.' To the personal attacks made on him by the German press Chirol affected public indifference, but in his private letters he admitted his 'disgust' that the German government through its Press Bureau could conduct a campaign against someone with whom they had enjoyed such close relations over a period of four years. Chirol recognised that his anger might prejudice the views he expressed and told Wallace that they probably needed 'correcting for altitude and temperature'.[19]

The British Foreign Office seemed inclined to think that Anglo-German relations had now 'again become dove-like'. The Kaiser, though offering no public avowal of regret for sending his telegram, implored Lascelles to 'Tell Granny [Victoria] I didn't mean it.'[20] While no one would have told him so to his face, everyone knew that the Kaiser was a pathological liar. Salisbury was prepared to accept the telegram as nothing more than yet another aberration perpetrated by the febrile temperament of the Kaiser who, in his heart, wished to remain England's friend. In the circumstances it was probably best to say nothing. 'I wish the newspapers would be quiet,' Sanderson wrote to Lascelles, a sentiment heartily reciprocated by the embassy staff.[21] Spring Rice felt obliged to explain to one friend, Francis Villiers, the all too obvious resentment of another friend, Chirol, towards the Germans. 'He is a rather warm-hearted man and takes things seriously. . . . He is still very sore [and] believes in the existence of a determined hostility which takes a brutal and cowardly form.'[22] Chirol was not disposed to accept German assurances of friendliness. He wanted 'concrete proof of their sincerity before our confidence, which has been subjected to such severe shocks by recent incidents, can be fully restored'.[23] He was about to suffer a yet further indignity.

Without any prior notice Chirol suddenly found his familiar access to Holstein and Marschall forbidden. It was a grievous blow to his self-esteem.[24] He had supposed his position among British correspondents in Berlin was unique yet he was treated like any other journalist who had offended or caused official displeasure. To rub salt in the wound he was the target of personal jibes in the German press which he recognised as inspired by his 'friend', Holstein. Even someone less easily disposed to take offence than Chirol might have been excused feelings of betrayal and bitterness. Here was proof of German perfidy and insincerity. First they used and then they abused him. His crime: to give the lie to their official protestations of an intense desire to restore the former good relations between England and Germany, protestations which the guileless British government seemed intent to accept at their face value despite them 'not finding the slightest echo in the semi-official press'.[25] He had often enough recently told Wallace how much he wished to leave Berlin,[26] wishes that now were strengthened when he learned that Marschall was making offensive remarks about him to various senior diplomats.

Wallace had never allowed Chirol's too obvious personal pique to intrude upon or colour the tone of the leading articles he had written on Anglo-

German relations. Wallace visited Berlin a few months later and when Marschall complained of British press attitudes he retorted that 'The Times *had* tried to be friendly to Germany . . . but that experiment had been a dismal failure as the German papers had immediately said that England was begging pardon.'[27] Wallace was well aware of the game that the Germans were playing. The comments in their 'kept' press were intended for domestic consumption and more accurately reflected the government's true intentions with their unbridled hostility towards England than any official sentiments of friendship. When Hatzfeldt said to Wallace that relations between the British and German governments had never for a moment been troubled and all the harm had been done by the press, Wallace agreed, expressing his astonishment 'that organs in constant touch with the Wilhelmstrasse should have so misrepresented the views and feelings of the Government'. Hatzfeldt did not like this, Wallace told Chirol, 'and sailed away from it on some general remarks about the so-called inspired organs in Germany having often views different from the views of the Government. In reply to this, I confess myself to *looking* a little incredulous.'[28]

Chirol did not have Wallace's ability to make his own view plain while maintaining a perfect and correct friendliness. Recognising that his own bruised feelings ought not to prejudice 'relations between the two countries', Chirol suggested to Wallace that he be 'offered up on the altar of reconciliation as in the present state of affairs any special usefulness that my services in Berlin may have had has ceased. Anyone else could do as well or better.'[29] Having earlier refused Chirol's requests to be released hoping that matters might improve, Wallace now agreed that a replacement should be sought. At the end of April 1896, Chirol returned to London and Printing House Square. A new tenant would have to be found for *The Times*'s Berlin office at 66 Dorotheenstrasse.

What was the true significance for Anglo-German relations of the events precipitated by Jameson's foolish and ill-fated escapade? At the time it had seemed to offer German diplomacy a tantalising variety of attractive possibilities, but the Kaiser probably entertained only two considerations when he contemplated sending his telegram to Kruger. First, he thought that he had been presented with an ideal opportunity to humble England; the perfect retort to the insulting behaviour of Salisbury and the British press in the previous year. Second, it seemed to afford an excellent chance to stimulate a climate of German opinion that would not only justify but applaud a claim for increased spending on the imperial navy. William's thinking was dominated by the fortunes of his nascent navy. For example, his considered reaction to Malet's indiscreet threat in October had been to insist, 'We must make all the capital we can out of this business perhaps for a demand for an increase of the Navy.'[30] Thus it was no accident that when William drafted his telegram to Kruger, among those advisers present were the Head of the Imperial Naval Office, von Hollmann, the Chief of the Imperial Naval Cabinet, von Senden, and the Imperial Navy's Commander-in-Chief, von Knorr.

The intentions of Marschall and Holstein had been somewhat different. Chirol correctly guessed their purpose in a telegram to *The Times* as 'a bid for popularity at home ... and ... a warning to England that she could only find salvation in closer contact with Germany and her allies'.[31] Within a week of the publication of the Kruger telegram, Holstein had to admit that the best Germany could now expect would be 'a small diplomatic success' and to teach England 'a small political lesson', modest and modified aims that were to be disappointed.[32] Not only did Germany utterly fail to halt British 'absorption' of the Transvaal, but the stratagem designed to push Britain into the orbit of the Triple Alliance achieved the opposite effect. Though the Germans never seriously intended to threaten the integrity of the British Empire this was precisely how their nicely calculated scheme was interpreted by the British public.

Wilfrid Blunt, as might be expected of a determined anti-imperialist, described the reports and comment in the British press on the Jameson Raid and the Kruger telegram as 'a mixture of swagger and poltroonery'. First the newspapers had reflected, then exacerbated the passions of their readers. Now even the meanest Cockney ragamuffin affected as much imperial hauteur as any choleric colonel from Cheltenham or mindless patriotic firebrand from a Pall Mall club. 'England was greatly angered', Blunt reflected, because the country was 'infected by the gangrene of colonial rowdyism', a judgment endorsed by Hatzfeldt in a letter to Holstein.

> It is not a question of annoyance on the part of the Government, but of a deep-seated bitterness of feeling among the public, which has shown itself in every way. ... The suggestion that we could make real trouble for England in other parts of the world counted for absolutely nothing amongst the ignorant masses of the people. England's alleged isolation made no impression. They boasted proudly of it and felt that England was strong enough to defy all her enemies.[33]

What Hatzfeldt described was not the kind of public opinion which democratic theorists so fondly talk of as the best guide for political action, but the visceral prejudices of a mob whose passions had been enraged. It was this unreasoning, universal prejudice that so impressed Moberly Bell; that '*all* classes' had joined in the 'hisses for "Bumptious Bill of Berlin".'[34] If this was how the manager of *The Times* felt, did it really signify that Wallace was judiciously toning down some of Chirol's more inflammatory observations? Wallace might have worried about 'balance' in *The Times*'s presentation of news and opinion, but in this instance the same fine concern was not evinced by the newspaper's editor or manager. Just as impetuously as the rest of the British press and with an evident enthusiasm, *The Times* lifted its ancient petticoats and partnered public prejudice in the wildest of tarantellas, demonstrating along with its more popular contemporaries an eager willingness to engage in verbal abuse, to manipulate stereotypes and substitute emotional rant for rational discussion.[35] There was, therefore, more than some justification for the Kaiser's plaint that he was 'disappointed and indignant at the deplorably misinformed and disgraceful attacks of the Times which hitherto he had understood to be conducted by men of repute and responsibility'.[36]

For all Salisbury's apparent imperturbability, the British government was not entirely immune to the general atmosphere of hysteria. The queen, with a strange slip of the pen, demanded that her Prime Minister should 'pour oil on the flames', to which Salisbury replied he 'strongly discouraged violent language and precipitate action'. Yet, at the behest of Goschen and Chamberlain, he had agreed to establish a 'flying squadron' of ships for any emergency. When the queen learned of this from a report in *The Times*, she addressed a thunderous interrogatory to Salisbury. Why had she not been told of the squadron earlier? The premier could only weakly reply that the 'emissaries of the press were swarming all over the public offices and it is very difficult to keep anything from them'.[37] When it suited his purpose, Salisbury was fond of suggesting how inordinately difficult it was to conduct foreign affairs in a democracy where public opinion had to be taken into account. Baron Eckardstein reported that Salisbury had suggested 'no government in England could have withstood the pressure of public opinion, and if it had come to war between us then a general European war must have developed'.[38] Eckardstein was never a reliable witness. If Salisbury did speak to him in those precise terms it was prompted more by the premier's sense of the absurd than reality. When the mood suited, which was often, Salisbury ignored everyone and everything and pursued his own course with a fine patrician disdain.

Salisbury's friend, Alfred Austin, had played his part in the drama. On 11 January, *The Times*, together with a supporting editorial had published the Poet Laureate's first official verses, 'Jameson's Ride'. The queen was not amused, considering Austin's spirited doggerel a 'regrettable blunder'. Salisbury was embarrassed by his nominee's verses. Liberal newspapers, like the *Daily News*, were scornful, but the audience at the Alhambra Music Hall cheered the words to the echo before joining in a spontaneous rendition of the national anthem. Sanderson wearily expressed the frustration felt by the Foreign Office at Austin's most recent incursion into their concerns. 'I wish', he told Lascelles, 'the Poet Laureate would put his head into his butt of sherry or whatever the Laureate's wine is. . . . And if he must write verses, why doesn't he write better ones?'[39] This was not to be the last occasion when *The Times* would give its editorial support to poetic effusions that caused a mixture of embarrassment and weary resignation in Whitehall and Westminster and apoplexy in Berlin.

The Times was only one, though an important voice among many that chose to sing in raucous harmony the same imperial paean: damn the foreigner and the consequences. But had a contrary spirit existed at Printing House Square, it would have been very difficult to withstand the pressure of metropolitan public opinion.[40] That *The Times* had demonstrated an ability to bluster with the worst was not so important, for the circumstances surrounding the Kaiser's telegram to Kruger had been exceptional. In the long term, much more significant was the way that Chirol harboured his sense of personal grievance against the Germans. This was to colour his appreciation of Germany's intentions towards England and was particularly important when he succeeded Wallace as head of *The Times*'s foreign department. It made him more sympathetic than he might otherwise have been to the approach of his eventual successor as Berlin correspondent, George Saunders. When Saunders would quote from anti-British articles in the German press rather than from official

Wilhelmstrasse communiqués, and argue that he did so because they better reflected Germany's true intent, Chirol understood and agreed. Had he not suffered an intolerable slight; had not his good faith been betrayed by the disjunction between official and press expressions of opinion in Germany? Chirol knew from harsh personal experience that the Germans were not to be trusted. It was as well that everyone should understand that their 'kicks in the street' were a more sincere token of their regard and intent than any 'kisses in the cupboard'.[41]

The new tenant at 66 Dorotheenstrasse

We too have our feelings. . . . Imagine the cumulative effect produced by the steady stream of insult and abuse which has poured in for the last two years. . . . Nothing of the kind comes to us from other countries, but only from Germany. Consider the atmosphere of resentment which this creates, and how enormously it adds to the difficulty of those who want to prevent at least any widening of the breach. . . . I cannot altogether acquit your official world of some responsibility for it. I have been too long in Berlin not to be aware of the splendid machinery the German Government disposes of for guiding and instructing the Press, especially as to foreign affairs.

Chirol to Holstein

A not unimportant obstacle to the improvement of Anglo-German feelings is the present 'Times' correspondent, Saunders. Twice or three times a week he collects bitter criticisms of England and sends them to London . . . and the 'Times' writes sour leading articles, which are answered from here in the same tone. It may go on for a long time like this if Saunders remains here.

Bülow to Hatzfeldt

Chirol recommended George Saunders, Berlin correspondent of the *Morning Post*, as his replacement, and this was agreed at Printing House Square. As Saunders could not be released from his contract with his employers until January 1897, a temporary appointment had to be made. Henry Wickham Steed, then aged 25, was offered and accepted this posting. Able, determined and very ambitious, Steed had an intimate knowledge of Germany, having spent his final year of university studies at Jena. When he returned to Germany in May 1896, he discovered the general atmosphere much changed from his student days. German liberalism was in its death throes crushed between the forces of social democracy and nationalist militarism. Steed became 'profoundly convinced that nothing save a complete change in German methods and tendencies or a complete abdication by England of her place in the world could, in the long run, prevent an Anglo-German conflict'.

Though his appointment was for eight months only, Steed very quickly established himself as a perceptive commentator on the Berlin scene. His tenancy of The Times's Berlin office in Dorotheenstrasse was notable for the substantial 'scoop' of identifying Bismarck as the author of a newspaper article that revealed the 'Reinsurance' Treaty with Russia had been signed behind the backs of Germany's Triple Alliance partners. Steed also discovered that Caprivi had refused to renew the 'Reinsurance' Treaty. The last months of Steed's tenancy coincided with the scandalous Leckert von Lutzow libel case that discredited not only the German secret police, but also the Kaiser, his Court and the Foreign Office. It was as a direct consequence of the trial that Marschall was effectively banished to the Constantinople embassy and his position as Foreign Secretary fell to Prince Bülow. The tensions in Berlin did not make life easy for a correspondent, but Steed managed to maintain correct relations with German officials. It was the mutual desire of Printing House Square and the Wilhelmstrasse that the fences broken in Chirol's last months in Berlin should be mended. On a visit to Steed, Moberly Bell emphasised that on no account was friction to be risked between official Germany and *The Times*. Steed was not unhappy to hand over his difficult charge to Saunders. He later wrote: 'The thought of leaving to another the uncongenial task of recording German manifestations of ill-will towards my own country was not displeasing.'[1]

Though almost the same age as Chirol when he had been appointed *The Times*'s Berlin correspondent, George Saunders was strikingly different in appearance, manner and temperament. Tall and handsome, his broad features were dominated by piercing blue eyes and a magnificent handle-bar moustache. From his education at Balliol and at Glasgow, Bonn and Göttingen universities he retained a life-long passion for the classics. From his father, editor of the *Christian Democrat*, he inherited a zealous attachment to Christian tenets and pride in his profession. He had been appointed Berlin correspondent of the *Morning Post* in 1888, before which he had served a valuable if unconventional apprenticeship under the remarkable and erratic W. T. Stead. Saunders's marriage in 1893 to Gertrude Hainauer, daughter of a prominent Jewish Berlin banker and art collector, gave him familiar and privileged access to all save the highest ranks of Berlin society. Among his well-placed and well-informed contacts at the Wilhelmstrasse was Friedrich von Holstein. A student of German history, folklore and custom, Saunders was, in J. L. Garvin's admittedly biased judgment, 'a singularly acute and well-informed student of German politics'.[2] Saunders's writing was characterised by a vital mixture of missionary zeal and native canniness. At first his natural caution deceived the German government into supposing that if he could not be frightened then he might be flattered into compliance with its wishes. Saunders, who never arrived at any opinion lightly, would then hold to it tenaciously and propagate it with a relentless will. Despite his German wife and two decades' residence in Berlin, he remained a foreigner who advertised his distaste for 'the city of the plain'. He emphasised a fierce pride in his patrimony by enunciating his fluent German in an excruciating Scots accent and exercised in the winter, to the vast amusement of Berliners, by playing at curling.

Nowhere was his disenchantment with Germany, and particularly the Kaiser, more apparent than in his frequent letters to his father. He spoke often of Germany 'bristling with an ominous energy' while an irresponsible political leadership committed to expansion wasted the country's ample resources upon schemes of imperial *folie de grandeur*.

> I don't think that the basis of Germany is sound. It is the desire for material well being, corn and wine. That is *not* the case with us. . . . We shall still outlast the German Empire, I am sure, but we shall have to fight one day. . . . The policy of the German Emperor is to take in hand all the bankrupt states – China, the Sultan, Spain – and to work them *cheap* for his own advantage. He will burn his fingers someday.[3]

Careful always to distinguish between the German people and their government, Saunders's judgment of the latter was damning. 'Germany is a parvenu power with a parvenu's faults – stilted, affected, envious, sensitive, ambitious, discontented, ill-mannered, self-conscious.' The German Empire was 'a fraud against civilized humanity'.[4] In a book that he wrote shortly after the outbreak of the Great War, Saunders stated that 'his view was formed in all essentials about the time of Count Caprivi's fall in 1894 . . . and confirmed during long residence in Berlin'.[5] It remained his fundamental belief that Germany's imperial ambitions and British interests were totally incompatible. Therefore he considered that it was his 'imperative duty . . . to expose certain German ambitions', to alert Britons to the implications for them of *Weltmachtpolitik* and the *Neue Kurs*.[6] Purposely choosing a military metaphor he described himself as 'a soldier of the ranks . . . a scout who has got through enemy lines with the result of his observations'.[7]

Allowing for the heightened emotions engendered by the outbreak of war with Germany, a letter Saunders wrote to his sister in August 1914 clearly indicates his sense of personal involvement and the single-minded commitment with which he invested his pre-war journalism. 'I began my little campaign . . . close upon twenty years ago, before I left the "Morning Post", and I should never for a day or a week have desisted from it if the management of those papers had allowed me.' His censures of the Kaiser were almost paranoid in their intensity. 'I have hated him with all my soul ever since I saw into the monstrosity of his soul and mind more than twenty years ago. It is he, he, he who is the villain of this whole business.' In particular, it was the Kaiser's telegram to Kruger that had convinced Saunders of William's nefarious designs. He was to describe it as 'the greatest mistake of William II's reign . . . for he had awakened in England suspicions which were never to be wholly eradicated'.[8] In a contemporary despatch to the *Morning Post* he had claimed that it would 'never be forgotten by the nation which will always bear it in mind in the future orientation of its policy'.[9]

The traditions of the *Morning Post* were High Tory and patrician, self-consciously English and imperial.[10] Affairs in Africa most frequently stirred its editorial writers to ardent jingo declarations. In 1896 its chief leader writer on imperial and military affairs, Henry Spenser Wilkinson, was particularly concerned that no one in the government had thought through the relationship between policy and naval and military preparation. His influence is clear in the *Post*'s editorial injunction that the government should respond to the Kaiser's 'piece of gratuitous mischief' not merely with a flying squadron but by recalling the Mediterranean fleet to join with the Channel fleet. Saunders did not share Wilkinson's informed concern about the strategic implications of foreign policy decisions, but his messages from Berlin were pitched to harmonise with the shrill tone of Wilkinson's leaders. 'For England's honour, England, peace-loving, commercial England, will fight. . . . Every Englishman and every English woman breathes freely. We are ourselves again.' Saunders wittingly heaped coals on the *Morning Post*'s fires of passionate polemic. 'Be prepared not only for violent or subtle acts of aggression, but for hostile manoeuvres and the tortuous methods of the new German diplomacy which may have many surprises in store for us.'[11] As Saunders served out his period of notice with the *Morning Post*, it could not have escaped the attention of his future employers that his reports from Berlin displayed an overt hostility to the German government's policies.

It happened that immediately before Saunders took over the Berlin office, *The Times* published a series of fiery articles condemning the German press. At the Foreign Office, Sanderson noted wryly that 'after taking a little space for hesitation and reflection', the newspaper had 'gone off with an explosion like a fifty ton gun'. The Germans were not likely to ignore such an outburst. 'We shall, I expect, see some choice expressions,' he told Lascelles. Sanderson had little faith in *The Times*'s ability either to understand or correctly interpret any hints from the Foreign Office about the best way to conduct itself. 'I remember one occasion on which Lord Granville saw Buckle, gave him some information and suggested an article. He went away under what inspiration I know not and wrote an article in the exactly contrary sense throwing contumely upon the Government and all its works.'[12]

Whatever the reservations of the British Foreign Office, the Wilhelmstrasse wanted to enjoy better relations with *The Times*'s Berlin correspondent. Holstein made this very clear in a two-hour discussion with Saunders in February 1897. The newspaper was also determined that its new Berlin correspondent should not be prejudiced by previous events and therefore was equally anxious that relations henceforth should be as smooth as possible. Statements were solicited from the Wilhelmstrasse on points of possible discord and Saunders was instructed to avoid official ostracism by not criticising the Kaiser. This left Saunders a carefully circumscribed area within which to exercise his discretion. However, by analysing the German press Saunders could claim he was sticking to the letter of his instructions and yet keep his readers informed of the true sentiments of the most active and politically effective sections of German opinion. He supplemented this information with long, detailed letters to Wallace and Chirol which invariably were also read by Moberly Bell.

In their February conversation, Holstein had talked not only about press and government relations but had enlarged upon the general diplomatic scene, claiming that Germany had no reason for concern about Egypt. Should England, to further her schemes there, make friendly overtures to France, 'the result would be that Russia would only want *us* more than ever'.[13] This confirmed Saunders's view that Germany was manipulating Anglo-Russian relations to her own advantage. Saunders, unlike Chirol, was not particularly concerned about any Russian threat. He had long believed it was Germany's purpose 'to keep England at loggerheads with Russia and to keep Russia busy in Asia. . . . The Germans succeed in this as the Russians have no great confidence in us or we in them.'[14] Saunders thought the solution was obvious, and Wallace agreed. 'As the Germans hate us like poison an accommodation with Russia is the sensible thing to aim for.' It ought to be 'easily obtainable . . . either now or in the future'.[15]

Holstein had seemed particularly preoccupied with the Kaiser's demands for more money for his navy. William wanted not only more and bigger ships, he wanted them built more quickly. The previous month he had talked quite casually of ' "several" hundred million in additional appropriations for the navy'. Holstein dreaded the prospect of the damage such demands might have on Germany's domestic politics. There might even be a *coup d'état* and the Kaiser compelled to yield.[16] Saunders could say nothing openly about this in *The Times* for Bell had obliged him to keep his sharpest comments on the Kaiser to his private correspondence. Saunders now warned Bell, 'The Emperor, like many emotional people, often consciously or unconsciously manifests emotion in order to awaken it in others, with the ulterior object of smoothing the way for some policy which he wishes to initiate.' Far from endangering his position, the Kaiser's big navy programme would strengthen it. Effectively William was challenging his people. 'Are you prepared to stand up to England on equal terms? If so, you must pay for the big fleet.' Germany had the skills and the resources to support such a programme. Saunders had earlier argued persuasively in a letter to Wallace that if the Germans were not offered the prospect of a *Weltmachtpolitik*, then they would employ their energies 'to propose reforms, criticise the situation and assail the privileges of the Army and other classes'. He had concluded with the warning that 'England must reckon with these things', and the injunction that she should 'answer German naval expansion with energy and speed'.[17] A similar but even more explicit statement about Germany's ambitions Saunders addressed to his father in the early days of the Boer War. 'England is the next big nut the Germans want to crack. They are building many ships, and they build and man them just as well as we do. In twenty five years they will be a first rate naval power. . . . The best we can do is to be "strong".'[18]

Though *The Times* was disposed to refrain from any unnecessary criticism of Germany's policy in general and of the Kaiser in particular, similar restraint was not shown by much of the patriotic English press. 'Your people do not realise how monarchs are looked upon on the continent,' the Kaiser had snapped at Grierson, the British military attaché. William had been much put out by a cartoon in *Punch* representing him as the Emperor of China. 'While these personal attacks are made upon me you cannot expect the German press to remain quiet.'[19] The Kaiser would frequently expatiate on this theme to British embassy staff. A fortnight later it was the Ambassador's turn to be harangued. Had he not done everything in his power to create better relations between their two countries since he came to the throne? What had been the result? 'On the last occasion of his visiting England he had been assailed by the press directly and personally, and since then the personal attacks against him had so much increased and become so violent that it had become impossible for him to return to England. He had therefore been compelled to change his tactics and do his best to further German interests alone.'[20] When Lascelles suggested that the tone of British press had improved, the Kaiser grudgingly agreed, but insisted that this was because its energies were presently engaged in promoting hostility against him in America.[21] The Kaiser's morbid fascination with the British press was chronic. When Lascelles insisted that the government could do nothing about it, he was met by the flat rejoinder, 'Grandma did it.'[22]

When Chirol succeeded Wallace as head of *The Times*'s foreign department, this did not lead, as might have been expected, to a sharpening of critical editorial comment against Germany. Although Chirol remained suspicious about German intentions he was more immediately concerned with fears of possible Russian aggression in the Middle and Far East. To Chirol it seemed that Britain needed an international friend, or at the least, the willing compliance of another Great Power. France for the moment was useless. She had revealed her moral bankruptcy by the disgraceful Dreyfus case, while the Fashoda crisis had demonstrated beyond any doubt that France's military and naval strength did not, for the present, constitute an effective counter in the diplomatic game. In Anatolia, therefore, Chirol suggested it might pay Britain to support Germany in seeking concessions. 'Better Germany should step in if we stand out, rather than Russia or France,' he argued. Saunders was not persuaded. 'The less we have to do with [Germany] the better. . . . We shall soon enough have to come to close quarters. . . . I feel that, as I feel the change of weather in my bones.'[23] What Saunders wanted was an alliance with Russia – a bold, even premature move. But, as he wrote to his father:

> We make a great mistake in supporting Germany against Russia. We ought to make friends with Russia. Our patronage of the German Baghdad Railway scheme is a mistake. If once we let Germany into Persia she will conspire with Russia against us and with us against Russia and will exact a heavy commission from both Powers. Hatred and jealousy of our power are the leading motives of German policy. Other nations feel the same, but Germany is the most dangerous.[24]

The divide between Chirol and Saunders was nowhere more clearly reflected than in their very different appreciation of Germany's naval ambitions. In a leader published in the middle of the month that elapsed between the outbreak of the Boer War on 12 October 1899, and the signing of the Anglo-German agreement over Samoa on 14 November, Chirol suggested the rationale of Germany's Naval Bill was that 'the German Empire has a great and growing commerce, and large colonial interests, which, though not yet very prosperous or progressive, claim protection from a State of the first order'.[25] To Saunders it seemed as though Chirol was anxious to demonstrate the same gullibility as the British government had shown at the time of the Kruger telegram and now he was swallowing wholesale German official assertions of good will. How could Chirol doubt Germany's true purpose when it was manifest in the vicious attacks on England printed every day by the semi-official press? To dismiss these as mere newspaper vapourings was absurd. No less well informed a commentator than Count Posadowsky, the recently appointed nominee of the Kaiser as Deputy Chancellor and State Secretary of the Reich Ministry of the Interior, had 'very emphatically admitted' to Saunders, 'the *influence* of the German press in Germany was *"enormous"*. "People", he said, "are too busy or too lazy to seek impartial information so they read the Lokal Anzeiger and *believe what they read."* He admitted the conduct of the German press towards England just now . . . was scandalous.' Naturally, Posadowsky had repeated the usual solemn assurance that the ravings of the press were strongly disapproved of in official quarters, but Saunders dismissed that all too familiar and patent disclaimer.

> My theory [he told Chirol] is that, to take the most charitable view, the Government at least tolerates the attacks upon England in order to get wind for the sails of the New Navy Bill. It is true that the Berliner Neuste Nachrichten protested the other day against a violent article in the Munich Allgemeine, which had urged an increase in the Navy as directed against England. But the ground of protest was that England would be moved by these attacks to take her own precautions.[26]

Saunders had not been pleased to have to read leaders in *The Times* that spoke of friendship with Germany.[27] For the moment, Bell, Chirol and Buckle were determined that together they should encourage a better understanding between the two Powers, but this did not prevent them from publishing Saunders's Berlin despatches which demonstrated the opposite temper.

In the three key months from October to December 1899, *The Times* published fifty-four despatches from Berlin, more than three times as many as in any other British newspaper.[28] As Saunders drew heavily upon material in the German press which was available to all journalists, this at least suggests that he discovered more than the other Berlin correspondents considered worth bringing to the attention of their readers. In *The Times*'s news columns, Germany was accorded more space than Russia and France combined, a ratio that was reversed in papers like the *Standard* and the *Morning Post*. Neither of these newspapers was ever pro-German, yet they gave space to pro-British comment in the German press which Saunders either excluded or made appear insignificant. Saunders's despatches had not gone unnoticed and Bülow recognised him as 'a not unimportant obstacle to the improvement of Anglo-German feeling'. Bülow strangely supposed that Saunders's 'bitter criticisms' were inspired solely by an enmity for Chamberlain. He therefore instructed Hatzfeldt to tell Chamberlain this 'in as undiluted a form as possible'.[29]

It was while he was accompanying the Kaiser on a visit to England in November that Bülow reported how he had pointed out to Balfour that

> Saunders . . . was amusing himself by collecting every attack on England from the most obscure German papers and laying them before the British public each morning. This tendencious method of reporting made it very difficult for us to keep up good relations with England which were

desired on many sides. Mr Balfour is ready to try whether it is not possible to effect a change in the representation of 'The Times' in Berlin.[30]

Balfour, whenever his uncle Salisbury was indisposed, took over for him at the Foreign Office. He had generously supported Chamberlain when the Colonial Secretary had impulsively made a bid for Anglo-German-American friendship in a speech at Birmingham in May 1898. Salisbury, who was less than fond of the Kaiser, deeply distrusted 'amateur diplomats' whether of the German imperial or Birmingham demagogue variety. Balfour, however, shared Chamberlain's desire for a rapprochement with Germany. When the Kaiser came to England in November 1899, Balfour once more substituted for the British Prime Minister then still mourning the recent death of his wife. Balfour supposed that the Kaiser demonstrated on this visit a 'wholesome' state of mind. Chamberlain was even more impressed. Two conversations were sufficient to confirm for him 'the Emperor's extraordinary grasp of questions of European politics'.[31] Excited and encouraged, to a great public meeting at Leicester on 30 November, Chamberlain advocated an alliance with Germany as 'most natural', an over-hasty action that caused much embarrassment to his Cabinet colleagues and to the Foreign Office. Saunders retailed to Chirol a conversation between Lascelles and Balfour on the subject of this initiative.

> Sir F told Balfour the misfortune was that Chamberlain had blurted out the very thing the Germans longed for and they would chuckle over it. Balfour seemed surprised to hear that the Germans would be pleased, but observed, 'It is extraordinary. In private Chamberlain is so tactful and so prudent. But very often when he gets on his feet either in the House or elsewhere, he seems to have left all his tact at home.' Several other Ministers spoke in the same way.

Saunders concluded his letter to Chirol with a warning. 'If the German Government thinks that Joe is to emerge as a kind of dictator, it will hasten to press its "alliance" upon us and so bind us hand and foot for the next five or six years. Imagine Joe as Prime Minister controlling foreign policy. *Quod Di avertant omen!*'[32]

Saunders thought Chamberlain was a dangerous amateur in the field of foreign affairs. Nor did he have a good opinion of Balfour's skills as a diplomat. For the Germans to suppose, however, that either minister might in some way effect Saunders's dismissal from Berlin, as Bülow had hinted, was absurd. Several years later, in a letter to Charles Hardinge, Chirol referred to the second occasion when attempts were made to remove Saunders.

> Arthur Walter happened to meet Lascelles in England and mentioned the matter to him. Sir Frank told him he need have no anxiety on that score, to which AW replied that it was no matter of anxiety to him, but it might perhaps be as well for the German Government to realise that if Saunders were expelled there would never again be a Times' Correspondent in Berlin and German affairs would be dealt with in London. Lascelles remarked that they would in that case probably not be dealt with in a very friendly spirit. AW said that that was altogether another question. The

policy of the paper was governed by considerations of public interest. The expulsion of the Times' correspondent would not necessarily affect these considerations: it was a matter which affected the dignity of the Times and would have to be regarded as an entirely separate issue.[33]

The Kaiser and his ministers retained an unshakeable conviction that the British government could, if it wished, directly influence the British press. No matter how frequently Lascelles sought to disabuse them of this notion and asserted the press enjoyed 'perfect freedom and entire independence of any sort of government control or even influence',[34] it seemed to make no difference. Salisbury had often enough muttered deprecatingly, 'the vagaries of newspapers are entirely beyond my control', and informed Hatzfeldt that his time was sufficiently engaged in 'reckoning with the changing opinions and impression of the multitude and humouring the differences of view in his own Cabinet'. Yet, in a moment of weakness, he once sought to humour the Kaisser's *idée fixe* by telegraphing to Lascelles, 'Since the Emperor seems to attach great weight to our influencing the attitude of the Press ... I will communicate with Sir Donald Mackenzie Wallace ... with whom I have a slight personal acquaintance.' There is no evidence that Salisbury did speak to Wallace. In a letter to Lascelles in March 1900, Sanderson summed up the position. 'The Times is not really friendly to Lord Salisbury or to this government. Mackenzie Wallace was on the whole so and, I believe, was a good deal annoyed when The Times attacked Lord Salisbury ... Chirol is much less so.'[35]

Relations between *The Times* and the Foreign Office were close.[36] This did not imply, however, that any ministerial fiat operated in Printing House Square, or that *The Times*'s representatives necessarily abandoned their own views at the government's behest. Sanderson, as he was the member of the Foreign Office permanent staff who most frequently met and talked with Chirol, was well placed to describe the foreign editor's independent attitude.

> Chirol said to me one day that he would avoid something ... because he thought it might prejudice the interests of the country, but whether it was or was not for the advantage of the Government was a matter of indifference as he was not particularly anxious to support them. He comes to see me as an old friend and can be trusted not to publish anything you tell him in confidence – but I know he is always looking out for anything which he considers weak or even conciliatory – and is prepared to have his knife into us immediately. As to Buckle and Moberly Bell, I believe them to be much worse. ... Lord Salisbury ... every now and then warns me when I tell him of a conversation with Chirol, 'Remember you are talking to a critic and not a supporter.'[37]

Chirol's constant anxiety was that the Germans should think that the government exercised any authority over what was said or who should say it in *The Times*. In May 1902, he wrote to Sanderson: 'I would venture to suggest that in your interest as in ours, it would be desirable that Lascelles should convey to the German FO in some shape or other that HMG are *unable to exercise any influence over the action of the Times in this or in any other matter.* I am sure that you will understand my meaning.'[38] Chirol was well enough informed of what went on in other departments of *The Times* to have had his tongue firmly in his cheek when making so sweeping a disclaimer.[39] But as far as foreign affairs were concerned, while maintaining close relations with the Foreign Office, *The Times*, never allowed that intimacy to become the arbiter of editorial comment. Nor did the paper ever strive for a monolithic presentation of news and opinion. Different emphases were on occasion deliberately reflected in editorials and the reports of correspondents.[40]

The *Bundesrath* incident conveniently illustrates the relationship between the British Foreign Office and Printing House Square at this time. Acting upon what proved to be false information, a German mail steamer, the *Bundesrath*, was detained by the Royal Navy and brought before a prize court at Durban. A similar incident also occurred at Aden. The British, as they were at war with the Boers, considered themselves entitled under international law to stop and search neutral shipping they suspected of carrying aid to the enemy. Bülow's notes on the subject were less than diplomatic, but the Germans were anxious not to cause a major incident. The crisis seemed to have passed, especially when the Kaiser made friendly noises about England as a consequence of some flattering remarks made about him by the Prince of Wales. This touching scene of international and family amity was rudely shattered by *The Times*. Two letters from Sanderson to Lascelles tell their own story.[41]

> It is unfortunate that just at the moment when the Emperor has shown himself particularly friendly, the Times should have gone off with a loud explosion. . . . I need not say that they never consult us before they go off into one of these tantrums. Nor, if they did so, do I think there would be any chance of their taking our advice. . . . I confess I thought the Times had blown off all its steam on the subject some time ago. Yet there is always a supply of hot water on the hob at Printing House Square.

> Chirol came to see me on Thursday last and said he heard that I disapproved of the Times article the day before on Germany and he had 'come to have his head washed'. I said that was amiable of him, and I must confess I thought it singularly inopportune to have gone off with a fresh bang. . . . Though I produced no penitence, I think he is likely to be quieter, and with the exception of calling the German answer to Kruger 'Pecksniffian', and a patronising article . . . the Times has gone tossing and goring elsewhere.[42]

When Bülow made a threatening speech in the Reichstag about the *Bundesrath* which Chirol thought unnecessary, he said as much in a sharply critical leader. Then, from de Blowitz in Paris, came disturbing news of secret negotiations between France, Germany and Russia seeking to take advantage of Britain's difficulties in South Africa. When Monson, the British Ambassador at Paris, passed on the information to Salisbury it was ignored. De Blowitz, so it was thought, had been the victim of a hoax. But Chirol had the same story confirmed from another source. Reluctantly he admitted, 'There is no longer any room to doubt the profound hostility and duplicity of Germany. She will not commit herself openly against us, but in every direction she is doing her best to obstruct and thwart us.'[43] The divide between Chirol and Saunders occasioned by their very different apprehensions concerning Russia was now temporarily healed. In a letter which must have given Saunders much satisfaction, Chirol admitted that 'we should not allow [France and Russia] to be wire-pulled from Berlin'.[44]

Despite his difference with Chirol, Saunders had never for a moment weakened in his resolve 'to expose certain German ambitions', and, as he told his father, 'Above all to disillusion people like Chamberlain. His Leicester speech showed that my persistent warnings were not superfluous.'[45] The Germans had several times tried to gag Saunders, first by getting at Chirol through von Eckardstein, and when that failed, by employing the more than willing Rothschild. The Kaiser had played his part as usual, firing off a telegram to Lascelles when particularly incensed by a report in *The Times*. The British government should stamp on their press. 'Disaster may come out of it if this is not stopped.' The 'unmitigated noodles' (as the Kaiser had recently referred to the English Cabinet) could do nothing, and said as much in the usual diplomatic language.[46]

Chirol in London was more or less immune to German attacks. Saunders, however, was obliged to suffer a stream of obloquy in the German press, particularly after a contribution of his that surveyed the year's foreign policy. Almost with a triumphal note he wrote to his father, 'They were not pleased with my four columns here and attacked me by name in the press saying that I wish to sow discord between England and Germany.' Though the Wilhelmstrasse showed him an 'alarming civility', Saunders continued to concentrate his attention upon the German press as the true measure of Germany's feelings and intentions. As he explained, 'The German newspapers occupy a quite different position from ours. There are few public speeches such as our politicians deliver and when the Government wants to influence public opinion it does so through the press. Consequently, one must be always on the watch for indications of the drift of Government opinion on the popular opinion that influences it.'[47] Had it been needed, Spring Rice had provided Chirol with an independent confirmation of the virulence of the German press. The Germans were pursuing 'a systematic campaign of slander which sometimes goes into winter quarters, but never makes peace.... The public press of Germany ... is an engine of concentrated and studied malignity which makes one long to give the answer which it deserves. To go to war for newspaper articles! It sounds absurd; and yet that is what almost every English resident in Germany must be inclined to wish.'[48] In personal letters, Bell and Chirol acknowledged Saunders's difficulties and the debt that *The Times* owed its correspondent for his courage in working 'under circumstances of peculiar difficulty' in order 'to place before the British public facts with which it was of the highest importance it should be made acquainted'.[49] Chirol wrote to the British Ambassador in Berlin:

To my mind [Saunders] deserves very great credit for the fearlessness and ability with which he has exposed – and always in a studiously temperate form – the true inwardness of German feeling towards this country. It would be easy for him – and of course in every way much pleasanter – to allow our readers to remain in a fool's paradise with regard to Germany's attitude. I can quite understand that Bülow would like to see him removed, for the excellent work he has done for us has attracted much attention over here and with results, I trust, by no means palatable to the Germans. So long as I have any influence with the Times Bülow will have to put up with the 'calamity' of his presence in Berlin. To sacrifice him would be not only a gross injustice but a gross blunder.[50]

If anything, the international scene grew more menacing. A German expedition was despatched to China to seek retribution for the murder by the Boxers of the German minister at Peking, Baron von Ketteler. Matching his rhetoric to the moment, the Kaiser addressed his troops at Bremerhaven. 'Just as the Huns . . . created for themselves a name which men still respect, you should give the name of German such cause to be remembered in China for a thousand years that no Chinaman, no matter whether his eyes be slit or not, will dare to look a German in the face. . . . Open the road for culture once and for all.'[51] The Kaiser was to have cause to regret that speech perhaps more than any other. Constitutionally incapable of stopping himself from either saying or writing the first thing that came into his head, William marked his career with a series of oratorical and epistolatory embarrassments.

On 1 September 1900, Britain annexed the Transvaal. Within two weeks Parliament was dissolved and a general election called, ostensibly to provide a mandate for the annexation. In a long letter to L. S. Amery, temporarily in charge of *The Times*'s foreign department, Saunders commented upon recent events and German hopes concerning the general election.

> The Emperor's speeches, if they sometimes embarrass the Foreign Office are also skilfully turned to account on occasion. Do you remember that Bacon in his essay on 'Negotiating' recommends the employment of 'Frorward and Absurd men for business that doth not well bear out itself'. The 'froward and absurd' Emperor . . . makes proposals that no sensible FO would ever venture upon. . . .
>
> The Germans are very eager to re-establish the old balance they held between England and Russia. They further seem to think that the exigencies of the General Election in England will make Chamberlain, Balfour & Co emphasize our good relations with Germany, as the Englishman always foolishly wants some *fact* which seems tangible to go upon. To assert identity of interests between Germany and England will please the English elector and make him believe that foreign politics are being admirably managed. . . . He is always wanting to hear that we are on terms of the closest friendship with some Power or other – a most vain ambition![52]

His sharp comments on the naivety of the British electorate in foreign affairs was a true measure of Saunders's immediate concern. He had just returned to Berlin after his annual six weeks leave in Scotland where he had conversed with Rosebery, 'fully alive to the necessity of keeping our powder dry'. Saunders feared that British electors could be led astray by the international action in China and 'become enthusiastic over this temporary cooperation with Germany . . . and may acclaim her as our ally for all time'.

> We all talk as if what were important were that *we* should not be isolated. Only think of the danger Germany incurs of being isolated. Dependent as she still is on our naval stations she cannot openly move a finger against us in China without risking that we shut the trap. But she knows that we won't, that we are in a great funk of Russia and that we will allow her to talk big and make the Orientals think that she is a Great Power of the world. It is impudent, but it is clever. When the new German Navy is ready she will speak in a somewhat different tone to us and by that time she will also have increased her vested interests all over the world. We ought to treat her . . . with friendliness and firmness but never commit ourselves in general terms to her big plans.[53]

Saunders's message had remained unchanged for almost four years. He would continue to watch the German government carefully, making certain that his readers were apprised of the Wilhelmstrasse's true intent. But the question remained, who was to keep an eye upon wayward British politicians who, to sate their ambition or flatter their self-esteem, might discount German vindictiveness towards Britain as immaterial? Saunders addressed his doubts to the editor of the *National Review*, L. J. Maxse. He could not have chosen anyone more sensitive or receptive to such fears. Maxse had long been convinced that the British public, like its government, needed to be told repeatedly that Germany was never to be trusted.

Leo Maxse's ABC of better relations with Russia

The *National Review* is poisonous and its editor a palpable and malicious liar.

Kreuz Zeitung

Maxse said I must be a hypocrite because I said friendly things about England.

Count Bernstorff to H. A. Gwynne

Born in November 1864, Leopold James was the second child and younger son of Admiral Augustus Maxse. Educated at Harrow and King's College, Cambridge, he was President of the University Union and gained a second in the historical tripos. After a world tour, Maxse returned to England in 1887 a confirmed and particularly ardent imperialist. When plans to pursue a career at the bar and in politics were frustrated by prolonged illness, for £1500 his father bought the *National Review*, supposing that a little dilettante journalism would not make undue demands upon his son's frail constitution. The *National*, a monthly review of no particular merit, influence or importance, had sunk into premature decrepitude under Alfred Austin's editorship. Leo, as the new proprietor and editor, had considerable ambitions for the future of his new property, and his enormous capacity for hard work, considerable talents as a writer, and the inestimable advantage of easy and familiar access to those with influence and power in the conduct of the nation's affairs soon established both editor and the *National Review* as of some consequence and certainly not to be ignored in the world of political journalism. In 1899 Alfred Milner, then the friend, later the husband of Maxse's sister, Violet, Salisbury's daughter-in-law, suggested that Leo should become editor of the *Cape Times*. Maxse refused this flattering offer because, according to Violet, he had decided 'he must stay in England to warn the people of the German danger'.[1]

In 1915 Maxse published a collection of articles previously published in the *National Review*. Presuming 'to trespass once again on the exemplary and unmurmuring patience' of his regular readers, he thanked them for enduring in the past 'the wearisome iteration and reiteration of the obsessions of a crank'. With a passion and consistency certainly unrivalled by any other British journalist, for almost two decades he had warned of German ambitions and their consequences for the safety of Britain and her empire. He had stated bluntly that if war was to be avoided between 'the two great Saxon Powers', then Britain's military, naval and political leaders needed to make effective preparations. His advice had been ignored. Only Providence 'which protects fools and knaves' had allowed Britain 'to stumble at the twelfth hour into the Triple Entente', so that now the British confronted 'the *Furor Teutonicus*' in the company of 'redoubtable Allies'. He pointed the finger of scorn at three particular 'statesmen' – Haldane, Lloyd George and Esher. How extraordinary were their 'powers of self deception when for many years a war against the barbarous Boches has been staring us and striking us in the face'.[2]

Anything or anyone Maxse opposed, he criticised with an 'unremitting and caustic pen'.[3] Friends applauded the buffets that he bestowed so liberally, treasured his considerable skills as a writer and enjoyed his sardonic wit. Understandably, those Maxse savaged took a different view. Nursing the latest of many wounds, H. W. Massingham, editor of the Radical weekly *Nation*, described Maxse as 'the most egregious gobemouche ever'. Yet even Maxse's victims had to admit his criticism was fine-tuned by an undoubted literary talent. As Asquith tiredly confessed to Loulou Harcourt, the man's style was 'diverting'. Asquith's wife, Margot, admitted that 'she could never be angry with my beloved Admiral Maxse's son, or Violet's brother', even if he did 'get *hundreds* of facts wrong. . . . You always wanted war with Germany and I must say you were *most frank* about it.'[4]

'Episodes of the Month', the *National Review*'s invariable opening, was Maxse's idiosyncratic commentary on domestic and foreign political events. To some it afforded delight and inspiration. In others it prompted contempt or apoplexy. 'I have been reading Episodes of the Month with the usual great interest,' wrote Lord Roberts, 'and I am delighted that you keep on hammering away at the German Peril and the absence of anything like proper Home Defence.'[5] The old warrior's good opinion was to be expected for Maxse was an enthusiastic advocate of national service, not only writing but often speaking on public platforms in that interest.[6] He was also one of that small band of scribes who drafted the notes for Roberts's many speeches and letters to the press.

Never the cause, idea or policy, but the man who best personified it earned Maxse's praise, or, most often, censure. Journalist friends, like Charles Repington, frequently took him to task for this foible:

> Individuals count little. I ask you not to lower yourself to these trivialities and to hold fast to the great principles which have been established by history and cannot be much changed by the personal experiences, likes and dislikes of twentieth century pigmies. If you take the other course you exchange the searchlight for a miserable tallow dip which will serve you not at all save to show you that the road is damnably dark.[7]

Maxse paid no attention. Tweedmouth's appointment as First Lord of the Admiralty was greeted with the assertion that he was 'better fitted to serve as Astronomer Royal'; and when Tweedmouth's nephew, Churchill, went to the same office, Maxse dismissed him out of hand as 'a wind-bag and self-advertising mountebank'. Maxse's sting was so sharp because his opinions of men were often a good deal nearer the truth than the unfortunate victims would care to admit. The Liberal press – Maxse invariably described it as 'radical, flatulent fools forever on the peace path' – was personified by the Quaker Cadburys, 'our cocoa contemporaries who are intent upon throwing the whole of Europe into the arms of Germany'. But no person suffered more from Maxse's attentions than Richard Haldane, Liberal War Minister and later Lord Chancellor: the 'great Haldane humbug', the 'prodigious gas-bag' who 'abandoned the law for seven years in order to play ducks and drakes with the British Army'. Haldane earned Maxse's final accolade of contempt. 'We devoutly wish that he would take up his permanent abode in Germany.'[8]

Ever intent upon 'pursuing my own particular bug-bear', Maxse admitted to his friend Northcliffe, 'there is no place for me in the middle ground'.[9] Garvin, who contributed on an irregular basis to the *National Review*, chided Maxse in the early years. 'I feel strongly we should follow Bismarck's formula about being civil to an opponent "up to the foot of the gallows and hang him all the same". But that is the merest detail.'[10] There was never anything mealy-mouthed about Garvin's approach to journalism, but he did have to take account of profit and loss in a way that never concerned Maxse. When, in 1912, Garvin compared their different approaches to the Anglo-German issue, he wrote in a spirit of understanding, even approval. What makes the letter particularly interesting is that it is a comment on *educating* public opinion by a journalist who was generally recognised by his contemporaries as a supreme exponent of his craft.

> A philosophic tone in discussing these issues is a real help to me in securing more of the wavering margin of mankind. . . . Your situation is different as your readers are mainly those who agree with the strong imperial policy already, whereas I have to build up circulation by means in which persuasion must play its part with directness and force. It was the same on the 'Observer' at first, and then in time, the stronger the medicine was, the more they liked it.[11]

Yet there were those who began as friends, or at least allies, who eventually were alienated because Maxse would insist upon measuring men by whether their opinions happened to coincide with his own. If he agreed with an opinion, he would describe it as 'rational' or 'national' (two adjectives which were as one in his polemical writing). Opinions he did not share attracted, at the best, the epithet 'wobbling', but more usually 'anti-national', 'dangerous nonsense', 'gush', or, 'perilous twaddle'. Valentine Chirol deftly pierced the heart of Maxse's strength and weakness as a commentator on men and events:

> I had hitherto fondly imagined that the earnestness, I might almost say, the fierceness of your political convictions, did not preclude altogether a larger view of the ethics of journalism and of public life generally. I can only assume that a sense of dogmatic infallibility, to which I never attained, in matters political carries with it the same irresistible impulse towards 'comprehensive damnation clauses' of which dogmatic infallibility in matters theological has left us so striking an illustration in the Athanasian creed.[12]

Chirol was upset with Maxse because he had said less than kind things about *The Times* and had been particularly hard on a mutual friend, Thursfield, for his support of Admiral Fisher. Thursfield was no good, and neither was *The Times*, Maxse asserted, for the opinions of both were 'wobbling'.[13] Chirol's observations – made at some considerable length – did not change anything. But why should they have when Maxse so often in the past as in the future earned private plaudits from the Printing House Square fraternity? Lovat Fraser declared that he was prouder of his association with the *National Review*, 'the one absolutely fearless voice in the country today', than with *The Times* which, 'though I can only say so privately, seems to me to be often guilty of moral cowardice'.[14]

There were qualities in Maxse's political thought that he shared with Kipling, another critic loudly and constantly concerned about Germany's aggressive intentions. There was certainly insight but also bigotry. Ideas once formed were petrified in marmoreal permanence. From time to time, most of the British press lapsed from its minatory spirit towards Germany, in the *Daily Mail*'s case going so far as to write a boot licking editorial when the Kaiser visited England during the Boer War – 'A friend in need is a friend indeed.' Maxse, like Kipling, kept the 'real enemy' permanently in his sights. Neither man forgave easily friends who had strayed even momentarily from the path of righteousness. If Germany was to be faced successfully, then England should be always 'bloody, bold and resolute'. Instead, as Kipling observed with disgust to his friend Charles Norton, 'England is still engaged in saving the peace of the world, pretty much as the lady passenger saved the Cunarder – by offering her virtue to the excited man who was about to sink the ship if he didn't get it. . . .'[15]

In his attacks upon Germany in the *National Review*, Maxse's closest associate was Sir Rowland Blennerhassett. The measure of Sir Rowland's 'ripe judgment and abounding wisdom' concerning Germany's evil intentions, Maxse insisted, 'might be gathered from his frequent remark: "I can't give you the precise date when Germany will make war, but I don't see how it can be later than 1915." '[16] Blennerhassett, who had completed his university studies in Munich where he became acquainted with Bismarck, took a particular interest in foreign affairs. He had many close friends in French government circles, travelled frequently in Europe and contributed numerous articles to British and German newspapers and journals on political topics. Towards the end of his life – he died in 1909 – most of his published writing was confined to the *National Review*. His early admiration for Bismarck had 'engendered a faith in the superiority of German to English methods of progress. His early wish that England should learn from Germany metamorphosed into a strong desire that she should prepare herself for the rivalry which the new Germany's ambitions made inevitable.'[17] Maxse 'during the dark days of the Boer War' was delighted to hear from George Saunders, whom he counted as the friend who 'most notably warned me against Germany and educated me in German policy', that articles contributed by Sir Rowland had 'made [the Germans] very wild and there were several attacks upon the "National Review" in the "Post" &c.'[18]

When Joseph Chamberlain, in his Leicester speech, declared his support for the idea of an Anglo-German alliance, even though Chamberlain was a long-standing family friend whom Maxse admired, the editor was quick to make a public rejoinder.

> We do not believe it to be either the desire or in the interests of Great Britain ... to enter into any kind of alliance with Germany.... Allusions to Germany have become frequent and flowery in the utterances of British Ministers, but official German references to England remain just within the bounds of frigid politeness.[19]

By Maxse's usual standards, the tone of the article was restrained. The arguments betray the considerable influence George Saunders's thinking exercised upon him. In July there was an exchange of letters, Maxse seeking Saunders's aid to unravel the 'workings of the semi-official press system' operated by the Wilhelmstrasse. Since the Jameson Raid, the German press had published a constant stream of mendacious attacks on England, 'so scandalous and disgraceful that for the most part', Saunders argued, 'it seemed too absurd for Englishmen to pay attention to them'. Nevertheless 'they altogether corrupted German opinion and the lies were swallowed wholesale in Russia and in Austria'.[20]

Maxse wanted to pin the blame for the anti-British campaign where it really belonged. 'It is quite childish to imagine that persons in the highest authority in Germany are not largely responsible for the hostility to England which is shown throughout the German Empire,' Blennerhassett had written in March 1900. 'We all know how Prince Bismarck managed the Press, and everyone moderately well informed about German matters is perfectly well aware that many newspapers in every part of the Empire are directly or indirectly inspired by the Government.'[21] Chirol shared this opinion, as is clear from his contemporary letters to Lascelles.[22] He did not admit as much to Maxse because he feared his hot and notoriously indiscreet temper. Not that Maxse lacked for allies in the British press. John St Loe Strachey, owner and editor of the *Spectator*, happily joined with Maxse in censuring Chamberlain for making up to Germany. For his pains he received a letter from Chamberlain who, very much upon his dignity, drew attention to his 'second speech at Manchester ... in which I tried clearly to indicate our policy.... We do *not* want ... the Germans to pull chestnuts out of the fire for us – but to cooperate in the protection of joint interests. This policy ... would prevent even Russia from playing false.'[23] The last part of this argument would have appealed particularly to Chirol. The cause of the rift between Chamberlain and his usually faithful press acolytes lay in their different appreciations of the threat posed by Russia. Chamberlain did not trust Russia. Strachey believed, as did Maxse, that English fears of the Russians were played upon by the Germans to their advantage. Chamberlain did not or would not accept this interpretation. Because of his growing dominance in the councils of the Unionist party and Salisbury's obviously diminishing powers and influence, Maxse and Strachey, like George Saunders, feared that a general election might perhaps allow Chamberlain 'to emerge with the allures of a dictator'.[24] There were politicians who shared the concern of these journalists.

Sir Edward Grey, the Liberal Imperialist, when Rosebery's second-in-command at the Foreign Office, had begun an occasional correspondence with Maxse. In a letter of October 1901, he was as blunt about Chamberlain's limitations as he was scathing of the government's handling of its foreign policy. 'Lord Salisbury, who thinks deeply, does so without purpose, and Chamberlain, who is full of purpose, doesn't think deep. They would make a formidable combination but they don't combine, and so we suffer from the defects of both.'[25] This comment had been prompted by Maxse sending to him the first proof of an article he intended to publish pseudonymously. Maxse was by now convinced that Britain could no longer afford a policy of isolation. Rapprochement should be sought, not with Germany and the Triple Alliance, but with France and her ally, Russia. Maxse, though not blind to that nation's weaknesses, had never made any secret of his great and abiding love of France. For the moment a broken reed, France would not always be so. The nation's true spirit was evinced by his close friend, Clemenceau. There would come a time when, with their morale restored, 'the French will bite and our German friends will be astounded by the consequences'.[26] Maxse's view of France was shared by William Lavino, soon to replace de Blowitz as *The Times*'s Paris correspondent. As Maxse told Strachey, 'For a correct view of France you cannot do better than put yourself in the hands of Lavino ... most obliging, helpful and knowledgeable.'[27] Lavino not only supported better Anglo-French relations, he as keenly sponsored an Anglo-Russian agreement.

Maxse's view of Russia was dictated by George Saunders's insistence that Germany was playing the part of 'dishonest broker' between St Petersburg and London. Blennerhassett similarly subscribed to this interpretation of Germany's purpose. 'German incitement of Russia to pick a quarrel with England', he had written in the *National Review* for February 1900, 'has been daily addressed by Berlin to St Petersburg for the best part of a generation. . . . Germany has no ambition to beard the British lion singlehanded. . . . She will play the jackal round the combatants and, ultimately, the hyena when the contest has been decided. That is what Germany calls the policy of *Weltpolitik*.' Blennerhassett contributed considerably to the early drafts of Maxse's proposed article on foreign policy.[28] He wrote to Maxse, 'Please without *any hesitation* use any portion of what I have written exactly as you like. I only want to help the cause.' Though it contradicted what he had written in his March article in the *National Review*, Sir Rowland persuaded Maxse to play down references to the role of the German press in poisoning Anglo-Russian relations. They were, perhaps, 'giving the German Press too much notice'.[29]

When Grey received Maxse's first proof he immediately discerned what would attract criticism. 'They will say that the anti-German bias is too apparent.' Nevertheless, he applauded the point of the exercise: 'to establish confidence and direct relations with Russia and to eliminate in that quarter the German broker who keeps England and Russia apart and levies a constant confusion upon us while preventing us from doing any business with Russia'. This gives a fascinating clue to the thinking of the future Foreign Secretary who, despite much criticism from his Radical backbenchers, in 1907 would successfully negotiate the completion of the entente policy by an Anglo-Russian agreement. His nature being what it was, Grey attached a caveat to his approval. 'This will have to be done quietly and cautiously.'[30] Grey could not seriously have supposed that, of all people, Maxse would accept such advice! Yet the fire-eating Leo did seem, for once, to be unusually cautious, which suggests the degree of importance that he attached to the exercise. Edward Tyas Cook, editor of the *Daily News*, had, like Grey, received a first proof, and suggested an important addition that Maxse duly incorporated. 'Foreign statesmen are supposed to say, "It is impossible to do business with England for one Government reverses the foreign policy of its predecessor." Might it be worthwhile to include a reference to the growing perception of the importance of continuity – which Rosebery has done so much to popularise?'[31] An amended second proof of the article was now sent to Grey who noted the new section added on France that had originally been suggested by Blennerhassett.[32] 'I am glad you have put in a word about them,' Grey wrote. 'It is a pity that the suspicion of instability always attaches to them.'[33] In a last minute addition, Maxse incorporated Grey's exact words into his text. George Saunders, who had seen earlier drafts of the article, declared that it was now 'much improved, and there is nothing I can think of to add to it'.[34]

Advance copies of the article were sent to all British daily newspapers, most leading German papers (Saunders had provided Maxse with a list of names and addresses), continental writers on foreign affairs, and to Maxse's many contacts including senior members of the British Foreign Office. The introduction covered events in foreign policy 'from the moment a too famous raid provoked a no less famous telegram'. Britain now lived in 'an entirely new world', and, 'The main fact which should impress itself upon Englishmen [was] the extraordinary growth of Germany . . . as a Sea Power.'

> The official advocates of the Navy Bills which have been introduced into the Reichstag during the last three years have made no concealment as to the objective of the modern German Navy and the portion of the German Press which takes its cue from the Government has told us in language impossible to misunderstand that Germany aspires to deprive us of our position on the ocean. 'Unsere Zukunft liegt auf dem Wasser' [Our future lies on the seas], such is the swelling phrase of the Kaiser; but like all his rhetoric, there is serious purpose behind it. . . . Great Britain is therefore confronted with the development of a new sea power founded on the same economic basis as herself, and impelled by a desire to be supreme. . . . We have secured in the past the sovereignty of the seas, and our sceptre cannot be wrested from us without a bloody struggle.

So much and more on the German navy as a threat to England would have been quite familiar to Maxse's readers; but then he addressed himself to his major proposition.

> We venture to sketch in outline some suggestions for a comprehensive settlement between Russia and Britain with the object of demonstrating to sceptics that at any rate the raw material for an Anglo-Russian agreement abounds. . . . In seeking to close our prolonged contest with

Russia, we are desirous of doing something which would be for the
advantage of civilisation, and should it be effected, it would not be the
less welcome because it brought us back into friendly relations with France
– a country whose history is closely interwoven with our own, and with
which we share so many political sentiments. The French are perhaps the
only nation which will make sacrifices and run risks for the sake of those
who enjoy their friendship. They are capable of sentimental attachment
as well as sentimental hatred.[35] ... No one familiar with the personnel
of our politics can seriously suggest that if Lord Salisbury and Lord
Lansdowne were to pursue the policy set forth in this paper, their successors
would fail to keep the engagement they might inherit.[36]

In two letters to Captain Mahan,[37] the American naval historian who occasionally contributed articles to the *National Review*, Maxse enlarged on the
content of his essay.

The settled hostility of Germany aims at the heart of the British Empire
and will be content with nothing less than taking our place as the first
Sea Power. It is this which necessitates a revision of our foreign policy.
An arrangement with Russia ought to be within the range of practical
politics. . . . German hostility is far more serious because it will be so
infinitely better equipped than the amorphous advance of Russia in Asia.

Maxse obviously considered that friendship with Russia was the better choice
of two evils. Germany was resolute in her enmity, but Russia could be
dissuaded by a stern statement of unflinching intent. The trouble was,

Our Cabinets are composed chiefly of persons of the Mandarin type –
believers in shams and make-shifts and phrases – and are not capable
of steadily and resolutely upholding the policy of 'Hands Off the Persian
Gulf'. . . . In my humble opinion, things being what they are and Statesmen
what they are, it might be wiser to come to terms with Russia, who would
agree to the exclusion of Germany. We cannot come to terms with
Germany because the key to her policy today, as in the days of Bismarck,
is subservience to Russia.[38]

The publication of 'ABC's' thoughts on foreign policy elicited a variety of
responses. In Germany, much time and trouble was spent unavailingly to
discover exactly who the authors were.[39] While nothing was said openly, the
German fear was that the article was a 'kite' being flown by the British Foreign
Office. Thus, when the Anglo-Japanese agreement was signed, Bülow wrote
with delight to Metternich that at least for the moment it had thrown a spanner
into any work for rapprochement with Russia.[40] Of Maxse's friends and
acquaintances who knew that he was the author, Chirol's comments were the
least friendly. He carped at 'the very offensive tone you assume with regard
to Germany', and questioned whether it had been 'politic'. Knowing Maxse's
good opinion of Lavino, Chirol malevolently cited that correspondent's grumbles that the article would have been better received in Paris 'had it not

appeared to be inspired by hatred of Germany rather than by a desire merely to promote better relations with Russia'.[41]

Chirol was being difficult as only he knew how to be. He did not entirely share the Saunders/Maxse view that Russia would be tractable, fearing that country's influence for evil and ambitions in the Middle and Far East as a more immediate and real threat than either Saunders or Maxse appreciated. What was more, his letter was written after a visit to Berlin where, to his immense gratification, he had been received as of old by Holstein and Bülow. Nevertheless, Chirol's attitude towards Russia was changing, as is clear from a letter he wrote at that time to Charles Hardinge, a diplomat already marked by ability and royal favour to rise high in his profession, then Secretary at the St Petersburg embassy. 'Do you think there is any serious desire in influential quarters to come to any sort of serious agreement with us about Asiatic questions?' Chirol had inquired. 'We are sick over here at the slipperiness of our German friends and I think there would be a much greater disposition over here to respond to any such desire on the part of Russia than at any time within my memory almost.'[42]

Hardinge, who had been privy to Maxse's planned article and had offered advice while stressing, in the usual Foreign Office format, that his opinion was '*private* not official', applauded the finished work. 'I thoroughly agree with you,' he wrote to Maxse, 'both upon the opportunities and the necessity of such a policy as you have sketched.' Replying, Maxse could not resist boasting that the article was 'making a very considerable hit' with certain Russians in London.[43] That George Saunders was 'in sympathy' with Maxse's article was only to be expected since it was he who had emphasised that 'above all' it 'should be brought under the nose of influential Russians'.[44]

Much the most interesting immediate response Maxse received was from Joseph Chamberlain, who wrote, 'I wish to be on good terms with all the world – but if this is not possible I do not believe that Russia is the strongest or the most useful of political allies. I do not however mind an attempt to frighten Germany a little, and I admit that Bülow has not behaved very well. But if you think he has got the better of us in recent negotiations, I beg leave to differ.'[45] This letter was written less than a week after a speech made in Edinburgh where, responding to attacks in the German press on the conduct of British troops in South Africa, Chamberlain asserted that other armies, particularly the Germans in 1870, had behaved in a worse manner. The German press took Chamberlain to task. Little might have come of this fratch had not Bülow, despite the earnest warnings of his advisers, in January 1902 rebuked Chamberlain in the Reichstag. He had been clearly warned by Hammann, Richthofen and Holstein that it was better to say nothing, but Bülow had nevertheless insisted to Metternich, 'all would soon be forgotten'.[46] The Chancellor could not have been more wrong in his estimate. Bülow, to the delight of the Reichstag deputies, quoted Frederick the Great: 'Let that man alone and do not excite yourselves. He is biting granite.' Chamberlain's reply in a speech at Birmingham made him the popular hero of the hour in Britain. He was intent on demonstrating to everyone, not least to Bülow, his own adamantine nature. 'What I have said, I have said. I withdraw nothing. I qualify nothing. I defend nothing. . . . I do not want to give lessons to a foreign minister and I will not accept any at his hands. I am responsible only to my sovereign and my own countrymen.'

Unfortunately, Chamberlain's true character was misunderstood by many, not least the German Chancellor. People judged him by his outward appearance to be cool and passionless. On the contrary, he was proud, rash, impulsive, a political gambler and quick to take offence. Between October 1901 and January 1902, Chamberlain changed his mind. He abandoned thoughts of agreement with Germany, the idea that since 1900 he had so assiduously peddled to his Cabinet colleagues. While he had advocated friendship with Germany, his journalist friends (Garvin's description of them as 'the new and growing school of English thinkers' was somewhat grandiloquent) had been advertising their distrust, even their hatred of that country. As Garvin wrote in his biography of Chamberlain, 'We could not allow the fate of the Island and the Empire to become dependent on the casting vote of a super-armed Germany.'[47] Wilfrid Blunt had been sufficiently impressed by a vehement article by Garvin in the *Fortnightly*, written under the pseudonym 'Calchas', to record it in his diary. 'It was about the coming struggle of the Empires to eat each other up.'[48] Eagerly prompted by Maxse, Garvin wrote articles that were uncompromisingly hostile towards Germany and proposed agreement between England and Russia. He seems to have supposed that he, Maxse and other like spirits were engaged in a crusade against evil for which time was fast running out. 'German diplomacy is clever,' he wrote to Maxse, 'and will not be idle while we are at work. Time from my stand-point is valuable in this matter and if we are not bold in making up our minds as to how far we are prepared to go we may find other arrangements made for us.'[49]

Never alone, but invariably at the forefront of those publicists intent on imbuing the conduct of British foreign policy with a new direction and sense of purpose, Leo Maxse worked tirelessly in the next eighteen months for an end to any future possibility of cooperation between Germany and Britain. Within the Cabinet these publicists now had a powerful ally in Joseph Chamberlain. Soon a campaign for economic protection would be launched upon an anti-German platform. Germany's diplomatic chicanery, combined with the supposed economic threat she posed as a trade rival, would be the most frequently shouted slogans offered in the country-wide promotion of imperial preference. These various themes, synthesised by the publicists, were, after some initial delay, promoted by Chamberlain and his cohorts in Parliament and throughout the country. Over the next two and a half years the official line on foreign policy was obliged to match that represented by the earlier trumpetings of a section of England's right-wing press. The signing of the Anglo-French entente in 1904 confirmed 'the association of official policy with altered publicity stereotypes'.[50] It anticipated by three years the Anglo-Russian agreement that Maxse had first suggested in print in November 1901, but the logic of the entente policy, as Grey was to recognise, was indivisible. He would have argued with Maxse on that score only over the proposition that German hatred, envy and enmity was the *necessary* corollary of cooperation with the Dual Alliance of France and Russia.

To league with the shameless Hun

Apparently the modern fashion is to be perpetually either snarling at or prostrating yourself before your neighbours. That does not seem to the on-looker either dignified or very sensible. A public opinion which is always in extremes, and never consistent with itself, is tiring to watch, even from afar.

Milner to Selborne

And ye tell us now of a secret vow
Ye have made with an open foe!

The dead they mocked are scarcely cold,
Our wounded are bleeding yet –
And ye tell us now that our strength is sold
To help them press for a debt!

In sight of peace – from the Narrow Seas
O'er half the world to run –
With a cheated crew, to league anew
With the Goth and the shameless Hun!

Kipling 'The Rowers'

The change in Chamberlain's mind is most remarkable. The last time I saw him he was a mad philoGerman. And now!

Spring Rice to Florence Lascelles

In November 1900, Lord Salisbury made a number of changes in the Cabinet. 'Dear me,' observed Spring Rice. 'Here is the old ship on her beam ends, engines out of order and compass gone wrong, and she goes into port – to receive a set of officers in kid gloves and a new suit of white paint!'[1] Lansdowne assumed Salisbury's duties at the Foreign Office and the overall effect was a strengthening of the pro-German faction in the administration. This change of ministerial temper, together with the Kaiser's solicitous behaviour when his grandmother died in January 1901, seemed to augur an improvement in Anglo-German relations. Certainly Lansdowne was disposed to find a way of working amicably with the Germans but it proved extraordinarily difficult to discover suitable grounds for cooperation. Every proposal that seemed to offer that possibility failed. A draft alliance for joint action with Japan in the Far East collapsed when the Germans claimed that they were no longer interested in the fate of Manchuria. What they wanted was Britain to join with them against France and Russia. Sanderson told Lansdowne that such a convention, no matter how it might be worded, would 'practically amount to a guarantee to Germany of the provinces conquered from France, and that is the way the French will look at it. I do not see exactly what Germany will guarantee to us.'[2] Talks continued fitfully, but those who had earlier sought agreement with Germany now began to think that the Germans could not be trusted: they were insisting on their pound of flesh but offered nothing of real value in return. So marked was this change in attitude that Sanderson, an eminently fair-minded man who 'earlier had to explain often enough there were certain things we could not expect of the Germans, however friendly they might be', now had to emphasise repeatedly to the same ministers 'that the conduct of the German government has in some material aspects been friendly'. He told Lascelles that among Cabinet members there was 'a settled dislike of the Germans and an impression that they are ready and anxious to play us any shabby trick they can'.[3] Attempts to improve relations seemed only to achieve the contrary effect.

Holstein, in a memorandum for Bülow dated March 1901, encapsulated Germany's aims in the talks with Britain. He proposed that 'England should make up her mind to link herself at some time with the Triple Alliance' bringing in Japan 'as a pendant'.[4] He was convinced that circumstances would eventually oblige England to join with Germany. Meanwhile, all that had to be done was to keep Britain in a receptive mood. It was this last condition that was proving the problem. Holstein argued that two obstacles had to be surmounted. Time would soon solve the first – Salisbury. He was old and his resignation could not be delayed much longer. The second, British public opinion, was more difficult, but the careful cultivation of the press would help to undermine resistance. But who was to effect this purpose? Holstein could think of no one better qualified than his old 'friend', Chirol. Most conveniently, Chirol was at that moment visiting Berlin. Using Friedrich von Rosen as his intermediary, Holstein arranged a meeting with Chirol. Conversations followed, first with Holstein, and then with Bülow. A subsequent exchange of letters continued into the new year. Chirol was not only delighted, he was flattered that the 'old relations' were once more happily restored. He seems to have thought that the talks might 'bear some fruit in promoting a better understanding' between Germany and England. At the very least, they would certainly serve 'to clear up several points which had hitherto remained obscure to me in the policy of Germany'.[5]

During their first conversation, Holstein reviewed the recent course of Anglo-German relations. To Chirol's evident surprise he produced 'documentary proof' that indicated the main stumbling block to better relations between their countries had been Salisbury. Holstein knew that Chirol was 'not fond of Salisbury and [was] always ready to suspect him of inertness'.[6] Holstein argued that as long as Salisbury remained in office there was little likelihood of agreement. Nevertheless, the long-term prospect for Anglo-German rapprochement was excellent. He insisted that this view was 'shared in the highest positions in Germany, namely by His Majesty and the Chancellor'. Chirol thanked Holstein for the assurances he had been given and affirmed that he now 'took a more hopeful view of Anglo-German relations than before'. Holstein sent a memorandum of what he proposed to discuss in his next conversation with Chirol to Bülow who expressed his complete agreement. The conversations were to concentrate upon the 'future perspective of a German-English alliance'. It was after this second meeting with Holstein that Chirol spoke to Bülow who suddenly offered an unexpected *quid pro quo*. If Chirol agreed to use his influence with *The Times* to help restore Anglo-German relations to a position of confidence and intimacy, then Bülow promised, upon his honour, he would 'never countenance hostile attacks against Britain in the German press, nor allow himself to be deflected by the anti-British sentiments of an ignorant public from the policy of true friendship which lay nearest his heart'.[7] With this assurance Chirol returned to England in cheerful and optimistic mood. He even wrote to Wickham Steed that the Germans were far from happy and apparently apprehensive that they had been altogether too tolerant of pro-Boer demonstrations and the Anglophobia expressed by pan-German elements.[8]

Chamberlain's Edinburgh speech in late October that year promoted a frenzied response from the German public, painstakingly and faithfully recorded by Saunders in his telegrams to *The Times*. The rest of the English press remained reserved and calm. Domestic political loyalties explain the attitude of the Liberal press, but not the uncharacteristic reticence, even caution, of their 'patriotic' contemporaries. 'Many people here', Metternich, the newly appointed German ambassador to London, wrote to Bülow, 'look upon Chamberlain's remark as clumsy and tactless', but he warned the Chancellor not to attack Chamberlain, for undoubtedly the public would side with the British minister.[9] The vitriolic criticism of Chamberlain in the German press continued unabated and eventually Chirol felt obliged to comment upon 'their extraordinary outburst', which was quite out of proportion to its initial cause. Saunders had suggested, and Chirol agreed, that Bülow ought to define the official attitude in the Reichstag. The Chancellor should not allow the belief to gain ground in England that 'the passionate enmity of the German people must be regarded as a more powerful and permanent factor in moulding the relations of the two countries than the wise and friendly statesmanship of German rulers'.[10] Bülow was being gently reminded of his promise to curb the German press. Holstein knew that Chirol's intentions were conciliatory but he did not seem to realise that Chamberlain's offensive words justified German anger. Chirol's response, by telegram and a long letter, pointed out that the German Government could not 'altogether be acquitted of some responsibility'. Holstein was impressed, but Bülow remained unmoved. 'Nothing could be more stupid', he blustered, 'than the request for repression of the anti-English trend from above.' Bülow thereby conceded that he would rather bend to German public opinion than attempt to honour his freely given pledge. All Holstein's attempts to disarm Chirol with friendly letters were unavailing. The response was courteous enough, but the message depressing. 'I am reluctantly driven to the conclusion ... that all one can hope to do for the present is to avoid anything which should widen the breach.'[11] The faint hope was shattered when Bülow spoke in the Reichstag on 8 January 1902.

Though Holstein's attempt to use Chirol to further Germany's diplomatic aims had failed because of Bülow's actions, this did not altogether exhaust the resources of the Wilhelmstrasse in the move to bend *The Times* to their purpose. In London, at a private dinner party given by Sir Ernest Cassel, Metternich attempted to capture Moberly Bell's sympathies for an Anglo-German alliance. As the interests of their two countries were clearly identical, why not have an alliance, asked the Ambassador? Precisely because our interests are identical there is no need for an alliance, Bell countered; and for the rest of the evening stolidly rejected all Metternich's blandishments and arguments. The manager of *The Times* was not to be persuaded that Britain should ally herself with Germany.[12] On 7 January 1902, in a leading article, *The Times* made public its considered opinion on the question of alliance. Holstein was reluctantly obliged to share Chirol's view and admit 'the time for an Anglo-German agreement has not come'. Bell had demonstrated to Metternich beyond any doubt his belief that such an agreement was not needed. Sanderson informed Chirol privately that the British government, 'at least for the time being, has abandoned any thoughts of agreement and has informed the Germans as much'.[13] Now *The Times* had publicly pronounced its own *non possumus*. For the moment *pourparlers* between German diplomats and British journalists ceased.

If Bülow sincerely sought better relations with England, he could not have made a greater mistake than his speech to the Reichstag. The *Daily Mail*, hitherto silent, now avowed, 'We are not prepared to accept foreign rebukes, administered with even less tact and discretion, to our public men, or to sit in sack-cloth and ashes at a foreign censor's behest.'[14] With the exception of the Liberal dailies, the rest of the English press assumed this same truculent attitude. *The Times* went overboard. Chirol's leading articles were but counter-point to readers' letters which unrestrainedly denounced Bülow in particular and all Germans in general. From Berlin, Saunders stoked these xenophobic passions with his despatches and, in particular, two articles on 'The Literature of Anglophobia' that reviewed with painstaking detail the very worst scurrilities published by the German gutter press, particularly emphasising the lampoons of the royal family and the slanders against the conduct of the British army in South Africa. Complaints concerning Saunders's latest literary endeavours showered upon the innocent head of the British Ambassador. The German press howled for his dismissal, but the government was intent not to repeat the mistake it had made with Chirol. Its pose of frigid official politeness, however, sometimes broke down. At a private meeting at Posadowsky's house, von Richthofen lost his temper and in general hearing 'inveighed against Saunders pointing out his intense iniquity'.[15] The German press praised Richthofen fulsomely and defamatory stories about *The Times*'s Berlin correspondent bounced around the various chancelleries. Saunders did not complain to Printing House Square about the treatment he was receiving, but when, eventually, Moberly Bell learned of these attacks that daily filled the German press, he wired straightaway to Saunders, *en clair*: 'I congratulate you on the attacks of the reptile press whose praise would be blame.'[16]

The signing of the Anglo-Japanese treaty in January, and then the Peace of Vereeniging in May 1902 ending the Boer War, altered the diplomatic climate. Two particularly sensitive questions – the future of the German navy (upon which subject Saunders commented *ad nauseam*), and Germany's relations with Russia – caused the Wilhelmstrasse urgently to review Anglo-German relations. The recent press polemics in both countries had not served Germany's best interests. Metternich suggested to King Edward that *The Times* was the main culprit in unnecessarily fomenting ill-will between their two nations. Edward mentioned this to his friend Rothschild who invited Bell to dine with him at his London house. After dinner, with cigars came the inevitable talk of an Anglo-German agreement. Bell prevaricated, for this attempt by Rothschild to get at *The Times* through him was much too obvious. Rothschild's sympathies for Germany were notorious and Bell was not unduly impressed by his gauche advertisement that their meeting had been at the wish of 'an august person'. Bell claimed that there was nothing he could do until he had consulted with Saunders. He did, however, promise Rothschild that once he has canvassed Saunders's opinion he would give him 'something in writing'.

As soon as he received Bell's 'deeply interesting and indeed momentous letter', Saunders set down a long and detailed reply, admitting that he felt himself to be 'in the position of Colin Campbell at the Alma when as Brigadier he was asked by his Divisional General, the Duke of Cambridge, for his opinion. My answer is *mutatis mutandis* the same as Colin Campbell's. "Better that the Guards should lie dead to the last man than that they should retire!"' Saunders's whole letter reflected this uncompromising spirit. It merits extensive quotation as a definitive statement of his thoughts on Anglo-German relations in this period, summarising as it does those opinions he so frequently rehearsed in letters to his friends.

The question is: 'Are we to ignore the whole tendency of German policy during the present reign, are we to pass a sponge over every indication of German plans and ambitions and to range ourselves definitely on the German side, accepting for ever the lead of the Foreign Office in Berlin, which is far from vigorous and alert (alas!) than ours and which will take us in tow?'

Consider, please, what this *means*. I take the least evil (though God knows it is serious enough) first. It means (1) the alienation of our immediate neighbour France. Say against France what you will [she] is a country and a nation whose ideas, whose ambitions, whose ideals, we can understand and know the *limits* of. . . . Germany the British public does *not* know. . . . Can you consent to place British foreign policy in German leading-strings? That is what it comes to. . . . England does not *need* to enter into this bondage. She is too great, too old, too strong. (2) It means permanent 'separation' from Russia with the cunning, assiduous German broker ever between. . . . Any arrangement, any policy, any *tendency* which caused England to make a final choice for Germany against Russia and

France would be a *fatal, irrevocable* step. The Times ought to and I trust *can* prevent it. . . . (3) Rothschild's Berlin friend, Dr Paul Schwabach, once said to me: 'You must inevitably *quarrel* with America.' One of the great objects of German endeavours is to detach us from America. . . . Let us not alienate ourselves from our American brethren – bone of our bone and flesh of our flesh! . . . (4) The *insistence* of these German overtures to you, to Chirol and to me is (to me at least) easily explicable. Germany is face to face with a crisis. Her Imperial Revenue is at a standstill; her Imperial expenditure increasing by leaps and bounds. . . . So far as Germany is concerned, we hold the keys of the Atlantic Ocean and indeed of all the Seven Seas. Let us keep them! Germany is a parochial Power and, if we are firm and not foolish, will remain so. . . .

I know the power of German influence. . . . There is temptation . . . because there is a flashy schoolboy of an Emperor, a vast, though mostly impoverished nobility, snobbishness like that of Thackeray's 'Vanity Fair' (not like modern England's foibles and vices), an army with a record and a system, dynasties allied (what a tragedy) by marriage; education (artificial to a degree and, believe me, also essentially unsound). . . . It is not business. It is cant, talk, appearances. . . .

I summarise my essentials of British Foreign Policy as follows
(1) Absolute independence of Germany. No closer relations with Germany than with France. Friendliness, politeness, where friendliness is possible, but above all, alertness and political aloofness. . . .
(2) Friendly, neighbourly relations with France. . . . There is no fear now of sentimentality on either side. . . . France has become bourgeois . . . sensible, prudent, *cautious* in her old age. . . . They are no longer *moqueurs*; they are students. (3) Above all we must go hand in hand with America in good and evil fortune. This is absolutely essential. . . .
(4) A *steady* object of British policy ought to be the ultimate settlement of our relations, territorial and political, with Russia. Very gradual it must doubtless be. . . . But settle we must and can. . . . Entanglements with Germany will do more than anything else to prevent it. . . .

My final word is . . . Germany at present finds herself in desperate straits, eg (1) an insoluble economic problem at home. . . . (2) no statesman at her disposal. Bülow, by universal consent, a perfect imposition and mountebank. (3) The Emperor, a wayward boy (at 44!) with the vastest of ambitions altogether out of proportion to his means. Insane jealousy on his part of England, even of the Coronation ceremony. He is sure to try some diversion, eg (1) a telegram virtually offering an alliance, or (2) a menace, or (3) some foolish pageant in Germany. Vanitas vitatum! . . . Total result: a desperate desire to make a last bid for England. Lesson for England: reserve, aloofness, especially as we have great and purely British tasks before us.

P.S. I feel sure, not cocksure, but *sure* of the rightness of what I say.[17]

How much of this letter Bell used in his own to Rothschild is not known. The initiative for an agreement, however, was not renewed.

Saunders's sentimental references to Anglo-American relations reflected a growing official British concern with the influence of German propaganda in America, highlighted by the German Crown Prince's visit to the United States. Spring Rice angrily reported how the German Ambassador in Washington, Holleben, 'pursuing the customary game', had established 'a regular press bureau which distributes anti-British calumnies'.[18] For a number of years, relations between Britain and the United States had been difficult. The peremptory message President Cleveland had despatched in December 1895 about the long-standing boundary dispute between Venezuela and British Guiana had been scarcely less happily phrased to placate British sensibilities than the Kaiser's more notorious telegram to Kruger. Arthur Balfour, in a flippant letter to Strachey in 1898, neatly formulated the problem that faced any British politician wishing to promote better relations with the United States: 'From the nature of the case, American patriotism must be fed on histories of the War of Independence, and the most stirring memories must be of conflicts with this country.'[19] Leo Maxse was particularly concerned that troubled Anglo-American relations were attracting Germany's attention. 'The appointed role of Germany', he wrote to Mahan, 'is simply that of marplot . . . to set each at the other and take blackmail off both, as she has done with Russia and England for the last thirty years. We earnestly hope that people on your side will be too shrewd to further her little game.'[20]

In July 1902, because Balfour had succeeded his uncle Salisbury as Prime Minister, the Germans were encouraged to attempt to restore better relations with England. One manifestation of this was a twelve-day visit by the Kaiser. Initially Maxse was concerned that William would be 'clever enough to keep up his pose as a friend and use his influence, which unfortunately is still large with our Court, to bamboozle the British public, as he realizes that the German naval programme is not yet sufficiently advanced to make it safe for him to throw off his mask'.[21] He need not have worried. The British press at best was guardedly hostile towards the Kaiser, an attitude that matched general opinion in the country. Eckardstein reported a conversation with Chamberlain who had 'launched out against Germany and especially Bülow. . . . After the abominable way in which Bülow especially behaved . . . there could no longer be any question of an agreement. . . . Nothing would be more popular in England than war with Germany.'[22] Shortly after this conversation with Eckardstein, Chamberlain visited South Africa. 'But for that journey', Chirol later informed Strachey, 'his influence would have been exerted . . . to avert the Venezuelan imbroglio.'[23]

From 1898 to 1900 there had been a civil war in Venezuela. Attempts by the British and German governments to secure compensation for the lost property and money of their nationals had come to nothing. In December 1902, quite unexpectedly, Balfour told the Commons that British and German warships were blockading the coast of Venezuela. Startling as this news was, the subsequent reports that the Germans had bombarded forts and sunk several gunboats caused a public furore. All the British press, without political distinction, joined in. If the Liberals feared that relations with the United States had been unnecessarily jeopardised, with the notable exception of the *Daily Telegraph* Tory newspapers thundered at the way Britain found herself 'Tied to Germany's Tail'.[24] On 22 December *The Times* printed a poem by Kipling, 'The Rowers', which described the Germans as 'the shameless Hun' who was Britain's 'open foe'. *The Times*'s editorial observed that Kipling's poem 'expressed sentiments which unquestionably prevail far and wide throughout the nation'.

The Kaiser was inordinately vexed by the behaviour of the British press. He particularly resented Kipling's verses 'as hitherto he had been a great admirer of that individual's work'. Frank Lascelles, offering this crumb of literary intelligence garnered from a conversation with Richthofen, had other and more important news for Sanderson.

> The German Government are quite as anxious as we are to finish the Venezuelan-business and have been frightened by the tone of the English press. They will therefore agree to anything we propose as they certainly do not wish to increase our difficulties with public opinion in England. . . . The Germans are very sensitive about our press which they believe has far more influence than it really has.[25]

In the face of the public's implacable ill-will, the British government was obliged to scramble out of the Venezuelan 'mess' with as much dignity as it could muster, its embarrassment made worse by the Germans dragging their feet over arbitration. Lansdowne, described by Metternich as 'a man of honour who sticks to the promises he has made', had reluctantly to admit to the German Ambassador that his actions were being dictated by 'public opinion . . . which will not tolerate the present situation being prolonged'.[26] On 13 February 1903 a protocol was signed that settled the issue. Maxse's response was to write triumphantly to Mahan:

> I think one may really regard our deplorable Venezuelan enterprise as a blessing in disguise. It brought out a display of independence towards our Government indicative of the virility and vigour of public opinion in this country. . . . The Venezuelan 'mess', as it is popularly called and officially described, has dealt a heavy blow at the policy of cooperating anywhere with Germany. . . . Those of us who are at close quarters with the slip-shod methods of British statesmen know that such cooperation would always be detrimental to our interests. Germany is perfectly prepared to exploit us wherever she can. . . . I know you think the National Review has taken a rather extreme line upon the German question, but I venture to say that it is justified by the events which are passing under our eyes in the world. For the moment, pending her naval preparedness, Germany is no doubt willing to make use of us wherever she can, and even possibly keep a civil tongue in her head, but it is our duty to keep her at arm's length because she is not to be trusted anywhere.[27]

Maxse had earlier declared his 'anxiety' that Mahan should not think he was being 'carried away by a fad' in his opposition to Germany. Mahan affirmed that he entertained no such thoughts about Maxse's opinions 'which I know are shared by a great many of your people. I have not the least doubt, either, of the hostile feeling of the German people towards you and, in a slightly less degree, towards ourselves.'[28]

Lansdowne angrily but unavailingly deplored the excesses and prejudices of uninformed opinion. Yet the temper of the majority of his Cabinet colleagues, as well as of the Foreign Office's permanent officials, was to agree entirely with Kipling's bitter and outraged response to the idea of cooperating with the Germans. 'Everyone in the office and out talks as if we had but one enemy in the world,' Spring Rice confirmed. 'It is no manner of good trying to assure us unofficially or officially that they [the Germans] are our friends. No one believes it now and the only effect is to disgust.'[29] It seemed as though Lansdowne alone required proof that there was no possibility of cooperation with Germany in the existing climate of public opinion.[30] In less than two months he was given that proof in a sharp and embarrassing manner.

In February 1903 the financiers Sir Ernest Cassel and Sir Clinton Dawkins met Lansdowne to discuss the British Government's attitude to the joint financing with the Deutsche Bank of an extension to the Baghdad railway. At an earlier stage of the negotiations, Lansdowne had said he thought 'it would be a great misfortune if the railway were to be constructed without British participation'. Now he confirmed to Cassel and Dawkins that the government itself was 'favourably disposed towards the project'.[31] The public first learned of British involvement from an answer Balfour gave to a questioner in the Commons on 7 April.[32] Little more than two weeks later he was obliged to tell the House that the government no longer supported the scheme. This *volte face* came after a furious campaign in the press prompted initially by Leo Maxse and John St Loe Strachey.

It is not clear how Maxse first heard of the proposed arrangement. Possibly it was Dawkins who told him, for they were close friends. Financiers were one of Maxse's pet aversions but he exempted Sir Clinton as he was 'sound' on the question of compulsory military service. In the April issue of his *Review*, Maxse launched a slashing attack on the whole project: 'No sooner are we clear . . . of the miserable [Venezuelan] episode than we are plunged headlong into the Mesopotamian mess, which is far more serious because more lasting, and from which a very determined and vociferous expression of public opinion will be required in order to release us.' Maxse was scornful of both Balfour and Lansdowne. 'The withdrawal of the late Premier has left the Cabinet alarmingly deficient of knowledge or instinct in foreign politics and the Kaiser has encountered little, if any, resistance to his projects. Downing Street has become a mere annex of the Wilhelmstrasse and it would make for economy and efficiency if we put up the shutters of our costly Foreign Office.'[33] Though the campaign was not coordinated, Strachey promptly complemented Maxse's efforts in his *Spectator*.

Strachey considered that it was his special responsibility as a journalist 'to play the watchdog, even if the barking did annoy the neighbours'.[34] Though totally opposed on the issue of protection, Strachey and Maxse both believed passionately in the inevitability of an European war. Strachey first learned of the move to finance jointly the Baghdad railway from two well-placed Foreign Office sources: Spring Rice, who was not too busy, despite preparations for his new posting as First Secretary at the St Petersburg Embassy, to write a long letter – 'I want you to take this letter as a guide. Use as much as you like, but do not *quote* any words or phrases exactly' – and Louis Mallet, then Assistant Clerk at the Foreign Office, a man who was always virulently anti-Germany in his attitudes. The German Foreign Office was convinced that the campaign by Maxse and Strachey was prompted by the Russians who 'of course were interested in thwarting the arrangements which were virtually settled'.[35]

The first time Maxse mentioned the Baghdad railway in his correspondence with Strachey was in a postscript to a letter dated 20 April 1903. By that time almost all the British press was in full cry against the British government's support for what was now called 'The Baghdad Bungle'. The *Spectator*, in Maxse's opinion, had been 'magnificent'. He claimed that had he and Strachey not ' "blown the gaff", the British public would have been presented with a *fait accompli* and the war between Russia and England, for which Germany has worked for the last twenty years, would have been brought a step nearer. We are by no means out of the wood, but I think we have a chance of defeating Lord Lansdowne's latest.'[36] Maxse need not have worried. The Germans unwittingly delivered the *coup de grâce* to the scheme. Gwinner supposed public opposition might be disarmed if someone published the text of the convention by which the Turkish government granted the original concession to the Deutsche Bank. He therefore gave it to *The Times*, who published it on 22 April, but together with an intemperate editorial which fiercely attacked any idea of British participation. The rest of the British press blithely ignored the terms of the convention and instead quoted with approval from the critical editorial. Thoroughly intimidated, the government gave way.

There were some who regretted the government's hasty retreat. Esher, who through his friend, Cassel, had been associated with the financial negotiations, was furious. There had been 'a lot of money to be made in it', but 'a frightened government ran away . . . from a press campaign stimulated by stupid fools. . . . The English people, led by a foolish, half-informed press, are children in foreign politics. They have always been so and have paid dearly.'[37] Esher's instinct had warned him the government was likely to 'flinch'. Chirol claimed it had been 'Mr C[hamberlain]'s determined oppositon' that had 'settled the fate of the Baghdad Railway in Cabinet'.[38] In later years Lansdowne grumbled privately of how he had been 'forced to yield to an "insensate outcry" '. A letter he wrote to the Indian Viceroy shows how angry he was that a 'worthwhile scheme' had been discredited by a 'sharp recrudescence of the anti-German fever. . . . I am afraid that in the long run our attitude will be somewhat difficult to explain.'[39]

That Lansdowne chose to write to Curzon to vent his frustration reveals just how out of touch with opinion he was. The notoriously sensitive viceroy had written to another member of the Cabinet, Selborne, to say he had 'always been opposed to the Baghdad scheme', adding frostily, 'Although the matter is apparently discussed from its bearing upon Indian interests . . . no one has ever thought of asking my opinion on the subject.'[40] Lansdowne seems to have supposed that had Balfour backed him even more strenuously in Cabinet against Chamberlain, he might have won the day. As to the press campaign, the Foreign Secretary had not considered the attack by Maxse and Strachey to be particularly formidable. Their arguments were 'paltry' and he was not to be intimidated by the two editors 'proclaiming in London and Paris that they had "nobbled" Joe'. When Chirol had called at the Foreign Office it had been Sanderson's distinct impression that 'while he did not care for the project he was not actively hostile'. With a little effort, Chirol's favour and presumably the support of *The Times* might have been successfully courted.[41]

More than a year after these stirring events, Maxse wrote to tell Garvin of a dinner party he had recently attended where the only other male guest had been Balfour. With their host, Prime Minister and editor had talked until midnight 'on all sorts of things but mainly of foreign policy'.

> The impression I got was that if only Balfour saw 'white men' he might become a white man! He seemed to me to be curiously receptive, though of course one may be misled by that very delightful and appreciative manner, but I had it out with him over the Baghdad Railway and other things and came away regretting that he lives so much among sycophants and rotters. . . . In the course of argument he did admit that 'the German Navy is directed against England', so I think we have not wholly laboured in vain, because only a year ago he was laughing at this idea.[42]

For Strachey, the passage of time was to effect a strange reinterpretation of the Venezuelan and Baghdad affairs. In an article in the *Spectator* in October 1906 he argued that the two incidents had been 'efforts to conciliate the Germans'. This prompted swift reproval from J. A. Spender.

> The Germans regard [these two incidents] as fresh wounds . . . instances proving the impossibility of working with a British Government. Is this surprising? Our Government pledged itself to the German, or practically so, then backed out and left the Germans to suppose that the anti-German feeling over here was so strong that nothing could be done about it. . . . I don't see how we can expect Germans to put that affair to our credit. The mischief was that we went into it at all, but necessarily the backing out is what the Germans remember. The belief apparently in Germany is that we promised our cooperation as part of the price for Germany's official correctitude during the Boer War and for turning Mr Kruger away from the gates of Berlin, and they kept saying that when they have done their part, we failed to deliver ours.[43]

No German diplomat would have argued with Spender's account of why Germany nursed injured feelings about Britain's actions, first in Venezuela and then over the Baghdad railway scheme.

The last words on these two events were not spoken until February 1907, and then by two senior permanent officials of the Foreign Office. Eyre Crowe, by then Senior Clerk, circulated a memorandum on Britain's relations with France and Germany. In tone and content, it was extremely critical of German policy and diplomatic methods. Sanderson, who had recently retired as Permanent Under Secretary, responded with a memorandum of his own that, if it was not intended to question, at least suggested a modification of some of Crowe's more trenchant criticisms. Sanderson observed that, 'While the British Government has remained calm and conciliatory, the press and public opinion here have interfered seriously with our working so much together [with the Germans] as would otherwise have been desirable.' Eyre Crowe commented in the margin:

> I cannot recall any such instance. Venezuela and the Baghdad railway are the only two cases known to me where the foreign policy of HMG seemed to be directly influenced by public opinion as expressed in the newspapers and magazines. As regards Venezuela, events showed that cooperation with Germany was certainly not 'desirable' in British interests. And the conditions offered by Lord Lansdowne for British participation in the Baghdad railway were clearly unacceptable at the time.[44]

New friends and old enemies

The arrangement with France is a very good score it seems to me.
Milner to Selborne

Germany's prestige has shrunk in the last few years while our opponents
and rivals are on the point of encircling us. Difficult situations must
therefore be expected to arise for which I would prefer not to take the share
of moral responsibility which every collaboration bears.
Holstein to Hammann

I hear that there is complete estrangement, at any rate for the moment,
between the highest circles in Germany and Great Britain, at which I
frankly rejoice because their friendly relationship has always involved
something detrimental to British interests.
Maxse to Spring Rice

'A curious combination,' mused Esher to his son. 'The King is at present a
Chamberlainite.'[1] Edward had publicly demonstrated his antipathy towards the
Germans and affection for the French. Largely on his own initiative, and with
only grudging approval from Lansdowne, the king had visited France early in
May 1903. Radolin, the German Ambassador, had told his masters he thought
such a visit might 'lead to détente in the up-to-now not very favourable
relations between France and England at which they aim strongly at the Quai
d'Orsay'. The visit was a triumph for Edward. Within hours he had won over
the Parisians. He had spoken of 'friendship' between their two countries.
Elements in both French and British press talked instead of 'alliance'. Metternich noted such ideas were prompted by a general aversion to Germany.
'Without the Anglo-German estrangement an Anglophile atmosphere in
France would be impossible, and M. Delcassé would have to wait a long time
for the fulfilment of his wish. Without the aversion to Germany the English
press could not have worked for months towards a reconciliation with France,
nor could M. Cambon have made his reconciliatory speeches.'[2]

In July, President Loubet, together with the French Foreign Secretary
Delcassé, visited England. Both were fêted and paid every attention. In conversation with Lansdowne, Delcassé lightly sketched the outline of a possible
treaty between their two countries. After the Foreign Minister's departure, the
French Ambassador, Cambon, continued the initiative. The negotiations went
so well that by September, Lansdowne was drafting a confidential minute for

the Cabinet's consideration. Very considerable difficulties remained, but the will to overcome them was apparent on both sides of the Channel. Central to the negotiations was what amounted to a proposal for a colonial trade-off between the two principals. If France recognised England's claim to Egypt then, subject to certain restrictions, England would acknowledge French predominance in Morocco. Lansdowne allowed himself the anticipatory reflection that 'A good understanding with France would not improbably be the precursor of a better understanding with Russia.'[3]

Despite these private reflections Lansdowne treated the new Russian Ambassador, Benckendorff, with a frigid reserve, so much so that the Count was moved to describe a conversation with Delcassé during his London visit as 'a refreshing drink' in the 'Saharan climes of the Court of St James'. The attitude of *The Times* did not help. It chose to repay the Russians for dismissing their St Petersburg correspondent by publishing a series of clandestine despatches that emphasised Russian disorder and corruption. *The Times* was informed and approved of the Anglo-French negotiations, yet continued to report on France's diplomatic partner with some spite. As a major priority of his new posting to Russia, Charles Hardinge determined that through his old friend Chirol, he would do what he could to change the attitude at Printing House Square. In a letter to Chirol, Hardinge told him that he could have little idea how *The Times* was regarded in Russia; of its

> power for good and evil as a political weapon, and the harm it has done
> our country and our individual countrymen during the past few months
> by embittering our relations with the Russians. . . . You know, our policy
> is to maintain friendly relations with the Russian Government. . . . It is
> necessary to lose no time in preparing public opinion for it. . . . If the
> Times continues to maintain its present tone of hostile criticism, the
> difficulty of my task will be infinitely greater. . . . I am very anxious *pro
> bono publico* that these newspaper polemics should cease, and if you will
> hold out to me any prospect of sending a properly qualified correspondent
> here, I will myself take the initiative of sounding the Russian Government
> as to their willingness to accept him.

But Chirol returned a dusty answer to Hardinge's appeal.[4]

Suddenly the Anglo-French negotiations seemed imperilled by the enmity of their respective alliance partners. Chirol, who had long considered war between Russia and Japan inevitable, suffered no qualms when hostilities broke out in February 1904. His only anxiety was that English public opinion should support the Japanese. Would French opinion change towards England? In a state of considerable alarm, Leo Maxse scurried over to France to consult with his many friends there in high places. Despite a débâcle on the Paris Bourse prompted by news of the Japanese victory at Port Arthur, he was reassured. The French recognised English sympathy for the Japanese, but there would be no recriminations. The danger feared in Paris was that the Germans might seize the opportunity to make trouble. The risk of difficult incidents was inseparable from a state of war anywhere on the globe. Chirol told Spring Rice that another, 'better informed' visitor to France than Maxse had reported the French feared the English might deliberately engineer an incident as an excuse to 'Port Arthur' the French Fleet, 'a not unnatural suspicion given the conviction that prevails on the Continent as to our Machiavellianism'. The circumstances were so delicate that even a minor infraction of neutrality might spell disaster. The farcical element in the drama was provided by those English newspapers who, while claiming they keenly supported better Anglo-French relations, by their 'stupid chatter' were likely to provoke an incident.

> They have no responsibility whatever, and their ignorance is stupendous. . . . The St James's Gazette started the yarn about the Japs having used Wei-hai-wei as a base, and blithered about our 'benevolent' neutrality etc. As for more harmless 'fakes', there is no end to them. The Daily Mail published in the same column that Kuropatkin had been received by the Tsar and that he had arrived at Harbin! Another, that troops were passing through Irkutsk by train at more rapid intervals than the trains at Clapham Junction! It is the levity of the whole thing that is so scandalous.[5]

Northcliffe was blissfully unaware that his beloved *Daily Mail* was being taken to task by Chirol. The *Mail* had confidently forecast a rapid end to the war on the dubious ground that 'war reconciles rather than permanently divides nations'. It also more pertinently pointed out that the only beneficiary of the weakness of either combatant would be Germany.[6] Ever sensitive to the mote in the eye of another while resolutely ignoring the plank in his own, Northcliffe smote the 'ridiculous nonsense' published by rival newspapers. 'If I had done as much', he told Strachey, 'there would have been a panic.' With mock modesty he complained that the trouble with his vast circulation was that 'an immense number of people see everything that appears in it and the comment they make magnifies every utterance. We have been obliged to reduce the tone and colour of the paper to far below that of any morning newspaper except the Times, and even then such remarks as I make will get magnified by hearsay. The position is a new one and a difficult one for a newspaper owner.'[7] Northcliffe never ignored an opportunity to massage his massive ego.

Less intent on self-advertisement than Northcliffe, yet just as vigilant to perceive German duplicity, Maxse was busily engaged in following up 'hints', volunteered by Spring Rice, that the Germans 'who have manoeuvered us twice to the verge of war during the last month are quite capable of reproducing the crisis until it terminates fatally. The trouble is that newspaper editors are absurdly sensitive to the suggestion that they have been "had" by the wily Teuton.'[8] Chirol would have agreed with this, at least to the extent that the Germans, to discredit the Japanese, were emphasising the 'Yellow Peril'. That calumny, he informed Strachey, was 'manufactured in Germany to serve German purposes', and the great apostle of the doctrine was the Kaiser. On a Mediterranean cruise, the emperor's 'violent tirades against Japan were considered to be in rather bad taste – like many others things he said and did.' Strachey was amazed to learn that his uncertainty as to what view he ought to adopt in the *Spectator* had 'rehabilitated' him in William's eyes as one editor who was 'taking the good European line'.[9] But Louis Mallet and Spring Rice were quick to provide sufficient hints and promptings in their 'extremely pessimistic' letters to guide St Loe's wayward steps once more into the path of correctitude and righteousness. 'I hope I have not overdone it,' Strachey anxiously inquired of Mallet, while apologising for the rude remarks he had felt obliged to make about the British government. How could anyone feel secure with 'an exhausted and discredited Premier and a Cabinet of inferior men'?[10] Strachey's mind was more exercised by domestic than foreign politics; as an ardent Free Trader he was not inclined to join, other than warily, a band-waggon associated with Chamberlain.

The signing of the entente between France and England on 8 April 1904 was greeted with jubilation at Printing House Square. In Germany, however, there was no sign of rejoicing. Bülow asked the Reichstag to give him time to consider Germany's position. The agreement had been reached without any attempt to consult with them. *The Times* pronounced that British isolation was now a thing of the past. In Paris, Lavino urged that an Anglo-Russian agreement should follow and his newspaper spelled out the implication of this in a bold headline – 'The Isolation of Germany'.[11] Germany's first move was for the Kaiser to invite his uncle Edward to Kiel. Like others at the Foreign Office, Louis Mallet was riven with anxiety. He wrote tremulously to Balfour's secretary, Jack Sandars, that if the visit could not be avoided then at least Lansdowne must 'give a good talking' to the King and every effort should be made to limit the visit to 'a mere family meeting. The Germans will do all in their power to give the visit an international and political character. . . . It is not likely that the Emperor will propose an understanding with England at present, but if he did the King should answer that we should be agreeable if he will add no more to his fleet – until that day we must remain on guard.'[12] Despite misgivings, the visit was concluded without too many complications.

When King Edward had described how Englishmen in Germany were full of praise for German energy, efficiency and knowledge, Bülow allowed himself the indulgence to interrupt the royal disquisition and insist with a smile that an exception would surely have to be made for George Saunders of *The Times*. It was Saunders who constantly emphasised in his despatches, as in his private letters to Bell, Chirol and Amery, that the growth of the German navy was the central issue governing relations between the two Powers. The Germans were undoubtedly anxious about rumours that the British were contemplating a pre-emptive strike against their fleet. Arnold White, a naval correspondent known to be very close to Jack Fisher, the recently appointed First Sea Lord, had been advertising schemes to 'Copenhagen' the German fleet. Plans for 'springing at the enemy's throat' were very popular after the successful Japanese attack on Port Arthur. 'If only we had such a plan', Strachey had written wistfully to Mallet, 'and acted on it instantly, I should not be afraid of war.'[13] But it was to be the Russians and not the British or the Germans who provided an unexpected naval 'action'.

On 23 October 1904, the news was received in London that the Russian Baltic fleet, while passing through the North Sea on its long journey to engage the Japanese in the Pacific, had fired on the Hull fishing fleet. Two ships had been sunk and a number of lives lost. The immediate Russian explanation was that they thought they were being attacked under cover of night by Japanese submarines. The British public reacted violently to this incredible story. Even within the Cabinet, the Prime Minister and Foreign Secretary found it was not easy to restrain some of their more belligerent colleagues. Goschen, in a letter to Milner, praised Balfour and Lansdowne for remaining cool. 'They have managed well in extraordinary difficult circumstances. . . . Of course the supreme object was to carry France along with them, and that they have *thoroughly* done.'[14] For the British press, as Chirol told Spring Rice, it had been 'a pretty toilsome week'.

> I had some trouble to hold myself in check – not to speak of yet angrier spirits in Printing House Square. . . . When the unspeakable Admiral's report came through, we very nearly took the bit between our teeth. . . . With me the main consideration was to carry France with us. Another consideration was that war would have played into the hands of Germany. Her share in the business is still obscure. . . . Where did the reports come from which started the scare in the Baltic Fleet? Our Admiralty is convinced that they came from Germany possibly by way of Denmark.[15]

Chirol told Lascelles he was certain that the 'outrage was deliberate'. The single comforting feature was that the British Home Squadron had been moved to cover the German fleet at Kiel. 'The Admiralty have at last come to realise that the German Fleet is a potentially hostile factor.'[16] Lascelles was most anxious to quash the rumour that it was the Germans who were behind the Russian action, but the general attitude in the Foreign Office was to discount Lascelles as 'very pro-German'. Mallet writing to Sandars ridiculed Lascelles's gullibility. 'He disbelieves the stories that the Germans were the people who warned Russia because Bülow – who is the greatest liar in creation – assures him on his honour that they did not do so. . . . We all know that Germany is anxious to see us at logger-heads with Russia, although Lascelles does not admit as much. . . . History repeats itself, the German methods are always the same.'[17]

Foreign Office suspicion of Germany was well illustrated by its paranoid collective reaction to a trivial incident concerning the booing of the Russian Ambassador at Victoria station. The police reported that most of the crowd were Germans. How could they have known that Benckendorff was due to arrive at that precise time and place? 'The tip must have been given to the crowd by somebody "in the know". Fortunately B kept his head and the incident assumed no grave proportions. But there *was* a method in it and it *might* have had a very serious result.'[18] For several days there was a real danger of war between Russia and Britain, but the crisis was weathered at the cost of a further deterioration in Anglo-German relations.

Either side of the North Sea a newspaper war was declared, fuelled by the careless remarks of politicians and the jingo posturing of naval personnel. There was a panic in Berlin, even among the highest and best informed social circles. This time, they supposed, the British would surely descend upon their fleet at Kiel. Consequently there were few Germans who did not support the

emperor's call for greater naval armaments. Count Bernstorff, Baron Eckardstein's replacement as German press officer in London, vainly tried to stem
the tide of insult and calumny in the newspapers, but his assurances were
either ignored or dismissed as patent fabrications.[19] Chirol wanted to know
why the Wilhelmstrasse continued to pretend that they were not interested in
a Russo-German rapprochement when they were all too obviously using the
Russo-Japanese war to that end. 'I don't resent this,' he told Bernstorff, 'for
every nation is the best judge of its own interests. But I cannot make myself
a party to your endeavours to disguise the dominant tendency of Germany's
present policy.'[20] Despite his best efforts, Bernstorff achieved nothing. No
British journalist was impressed by the palpably false assertion that the German
government had 'absolutely no power to prevent anything being written or
printed', nor would they accept Bernstorff's plea that 'attacks in our comic
and satirical papers are no worse than those I have in the last four years read
here constantly against Germany in the Times, Daily Mail and National
Review, not to mention others. What about the continual lies told about
Germany in the English press?'[21] His pleas fell upon deaf ears.

Because it was racked by the internal divisions prompted by the arguments
for and against tariff reform, Balfour's administration was particularly vulnerable to pressure from a public opinion excited by the anti-German campaign
in the press. Lascelles loudly and frequently complained about the excesses of
the Fleet Street warriors, but Lansdowne was quite unmoved, even when the
Ambassador reported that the Germans were convinced by these constant
attacks that 'HM's Government have concluded a defensive and offensive
alliance with France against Germany'.[22] Balfour, who was fond of claiming
that he never read the newspapers, felt that it was time for him to put a stop
to Lascelles's constant complaints.[23] The Prime Minister admitted that he, like
the Ambassador, often had cause to regret the way in which British newspapers
chose to express their suspicions about Germany. But Lascelles would 'not
find even the faintest suggestion that England either desired war with Germany
or had anything to gain from it'. He did not deny that many Englishmen
entertained a 'deep distrust of German policy' but that was easily explained
by 'certain diplomatic events in Germany which have produced a painful
impression'. Balfour instanced 'the arguments by which the German Fleet was
brought into being', and the way that 'a whole school of political thinkers has
preached ... that it was Britain alone who stood between Germany and the
realisation of the German ideal of colonial expansion'.[24]

Despite all his earlier disappointments, Bernstorff still tried to improve the
tone of the British press towards Germany. So inept were his efforts that he
even alienated one of his few allies. Lucien Wolf, a staff member of the *Daily
Graphic*, was a prolific writer on foreign affairs. His articles, which appeared
in many British newspapers and journals of opinion, had in the past often
demonstrated his willingness to advertise the 'official' German attitude. Now
he returned the draft of an article that Bernstorff had sent to him. Wolf
explained that although he was 'glad to assist in placing the German view of
public questions before the British public, and even defend them', he was not
prepared 'to put forward as English what is really a German opinion'. Mallet

got hold of a copy of this letter which he sent immediately to the Prime Minister's private secretary. He told Sandars, 'if they are trying that game on here it is certain they are doing so in Paris where the press can be more easily bought. It is notorious that Berlin news agents are responsible for the dissemination of anti-English views in St Petersburg.'[25]

The Germans supposed that the hostility of the British press was easily explained. The Teutophobe journalists were in the pay of Russian agents. Rothschild learned from Paul von Schwabach that it was 'foreign agents, especially Russian' who were propagating the 'absurd' idea that Germany was only waiting for the moment when she felt strong enough to launch an attack on Britain. Schwabach suggested that the British government ought to take 'careful measures against these spiteful utterances. . . . A direct English attack upon Germany may be brought about by no better reason than aggressive articles written by Russian journalists in English papers.'[26] Rothschild immediately passed on this report to Balfour. Schwabach's argument might have been more impressive had his examples been more convincing. He suggested that an article written by J. L. Garvin was actually the work of two Russian agents, Tatischeff and Wasselitzky. The British Foreign Office was not unaware that the 'Schwabach-Rothschild Channel' was regularly used by the Wilhelmstrasse in its attempts to influence British opinion. Effectively, Schwabach was Holstein's tool.[27] An inveterate and vicious gossip, Schwabach, a close friend of the Kaiser, was generally an unfortunate influence upon Anglo-German relations. In particular, by embroidering and broadcasting stories about King Edward, and exaggerating out of all proportion supposed royal slights, he did nothing to soothe or lessen William's envy of his uncle. He told George Saunders at the time of the first Moroccan crisis that he knew 'from one who witnessed the incident' that King Edward and Delcassé had wanted war with Germany.[28]

George Saunders had never hidden from his friends his belief that the Germans would not willingly accept the Anglo-French entente, and predicted that Germany would attempt to sunder the agreement by exerting pressure on France. In January 1905, when Port Arthur finally fell to the investing Japanese troops and Russia tottered under the double blow of crushing military defeat and revolution in the streets of St Petersburg, Bülow decided the moment had arrived to strike at France just as Saunders had predicted. Bülow thought that the blow might be dealt most effectively in Morocco. He chose as the instrument of his policy the Kaiser, then enjoying a Mediterranean cruise. Initially, the 'All Highest' was not over-enthusiastic about his commission, but cajoled by Bülow and assured that his life was not in any danger, he agreed to land at Tangiers where he delivered a series of quite remarkable orations. Bülow telegraphed his master.

> Your Majesty's imposing demeanour, the weighty speeches, especially
> those to the French chargé d'affaires and the German colony, have as
> a guarantee of Moroccan independence made a deep impression both in
> and out of Europe. . . . Part of the British press still indulge in wild
> ideas. But even this section of the British press will become more

reasonable when they realise that Germany genuinely seeks no special advantage.[29]

Bülow supposed that the British press, its sense of 'fair play' roused by Bernstorff's judicious promptings, would recognise that Germany had a sound legal argument for interfering in Morocco. The Chancellor's optimistic expectations were further raised by the attitude of *The Times*'s Morocco correspondent, W. Burton Harris. He strongly supported the Kaiser's visit. He had even promised to show to Kühlmann, Bülow's special envoy to the Tangier legation, 'all telegrams of political interest before sending them off [to London] so that they might contain nothing contrary to [German] wishes'.[30] Chirol was not pleased that Harris was cooperating with the Germans and sharply reminded him that 'the policy of the Times is to support the French in Morocco'. When this did not have the desired effect, Harris's despatches were either modified or suppressed. *The Times*'s editorials unequivocally declared that the Kaiser's visit had been a 'provocation' and William was denounced as 'an imperial agent-provocateur'.[31] No Unionist paper accepted that Germany had any legal right to support her action. They insisted that the Tangier episode had been designed specifically as an unwarranted and brutal attack upon the entente. With one voice the patriotic press asserted France's right to Morocco. *The Times* angrily insisted that 'Germany had covertly impugned the British character's staunchness and loyalty' if she supposed that Britain would not stand by France.[32] There was enormous excitement in the Foreign Office. With Balfour's agreement, Lansdowne sent a telegram to the British Ambassador in Paris to be given to Delcassé. 'Without actually committing Britain to the use of armed force [it] certainly implied its possibility.'[33]

Bülow vented much of his immediate anger and frustration on the unfortunate Bernstorff whose efforts to win over the British press had been such a dismal failure. What particularly upset the Chancellor was that it had been his suggestion that Bernstorff should go to London. He had confidently supposed Bernstorff would be able to repeat his earlier successful cultivation of the press in Munich. Falteringly, Bernstorff told his mentor of the difficulties he faced. 'After one has spoken to the journalists, one's ideas can be found in the next leading articles, but such influence lasts only twentyfour hours. Then the stream continues as of old and the single favourable editorial disappears without a trace in the torrent.'[34] Bernstorff was not entirely to blame for his failure. There had been other, more persuasive voices talking to British journalists. Count Götz von Seckendorff, who had accompanied the Kaiser on his Tangier visit, told Chirol that Albert Ballin had been the key figure in persuading the Kaiser to adopt Bülow's plan. Seckendorff emphasised that the commercial and industrial classes in Berlin were as anti-British as the Junkers and even more passionately committed to a policy of aggressive imperialism.[35] Maxse, given this information by Chirol, used it to some effect in the next issue of the *National Review* so that when Lansdowne met Metternich he reported that the German Ambassador was 'loud in his lamentations' and 'had the National Review on the brain'.[36]

Part of Bülow's plan had been to 'embarrass M. Delcassé and traverse his schemes'.[37] Lavino was busily reminding the readers of *The Times* that regretfully the entente was not an alliance, while the author of an article in the *Nineteenth Century* argued that only an alliance could 'provide a sufficient guarantee of mutual assistance and national security to both France and Britain'.[38] Some writers talked as though an offensive and defensive alliance with France already existed, a claim the Germans took seriously enough for both Lansdowne and Lascelles to have to deny it strenuously.[39]

Even though the usual 'patriotic' journalists were disposed to make brave statements about French rights in Morocco and possible alliances, there were many Frenchmen who dreaded a German attack, not in Morocco but through Belgium. What use would fine words, or even the British navy, be then? Doubts about German intentions even invaded the British Cabinet. Baleful rumour replaced sanguine certainty. Midleton later recalled to Selborne, thousands of miles away in South Africa but anxious for news from home, 'There is practically no doubt that the Germans were at one moment on the point of mobilisation in regard to France. At all events, they persuaded everybody of it.'[40] French concern was heightened by the crushing reverses their Russian ally had suffered at the hands of Britain's partner, Japan. What if the Germans, enraged and provoked beyond endurance by British press polemics and unhindered on their eastern frontier because of Russia's weakness, should choose to fall upon France in the west? As rumour and fear multiplied in Paris, the opportunity was seized by disaffected elements who had long hated Delcassé to remove him from power. His successor, Rouvier, immediately accepted German demands for a conference to settle the Moroccan problem. Suddenly, some of the Hotspurs in the English press, like H. W. Wilson, began to have doubts. 'Is it wise to add fuel to the flames?' he asked Northcliffe.

I have always held that war between England and Germany would be terrible, and I am very doubtful of the probability of our success in it. Even with France on our side, I would not lay much money upon a British victory. . . . If the recent political history of France is studied, it will be found that she has constantly given way to German susceptibilities and changed her Cabinets to suit Germany. In short, as an Austrian put it to me, the entente is 'two rotten nations leaning against each other in moral terror of Germany'.[41]

Thus in some pusillanimous English minds, the Kaiser's appearance at Tangiers 'in shining armour' altered the whole complexion of the Anglo-French entente.

So tumultuous and swift were the changes that engulfed the diplomatic scene that the confusion and uncertainty of some journalists was not to be wondered at.[42] With the meeting of the Tsar and the Kaiser at Björkö, German prestige rose alarmingly and men talked of a renewal of the *Dreikaiserbund*.[43] Spring Rice, writing from St Petersburg, told Strachey what a great success the meeting of emperor and Tsar had been and how William had made 'a most agreeable impression as Russia's one true friend in her hour of need'.

The Tsar will at last consent to take the Kaiser's advice which he has hitherto steadfastly refused to do. . . . The Court is extremely German and Germany seems to have regained all the ground lost during the last reign. . . . What is ever in the Kaiser's mind is that nothing in the world should happen without his knowledge and consent. . . . To obtain this end he is perpetually inventing a common danger which can only be confronted successfully by an association headed by the Kaiser. The common enemy at present is England, combined with the Yellow Peril, which evil combination now is menacing the world.[44]

It seemed that the Kaiser's singular vision of world affairs was confirmed when in August the Anglo-Japanese Alliance was renewed. In September, by the Treaty of Portsmouth, Russo-Japanese hostilities ceased. Immediately, if unexpectedly, it was *The Times* that led the way in campaigning for better Anglo-Russian relations.[45] Russia was, after all, France's ally. Something would have to be done to shore up the entente. Another factor increasingly impinged on the minds of journalists and Foreign Office personnel alike. Balfour's tenacious grasp on power must soon relax. What might happen, as seemed likely, if the Liberals formed the next government? Their hatred of Russia and their sentimental attachment to Germany were notorious. Chirol had observed to Charles Hardinge a year earlier that many supported the Unionists 'only because they believe a Radical Government would be a public danger in the present situation of Weltpolitik. If their confidence is shaken the life of the present Administration would not be worth much.'[46] By July 1905, Chirol thought that the one small reason for optimism was the hope that the Liberal Imperialists might capture the key portfolios in the Liberal Cabinet.

> I think it may now be taken as indisputable that Germany has lost much more than she gained by her anti-British campaign in France, and even Rosebery, if he should come in as Foreign Minister would find it difficult to carry out a pro-German policy in this country against the weight of public opinion. . . . If Edward Grey and his friends were certain to rule the roost when the other party comes in there would not be much cause for anxiety. But will they? . . . Charlie Trevelyan, one of the leading spirits of the young Radicals, was down here yesterday and his ignorance of foreign affairs was only equalled by his cocksureness. . . . You will have a jolly time if its Radical tail wags the next Administration.[47]

Chirol had noted 'a certain tenderness for Germany' in the Liberal press. Commentators on foreign affairs as anxiously focused their attentions upon J. A. Spender, the most powerful and influential journalist in the councils of the Liberal party, as upon his close associate, Edward Grey, recognised as a leading contender for Lansdowne's office. Spender was not averse to the idea of better Anglo-German relations, but he had never fallen for Bernstorff's ploys and refused to advertise Bülow's view of what should be England's 'beau rôle at the forthcoming Morocco Conference, [to] try to satisfy everybody by friendly mediation'.[48] Spender had assured Strachey that a Liberal government would not mean 'any change of *policy* as regards Germany, and least of all any weakening of our agreement with France'. The most immediate problem, however, was the 'urgent need for a change of *feeling*'.

> You probably have had just the same experience as I in regard to the French during the last few months. (1) Agitated appeals to do anything possible to damp down the anti-German agitation in this country, since the French public were in a fright lest we should involve them in *our* quarrel with Germany, and then, (2) when something quite modest was done in this direction, nervous warnings to stop lest the same public should think that we were going to desert them. We can't live perpetually on this razor edge between doing too much and doing too little but shall infallibly topple over on one side or the other unless feelings grow more stable. Then, after the Morocco affair and the nervous incompetence of the French in handling it, the Germans will pinch France whenever they want to get at us, and if the quarrel goes on, the French will by and by ask whether the understanding with us is worth the practical inconvenience of this fiction. . . . I am no pro-German and greatly dislike the German diplomatic method, but it seems to me that we are in danger of cutting off our noses to spite our face. . . . France's chief motives are (1) to avoid invasion, and (2) to secure and keep a *continental* ally in case of invasion. If the English understanding means chronic friction with Germany and estrangement from Russia, it will not last, and Germany with Russia's aid, can make it both things.[49]

Grey had a particular regard for Spender. His articles, he considered, were 'like the opinion of a valued colleague'. In 1908 Grey was to write, 'You manage to combine independent thought with unswerving support of the party in a way which is very rare.'[50] Spender had a coolness and detachment that allowed him to assess problems and personalities in a manner quite unlike that of any other contemporary Liberal journalist. Thus he was neither particularly surprised nor unduly worried when, in August 1905, he received an hysterical note from Spring Rice. 'Some of my foreign acquaintances might resent what I write,' Spring Rice began, counselling Spender, unnecessarily, not to mention his name as the source of the 'certain knowledge that in order to win Germany's favour the Liberals are prepared to throw over the French'. This information was common knowledge in Germany, America and France. Would Spender abjure the Liberal leaders 'to do nothing to encourage such an idea'?[51] Grey had heard the same story. In his speeches he spoke of 'continuity of foreign policy', no matter who should succeed Lansdowne. He made it plain that he not only supported France, but also the logical extension of the entente policy to embrace Russia. Such words were calculated to rouse the indignation of all Radical Liberals, but Grey received loyal support from Spender in the *Westminster Gazette*. Grey had told Spender he would do anything to combat the idea that the Liberals would abandon France. Otherwise they would run 'a real risk of losing France without gaining Germany who won't want us if she can detach France from us'.[52] Grey, in Maxse's words, was 'playing the white man'.

Balfour's uncanny ability to delay the inevitable demise of his administration heightened the fears of those anxious to see Grey established as Foreign Secretary. Louis Mallet, one moment prostrate with nervous exhaustion, the next flapping like a wet hen, impressed Grey 'with all the force I could, that if Germany means war, it lies with us to prevent it.' He urged anyone he thought might be able to exercise some influence 'to make every effort to get Grey in the Foreign Office or everything will go to pot. Can you get at Campbell-Bannerman *otherwise than* through the Asquiths?' he asked Strachey. He was almost deafened by the imagined sound of war drums and trumpets. 'Things are critical abroad. Germany is going to make a determined effort to capture the Liberals and thus ensure our quiescence in the event of their attacking France.'⁵³

Despite the impression he gave in public, Grey had not been altogether disinterested about his political future. In concert with Haldane and Asquith, and with the King's secretary as their eager aide, a private contract had been made between the three Liberal Imperialists in September – the Relugas compact.⁵⁴ This was intended to bind the hands of their party's Little Englander leader when constructing the Liberal Cabinet. The scheme faltered and then failed in the face of Sir Henry's resolution and Asquith's ambition to secure the reversionary title to his party's leadership.⁵⁵ There was more than a hint of desperation in Hardinge's note to Maxse: 'I believe there is now no question of Grey coming to the Foreign Office. You can understand my anxiety as to who is to be the occupant of that Department.'⁵⁶ An exhausting, frenetic week elapsed between Balfour's resignation and the announcement of Campbell-Bannerman's Cabinet.

'It is a strong Cabinet and a good Cabinet . . . symmetrical, well-balanced and very representative,' purred W. T. Stead in his *Review of Reviews*. The Liberal press seemed tolerably happy that it was not, in the *Manchester Guardian*'s words, 'the Cabinet of any section [but] of the party'. Typically Leo Maxse railed against 'the predominance of pro-Boers'. One appointment, though for different reasons, seemed to please everyone. Grey had been given charge of the Foreign Office. The officials there, Margot Asquith recorded, for once without exaggeration, had 'trembled lest he should stand out'. Sir Edward was Foreign Secretary, 'the strong silent man that a generation brought up on Carlyle earnestly sought', Lloyd George later observed, Radical tongue very firmly in cheek.⁵⁷

It was almost Christmas. The New Year would bring a general election. Men's minds most naturally turned to thoughts of home, but foreign affairs refused to recognise a hiatus whether promoted by the season of good will or the demands of the hustings. The Kaiser, even when receiving gifts from Alfred Beit, felt obliged to turn their conversation away from the subject of art to the much less anodyne topic of Anglo-German relations and especially the evils of the English press that continued to poison the wells of public opinion. Beit promised the Kaiser he would do his best to improve matters.

'Go for our chief opponents there, Moberly Bell, and Harmsworth, whom His Majesty is making a Lord,' urged William.

'Do not forget Saunders,' prompted Beit. 'Only the other day he wired

London that he had heard from an unimpeachable source that within two months Germany will have declared war on England.'

'That's a fat lie and a good one,' the Kaiser responded.

When he reported his conversation with Beit to Bülow, the Kaiser could not resist embroidering his last observation. 'That Mr Saunders is a first class swine.'[58] Had he known, George Saunders would have accepted cheerfully the Kaiser's estimate as a belated but thoroughly well-earned and deserved Christmas box.

Einkreisungspolitik – encirclement

The modern growth of Germany in population, in territory, in trade, in industry, in organisation for peace and war alike, has brought about a change in British sentiment in favour of Agreements. There is a vague feeling that Germany may in the twentieth century play the role that Spain played in the sixteenth and France in the seventeenth and eighteenth centuries, and this apprehension has made us more ready to welcome any negotiations by which cooperation with other Powers for a common defence in case of need might be facilitated.

Morning Post

Our attitude towards the Germans is not unfriendly, but they have forced us to make it defensive.

Grey to Strachey

The Radical papers are up in arms at last against Grey, who has just concluded an arrangement with the Russian Government.... The whole thing, of course, is abominable, but what fools the Radical members are to have put up with Grey these two years since the General Election.

W. S. Blunt's Diary

Rapprochement between England and Germany I hold to be entirely fictitious.

Chirol to Strachey

Beit, during his Christmas conversation with the Kaiser, observed that if the Germans generally supposed England wanted war, the English seemed equally convinced that it was the Kaiser who was spoiling for a conflict. William repeated his familiar disclaimer. He had done his best for the past eighteen years to preserve the peace of Europe. Why should he now want war, especially over Morocco? The real problem was the bellicose temper of the British. What else could explain the irrational behaviour of Francis Bertie, British Ambassador in Paris? At a private party the previous July, Bertie had abused the German Ambassador, Radolin, and then truculently asserted, 'You won't and shan't have this conference.' His tone had been so offensive that 'Prince Radolin would have been justified in challenging him to a duel, but he restrained himself.'[1]

For the six months before the delegates of the Powers met at Algeçiras on 16 January 1906, Anglo-German relations were extremely tense. In part, the

Kaiser was responsible for this. His public speeches oscillated violently between peaceful platitudes and defiant belligerence. Every war-like speech seemed to promote a fresh outburst of calumny against George Saunders in the German press. With justification, Saunders in a letter to Walter quoted Horace, *quidquid delirant reges plectuntur Achivi* – 'for every folly of the princes the Greeks feel the scourge.' Saunders suggested 'the German temper' explained the Kaiser's extravagant language.

It is essentially irreconcilable and even the most far-reaching concessions on our part would not be oil on troubled waters but oil upon flames.
The upper and middle classes in Germany are consumed with ambition, restlessness and envy. The lower classes want no war, but almost compel the Emperor to engage in an exciting Weltpolitik in order to distract attention from internal discontent.

The Germans could not forget and they would not forgive the signing of the Anglo-French entente. Had Berlin brought about a continental coalition against England, Saunders argued, 'it would have been lauded as an eminently pacific achievement designed to put an end to British predominance of the seas. ... Our entente with France, and even our alliance with Japan is regarded as nothing short of a crime, and the Emperor ... has lashed himself into a perfect fury against England.'[2] Saunders was being purposely ingenuous. The inexorable logic of Britain's new stance in foreign policy was as obvious to him as it was to the Germans. A successful entente with France was the stepping stone to an arrangement with Russia. Then where would Germany be? Charles Repington, writing to his friend Raymond Marker, Kitchener's ADC in India, put the matter in a nutshell.

You folk in Simla ... I am sorry you are so anti-Russian. The question for us is whether Russia shall join the Triple Alliance or whether she shall join us. ... Germany is now our most dangerous rival and our business is to detach every Power from her that we can influence. The French entente is the basis of all our policy in the West and the Jap Alliance in the East and I do not see why these policies should conflict.[3]

Saunders told Maxse that the Germans hoped the change of British government would be to their advantage. 'The Liberals will want to try to settle the German political and personal quarrel and will make overtures. If they do the Germans would at once taunt the French with British "defection" and try to make them nervous.' France required strong backing by Britain. Could 'the present nondescript Government' be counted upon to provide it? 'In Grey', wrote Saunders, 'I have complete confidence but what pressure may not be put upon him in the Cabinet?'[4] The part that Grey chose for England to play at the forthcoming Algeçiras Conference would be crucial. The instructions he gave to the British delegate, Sir Arthur Nicolson, were precise.

As far as I can discover the Germans will refuse altogether to concede to France the special position in Morocco which we have promised France not only to concede to her but to help her by diplomatic methods to obtain. ... Our main object therefore must be to help France to carry the point at the Conference. In return for this it is essential that we should be in her confidence both before and during the Conference and we are telling the French Government this. . . . If France does begin to talk of concessions to Germany they must be such as do not infringe the conditions of the Anglo-French declarations.[5]

'Any attempt to capture the Liberals [by Germany] will fail so long as we have Sir Edward,' Louis Mallet had confidently told Nicolson.[6] With the members of the Liberal government scattered all over the country electioneering, effectively Grey had enjoyed a free hand to determine British policy at Algeçiras.

Nicolson was Britain's sole delegate to the conference. While the other Powers' delegates crowded into the Reina Cristina Hotel, Nicolson was ensconced, immune and isolated, in a handsome villa. Though a small man, frail and twisted by rheumatism, Sir Arthur could inspire such awe in even the boldest newspaper correspondent that, as the *Daily Mail* admitted, 'none would have the temerity to buttonhole him'. Nicolson, however, was 'very glad to enjoy . . . the company and advice' of Mackenzie Wallace, attending the conference not only to report for *The Times*, but also to keep an eye on how matters developed for King Edward. He had been urged by the King 'to use every effort to bridge over the differences between Germany and France'. To Wallace, Nicolson spoke 'freely . . . feeling absolute confidence in his discretion. He has a cool head,' he told his wife, 'and his opinion is worth having.'[7]

Saunders described the appointment of Radowitz and Tattenbach, the German delegates, as 'nothing less than a provocation' to the French, 'intended to tighten the screw upon them and make them panic'.[8] The English Liberal press noted that despite all her difficulties – a change of government and Russia disabled as an effective ally – the French remained as resolute as ever in their stance on Morocco. Was it possible that Britain had offered France her unconditional support? That might explain why papers like the *Daily Mail* talked of troop movements and described the entente as an alliance. H. W. Massingham voiced the concern of English Radicals, their dislike of the notion that Britain had been 'drawn into playing with a situation of great gravity without being able to influence it for good'.[9] As to the Unionist press, Bernstorff complained to Spender, they were 'not only supporting France but egging it on'.[10] The editorials of the *Daily Mail* in particular were highly coloured and every bit as inventive as the reports it printed from its special correspondent in Algeçiras, Edgar Wallace. Lucien Wolf was persuaded to write an article in favour of Germany, but Tyrrell dismissed it as 'contradictory'.[11] Otherwise, Germany's legal claim went by default and, as Metternich told Bülow, in London, 'Our Morocco policy is seen as an attempt to smashup the Anglo-French entente.'[12]

At last the conference wearily wound to its conclusion and on 8 April 1906 an agreement was signed between France and Germany. English commentators of every political persuasion seemed to find reason to be pleased with the result. Even the dilatoriness of the delegates in reaching a settlement found an apologist in *Concord*. 'The slow methods of the law are certainly preferable to the scramble of unchecked private interest, ambition or revenge.'[13] While the entente had emerged strengthened by fire, Germany had suffered a diplomatic reverse. Italy's unexpected defection had left Germany with only Austria's support to count on. With obvious relish, in a report to *The Times* Saunders quoted the admission of the *Frankfurter Zeitung* that 'Germany cannot face the new aspect of affairs with very brilliant anticipations. . . . We can hardly face the new century arm-in-arm with Austria-Hungary alone.'[14]

There was another and unexpected item of news from Germany that completed British satisfaction: Holstein had been dismissed. Bülow had made Holstein the scapegoat for the failure of his Moroccan venture. In a desperate last-minute attempt to avoid dismissal Holstein had tried to conjure the sympathies of the British Ambassador for his undeserved plight. Crowe laconically minuted Lascelles's letter reporting this extraordinary event:

> Holstein has not, I think, been a friend of this country. . . . It is not unjust he should now pay the penalty for having persistently failed to appreciate the position which England really occupies in the world – (so long as she is strong).
>
> There is some grim humour in the fact – if it is a fact – that Herr von Holstein's fall is brought about by his own Press Bureau, that pet institution of Bismarckian policy.[15]

As befitted an 'old friend', Chirol paid Holstein a handsome tribute in *The Times*. His 'strong will, great abilities and unequalled knowledge and experience' would be missed. But there was no hiding the general satisfaction that Bülow's *éminence grise* had fallen from power. The question was, did Holstein's dismissal presage better or worse relations between England and Germany?

In the press of both countries the spirit of distrust and mutual hatred grew. No British popular newspaper engaged more eagerly in stepping up anti-German feeling than the *Daily Mail*. The newspaper's Berlin correspondent, F. V. Wile, was 32 when he resigned from the *Chicago Daily News* to join the *Mail*. He worked four years in Berlin for that paper and was paid the highest salary of any American newspaper man in Europe.[16] Lascelles reported to Hardinge that this 'clever little American Jew' had told Aubrey Stanhope of the *New York Herald* that he had been instructed by Northcliffe 'to send home sensational news at any cost. He was not to be particular about its accuracy as it was easy to contradict it afterwards.' Lascelles was furious.

> Wile seems to be acting pretty faithfully on these instructions as he has invented a speech by the Emperor . . . and is, I believe, responsible for the ridiculous statement that the Emperor declared that he would never again put his foot in Berlin if a Social Democrat were elected for the first division of Berlin, a remark which he was stated to have made many years ago about the election of a Burgomaster.[17]

The Ambassador had good reason to be angry with the *Daily Mail*. A month earlier there had been a minor panic in the Foreign Office when a secret despatch from Grey had been quoted verbatim in the *Mail*. Hardinge insisted the Berlin embassy was the source of the leak. Lascelles had been obliged to undertake a thorough and tedious investigation with no success. He had then insisted that the leak must have originated in London. 'What other information might they have?' Hardinge inquired anxiously. The *Daily Mail* enjoyed a certain notoriety among government departments for its record of publishing 'secret' information. Previously the War Office and Admiralty rather than the Foreign Office had suffered most from these depredations. To do something in the circumstances was better than nothing. Hardinge insisted the locks on all diplomatic pouches should be changed.[18]

Northcliffe was delighted by the enterprise his Berlin correspondent was showing. He later admitted to Kennedy Jones that Wile was not ideal in every particular 'but as a news gatherer he is easily the best in Berlin'.[19] Wile claimed Lascelles's charge against him was 'an infamous lie'. He intended to tell the Ambassador as much, though 'naturally employing more parliamentary language'. Wile knew how to secure Northcliffe's favour. 'I have borne vividly in mind your injunction,' he wrote, 'given in the midst of our walk through the grounds of Sutton Place last September, that the Daily Mail's representative in Berlin is not expected to get his political inspiration from HM's Embassy.'[20]

In an attempt to defuse the explosive atmosphere created by the British and German press, a group of German editors and correspondents were invited to London. To his friends' great surprise, St Loe Strachey attended a reception given for the Germans in June. There were friendly speeches of welcome by ministers, and Grey had not been above improving his status with his own backbenchers by making friendly references to the visit in Parliament.[21] But Sir Edward revealed his true feelings to Chirol who, in turn, told Strachey, now rehabilitated because he had contributed a sharp note in the *Spectator* scolding Germany for attempting to bedevil Anglo-French relations. 'May I say how glad I was to see you speak out so firmly,' Chirol told Strachey.

> Some of the speeches made by Cabinet Ministers were to my mind extraordinarily impolitic and must have been very embarrassing for Grey who did not conceal from me the other day his annoyance at the whole business. . . . This pro-German gush is very undesirable. . . . It will look like putting the seal on a popular rapprochement between the two countries which I hold to be entirely fictitious. As Grey said to me, 'the relations between Berlin and Paris must largely govern relations between Berlin and London, and as yet I have seen no indications whatever of any desire on the part of Germany to improve the former.'[22]

Through Saunders's indefatigable efforts *The Times* was able to neutralise the visit by the German editors. An article from the *Kölnische Zeitung* was quoted at length. This admitted that despite the honeyed words of international amity at the Guildhall Germany's true intention was 'to smash an understanding between France and England', and to take advantage 'of any incident likely to prove serviceable for this purpose'.[23] Crowe attached his own scathing minute to *The Times* account. 'If this fraternizing were really likely to lead to improved relations . . . something might be said for it. [But] the German Press does not influence the German Government. On the contrary, the German Government influences the Press. . . . Germans are essentially people whom it does not pay to run after.' Grey added his own cynical observation. 'There is nothing more in what has been said about Germany lately in this country than a gratification of the desire to gush, which is very strong just now.'[24]

Eyre Crowe valued the work of his brother-in-law, Spenser Wilkinson, leader writer and military correspondent of the *Morning Post*, but was not disposed to subscribe to the generally accepted dictum that the press materially affected international relations.[25] That, he maintained, was a newspaper fiction believed in by journalists and well-meaning but weak-minded politicians. His own estimate he advertised in an exhaustive memorandum, 'On the present state of British relations with France and Germany'.

> It is exceedingly doubtful whether the campaign [carried on against this country in the German Press and in some measure responded to in the English papers] has any share whatever in determining the attitude of the two Governments, and those people who see in the newspaper controversy the main cause of friction between Germany and England and who consequently believe that the friction can be removed by fraternisation of journalists . . . have not sufficiently studied – in most cases could not possibly be in a position to study – the records of the actual occurrences which have taken place, and which clearly show that it is the direct action of the German Government which has been the all-sufficient cause of whatever obstacles there may be to the maintenance of normally friendly relations between the two countries.[26]

Eyre Crowe's view was certainly blinkered but it cannot be ignored for it was the opinion of the professional diplomat *par excellence*. The consistency with which he maintained his view is clear from a letter he wrote to Sir Charles Dilke later that same year from The Hague, about an article by Sir Thomas Barclay in the *Fortnightly*. Crowe dismissed Barclay as one of that 'confraternity of international busybodies who believe they are leading the world, whilst in reality they are merely the tools of those Powers who find it useful to encourage [them]'.[27] Other permanent members of the Foreign Office staff, while they admired Crowe's Olympian view of his profession's untrammelled importance, nevertheless paid more than cursory attention to courting the favours of the press, if for no better reason than insurance. Charles Hardinge, for example, during the course of the negotiations for the Anglo-Russian agreement, wrote to tell Nicolson in St Petersburg that he had 'been endeavouring to work the press . . . It will all help on the good cause.'[28] As Saunders had told Walter before the Algeçiras conference, if only in a negative sense, German attempts to persuade their public to support a *Weltpolitik* had been enormously enhanced by *Le Matin*'s revelation of supposed secret clauses in the entente, and a foolish article contributed by Admiral Fitzgerald to the *Deutsche Revue* advocating a pre-emptive strike against the Germany navy.

> These really distorted revelations were a perfect God-send to the German chauvinists. . . . William II . . . could not persuade people that there was any real danger of an attack from our side as all they were able to adduce (and constantly did adduce) was an article which appeared . . . [1898] . . . in the Saturday Review then at the lowest ebb of its fortunes, entitled 'Delenda est Germania'. This article – written, I believe, by the then musical critic of the Saturday! – they continued to cite ad nauseam until the other day.[29]

Despite Crowe's disdainful opinion, others believed that some good might come from the exchange of journalists. A German invitation to Berlin for British press representatives was accepted by many distinguished newspaper men. Leo Maxse was quick to point out that among 'the peripatetic host marshalled by Mr Spender' to pay 'a pious pilgrimage to Potsdam and other Anglophobe shrines in Germany', there were 'no representatives of *The Times, Morning Post, Daily Mail, Evening News, Globe, Spectator, Observer, Nineteenth Century & After, Fortnightly Review* and other organs of light and learning'.[30] Modesty presumably dictated he should not number his own *National Review* in that company! W. T. Stead, who was going to Berlin, attempted to persuade Strachey to change his mind. 'The French are most absurdly sensitive as to any rapprochement between us and Germany ... but, any danger that might be feared from the German visit might be counteracted by an invitation to French editors to visit this country.' Strachey was unmoved by Stead's proposal of an endless exchange of editors. His reply was disconcertingly chilling. 'I do not think that relations are likely to become more friendly by the artificial creation of social niceties. On the contrary, they are likely to be made worse.'[31]

The German welcome quite outshone the one they had received a year earlier in London. There were banquets and fulsome speeches by various ministers, but it was the Kaiser who provided the high-spot of the junketing. On his birthday, resplendent in the full dress uniform of the Prussian Guard, seated astride an enormous steed, with suitable condescension, William summoned select journalists to converse with him in turn. Spender, as leader of the group, was afforded the further privilege of an interview with the Chancellor. The one startling piece of information he returned with was that Bülow had introduced him to Holstein, news that Metternich dismissed as 'impossible'.[32]

It was hardly surprising that Metternich should have been amazed by Spender's story. Chaos ruled among Germany's leaders. 'The muddle in the Foreign Office', Charles Towers of Associated Newspapers wrote to Strachey, 'is perfectly intolerable. Nobody seems to know what anyone else is doing.' It was enough that the Germans were acutely sensitive about their lost prestige over Morocco, but Lascelles admitted what concerned him was that at any moment some rash action by the Kaiser, who was in a highly excitable and irritable temper, might further complicate the already troubled international scene. Bülow was also behaving very strangely.

> Several departmental ministers have told Sir Frank that they could get nothing attended to by the Chancellor who seems to write speeches and then go away. Von Zedlitz ... told the correspondent of the Zeit the other day that Bülow 'seemed to have more time than ever for extraneous interests and pursuits,' which from what Sir Frank said would seem to be true enough, but not exactly as Zedlitz meant it. Altogether things are confused and there is a possibility that the winter season will bring some kind of climax. Maximilian Harden ... who just now is on good terms with Holstein says ... there are storms about to burst.[33]

The storms that Harden had in mind were of his own making. Holstein, still sore about his dismissal, was convinced that it had been engineered by the Kaiser's friend, Eulenberg. Harden, with Holstein as the eager abetter of his schemes, wrote a series of articles in his newspaper, *Die Zukunft*, accusing certain intimates of the Kaiser, including Eulenberg and Count Moltke, the City Commandant of Berlin, of taking part in homosexual activities. The consequent furore continued for months and was enormously damaging to the credibility of the German ruling class. The Kaiser, beside himself with frustration and rage, was forced to abandon Eulenberg to his fate. Bülow roused himself from his other pursuits to take a hand in the affair. The removal, first of Eulenberg, and subsequently of Posadowsky and Tschirsky, conveniently disposed of a trio of possible rivals to the chancellorship. When Moltke successfully sued Harden for libel, the editor was handsomely compensated by Bülow out of public funds. The significant feature of the whole tawdry business was that at its end the Kaiser was even more isolated from his advisers than before. The prospect of William acting on his own initiative without any professional advice was sufficient to worry anyone interested in the rational conduct of Germany's foreign policy. Lascelles believed that the '*jeu des beaux yeux*' had been played out, 'partly to still the insistent warnings of the staider German press, but chiefly to gain time to clear things up at home'. For the same reason, the German government was 'really anxious to reach a state of détente even with France'. If Lascelles's estimate was correct, then the persistent snarling about German ambitions that continued in sections of the English patriotic press could only be counterproductive. They were 'carrying England's attitude towards Germany onto a wholly false plain'. Towers shared Lascelles's opinion. 'It is one thing to "keep your powder dry",' he concluded his letter to Strachey, 'another thing to be continually sniping. The result of the latter is more than likely to precipitate the events which one desires to avoid, namely a campaign on false issues and off the strategic line.'[34]

Bernstorff, who had now left the London embassy for Cairo, had constantly drawn the Kaiser's attention to the more violent diatribes in the English press so that William entertained 'very mistaken impressions as to the relative importance and circulation of certain newspapers and magazines'. Lord Edmond Fitzmaurice, Liberal Under Secretary of State for Foreign Affairs, who deplored the extreme anti-German line pursued by some writers, told Lascelles that he 'quite understood the irritation in Germany at the constant anti-German press campaign in England conducted by Rowland Blennerhassett', but the Germans 'ought not to exaggerate its importance'.[35] Sir Rowland was busy informing Grey that, in his opinion, 'Anglo-German relations have never been so good as during the last three years.' He was not trying to be amusing, merely advertising his recipe for a successful British foreign policy. 'Stick close by France ... otherwise we shall drift into the worst possible relations with the Government at Berlin which will be encouraged by our cowardice and folly to become unbearably aggressive and violent.'[36] Blennerhassett's view was simple: emphasise German faults, cling to the entente at any cost, arm to the teeth and remain on guard constantly against likely German perfidy. Maxse shared these views. When the British Prime Minister actually proposed a peace initiative, the apoplectic response of the *National Review* was only to be expected.

Sir Henry Campbell-Bannerman had frequently declared his concern that the ever-increasing pace and cost of the armament competition between the Powers threatened European peace. He determined that the British government should at least attempt to effect a reduction, but it was only after consultation with Grey that he wrote an article for the first number of the new Radical weekly, the *Nation*, on 'The Hague Conference and the limitation of armaments'. The general tone was anodyne, but Sir Henry promised that Britain would do more than she had done already to reduce military and naval expenditure, 'provided we find a similar disposition in other quarters'.[37] His words had been carefully chosen to cause neither offence nor misunderstanding. The *Albany Review* supposed Campbell-Bannerman had voiced 'the great but inarticulate aspiration of the common people', but the *Daily Mail* bluntly reminded the Prime Minister he had not been given a mandate by the nation 'to weaken its Navy for the sole purpose of providing funds for doles to the Socialists'. Maxse exploded in the *National Review*. It was 'monstrous' that a British Prime Minister could write such 'perilous twaddle', and at a time when the Kaiser had won an electoral victory in the Reichstag for his big navy policy.

> It is insane of British statesmen to go whining for disarmament, all the more as it is exceedingly distasteful to the French Government . . .
> though no doubt the British Premier . . . is too fatuously self-complacent to realise the ill-concealed indignation he has aroused in responsible circles in Paris. The only effective reply to German preparation, which is undoubtedly directed against this country . . . is adequate counter-preparation.[38]

It was upon such stony ground that Campbell-Bannerman's noble initiative withered and died. The applause of the British Liberal press was scarcely audible in the din created by their patriotic, Conservative contemporaries. Only *The Times* advertised its singularity by affecting a contemptuous indifference. In Europe, the Germans were not alone in supposing that the Prime Minister's article had been nothing but a 'transparent hypocrisy . . . part of a Machiavellian design and a step towards the destruction of the German Navy'.[39]

To laughter and cheers, Bülow announced in the Reichstag on 30 April 1907 that Germany declined to discuss the question of disarmament at The Hague. 'We confine ourselves to allowing those Powers which look forward to some result from that discussion to conduct the discussion alone.' After such an overture six weeks before the delegates were to meet, even the keenest British supporters of arbitration and disarmament reluctantly admitted to themselves that they should not expect too much from The Hague Conference. By a strange, but in the circumstances entirely appropriate paradox, H. W. Nevinson, retained by the *Daily Chronicle* as a war correspondent, found himself assigned to the Second Hague Peace Conference. The delegates, he noted, were not exactly those one would have chosen to usher in a new era for mankind. As to the international propagandists of pacifism, among that strange crew the strangest was the ubiquitous W. T. Stead, 'bouncing with vitality and running over with human kindness towards Emperors, Kings, peoples, and a bevy of girls alike; exuberant for peace, and in the end calling for as many battleships as we could possibly build'.[40]

Though the sessions were held in secret, this did not deter Stead from publishing a 'daily chronicle of the debates of the first Parliament of the World', his *Courier de la Conférence*. Stead was already in bad odour with the British Foreign Office. His inclination to be carried away by his own enthusiasm sometimes prompted a cavalier approach to the truth. In January, he had written in *Le Matin* that he had been 'authorised by the Prime Minister and Foreign Secretary to make certain declarations concerning Government policy at the forthcoming Peace Conference'. Sir Henry indignantly denied the claim. Grey merely informed Bertie that he saw no reason to volunteer a public contradiction 'unless serious notice is taken of Mr Stead's statement'.[41] Grey was not unduly worried by Stead's fabrications. Neither was Eyre Crowe who attended the conference and reported, 'Mr Stead has been encouraged by Germany, Austria and Russia to disseminate under the pacifist flag of his exceedingly scurrilous paper . . . daily attacks on England and all her works, to the intense delight and satisfaction of all who enjoy this popular representation.'[42] Stead was generally recognised as the licensed clown at such international jamborees, and Crowe could afford to be dismissive. Not so, however, about Germany's chief delegate, Marschall, 'the embodiment of the double-faced spirit of intrigue' who apparently had set his sights upon his appointment as Ambassador in London. 'He seems to me', Crowe wrote to Tyrrell, 'cunning and false to a degree, very plausible, very determined, a most dangerous person, deep in all newspaper manipulation. He has here a regular press bureau installed in his hotel. Even Saunders of the Times is not proof against his tricks. He *certainly* works several English newspapers from here.'[43]

The Hague Conference never recovered from its bad start. The formal opening coincided with the dramatic news that the Russian Duma had been dissolved. 'The genius of Aeschylus', pronounced *New Age*, 'could not have created a more tragic chorus.'[44] So mercilessly did Stead revile and ridicule the British delegation that Grey, much against his inclination, was obliged to remonstrate. Characteristically, Stead paid no attention, pronouncing the conference 'a miserable and scandalous débâcle'.[45] Nevinson thought that to call it a peace conference was, at best, 'an amusing instance of ironic mockery'. It was as though 'two farmers, long accustomed to confirm their neighbour-liness by burning each other's ricks, had met for a conference upon their future behaviour and had parted amicably with the agreement in future to use safety matches only'.[46] Equally jaundiced, but for different reasons, Crowe summarised the achievement of the conference. It had accentuated the serious differences that divided the Powers. 'Our disarmament crusade has been the best advertisement of the German Navy League and every German has by now been persuaded that England is exhausted, has reached the end of her tether and must speedily collapse if the pressure is kept up. You will find that this impression now prevails all over Germany.'[47]

The Conservative press indulged in a great outburst, addressed to their Liberal contemporaries, of 'I told you so.' There was some justification for this behaviour. The Berlin *Post* had dismissed Campbell-Bannerman's initiative with the flat assertion that war between England and Germany was now *inevitable*. 'Nobody in Germany doubts England's abhorrence of war, but abhorrence of war has nothing to do with Anglo-German relations. The conditions of Germany's development and her rivalry with England for world power would of themselves bring about a fatal collision.'[48] Austin Harrison, formerly in charge of Reuter's Agency in Berlin but now drama critic of the *Observer*, contributed two widely noticed articles on Anglo-German relations. Old Germany, he asserted, was dead, and in its place stood

> New Germany in mailed coat, defiant, exasperated, determined, at bay, with her right hand on the scabbard. . . . The new generation is saturated in world-political dreams and ambitions and has been educated to the understanding of a forward maritime policy. . . . Believing, as the German Government does, that a final struggle for world power with England is inevitable, it is paving the way for that struggle by representing England as the enemy and the aggressor. It is thus in advance ensuring the full support of the German nation for any blow which it may suddenly deal.[49]

Quoting Dr Johnson, with evident relish the *Daily Mail* insisted, 'Let us clear our minds of cant.' Peace conferences were so much 'humbug'. The world was now 'an armed camp; rumours of war come from both east and west, nor are the sparks wanting that may at any time ignite the loose powder that has been so carelessly strewn in bountiful profusion'.[50]

The ultimate irony of the Second Hague Peace Conference was that when it ended Anglo-German naval rivalry had reached new heights of intensity. From the beginning there had been an unbridgeable lacuna in Campbell-Bannerman's argument. To satisfy some he had said, 'We will ask at The Hague for a measure of disarmament.' To satisfy others he had asserted, 'Such disarmament as we might be prepared to undertake will not endanger the nation's safety or naval supremacy.' It was impossible to satisfy both groups of opinion, nor would it have been any defence to plead that the same argument had been earlier employed by that master of logic-chopping, Balfour. Whatever hopes Sir Henry might have entertained, Grey had no illusions about what the conference might achieve. So much is apparent from the instructions he had given Sir Edward Fry. 'The Government cannot agree to any resolution which would diminish the effective means which the Navy has of bringing pressure to bear upon the enemy.'[51] It was too much to suppose that the Germans would accept British assurances that the navy was a purely defensive force.

Grey's attentions had been focused not so much upon The Hague as the negotiations to achieve agreement with Russia. The prospects had been bleak, with the pro-German party dominating Russian court and government circles, but as early as March 1906, he had won the tacit agreement of Benckendorff to work for understanding between their two countries. Grey had clearly defined his hopes in a letter to Knollys, the King's secretary. The agreement was 'a thing most to be desired' for it would 'complete and strengthen the entente with France and add very much to the strength and comfort of our position'.[52] After his triumph at Algeçiras, Nicolson was the obvious choice for the crucial post of Ambassador to St Petersburg. At a dinner party Grey gave for Nicolson on the eve of his departure for Russia, 'for more than four hours' they talked 'entente, in and out, up and down'. The little Ambassador admitted that he undertook his new task 'with great diffidence and considerable misgiving'.[53] Nicolson's most invaluable aide at the Foreign Office was to be Charles Hardinge who had recently returned from Russia determined to bring about Anglo-Russian agreement. He was convinced a revived Russia would provide a real continental check to any German threat. Fear of Germany and the possibility of Russo-German rapprochement dominated English thinking throughout the negotiations.[54]

The problems to be faced were formidable. Many Liberals were resolutely opposed to any dealings with Russia. When Grey told the Commons he had decided to send the British fleet to Cronstadt during its Baltic cruise, he was loudly denounced by his own backbenchers. Only the Russians' tactful request that the visit he abandoned saved Grey's face. The dissolution of the Duma in July was another crippling blow. Grey knew that the best way to placate his critics was some measure of success for the Russian reform movement. Hardinge was desolate. This latest blow had undermined 'the edifice which we have been building up with so much care'. Nicolson was equally distraught. 'Two months ago there was every hope and now very little.'[55] The Radical press was cock-a-hoop supposing that even Grey would not now have the temerity to support Russia knowing that England's friendship would be 'seized as a prop by the tottering despotism still red with the fresh blood of Bielostok'.[56] In contrast with the loud lamentations and protestations of the Liberal press, Conservative newspapers either ignored or played down Russia's internal problems in their occasional forays to defend Grey against his own party.

The Radicals had sharply criticised the countenancing of any financial loan to Russia quoting Milyoukov, the Cadet party leader, who insisted it would be 'bitterly resented by the Russian people'.[57] Nevertheless, in April, a joint Anglo-French loan was raised. Criticism by the Radical press was expected, but what concerned the supporters of Anglo-Russian rapprochement was the attitude adopted by *The Times*. When the Duma was dissolved, *The Times* not only criticised the Russian 'despotism' but added the stinging observation that it 'justified those who had besought the friends of constitutional liberty not to lend more money to the autocracy'.[58] There were members of the Russian government who did not care a fig for the good opinion or otherwise of *The Times*, but Benckendorff assured Isvolsky, Russia's Foreign Minister, that 'A telegram regarding general foreign policy in that newspaper has a thousand times the importance of a similar one in another newspaper, and it is the same in the realm of foreign finance.' The Ambassador argued that his government would do well to recognise such influence and do everything it could to restore good relations with Printing House Square. Benckendorff busily curried favour with as many English newspapers as possible. He boasted of his close rapport with the *Standard* and *Daily Telegraph*, but admitted that his contacts with *The Times* were unfortunately both intermittent and indirect.[59]

At Printing House Square there was little if any sympathy felt for the problems of the Russian government. Walter simply dismissed the country as 'outside the pale of civilisation'. Both he and Moberly Bell had never forgiven the Russians for expelling *The Times* St Petersburg correspondent.[60] The British Foreign Office, then and subsequently, had done everything it could to persuade them to be a little less intransigent. Despite Hardinge's best efforts with Chirol the position had not materially altered since October 1903 when Sanderson had admitted to Spring Rice that as *The Times*'s owner and manager were so resolute, he did 'not imagine that benevolent advice would have any effect'.[61] If there was to be a change, the initiative would have to come from the Russians. Yet, in Chirol's words, when 'a very substantial olive branch was held out', Walter and Moberly Bell gave in only with the greatest reluctance. After protracted negotiations, on 17 December 1906, *The Times* announced 'with satisfaction':

> The Russian Government has withdrawn the administrative measures directed, as we have always held, without justification against our former Correspondent, and the whole incident henceforth belongs, we trust, to a past phase in Russian affairs, which has, we know, been long regretted by many Russians.

This graceless, sanctimoniously smug tone was not enhanced by the absurd claim that because they had re-established their correspondent in St Petersburg, this would 'naturally tend to promote an intelligent knowledge of Russian affairs in England'. The assertion was pure humbug for there was considerable confusion in the minds of *The Times*'s staff how they should best treat Russia. Naturally, Lavino was delighted for he had long been an enthusiastic protagonist of an Anglo-Russian entente. Wallace was not unsympathetic to that idea either, but for the moment was not prepared to commit himself one way or another. Bell and Walter remained aloof but suspicious. Chirol was not at all certain what good, if any, might come from negotiating with the Russians, but, as a long letter to Nicolson makes clear, he gave his tacit support to the negotiations because he was apprehensive about German intentions.

> I am following with the keenest interest the progress of your negotiations which seem at last to have entered on a really promising phase, and the more closely I study the situation created in Germany by the last elections, the more I feel disposed to welcome any agreement with Russia which offers a fair prospect of permanency. . . . I feel convinced that when William, in his torch-light speech after the election, talked about riding down whatever obstacles are placed in our way, he was not thinking merely of his Social Democrats.[62]

The Radical press continued to express its concern about rapprochement with Russia and censured public apathy.[63] Wallace was not concerned about public indifference so much as that shown by Unionist politicians. That *was* worrying. He was exercising what influence he had upon Chirol, and told Nicolson he thought he had 'opened his eyes a little'. But, for the most part 'people have made up their minds – *leur siège est fait* – it is no use trying to convert them to a truer conception of the state of things. Still, I do what I can in private ways.' Whatever happened, the Unionists would not be able to deny 'that this Government has simply carried out their policy, and that if we do not get as much as we would like, the fact is due mainly to their inactivity in office'.[64]

Grey's Radical opponents would have heartily agreed with Wallace's estimate.

The *Nation* warned its readers that 'a certain mobilisation of Powers is proceeding with England and France at its centre, always with Germany outside'.[65] They could hardly admit that a *Liberal* Foreign Secretary was pursuing such a policy *voluntarily*. Nor, because they advocated retrenchment in armament expenditure, would they accept Garvin's explanation in the *Fortnightly Review*, that British policy was the necessary response to 'Germany's challenge to our naval supremacy which is the life of our race'.[66] George Saunders had been saying and implying as much by his reports from Berlin in *The Times* for years. The Radicals were left with a conspiracy theory. Stead argued in his *Review of Reviews*, Grey behaved as he did because he was 'the prisoner of the Tchinovnik of the Foreign Office', by which he meant Charles Hardinge. Strachey rebuked Stead for this in private. He reminded Stead that Grey was his personal friend and that they had been at Balliol together. Strachey knew Grey to be high-minded, scrupulously honourable and nobody's poodle. Not satisfied with this Strachey wrote a long article in the *Spectator* arguing that Unionists like himself supported Grey because of his 'practical wisdom and high sense of responsibility in the management of foreign affairs'. It was 'absurd' for anyone to suppose that 'Grey was eclipsed by Sir Charles Hardinge, or that he [was] a puppet in the hands of his Foreign Office officials.' But Strachey was too close to Grey ever to be entirely convincing as an unbiased commentator on his stewardship of the Foreign Office.[67]

St Loe was among the first to congratulate Grey on the signing of the Anglo-Russian Convention. 'I am sure', he wrote, 'that no better piece of work has been done for the safety and welfare of the Empire and the peace of the world for many years.'[68] Strachey's order of priorities is interesting. The removal of the Russian threat to India was enormously important to any imperialist as Grey's Radical critics were only too well aware. They concentrated upon the European implications of the convention, how it altered what they called the European Concert. Agreement between Russia and England was 'not a guarantee of peace but an anti-German design to restore the influence of Russia as a counterpoise to Germany in the interests of *British Weltpolitik*'.[69] Radicals wanted a Liberal Foreign Secretary to pursue a Liberal foreign policy. Leo Maxse, on the contrary, was forever blustering that foreign policy was not a party concern. What otherwise, he asked pertinently, might be meant by the notion of 'continuity' in foreign policy? Leo insisted that wise men would ignore the 'ignorant sentimentalists', and, 'the Potsdam Party in the Cabinet', and instead give their whole-hearted support to Sir Edward Grey who, 'in a remarkably short space of time ha[d] succeeded in securing the confidence of Europe by his sincerity and loyalty'.[70]

When the news was made public that an Anglo-Russian agreement had been signed, Mackenzie Wallace wrote to his old friend Nicolson congratulating him upon 'the successful termination' of his 'great work'. The news had been sudden and a 'great surprise for it always seemed to me that you were too sanguine'. Wallace was 'delighted to find that I was wrong'. The convention was 'an historical event of considerable importance'.[71] Chirol was much less enthusiastic and admitted there were 'many things in this by no means ideal Agreement that go desperately against the grain'. He could not find it in his heart to become an ardent Russophile overnight.[72] Nevertheless, for the moment, he was prepared to give the agreement his public support. *The Times* claimed the convention 'would lead to closer and more intimate relations all over the world'.[73] Spender in the *Westminster Gazette* also adopted this 'official' line and explicitly denied that there had been 'any European motive'.[74] The *Nation* was not blind to these specious assurances. When the convention was debated in the Commons, Massingham asserted Russo-British rapprochement was 'a development of the ties created by our French entente. That is its real genesis. We have carried out M. Delcassé's idea and isolated conservative Germany by embracing reactionary Russia.'[75] In a letter to *The Times*, H. N. Brailsford put the matter more shortly. 'Had peace been our object we should have sought it rather in Berlin than in St Petersburg.'[76]

The diplomatic scene had suffered a revolutionary change. With the Balance of Power in Europe transformed, Anglo-German relations were bound to be affected. Maxse, always anticipating trouble, was concerned about the constrained attitude of the German Foreign Office. He solemnly warned his readers that they should prepare themselves 'for the usual mischief-making. . . . That England and Russia have publicly shaken hands is anathema to the powers-that-be in Berlin.'[77] As he had been among the first to propagate and publicise the idea of rapprochement with Russia he was delighted with the convention and wrote of it in the *National Review* as strengthening Anglo-French ties. In his private correspondence, however, he described its *raison d'être* as a guarantee against German aggression.

German diplomats naturally were guarded in their response to the convention. Von Miquel, chargé d'affaires at St Petersburg, analysing the true inspiration behind the agreement noted that if it could not be ascribed to any anti-German tendency, nevertheless, it was Germany that was most affected. The Kaiser minuted this observation, 'Yes, when taken all round, it is aimed at us.' German politicians were not so circumspect as their diplomats when making statements. The Nationalist deputies in the Reichstag regarded the implications of Anglo-Russian reconciliation as considerably more sinister and disquieting than any Anglo-French entente. It was the crowning success of *Einkreisungspolitik*. Germany was encircled, isolated from the other major Powers.[78]

For Saunders, Maxse, Garvin and all the other so-called 'Teutophobes' of the British press, Europe offered a distinctly pleasanter prospect in the autumn of 1907 than it had a decade earlier. The British government had changed and a Liberal politician now had charge of the Foreign Office, but their warnings had apparently been heeded, their advice accepted. Where Britain had been isolated, the target of Germany's scheming, she now was a member of the Triple Entente. Germany's diplomatic position had been weakened considerably since William could count with certainty only upon the tattered Austro-Hungarian Empire as an ally. At that moment, as they contemplated the diplomatic revolution they had so ardently sponsored, those journalists could not have been aware of the baleful consequences that would follow, or of the fragile nature of the newly forged entente of Russia, France and England.

•••••••• PART 2 ••••••••

Alarums and excursions:
the admirals
and the generals

7

Dies irae, dies illa

The *Daily Mail* is the embodiment and the mouthpiece of the Imperial idea. We know that the advance of the Union Jack means protection for weaker races, justice for the oppressed, liberty for the down-trodden. Our Empire has not yet exhausted itself. Great tasks lie before it, great responsibilities have to be borne.

It is for the power, the greatness, the supremacy of this Empire that we have stood. In the heart of every Englishman has dawned the consciousness that a still greater destiny awaits us.

Daily Mail's *Fourth Anniversary Editorial*

What will the twentieth century be? What will be its distinctive note? What does it bear in its awful womb? Of one thing only we can be certain – that it will be a period of keen, intelligent, almost fierce international competition. How then should we prepare for such an epoch, such a conflict?

Rosebery's Address as Glasgow University's Rector

I was probably right when I told Herbert Spencer I thought it would need a foreign army landed on our shores to bring us quite to our sober senses.

W. S. Blunt's Diary

The Liberal party was hopelessly distracted and divided over imperial questions. Their Unionist opponents suffered no such damaging doubts and their electoral victory in 1895 was recognised as a sign that the nation wanted a policy of imperial expansion. For Unionists like Joseph Chamberlain it was a time of optimism and boundless opportunity. As he told the Duke of Devonshire, 'We have a chance now of doing something which will make this government memorable.'[1] Like a giant refreshed, Britain joined with other European powers, in Asia but more especially Africa, 'pegging out claims for the future'. For the most part the British public enthusiastically endorsed these adventures. Few then seemed disposed to count the possible future cost. Wilfrid Blunt simply recorded in his diary for January 1896: 'In just six months Britain has managed to quarrel violently with China, Turkey, Belgium, Ashanti, France, Venezuela, America and Germany. This is a record performance.'[2]

People's ideas about imperialism were invested with much sentimental humbug. The public in its enthusiasm ignored uncomfortable facts; they displayed attitudes that would have been more appropriate in the acolytes of a novel religion than the arbiters of a political policy. The patriotic press signalled its unalloyed enthusiasm with brashly vulgar propaganda and prophecies of unadulterated optimism. *The Times* proved on occasion to be as adept as the *Daily Express* or *Daily Mail* at sonorously hymning meaningless imperial slogans. Imperialism was excited in the theatre, celebrated in the music hall, and exhorted in the novels, histories and poems of writers like Henty and Stevenson, Haggard and Conrad, Fitchett and Newbolt. But imperialism's supreme public advocate and popular exponent was Rudyard Kipling. For him, the British were, in the Old Testament sense of that word, a *chosen* people. Their privilege was to rule a quarter of the globe, their task to 'carry the white man's burden'. If the nation was to fulfil adequately its great imperial destiny, it ought to be dutiful, obedient and sober. Scarcely aware that privilege implied responsibilities, the British were 'bung-full of beastly spiritual pride, material luxury and over-ease, unconsciously turning ideals to a mean and easy life ... and making civilization another name for shirking'.[3] Although he censured this laxity unmercifully, Kipling discerned little evidence of a new, sterner spirit informing the British nation. 'Like you,' he wrote to his friend, the naval journalist, Leslie Cope-Cornford, 'I ain't happy – but gravely disquieted in my innards. Like you I see no hope, neither any escape from our imbecile apathy.'[4]

In a strange way, the initial shock administered to British complacency by the Boers in 1899 was welcomed by anxious imperialists as a salutary lesson that might, at least, impress the nation and rouse it from apathy. Edward Levy Lawson, principal proprietor of the *Daily Telegraph*, wrote to J. L. Garvin, 'We want discipline as a nation. We have been living, for years, too much in idleness, in luxury, in a condition without any of the painstaking spirit by the influence of which nations have maintained and increased their power.... The war, whatever its issue, must give us a new impulse and a new ideal that will be invaluable to the Empire.'[5] There was another lesson that the war might profitably teach. As Spring Rice told Chirol in December 1899: 'We cannot separate our politics from knowledge of military conditions. The intimate connection of the two departments has been one of the main causes of German success. They learnt it in a hard school and we shall have to learn too.'[6]

The public's appetite for the literature of war and tales of military adventure was insatiable – a fact that the newspapers recognised. But the press was always more mindful of profit than principle. 'The instruction it furnished its pupils', in the opinion of Sir John Ardagh, Director of Military Intelligence, was 'not only ignorant but partial, and [the press was] disposed to pander to its pupils for the sake of popularity.'[7] The public wanted to be amused and diverted, not instructed. It was at best indifferent and frequently hostile to the private soldier.[8] The people were uncaring of the army's condition and supposed it was enough that as wars were invariably fought to distant lands they should cost as little as possible and cause no inconvenience to everyday life. As Spring Rice bitterly observed to R. C. M. Ferguson:

Imperialism is not so bad a thing if you pay for it in your own blood, but

spending 3 per cent out of your stock-exchange gains to buy people to
fight for you in picturesque places in order to provide you with interesting
illustrated papers (or new investments) is a different thing. . . . Are we
like a man who dreams of being a great admiral and goes on shore at
once because he is sea-sick? I wish we hadn't boasted and shouted so
much and spoilt our own game and turned the whole thing into a burglar's
prowl.[9]

Wilfrid Blunt claimed that militarism reigned supreme in Europe. In England
it seemed to manifest itself in posturing, hideous swagger, a lust for glory and
a lack of moral proportion. Was the public so blind as not to see that 'the
amusements of Empire would some day soon demand their price'?[10]

The Liberal member for West Newington, Captain Cecil Norton,
complained that in ten years in the Commons, in any debate intended to
improve army conditions, speakers invariably addressed 'a practically empty
House, an empty press gallery and an unsympathetic public'.[11] St Loe Strachey
castigated politicians for being so spineless when it came to military reforms.
'It is a discreditable thing that a press campaign should be necessary before
the commonest precautions are taken.'[12] Strachey's criticism was valid but hid
a more significant truth. Military questions are exceedingly complex and to
answer them requires considerable technical expertise, planning in the long
term, strategy and organisation. Public and parliamentarians had neither the
time nor the inclination to master the intricacies involved. Consequently a
campaign to effect any change – except at a time of national crisis, real or
imagined – fell easy victim to the stone-walling tactics of conservative minded
'experts'. Should this frustrating hurdle be negotiated there remained the even
more imposing barrier of an ever-vigilant Treasury wedded to economy. A
scheme's importance or necessity was never an adequate defence against it
being 'whittled down by a Treasury *non possumus*'.[13]

Before the outbreak of war with the Boers a few voices only had cried in
the wilderness of public indifference for a serious consideration of the military
and strategic implications of Britain's changing position in world affairs. None
had spoken more urgently or cogently on this subject than Spenser Wilkinson,
military correspondent of the *Morning Post*.[14] He complained frequently and
bitterly that nobody in Salisbury's Cabinet had 'thoroughly thought out the
relations between policy, war and naval and military preparations'. He insisted
not the army but its political masters were at fault. At the beginning of its
campaign in South Africa, the army had been 'deliberately handicapped' by
the government who had conceded the strategical advantage to the enemy by
sending too few reinforcements too late. Nevertheless, Wilkinson thought the
war might achieve some good. 'It is giving us the beginnings of political
education in a department that has been utterly neglected!'

Wilkinson had powerful and influential friends. At the Foreign Office, his
brother-in-law, Eyre Crowe, owed him his education in military matters.
Another of Wilkinson's disciples, H. O. Arnold-Forster, succeeded Brodrick
as War Minister in 1903. A particularly close friend was Lord Roberts. The
two men had campaigned together and Roberts frequently sought Wilkinson's

advice. Sir William Nicholson, appointed Ardagh's successor as Director of Military Intelligence, was so impressed by Wilkinson's ability and his profound knowledge of military history, administration and tactics that he had wanted him appointed as his assistant. The proposal failed when it fell foul of Treasury parsimony. General Hamilton supplied Wilkinson not only with official reports but also a stream of trenchant opinion, usually less than flattering about the British high command in South Africa, particularly Sir Redvers Buller. 'Use this information,' 'Johnny' Hamilton had instructed Wilkinson, 'provided you contrive to turn the actual wording a little.'[15]

Initially, the popular Unionist newspapers had chosen to treat war with the Boers with derision. Sir Almeric Fitzroy, Clerk to the Privy Council, was appalled by the levity and irresponsibility. 'At a moment when the public mind is excited, its nerves unstrung and its credulity omniverous ... the patriotic press from a vulgar love of sensational headlines and a desire to be the first to disseminate anything that can astound or appal the popular imagination ... show an utter indifference to the correction of impressions that rest on imperfect information for the spread of which they are themselves responsible.'[16] The *Daily Mail* had declared its uncertainty whether to laugh or to weep at the effrontery, the presumption of 'so trumpery a little state' daring to make 'so grotesque a challenge'.[17] A similar, more dangerous complacency ruled at the War Office. George Wyndham, the Under Secretary, boasted to his mother that the army was 'more efficient than at any time since Waterloo'.[18] On the eve of mobilisation, the 'experts' seemed agreed that England was well prepared. General Buller, who was to command the troops in Natal, told Lansdowne that within six weeks he would be in Pretoria, capital of the Transvaal. Little wonder, therefore, that the popular press should have been wildly optimistic. Equally inevitable, when harsh reality showed that their early euphoric rhapsodies had been built upon false and foolish estimates, those that had fed their readers' appetites for aggression most assiduously by extolling imperial pride, pomp and military might, sought to spare their own transgressions by savaging the government for its inept prosecution of what had now become the 'unnecessary' war.

In the spring of 1900, after news of nothing but disaster, the relief of Mafeking was greeted by the public with a perfect delirium of delight. As wildly celebrating crowds surged through the streets of London, the bulletin board outside the War Office baldly pronounced 'No News'. As usual, the War Office had been taken by surprise. Yet, as from a battered sieve, rumour, scandal, plans, memoranda, all manner of inconvenient, secret and embarrassing information flowed from that office to be gratefully reproduced by the press. By 1900, the infection of unofficial 'leaks' to the press had spread throughout the military hierarchy.[19] The War Office's channels for disseminating unofficial information were more efficient, much more frequently used, than those that were officially approved. Official relations between the War Office and the press were very different. These were conducted reluctantly, suspiciously and usually incompetently. Even the granting of licences to war correspondents generated the maximum confusion and ill-will.

The rules that governed 'newspaper correspondents at the seat of war' were quite explicit. Thirteen detailed, tortuously drafted paragraphs obliged editors, managers of news agencies and correspondents to sign a declaration that placed them under the Army Act. All communications had to be vetted by a staff officer, and the military were required to supply only 'as much information . . . as they may consider advisable and consistent with their duty'. The field commander retained an absolute power 'to revoke at any time, any licence granted'.[20] These were formidable powers to limit journalistic enterprise, yet Buller had told Wyndham he hoped that 'licences [would] be refused all foreign correspondents. They are only spies. . . . Everyone knows correspondents are a great trouble and I hope the War Office will limit them as much as possible.'[21] Roberts, unlike Buller, recognised how important the press could be during wartime and freely gave his confidences to a wide circle of journalists. Lawson was one newspaper owner quick to appreciate not only how relations between military and journalists improved when Roberts assumed command, but also the better tone of official despatches. 'The true spirit of English grit comes out most magnificently in the simple, modest, statesmanlike wording of Roberts' despatches, in striking contrast to the despatches of his predecessor in the field . . . which were in tone and language against the grain.'[22]

Roberts's attitude was far from typical among the British high command. The problem of licensing war correspondents was never satisfactorily resolved. It was the subject of a trenchant note from the War Minister to the Adjutant General in November 1904. 'My own view', Arnold-Forster wrote, 'is that the practice hitherto has been altogether wrong and that correspondents have more often proved an embarrassment than an aid to the army in time of war. It is difficult to make a change because the idea that war is conducted for the benefit of the newspapers has taken a very firm root in this country.'[23] In short, the War Office's attitude to war correspondents was paranoid. It was thought that journalists were the unwitting agents of any potentially hostile power. An unsigned minute attached to yet another draft of 'Rules for Press Correspondents' noted how frequently information was printed that was 'of incalculable value to a possible enemy' but 'not the slightest interest to the general public for whose edification it was published'.[24] As with other departments of government, then and since, the War Office would not recognise that a newspaper's public role depends as much upon the character of the political system within which it operates as upon its own aims and ideas. Deeply ingrained aristocratic attitudes dictate that the way government works should be viewed, not in the spirit of inquiry but with blinkered respect, or, better, awe. Consequently, official contacts with the press are kept to a minimum and then channelled through regulating peep-holes. The system was and remains inefficient, and needlessly offensive. Northcliffe, in a letter to Roberts written eight years later, accurately summarised the inefficiencies and ineffectiveness of press control during the Boer war. 'The management of the press in South Africa was scandalous. To my knowledge the censors allowed dangerous messages to pass, withheld interesting but quite safe messages, and, worst of all, interpolated the names of friends in action, in order to attract public notice to them.'[25] Roberts could not and did not deny Northcliffe's charges.

The attitude of the War Minister had not helped. Brodrick had some early if financially ill-rewarded experience as a journalist, but this did not make him a minister who could handle the press diplomatically, sympathetically or efficiently. His successor was even more inept. After a meeting with the Adjutant General, R. D. Blumenfeld of the *Daily Express* wrote in his diary: 'When I left the War Office, Sir Evelyn came out of the door with me and whispered that Mr Brodrick . . . was not at all agreeable to the visits of myself and one or two other editors. In fact, he was arranging to put in a sort of super-Press agent to whom all journalists will have to go in future.' The 'military intelligence' that Blumenfeld unavailingly had sought was the colour of the plume in the bearskin hats of the newly formed Fourth Guards Regiment of the Household Brigade.[26]

In February 1901 the *Daily Mail* published the gist of a scheme of army reform that Brodrick had submitted to the Cabinet. This information had earlier been offered to the *Standard* which had not accepted and told Brodrick. The source of the leak was subsequently traced to a junior clerk in the War Office who was dismissed. Five months later the *Daily Mail* published the contents of telegrams that had passed between Kitchener and Roberts. This information had earlier been offered to the *Daily Telegraph* which had refused to publish it. Brodrick's reaction was to try to stop news from official agencies, touching not only his own but also other departments, from being given to the *Mail*. Charles Watney, Foreign Editor of the *Daily Mail*, learning of Brodrick's intention, published a leading article which affected a nice balance between injured innocence and truculence. It stated that the *Mail* 'was in a position to publish much other official information despite Mr Brodrick'. Relations between the *Mail* and the War Office had deteriorated disastrously in the previous months. At the start of the war it had been uncritically adulatory about the War Office. Then had come, at first, tempered criticisms of obvious muddles and half-measures followed by the disclosure of the serious weaknesses of British artillery and the demand for more and better guns. On Northcliffe's initiative the *Mail* had called for an investigation into the medical services in South Africa which were soon to be revealed as totally inadequate.

Brodrick's stupid and hasty initiative led to a private notice question being asked in the House by Reginald Lucas. Brodrick told the Commons of the two earlier occasions when stories in the *Daily Mail* had earned his displeasure. He concluded, 'while taking such steps in regard to guilty individuals as may be necessary, I cannot justify leaving men of moderate income to temptations which may be offered them by a prominent journal'. Immediately and vehemently, Northcliffe repudiated the charge of bribery though, as he well knew, this was not an uncommon method of obtaining military and naval information from lowly officials. After an unsuccessful attempt to summon Northcliffe to the bar of the House for breach of parliamentary privilege, both minister and newspaper proprietor were obliged to climb down, although it was Brodrick's dignity that suffered the harder fall. The press agencies insisted Brodrick could not single out the *Daily Mail* and treat it as a pariah. He was obliged to acknowledge publicly that he had made an error of judgment. Northcliffe subsided somewhat more noisily in a spluttering leader in the *Daily Mail* that 'strongly object[ed] to Mr Brodrick's baseless and mean retort that this journal is in the habit of offering pecuniary temptations to War Office clerks for the purpose of obtaining news'.

Balfour played the part of peacemaker, for he was 'very anxious' that the breach between Brodrick and Northcliffe should be healed as swiftly as possible. 'I know this is very inconvenient for you,' he wrote to Brodrick, 'but I am sure it would be desirable in the public interest that the whole matter should be put upon a sound basis.' What Balfour wanted to avoid was any more comment such as the *Daily Mail's* suggestion that the War Minister was being urged 'by the peace at any price party in the Cabinet deliberately to hush up stories ... lest their publication irritate the Boers'. What finally decided that the *Daily Mail* should cease sniping at Brodrick was the sudden death of his wife.

A month after the affair was over, Northcliffe called upon Brodrick at the War Office. Now his behaviour was very different from his earlier public pose. He claimed that at the time he had not known the information the *Daily Mail* published had been improperly obtained. The contributor had been subsequently discharged. He wanted Brodrick to write a letter 'which he would one day show if he ever stood for a constituency and it was urged against him that he had knowingly purchased secret documents'. As Northcliffe had not then altogether abandoned the idea that one day he might wish to become a member of the Commons, he thought it politic to make his peace with the minister. Before Brodrick quit the War Office, he was to write 'cordial letters of thanks' to the *Daily Mail's* owner, 'for cooperating with us'.[27] This new-found amity even survived Brodrick's move to the India Office. There, the minister had the *Daily Mail* reinstated on the list of those newspapers to be sent departmental news, an action that elicited from Watney a series of grovelling letters that could as well have been penned by Uriah Heep. 'I am keenly responsive to your mark of good-will. . . . Very many thanks for your kind notes and guidance. . . . What I can do I will.'[28] This, Brodrick assumed, was a 'proper' and 'responsible' relationship between a minister and a newspaper. The *Daily Mail*, for its part, was more inclined to play friend than foe to Unionist governments and politicians.

The early months of hostilities in South Africa thoroughly disabused the British public of any notion it entertained about the army's fitness for its task. 'Rich and poor alike,' wrote young Bertha Synge to her friend Milner, the true architect of the war, 'we are all plunged in gloom.'

> Picture the newsboys at the corners. . . . Imagine the rush for newspapers. . . . Carriages stopped at the corners for papers to be bought – bus conductors rushing with handfuls of pennies as deputations for their passengers. There was a perfect sea of newspapers and anxious faces behind – intense gravity prevailed.[29]

Though news from the front eventually improved, as the campaign unfolded it revealed a sad, shaming story of ineptitude by generals, incompetence and confusion by government, and inadequate medical provision. Despite stirring tales of individual heroism, Britain was not spared the indignity of learning that officers in the Army Service Corps had been guilty of fraud in the sale and repurchase of goods and stores. The *Standard*'s 'Tea-time war' of October had become by December a 'costly, sanguinary shambles'.

When exaggerated hopes had taken such brutal knocks, people sought a culprit to blame for their unexpected misfortunes. Wolseley thought that the Almighty had been rather partisan. He wrote to his wife that 'God seems to be with the Boers and against us.'[30] Only a little less metaphysical, Salisbury censured the inadequacies of the British constitution. He told the House of Lords, 'As an instrument of peace it has not yet met its match, but for purposes of war there is more to be said.'[31] If that was the way the Prime Minister felt, Lawson thought it would have been more becoming and appropriate had he communicated his dissatisfaction to the country by resigning.[32] There was no disposition among the patriotic press to allow Salisbury to get away lightly with such an unlikely disclaimer.

Even among his Cabinet colleagues, the 'masterful inactivity' and 'steady decline in power and grip' of Britain's aged and tired Prime Minister inspired little confidence.[33] Presumably following the principle that in politics it is better to be seen doing something rather than nothing, Salisbury reshuffled the Cabinet offices. Lansdowne vacated the War Office for Brodrick, and Goschen the Admiralty for Selborne, Salisbury's son-in-law. The moves reflected better on the Prime Minister's sense of humour than of political priorities, Maxse suggested, but it really was not a suitable time for Salisbury 'to perpetrate a joke on the nation'. With the confidence that only sublime unoriginality can inspire, Maxse proclaimed the nation required 'efficient' government. In its hour of need the country should be led 'not by a politician . . . but a man who has thought, who has seen and who knows – a man with an iron will'. Instead, it suffered from '[a]n assemblage of sexagenarians . . . bound by the shibboleths of a bygone era . . . blind to the salient tendencies of modern life'.[34] A year earlier, Spring Rice had said as much in a letter to his cousin. 'Our leaders are too old, or too tired, or too busy to think, there is no proper organisation and we are like Swift, dying at the top. If only some young, strong man would come and clear it all up! We must reform or perish.'[35] It is a measure of the desperation men like Maxse and Spring Rice felt that they should hint to each other the 'man of the moment', their 'young Caesar', should be none other than Lord Rosebery. In his book, *Lessons of the War* (1900), Spenser Wilkinson wrote, 'There is no other public man who commands such general confidence. . . . Lord Rosebery could make a Government tomorrow if he would ignore parties and pick out the competent men wherever they are to be found.' In the presentation copy that he sent to Rosebery, Wilkinson coyly inscribed on the fly-leaf: 'Art thou he that should come or do we look for another?'[36] As usual, Rosebery said nothing.

Rosebery's appeal was that he was thought to be, not a party politician but 'the advocate of the Nation'. Anxious commentators anticipating the decline and fall of the British Empire were decidedly conservative by disposition, but they did not suppose that the Tory party was any more efficient, better informed or disposed to accept that Britain was weak and vulnerable than was the Liberal Opposition. The war with the Boers had confirmed their most pessimistic estimates. The actions of a few tattered commandos of Boer farmers had exposed Britain's impotence and incompetence to the world. The intensity of hatred shown by the other major Powers towards England was 'really astonishing. If we fall we shall have a hundred fangs at our throat.'[37] Yet the Prime Minister seemed to suppose it was enough that he should shuffle members of the 'Hotel Cecil' into new governmental slots. Lansdowne had not been impressive as a War Minister but could better be expected of St John Brodrick? Could it seriously be supposed that an adventurous foreign Power, recognising Britain's chronic weakness, would hesitate to seize the prize because the Prime Minister's son-in-law had taken over the Admiralty?

Milner, known to have a certain sympathy for Germany, was not yet ready to admit to Maxse that the Germans 'want to take away our Empire. But if they did I think they would have considerable excuse. The fact is that in our present state of preparation and *state of mind*, we really are a flagrant temptation to any enterprising neighbour.'[38] Not their hatred but their admiration for Germany convinced men like Maxse and Milner that Germany's ambition was Britain's greatest danger. Milner contrasted Germany's autocratic government with Britain's parliamentary democracy to the latter's marked disadvantage. He had written to a young friend in December 1901: 'Unless and until party can be got out of Imperial politics, it is no use trying to make or maintain Empires. Party is all very well for things which are not vital and which you can afford to settle *more or less*. But for a really big and crucial thing, the weakness and the compromise which it involves even with the strongest government *must ruin any settlement*.'[39] If the British remained content with their muddling ways they would be taught a harsh and final lesson, for the Germans were scientifically building up their strength, planning for *Der Tag*, the day when their preparations would be crowned by the successful invasion and conquest of Britain.

Is the Kaiser coming for tea?

Bebel said again the other day plainly that the increase of the German
Fleet was directed against this country. Of course it is, and the whole
plan of attack is quite ready.

H. M. Hyndman to L. J. Maxse

Did you ever see such confused meddling as the discussions in the
House last night? No one seems to have a clear conception whether a
dinghy with five men, or a Fleet with an Army Corps is the minimum
which the inhabitants of Clacton may have to entertain one day with tea
and shrimps.

Clinton Dawkins to Maxse

Would the Kaiser invade Britain and succeed where even Napoleon had failed?
To many people such a question seemed altogether too fanciful and theatrical.
Surely, only hysterical super-nationalists could convince themselves that such
a far-fetched danger was a reality. Yet right-wing publicists were not the only
ones who were concerned. H. M. Hyndman, the prophet of socialism, wrote
to Maxse, 'If you ever look at "Justice" you will have seen that we English
Social Democrats have no doubt about German policy.' Hyndman had been
told by the leader of the Social Democrats in the Reichstag that Germany's
plan of attack was already prepared. Hyndman believed that England was in
much greater and more immediate danger of invasion than France. 'It costs
£35,000,000 at least even to mobilise the German army. It will cost nothing
approaching that sum to raid the Essex coast when the German Fleet is ready.'[1]
Such opinions were not confined to amateur strategists. Admiral Fitzgerald
was convinced that sooner rather than later the Germans were certain to
attempt to wrest power from Britain by invasion. 'Germany's ambition is to
attack by force of arms upon the first suitable opportunity. The provocation
that we give her is that we stand in the way of her declared ambitions. That
is all, but that is enough.'[2]

German politicians and diplomats constantly told their British counterparts
that a 'German invasion exists only in the British imagination', or that, 'No
reasonable being in Germany ever thought of it.'[3] But there were those with
eyes that saw behind Germany's disarming diplomatic falsehoods sufficient
evidence to satisfy them that Germany was preparing for invasion. The years
went by and Germany did not invade, but those who believed in the theory of

the 'bolt from the blue' saw no reason to change their ideas. A letter that Cecil Spring Rice wrote to Maxse in June 1908 may serve as an example, typical of its kind.[4]

Spring Rice was convinced that the Reichstag elections of the previous spring had been stage-managed in order to secure a patriotic majority that for the next five years would comply with all the Kaiser's plans. This had been implicit in the Kaiser's successful appeal to the German electorate. 'If you desire Germany to be a world power then you must give me a Reichstag that will make the necessary sacrifices without flinching.' Of course, the appeal had been made covertly, but as usual, the Kaiser had given the game away by his boasting: 'Now that Germany is in the saddle we can ride down our enemies.' A pliant majority in the Reichstag probably meant there would be a new Army Bill in 1910 that would last for six years instead of four and provide for two new Army Corps – one for the east, the other for the west. The great Slav population on Germany's eastern frontier, that posed a threat to Danzig and Berlin, would be forcibly removed or otherwise made innocuous. A compliant Prussian Landtag could be counted upon to raise the necessary loan to finance such an operation. On the western frontier the work had already begun upon huge military fortifications near Metz. In the north, military and naval preparations were being pushed on apace. In 1911, a year before the next election to the Reichstag, a new Navy Bill would be approved. This would be designed to place Germany on an equal naval footing with Britain. When all these plans were brought to fruition, Britain would be left with two hopeless alternatives. Either she could accept the new circumstances, thus effectively acquiescing in German hegemony over Europe, or, with almost no hope of success, she could run the enormous risk of armed conflict. There were some who would prefer England to accept Germany's hegemony without a struggle, but the majority looked forward to a war which they supposed could only end very rapidly with victory. Britain would then have to pay an enormous indemnity that would effectively crush her industrial strength and make the maintenance of a great navy for the future impossible.

If the German plan was to succeed, then, Spring Rice argued, British resistance would have to collapse rapidly. A long and desperate encounter would lead inevitably to a great European war. Thus, the blow against England would have to be sudden and final. The Germans would entrust the war to their navy and a compact invasion force of some three or four hundred thousand adventurers, numbers that would hardly affect national comfort. Any temporary commercial loss would be more than recouped by the indemnity. Germany's industrialists were convinced by the tantalising prospect held out by their government. They accepted the idea of England's invasion with eager anticipation. The glory might go to the army and navy, but theirs would be the more tangible prize of huge profits and their great industrial competitor broken.

The one question that remained to be answered was not whether Germany would invade Britain, but *when*. According to information he had been given by the British military attaché in Berlin, Spring Rice believed that their army had completed its preparations. They had all the information they needed about England, for trained men had long been placed strategically to spy out the strength and weaknesses of Britain's defences and to inform the German General Staff of any late change. When the time came, they would cause disruption and confusion by acts of sabotage. In Germany, large holdings of quick-firing guns were ready for transit. They had eliminated the need for draught horses to pull the limbers by using mechanised transport. Naturally the final preparations were being kept secret by rigorous security. While German intelligence had all the information it needed, the British, as usual, knew next to nothing.

Spring Rice was quite prepared to admit that Captain P. W. Dumas, the British naval attaché in Berlin, did not agree with this estimate, but the difference between his assessment of Germany's intentions and preparations and the military attaché's was easily explained. It reflected the division and antagonism between their two Services. Why should greater credence be given to Dumas when among informed people the inaccuracy of his intelligence reports was notorious?[5] In any event, Dumas admitted that if for any reason the British navy should move from the North Sea, then the Germans would immediately put into effect their invasion plans. On this reading of the circumstances, Spring Rice reasoned that the object of German diplomacy would be to create a diversion somewhere in the world – Egypt was a likely target – and thus draw away the British fleet leaving Britain naked and defenceless. Perhaps the Kaiser, like Napoleon and Francis I before him, counted upon the Turks to create the necessary diversion? But, whichever way one looked at the diplomatic strategy, it remained that the differences between the estimates of naval and military attachés were reduced to a single factor – time. The not unlikely combination of German diplomatic chicanery and British naval incompetence might, at any moment, create the ideal opportunity for Germany to strike.

The Germans had every reason to be confident in their strategy. Wild talk by the First Sea Lord, Admiral Fisher, that he would 'Copenhagen' their fleet at Kiel had been exploited by German diplomats to hide their own country's intentions while advertising a spurious notion of British aggressive intent. It had also helped to confirm the official whine that the British wanted to isolate Germany in Europe and surround her with hostile Powers. Not only was this manifest nonsense, claimed Spring Rice, but it gave an entirely false picture of the real military capability of Britain's entente partners. France was so demoralised that she could be insulted with impunity. Russia with its broken-backed bureaucracy would present no problem. Even discounting the possibility of the recreation of the *Dreikaiserbund*, Germany had as little to fear from Russia as Louis XIV's France had cause to be concerned about England when Charles II was king. And, if necessary, Germany's armies could easily hold the French and the Russians on their respective frontiers. It was England that was Germany's prime target. It would not profit her to dominate continental Europe if England remained as a centre of resistance in her island fortress. To take Europe without England was to risk, as in the past, Britain becoming paymaster and inspiration of a hostile coalition. But if England were invaded and taken by storm, then Europe would collapse into Germany's arms. Thus,

Spring Rice, and all those who, like him, believed in Germany's intention to invade England – the 'bolt from the blue' advocates – fashioned their ideas.

That Britain might be invaded was not a new idea.[6] The element of novelty this time was the casting of suspicion upon Germany rather than, as in the past, France. Changing the villain of the piece had caused a certain amount of confusion during the Boer War when anxiety among the public had been raised to fever pitch. When Rosebery told the Lords, 'We are surrounded by an atmosphere of hatred unprecedented in the history of this country,'[7] there was hopeless confusion in many minds as to which European Power was the most likely to attack England. The *Daily Mail* abandoned Teutophobia and as quickly discovered Francophobia, so that when the Kaiser visited Windsor he was described as 'A Friend in Need'. Those who 'for four years had abused and laughed at the Emperor William' now proclaimed him a 'hero and were busily licking his boots'.[8]

The national neurosis about invasion was not soothed by the so-called 'blue water' advocates asserting that there was nothing to fear so long as Britain ruled the waves. Could the navy be trusted? Might it not prove to be a broken reed when put to the test? The army's recent débâcle suggested a probable and far from comforting precedent. Leo Maxse, who admittedly had something of a penchant for invasion theories, declared that he was not prepared 'to sit like a fatalist and accept a foreign yoke' because 'some simple-minded absolutist of the Blue Water School supposes the Navy is sufficient guarantee of England's safety from invasion.'[9] Strachey was advertising similar sentiments in his *Spectator*.[10] Both men seemed convinced that national salvation would be best secured by supporting the Volunteers. That body's most effusive parliamentary coadjutor was the amazingly vigorous octogenarian the ninth Earl of Wemyss who frequently addressed the Upper House on the merits of 'England's one certain protection against invasion'. As often, the irrepressible earl peppered the correspondence columns of the Tory press extolling the same specific for all known invasion ills.

In the appropriate month of April 1900, Maxse affirmed as a certainty to his readers that the French General Staff *knew* that they could land 50,000 troops in England. What was more, the military attachés of a number of foreign nations were busily telling their governments that England was practically defenceless. Following the inexorable laws of invasion arithmetic, Maxse's 50,000 became in the *Daily Mail* 80,000 with 400 guns thrown in for good measure. Then *Public Opinion* unblushingly told its readers that it had been reliably informed by a French naval captain that the true figure was 90,000.[11] Suddenly elderly gentlemen in the home counties became aware of a veritable plague of French military cyclists choking the country lanes while the suburbs of London groaned with hordes of highly suspicious aliens obviously waiting only to be summoned by an invader to commit countless acts of sabotage. The *St James's Gazette*, the journalistic epitome of the British stiff upper lip, remained unruffled by the fearful revelations of its contemporaries and instead offered a simple solution. A Home Guard should straightway be constituted and London's fire-fighting appliances converted to make mobile gun platforms. To discourage any unwonted complacency that might have been induced by these simple, practical remedies, the numbers of the invading force were increased to 115,000, while its military expert, F. N. Maude, insisted that such a force could only be repelled by a defensive army of not less than three million.[12]

The most dramatic manifestation of apparent government concern prompted by these ever-mounting newspaper statistics came from a most unexpected source. Salisbury, no lover or supporter of invasion scares, to a meeting of the Primrose League in May delivered an encomium on the virtues of every Englishman making himself fit to meet any invader by joining a rifle club.[13] Rifle shooting as a hobby was an obsession of most invasion polemicists, reaching its apogee with a national campaign by Lord Roberts in 1905. Supporters were for ever drawing parallels with the longbow men of Crecy. Kipling, who was as keen on rifle shooting as he was contemptuous of spectator sports, poured scorn on 'the flannelled fools at the wicket or the muddied oafs at the goals' who, if England were invaded would presumably hope to 'even the odds, with nets and hoops and mallets, with rackets and bats and rods'. The real attraction of rifle shooting was that it was cheap and a much more readily acceptable alternative than compulsory military service which ideally these Hotspurs would dearly have loved to impose on England's young men.

Leo Maxse, not inclined to look a gift horse in the mouth, welcomed Salisbury as the latest but much the most distinguished convert to the ranks of the bolt from the blue school, and thus emboldened, hurled defiance at any and all possible invaders while proposing Arthur, Duke of Connaught, who with fifty thousand veterans would see off any Kaiser, Tsar or French President.[14] Other responses to Salisbury's injunction followed a familiar pattern. In the press, advocates of different panaceas either used or abused Salisbury's plea as best suited their own priorities. So Strachey, who was a keen advocate of rifle clubs, welcomed Salisbury's patronage, while the *Daily Mail*, because it was engaged in its annual naval scare, employed the premier's argument for rifle shooting to make a case for a larger fleet. The various protagonists vociferously multiplied confusion and, as Maxse despairingly noted, at the end of the day the nation rather than being better prepared presented an even greater temptation to any invader.[15]

Once an immediate problem has been overcome, the British have always had a notorious record of forgetting about it as quickly as possible and doing nothing. Sir Clinton Dawkins, who had chaired one of the three commissions that examined all aspects of British military organisation during and after the Boer War, was delighted to tell his friend, Milner, 'Curiously enough there is perhaps more interest at the present time in military reform than during the war. . . . The ground is pretty well prepared for changes.'[16] A more cautious person than Dawkins would have excluded the Volunteers from his assertion. They neither recognised nor accepted the need for change. Any attempt to discuss the Volunteers merely restoked the fires of invasion panic. Brodrick was generally sympathetic towards them, but when he attempted to enlarge their establishment, numbers perversely decreased. The Norfolk Commission's flat pronouncement that the Volunteers were 'unfit to take the field',[17] clearly implied that something had to be done about them. The question remained, what exactly? Arnold-Forster, Brodrick's successor as War Minister, proposed a reduction of the Volunteer establishment while improving their training so that they might constitute an adequate first line of home defence against an invader. The secretary of the newly formed Committee of Imperial Defence, George Clarke, who had an excellent opinion of his own talents as a military and naval expert, pronounced Forster's scheme 'a grave mistake' though he admitted that the Volunteers were in need of 'regeneration'. Much of their training was simply 'idiotic'. A lieutenant colonel in the Militia had told him that at a recent camp they had been unable to arrange a field day after the Derby because so many officers were still at Epsom. Esher, to whom Clarke had addressed his complaints, decided that he must make a speech on the Volunteers. Clarke thought it 'admirable. Many thoughtful people would echo all you said. Unfortunately hardly anyone has the courage to say the truth. Even MP's have told me that they could not speak out. "The Editor of the local paper that supports me is a sergeant in the Volunteers," and so on. It is now an influence in politics which goes much further than is generally understood and which works evil in many ways.'[18]

Arnold-Forster had very soon discovered that when tangling with the Volunteer lobby in Parliament and the press, it was not enough to have a good scheme or even the more cogent case to argue. 'Touch a single unit of the Auxiliary Forces,' he told Balfour, 'and it is enough to raise screams from half the House of Commons.'[19] But even before Forster's ideas reached Parliament they were doomed. He only had his way in Cabinet after a dreadful struggle, and Balfour made it clear that at best he proffered his Minister for War half-hearted support. There were the usual 'leaks' published in the *Daily Express* and *Standard* and these were followed by the threat of a back-bench revolt by Militia supporters. Balfour scampered for cover and Arnold-Forster was left to present his scheme effectively without any support from his own front bench.[20] Then and subsequently, he was given such a roasting by his critics that, in a desperate attempt to win the war having lost every battle, when introducing his Army Estimates in 1905, he cited the Committee of Imperial Defence as his authority for the claim that given a sufficient navy the largest possible invasion force that could reasonably be anticipated would be no more than five thousand. Because prescription has always enjoyed a compelling authority in British political argument, Forster quoting the conclusions of a new-fangled committee was either ignored by his critics or buried by the repetition of old and very familiar assertions. The Volunteers trained the country's best spirits. They were the best protection against any unexpected event that might occur – the Dogger Bank incident was frequently cited as an example. Most convincingly, however, the familiar platitude was reiterated that the Volunteers were the nation's best guarantee against the adoption of the continental scheme of conscription.

Poor Arthur Balfour, delicately husbanding the dwindling fortunes of his administration, was well aware that the failure of Forster's schemes and that minister's acerbic manner with his critics further undermined the government's uncertain future. He appreciated Arnold-Forster's good qualities but had never been a keen supporter of the War Minister and it had been Chamberlain who had insisted upon his appointment.[21] Forster was the author of many of the ills that beset him, but there was good reason to sympathise with his wish 'that everyone else would not try to run my Department for me'.[22] Brodrick constantly interfered; Clarke and Esher were always plotting against him, and most of the senior army officers were hostile. All his critics busily retailed the War Minister's faults to the press. While they successfully puffed their schemes, Arnold Forster failed to win the confidence of the press. Even so, Esher unkindly suggested that he ought to be 'muzzled with an iron mask'.[23]

The Admiralty now decided to take a hand in affairs. Always jealous of any attempt to improve the army lest it should deprive the Senior Service of funds, the First Sea Lord, in his usual exaggerated style, wrote to Sandars imploring him to urge his master '*instantly to publish his great paper on Invasion.* . . . If you don't tell these truths . . . we'll sweep the country with the cry "Down with Balfour and his Bloated Army." '[24] In May 1905 Balfour gave the Commons a complete account of the CID's investigation and findings of the invasion issue. He was complimented by the leaders of the Opposition for pacifying the country's alarmists. From the government back benches, a notorious 'blue water' supporter, Sir John Colomb, supposing his views to have been completely vindicated by Balfour's speech, delivered an eloquent *nunc dimittis*. 'I rejoice at having lived to hear an explicit statement . . . upon principles of policy giving clear and distinct reasons why those principles should be followed.'[25] But whatever others might think, the Volunteer lobby remained unimpressed and continued their carping and putting down of stale, familiar questions.

Though Balfour's statement had been welcomed in the editorial columns of *The Times*, its military correspondent was critical and urged revision. For a comparative newcomer to Printing House Square, Charles Repington was less than polite in the opinions he expressed in his private correspondence about the editorial views of *The Times* on India and the army. He told Esher that they were 'Not arguments but pails full of blather, blarney and bumcomb.' Esher did not agree, and was angered by Repington's criticism of Balfour for that implied criticism of the CID of which he was a permanent member. Esher sharply rebuked Repington for the likely 'ill effects of your critical examination. . . . Was it worthwhile [as a patriot] to employ the dissecting knife so thoroughly. The impression produced by *your* article is that AJB (Balfour) is a mere amateur fumbler.'[26] Spenser Wilkinson in the *Morning Post* had been even harsher than Repington, pronouncing Balfour's statement 'a national calamity'. A year later he was still reminding his readers of Balfour's 'calamitous invasion statement'. Clarke considered this both 'stupid and unjust'. But, as he told Esher, the problem was that 'it might impress the people who never read the invasion speech. If I draft a short answer, could you put anyone on to father it – someone to whom the M Post could not refuse admittance?' Clarke also pointed out that the Director of Naval Intelligence, Charles Ottley, thought that Wilkinson's 'absolutely false statements' ought to be answered. 'I rather think', Clarke concluded, 'SW does much harm.'[27]

Dawkins had written to Maxse that he feared the effect of Balfour's statement would be 'most deplorable. . . . It will lull people into a sense of false security. It will give an excuse to every idle and sleepy person to turn over on the other side; it will frustrate any attempt to make something out of the Auxiliary Forces.'[28] Maxse did not need Dawkins's encouragement to 'tear Balfour's statement to pieces in the National Review'. When he did, he received the praise not only of Dawkins but of Milner. 'I am so glad you went for the "no danger of invasion" theory. I was really terrified when I read it, especially seeing the quarter from which it came.'[29] Repington wrote to Maxse to tell him that Balfour's statement had been far from impressive as it had revealed the Prime Minister had no grasp of the real problems. What else could have been expected? 'The PM has taken to the study of strategy late in life, and has only a half-fledged intuition to guide him. It will be the affair of many years to sort out all his ideas and get them in order.' Repington also insisted that Balfour was not the *real* influence on the invasion issue. He was merely the mouthpiece; the brains belonged to the CID's Secretary, George Clarke.[30]

This was a dangerous line of argument for Repington to pursue with Maxse. He had spent much time and effort in an attempt to persuade Leo that the CID was a necessary and much-to-be-desired improvement. There was always a danger when stepping near, not necessarily upon, one of Maxse's corns, that it might inspire a 'fountain of damnation clauses'. George Clarke had also been trying to persuade Leo of the CID's virtues. When Maxse published his outburst against Balfour, Clarke was coolly dismissive. 'I will not argue about Balfour's speech, the main principles of which will certainly be acted upon by this and every other Government we are likely to have.'[31]

Clarke was a 'blue water' advocate. He supposed any raid, whether a full invasion or a more limited incursion, was impossible so long as the navy maintained sufficient strength and efficiency. He believed that invasionmongers were merely intent to put money that was better spent on the navy in the army's coffers. Though Clarke thought he saw through their schemes it did occur to him that it would be politically useful to turn all the invasion propaganda 'to serve as a peg on which to hang a justification of an intelligible organisation of the Volunteers. Numbers could be cut and considerable sums of money saved.'[32] He gave this wise advice to Balfour who rejected it. The Prime Minister also gave short shrift to the pleas of Admiral Fisher who declared, on the basis of a paper drawn up by Ottley, his conviction that a dinghy with five Germans aboard represented Britain's maximum possible invasion risk. Why squander money upon useless fortifications and to keep 170,000 men kicking their heels in enforced idleness as a supposed force for 'home defence' when the money could be better spent on the navy, he asked the Prime Minister? The last wish was all too clearly the inspiration of Fisher's thoughts and Balfour ignored the pleas of the ebullient First Sea Lord. Balfour could not, however, gag the press.

Quoting examples from the *Daily Mail*, Ottley had written to Clarke suggesting that it would be

very desirable, if practicable, to put a stopper to the published hysteria with which some of our newspapers at present (in a time of peace) regale their readers. . . . Could we tell Chirol, or some other sane newspaper authority, our views and beg him to work the oracle in such wise as to moderate the rhetoric and the transports of our less responsible journalists?

As an old newspaper hand himself, Clarke could tell Ottley that nothing would be done to prevent 'this great evil'. The real source of the problem was not the press but government. If 'it would treat the responsible part of the press wisely and generously, the effect would at least be remedial'. Clarke passed on Ottley's letter to Chirol, admitting that 'the attitude of the Admiralty and War Office to the press is the most stupid and impolitic' of all government departments.

> When hard up they try to use it. Ordinarily they keep you at a distance and wrap themselves in a cloud of silly mystery. I should like to see a discreet official told off to meet accredited representatives of the great papers and tell them frankly all that can be made public. Most things can.[33]

The advantage of having a well-disposed and cooperative press should have been obvious, yet governments, whether Unionist or Liberal, seemed incapable of grasping this simple truth. Departments vied with each other and individual with individual, everyone busily seeking the attention of a sympathetic editor or journalist to whom they might unofficially 'leak' confidential and usually contradictory information. Clarke told Sandars that the press had every reason to distrust governments whose negligent, uncaring attitude was the real reason why irresponsible persons gained access to editors with evil consequences. It was too easy to blame the press for publishing 'inaccurate information' or censure 'the conspicuous lack of any form of conscience on the part of editors'. The government was in large part to blame for 'the fact that almost anyone with a tolerably facile pen is now permitted to air opinions which he has no means of forming'.[34] The reason why so much 'inaccurate information' was published about the army and the navy was because 'few men in those two Services learn to think or to set out reasons for policy in logical form. . . . Their ideas are often based upon nothing more solid than crude impressions.'[35] The problem as outlined by Clarke in his letters to Sandars and Balfour was never satisfactorily solved. In 1912 Ottley, in a letter to Esher, instanced as an outstanding example of the faults Clarke had described the recent complaints of Admiral of the Fleet, Sir Gerard Noel, in a letter published in the *Standard*, about the CID's baleful influence upon naval affairs.

> Noel's authority on this question is mathematically expressed by the square root of minus one: a quantity impossibly small. . . . But I do not think he is singular in that respect. . . . There is a numerous army of scribes who, knowing nothing of what the Defence Committee does, ascribe to it noxious characteristics of a purely imaginary kind.[36]

The problem of 'editorial conscience' was extremely complex for, as Clark later admitted to Chirol, 'Questions of policy are questions of opinion.'[37] It was not necessarily simple perversity that dictated that an editor should interpret an incident or set of facts in a way that displeased the government. H. A. Gwynne, not long after he became editor of the *Standard*, had discussed the invasion issue with Raymond Marker who was then Arnold-Forster's secretary.

> I will admit to you that I go rather beyond the extreme probabilities of the case because I want to rouse England to the fact that she is in danger.... I want you to understand that it is no carping spirit which prompts me to unsettle the country as far as I can on the question of defence. It is simply because I feel that we are in a bad way, and I am determined to do my best to remedy the matter.[38]

Any 'blue water' advocate would have been distressed by 'Taffy' Gwynne's fulminations on the invasion issue but they were inspired by a genuine if mistaken sense of patriotic and editorial duty.

There was, in any case, good reason for confusion concerning the question of invasion. The divide between Admiralty and War Office opinion on that subject was partly inspired by inter-Service jealousy, and the competition for financial resources. But while 'blue water' advocates ridiculed the 'bolt from the blue' claim that Germany might invade Britain, they were not averse to the idea of a British naval-borne invasion of Germany. Rumours of such thinking circulated widely in Society. Arnold-Forster found himself charged by a fellow dinner guest with being the author of a scheme to land 100,000 men in Schleswig-Holstein, and that he had said as much to Moberly Bell. 'Of course the thing is utterly absurd and untrue,' Forster wrote in his diary. 'The idea of my supposing we could land troops on the German coast is really ridiculous.'[39] But many senior naval officers, not excluding the First Sea Lord, thought such a scheme eminently practicable. When the military pointed to the published opinions of young German General Staff officers as 'proof' that the Germans were contemplating an invasion of Britain, these were airily dismissed as 'lucubrations', kites flown by enemy publicists 'anxious to divert British expenditure from naval into military channels'. The intention was obvious, so Clarke thought, but 'because these rumours are treated seriously by ignorant British journalists' they were having a sad influence 'upon the feeling among the masses who neither reason nor read history'.[40]

The press was frequently blamed for exciting ignorant opinion with unnecessary fears about German invasion plans, but a more likely and generally persuasive source for convincing the public that the Kaiser was about to descend upon the shores of England was the activity of certain popular novelists. *Riddle of the Sands* by Erskine Childers was one of the earliest, best written and most convincing novels of the invasion genre, but the most widely read and influential was William Le Queux's *The Invasion of 1910*, serialised by the *Daily Mail* in 1906.[41] By any criterion, Le Queux was an extraordinary man. Born in 1864, he started professional life as a journalist and served a period as a special correspondent and as a sub-editor on the *Globe* before devoting himself to writing novels which he produced at a prodigious rate. He advertised himself in *Who's Who* as having 'an intimate knowledge of the secret services of the Continental Powers', a subject about which he was 'consulted by the British Government'. Le Queux inhabited his own strange world where fact and fiction, romance and reality were inextricably confused. *The Invasion of 1910* was not his first venture into invasion 'literature', for one of the three books he published in 1899 had a similar subject, *England's Peril*. In 1906, however, his literary genius had the inestimable advantage of Northcliffe as its handmaid. Northcliffe promoted Le Queux's story with every commercial and journalistic aid. As profit, in Northcliffe's scheme of values, came a long way before details of likely military strategy, the invading hordes of the story were obliged to follow a circuitous route through major cities that insured maximum publicity and improved sales for the *Daily Mail*. If readers were somewhat baffled by the adventure's confusing conclusion, Le Queux provided them with a stirring moral harangue that encompassed the inefficiencies of the War Office, the unwillingness of the public to accept universal military service, the spinelessness of the government, the perils of socialism and the neglect of the fleet. It is something of an anti-climax after this to discover that the author's specific that was to remedy such a plague of ills is the provision of rifle clubs, for, by this expedient alone the nefarious designs of the story's invaders were finally defeated.[42]

Le Queux's enormous commercial success inspired an industry of imitators. As their main inspiration was the thought of a quick and handsome profit, the plots became ever thinner and characterisation deteriorated into caricature. The Germans were beastlier, the complaints about the inadequacies of British politicians more strident, and a harsh note of political partisanship was directed against the Liberal government. So offensive did Strachey find A. J. Dawson's *The Message* that he urged Lord Roberts to bring pressure upon the National Service League to stop distributing the book which ostensibly was designed as a plea for conscription. Roberts complied with Strachey's request and, although usually not sensitive about such matters, so did the NSL.[43]

In the public mind, Lord Roberts personified the case for conscription against the perils of invasion. The old warrior had been a member of the CID when, in 1903, it had dismissed the possibility of invasion. This seems to have been but a temporary aberration on his part. For Roberts, invasion, compulsory service, reform of the army, the problem of the Volunteers, were not different questions but aspects of a single great issue that the nation refused to face and the government lacked the political will to solve. He complained that it had never been his desire to seek the limelight. 'None of the leading politicians on either side of the House seem to realise the necessity for making any serious effort,' he grumbled to Sir Dighton Probyn, an old military friend and a member of the royal household. 'Unless the matter is taken in hand in some other way, there will be no improvement in the present lamentable state of affairs.'[44] Roberts's most natural ally in his campaign should have been the National Service League, but although offered the presidency he refused.

The NSL, formed in 1902, wanted compulsory service but did not openly advocate as much for this would have meant asking the public to accept the difficult proposition that conscripted men would have to serve overseas. Instead, compulsory military training was promoted for 'home defence'. Membership of the league was predominantly middle-class and Unionist in its political sympathies. This overwhelming Tory and Establishment influence weakened what little appeal it might have had for the working classes and placed a large question mark against its often-repeated claim to be a non-party organisation. Press support for the NSL, with the exception of the socialist weekly, *Clarion*, edited by Robert Blatchford, similarly divided along party lines. The *Morning Post, Daily Telegraph, Daily Express* and *Standard* were keen advocates of the NSL's cause. The *Daily Mail*, while occasionally adopting a somewhat ambivalent stance, was usually encouraging. The league did not want to appear to discredit the navy's defensive role, but argued that a more efficient home army would release the navy from coastline duties. The fear of invasion was exploited for, in this way, it was hoped that ingrained national prejudice against compulsory service as a threat to an Englishman's traditional liberty might be overcome.[45]

A speech made by Roberts at the Mansion House in August 1905 greatly enhanced the influence of the league. 'Hardly any paper will now refuse to publish our opinions,' boasted the *National Service Journal*.[46] Roberts had sought to recruit as many prominent supporters as possible. Though he 'strongly sympathised' with Roberts, on this occasion Milner begged leave to decline. It was 'too soon' for him publicly to nail his colours to Roberts's mast. 'I shall be more use to you later on if I am less precipitate.'[47] Roberts's demands proved less than his keenest supporters might have wished – rifle drill for schoolboys and a 'home defence army' guaranteed to 'render any attempt at invasion out of the question'.

The speech was not well received in government circles. Balfour apparently shared Arnold Forster's view of its 'outrageous character'.[48] Even some of Roberts's allies were offended because they misunderstood what he had said. Strachey took Roberts to task in the *Spectator* for devaluing the Volunteers. Roberts replied that his 'sole object [was] to render the army fit for war in all its branches, not to do away with the Auxiliary Forces, but to make them efficient in a way they never can be so long as they are composed of only very partially trained men.' He concluded, 'No amount of sympathy will make a man a soldier.'[49] To avoid the possibility of any further unnecessary and damaging public dispute, a meeting was arranged between Roberts and Balfour at Balmoral. There Roberts promised he would say no more until there had been a meeting of the CID thoroughly to thrash out the whole issue. When the committee met in November, Roberts, in Brodrick's words, brought with him 'a most astounding proposal. . . . Conscription for a very brief period of training between seventeen and eighteen and a bout of shooting afterwards'.[50] Committee members were not impressed. 'Because I can be of no further assistance,' Roberts wrote to the King's equerry, 'I have tendered my resignation. . . . I now propose to take up the Presidentship of the National Service League.'[51] Three weeks later, the government resigned.

While the politicians of both parties hastened to the hustings, Roberts began a great public campaign for conscription. In January he was urging a 'million man standard' – a phrase suggested by J. L. Garvin – both as security against invasion and as the necessary military complement for the navy's Two Power Standard. Brodrick supposed that Roberts was being advised by General Nicholson, 'unemployed for months and in a very mischievous mood'. Arnold-

Forster would have agreed with Brodrick that Roberts was being manipulated, but, to his way of thinking, by a much more sinister influence than Nicholson. It was a 'thousand pities' the old man should 'lend himself to the transparent manoeuvres of A'Court'.[52] Forster's conjecture, that it was Charles Repington who was involved with Roberts's campaign, was the better-informed guess.

Enter 'the gorgeous Wreckington'

Repington has very many most splendid qualities, but, between ourselves, in spite of his birth and education, he is not a gentleman and is a most resplendent snob.

H. A. Gwynne to John St Loe Strachey

A Court makes a nasty covert attack on me in today's Times. Dirty brute. . . . A number of fellows came to see me and told me what they thought of a Court. I think the lying brute has over-reached himself this time.

General Sir Henry Wilson's Diary

Found a tiresome article by the Military Correspondent in the 'Times'. . . . The whole attack is absolutely unjust and the facts are all wrong, and the writer, Acourt, must know that many of them are wrong. The article is rather a base form of revenge on me. . . . The personal attack is dressed up in large type and fortified by animosity and this presented as a judgment based on the real consideration of public needs.

H. O. Arnold-Forster's Diary

Born to most comfortable circumstances in 1858, Charles à Court Repington[1] was educated at Eton and Sandhurst before entering his chosen profession. He proved himself an able, dashing, ambitious and hard-working young officer. He was also extravagant, handsome and had an eye for the ladies. This last was to bring his very promising military career to an abrupt and premature end. While serving in Egypt, he fell in love with Lady Mary Garstin, wife of a prominent British diplomat. Four years later, despite having given a written undertaking that he would never again see or communicate with the lady, Repington deserted his wife for Mary with whom he lived until his death in 1925. In her brave memoirs, Mary recorded what 'a terrible blow to Charley' his enforced resignation was, adding poignantly, 'the army then and always was the love of his life. All else came second to it.'[2]

Before leaving the army Repington had contributed an occasional article on military subjects to the press. He now turned full-time to journalism, rapidly and deservedly establishing an international reputation as a military expert. For a short period he served on Spender's *Westminster Gazette* before joining *The Times* as its military correspondent. In a letter to Moberly Bell accepting his new post, he gave an amusing description of the current chaotic state of the army and some of its senior officers. Kitchener was 'cantankerous', the army, 'generally very ill at ease'. Lord Roberts 'shirks all serious issues and talks to children while Wolseley has taken up poultry farming'.[3]

Repington retained many contacts at the War Office, and these he used to his considerable advantage. He never doubted for a moment that he was the best informed and the most able of all military correspondents and he expected *The Times* to recognise as much by the salary and the expenses he received.[4] He wrote with great facility in a lucid, simple style easily understood even by non-specialist readers. Absolutely convinced that his views on military matters were invariably correct, he never doubted that his writing exerted an enormous influence.[5] His many critics recognised though regretted the authority he commanded. Nevertheless, they were sometimes tempted to dismiss him too lightly. 'Who is Repington?' Admiral Fisher rhetorically inquired of Arnold-Forster. 'A man who has been kicked out of the Army and turned out of all his clubs.'[6] Repington was arrogant and conceited, but cheap jibes that he was 'a cad', 'a bounder', 'not quite a gentleman', were the salve with which critics, sadly wounded by the military correspondent in public debate, anxiously sought to re-establish their self-esteem and vanity. George Clarke, who had written much in the past for *The Times* on military and naval topics, at first had welcomed Repington's appointment for his support of the Committee of Imperial Defence and the concept of a General Staff. Soon, however, he was complaining to his friend Chirol that while Repington might be clever he was not a fair controversialist. 'He has not met his opponents at all though he may have dazzled the readers of the paper.'[7] Rapidly Clarke became convinced that it would be advantageous for *The Times* and the army if 'the claws of the military correspondent were clipped'.[8]

Among politicians, the long-suffering Arnold-Forster had perhaps least cause to evince any affection for Repington who ridiculed the minister's ideas as baldly in *The Times* as in his private correspondence. Forster's schemes were 'wholly bad ... not a point to recommend them.... Progress with A-F at the helm is hopeless.... It is useless to compromise to save A-F's face. I am sick of him and all his works.'[9] Though sadly wounded, Forster at least had the courage to grapple with his man in public debate and there were some thunderous exchanges between them in letters to *The Times*.[10]

Arnold-Forster explained to Balfour that although Repington was 'able enough' he believed that he was not a reliable guide to army reform as he suffered from two fatal limitations. He was 'always working for his own hand; much more intent ... on "scoring a point" than on constant advocacy of a truly national policy'. The second disqualification was more serious. 'He reminds me of Mahan's description of Bonaparte, "One of those wizards whose power ceases the moment they come into contact with water" – in this case, salt water. He knows nothing whatever about the sea and as far as I can make out, resolutely refuses to learn.'[11] In a letter to his friend Maxse, Forster claimed that Repington was 'a mere creature of Esher's. Every time Esher changes his plans, which is about once every six months, the Times' correspondent follows suit.'[12] Arnold-Forster was no fool and his criticisms therefore deserve careful consideration. But the charge that Repington was manipulated by Esher is easily dismissed, inspired as it was more by Forster's personal antipathy towards Repington and his frustration with the way Esher interfered with his plans than by objective criteria.

'It is always a great encouragement to me to have your good opinion upon any work of mine,' Repington wrote to Esher in October 1909. 'I am sure you know, I value your opinion highly.' Six months later when Esher had been ill, Repington wrote of 'how much I missed your shrewd and sagacious advice'.[13] Yet their opinions on military, naval and strategic problems frequently differed. When they did, Repington invariably, unhesitatingly and determinedly went his own way. As he had insisted to Raymond Marker, 'I take orders from no man and though what I write may have merit or none, it represents at all events my sincere conviction, independent of all personal, political and other bias.' His attitude towards Esher was the same as that he displayed to his employers. 'So long as the Times allows me to write with absolute independence I shall say precisely what I think: when I am asked to support some scheme in which I do not believe I shall stop writing in the Times.'[14]

Though markedly conservative by disposition, Repington was never averse to the idea of smiting Tories when he thought that they were in the wrong – which was often. Nor had he any prejudice against working with Liberals, so long as he thought that they were serving what he had decided was the national interest. All Radicals, however, he hated, for their 'dangerous sentimentalism'. They as fervently loathed the man they derided as 'the gorgeous Wreckington'. Repington had little respect for the 'genus politician', whether Radical, Liberal or Unionist. 'They know nothing of the Army . . . and almost as little of the Empire.' Cabinet ministers, for the most part, he supposed were 'too busy to read carefully and too ignorant to understand' any specialist papers that were put in front of them. In any event, 'They never move at all except under the lash of the press.'[15] He was prepared to make one exception to this rule. Repington discerned in Richard Burdon Haldane qualities that he thought worth supporting. When Haldane was appointed Minister of War in Campbell-Bannerman's Cabinet, Repington wrote, 'I hope much from him. He is the best Secretary of State we have had at the War Office so far as brain and ability are concerned . . . everything promises well.'[16]

In November and December 1905, the Germans, conscious of the approaching conference in Algeçiras, had sought to ingratiate themselves with the British public, an action described by Repington as 'the stock-in-trade of German militant diplomacy to appeal to easy-going, unsuspecting Britishers'. Quite incensed by the apparent gullibility of the public at a time of acute national danger, on 27 December 1905 Repington published a stern and angry article that warned the Germans, 'a Franco-German war might unchain animosities in unexpected quarters'. The next day he accepted an invitation to dine with long-time friend, Huguet who had been appointed the previous December, French military attaché in London.[17]

Huguet told Repington that his government was in a state of extreme anxiety. Sir Edward Grey, who had so recently taken over at the Foreign Office, had 'not renewed the assurances given by Lord Lansdowne'. The French needed to know what Britain intended to do if, as then seemed likely, Germany should attack France through Belgium. Though their conversation did not conclude until the early hours of the next morning, when he returned home, Repington wrote a summary of what had passed between him and Huguet and sent it by express mail to Grey. He received no reply until 1 January. The Foreign Secretary described the account of the conversation as 'interesting', and added, 'I can only say that I have not receded from anything which Lord Lansdowne said to the French and have no hesitation in affirming it.' On 3 January, Repington again wrote to Grey urging the need for military consultation with the French and Belgians. In the meantime he had talked with George Clarke, Esher, Admiral Fisher, and the head of the War Office's Operations Branch, General Grierson. Huguet had been wise to speak first with Repington. No other freelance agent would have had such easy and familiar access to leading members of the Cabinet, CID, War Office and Admiralty.

The obvious differences and consequent confusion between British military and naval planning, Repington found extremely disturbing. Admiral Fisher, supported by Clarke, refused to think beyond his own Baltic scheme to land troops on the German coast. Grierson talked of several British divisons being transported by the navy to Namur. It was this plan that Repington thought the more practicable, though it is clear from his letter to Esher, dated 14 January, that for him it was a novel conception that he considered important for its diplomatic rather than military effect.

> Now as to the employment of our troops on the continent alongside the French, *I think we are most of us opposed to participation in a land struggle on the continent if we can avoid it.* [My emphasis] But circumstances alter cases, and the circumstances at present are that the highest French authorities tell us that it is not the *amount* of our military support that they regard, but the *principle* of joint cooperation and the moral effect to be produced by the appearance of British troops. Can we allow our desires or prejudices to stand in the way of giving them the satisfaction they require?[18]

This letter was written to Esher *after* Repington had received from the French a reply to his eleven specific questions drafted in consultation with Clarke and Esher. Huguet had carried this interrogatory to Paris on 11 January, returning the next day with the answers. The French had politely but firmly vetoed the idea of a British landing on the German coast [Fisher's idea], and affirmed the importance they attached to a 'certain number' – if possible, two divisions – of British soldiers to fight side by side with their troops from the fifth or sixth day after mobilisation. The French wanted the British to plan and coordinate naval strategy while they wished to take responsibility for the military command. Repington considered the content and tone of the replies as most satisfactory but was horrified by Fisher's reaction when Huguet explained the French tactical plan. The First Sea Lord said the ideas were impossible. He would not look beyond his own plan to transport a large British force to the Baltic.

Grey and Haldane, busily engaged in electioneering, had managed a brief meeting. They decided that the military discussions, so propitiously begun by

Huguet and Repington, should be continued and placed upon an official footing. Haldane wrote to Grey on 17 January to confirm this. 'I sent on Sunday full instructions to Neville so that the French attaché will find Gen Grierson ready.' He wrote again two days later: 'I have carried out what you desire. General Grierson is in communication with the French military attaché – confidentially without prejudice. Preparation to land 105,000 men and 336 guns by end of January.'[19] Repington's part in the negotiations was now at an end.

The result of the general election confirmed the Liberals in power, invulnerable to immediate Tory attacks. The greatest danger to Haldane's schemes at the War Office was the suspicion and animosity of his own backbenchers. For the moment he enjoyed the wholehearted support of the Unionist press but within six months this had evaporated. H. A. Gwynne of the *Standard* was not the only Tory editor who regretted that he now had 'to turn round and go for Haldane. It is most unfortunate,' he told Raymond Marker. 'I have been doing my utmost to put the Army above party politics and now our almost unanimous condemnation of his scheme looks as though our hostility is a party move, which it is not at all.' A month later, writing to the same correspondent, Gwynne was even more angry and pessimistic. 'I have come to the conclusion (and only with much regret) that Haldane is nothing more or less than a humbug. He is a creature of circumstance and a compromiser of the worst kind. . . . He has given in to the extremists. . . . He has allowed himself to be swept off his feet by the Little Englanders of the Lloyd George type.'[20]

Repington did not share Gwynne's view, and saw no reason to alter his earlier estimate that Haldane was supremely fitted to be Minister of War, 'so long as, in my humble judgment he continues to play the correct game from *our* point of view'.[21] His services were still at the minister's disposal as a propagandist and also in the important covert role of negotiator with various intractable Tory groups. Nor was Repington unduly concerned about the 'antics' of Haldane's Radical critics. As he told Esher, 'They will never go in harness.' He noted with disgust that 'no one in the old days cared a fig for these extremists. Now the tendency is to bow to every breeze.'[22] He was much more worried about the minister's Tory critics whom he described to Haldane's mother as 'the tribe of Laodicians . . . particularly numerous and more harmful than open foes. . . . I have to pander to these gentry by criticising details of your son's policy otherwise I should be dubbed a partisan and the effect of my general support for his policy as a whole would be lost.'[23]

Haldane did not underestimate the value of having Repington as an ally, frequently drawing the attention of his mother or sister to articles written by 'the excellent Col Repington'.[24] Haldane's sister, Elizabeth, had been completely ensnared by Repington's charm, but the minister was never blind to the correspondent's impatience and, more importantly, to the ultimate balance of power between a journalist and a senior politician holding Cabinet office.[25] Both men respected each other, but given their very different tasks and temperaments they knew it was too much to suppose that their paths would never diverge. Repington supported Haldane because, 'He has the big idea which every other Minister of War has lacked.' But, as he admitted to Esher, he wished that the Secretary of State would be less secretive.

> This hole and corner business is useless in modern democracy. You must come out into the open, explain your policy, give details, lash people who disagree with you and carry your policy out with a strong hand. . . . Mr Haldane, I know, has the great gift of conquering all who approach him. His implacable serenity is a better shield than triple brass. He comes, he smiles, he conquers. . . . I want Mr H to succeed, but he cannot unless he takes a firm line and announces a clear policy. . . . Can't you get some lymph from a good pig-headed priest from the Propaganda College in Rome and inoculate the S of S with a single idea and purpose?[26]

Repington's sentiments would have been understood and applauded by most senior army officers. Major General John Spencer Ewart, appointed in October 1906 Director of Military Operations and Intelligence, was puzzled as to why 'high-minded and sincerely patriotic men' like Grey and Haldane, well aware of the strategic implications of the joint Franco-British military talks, should apparently refuse to divulge this information to other members of the Cabinet. The consequence of their secrecy was a 'Gilbertian state of military preparation [for] those members of the Cabinet not in the know are agitating for reductions which dislocate all our preparations'.[27] This allowed Radical ministers like Churchill and Lloyd George to create havoc.[28] But it was just because of the strength of the Radical reductionist lobby within the Liberal party and Cabinet that Haldane, just like Grey, was obliged to sell his schemes by stealth and deception. Repington, in the early days, talked of 'appealing to the national interest', to 'Patriotism', to 'a policy on which the Centre Party of both sides of the House will vote solid'.[29] But such hopes, Repington soon perceived, were chimerical so long as the Radical element among the Liberals was rampant and while the Tories remained a broken remnant after their election débâcle. Though he was occasionally betrayed by his impatience, Repington saw what Haldane was attempting and was wise enough to employ the minister's own tactics in a campaign to secure conscription that now began to form in his mind.

Repington explained his thinking to Ewart at a luncheon party in January 1907. Ewart said that he could not understand why a man as clever as Repington could advocate compulsory service for home defence when he knew perfectly well that in a war with Germany the fighting would be done not in England but on the continent.

> Repington replied that he knew that just as well as I did, but you had to take 'two bites at the cherry' first you had to obtain the principle of compulsory service for Home Defence and then hope for a Government strong enough to say that the Territorial Force must serve abroad if required to do so.

The general was not convinced by the argument. 'It would pay us better to tell the British public the whole truth.'[30] If Repington had revealed the whole of his strategy, as he did to Marker,[31] it would hardly have pleased Ewart, for it depended upon Haldane's scheme for the Territorials succeeding. Ewart's concern was with the military budget already cut back because of the navy's demands, money spent on the Territorials could only come from the Regulars who would form the Expeditionary Force to fight in France.

When it became known that Repington had joined the 'bolt from the blue' advocates, Fisher denounced him as a turncoat. 'Having fought on one side, he now fights on the other and is now the chosen apostle lying in Mr Leo Maxse's bosom.'[32] The pun on 'lie' was intentional. Arnold-Forster thought that Repington's change of mind was not so much a matter of 'miserable apostasy', as just another example of his 'purposeless vacillation'. He told Balfour, 'I have studied his writing for a very long time and I will undertake to say that there is scarcely any thesis with regard to defence which I could not defend or condemn by reference to them.'[33]

Three factors have to be borne in mind when we consider Repington's statements and actions on invasion and conscription. First, he viewed the two issues as inseparable in the strategy that he had devised. Second, his ideas, like his tactics, developed by stages. Third, his statements in *The Times*, and more notably in the *National Review*, were intended for general public consumption and dictated by circumstances over which he often had little or no control. He had once been a keen and persuasive advocate of the 'blue water' school and a supporter of the volunteer principle. That had been five years earlier, as he told Maxse in 1907, 'in our salad days'.

> Since then I have had the leisure to examine the theories. I have discovered the errors they contain and have become a convert from sheer lack of evidence to support the Blue Water case, and from the abundance of evidence on the other side.[34]

As late as April 1905, Repington, in an article in *The Times*, had criticised the invasion alarmists. After Balfour's statement to the Commons on invasion in the following month, Repington consistently supported the possibility of invasion in his public writings. In his private letters he did allow himself a rather half-hearted caveat when writing to Raymond Marker in June. 'Things look very dicky between France and Germany. . . . This will be the boltest of bolts from the blue if it falls and *at the back of one's mind one must think it impossible.*' [My emphasis][35] At the time of Balfour's speech he told Esher that he thought it an argument for both a weak army and navy. 'I would willingly undertake the invasion of England under the hypothesis of the Prime Minister and would lay 7 to 4 upon my success.'[36]

By January 1906, when he was the moving spirit in the establishment of the National Defence Association, Repington was convinced that the theoretical case for conscription was unanswerable. Yet at the same time he recognised that so keenly engrained was the public's prejudice against conscription that the only hope of changing it would be a properly orchestrated propaganda campaign. The National Service League would not achieve anything as, like Roberts, who was totally lacking in political finesse, they did not appreciate that the case for compulsion could only be won by stealth. It 'simply wasn't cricket' the way Roberts insisted on starting a debate in the Lords and mouthing the same, old, tired platitudes. 'He is admired but thoroughly distrusted by the mass of people. A good figurehead and voilà tout.'[37] Roberts was president of the executive committee of the NDA, but because that body attracted for its ostensible purpose – to lobby for the Territorial Army – as many supporters of the volunteer principle as compulsionists, it seemed to Repington to afford the ideal agency to break down the polarisation of the opposing factions. The first steps towards compulsion could only be short. 'We cannot go further yet as there is an ocean of prejudice against anything you call "military". But the compulsionists can help us to improve what we have got, and the voluntary school must go as far as to bring in physical drill and the use of the rifle.'[38]

In his writing in *The Times*, Repington, while supporting Haldane, fired warning shots over the heads of the minister's Liberal and Radical critics. 'If [they] do not support his policy and make it a success, a great many supporters of the voluntary system will be compelled to go over, bag and baggage, to the conscriptionists.'[39] Haldane appeared to be remarkably cheerful, as though he was convinced that he would succeed where his Tory predecessors had miserably failed. Attending a meeting of the NDA in August, he overflowed with bonhomie, even suggesting the NDA ought to change its name to the Imperial Attack Association. 'But that,' as Repington noted, 'was *after* dinner and if he had dared to repeat those sentiments in the House he would have been locked in the Clock Tower by his enraged party.'[40]

Being 'at daggers drawn with Chirol' and most of the senior staff on *The Times* did not make life easy for Repington. They were behaving 'no better than a set of brigands',[41] but this did not deter him from setting out to tackle the Admiralty. That department of state, and Fisher in particular, had been allowed to get away with too much for too long. Fisher Repington described as a 'cantankerous humbug' who made life 'd-d difficult'. The Admiral's 'frousy idea of strategy' was about as much use as 'trying to kill a tiger by tickling his tail. . . . Our sailors have thought out nothing and have the very vaguest idea of strategy on a large scale.'[42] Even though Roberts's arguments for invasion were 'admittedly fearfully weak', Fisher's complacent rejection of any invasion risk was inspired only by his selfish concern to insure the navy secured more than its fair share of the defence budget. Repington was convinced that for the good of the Admiralty and the safety of the nation he must 'hit them for six' and he would do so with a strong invasion argument that would win public support for conscription. All this he talked over with his editor, Buckle, who agreed that he would help even though it was 'bound to lead to a devil of a rumpus'. When Parliament rose for its summer recess, Repington would attack with an article that would finally 'destroy the effect of Balfour's pronouncement of last year respecting invasion'.[43]

The promised article appeared in *The Times* on 29 August 1906 and it prompted a furious exchange of correspondence that lasted for more than a month. Balfour, demonstrating his open-mindedness on defence issues, was obviously impressed by Repington's arguments, despite the best efforts of George Clarke to belittle Repington while reassuring the Tory leader. Clarke particularly emphasised the difference between the 'calculated thinking' of the

CID and the true purpose of Repington's 'scaremongering'. Could not Balfour see that by raising the invasion issue, the military correspondent was actually 'intent on frying other fish'? Surely everyone by now recognised that an invasion 'scare', real or supposed, was a powerful inducement to make public and politicians think more favourably about conscription, if only for home defence? It was 'an uncomfortable thought' that a man like Repington 'was capable of doing such a large amount of mischief'. Clarke's advocacy would have been more persuasive had his personal pique been less obvious. He resented the way Repington had replaced him in Haldane's affections.[44]

Repington's article proved to be, not the end of an old and familiar story, as Clarke so obviously wished, but the beginning of an entirely new chapter. To his great dismay Clarke learned in November that Balfour had agreed to attend a meeting of the National Defence Association where Repington was to give a paper on invasion and a critique of the Blue Water school. Clarke warned Balfour that Repington was bound to upset the arguments upon which the Tory leader's Commons' statement the previous year had been postulated. 'I need not remind you,' he told Balfour, 'that you then pointed out it was irrational to suppose that, at a period of tension, our organised fleets would be away from home waters.'

If people like Repington can succeed in persuading the country that the fleet is not a protection against invasion, then clearly we have no possible basis for military organization except compulsion, and this, all thinking people will agree, is utterly impracticable. And if we talk compulsion knowing we cannot adopt it, we shall discredit all organization which is reasonable with the result of perpetuating the aimless muddling of the past.[45]

Despite this jeremiad Balfour attended the meeting and, having listened to Repington's paper, spoke himself for three-quarters of an hour in which time he 'agreed with every positive proposition' that had been advanced. Balfour's speech was, according to Repington, the 'best he ever delivered'. Esher, who had read an early draft of Repington's paper about which he had been less than enthusiastic, now learned that a 'revised version' would be published in *The Times*. He did not need telling by the author that it would give George Clarke 'fits' and 'bring the whole flotilla of Navalists down on [him]. The more the merrier,' the military correspondent announced. 'Until we have put an end to all the damned nonsense that is written about sea power we shall never get our national army.'[46] There was every reason for Repington to feel pleased with himself. As he admitted to Roberts, Balfour had been 'pushed further than we could have dared to hope'.[47]

A few days later, he again wrote to Roberts, this time asking him if he would, 'Whip up the frock-coats and mutton chops.'[48] If there was to be any measure of lasting success for his plan then Repington knew he must win the support of prominent figures outside the military establishment. As he had said to Milner the previous July, 'How to get what is wanted is a national and social question and until the natural leaders of the people take the question up, the people remain puzzled and do not know to what saint to vow themselves. . . . If you could collect around you a certain number of independent men of mark of the type of Cromer, Curzon etc, and place the issue fairly and squarely before the people, I think we should make rapid progress.'[49] Unfortunately 'men of mark' showed an extraordinary reluctance to be recruited. Roberts certainly tried hard to fulfil his commission but with little success on this as on subsequent occasions. It was one thing to make encouraging noises in private, another to speak out on a public platform.

Repington was not a little surprised and discouraged that it should be left to him to carry the main weight of debate. *The Times* for a while became the arena for a gladiatorial contest between the military correspondent and a variety of Admiralty advocates. George Clarke proved a doughty warrior in the navy's interest, ridiculing the 'bolt from the blue' advocates and charging them with starting a 'mischievous agitation' because they 'never resorted to the process of thinking'. It was all good knock-about stuff, and no one was more delighted or applauded Clarke's blows more enthusiastically than Admiral Fisher.

By January 1907 Repington was convinced that his best course of action to achieve anything more positive than the exchange of verbal insults was, if possible, to force the Cabinet to investigate the issue of invasion. General Ewart was proving a most useful ally and Repington cultivated this contact through a mutual friend, Lord Lovat. The three men met frequently and there was a helpful exchange of information as well as ideas. Ewart's department was kept in a woeful state of penury as a consequence of Foreign Office and Treasury penny-pinching. Here, Repington was able to help him, informing Moberly Bell:

> I am on good terms with the War Office Intelligence People just now, and they give me all I want. A quid pro quo is advisable. . . . I wish to show . . . Ewart our Intelligence Department and allow him to apply to it in case of need. . . . It would be a recognition of his assistance to me.[50]

If reprehensible, Repington's smug tone is quite understandable. He had further good reason to feel pleased with himself when Sir Samuel Scott very generously financed trips by him and Lovat to Germany so that they might gather further information, the better to make their case.[51] While the spade-work of preparation was going on, Repington cultivated Roberts's favour. When the time was ready to act, the old warrior would be an unimpeachable figurehead.[52]

As Balfour had reacted so favourably to Repington's earlier paper on invasion, when they had gathered together sufficient evidence to make their case convincing, the conspirators approached the ex-premier to press 'certain considerations which induced them to think that there were important changes in the circumstances under which the Defence Committee in 1902–03 had arrived at the conclusion that invasion was impossible'. In short, they argued that Germany posed a different and greater threat than had France, that conditions were much more perilous than they had been five years earlier and that the public ought to be aware of these changes. Balfour's response could not have been more reassuring. He admitted his own conviction that there could never be a final conclusion on an issue like invasion and agreed, if they could produce sufficient evidence to prove that new circumstances had arisen since the CID had last drawn up its conclusion, then he would embody this in a note that he would send to the Defence Committee accompanied by his own comments. As good as his word, in July 1907, Balfour wrote a long letter to the CID's secretary, George Clarke.

> In the Memorandum of 1903 on Serious Invasion, the enemy was supposed to be France. In the enclosed Notes, the presumed enemy is Germany. The change no doubt corresponds in the minds of the writers with modification in the European situation: but evidently it is only important if invasion is really easier of accomplishment by a German than a French Army. The original Defence Paper went upon the opposite hypothesis. . . .
> In ultimate analysis, the question of Invasion on its naval side is from the invader's point of view a question of secrecy and speed. . . . Secrecy as well as speed seems more within [the Germans'] grasp. And though the distance to be traversed by the invaders is greater, the ships at their disposal are faster, and their course would probably be further from hostile fleets. The point to be determined is whether these differences in favour of Germany, if shewn to be real, constitute any sufficient ground for taking a less sanguine view of our immunity from serious invasion than seemed justified but a short time since.

Clarke agreed that a copy of Balfour's letter, together with the notes, should be printed. It was his opinion that the new material did not affect the conclusions reached in 1903. Nevertheless it would be a worthwhile exercise for the CID to examine the evidence anew. He had come to this decision reluctantly as, although still a keen 'blue water' advocate, he recognised that the Admiralty's behaviour gave some cause for concern. He admitted to Balfour, 'It has long been difficult to secure proper treatment of any naval question. The Admiralty is inclined to set itself above the Cabinet.' Only 'in deference to Press clamour' had the Channel fleet been recently increased.[53]

Repington could not have been more pleased by the way in which Balfour had presented their case. What he wanted to do now was to prepare the public's mind for the coming inquiry by giving them a full account of his own views on the invasion issue. However, this was impossible because of the influence of 'the "blue water" men in the Times'. So he was obliged to turn to Leo Maxse to ask if he might publish a long article on the subject in the November issue of the *National Review*. Repington also wanted to make sure that Maxse did not inadvertently spoil the case by making contumacious remarks about Balfour or charging off on one of his frequent insolent and ill-informed forays against the CID.

> It will be better to say nothing about the Inquiry which Roberts, Lovat, Sammy Scott and I have wrung from the Government and from a very hostile Admiralty. It will begin about November 20. Do not run down Arthur Balfour on this question. We have made great efforts to convert him this year and he has written an admirable letter to the Defence Committee forwarding our views and will, I think, come over to us. This

is all very confidential for your personal information and the less said about it the better.[54]

Until he received an absolute assurance from Haldane, Repington continued to worry that all his carefully made plans would come to nothing, frustrated by the efforts of Fisher or one of the Admiral's acolytes.[55] By a strange irony, it was Fisher's exaggerated opposition to the idea of an invasion investigation that finally insured that the CID would act.

The last thing Fisher wanted was an investigation into the topic of invasion. The Senior Service was deeply divided between his supporters and those of Admiral Lord Charles Beresford. Sir John and Lord Charles had been at each other's throats for years, and Fisher had a shrewd suspicion that somehow or other Beresford must have something to do with this latest pestilential inconvenience.

A discordant band of brothers

Fisher forced every department of the Naval Service to review its position
and question its own existence. He shook them and beat them and
cajoled them out of slumber into intense activity. But the Navy was not a
pleasant place while this was going on. The 'Band of Brothers' tradition
which Nelson handed down was for the time discarded.

W. S. Churchill, The World Crisis

The Press was used to delude the public as to the efficacy of certain
reforms which were pressed through without debate, thought or
consideration by Sir John Fisher, aided by such people as Captain Bacon
who used espionage, intimidation and favouritism in order to silence Naval
opinion in the Fleet on these mad schemes.

Beresford to Strachey

The fortunes of the Royal Navy before the Great War were dominated by
Admiral Sir John Arbuthnot Fisher. In a few acrimonious years he successfully
effected a revolutionary reorganisation of that most conservative Service, an
undertaking that compelled a response from all who were involved. Some were
devoted to Fisher and admired his schemes. Others thought him arrogant and
his ideas wrong-headed. Time and malice nurtured the envy Fisher's critics
felt for his many social, political and professional triumphs. So uncompromising
was their hostility that they dismissed the man and all his works, questioned
his purpose, denigrated his methods and arraigned him before the world as 'a
dangerous lunatic' and 'the wrecker of the navy'. That everyone did not share
their views they supposed was because men's ears were stuffed with Fisher's
'noisy, blatant, popularity-hunting, self-advertising buncombe and blather'.[1]

Fisher's most ardent disciples within the Service – the favoured members
of what was known as the 'Fishpond' – were the younger naval personnel. Few
senior officers shared their enthusiasm, but Fisher merely dismissed them in
his cavalier fashion as 'prehistoric', 'Yellow Admirals', 'naval Rip van Winkles',
'fossils'. When Admiral Noel had protested Fisher's unfitness to be appointed
as First Sea Lord, he claimed that his opinion was shared by 'practically all
the most reliable men in the upper ranks of the Navy'. Admiral Custance
believed that Fisher lacked any grasp of fundamental principle. The fellow
was determined to run himself to the front at any price. He was a time-server,
superficial, a desk-bound warrior whose only noteworthy quality was a capacity

to deceive others who ought to have known better. Admiral Fitzgerald warned that if the First Sea Lord's hypnotic powers were not rapidly curbed he would 'surely wreak some dreadful mischief upon the Navy'.[2] Fisher disdainfully dubbed this formidable group of senior naval officers and the journalists whose support they commanded 'the Syndicate of Discontent', 'the Adullamites', or, using his friend Arnold White's phrase, 'the Blue Funk School'. Towards one senior officer, Admiral Lord Charles Beresford, Fisher demonstrated an enmity of pathological intensity that was as heartily reciprocated. Edmond Slade, an eminently fair-minded man and well placed to make a judgment, believed there was nothing to choose between Fisher and Beresford as far as their absurd personal vendetta was concerned. They would continue their undignified and damaging squabble so long as they remained in their respective commands.[3]

At the turn of the century Beresford was better known to the general British public than Fisher.[4] In 1882 his audacious and heroic conduct at the bombardment of Alexandria had earned him universal admiration and recognition. Subsequently, for one reason and another, he had scarcely been out of the public eye; first as intimate, then enemy of Edward, Prince of Wales; as socialite, prankster, senior naval officer and the Commons' outspoken 'Member for the Navy'. Lord Charles was an impulsive, warm-hearted, generous, larger-than-life, egotistical Irishman. At sea he was not the greatest of strategists but had shown a capacity to handle fleets and to fight with care and cunning. On land he was not seen to best advantage, 'especially when attempting the role of statesmanship of which he is particularly fond'. The author of this tongue-in-cheek observation was Sir William White, the distinguished naval architect, who succinctly concluded his pen-portrait of the Admiral in a letter to Strachey: 'Beresford is by nature most outspoken.'[5] Brodrick, who knew Beresford even better than White, thought that although there was a good deal to be said for him, 'Charlie B's propensity to say too much too often has ruined his prospects.' He had been more than insubordinate, he had been exceedingly foolish to talk slightingly of Fisher, his superior officer, 'to so many people'.[6]

For two years, from 1900 to 1902, Beresford had served as Fisher's second-in-command in the Mediterranean. Because they both wanted to increase the size of the fleet, they campaigned together with a certain degree of amity. But once this problem had been resolved, the underlying tension in their relationship reasserted itself. Commentators, then and since, have canvassed a number of causes to explain the final rift, but it seems best to conclude that not one but a number of incidents, compounded by the antipathetic characters of the two men, combined to make Sir John and Lord Charles irreconcilable foes. Sadly, their mutual ill-will was supplemented and envenomed by the frequent promptings of 'friends' who, while lauding the one, maliciously slandered the other. Universally acknowledged as the chosen champions and the personification of two bitterly opposed naval factions, both men were almost as often sinned against as sinning. If Fisher was the greater, more able man, Beresford was never less than Sir John in love of self, country and navy, to which Service both men gave unstintingly the better part of their lives.

Valentine Chirol, writing to Spring Rice in October 1904, had enjoyed poking fun at the Liberal party's ignorance of the navy. In a recent article in the *Nineteenth Century* which had discussed the future membership of a Liberal Cabinet, the author, Henry Lucy, 'forgot all about the First Lord of the Admiralty! which has caused much scoffing on "our side" as an indication of what the Navy can expect if they come in!'[7] With Fisher as First Sea Lord, political charge of the Board of Admiralty was no sinecure. Cawdor admitted that as First Lord he had found controlling Fisher 'a duty that taxed his vigilance to the utmost', and he doubted whether his Liberal successor, Lord Tweedmouth, would be 'strong enough to keep Fisher under adequate control'.[8] Subsequent events were to justify this anxiety.

As First Lord, Tweedmouth was more hopelessly distracted than had been either of his immediate predecessors by the incessant public and private feudings of the Fisher and Beresford cliques. In July 1906, he proposed Beresford for the Channel fleet, the chief command in home waters, with the responsibility 'to organise the fleet for war and immediate action'.[9] The offer was accepted eagerly. Fisher was outraged, his anger made worse by the noise Beresford's friends were raising in the press. It was not enough that they should proclaim Lord Charles's unique fitness for so onerous, prestigious and honourable a command, but they were suggesting that should he replace Fisher as First Sea Lord 'assuredly nothing would be more popular in the eyes of the nation'.[10] Fisher's response was to bombard Tweedmouth with a barrage of arguments – strategic, diplomatic and political – that the Channel command ought to be divided. Never once did Fisher declare his jealousy of Beresford, though this was at least an important reason for his action. Eventually, Tweedmouth succumbed to Fisher's pleas. When informed that his command was to be divided, Beresford was furiously indignant. How dare the First Lord strip him of two-thirds of his fleet's complement at the instigation of a jealous rival. There followed a torrid period with much acrimonious bargaining, a distraught Tweedmouth attempting to hold the ring between an outraged Beresford and an implacable Fisher. In the end it was Beresford who won a limited victory. He accepted his attenuated command but upon the understanding that at any time, for war exercises or manoeuvres, he would have at his disposal the original Channel fleet. Fisher retired from the fight, his feathers ruffled, suggesting to his cronies, with an uncharacteristic lack of gallantry, that Beresford had caused the trouble because 'he funked the Channel . . . Fogs and short days and difficult navigation very different to Mediterranean and white trousers!!!'[11] He knew that this aspersion, aimed at Beresford's notorious fondness for 'spit and polish' and running an 'exceedingly flag-shippy flag-ship', was quite without foundation.

Fisher's ill-humour may in part be excused because throughout the previous year he had suffered a vitriolic press campaign orchestrated by 'Leo Maxse in the "National Review", et hoc genus omne . . . and the pessimists and the "washing-dirty-clothes-in-publicists" '.[12] Fisher's allies in the press had good reason to be concerned about this constant carping. James Thursfield, senior naval correspondent of *The Times*, in a letter to Buckle, compared these present unfavourable opinions with the recent past when Fisher and the Admiralty had commanded the confidence of a united country. Was there, he asked rhetorically, 'any substantive ground for the change of attitude'?[13] Though not directed to him, the question was answered by H. W. Wilson, the *Daily Mail*'s naval expert, once an enthusiastic supporter of Fisher. A few months earlier he had published in the *National Review* an article highly critical of the First Sea Lord. He wrote to Arnold White who, at Fisher's request, had been 'firing broadsides . . . hitting between wind and water . . . the silly idiots whom the uninformed and ignorant editors allow to disport themselves in their papers in big print'.[14] What he wanted, Wilson told White, was to 'secure the concentration of an overwhelming force in the North Sea'. He charged Fisher with giving a spurious rationale for the division of the Channel fleet. It had been his personal pique at Beresford's advancement that had prompted his 'glaring infringement of every principle of strategy'. Now Fisher would have to pay for his ill-conceived action.

> If Fisher is angry with us I am sorry. He is angry with those who might
> have been and were prepared to be his best friends; who have fought
> for him through thick and thin and who believed in him two years ago as
> you do now. But supposing anything should happen in the North Sea
> through his dispositions; where would we be, and what would be my own
> feeling if we and I had sat still and never uttered a protest against changes
> which fifty per cent of naval officers condemn?[15]

It was this last point that was so damaging to Fisher's credibility. Even an admirer like Louis Battenberg described Fisher's disposition of the Channel fleet as 'simple topsey-turveydom' and opposed to all his previously accepted strategic principles.[16] Could you trust the man who was virtual dictator of the navy when he was prepared to put the nation's safety in pawn merely to satisfy a personal grudge?

Beresford, encouraged by R. D. Blumenfeld of the *Daily Express* and H. A. Gwynne of the *Standard*, cultivated his resentment for Fisher and provided a series of ever more indiscreet and inflammatory squibs about the First Sea Lord. It was his 'considered' opinion, he wrote to Blumenfeld, that,

> the safety of the Fleets is in the hands of a man who was lamentable as
> an Executive and is criminal as an Administrator, all his efforts being
> for personal grandisement and pecuniary advantage. He has, I believe,
> over £5,000 a year. More than a Cabinet Minister rank for ruining the
> Navy, demoralising it all round, causing irritation and disloyalty among
> the officers and disaffection and insubordination among the men.[17]

This last was an outrageous example of the pot calling the kettle black, for not only was the popular press loud with Beresford's disloyal observations suitably embroidered and disguised by willing editorial pens, but the navy also reverberated to his complaints; his canvassing for support against Fisher among his brother officers and his slanderous ward-room conversations, while by almost every post, a bemused Tweedmouth received a consignment of letters in Beresford's distinctive, large, illegible hand, complaining about the First Sea Lord.

Fisher did not stand naked among his enemies, nor were his supporters without influence in the councils of the nation. To Thursfield, from whom he was anxious to solicit a series of friendly articles, Fisher quoted Esher's assertion that all the senior members of the Liberal Cabinet, Balfour and Lansdowne, the king and his secretary, Knollys, Burnham, owner of the *Daily Telegraph* – not to mention Esher himself – to a man, were supporters of everything he had done at the Admiralty. Yet, the confidence of this congeries of the united Establishment apparently was not enough. '*The time has now arrived*', he wrote to Thursfield, 'for a "Justification Pour" as the French would say, and I suggest to you to see Mr Buckle, trust him implicitly, show him *everything* and let the Times prepare its own series of articles . . . your papers will assure him he is on the Bedrock of Certainty in all he says – This *infinitely* better than any Admiralty Minute and official "exposé des motifs" and the Times *the only vehicle and the authority that will be accepted*. . . .'[18]

The reputation of *The Times* had waxed fat on the crumbs of intelligence that were purposely dropped into its lap from the tables of the great. Buckle did not wish his naval correspondent to be accused of being Fisher's sycophant, but was reassured when Thursfield told him that it was not his intention 'to write an apologia for the Admiralty'.[19] Nevertheless, the articles entitled 'The State of the Navy', based as they were on notes provided by Fisher, constituted a piece of special pleading for Sir John. Not that Fisher was particularly pleased or impressed by Thursfield's efforts on his behalf. He had much preferred Julian Corbett's essay in the *Nineteenth Century* – also based closely upon notes thoughtfully provided by the incorrigible Fisher. Thursfield had been too dispassionate. He had not, like Corbett, 'hit out' sufficiently at his enemies. Thursfield might have recalled with profit one of the Admiral's more favoured scriptural apophthegms: 'The Kingdom of Heaven suffereth violence and the violent take it by force.'[20]

Fisher's tribulations were multiplied because everyone knew how he dominated the Board of Admiralty. It was appropriate, therefore, that he should suffer most of the opprobrium visited upon that department. 'Fisher's dictatorship . . . is not the Admiralty system', Selborne complained in August 1905.[21] Selborne blamed his successor as First Lord for this state of affairs, but Admiral Fitzgerald thought Fisher had kept all his First Lords completely under his thumb and made the other members of the Board his creatures. 'It is', he wrote to Maxse, 'autocracy pure and simple – or at any rate, simple.'[22] Arnold-Forster said the trouble was Sir John's disposition to regard the navy as his own property. The Admiralty was 'always inclined to be a little above its boots'. With the present First Lord, Tweedmouth, 'manifestly quite incompetent',[23] there was good reason for even an ex-minister like Midleton, who usually 'would not have a word spoken against Fisher who has done great work', to have pause for thought.[24] Fisher was such a swashbuckler, there was a very real danger of a reaction. 'A serious prospect,' Arnold-Forster sanctimoniously intoned to Balfour, 'for when battle is once joined the extremists will prevail.'[25] With the typical reservation of a cautious spirit, Austen Chamberlain summed up these feelings of disquiet among former Tory ministers, once wholehearted Fisherites. 'I've grown to distrust Fisher's ways,' he admitted to Maxse. 'His speeches and intrigues are deplorable and shake all confidence. And of course he may be wrong on many points, tho' he is a very clever man.'[26]

Esher thought that because Fisher was the target of complaint by groups within both political parties 'presumably he ha[d] found the *juste milieu*'.[27] This he knew was to beg the real question. Why were so many men of different political sympathies bent upon Fisher's humiliation and destruction? Even Beresford could admit that 'some of the reforms of the last four years at the Admiralty have been good in themselves'.[28] What infuriated many of Fisher's critics was the way he had engineered and publicised his reforms. From time to time this most autocratic of Sea Lords would indulge a wayward, democratic daemon and cavort and flirt indecently with his press 'jackals'. He had been 'playing the fool for four years . . . indulging in a superficial and provocative policy', William White told Strachey. 'So long as the half-penny newspapers, through the agency of men primed by Fisher himself, declare that all is well and that there never was such a capable administrator, Fisher is satisfied. The policy throughout is best described as "After the Deluge".'[29]

What distinguished Fisher from other men of affairs in his cultivation of the press was the gigantic scale of his unrelenting effort – for the most part successful – to recruit journalists to create a welcoming and favourable public opinion for himself and his measures. Though almost all the so-called 'Silent Service' seemed inspired by similar intent, Fisher was always the supreme exponent. One of his biographers has claimed that, 'He was the first of our Admirals to make an intelligent use of the press for the benefit of the Navy. . . . Fisher felt that publicity was essential to success and having gauged the consequent disadvantages he boldly faced them.'[30] Another, less friendly commentator, in a letter to *The Times*, declared that he had 'never known such elaborate attempts to influence the newspapers . . . not even by a politician whose career depended upon it'.[31] Fisher insisted that the press provided him with 'the only engine that could effect the vast revolution' he desired in the navy. 'Without the press it could not have been done.'[32]

The corridors of the Admiralty buzzed with the susurration of a thousand 'exclusive' hints and rumours offered to the conveniently credulous cohorts of attendant journalists. For those, not so few, that Fisher particularly favoured, by post or special messenger came prints and plans, documents of every description, bearing the latest confidential intelligence from the Cabinet, usually accompanied by one of Fisher's extraordinary holographs, underscored in coloured pencil for emphasis, littered with exclamation marks, with the repeated fervid assurance that the information was for his correspondent's eyes alone, and invariably headed with the legend 'most' or 'very secret'. Given his prodigal gifts of classified information and his extravagant charm, it is not too difficult to understand why Fisher enjoyed so much success in his promiscuous pursuit of journalists. 'He cultivated the Press unblushingly,' wrote J. A. Spender, but as one who had surrendered frequently to Fisher's blandishments was quick to add that the Admiral's motives were invariably 'lofty' and 'patriotic'.

He took such pains with each of us, was so intimate and affectionate that we never could resist the notion that we were the chosen repositories of his special confidence. He gave with both hands to each in turn, and we rewarded him with such an advertisement of himself and his ideas as no seaman ever received from newspapers.[33]

Of all Fisher's distinguished allies in the press, J. L. Garvin was the closest and most important, especially in the crucial two years, 1908 and 1909.[34] Their association had begun in 1904. By March of the following year Fisher was writing, '*We have done much*! **We are going to do more**! but we must have public opinion as an avalanche to hurl and dash the pessimists into the bottomless pit of perdition, out of the way of progress.'[35] When Garvin was appointed editor of the *Observer* both men immediately recognised how this enhanced the possibilities of working together to their mutual advantage. So great was Fisher's trust in Garvin and his estimate of the influence the *Observer* could exercise under that editor that he risked his professional career in order to provide information of a most secret and confidential nature. Garvin welcomed this extraordinary confidence shown in him and returned Fisher's trust and friendship with loyalty and dedication.

With the merest hint of the envy of someone much less successful at working the press to serve his own ends, Arnold-Forster observed unctuously to Balfour, 'Sir John has put himself entirely in the wrong by his methods, his newspaper log-rolling, his "confidential" documents communicated under the seal of secrecy to the Town Crier!'[36] On one occasion, Forster bearded Fisher on this subject, opening their conversation in his usual unvarnished fashion by telling him he did not like what he was doing. Fisher disarmingly accepted Forster's censure and told him that he was not alone in his opinion, instancing as another who shared his view Pretyman, successively a Civil Lord and then Secretary to the Admiralty during the Balfour administration. Fisher knew that he could as well have cited a hundred names. He insisted that he was 'absolutely compelled to use the press so as to get public opinion with him to carry through such far-reaching reforms'.[37] But there was always an element in Fisher's make-up that drove him to court extremes; it was as though he could not help himself. Indiscretion was as much part of his nature as secrecy and cunning. In the excitement of the moment he could be betrayed by his own exuberance and say things that were better left unsaid. Nevertheless, his urgent injunction to editors after a *tête-à-tête*, 'kindly do not remember anything I said', was repeated too frequently to suggest that he had suffered a genuine lapse of discretion. That he was not betrayed by those who shared his confidences was testimony to their conviction that, despite his obvious faults, Fisher was a great public servant whose foresight, ability and energy was the best guarantee of Britain remaining mistress of the oceans of the world.

The Admiral's critics too readily accepted simple explanations to account for his hold upon the loyalties of his press supporters. It was not just the information he supplied but the way he emphasised how much he valued their contribution that was a crucial factor in his success. 'I write to you', he told Thursfield in 1903, 'because public opinion has far more weight than the strongest representations of even the fighting Admirals.' Fisher was never restrained in expressing opinions about his friends, enemies, the state of the world, or heaven and hell. The blazing enthusiasm of the moment was never to be cabinned by the merest hint of a cautionary caveat. Praise, like blame, should be distributed extravagantly with an unself-conscious largesse. It was not enough, for example, to provide Thursfield with detailed notes from which to construct an article, but when the work was finished Fisher hastened to despatch a handsome eulogium. 'I can sincerely say I know no man who has done the Navy more service than you have done by your admirable perception. . . . Your leading article in the Times was, I fear, too kind.'[38] How difficult for anyone to resist such child-like artlessness. What a delightful, incorrigible, rogue not only to break all the rules but never to forget to acknowledge the help that he had been given.

Fisher's ubiquitous influence in the press meant that his voice was heard loudly and frequently in every part of the country. To insure that it was the authorised version of the truth that was disseminated, Fisher did not hesitate to supply even the exact words he calculated would best achieve his desired effect. Parliament would never give 'the blank cheque to the sailors' that he wanted unless he 'shoved for all [his] worth', and the press did its part. '*Agitate, agitate*! . . . If there is a hell of a row outside, they'll give way inside.'[39] Excluding Garvin, Fisher generally favoured a journalistic broadside to the single shot, no matter how well aimed. Sir John's foibles were a familiar and accepted part of the game, even as his frequent injunction, '*This is a secret and not to be mentioned*', was the usual overture to a desired cacophony of publicity. His gratuitous advice, 'Reiteration is the secret of conviction! Repetition is the soul of journalism! *I do hope that you will keep on hammering*!' was readily accepted by those who devilled earnestly at his behest because it was almost invariably accompanied by a suitable titbit of news as a *pourboire*.[40] Arnold White once likened Fisher to the Messiah. The only drawback was his overweening desire to make an entry into Jerusalem twice weekly and to postpone his crucifixion indefinitely.

> 10 Dreadnoughts in 18 months, and the 'Globe' etc, call me a 'Traitor' etc. However, the truth is we do not want anyone to know the truth as it mystifies the foreigners. They can 'crucify' me now, but when, by and bye, they see Dreadnoughts coming up like mushrooms they'll sing out 'Hosanna'. *Do not say anything. I only want you to know*.[41]

A confusing message certainly, but one hesitates to call it blasphemous when in 1914 the author was to experience a truly remarkable resurrection.

Beresford never enjoyed the same quality of support from his journalist acolytes as Fisher. It was not that he was any less assiduous in firing off instructions and information, but he could never establish a like degree of mutual confidence, loyalty and trust. He was forever seeking impossible guarantees that his confidences would not be betrayed, even from a long-time and faithful ally like H. A. Gwynne.[42] Beresford's influence on the press was mainly negative, the support he enjoyed more often a reflection of dissatisfaction with Fisher than a positive endorsement of him or his ideas. He tried to woo

Northcliffe a number of times but his suit was spurned with the hollow excuse that he did not need extra support when he was already 'encompassed by a steel ring . . . of a powerful cabal'. Relaying this disappointing response Beresford sadly noted that he had 'only two strong supporters . . . in the press'.[43] They were R. D. Blumenfeld of the *Daily Express* and H. A. Gwynne of the *Standard*. Both newspapers – Fisher described them to Tweedmouth as 'mendacious, drivelling rags' – were owned by Arthur Pearson.

Gwynne, Beresford's most consistent and loyal apologist, 'for a long time bore the burden of the day almost single-handed'.[44] As a friend of the Chamberlains Gwynne was little loved by the free trade Unionists, but they dismissed him too lightly as 'a fool prone to talk with great recklessness'.[45] Pearson never doubted his editor's capacity and advertised his appointment as proof of his jealous concern for the *Standard*'s existing reputation and determination to increase its authority in the future.[46]

Fisher had not taken long to recruit both Gwynne and the *Standard*'s new naval correspondent, Leslie Cope-Cornford, to support his schemes. In December 1905 Fisher was busily advertising his excellence as an economist to them, implying that by his astuteness he had actually squared the financial circle and achieved more for the navy by paying less. He prefaced this account of his achievement with typical hyperbole: 'The Empire floats on the Navy, and the Navy floats on the "Standard".' In one year he had saved ten million pounds yet 'left the Fleet immeasurably stronger and more efficient'.[47] Gwynne was not altogether persuaded of Fisher's genius as an economist and thought it more likely that Fisher had given in to the dictates of politicians. Maxse, in his inimitable style, was already bellowing that Sir John had become 'the willing instrument of a cheese-paring Cobdenite Cabinet'. In January 1906 Fisher was still writing to Gwynne congratulating him on an article in the *Standard* written by Cope-Cornford from notes supplied by the First Sea Lord. 'I say to you *absolutely without flattery* I never in my life read anything better. *Never!*'[48] A year later it was Beresford who was writing to congratulate Gwynne on the *Standard*'s attitude to the navy. He pronounced himself to be 'in hearty sympathy and agreement with your statements which have been absolutely true in substance and in fact'.[49] Beresford's approval was hardly surprising. For months he had been supplying Gwynne with a regular budget of information and opinion.

Gwynne never doubted he was right to champion Beresford's cause against Fisher. Merely to satisfy his jealousy and vanity Fisher had made Britain unnecessarily vulnerable to a German invasion threat by dividing the Channel fleet. As he told Beresford in May 1907, 'If Germany should make an incursion during the next three months and should land 100,000 men in England who could walk up and down the country as easily as a hot knife through butter, the weakness of the Channel Fleet would be their temptation.'[50] Nor was such concern limited to invasion alarmists or jingo hotheads. George Clarke, who deplored the mounting campaign of the 'bolt from the blue' scaremongers, admitted, 'We have not got the organization or the distribution we require and the Navy generally is far from being in a satisfactory state.'[51] The absurd maldistribution of the Channel fleet apart, Clarke knew there was good reason to distrust Fisher's strategic sense. At the time of the first Moroccan crisis the First Sea Lord had shown a lack of both grip and urgency. Repington, who had been closely involved with those events, had at the time recorded his disillusionment with Fisher. 'Sir John has no plans to offer. . . . I thought that we had a St Vincent at Whitehall but apparently I was mistaken.'[52] Putting the invasionist case bluntly to Esher, Repington argued 'that no naval precautions we take, short of those which would throw an unendurable strain upon personnel, can safeguard us against a naval surprise. . . . I have no confidence in our naval shield against an enemy who gives himself the overwhelming advantage of the initiative and surprise.'[53] What Repington did not divulge to Esher was that he had been supplied evidence by Beresford that clearly implied the navy would be hard pressed to contain the German fleet even if given advanced notice of any intention to attack.

Fisher was always reluctant to spell out his strategy, even to senior naval colleagues. He later maintained this was because Beresford was 'more or less off his head, or at least brainless and irresponsible for his language. How could one trust deep strategic and war secrets to such a man?'[54] This was special pleading of a kind Repington had already hit firmly upon the head. Fisher's attitude was not excusable even if it was understandable. Like all strong men he wished to do as he pleased. 'It is alright for an Admiral or General in war with a distinct mission given them, but for such a vast business as peace strategy, so huge and so all embracing . . . it is not safe to confide the fortunes of our Empire to one man however able.'[55] Fisher's unfortunate disposition to threaten and bluff was another fatal weakness. Germany simply was not the sort of Power one could afford to trifle with, or 'tease and promise to bully a year hence with impunity. . . . Sir JF is gambling on William's cowardice. It is unsafe to do that with a man who acts on the impulse of the moment.'[56]

Gwynne, convinced by his meetings with Repington, Roberts and Beresford that so long as Fisher remained at the Admiralty no adequate preparations would be made to repel a German invasion, decided there should be a double-headed campaign against the First Sea Lord – in Parliament and in the press. He wrote to Beresford:

> We are confronted with the most astute cunning devil who ever sat at the Admiralty. . . . The campaign has now to be organised. We must no longer beat the air with unnecessary questions but concentrate the whole of our efforts towards definite objects.
>
> I am seeing Balfour possibly this week but at any rate next week. I shall lay before him all the facts as I know them and shall urge upon him most strongly the necessity for action. But I must tell you frankly that I am not particularly optimistic. He is *not* a big man. The party does not seem to have any pluck left and while an energetic Opposition would have riddled the Government through and through, they sat silent and useless. However, if I fail with Balfour I will try Walter Long and A. Chamberlain.[57]

The plan was bound to fail. The parliamentary tactics of the pro-Beresfordians were easily thwarted. They spread their shot so widely that though they hit many targets none was seriously disabled. To bring about Fisher's downfall alone would have been a sufficient and formidable task to accomplish. But they sniped at Balfour's leadership of the Tories while making desultory attempts to undermine Esher's influence and questioned the value of the Committee of Imperial Defence.[58] Totally insensitive to the nuances and subtleties of parliamentary life and loyalties, one of the few attitudes they did share was a general contempt for all politicians.

The choice of Walter Long to oppose Balfour was particularly inept. Long welcomed their deputation by promptly kicking it down the stairs.[59] Similarly, Austen Chamberlain was a hopelessly broken reed with which to beat Fisher. Approached by Leo Maxse on behalf of the Beresfordian malcontents, Chamberlain admitted to 'feeling a little mean' in not showing more enthusiasm for their cause, but 'standing as I do in my father's absence rather conspicuously for Tariff Reform, I think I am right not to burden myself with another great question.' In any event Chamberlain had already indicated to Maxse that he would be, at best, a cautious and reluctant opponent of Fisher. 'Our naval supremacy must be maintained no matter to what methods we have to resort. . . . Yet I find it hard to believe that [Fisher] would sacrifice the efficiency of the Fleet.'[60]

Though the campaign was a complete failure, the attacks fizzling out like so many damp squibs, Beresford did not seem unduly perturbed. He merely urged his journalist allies to even greater efforts while praising their 'yeoman service for the Empire'. If only they would 'keep on as strongly as you are now', then eventually they must 'confirm the doubts in the minds of all sensible men'.[61] This was all very well, but the minds of most men were already made up, their prejudices committed. Fisherites and Beresfordians were not inclined to be persuaded by the arguments of the opposing faction. There was no longer any place in the press debate for anyone attempting an objective, non-partisan stance, something Strachey discovered when charged by a reader with having 'been had by Lord Charles Beresford' for publishing in the *Spectator* several letters critical of Fisher. His angry, reasoned riposte probably fell upon deaf ears. 'I refuse absolutely to admit the notion that criticism of Fisher on public actions is the equivalent of hating him. . . . I shall always refuse to give way to the notion that to speak of Fisher except in terms of praise is an action of Lèse Majesté.'[62]

If some editors recognised their advocacy was further polarising rather than resolving the conflict, that their propaganda was winning few if any converts, neither Fisher nor Beresford seemed to lose faith in the ability of journalists to sway opinion. In Beresford's mind there seems to have been some confusion whether it was Fisher or his press minions that determined Admiralty policy. 'He has altered his policy times innumerable through the Press making him do so – in fact, the Press has dictated his policy for sometime, these constant changes causing great expense.'[63] Nor did he confine such diatribes to journalist friends but told Balfour that the Admiralty under Fisher was being ruled by Fleet Street.[64] Beresford was never short of an audience for the stream of calumny and complaint he directed at Fisher. To journalists, politicians, society friends and brother officers, he rehearsed the complete range of Fisher's supposed mistakes: the choice of the Dreadnought, the economies, the scrapping policy, but above all, the division of the Channel fleet and the lack of war plans. Tweedmouth was also a frequent, unwilling auditor of Lord Charles's campaign of complaint and calumny. In an attempt to seek at least temporary relief, he called a conference in July 1907 between himself and the two warring Admirals. The experiment proved futile. Beresford's answers to questions put by Fisher and Tweedmouth were evasive, clumsy and frequently contradictory. Yet, not one wit disturbed, he carried on much as before, save to add a new boast that now he 'held the Admiralty in the palm of his hand, the country was with him and he was only waiting his time to crumble them up'.[65] His bitterness towards Fisher dominated his every conversation.

There was talk that Beresford might resign and stump the country the better to advertise his complaints. Fisher told his friends he wished that Beresford would do just that. 'My own firm belief', Fisher wrote to Cawdor, 'is that Beresford would fizzle out in a week.'[66] Esher, now aware that Repington was in frequent contact with Lord Charles, asked the military correspondent why he had not urged Beresford to resign. Repington replied, 'I did so because I thought the public interest and the [invasion] inquiry promised would be better served by Beresford appearing in his capacity as C-in-C of the Channel Fleet and Admiralissimo designate in war. . . . I want the sub-committee to have his views while he is in a responsible position. That is all I care about.'[67]

The Committee of Imperial Defence investigates

Invasion is not only possible but probable if the Germans take the right line. ... The Dreadnought when full up with stores would be shut up in the Medway at low water. ... I will send you the detailed list of Distribution of Ships in Home Waters as far as I can get it.

Beresford to Repington

Meynell, who dined with me tonight, professed to know what the King thinks about the danger of war with Germany, and what the Kaiser Wilhelm's plan is. Wilhelm, as soon as he is ready for it, will throw a *corps d'armée* or two into England, making proclamation that he has come, not as an enemy to the King, but as grandson of Queen Victoria, to deliver him from the socialistic gang which is ruining the country. He will then in conjunction with the King dissolve Parliament, and re-establish the King's autocratic rule as feudatory of the German Empire. Such is the programme, and the King believes in it as true.

W. S. Blunt's Diary

Since he has been ashore, the First Sea Lord has developed an unspeakable contempt for 'scaremongers', but when he was afloat he was a public-spirited and patriotic promoter of 'scares', and he would hardly deny that the present British Navy, which *ex hypothesi* is *nulli secundus*, owes its existence exclusively to the efforts of the 'scaremongers'.

Maxse to the editor of The Times

'Can you not disabuse Fisher of the foolish idea that we desire to attack him?' Repington asked Esher. 'Our target is to expose an invertebrate and huckstering Government which fails to give the consideration to defence questions which circumstances require.' Fisher had been caught up in the invasionist campaign because he still indulged a selfish departmental myopia and refused to take a dispassionate, general view of the country's defence needs. The Admiralty were always 'stuffing up the Cabinet with fallacies to suit their own book', but this time they would be left 'without a leg to stand on'.[1] Fisher had hoped to stop any CID inquiry by constant public and private assertions that invasion was a matter that concerned the Admiralty alone and it was their right and duty to keep their own counsel on the subject. This line of argument the First Sea Lord complemented with the flamboyant assertion that a German invasion was 'an impossibility', a 'chimera'. The way Fisher behaved, Haldane told Esher, there was no alternative but to call a meeting of the CID to investigate the whole issue thoroughly. When Esher rebuked Fisher for adopting so high-handed and stupid an attitude, the Admiral responded with suitable contrition, 'I quite expected to be slated by you and *I've got it.* Also I fully expected you would have your wicked way *and you've got it!*' Fisher correctly suspected Esher of having a considerable stake in the Roberts-Repington camp.[2] Although Esher was not averse to hunting with the army hounds he would still encourage the Admiralty hare by cheering Fisher with the thought that an inquiry could operate to his benefit rather than disadvantage. Suppose the case for invasion was proved: that would mean more money for defence. Why should not most of the extra money go to the navy? Did not Fisher perceive that 'an invasion scare is the mill of God which grinds you out a Navy of Dreadnoughts and keeps the British people war-like in spirit'? The conclusion was obvious.

> Do not be scornful and sit down with the Pharisees! Your functions are not only to believe that you possess a Navy strong enough to defeat the Germans at all points, but to justify the belief that is in you, wherever and whenever required! Tiresome perhaps, but part of your day's work. So don't be querulous![3]

Not everyone saw the issue as clearly as Esher. In the simple accountancy of inter-Service rivalry, if the invasion scare should prosper, then there was a chance that compulsory service would be accepted. This would mean more money certainly – but for the army and not the navy. It was along these fixed grooves that, Repington insisted, the minds of the 'blue water' men at *The Times* ran. Robinson, Thursfield, Capper and Buckle, they were all 'perverts on the whole subject', Repington complained to Moberly Bell. 'I have not had one syllable of Editorial support in my campaign. . . . I wanted the Times to have been the lever and to have got the credit, but failing the Times I have got where I wanted without it.'[4] To Leo Maxse, Repington had boasted that although the 'blue water' men carried 'many guns, I shall knock them all out'. When *The Times* would not absorb the flood of its military correspondent's writing on the invasion threat, Maxse's *National Review* offered a haven for his orphaned thoughts.[5] In November and December 1907 the combined though very different literary talents of Maxse, Repington and H. W. Wilson of the *Daily Mail* belaboured Fisher and raised a fine dust about the imminence of invasion.

Given his notoriously volatile disposition, how might Fisher react to all these painful and well-placed public pinpricks? What exercised Midleton's mind was the likely effect upon the credibility of the previous Tory administration. What if Beresford was in cahoots with Repington? He had spoken to the Admiral and to Roberts. If the two groups combined, the consequences for the Tories could be disastrous, he told his friend Selborne. Circumstances had undoubtedly changed since the 1905 invasion statement. Nevertheless, by supporting the principle of 'no invasion' Balfour had effectively paralysed attempts to organise home defence at a time when he knew that Fisher had virtually gagged all naval personnel who disagreed with him. From what Beresford was saying, or rather had 'categorically insisted', the present disposition of naval and military forces meant that 'the Germans could land without difficulty'. Midleton poured out his concern to Balfour.

> If we have been misled by Fisher then *we are accountable for his action*[my emphasis]. At any moment a serious crisis might break out. If C B [Beresford] gives up his command he will make an all round appeal to the public attacking all [Fisher's] tyrannies during the last few years and going most vehemently for Esher and the King. I ascertained from Beresford what portion of the Press he could command and it is considerable.[6]

Arnold-Forster was another ex-minister who wrote to Balfour expressing his extreme disquiet at the same prospect that troubled Midleton. Forster's apprehension was not tempered by what seemed to him a feeble response by Balfour. 'We are living over an explosive mine, and either Charlie Beresford or some other less important person may at any moment light the fuse: but I think among us, by absolutely refusing to treat the matter on party lines we ought to be able to prevent much damage being done.'[7]

Repington's preparation of ammunition for the forthcoming inquiry was helped by Beresford and his chief of staff, Sturdee. Beresford warned Repington against any complacency. Fisher was a 'slippery old fish' to try and catch. If he could he would 'pack the committee of investigation with his own people ... and then say he had a committee of responsible people and that there was nothing in the statement made by us'. Generally, however, Beresford was pleased with the way Repington was preparing the invasionist case. 'I am sure you are going on the right lines and I'm coming up shortly to see Lord Roberts.'[8] A week later, and Beresford once more confirmed his confidence that 'the Germans could hold the Straits of Dover for forty eight hours'. He was more than prepared, he was eager to tell the committee that the Germans could invade England. With obvious satisfaction Repington retailed this and Beresford's other observations to Roberts while admitting he was also getting considerable help from various friends at the War Office, particularly Rawlinson, Aston, Stackpole and Strachan.[9] Would Roberts now begin to compile a list of witnesses whom they might call to testify on their behalf before the committee? The old man set to his new task with a will. The names of admirals jostled with those of ambassadors, consuls, attachés, concluding with the incongruous pairing of Rothschild and the Prince of Wales. Esher, the familiar of princes and potentates, was not impressed. The list was 'very long and rather absurd'.[10]

For Fisher, the period before the committee of investigation met was an agony to support. While his enemies plotted, it would have been better had he continued to affect that same amused indifference with which he greeted Arnold-Forster's observation that the War Office was 'fooling away millions upon the avowed ground that invasion was possible', while the navy on the opposite hypothesis was 'busily dragging up all mines and dismantling all the coastal forts'.[11] Fisher had to make, if only once, a dashing public contribution to the debate. He entered the lists with a speech at the Guildhall banquet in

November that was as unwise as it was full of pluck and bravado. To the laughter and cheers of his audience he instructed them they might sleep quietly in their beds and not be disturbed by recently resuscitated invasion bogeys. Though not referring to Leo Maxse by name, to the vast amusement of his audience he described him as 'a red-hot and most charmingly interesting magazine editor'.

Fisher's press lieutenants were very angry. They had besought him never to rise to the bait of Maxse and Repington and yet, encouraged by cheap applause, he had taken the lure, hook, line and sinker. 'I regret it more than I can say,' wrote Arnold White. 'You have wholly misunderstood what it is your countrymen want from the Head of the Navy.'[12] Garvin, in two articles in the *Daily Telegraph*, made the best he could of 'our great Admiral's one great mistake at the Guildhall', but in a private letter to Fisher censured him for his emotional outburst. Like a chastened schoolboy Fisher replied, 'Had you been present at the Guildhall you'd have forgiven me. I spoke without a note and from the abundance of my heart and the enthusiasm all around me swept me clean away and yet all is true what I said.'[13]

Fisher's incursion was doubly unfortunate for it coincided with not only the opening of the CID investigation but also the next public phase of his quarrel with Beresford. He had admitted to Garvin he knew 'full-well that it is not Maxse who ought to be hung' and that he was 'biding [his] time for the real culprit', yet the First Sea Lord did not even have the satisfaction of the last word. That was to be Maxse's in a letter published three days later in *The Times*.

> Although we are exhorted by Sir John Fisher to sleep quietly in our beds so long as the present regime endures, the blustering tone of his speech, which is somewhat out of harmony with the modest and manly traditions of the great silent Navy, is calculated to have the opposite effect. It may tickle the ears of the groundlings at a banquet but it leaves a nasty taste in the mouth next morning, because it is so painfully reminiscent of the tragic swagger of inefficient War Ministers on the eve of historic disasters. That our politicians are self-complacent, goes without saying, and that the British public are self-complacent, but it is painful to find that same perilous spirit pervading Whitehall; and, so far from increasing confidence, Sir John Fisher's speech will encourage the critics to remain *toujours en vedette*.[14]

Fisher's speech and Maxse's rejoinder – signed, with singular incongruity, 'Yours obediently' – provided a suitable ceremonial salute between enemies as overture to the first deliberations of the committee on invasion.

The degree of importance the government attached to the investigation may be deduced from the committee's membership. Asquith, then Chancellor of the Exchequer but soon to succeed Campbell-Bannerman as Prime Minister, took the chair. The secretary was Captain Sir Charles Langdale Ottley. The government's other representatives were the Lord President, the Foreign Secretary, the Minister of War and the First Lord of the Admiralty. The navy was represented by Fisher and the Director of Naval Intelligence, Captain E. J. W. Slade. Numerically, the army carried rather more guns; no less than three full generals – Lyttleton, Nicholson and French – and the Director of Military Operations, Major-General J. S. Ewart. Inevitably, Lord Esher made up the quorum. The committee met sixteen times between 27 November 1907 and 28 July 1908. Its report was completed and signed on 22 October 1908.[15]

At the first meeting, Roberts read a statement of general principles written for him by Repington.[16] The presentation was eloquent and what impressed Esher particularly was 'the peroration delivered with rhetorical emotion and very well done'. Repington, who followed Roberts, described a possible German attack, landing at Edinburgh and Leith, seizing the north and then moving southwards upon a broad front, living off the land, ravaging towns and citizenry.[17] This description concluded with a series of pointed questions. How many troops were assigned to home defence? How long would it take to collect them? What arrangements had been made for their transportation and supply? Had a central authority been constituted to deal with the problems of home defence? Behind these questions lay the clear implication that because invasion had been rejected as 'an impossible contingency . . . our brave young fellows at home will fight under conditions of extreme disadvantage'. When Repington had earlier rehearsed an outline of his evidence, Esher had thought the committee would never accept the general hypothesis. Now he was no longer so certain. Despite himself, he was impressed by 'the mass of information and carefully compiled details'. That evening he entertained Repington as a guest at his country house, Orchard Lea.[18]

Repington was not convinced that either he or Roberts had done sufficient justice to their case. The irascible Fisher who, from the first moment, had made his anger with the invasionists obvious, would thwart them somehow.[19] He would not be comforted by Lovat's argument that the First Sea Lord's petulant display was likely to alienate any sympathy committee members felt for the Admiralty's case.[20] Fisher had been rude to everyone and had made it obvious that as far as he was concerned any inquiry was a complete waste of time. Now he claimed it would be sufficient for the Admiralty to enter written responses to the Repington Roberts evidence and there the matter should end. 'Without the power of cross examination . . . no enquiry is worth much. What has he to hide?' Esher asked himself.[21]

Outside the meetings Fisher continued to fume. He vowed to Balfour that he would 'smash the invasion bogey for ever' and bring eternal discredit down upon the heads of Repington and Roberts.[22] Slade did not share all the Admiral's prejudices against the army. Rather than rely like Fisher on the negative huffing and puffing of empty threats he perceived by close examination that the invasionist case, for all its extra details, was the same old story even if writ larger. He worked hard to produce for the next meeting of the committee an Admiralty statement which reflected his, not Fisher's strategic appreciation of the problems of invasion. He argued for 'a combined strategy . . . a reasoned understanding between the two Services as to their respective functions in that behalf'. Only after considerable debate did Fisher and Tweedmouth reluctantly agree to its presentation. When, however, it achieved considerable success with the committee's members, Fisher sent a copy to Balfour claiming that it had *'swept the Board'*.[23] He did not admit that he had been a reluctant convert to Slade's scheme. That Tweedmouth still entertained doubts was reflected in his gratuitously offensive cross-examination of Roberts, described without exaggeration by Repington as 'a vicious and deplorable attack'.[24]

Slade's memorandum had impressed the committee members and required answering. For once, the counter-offensive Repington launched proved inadequate. Cross-examination was postponed until the new year giving Repington a further opportunity to prepare another, more effective counter-blast. His great hope as the one source of information that could damage the Admiralty's credibility was Beresford. To anyone who would listen, Lord Charles was thundering about the criminal shortage of cruisers and destroyers ready for action in the North Sea and how he ought to be called to give evidence to the committee. The trouble with Lord Charles's limitless invective as far as Repington was concerned was 'the paucity of precise statements'. He pleaded with Roberts to see whether he could prise the essential details out of Beresford.[25]

Despite the success of Slade's memorandum, Fisher was not happy. Since late autumn there had been endless wrangles over the next year's naval estimates that had consumed much time and energy. There was a rumour that Balfour, whom he counted as one of his staunchest supporters, was apparently pressing for Beresford to give evidence to the inquiry. As though this was not enough there was the disquieting news that Tweedmouth, very much in Fisher's pocket, was under attack from a Radical cabal in the Cabinet who wanted him removed. It was at this moment in Fisher's mounting ill fortune that Repington approached him and suggested there might be an accommodation between the Admiralty and the invasionists 'out of court'. They would support him in his battle for increased estimates if he 'would support our views for a strong Territorial Army and withdraw his pretensions to play the part of both Army and Navy'.[26]

This was not so surprising a move by Repington as at first it might appear to be. Slade's strategic view, that the 'Army and Navy ... should never be thought of as apart from each other',[27] was in essence shared by Repington. It was Fisher who supposed that anything given to the army necessarily damaged the navy. This was not a devious plot by Repington; his good faith was not in question. The offer was genuine for he had approached Fisher with a similar proposal in September only to be repulsed. Fisher then supposed Repington's was 'a purely party move. I said to him: *"Vade retro, Satanas,"* and he bolted!'[28] The second invitation was rejected with equal expedition. How can I trust that 'clever scoundrel', Fisher asked? What was the *real* motive behind his offer? 'We must be careful what we do.'[29]

According to Esher, when the hearing resumed on 27 January 1908, it proved inconclusive mainly because of Asquith's limitations as a chairman. 'He lacks some element of character; perhaps hardiness ... his chin *recedes* when an attack is possible or imminent.'[30] Though Repington, in the opinion of his chief interlocutor, Slade, was 'very good' for most of his examination, eventually he wilted under attack. Asquith did not allow Slade to press home his advantage. Had he done so Slade was convinced in another hour and a half at most he would have demolished Repington's case.[31]

Repington knew that it had been a close call. He was disheartened and his disenchantment was complete when he and Roberts were excluded from subsequent meetings of the inquiry. The tide of opinion seemed to have set against them. Roberts's response was to suggest the familiar, stale pattern of a speech by him in the Lords and 'inspired' articles by friendly journalists 'to help to enlighten the public as to the possibility of invasion'.[32] Repington, however, was convinced that their game was lost unless they could think of some bold, novel initiative. It was at this moment that he first learned of an exchange of letters between the Kaiser and the First Lord of the Admiralty.

In a letter refusing to join the pro-Beresfordian Imperial Maritime League,[33] Esher had written that the Germans and the Kaiser were most anxious to see Fisher dethroned as First Sea Lord. A week after this letter had appeared in *The Times*, the King received a note from the Kaiser that stated he was writing to Tweedmouth to reject the despicable assertions made by Esher and to set at ease any remaining British concern about German naval intentions.[34] King Edward was furious with his nephew's latest interference in the fortunes of the British navy, but there was nothing he could do.[35]

Tweedmouth's morning mail on 18 February 1908 included a blue, crested, registered envelope bearing the imperial message. In his typically rambling letter, William dismissed Esher's opinion about the likely German reaction to Fisher's fall as 'a piece of unmitigated balderdash' written by the 'supervisor of the royal drains'. It was 'absolutely *nonsensical and untrue*' to suppose that the Supplementary Naval Law was intended as a challenge to British naval supremacy. 'The German Fleet', he avowed with stunning insouciance, 'is built against nobody at all,' and concluded, that for the British perpetually to quote 'the *German Danger* [was] utterly unworthy of . . . a great nation . . . and its mighty navy which is about five times the size of the German navy; there is something very ludicrous about it.'[36]

Tweedmouth was ecstatic about his new-found pen friend, supposing he had been paid an enormous compliment. Accounts of Campbell-Bannerman's ministry usually dwell upon its collective brilliance. Even in a less corruscating assemblage Tweedmouth would never have been thought of as capable of more than an intermittent twinkle. Midleton cruelly listed the First Lord's weaknesses while offering an interesting explanation for at least some of his failings as a minister.

> He is practically useless as a speaker and his colleagues seem to think he
> has neither judgment nor discretion. It is an example of how little good
> the Whips room is as a training except for a few months at the start.
> There are very few who have lived the life of a whip for a long period who
> are much use afterwards in higher posts.[37]

Poor Tweedmouth, even his representatives in the Commons were so weak that they did not help his cause. Arnold Forster dismissed them as 'Two congenital idiots: Robertson doesn't even know what he is saying, and Lambert does not know, or pretend to know, the difference between a battleship and a cow.'[38] Tweedmouth's problems were compounded by the feuding between the Beresford and Fisher factions while his Cabinet colleagues neither sought nor valued his opinion on anything.[39] His threats of resignation, just as his advice, were blithely ignored. Not unnaturally Tweedmouth sought consolation for his bruised ego elsewhere than at Westminster. When he received the Kaiser's letter he could not wait to tell his friends and cronies about his deserved if unexpected honour. As Rothschild's weekend guest he read the imperial epistle to a suitably impressed audience. Before this and other impromptu and impolitic public readings, Tweedmouth had shown the letter to Grey and King Edward. National as well as personal interests would have been best served by a discreet silence, but Grey approved a draft reply by Tweedmouth and, what was more, agreed that the naval estimates, not yet debated by Parliament, should be enclosed for the Kaiser's information and comfort.[40]

As everyone seemed intent on behaving with the maximum indiscretion it was hardly surprising that Fleet Street very soon learned of the letter and its contents.[41] With the exception of Repington, all agreed to keep their silence. When Repington told Esher he thought the letter ought to be published, Esher did what he could to dissuade him. It would be 'unfortunate', he wrote in his 'Journal'. Repington should 'take an example from Delane, in the old days of the Times, who would never have embarked on so perilous an enterprise without warning Lord Palmerston'.[42] Buckle, despite stern contrary advice from senior editorial colleagues, decided *The Times*'s readers should be alerted to the wickedness and impropriety of the Kaiser's action. He published a letter from Repington prefaced with the claim that its author considered it was 'his duty' to draw public attention to a matter of such grave importance,[43] and supported it with a strongly worded editorial which he dictated to J. C. Ross. The combination of leader and letter was intended to make the maximum impact.[44] Esher had been warned in advance what to expect. 'I shall throw my bomb tomorrow,' Repington had written. Buckle had made inquiries at the Foreign Office where he discovered that 'the Kaiser's action is greatly resented'. Repington anticipated 'a pretty racket'.[45] He was not disappointed.

The 'revelation' caused anger and amazement in every quarter of the political and social establishment. Asquith, if he was to be believed, said he knew nothing about the incident until he read Repington's nasty squib in *The Times*.[46] His and every other mind was exercised by the question, what exactly had prompted Repington's action? J. A. Spender admitted to Tweedmouth that he was 'astounded . . . I thought Repington was a man of discretion and good sense yet this is one of the worst pieces of deliberate mischief I ever saw made even in the yellow press.'[47] The Kaiser thought *The Times* had been put up to its trick by his uncle Bertie, 'anxious lest my letter should produce too tranquil-lizing an impression'.[48] But Edmund Slade's explanation was nearest the truth. He supposed the letter had been prompted by a mixture of revenge and frustration. Repington knew the invasion inquiry was slipping from his grasp. Malice towards Tweedmouth was understandable for he backed Fisher quite uncritically and his hectoring interrogation, particularly of Roberts, with its barely disguised, vicious innuendoes would hardly have endeared him to Repington.[49]

The true purpose in publishing his letter Repington admitted to Roberts. He hoped that his 'calculated indiscretion [might] do good to the cause we have at heart'.[50] The Admiralty might be swept away upon an irresistible tide of public concern, its credibility destroyed because it would be supposed the Kaiser was exercising an undue and direct influence, undermining the navy's ability to resist the German fleet. Fears of invasion in the public mind would be so multiplied that at best conscription would be accepted. At least there was certain to be overwhelming support for the army in general and the Territorials in particular. Haldane, his hand immeasurably strengthened in the Cabinet, would easily resist the carping of his Radical critics while the Admiralty's insidious and dangerous propaganda that economies should be borne entirely by the military would be sunk without trace.

The scheme was large and bold: it ought to have worked and yet misfired. Opposition politicians and patriotic press should with one accord have chased the hare so carefully raised. Yet they chose to remain silent and aloof. Maxse, Repington's closest aide in his scheme, angrily demanded of Northcliffe why the *Daily Mail* had not joined the hue and cry. Was it because it shared 'the jealousy of the Times felt by other papers' so that the occasion was used 'simply to abuse the Times'?[51] Northcliffe attempted to turn away Maxse's wrath with a soft answer. 'My Daily Mail had to take that line about the disgraceful Tweedmouth matter to put the Germans off the scent.' Then in the final stages of his ultimately successful negotiations to buy *The Times*, Northcliffe suggested that had the *Mail* acted otherwise a German syndicate would have been 'certain of my identity and beaten my price which is steep enough'.[52] Despite the hint of 'patriotic duty', the excuse was dreadfully thin. What Northcliffe did not tell Maxse was how impressed he had been by the way Garvin had treated the Tweedmouth affair in his *Observer*. He wrote to Garvin of his pleasure that the *Observer* was being 'very widely quoted abroad. . . . I have noticed how suggestions you have made on a Sunday have been frequently carried out by the Government.'[53] Northcliffe was delighted with the way Garvin was fulfilling his highest hopes for the *Observer*. Without detracting from Garvin's supreme gifts, what Northcliffe did not know was that the editor had been privy to all the early moves in this particular little game from the moment in late January when the First Sea Lord had sent him a copy of the Esher letter that had sparked the whole incident, with corrections made by himself and Knollys. Fisher had written, without exaggeration, 'I think that the enclosed from Esher will interest you.'[54]

Repington was left to nurse his hurt and anger at the reaction of the Tory press. 'It has been rather a revelation to me,' he wrote to Maxse, 'showing as it does that a number of papers care more for their own than for national interests.' But the press did not distress Repington half so much as the somnolence of the Tory Opposition. 'I presented them with an unequalled chance. They all remained as tame as tomcats. What can you do with such a crowd?'[55] There was a very simple explanation for their conduct. Asquith, acting with what was for him amazing alacrity, had taken the Tory leaders into his confidence. Entering fully into the spirit of the exercise – it would not be in the general interest of the nation for the public to learn that Tweedmouth had revealed the content of the naval estimates to the Kaiser *before* they had been debated in the House – the Tory leaders gave assurances of their compliance in (to use the now familiar term) the 'cover-up'. When Maxse pressed Balfour's secretary to explain Tory tameness, Sandars's reply was too offhand, too casual to convince. 'I am sorry you think the Opposition ought to have made more stir ... but the affair was taken with a philosophic indifference.'[56] It was all too obvious to Repington now that it was also too late. 'Balfour silenced the rabble seeking office and rewards ... the Tapers and Tadpoles shivering for their shekels. You and I they cannot square', he boasted to Maxse, 'unless they convince us, and that is why they will always hate us like the devil. What a blessed thing is independence.'[57]

With this affirmation of their incorruptibility Repington was prepared to accept defeat. Not so Maxse who never knew when a fight was over. In a speech at Brighton he asserted categorically that the refusal to publish Tweedmouth's letter was not because, as was claimed, it was a private communication. That was merely the government trying to save its blushes. The real reason was Tweedmouth's reply had been so abject that had it been published public indignation could never have been assuaged. When Maxse correctly charged Tweedmouth with sending the Kaiser the naval estimates, Ernest Villiers, senior member for the Brighton constituency, wrote threateningly demanding 'proof of these grave assertions', but very soon subsided.[58] Repington thanked Maxse for his 'good national service' which unfortunately had been 'burked by the papers save the Times'.[59] When, reshuffling his Cabinet the following month, Asquith rather shabbily removed Tweedmouth from the Admiralty,[60] replacing him with Reginald McKenna, *The Times* claimed the credit. It was poor consolation for the failure of the original plan.

Against this excited public background, the invasion inquiry continued its work. Major-General Ewart and Captain Slade, despite the antipathies and prejudices of the leaders of their two Services, had managed to give to the inquiry a spirit of reason, compromise and cooperation which was enhanced by the novel decision to invite the Leader of the Opposition to address its members. 'Such masterly knowledge of the subject, so perfect a manner of exposition. ... Dear Arthur,' simpered Esher to Balfour, 'Pray believe there is not one word of exaggeration as to the effect you produced.'[61] So brilliant was Balfour's speech it probably deserved all Esher's hyperbole. It certainly defused the warring camps temporarily. When he sat down, he was not asked a single question. Balfour's speech should have set the tone for the final work of the committee. Instead there was sufficient time for another quarrel between the Services in the persons of Nicholson and Fisher. The committee's final report was weaker than it need otherwise have been.[62]

Much that had passed in the committee necessarily was out of public sight and hearing. But now the battle between the rival advocates of 'blue water' and 'bolt from the blue' once more entered the public arena, an unintended consequence of that summer's unfortunate naval manoeuvres. Dwarfing in scale an earlier German exercise, it had been hoped the operation would help restore public confidence in the navy's capacity to defend Britain's shores on the grounds of size alone. The exercise was intended to test the fleet's ability to prevent an enemy invasion. A small force managed to elude the defending fleet and to scramble ashore at Wick in the north of Scotland. Because the Admiralty refused to release any information about this insignificant incursion, rumour happily rushed to fill the void. By December, the First Lord found himself in the Commons denying that 70,000 men had landed at Wick. Naturally few were disposed to believed the minister's disclaimer. That same day, the *Daily Mail* revealed that despite the very latest in mechanical transport – a steam engine and a couple of charabancs – during a simulated invasion exercise a group of Territorials had taken more than three hours to deploy upon the appropriate stretch of coast. These events which prompted heated public exchanges, charge and counter-charge, were farcical counter-point to the international scene which that autumn suddenly took a tragic and ominous turn for the worst. Between September and November war threatened to engulf France and Germany and it seemed not unlikely England might also be involved. When Austria annexed Bosnia-Herzegovina, it was generally believed Austria's Triple Alliance partner, Germany, was the guilty party who had encouraged the coup. As a result, in the 'patriotic' press, talk of German invasion became even wilder and more animated.

Publicising the imminence of invasion made for some strange alliances. Leo Maxse's *National Review* was keeping incongruous company with H. M. Hyndman's *Justice* and Robert Blatchford's *Clarion*. Both Hyndman and Maxse agreed that 'statesmen' – a word which even in their private letters they managed to invest with opprobrium – would 'do their best to lull us all to sleep'. Both men were convinced that 'Germany, from the national and imperial point of view, has everything to gain by attacking us.' Both wanted a system of compulsory national service introduced in Britain though, as Hyndman admitted, to serve very different political purposes.

> I want a citizen army for reasons other than mere resistance to the German invasion which will assuredly come when we least expect it. . . . I hope and believe that things will get hot here before I go over to the majority and we shall probably be shouldering arms then on opposite sides. But, at any rate, we don't want Germans to come over and keep the peace between us.

Hyndman also told Maxse of his pleasure that he and Blatchford had achieved exactly what they had set out to do. 'We have brought the whole discussion [about conscription and invasion] down into the street, and it will not die yet awhile, I'll take care of that.'[63] Certainly there were enough credulous targets for this kind of scaremongering in almost every home in the land – not excluding Buckingham Palace if what Wilfrid Meynell told Wilfrid Blunt was true.[64]

It did not require much wit for anyone to recognise how advantageous it would be for the invasion propagandists if they could cash in upon this new, widespread wave of public apprehension. As soon as he knew the invasion committee's report was completed and signed, Repington exerted every ounce of pressure that he could muster for its publication. He wanted the public to read and have its imagination further excited and stimulated by the evidence that he, Roberts and their associates had presented. The government demonstrated considerable reluctance about releasing the report, and Balfour apparently shared its concern. It would be 'highly inexpedient' to publish such a document 'at a time of acute international tension'. Back and forth the letters flew between Asquith, Haldane, Balfour, Roberts and Repington. Balfour, finding himself as mediator between government and those who cried, 'Publish and be damned', told Asquith, if it was announced that 70,000 was the officially agreed estimate of the size of an invading force then that might satisfy the invasionists.[65] If they expected Asquith to follow this advice, they waited in vain. The ideal opportunity would have been for him to have included it in his November Guildhall speech. Repington reflected angrily on the omission. The Prime Minister's words had suggested he was convinced the navy massed about England's shores was sufficient protection – a notion that touched the most sensitive nerve of any 'bolt from the blue' advocate.[66]

Having failed to force Asquith to publish, the next move was to threaten a debate in the Lords – always Roberts's favourite ploy. Repington, adopting the role of a reasonable man hostage to rather wild accomplices, negotiated with the Cabinet through Haldane. 'Subject to the figure [70,000] being given in the Lords ... we are all prepared to be tame enough to eat out of your hand. ... The more I think about it, the less reason I see why you should not give us the figure, and this is also Balfour's view.'[67] When Haldane's reply failed to satisfy 'the three noble Lords, Roberts, Milner and Lovat', Repington again took up his pen.

> Roberts ... is writing to Lord Crewe today to say that if the latter will state definitely that we have to be prepared to meet an invasion by 50,000 or 100,000 men, he, Lord R, will abandon the debate. ... If the Government do not see their way to make such a statement the debate will come off; every 'I' will be dotted and every 'T' crossed, and Germany will be directly implicated. I could not meet Milner's argument that Germany is mentioned every day in relation to our naval policy and cannot therefore be kept out of our military policy and discussion thereon.[68]

It did not require a lawyer's eye to see that the invasionist lobby was raising its terms. One final desperate throw to forestall the conspirators was to recruit the king to command Roberts not to initiate the debate. Roberts refused to be brow-beaten.[69]

In his speech moving the resolution Roberts demanded that the government should 'state definitely the conclusions arrived at as a result of the recent inquiry'. He proceeded to claim that there were 80,000 Germans harboured in England, 'almost all of them trained soldiers. ... If a German force once got into this country it would have the advantage of help and reinforcement such as no other army on foreign soil has ever enjoyed.' Roberts concluded with his now very familiar appeal for a citizen defence force of a million men.[70] During the subsequent debate, most of the speakers – including Lovat, Milner, Wemyss, Cawdor and Midleton – merely underlined Roberts's warnings and repeated his appeal. When put to the vote, the resolution was accepted by a handsome majority.[71]

The following day the newspapers were full of Roberts's speech. To judge by the praise bestowed on the Field Marshall by *The Times*, its 'blue water' men had been sunk without trace. 'Your shaft has gone home,' Repington wrote gleefully, and added his own dart in a long article that reiterated the demand for 'the million man standard'. Few Liberal newspapers dared question the wisdom of what Roberts had said. Those that did were smacked down perfunctorily by the Tory press as 'unpatriotic' and 'pro-German'. The melancholy Metternich wrote from the German embassy to Bülow, 'A year ago the old Field Marshall's speech would hardly have been possible. It would have been held to be such a violent exaggeration that it would have left no impression whatever. Today, it is taken more seriously; at any rate, it is not laughed at, and the exaggeration is not remarked upon.'[72] When Roberts's speech was denounced in the Reichstag this was seen as certain proof that his claims were correct. Admiralty supporters huffed and puffed in a vain attempt to regain the limelight, but their best efforts were nullified by a widely reported speech of Rosebery's. He warned that Britain no longer could afford to take lightly the risk of invasion. Balfour's 1905 'no invasion' statement was obsolete. In 1908 it was sensible to be concerned about German invasion plans. Fear of Germany's intentions was well founded.[73]

In December, among many other journals of opinion, *Nineteenth Century*, *Fortnightly* and inevitably the *National Review* stoked the fires of invasion panic. The *Pall Mall Gazette* considered it suitable to celebrate the 1908 festive season with an offering entitled 'A Disquieting thought for Christmas'. Public opinion was thoroughly aroused, a factor that the ever malleable politicians could not afford to ignore.

When the tide of opinion in the invasion inquiry had turned against the 'bolt from the blue' advocates, Repington had taken the only course left open for him to pursue – to drum the invasion scare to suitable heights, or depths, in the press. The Kaiser's indiscreet letter to Tweedmouth had afforded unlooked for but useful ammunition. However, it had been the government's unwillingness to publish the findings of the invasion inquiry that had allowed the Repington/Roberts cohort to achieve a massive publicity victory for their cause. Once more the government's paranoid attitude to publicity, its fear to tell the public anything, had misfired and allowed Repington and his friends to snatch an unlikely victory from the edge of defeat.

Of secrets, spies and saboteurs

I have received a letter which purports to come from a German General
Staff Officer offering to sell me the German plans for the Invasion of
England. . . . What we want is a secret service bureau organised on lines
similar to the German one, at present we have no such thing: I mean to
get one started.

Major General Ewart's Diary

4 m[iles] inland from Stranraer a private firm have meadows but this is
a blind. There are German experts [and a] depot for 2 Zeppelin ships –
being tested in a suitably hilly place. . . . For 3 years a wooden airship
has been building in a factory at Friern Barnet in London. Germans are
opp[osite] an Institute called the Freehold.

Roger Pocock's Pocket Diary

There are those among us who appear to be able to detect foreign
emissaries in every coppice of our fields and behind every sand dune on
our shores. . . . Apprehensive publicists invite us to believe that at a given
signal, the foreign servants who throng some of our hotels will suddenly
be revealed as a far more formidable phalanx of warriors than the wooden
horse disclosed to the disconcerted vision of the people of Troy.

Leader in The Times

There is a strong prejudice against trusting any form of censorship to
unqualified and incompetent military officials. If the publication of news
is to be in any way interfered with, there must be some assurance that
such a responsible duty shall be discharged by men of intelligence and
good common sense.

Sir John Leng to George Clarke

On 11 September 1908, under the headline 'Imperial Espionage', the *Daily
Mail* informed its readers, 'A significant and cynical proposed motor tour by
the Kaiser is to include a visit across the French frontier "to see the view"
from the Schlucht, a famous strategical pass of the Vosges.' Readers of the
Daily Mail would not have been at all surprised to learn that William and the
members of his entourage were engaged in spying, the better to encompass
the defeat of England and her allies. According to the *Mail* and other patriotic
newspapers and journals, spying and espionage were a German national

preoccupation. Stories about spies were a regular feature in the columns of the *Mail*. They were the inevitable publicity adjunct of any invasion scare and had been so since the *Daily Mail*'s first appearance. In those innocent days the newspaper had evinced a particular concern about pigeon spies.

> It is not obvious why we should tolerate foreign pigeon cotes. A Bill should be introduced forbidding the flying of pigeons within a certain distance of all fortresses and only permitting the introduction of foreign pigeons where British pigeon fanciers are granted corresponding facilities.[1]

In 1898 spies, whether feathered or otherwise, were sometimes French or Russian. By 1900 the editorial wizards of Carmelite House had decided that all spies in England were now German, preparing for the invasion of Britain. Readers were instructed to 'have no delusions on this point'. For eighteen years German Intelligence had been spying out the land. 'The invasion of England is one of the stock military topics in Germany. Every German officer has his own little bit of England marked off upon which he has been examined.'[2]

The *Daily Mail*'s most regular and active companion in this kind of story was the *Daily Express* whose editor, R. D. Blumenfeld, by 1908 had become an enthusiastic pursuer and reporter to the authorities of 'Germans "mapping-out" East Anglia for future reference'.[3] Leo Maxse was another keen spy hunter, as was his 'twin brother in blatancy and balderdash', Arnold White. Charles Lowe, once Berlin correspondent of *The Times* and the author of this unkind description, was inclined to dismiss stories about German spies as 'either the invention of sensation mongers or the hallucinations of hysterical old women of the male sex';[4] but Arthur Balfour was moved to show a discreet concern.

In the summer of 1903, Balfour, in order to test the vigilance of local defences against potential enemy agents and saboteurs, sent his own spy to Dover. There, 'without the least interference from the military authorities on the spot', he was able to 'bring away a complete survey of the defences with their armaments and weak points accurately noted'.[5] In January 1905, the secretary of the Committee of Imperial Defence, George Clarke, provided the Prime Minister with a 'memorandum on Foreign Espionage at Naval Ports'. There had been a series of reported 'suspicious activities' at almost every important British naval installation. Clarke concluded it was impossible to prevent foreign governments from obtaining information but, as a convinced 'blue water' advocate, he was not unduly perturbed. 'Until they have over-powered our fleet, knowledge of the defences of Portsmouth will avail them nothing.' The best that could be done, realistically and economically, was 'to make their investigations unpleasant and expensive [and] let it be known that we are aware of what is going on'.[6] Several years later in conversation with Metternich, Balfour told the German Ambassador that he did not think it very important that the public was concerned about German spying, as all countries employed agents. When Metternich told him that the German spy system in England was 'simply a dream picture in the minds of frightened Englishmen', Balfour managed to look suitably astonished.[7]

In part, Metternich's claim was true. Even by 1914, the German General Staff had no organised secret service operation in England as in France and Russia. The Reichstag voted a niggardly 300,000 marks each year for all espionage and counter-espionage activities. The status afforded this branch of the General Staff's work was reflected in the appointment of a comparatively junior officer, Colonel W. Nicolai, as Head of German Intelligence in 1913.[8] German naval intelligence was an altogether different matter. From 1902, spies and agents were regularly employed in England, and their numbers were increased after 1909. At first they were required to elicit information on armaments, gunnery tests, torpedo trials; later, to obtain Admiralty charts, plans of important naval bases and to reconnoitre suitable landing places for an invasion force along the east coast of England. Often the best source of this 'secret' information, as the War Office and Admiralty were only too well aware, was newspapers.

The publication of information 'likely to be helpful to an enemy' or 'damaging to national security' was governed by the 1889 Secrets Act. Designed to serve the interests of a different era, the Act was now hopelessly ineffective. Technological advances at the end of the nineteenth century revolutionised the materials of warfare and the government was anxious that new weapons and defences should not be advertised to any potential enemy. The trouble was that the Admiralty and the War Office could not agree among themselves what was the best course to adopt and so were unable to bring sufficient pressure to bear upon the politicians to make any changes. It was at Balfour's prompting that the new fangled Committee of Imperial Defence, on 12 October 1904, sat down to discuss the issue. Members of the sub-committee had before them a memorandum from the CIGS. This recognised that the need to control the press would decrease if better, more efficient ways of detecting and preventing espionage were available; but the Commissioner of Police, Sir Edward Henry, impressed members with the thought that this was not so much a time for self-criticism as for determining the means of 'subordinating the legitimate rights of private enterprise to a predominant national interest'.[9] Eventually it was agreed the one really effective measure would be 'to prohibit the publication of any intelligence except when supplied by the Government'. Strangely it was supposed that such a sweeping measure would be quite acceptable to 'the editors of the better class of London newspapers'.

While a suitable Bill was being drafted for submission to Parliament, George Clarke thought that it might be wise to confirm that the press would submit as willingly to censorship as the CID members had assumed. Clarke recruited Sydney Brooks who wrote for the *Pall Mall Gazette* and whose patriotism was above question or reproach. He was to conduct an inquiry among newspaper men, but in such a manner as to suggest the initiative was his and not the committee's. Brooks, thoroughly entering into the spirit of the enterprise, sent Clarke his 'plan of campaign'. He seemed to have convinced himself that it had been his idea from the beginning!

1 To ascertain what the War Office, Admiralty and Defence Committee think ought to be done.

2 To convert, if they need any conversion – I don't thing they need much – the leading London editors to the official view.

3 To arrange a Conference between the London editors and representatives of the Defence Committee, Admiralty and War Office.

4 To start a press campaign.[10]

Brooks worked with a will: there were letters to send to almost two hundred editors in the national and provincial press. They followed a common format and laboured, with apposite quotation and examples, the patriotic duty of editors. They all ended with three questions.

I should be glad to know whether you are prepared to support a Bill making the publication of all news of naval and military movements not authorised by the responsible authorities penal?

Are you also prepared to accept and advocate the principle that such a Bill should be passed to make it operative by Order in Council when the Government of the day so decides?

Finally, may I ask whether you would be willing to attend a Conference between the Editors of the London Press and the Committee of Imperial Defence, should such a Conference be thought advisable for the fuller discussion of the details of the Bill in question?[11]

Brooks was not only an enthusiast, he was a born optimist. Although few of the answers he received promised unequivocal support, this did not stop him from implying that almost all the answers were favourable. 'We should hardly agree to setting up such restrictive machinery as you propose,' R. J. Walling, editor of the *Western Daily Mercury* had replied. As befitted a journalist serving an area where the navy was of some consequence, he insisted that 'Any blame for indiscreet revelations of Service news probably rests with the Admiralty.'[12]

A sub-committee of four members of the Newspaper Society, meeting in February 1906, accepted that in time of emergency or war only official news should be published. They summoned a full meeting of their society for June to ratify this proposal. Sir John Leng, the elderly but influential editor of the *Dundee Advertiser*, could not be present at the meeting but he sent a letter which, when read to the members, effectively curbed any desire the society might have had to ratify its sub-committee's proposal. To do so, Leng argued, would mean 'a state press directed and controlled by not improbably incompetent and injudicious underlings of Government departments . . . altogether alien to my ideas of what an enlightened and influential press should be'.[13] After this broadside it was only with considerable difficulty that Fabian Ware, editor of the Ultra Tory *Morning Post*, managed to get the members to accept the original resolution with merely the phrase 'full endorsement' excluded. The natural consequence of this was the CID supposed that the press had given its 'general approval'. An enlarged sub-committee of the Newspaper Society was authorised by its members to consider any legislation that the government might propose.[14]

Leng was most unhappy with the society's decision. He recognised that the modified resolution did not express the real opposition of most members.

Therefore he decided he would publish in his own newspaper 'An Open Letter to the Press of the United Kingdom' to set the record straight.

> In effect the Newspaper Society has been induced so to act as to be represented as welcoming an unprecedented measure for placing the editorship of war news under State control, dictation and suppression. . . . It is a scare measure designed to let the armed forces do as they like. . . . We had a foretaste of what could happen in the stupid, fatuous, irritating censorship during the South African War. . . . I cannot withhold my protest against an attempt to facilitate the letting slip of the dogs of war by muzzling the press. The beginning of the twentieth century is not the time for subjecting it to such a degradation.[15]

Leng had retired as Liberal MP for Dundee at the general election, with an unimpeachable record as a temperance reformer and land taxer. As the owner of a number of popular journals in Scotland, he could not readily be ignored. Clarke was instructed by the Prime Minister, Campbell-Bannerman, to ask Leng to elaborate upon his claims. The most interesting point in his reply was his insisting that more than 'a comparatively few London newspapers' were involved in this issue – something that the CID constantly ignored. Nor was it a matter that concerned the press alone.

> The newspapers are largely dependent on the News Agencies – Press Association, Reuter, Central News and Exchange. Comparatively few journals have direct access to Government departmental intelligence. Some have high-placed political or official friends. . . . The News Agencies ought to be represented and taken into Conference with respect to any measure to be submitted to Parliament.

Leng concluded his letter with an impossible request. If there had to be interference with the publication of news, he asked for 'some assurance that such a responsible duty shall be discharged by men of intelligence and good common sense'.[16]

The CID was not one wit disturbed by Leng's impassioned plea for a more liberal and responsible approach to press control in the national interest. Leng's opposition was conveniently terminated by his death in December 1906,[17] and the general disposition among the committee's members to impose a draconian measure was stimulated and enhanced by concern about the supposed activities of German spies and agents. An attempt to extend rather than diminish the proposed powers of censorship under section one of the draft Bill was vetoed by Clarke who argued that its 'flavour was rather Prussian and bound to cause bitter resentment'. The Newspaper Society was showing considerable reluctance now that it could see the true temper of the government's purpose in the draft legislation. Meetings between the society and the CID prompted a draft of proposed amendments and the lack of enthusiasm was all too apparent at the Annual Conference of the Institute of Journalists at Scarborough in October. Harry Cornish, the institute's secretary, told Tweedmouth in November that 'some amendments may meet the objections of the Press without defeating the objects the Government has in view', but admitted he 'greatly feared ... there is very little chance of the Bill ... being accepted'.[18] It was not that journalists failed to recognise the need to prevent disclosures that might be helpful to an enemy, but they wanted assurance: first, that they would not be restricted in their comment and criticism of 'facts which are common knowledge'.[19] This posed immediate problems because of the unofficial information that leaked from the War Office and particularly the Admiralty. Their second concern was that there should be a right of appeal and that they would suffer no penalties unless it was proved that their offence had been committed 'wilfully'.[20]

At least the CID now recognised the journalists were not happy and the parliamentary draftsmen were given the impossible task of incorporating some of the doubts and hesitations in suitable amendments. Sydney Brooks was still rushing around all his many press contacts, tirelessly working for an effective compromise and affecting an absurd optimism.[21] But no amendment, short of destroying the original intention of the framers of the Bill, could possibly satisfy the journalists. This was made abundantly clear at a meeting of the CID with the Newspaper Society on 6 February 1908. The secretary of the Newspaper Proprietors' Association who was present at the meeting, condemned the amended, proposed Bill in the strongest terms, 'and in view of the hostile attitude of this Association, the Newspaper Society withdrew from any further negotiations with the Government.'[22]

The CID now began to consider by what means, other than statute, the press might be controlled. Both War Office and Admiralty continued to insist that some form of statutory prohibition was imperative. It was amazing that senior officers in both Services still clung to the belief that secrecy could be insured most effectively by statute when they were experiencing such difficulties in silencing their own men despite changes in King's Regulations and the imposition of a series of draconian orders.[23] General Ewart, chairing a committee at the War Office charged with considering the problem of recent leaks to the press, helplessly concluded, 'It is not sufficiently recognised in the War Office that no person in it who is not authorised to do so, is allowed to communicate with the press with regard to any matter which has been dealt with in the War Office.' What particularly concerned Ewart were the frequent stories in the newspapers about the work of his own directorate. If the Intelligence department could not keep its secrets, what hope was there for other branches of the Service?[24]

Bad as things were in the army, the state of the navy was considerably worse. Beresford, when 'Member for the Navy' in the Commons, had instructed the House that 'every increase and improvement of the Fleet had been brought about by public agitation, by the Press and outside pressure of public opinion'.[25] He complimented Arnold White (then as much his friend as Fisher's) on his 'ability to manipulate things ... just right to provoke the healthy curiosity and irritation which is necessary to make people think that all is not as they are told or as it should be'.[26] It was common knowledge that in the battle between Beresford and Fisher, journalists were given regular access to confidential and privileged documents. This, in part, was justified by the claim that as the navy was a national concern it was legitimate to appeal directly to the public.

Naturally such an admirably conceived 'principle' was enthusiastically endorsed by the press. On this 'democratic' view, when a journalist reported an 'inspired leak' he was doing nothing less than his patriotic duty!

With senior officers showing such a remarkable complacency about divulging secret information to their journalist friends it was to be expected their juniors would try to emulate their example. Newspaper correspondents who were not as favoured as some members of their craft but equally obliged by their editors to supply interesting copy, sometimes resorted to bribery. There were some senior naval officers who were particularly concerned about this increasingly frequent practice. Admiralty Instructions and King's Regulations were quite specific on the subject of relations with the press.

> All persons belonging to the Fleet are forbidden to write for any newspaper on subjects connected with the Naval Service, or to publish or cause to be published directly or indirectly in a newspaper or other periodical any matter or information relating to the Public Service.

It was a regulation that was honoured more frequently in its breach than observance, a suitably outraged Vice-Admiral Fawkes complained to the First Lord. With the examples of Fisher and Beresford undoubtedly very much in his mind, Fawkes insisted, the attitude of senior naval personnel determined that of their subordinates. A ship's company could be 'made as easily to dislike notoriety as unfortunately be led the other way'. But Fawkes's smug, moral effusion ended rather tamely.

> I am sure the people of England do not wish their favourite Service tempted by the Press to do wrong. . . . I see no difference between the newspapers which receive news improperly given and the man who receives stolen goods. Both are morally wrong and it is a pity that they both cannot be equally punished.[27]

Did the press deserve blame when its favours were so recklessly courted? Despite obvious abuses, there was little evidence that many officers genuinely wanted to stop trafficking in stories and information. Among newspapers, *The Times*, as ever, considered itself to be a special case, a little removed from and above the rest of the press. In its dealings with the Admiralty in the recent past it certainly had been.[28] Selborne, as enthusiastically as any naval member of the Board, had busily and frequently provided Thursfield with much excellent copy designed to demonstrate his wisdom as First Lord and the excellence of his proposed measures. In his turn Thursfield had given Selborne a homily on 'the impossibility of preventing the clandestine disclosure of information which you wish to keep secret'. It was as well that secret information should be given to *The Times* rather than allowed to get into less scrupulous and responsible hands. 'There are journalists who are paid to be indiscreet . . . and it is these who do the damage. . . . I hope I am not taking a liberty in writing in this sense, but I think I understand the ways of the Press better than they are understood at the Admiralty.'[29]

Certain senior personnel at the War Office and Admiralty, despite all the evidence to the contrary, convinced themselves that blame for the publication of 'inconvenient' information about the Services should be attached to 'irresponsible' and 'unpatriotic' journalists who insisted on publishing facts that could only be helpful to a potential enemy. For once, the two Services decided it would be best if they worked together. In January 1908, the Secretary of the Admiralty wrote to his opposite number at the War Office.

On several occasions and in particular with the experimental firing upon HMS Hero, Their Lordships have had reason to complain of the publication in newspapers of information derived from persons on board the ships present on the occasion, notwithstanding that it was the deliberate intention of Their Lordships that the proceedings should be kept out of the public press.

Under the Official Secrets Act as at present enacted there is no power to bring an action against persons who are responsible for the improper publication of official information and it is considered it would be desirable to incorporate in the present Bill a provision for dealing with this class of offence.[30]

The reluctant decision that the problem of curbing the press would have to be solved by statute was given further impetus two months later by an article in the *Morning Post* on the defences of Dover Harbour. This caused a frisson of horror and angry frustration at both War Office and Admiralty. The writer had correctly listed all the harbour's modern armaments with the exception of the quick-firing guns on the breakwater. Edmond Slade considered it 'a very bad case'. W. G. Greene, Assistant Secretary to the Admiralty, sought the opinion of Parliamentary Counsel and was advised that although a prosecution could be brought under the provisions of the 1889 Act, conviction would be most unlikely. F. F. Liddell suggested the inherent difficulty in such cases could never be solved by altering the wording of the Bill, 'unless the Government consent to shifting the onus of proof from the prosecution to the defence'. This would make it an offence to publish any information supposedly injurious to the interest of the state, unless the publisher could prove he had no reason to suspect the information he published had been improperly obtained or communicated. For the moment nothing could be done, but Admiralty and War Office agreed, the 'first suitable opportunity that arose' they would 'make the necessary alteration' suggested by Liddell.[31]

Effectively an impasse had been reached. The CID had hoped that the press would accept government control of information as its 'patriotic duty'. Journalists refused to see the matter in this simplistic light. The War Office, always the least patient partner to negotiations, pronounced it was a complete waste of time to seek any agreement with journalists. The government should demonstrate the courage of its convictions and behave responsibly by ending discussion and enacting the necessary legislation, the need for which had amply been demonstrated by recent stories in the press. Esher had suggested that it might be more practicable to seek agreement 'with the leading proprietors of newspapers who are fewer in number',[32] but the army supposed it would be quite useless to appeal to the proprietors' patriotism for this could hardly 'have much effect in an age of competition'. This was to misjudge the temper of some of the most influential of that august group. Northcliffe in particular had spoken often enough and written of his concern that there was 'no adequate provision or preparation to control the Press during war . . . a vitally important matter, not understood either by the authorities or by most of the newspapers'.[33] By a strange irony, the activities of a young army officer, Lt. Col. James Edmonds, eagerly abetted in his pursuit of German spies in England by a group of highly imaginative journalist friends, led to the next and more productive stage in curbing the enterprise of correspondents.

Not long after his appointment in October 1906, General Ewart transferred Edmonds to take charge of MO5. Edmonds discovered that his new office was rather run down. His predecessor in charge, a major more concerned with his parliamentary prospects than hunting German spies, had for months been nursing a difficult constituency. It was a relief to them both when a little later he was successfully elected. That left Edmonds with only one member of staff, a retired police detective. Edmonds discovered that there were hardly any records and none at all on Germany! Information he had received from German friends long resident in England, and his own observations – the head waiter at the Burlington Hotel, Dover, for example, was a German artillery captain whom he had last met at the Europeischer Hof in Metz[34] – made Edmonds pretty certain that the Germans had a spy system operating in England. The problem was that he had 'nothing to make much of a case' that he could put before Ewart, nothing that was until, as he admitted, he had 'two pieces of luck'.

> One of my friends, F. T. Jane (founder of 'The Naval Annual') who was on the look-out for spies, kidnapped a Portsmouth German in his car. . . . Another friend, William Le Queux . . . produced a volume called 'Spies of the Kaiser'. In both cases the outcome was that they both received dozens of letters telling them of the suspicious behaviour of Germans. . . . These communications they handed over to me.[35]

Edmonds's association with a writer of highly imaginative adventure and spy stories like Le Queux paralleled a similar fruitful association between Louis Battenberg when DNI, and Roger Pocock, the founder of the Legion of Frontiersmen.[36] Le Queux's latest fictional effusion, initially published as a serial in *Weekly News*,[37] revealed to his readers that the author 'knew' England was crawling with German spies, crouching under railway bridges, asking questions about water supplies and generally behaving in a most suspicious manner by taking early morning walks or bicycle rides to photograph Epping forest! Dozens of his readers rushed to tell Le Queux that they also had seen Germans behaving as suspiciously and these 'proofs' were straightway submitted to Col. Edmonds.

Le Queux had some time earlier been sold a bogus invasion plan by a group of German-American forgers who had set up a 'spy-bureau' in Belgium.[38] These enterprising gentlemen found senior army officers eager purchasers of their wares.[39] Baden-Powell, the hero of Mafeking, was one satisfied customer. 'One merely had to apply and state a price . . . to receive fairly good information before much time had elapsed.' One of his purchases in 1908 was an outline plan of a German invasion supposedly prepared by German spies resident in England. He soon convinced himself of its authenticity and gave a series of very successful lantern lectures to fellow officers, on how 90,000 German troops would land in Yorkshire once the Straits of Dover were blocked by mines and submarines. Reports about his little talks inevitably found their way into the newspapers. The resultant furore served only to convince Baden-Powell 'how nearly I had "touched the spot".... I was assailed with letters from Germans of most violent abuse from various quarters, high and low, which showed me I had gone even nearer the truth than I had suspected.'[40] Le Queux was convinced that his plan of invasion was genuine even though it was less credible than that sold to Baden-Powell. Unfortunately, those editors to whom he showed it were not impressed. He wrote to Lord Roberts to apprise the old warrior of his dilemma. 'My dear Le Queux,' Roberts replied, 'The world thinks me a lunatic also.' It had been in this spirit of comradeship induced by their joint affliction that they had bearded Northcliffe who always recognised a good commercial proposition when he saw one. The result had been *The Invasion of 1910*, serialised by the *Daily Mail* in 1906.[41]

Le Queux did not have the market for spy fiction entirely to himself, for his commercial success inspired an industry of imitators. In the winter of 1908 and spring of 1909, the popular press broke into a rash of serials with titles like *The Great Raid, The Invaders* and *While England Slept*. Nor was the youth of Britain forgotten or ignored. Their magazines and 'penny dreadfuls' were the regular stamping-ground for the fertile imaginings of authors who specialised in yarns about invasion and spies. Perhaps inspired by the awful enthusiasm of Baden-Powell's boy scouts whose good deed for the day often involved reporting perfectly innocent but 'suspicious-looking foreigners' to the police; or maybe, merely to show that despite all this literary traffic in patriotic tales the English had not altogether forfeited their sense of humour, the youthful P. G. Wodehouse splendidly guyed the whole invasion and spy genre in his story of *The Swoop, or How Clarence Saved England*. The hero of this tale, Clarence MacAndrew Chugwater, boy scout extraordinary, manages in remarkably few pages to save Britain from a concatenation of desperate and fiendish invaders: Germans in Essex, Russians in Yorkshire, the Mad Mullah in Hampshire, the Swiss Navy in Dorset, China at Lgxtpll, an inscrutable and unpronounceable Welsh village, Monaco at Auchtermuchty in the Kingdom of Fife and a group of Moroccan brigands at Brighton, while the Bollygolla chooses Margate to make his incursion. Not to be outdone, *Punch* happily inverted the familiar by sending Leo Maxse and William Le Queux to invade Berlin and then blow up the Kiel Canal and the German High Seas Fleet.[42]

The one feature common to all invasion stories was the ubiquitous activity of spies and saboteurs. Resident aliens, usually masquerading as waiters or barbers, would pave the way for an invading force by supplying vital intelligence. Nor was this theme confined to the lucubrations of febrile journalists in penny novels and the half-penny press, but appeared in articles in ostensibly serious journals of opinion. 'Germany already possesses in this country such an intelligence system as no other nation has ever maintained upon the territory of another,' wrote J. L. Garvin in the *Quarterly Review*. 'There are in this country some 50,000 German waiters. . . . The nakedness of our land is spied out. . . . The blow will fall when and where we least expect it.'[43]

By August 1908, *The Times*, thoroughly alarmed by the serious damage it supposed was being done by the national spy mania, published a long, cautionary editorial on the problems of 'recent absurd developments'. It was a 'put-up' job simply created by those who wanted to see the introduction of compulsory military service. Though it was entirely commendable 'to urge the importance of maintaining the efficiency of our defences . . . the spy mania actually hinders this very necessary agitation'. But to suppose, as the writer of *The Times*'s leader, that 'fears about suspicious foreigners and conscript waiters'[44] were confined to a gullible general public manipulated by unscrupulous profiteers and self-deluded military alarmists, was a piece of special pleading for the 'blue water' school.

When Dumas, the naval attaché at Berlin, in approved Admiralty fashion, deprecated as 'rubbish' the 'nonsense about invasion and spies' written by publicists 'inspired by invasionists like Lord Roberts', his despatches were firmly minuted by Eyre Crowe, Charles Hardinge and Edward Grey in the contrary sense. 'There is no doubt whatever that the Germans have studied and are studying the question of invasion. . . . We continue to work out the best methods of making any plans miscarry. . . . It is a danger to us to be borne in mind in all contingencies.'[45] Yet the Foreign Office, which controlled the funds for secret service work and counter intelligence, was always niggardly and Ewart was obliged to go cap in hand to Hardinge who 'supplied [him] with money as [he] needed it for special investigations. Strange to say,' Ewart recorded, 'I had not a penny piece at my own disposal.'[46] On minuscule budgets of a few thousand pounds a year – insufficient to finance professional agents in the field – the various sub-departments of Ewart's intelligence network supposed themselves to be struggling with a healthily financed and numerous German secret service.[47] Trying to put a brave face on the matter, in 1908 the War Office consoled itself with the thought that, 'Every foreign government implicitly believes that we have a thoroughly organised and efficient European Secret Service.' Ewart minuted this memorandum, 'Facts we have not got – thanks to the total absence of secret agents.'[48] A year later, in a private review of his six years at the War Office, Ewart wrote in his diary, 'With Edmonds' aid I have done something towards the development of our Secret Service work; in which we are lamentably behind other nations especially Germany which employs hosts of agents and spies through an SS bureau.'[49]

Ewart was not a particularly gullible man. Though he had some sympathy for the invasionist case he thought that 'Roberts and Repington overdid the beating of the invasion drum'.[50] If he shared many of the social and political prejudices of his class and profession he remained that truly *rara avis* among the higher ranks of both Services, one who refused to view every issue in a blinkered, myopic fashion. A friend of Ottley and Slade, he encouraged cooperation in strategy and planning between War Office and Admiralty. In a better position than any other man to form a judgment on the issue, he was convinced that the Germans were 'systematically reconnoitering the United Kingdom. The country is full of undesirable and suspicious aliens who might be a real danger in war.'[51] George Clarke, now safely distanced from the CID with his new appointment as Governor of Bombay, was wrong to suppose that spy mania was induced solely by 'the shattered nerves of Maxse and the Daily Mail which were never too strong'.[52]

If Maxse appeared to be a good deal more credulous than many another publicist in recognising foreign agents and spies, he was nevertheless quite clear in his own mind about the patriotic purpose he supposed he was serving, and was sometimes as much sinned against as sinning.[53] It was Maxse who was the first to compliment Northcliffe when the proprietor squashed any further stories in his *Daily Mail* about a German Zeppelin invasion. 'I was delighted by your timely letter,' he wrote. 'People were making pretty considerable asses of themselves over these imaginary airships and they required sitting upon as you have done. The real thing is so serious it is maddening to have people going off at tangents.'[54] By almost every post Maxse received 'proof', from his ever-alert readers, of German perfidy and deviousness.[55] What particularly angered him was that ministers who knew perfectly well what was going on would not tell the people the whole truth. In August 1908, he wrote to Northcliffe of how a Cabinet member had told a friend of his as they were going in to dinner together, ' "If the public knew what we know as to Germany's war preparations there would be a tremendous panic." An interesting commentary', Maxse added, 'on the public utterances of skunks of the Churchill and other types.'[56]

The key government minister who needed to be convinced about the reality of the threat to British security posed by German spies was Haldane. He was too astute not to recognise that behind many of the stories lurked commercial or propagandist intent. For that matter, he had been quicker than most to seize any advantage from these literary concoctions that happened to complement one of his own schemes.[57] He could not but be aware that there was a remarkable coincidence beween the 'undoubted facts' that were supplied to Edmonds by informers, and episodes described in certain stories and plays about spies and invasion. Whether the public's mind had been over-excited by a too-rich literary diet, or perhaps, because the Englishman's normal healthy disdain and disinterest in his neighbour's business was overborne by a sense of patriotic duty, reports of the dubious and bizarre behaviour of Germans continued to flood in to Col. Edmonds at MO5.

Edmonds was not so naive as to believe everything that fell conveniently into his waiting lap. The Germans were devious enough to 'plant' evidence to serve their own purpose. So, for that matter, were the French, which made matters confusing. There was, for example, the case of the German invasion plans left by mistake in a railway compartment of a train going to Berlin. There had been a mix-up over a passenger's bag which had not been retrieved for two hours, just sufficient time for a French agent to copy the plans. The French kindly transmitted the plans to London. Were the plans genuine? Had they been deliberately planted by the Germans, which Edmonds and Ewart were inclined to believe, or had they, as was Haldane's conjecture, been planted by the French government 'in order to wake us up and draw attention to our military needs'?[58] It was all very baffling, but it was a bonus that Haldane was now exercising his formidable mind along the right lines. When Edmonds first told Haldane of how a German officer had written to his English girlfriend in Bournemouth begging her to flee with him as England would shortly be invaded, the minister merely sniffed and asserted that MO5 had unearthed not military intelligence but proof of 'the apparatus of a white-slave traffic'. Edmonds almost lost his job on that occasion. Yet, surely if slowly, Haldane became convinced by the ever-mounting evidence Edmonds and his friends procured, that the Germans did have an espionage network operating in England and that something would have to be done about it. 'Early in 1909,' Edmonds records in his memoirs, 'Mr Haldane arranged that I should put the evidence which I had accumulated before a sub committee of the Committee of Imperial Defence of which he was chairman. . . . He gave me the tip "lay stress on the anarchist (demolition) motive".'[59]

The committee met three times between March and July 1909. Esher, inevitably a member, did not seem too impressed by Edmonds's evidence and later described him, less than fairly, as 'A silly witness from the WO. Spy catchers get espionage on the brain. Rats are everywhere – behind every arras.'[60] Edmonds, who had been enthusiastically listing German activities in mapping out British military and naval installations, was brought up short by a sharp question from Esher. Did not the British carry out similar reconnaissance on the German coast? Edmonds replied with terrible truthfulness, 'Only if their expenses are guaranteed.' In any event, he argued, it was practically impossible to get information about Germany, even information that was not secret! The Germans were highly suspicious of any foreigners, practically the whole male population was an intelligent and watchful auxiliary of the police and the act forbidding the collection of military information – the *Strafgesetzbuch* – was wide and drastic. Esher changed tack demanding rather pointedly whether Edmonds 'felt any apprehension regarding the large number of German waiters in this country'? Edmonds was ready for this, and stuck closely to the brief Haldane had given him. He 'did not think that we need have any apprehension regarding the majority of these waiters. . . . He thought that men who were to carry out demolitions would probably be sent over in time of strained relations, and were not likely to be resident in the country.'[61]

The evidence given by Captain R. C. Temple of the Naval Intelligence Department, with whom Edmonds worked closely and amicably, did not apparently rouse either doubts or anger in Esher's mind. Eminently sober and level-headed men, the committee's members showed neither surprise nor scepticism as in turn Edmonds and Temple revealed the extent of supposed German spy activity in the United Kingdom. No less than 'forty seven cases of alleged espionage [had been] reported to the General Staff' in 1908, and another twenty-four cases in the first three months of 1909. The report of the committee records that 'Edmonds laid great stress on the fact that none of these cases was reported by the police authorities and that he was indebted for information regarding them to private individuals.' If committee members had questioned Edmonds closely about these informants they would have received some very strange answers; but not as strange as the majority of the 'cases' listed in the appendix to their report.

The firm of Henri et Cie, barbers, Osborne Road, Southsea, is a German named Beck. He is a well educated man, has been eleven years in England but is not naturalized. He had until recently an assistant named Schweiger, another German, who was discovered by accident to wear a wig over his own thick head of hair. Schweiger is still living in Portsmouth. Both men consort with sick-bay stewards, officers' servants and similar ratings, and take much interest in navy gossip.

If German barbers figured almost as frequently as waiters in the listed cases, the other major category was cycling photographers. With an amazing obtuseness and perversity, the obvious *raison d'être* for their recorded behaviour was ignored, as in this case supplied by a Territorial captain in May 1908. 'Four Germans live in a small house near Epping. The men change every two or three months. . . . They have bicycles and photographic equipment. They are occasionally visited by women from London for weekends.'[62]

When Haldane opened the third and final meeting of the committee on espionage, he made the flat assertion, questioned by no other member, 'that there is no doubt that a great deal of German espionage is being undertaken in Great Britain, with a view to making a detailed study of our resources and of the topography of the country'.[63] We might well ask why Haldane and his fellow committee members accepted the extraordinary examples of supposed German espionage activity offered by Temple and Edmonds and yet, in the Commons, the Minister of War was quite scathing to questioners who put to him stories based upon similar evidence. When, for example, Sir John Barlow, Liberal member for the Frome division of Somerset, asked the minister whether he was aware that there were 66,000 trained German soldiers in England and that in cellars within a quarter of a mile of Charing Cross there were stored 50,000 stands of Mauser rifles with seven and a half million rounds of ammunition, Haldane thanked his inquisitor for exposing such a far-fetched story to the ridicule it so obviously deserved. The arithmetic of spies and 'trained soldiers in our midst' was following the familiar absurd multiplication of all the other components of the invasion story. So Roberts's '80,000 Germans in the United Kingdom almost all of them trained soldiers', was multiplied by Captain Daniel Patrick Driscoll DSO of 'Driscoll's Scouts' fame to '350,000 living in our midst under the protection of the British flag'.[64] Had this calculation been true it would have meant that more than half the entire strength of the German peacetime army was stationed in England. Driscoll's calculations amounted to more than the registered alien population in England and seven times the registered German aliens. This was lunatic arithmetic.[65]

Haldane's committee made five recommendations which when implemented had considerable impact in a number of discrete areas. First, a Secret Service Bureau was established with 'home' and 'foreign' departments. The 'home' department, dealing in counter-intelligence (known these days as MI5), was housed in a single room in the War Office. It remained starved of funds but was given a new head, Captain Vernon Kell, who had previously been Edmonds's deputy. The 'foreign' department, MI6, under the leadership of

Captain Mansfield Cumming RN, was equally penurious and consequently could afford to hire agents only upon a casual basis.[66] It should not be supposed that German agents were any better financed or more effective. At the end of a complex set of instructions sent to a German agent in June 1912 that had been intercepted by Kell's department, there was attached the following plaintive coda: 'A quick report will be most acceptable, but . . . only what is really seen or heard should be reported.'[67] It was easier, likely to be more accurate, less dangerous and certainly cheaper, for a German agent to get information by reading newspapers.

It was for this last reason that the committee proposed that the 1889 Official Secrets Act should be amended to stop the press publishing 'sensitive' documents. McKenna had lamented that under the existing laws the government could not prosecute the editor or proprietor of a newspaper that had published – as in the recent case of the *Daily Mail* – secret information regarding the construction of a battleship. The First Lord did not want the 1889 Secrets Act changed – earlier attempts had shown this would not work – but he suggested the drafting of a separate Bill. The committee members had agreed that the example he quoted and the general state of affairs was 'terrible', but reluctantly concluded that a separate Act would work effectively only with 'the prior approval of the press'. There was the rub. In the end, the usual 'solution' was accepted and yet another sub-committee was convened to examine the problem.[68]

The last meeting of the sub-committee on espionage coincided with the almost total disappearance of invasion and spy scares as the staple topic of the popular press. The summer of 1909, however, was only an apparent watershed, and invasion fears, with their inevitable spy and espionage concomitant, were to spring into life once more in 1913. Among the military it was now generally accepted that 'invasion scares and spies are only a means to an end: a stepping stone to that wider conscription most soldiers want'. It had all been a 'tongue in the cheek' exercise by 'Roberts and his most astute backers who speak of "Compulsion for Home Defence" '. It might have been thought that invasion would be the last topic to be discussed at the Admiralty, and yet, when not engaged in internecine warfare with Beresford, Fisher was still eagerly promoting his idea of a Baltic incursion. 'It is strange,' noted Ewart who, with Edmond Slade, had worked so hard for a commonsensical joint Service approach to strategy, 'that a man who has scouted the idea that Germany would embark 100,000 men in the UK, even by a sudden surprise, could argue that we could land 160,000 on the north coast of Germany.'[69]

The general public for the moment had had quite enough of reading about spies and espionage. It no longer wanted to contemplate the possibility that it might one morning wake up to find a troop of Uhlans trotting past the front door. The general relaxation of tension between Britain and Germany after the 1908 and 1909 alarms probably as much as anything helped the swift demise of such stories. There were also fresher and more immediate domestic topics to engage attention – the antics of the militant suffragettes or speculation about the possible consequences of Lloyd George's extraordinary budget that had been introduced in April. The newspapers that catered for the mass circulation market and who had been the most eager purveyors of invasion and spy stories recognised that variety was not only the spice of life but also the necessary if not sufficient condition of their survival as successful commercial properties. Their unsophisticated readers liked their news stories and opinions presented in snips and snaps. They were very easily bored. For the busy business man's breakfast-time read, three cheers for England and damn the foreigner had, if only for the sake of variety, to make way on occasion for a juicy murder or some other equally delectable fare.

So soon and so completely did the climate of opinion and concern change that even the ever-cautious Asquith, whose political motto seemed to be, 'He who hesitates may live to procrastinate another day', agreed that now was as suitable a time as any to announce at last to the Commons the conclusions reached the previous year by the committee on invasion. His statement was neither as bold nor as frank as Balfour's in 1905, but he excused his reticence by asserting the report was 'highly confidential' and that he did not wish 'to import any element of controversy into the debate'! Balfour, who followed Asquith, was a little more forthcoming, but claimed he did not want invasion to become a political issue that would divide the parties. In general, the press, both Liberal and Unionist, seemed to think these admirable and reasonable sentiments. 'The responsible leaders of both parties', piped *The Times*, 'are now substantially agreed not only as to the general standard at which our defensive forces are to be maintained, but as to the correlation of function to be henceforth established between them.'[70] The claim was as pious as it was premature. The events of August 1911 would give it the lie.

The public's palate for tales of invasion was jaded and the popular dailies, only too eager to cater to its every whim, demonstrated their sense of concern for the nation's welfare in matters of defence, by turning once more to the inexhaustible and fascinating topic of Britain's navy.

••••• 13 •••••

Hysteria navalis

There is, as you know very well, an impression in my party that you are more bent upon giving us further economies than additional strength. . . . If I could say that you . . . were determined in every sense to be Minister for the Navy . . . and you desired to maintain the unconditional supremacy of the Navy, *cost what it may*, I should be delighted.

J. L. Garvin to McKenna

The Prime Minister has brought about the grave uneasiness generally throughout the land by his statement only concerning one point i.e. 'Dreadnoughts' of the future. But it is in the present that the great danger lies, with Germany prepared and ready, and the British Fleet once more changed, shifted, disorganised and reduced. As a matter of fact, now is the time for the Germans to come, not in the future.

Beresford to Blumenfeld

Englishmen must insist on 'the Eight, the whole Eight, and nothing but the Eight' with more to follow, and break any man or faction that stands in the way.

Garvin in the Observer

'I see Sir W. White at it again in the Spectator last week,' Fisher wrote to his loyal ally Archibald Hurd of the *Daily Telegraph*. 'He cannot forgive me for not putting him on the Dreadnought Committee! And Strachey resents me for not lunching with him at Brooks!'[1] Strachey was the subject of Fisher's cheap jibe, more for the sin of association than commission.[2] He had given White the freedom of the columns of his journal for the pursuit of the Dreadnought controversy. In the prosecution of that same cause the distinguished naval architect and designer, using the pseudonym 'Civis', had also written extensively in the *Nineteenth Century*. Technically, White was probably the best qualified of all the critics who asserted that Fisher had made a disastrous blunder by supporting the all big gun battleship that had revolutionised naval design and ideas of naval warfare. The debate was of long standing and the arguments, though Fisher would have denied it, finely balanced. The suggestion that White's opposition had been inspired solely because it 'meant the scrapping of his creations' so that 'the first occupation of his greater leisure after retiring from Swan & Hunter [was] not to be friendly to the Admiralty', was neither true nor fair.[3]

The one practical test of the conflicting hypotheses for or against the Dreadnought – the attack on Port Arthur and the annihilation of the Russian Baltic fleet by the Japanese at the Battle of Tsushima – had resolved nothing. The opposing camps vindicated their opinions by citing the same incidents, a point made with clarity and restraint by Arnold-Forster to Garvin, who had never questioned that Fisher had been right to sponsor the Dreadnought. 'What you say about the King Edward VII and the Dreadnought is, I venture to think, far too dogmatic. There are some very good authorities who do actually hold the opinion that you deride; and I am bound to say they have very strong reasons to adduce in support of their belief. . . . It must not be forgotten that what took place during the Japanese war undoubtedly supports the contention of those who prefer "King Edward VII" type to the "Dreadnought" type.'[4] In the same week that Fisher became First Sea Lord, Admiral Custance had written to Admiral Bridge, 'There is a class of mind that sees a refuge only in fortifications . . . another class – or rather, the same – sees salvation only in huge ships . . . Heaven only knows what Fisher may not attempt to run. Any wild-cat scheme finds a supporter in him.'[5]

Fisher had determined that the future lay with the Dreadnought and rejected any contrary argument. His opinion had been confirmed by an independent Advisory Committee of Design, but his critics insisted that he had 'packed' the committee to achieve the result he wanted. Though the decision had been made the arguments did not abate. To put all your eggs in the basket of big battleships put England 'in a very dangerous position with regard to Germany', Beresford argued. 'The Two Power Standard is entirely chimerical as we have not enough small craft and TBD's. We have plenty of large ships, but we should not think very much of any military man who prated about his army and could only show us heavy artillery.'[6] Had Fisher made a disastrous blunder? Should his judgment be trusted when the Dreadnought was 'not universally or even generally accepted as the most efficient fighting battleship – the Lord Nelson, for example, being considered as good or even better'?[7] Fisher was notorious for his intemperate, sometimes conflicting enthusiasms, his eclectic delight in the latest mechanical invention, his capriciousness. His friends acknowledged among themselves that he was 'much too prone to assertions which are only rough guesses, and even when right is apt to overstate a case'.[8] Salisbury had once advised Selborne, 'Admiral Fisher is subject to some of those hallucinations of which Admirals are the victims which I had hoped he was cured by this time.'[9] Was his advocacy of the Dreadnought another such 'hallucination'?

The decision to build the Dreadnought involved much more than a technical argument. Where Britain led, other Powers with naval ambitions were obliged to follow that enormously costly path. As the initiators of a technical revolution the British navy gained a temporary lead in the new, monster battleships, but at the price of effectively sacrificing its overwhelming preponderance in pre-Dreadnought battleships. There was also a real possibility that the enormous extra cost to build these new ships would lead to a revulsion of opinion among the taxpaying public. Admiral Sir Cyprian Bridge wrote to Strachey, it was 'impossible to ignore the symptoms of general disquietude at the prospect of continued increases in our already considerable naval expenditure. This disquietude is felt and expressed by people who are friendly to the navy and who are really desirous of seeing it maintained at proper strength.... The policy involved in building the Dreadnought must necessarily, if it is persisted in, result in successively augmenting expenditure.'[10] This argument was particularly pertinent when the government's Radical supporters were insisting that armament expenditure should be reduced. The Liberals had been elected on a programme of 'Peace, Retrenchment and Reform'. Cut armament expenditure and there would be more to spend on the programme of promised social legislation. 'Pensions and not Dreadnoughts' was an appealing battle cry to many Liberals. The immediate, facile response of many naval publicists, Tories to a man, was to insist, 'Our Navy is not a party question', the tattered rag that Garvin flew at the masthead of his *Observer*. He told Rosebery, 'As long as I am editor, [the *Observer*] shall not know what party means to foreign and service questions.' It was his newspaper's 'historic cross-bench tradition' to support 'continuity of national policy'.[11] But all that this claim really meant was that he would support Liberal ministers like Asquith and Grey so long as their policies were indistinguishable from those of their Tory predecessors.

The increasing threat that the naval estimates might well be cut was serious enough to prompt a temporary truce between the warring Fisher and Beresford clans in the press. The outlook, Strachey thought, was grim. The Liberal Imperialist dominance of the government was slowly but surely being undermined by an unholy, unpatriotic alliance of Little Englanders, Labourites, pacifists and Radical economists. Divisions within the ranks of the 'patriotic publicists' made misrepresentation by their opponents that much easier. Strachey instanced Sir William White's recent articles on the Dreadnought debate. Although White was 'as keen as anyone can be to maintain an unquestioned supremacy for the British navy', A. G. Gardiner, the Radical editor of the *Daily News*, had twisted his words to reach the 'unfair deduction' that the navy ought to be reduced. 'Quite a number of people of the "Daily News" type would really prefer to have us weak at sea. They think if we have a strong fleet we may be tempted to use it, and they are quite prepared to run the risk of our being conquered rather than encourage what they call wicked Imperialism!'[12] Should the continuing, debilitating quarrel between the supporters of Beresford and Fisher end, then divided patriotic forces could unite and concentrate their efforts upon the navy's real enemies, the Radicals. McKenna, as First Lord, ought to dismiss both Fisher and Beresford. At one blow he would remove the source of all contention and reassert his proper authority as head of the Admiralty.[13] White agreed with this 'admirable solution'. McKenna neither possessed the personality nor did he have the support of his senior Cabinet colleagues for him to eradicate the naval cancer by radical surgery. Fisher, who had at first supposed that Asquith had replaced Tweedmouth with McKenna to effect his dismissal, had inveigled his political master into his net within a few days of McKenna taking up his new appointment.

Ardent Beresfordians were convinced that the economic toils in which Fisher was enmeshed were the consequences of his rule at the Admiralty rather than a measure of the success of the Liberal government's Radical economists. There was a heated exchange of letters between Maxse and Garvin in January and February 1908, about the progressive cutting of the naval estimates from 1905 onwards, and the First Sea Lord's dubious methods. Fisher was, according to Maxse, 'playing the game of the Cobdenite cheeseparers, endangering our Sea Power at the very time that we ought to be making a special shipbuilding effort'. He was 'the servant of a Radical government'. He had 'not justified the abandonment of the Cawdor Memorandum declaring four Dreadnoughts and Invincibles to be our irreducible minimum. The case is much worse now because of the two German programmes in two years. . . . I fear that Fisher is simply trying to please a particularly contemptible clique of politicians.' Maxse was prepared to admit that Fisher was 'undoubtedly a man of altogether exceptional ability, probably with a touch of genius who has rendered great service in the past'. Unfortunately, he had changed since becoming,

> a great courtier and social light. He has lost touch with the Service afloat and has become an administrative 'boss' who imagines that all difficulties are disposed of by his *ipse dixit*. By one gesture he sinks the German Fleet; by another the American Fleet. . . . The wicked bombast which he talks on all occasions encourages the English in their besetting sin of self-complacency. . . . He is so cunning in nobbling the press . . . including of course the Liberal press who do not care a twopenny damn about the Navy. He has done all this by nauseating flattery ours being the vainest of all professions. . . . His detestable spirit of bluster and bounce is our besetting sin as a nation. . . . Against such forms of insanity the Gods fight in vain. . . . I devoutly hope that your confidence in Fisher may be justified and that I may be wrong, but I confess to remaining anxious so long as he dominates the Admiralty.[14]

Throughout his tenure of office as First Sea Lord, Fisher had been under constant pressure to seek economies in the naval estimates. He had been instructed by Tory as well as Liberal ministers that savings had to be made; the estimates could no longer be allowed to climb to ever more dizzying heights. Characteristically, his initial response had been to hatch 'a big new scheme'.[15] This, in a nutshell, proposed to satisfy the need for economy in the navy by cutting the estimates of the army. Robbing Peter to pay Paul was the principle he reiterated constantly and sought to implement during his whole period in office. '*Strong at all points* we cannot be,' he informed McKenna in May 1908, 'and it therefore follows that our aim should be to concentrate our principal efforts upon the most vital point – naval defence – that is the pith of the matter.'[16] Financial orthodoxy reinforced his inherent prejudice against the army. It was supposed that any advantage the navy gained would have to be at the expense of the other great spending Service department. No one was more attached than Fisher to the concept that the interests of the two Services were mutually exclusive. Not only Fisher but Beresford and Fisher's successor as First Sea Lord, Admiral Wilson, were just as blinkered. Though it was Fisher's braggadocio that was advertised it hid less well known but real doubts and uncertainties.[17] If a Tory Chancellor of the Exchequer could proclaim, as Austen Chamberlain had, that the financial resources were inadequate 'to do all that we should desire in the matter of Imperial Defence',[18] and with his Liberal successors even more insistent that there should be a substantial fall in naval expenditure, Fisher often affected an imperturbability in public that he could scarce have felt.

'Public finance ... was of central significance to the politicians of the Edwardian era,'[19] and very special rules operated when the navy's finances were being discussed. Advertise a national danger and the public, swept along upon a tide of patriotic prejudice, would always support increased spending. To draw attention to Germany's apparent bid to challenge British naval supremacy touched a raw and sensitive nerve in the nation. Almost without exception, it was believed that England's immutable and sacred trust was to rule the oceans of the world, an article of faith that brooked no argument. Exaggerated advertisement was the normal part of lobbying for the naval estimates. The Cabinet began its considerations in November. By January at the latest, because of the squabbles and vendettas between competing interests, individuals and groups, the press would have been provided with more than enough material upon which to work its particular alchemy. Thereafter the eager cohorts of supporters would be recruited and drilled for the final clash when the estimates were published in March. From then until their acceptance, the naval estimates were *the* subject of public debate. Naval arithmetic was a popular diversion. 'Two Power Standard', just as 'an adequate margin of superiority', was never a matter of fact but the subject of endless debate and dispute. Like hares, in March Englishmen went mad. In the great naval panic of 1909, *The Times* wearily observed there would be a return to sanity in a fortnight. Meanwhile, 'The public always goes like this in March.'[20] With everyone infected by *hysteria navalis*, the peddlars of potions, the quacks with their dubious remedies, all had a field day. Naval estimates were always the happiest of hunting grounds for scaremongers, or, as *New Age* described them, 'the Directors of the Blue Funk Co ... the fraudulent contractor, the vampirical financier ... the astute shipbuilder, the pantaloon in putties and the champagne Admiral'.[21]

On 7 February 1908, Fisher wrote to Garvin: 'We are in a crisis.... Haldane is leading his colleagues to destruction in trying to get more for the Army and less for the Navy. Plain common sense says, "So much to spend. Give the Navy its irreducible minimum and give the balance to the Army." But alas! What happens is that the capable Minister gets the swag!' Fisher went on to tell Garvin 'a deadly secret'. He had been telephoned the previous night and told that Beresford had promised that if he were appointed First Sea Lord he would reduce the naval estimates from thirty-two to thirty millions. Fisher asserted, he did not believe a word of the story.[22] It was, however, true. Several days of hectic negotiation followed concluded by Haldane accepting an injunction from Campbell-Bannerman that the army estimates should be cut by £300,000, and a compromise was patched up over the naval estimates which amounted to their presentation on an instalment basis.[23] The Radical economists had forced the government's hand by insisting that either the estimates were reduced or they would vote against their own administration.

Their intransigence was even rewarded by the promise that they would be given a day's debate on their own motion for armament retrenchment. The Radicals and their press were overjoyed.[24]

The same day as Fisher told Garvin his 'deadly secret', the *Daily Mail*, with its customary brash confidence when making predictions, informed its readers that, 'The era of economy is over and finished. The nation must be prepared to see the naval estimates rise annually or else make ready to surrender the command of the sea and abandon the Empire.' As the alternative was impossible to contemplate, the obvious conclusion to be drawn was that there would be a sharp increase in naval expenditure. But the publication of the estimates on 24 February was a great disappointment greeted by the navalist press with howls of anger against Radical economists and groans of consternation for the future welfare of the empire. With its usual unerring ability to reduce any complex issue to a banal headline, the *Daily Mail* demanded to be told, 'Is Britain to surrender her maritime supremacy to provide old age pensions?'[25]

In an extraordinary series of leading articles on the navy that marked his first month in the editorial chair at the *Observer*, Garvin had said, without quibble or reservation, that the estimates would be 'a strong, far-reaching reply to the German naval menace'. Northcliffe, the *Observer*'s owner, knew that Garvin was fed his information by Fisher. In the circumstances it seemed very strange that the increase should have been so much smaller than everyone had been led to expect. A careful re-reading of Garvin's words, however, would have revealed that he had said not 1908, but 1909 would be 'the vital year' when 'four or five or even a larger number of Dreadnoughts will be laid down'.[26] But again, a memorandum accompanying the estimates made a mockery of this prophecy for it blandly suggested there might be no need to increase the 1909 capital ship building programme. What was the explanation for this uncomfortable disjunction between the confident forecast of future estimates by Garvin and the suggestion in the Admiralty appendix? The needs of the navy were obvious to any patriot and yet here was the Liberal press, with all too evident satisfaction, talking of the increase in the naval estimates as 'nominal' and boasting 'a victory over alarmist opinion'. Arnold-Forster suggested that Garvin, because of his too close attachment to Fisher, had been blinded so as not to perceive 'the true inwardness' of the Liberal government's tactics.

> Their one object ... is to put off all expenditure, and the proposed policy
> will inevitably mean an immense burden on future years. If a Unionist
> Government has to pay the bill, every one of the present lot will yap at it
> for increasing the Estimates.

The proper course, Forster argued, would have been to face the inevitable rise in the estimates at once by laying down two battleships. There was also the inexcusable delay over the naval base at Rosyth which the Naval Lords knew perfectly well was dangerous. 'The fact is that the Government having in a fit of financial purism put a stop to loans, doesn't put the cost of works upon the Estimates.'[27]

If Arnold-Forster's diagnosis of the government's purpose was correct, what confidence could be reposed in any future statement made by a Liberal minister? For example, what exactly had the Foreign Secretary, Sir Edward Grey, meant when he had told his constituents in January that the British navy was equal to any combination and that the government intended to maintain that position? It now seemed, in the light of the published estimates, that Grey had either been defeated in Cabinet or had purposely sold his audience a pig in a poke. Not every commentator on the Tory side saw the matter of the navy in these simple party terms. Spenser Wilkinson had written to tell Grey it was not so much a matter of finding more and yet more money to build even bigger, more expensive ships, but how best strategically to dispose Britain's existing fleets to thwart any German attack.

> England at this moment is almost at Germany's mercy. . . . We may have bigger ships, but for a campaign, more than that is required – the question is technical i.e. partly strategical and partly tactical. . . . The position is made far more dangerous to the State by your belief that the Navy is in a satisfactory condition. . . . If you base your policy on that belief (which I presume represents the views put before you by the Admiralty) and it comes to the test of war, then, if you are misinformed, what a disaster there must be.[28]

Wilkinson had explicitly disclaimed any association with the 'party' attack of his newspaper, the *Morning Post*. He did not admit that, in part, his letter was inspired by his deep distrust of Fisher. His comments, with their emphasis upon tactics and strategy, were most pertinent. The trouble with the popular press was that it never sought to engage the interest of its readers in such problems without dragging in the question of personalities. For the most part, when dealing with either of the Services, everything was reduced to the simplest, most easily comprehended equation. For the navy this amounted to a constant demand for extra money to build more and bigger battleships.

Similar considerations dictated the nature of debates in the House of Commons. The economists argued that if the government allowed itself to be misled by scaremongering and spent ever greater sums on the navy then it was putting in jeopardy its promised programme of domestic social reforms. More, it compromised the party's unity. The economists played straight into the hands of their opponents by concentrating on the financial issue while entertaining the naive hope that ministers would resist uncomfortable advice from 'so-called "experts" who are for ever dropping confidential documents about and popping in and out of newspaper offices. A very large proportion of our newspapers have for years been nagging at Germany,' insisted the Radical MP, Sir John Brunner. 'They live on sensations and scares, the more sensational the more profitable. . . . I object to government by scaremongers.' Nevertheless, Sir John insisted that the Liberal leaders were 'strong enough to decide policy for themselves and bear the responsibility'.[29] But what was the true measure of the government's independence? It settled for a compromise over the 1908 naval estimates that when suggested by Fisher a few days earlier had been laughed out of court. The government had been neither strong enough to stand up to the threats of the reductionist lobby of its own backbenchers, nor to challenge the intransigence of the Sea Lords. To the chagrin of most Liberals and the delight of the Tories, Edmund Robertson was obliged to admit as much to the House in an answer to Arthur Lee.[30] The government's position would have been virtually untenable had not the Tory Opposition been labouring under a handicap. Tory loyalty to the Admiralty case was dictated as much by fear as by conviction. They feared their own implication because of their past unquestioning support for Fisher and his schemes. This was why Leslie Cope-Cornford had earlier warned his editor, H. A. Gwynne, that it would be foolish to expect much from Balfour. 'He will not raise the question of inconsistency of policy. . . . J. F.'s policy with both Governments has been to establish his position by "economising with efficiency". He is excessively valuable to this Government as he was to Balfour.' Anxious to protect its own record in government, the Tory leadership would concentrate upon 'safe areas' for criticism.[31] Cornford's proved an accurate prediction of the line adopted by Tory spokesmen in the estimates' debates.

Balfour drew particular attention to a comparison of Britain's 'capacity for output' in capital ships with Germany's. Following an admission by Robertson that the Germans *might* accelerate their programme of construction, Balfour asked whether Germany would enjoy an advantage over Britain by the autumn of 1911 if the existing programme and building rates were maintained. Asquith responded immediately to the implied if unspoken suggestion. Should Germany accelerate her building programme then so would England. 'We do not intend in this matter to be left behind.'[32] The statement was accepted with relief by the Tory press.[33] Esher positively chortled: 'The government has been forced to give a pledge that in the next three years they will lay down sufficient ships to ensure our superiority.'[34] Asquith had issued the IOU but it would have to be picked up by a new Chancellor, for the death of Campbell Bannerman on 22 April gave Asquith the premiership and his first task in that office was to reconstruct the Cabinet.

The Radicals were pleased with the new Cabinet, most particularly Lloyd George's appointment to the Exchequer and the replacement of Tweedmouth at the Admiralty by the 'Treasury-trained' Reginald McKenna. The little Welshman, they supposed, 'could confidently be expected to speak plain words about extravagance and uneconomic expenditure to the Heads of the Spending Services'.[35] Although the leading exponent of the reductionist case in the Cabinet, Lloyd George was never an 'economist' in that same strict Gladstonian sense as was Harcourt or Morley. He was certainly not prepared to squander money 'on building gigantic flotillas to encounter mythical armadas', but he did believe in a strong navy and was always open to argument for greater expenditure provided the Admiralty could 'prove' that the nation's security would otherwise be endangered. Esher was quick to note that in a conversation with the German Ambassador, Lloyd George had affirmed his determination to maintain Britain's naval strength *vis-à-vis* Germany's 'even if it meant borrowing a hundred million for the fleet'. Esher concluded that 'L. G. in his heart does not care a bit for economy and is quite ready to face Parliament with any amount of deficit and to "go" for a big navy. He is plucky and an Imperialist at heart if he is anything.'[36]

The new Chancellor of the Exchequer's 'pragmatic' approach to the navy was to lead to some strange results. The navalist press was busy making capital out of the depression in the shipbuilding and engineering industries. As early as April 1908, the *Daily Mail* sought to use this argument as a lever to prise an increased naval building programme from the government. 'If the government is not composed of stoney-hearted pedants, the ship-building vote should be given out now. . . . 80 per cent of the cost of a battleship goes in wages to the British worker. A large ship-building programme is the best preventive of distress.'[37] The argument was well designed to cause embarrassment to a Liberal administration and, as the depression grew more severe, so the cry that something ought to be done became more insistent. In September, Lloyd George telegraphed McKenna. Would he consider building in excess of the year's estimates? 'The question requires serious and urgent attention.' McKenna's response was to ask whether the Chancellor was 'prepared for the consequences' of an action that would be unconstitutional and involve 'staggering increases in expenditure'? This confirmed Lloyd George in his poor opinion of the First Lord, but after reading McKenna a lecture on the impropriety of a newcomer to the Cabinet impugning a senior colleague's loyalty, he did not pursue his request further.[38]

It should not be supposed from this exchange that McKenna was living up to his promise as a stern supporter of retrenchment. Faced by the arguments of his naval advisers, his defection to the Admiralty case was both complete and swift. McKenna had been in office little more than a week when an exultant Fisher wrote to Esher:

> Yesterday with all Sea Lords present, McKenna formally agreed to 4 Dreadnoughts and *if necessary* 6 Dreadnoughts next year – perhaps the greatest triumph ever known.
> As he says, he has to eat every word he has said at the Treasury and Cabinet, but I am giving him some jam.[39]

Hints that he was entertaining second thoughts since coming to the Admiralty were apparent in a series of speeches McKenna made during October and November.[40] To the consternation of reductionists, his statement that he made 'no apology for saying that the cost of maintaining Britain's naval supremacy would inevitably be high', was repeated some days later by the Prime Minister. During November, in response to questions from Arthur Lee, the Unionist spokesman on the navy, Asquith twice defined the government's interpretation of the 'two power standard' as 'a ten per cent predominance over the combined strengths in capital ships of the next two strongest Powers'.[41] Because of its financial and political implications, the statement was a staggering blow to the Radicals.

The Times had welcomed the Prime Minister's assurance with an obvious satisfaction. If Britain were 'not to define her policy accurately, then some other Power might hope by persistent effort to tire us out in the race'.[42] There was no need to spell out who exactly was meant by this 'other Power'. As Grey wrote at the time, 'Never since I have been in office has opinion here been so thoroughly wide awake with regard to Germany and on its guard as it is now.'[43]

For months the patriotic press had been publishing scare stories about German plans of invasion and German spies. In October 1908, these home-spun effusions were dramatically enhanced by another unfortunate incursion into the public arena by the Kaiser when the *Daily Telegraph* published an interview given by William.

It was no ordinary capacity that the Kaiser possessed to perpetrate monumental indiscretions by speech or letter. Thus he was bound to remain, as the *Daily Mail*'s Berlin correspondent admitted to Northcliffe, 'barring perhaps only the navy, my greatest asset'.[44] Stories about the Kaiser 'of the right kind are always considered desirable at Carmelite House', wrote Wile, and later commented, tongue very firmly in cheek, 'None ever sent by me is deliberately unfriendly.'[45] No one at the *Daily Mail* paid any attention to the frequent complaints by the British Ambassador that these stories usually achieved nothing other than to exacerbate the already strained relations between Germany and England. Philip Dumas, now back at sea as commander of HMS *Hermes*, had been convinced by his period as naval attaché in Berlin, that the Kaiser 'truly love[d] England and wishe[d] to remain on good terms with the British people. . . . The perpetual personal attacks by the *National Review* &c, do unmixed harm, throwing him on the side of the Pan Germans and those who see in the increase of their sea power the means of destroying England and seizing her position in the world.'[46]

Colonel the Honourable E. J. Stuart-Wortley, former British military attaché at Paris, was an ardent admirer of the Kaiser. So impressed had he been by William's repeated expressions of friendly regard for England made on a visit to his house the previous autumn that he decided to draft an article in the form of an interview with his guest containing these amicable sentiments together with other imperial *bon mots* gathered during the German military manoeuvres at Saarbrücken. Harry Lawson, a friend of Stuart-Wortley, sent J. B. Firth, a member of the *Daily Telegraph*'s staff, to take down the colonel's dictated account. This was typed up on *Daily Telegraph* headed notepaper, and then submitted for the emperor's approval. For a variety of reasons, the draft was not as carefully scrutinised by the German Foreign Office as it should have been before it was returned to Lord Burnham. The 'interview' appeared in its full, naive glory in the columns of the *Daily Telegraph* on 27 October 1908. The impression made on English readers was not exactly that which the Kaiser or his admirers would have wished.[47] The Liberal and Labour press greeted this 'latest astounding exhibition of royal eccentricity' with amused toleration.[48] The Unionist press immediately seized upon the Kaiser's foolish remarks to make as much capital as they could for their naval campaign.[49] It was one thing for the Kaiser to declare that although the English were mad he remained their good friend. It was quite another to say that his affection was not shared by his subjects! This was hardly guaranteed to inspire confidence in his assertion that the German navy's sole purpose was to protect German commerce. The conditioned response of the navalist press was to insist that more British battleships should be constructed.

Hardly had the *Telegraph* interview been published when well-founded rumours began to circulate among diplomats and journalists that the Kaiser had given a much more indiscreet interview to an American called Hale. From information he had been given by Pichon, Francis Bertie told Charles Hardinge that the American correspondent had been 'disguised as a Methodist minister'!

> To him the Emperor is represented to have expressed the greatest contempt for the King of England and his entourage; to have stated that England was rotten and marching to her ruin and ought to be wiped out and that he considered war between Germany and England as inevitable and to have said, 'Let it come.' He also abused the Vatican; it is supposed because he thought that it would be pleasing to a Methodist Minister which he believed his interlocutor to be.[50]

This interview promised considerably more scope for making mischief than the *Daily Telegraph* article,[51] for the Kaiser was also supposed to have told Hale that Germany would support America in a war against the Japanese-British coalition accepting as compensation at the conclusion of hostilities, Egypt and Palestine. Still smarting from the embarrassment of the *Telegraph* episode, the Wilhelmstrasse moved swiftly, managing to suppress the magazine before it went on sale. The best efforts of certain British editors to secure a copy were unsuccessful.[52] No one was more diligent than Leo Maxse who had hoped, without avail, that his friend, Maurice Low, Washington correspondent of the *Morning Post*, might succeed where others had failed. Low explained:

> As soon as they yielded to the importunities of the German Government, they swept the office clean of every scrap of paper knowing how eagerly the hunt would be made for the interview. . . . Every New York paper is frantic to get hold of the article and will stop at nothing to obtain it. The *New York Herald* is willing to pay 10,000 dollars for it, but even that glittering bribe has failed to produce the much desired proof.[53]

Interview or no interview, the navalist press had every reason to be obliged to the Kaiser for his help in their campaign to maintain maximum pressure upon the government for increased naval estimates. Radical reductionists on the government's back benches, like Sir John Brunner, and economists in the Cabinet, like Churchill and Harcourt, condemned 'the windy agitations of ignorant, interested and excited hotheads', while Radical journals insisted, with a confidence that was more apparent than real, that Britain already possessed 'a broad margin of complete naval security', and that 'the fighting strength of the British Navy is no less than *four* times as strong as Germany's'.[54] Such arguments, however, did not affect the claim that was now deployed to create further anxiety in the hearts and minds of the public and the Cabinet.

The first hints in the British press that the German naval building programme was not all that it might seem to be appeared in *The Times* on 15 October, more than a month before the Germans published their new naval estimates. *The Times* claimed that the Germans had accelerated the pace of building their capital ships, and repeated this assertion in November.[55] In informed circles this was not a new fear for it had already been hinted at in an Admiralty memorandum a year earlier. The Director of Naval Intelligence, on the basis of reports from the British naval attachés and a careful reading of the German press, was personally convinced by September that the Germans were building quicker than they said they were. There was one problem. No one had experience of an armaments' race of the present intensity and expert opinion was divided as to how to interpret the available evidence. It could be argued the Germans had accelerated the speed of construction, but it might have been the size of the ships that had been increased. There was a natural temptation to employ whichever argument best suited the immediate purpose. Fisher, notorious for piling on technical details whenever he wished to carry a dubious point with any minister, employed both interpretations at different times.[56] Now, together with the other Naval Lords, he decided to plump for accelerated construction. What had been no more than 'an uncomfortable uncertainty' in their Lordships' minds early in 1908, by January 1909 had become 'a practical certainty' which they embodied in a memorandum. By 1912, the Germans would possess not thirteen Dreadnoughts, as the official schedule indicated, but seventeen – perhaps twenty-one! Therefore, they recommended a substantial increase in the British building programme that would match this covert German acceleration.[57] Fisher wanted McKenna to avoid giving the impression to his Cabinet colleagues that his professional advisers were leading him by the nose. He stressed to the First Lord 'the advantage of not allowing it to be supposed the Sea Lords are dominating the situation ... which would be disastrous and lead to resentment'. Instead, McKenna should tell the Cabinet that he had been convinced by his own enquiries and that the Sea Lords were standing by him.[58]

By January 1909, the debates on the naval estimates in the Cabinet that had been going on for months reached impasse. There was an unbridgeable divide between a 'big navy' group asking for six Dreadnoughts that was led by McKenna and Grey and towards which Asquith was inclined to lean; and a 'small navy' group led by Lloyd George and Churchill who insisted that four Dreadnoughts would be more than sufficient. Faced by the apparent intransigence of the Chancellor, McKenna, who by this time had been persuaded by Fisher the programme ought to be *eight* Dreadnoughts – though he dare not admit as much in public – was seriously contemplating resignation. Churchill, briefed by Admiral Custance and Sir William White, argued the technical case for a smaller construction programme, while Lloyd George reminded the Prime Minister that increased estimates 'would open all the old controversies which have rent the party for years and brought it to impotence and contempt'.[59]

Knowledge of the struggle going on within the Cabinet was retailed by the protagonists, blow for blow, to their journalist friends. Fisher, as usual, was busier than anyone, on occasion reporting hourly to Garvin as the battle lines shifted backward and forward. McKenna had also been recruiting press allies, most notably Buckle, who instructed Thursfield to prepare a leading article to strengthen the hands of the big navy group in Cabinet. This was followed by a sharp personal attack on Lloyd George, 'searching for hen roosts to rob', and Churchill, 'indulging his hereditary zeal in looking for economies especially at the expense of the defensive Services of the Crown'. If the Cabinet wished to allay the country's natural apprehension it should stick to Asquith's earlier interpretation of the Two Power Standard. 'The Board of Admiralty is known to have the will to do its duty. It must not be overruled.'[60]

The reductionist lobby was not backward in seeking the support of its own press acolytes, particularly the *Daily Chronicle* and *Daily News*. Asquith was moved to rebuke Lloyd George for this traffic. 'I greatly deplore the leakages into the press . . . of matters which at this stage ought clearly to be kept under the seal of the strictest confidence.'[61] Lloyd George, not one wit abashed by his leader's censure, retorted, 'I agree that it is most deplorable that whenever there is a controversy for Army & Navy there should be these disclosures. The Times, the DT, the Observer and West Gaz seem to have been fully informed as to what was going on inside the Cabinet weeks ago.' He naughtily concluded that it was 'most unfortunate' because other papers naturally had taken up the quarrel when they perceived 'a grave danger that a Liberal Cabinet may be rushed into a policy of extravagant expenditure on armaments.'[62] For once the small navy group enjoyed the better of the public exchanges and Garvin wrote to a friend of how, 'The campaign of the Little Navy press has caused so much alarm that nothing can be said or proposed at the moment which could escape suspicion.'[63]

Opinions apart, personal antipathies made Cabinet meetings wranglesome and abortive exercises. Fisher, in the best naval tradition of seeing only what he wanted to see, cursed Churchill to Garvin as a 'double-dyed traitor' for consorting with White and Custance. Could not Winston perceive their *real* aim was to get Charles Beresford installed as First Sea Lord? With Lloyd George and McKenna at daggers drawn, it was little wonder Asquith grew increasingly agitated. Fisher thought the Prime Minister's behaviour 'abominable' when compared with 'the much maligned McKenna' and the Foreign Secretary who was proving himself to be 'a rock'.[64] Yet Fisher had reason to be pleased because he was now confident that the case for six Dreadnoughts had been made in the Cabinet. On reflection he realised that all Asquith's 'dithering . . . was merely to play along the economists'. He wrote to Garvin: 'Well, you want me to tell you if the Six are secured. *YES YOU MAY!*' Had Garvin entertained any doubts about Fisher's claim, they would surely have been dismissed by the First Sea Lord's provoking and truculent parenthesis. 'The beauty of it is that though Six are sufficient I am going for EIGHT!!!'[65] It was on the basis of this letter that the *Observer* baldly announced on 14 February 1909 that Asquith and McKenna had adhered to their interpretation and pledge on the Two Power Standard and that six Dreadnoughts were secured in the Cabinet. This was two days before Parliament reassembled to hear the King's Speech opening the new session which made a passing mention only, in the vaguest possible terms, to 'an increase which has become necessary in the cost of my Navy'. This the Radical politician C. F. G. Masterman described as a *ballon d'essai* sent out by a divided Cabinet to test opinion within the Liberal party.[66]

The time taken to complete a Dreadnought type battleship was effectively determined by the speed with which the armour plate, guns and gun mountings could be supplied. Three years earlier, in May 1906, the managing director of the Coventry Ordnance Works, H. H. Mulliner, had informed the War

Office he had evidence which suggested that Krupp, the great German armaments combine, had recently enormously increased their capacity for producing
these particular items. On 19 February 1909, Mulliner met Asquith and in
the course of their conversation supplied the Prime Minister with information
Asquith subsequently admitted 'very much alarmed' him. Mulliner maintained,
'Krupp can turn out 54 turrets in a year – enough for 11 battleships.'[67] The
awful implication of this evidence was discussed four days later at a meeting
in the Prime Minister's room in the Commons. Asquith set the mood by
pronouncing 'the present condition' as 'parlous'. McKenna, evidently enjoying
the part of Cassandra, gloomily admitted that 'Britain is hopelessly behind the
Germans now'. All Lloyd George could offer by way of optimism to light the
gloom was the thought that Mulliner might have 'exaggerated, though not
deliberately'.[68] Buckle, because he was told what had passed at this meeting,
anticipated by more than a week the statements made subsequently to the
Commons by Asquith and McKenna. But, good as *The Times*'s source of
information was, it was nothing like as reliable or regular as Garvin's. As late
as 1 March, Buckle instructed Thursfield, who had been temporarily
withdrawn from the fray because of his notoriously close association with
Fisher, to 'poke-up McKenna' and stiffen his resolve, while Callender Ross
was to prepare a leader stating *The Times*'s determination that the nation should
be given six Dreadnoughts in the forthcoming naval estimates.

On 24 March, the day after the discussion of Mulliner's evidence, but a
fortnight after Fisher had told Garvin that six Dreadnoughts were certain and
that he was now pressing for eight, the warring fragments of the Liberal
ministry at last achieved a compromise over the naval estimates. Asquith
proposed that four Dreadnoughts should be laid down at once, and another
four if required. Acceptance effectively marked the total defeat of the Cabinet's
little navy group.[69]

The estimates were published on 12 March. They showed an increase of
three million pounds over those of the previous year. What the figures with
the cold assertions of alternatives and possible contingencies hid was an almost
hysterical urgency to implement the full eight-Dreadnought programme that
had overtaken more than one leading member of the government. The day
before publication of the estimates, Fisher had told Garvin to concentrate his
attention upon the footnote which dealt with the contingent, or extra four
Dreadnoughts.[70] In its 14 March issue, the *Observer* commented, 'As a lady's
letter puts its meaning in a postscript, the most significant feature of the
proposals is contained in the footnote.' Garvin explained, 'This stratagem has
been devised to save the reputation of certain Ministers and . . . to pacify the
pacifists in the House of Commons.' Garvin now wrote to Northcliffe clearly
spelling out his belligerent intent.

> The big fight on the navy seems unavoidable. . . . To run the accounts of
> two years together is a monstrous juggle. Still eight Dreadnoughts laid
> down in *a year and a day* will save the naval situation however fierce the
> fight for the remaining four ships. The only course is to defend Admiralty
> interests, to fight to have the additional clause made binding; and to

denounce all political hanky-panky in connection with the Navy. . . . It is impossible for a newspaper to weaken with the possibility of secret compacts. We must stick to the printed word of the Navy Estimates, the actual speeches of Ministers and to what Bishop Butler calls 'the plain and obvious'.[71]

This was not merely an expression of opinion, as Northcliffe realised. It was a call to battle and the master plan dictating how that battle would be fought and won by a group of newspapers with Garvin's *Observer* in the van.

The first day that the Commons debated the estimates, 16 March, it was not McKenna's cool statement, free of any rancour, that caused pain and amazement to the Radical reductionists on the government's back benches who had determined they would mount the strongest possible campaign of opposition,[72] but Asquith's response when Balfour claimed that Britain could no longer be sure of retaining her superiority in Dreadnoughts, for by 1912 Germany would have twenty-one of the monster battleships. This figure was the extreme projection given in January to McKenna by the Sea Lords, but Balfour was speaking to a brief which had been provided by Mulliner. Asquith questioned the 'absolute accuracy' of Balfour's alarmist prediction, but then admitted as a 'fatal and most serious fact' that Britain could no longer rely upon building her warships quicker than Germany.[73] The effect of this 'fatal' admission on the reductionists in his own party is vividly described in a diary entry of the Liberal MP, John Ellis. 'Our men scattered like sheep. I do not think at the moment five Liberals would have voted against increase. . . . The only thing to do was to tide it over. Next morning of course the Press joined in the hurricane. I went home sad at heart.'[74]

Fisher in a very different mood from Ellis, wrote that evening to Garvin.

We have engineered *8* Dreadnoughts this year. They can't be prevented!
– We have engineered the great Radical majority into an obedient flock
– Brunner & Co are wiped out! Nevertheless, don't desist. . . . *We have got to think in Dreadnoughts*! We can build 16 next year if required. . . .
I expect we shall build 8 . . . *and go on 8 a year*![75]

Garvin recognised that this letter was as much an exhortation from Fisher as a paean of exultant delight. It was a clear instruction that he should step up his demands in the next leading article he wrote for the *Observer*. Faithful to his naval mentor, Garvin passed on the command to Northcliffe. As four had become six and six had become eight, this was not the time to declare that the appetite of the navalist press for Dreadnoughts was sated.

Say that the truth lies between Balfour and Asquith. The truth is still black. Yet we can make all eight with certainty. . . . Well it is a great thing to have clear lines to fight on. *Eight Dreadnoughts for certain now*! But the eight not enough because the two power standard is no longer enough. It is that which has been misleading us all. Against Germany it gives no sufficient margin. The only possible *safe* formula is two to one – unless we make a somewhat smaller margin possible by adopting universal military training.[76]

What had amounted to an admission of national peril by Asquith was based not upon irrefutable evidence but upon assumption and suspicion, as Arthur Henderson and John Dillon were quick to tell the Commons. Few could or would hear reason. The Tory Opposition had been provided with the ideal opportunity to cripple the Liberals. Suddenly every Tory front-bench spokesman was a warrior anxious to thrust himself into the breach. 'Why, it is plain they have not done enough,' Austen Chamberlain insisted. Asquith's 'restlessness and irritation [was] the best possible evidence of his consciousness of the weakness of his case'.[77] It was true that the Prime Minister's colleagues were divided and unhappy, that McKenna was 'bitter against Lloyd George and Churchill' while Haldane, for attempting to patch the quarrels between his colleagues, was abused by everyone. Now, if ever, thought Esher, was the time to strike the government hard. A 'naval scare well engineered will bring us our eight Dreadnoughts'. Within days he had abandoned his normal reserve and was advocating the hanging of any naval member of the Admiralty Board who did not stick out for eight ships.[78] General Henry Wilson, no lover of the navy, thought this naval scandal the gift of a benign Providence. 'It is a perfect Godsend that this awakening has come now and not two years hence,' he confided to his diary. He seems to have supposed it insured the victory of tariff reform and compulsory service, for he expected the Liberal government to fall and be replaced by a Tory administration pledged to support the two measures he really cared about. You could not call Asquith and McKenna leaders when 'invariably they follow[ed] the tail of the hunt'. If Sir Henry had his way he 'would impeach Fisher and Asquith'![79] It was interesting how rapidly 'national' and 'patriotic' interests were overtaken in so many minds by calculations designed to serve less altruistic, less noble, more selfish ends. As always, Garvin in his *Observer* provided a splendid weathercock pointing the way in which the wind of change was blowing.

The leading article Garvin wrote for the *Observer* of 21 March was nothing less than a calculated stoking of the fires of what Fisher was pleased to describe as 'the heavenly panic now proceeding'. Should the government refuse to bow to public demand for the eight Dreadnoughts then, Garvin insisted, the House of Lords should enforce the national will by forcing a dissolution of Parliament. 'What impressive impudence,' wrote G. H. Perris in the *Labour Leader*. 'The lies of this Jingo editor who prefers poverty, war, any kind of anarchy to social reform ... must be choked in his throat.'[80] Garvin's polemic, his violent threats, were stronger than the invective even F. J. Higginbottom, newly appointed editor of the *Pall Mall Gazette*, allowed himself to print in the columns of his jingo rag. He did his best in an editorial for 22 March, headlined, 'The Sands are Running Out'. There Asquith was likened to the Jewish King who, 'When he asked "Who is on my side?" discovered only two or three eunuchs looked unto him'! By comparison, the *Daily Mail* was restrained, though at Northcliffe's command it borrowed extensively from Garvin and for days its news pages were choked with scare stories.

How idle are fine words about retrenchment, peace and brotherhood while we are open to the risk of unutterable ruin, to a deadly fight for national existence and to a war in its most destructive and cruel form. . . .

It is not the British people who are refusing the sheer needs of their Navy, but rather the Parliament of Britain which represents but faintly or not at all the voice of her thinkers and workers. . . .

Without the eight Dreadnoughts our Empire will be on the knees of the gods three years hence. . . .[81]

Behind the scenes every effort was made to coordinate the hysterical campaign. Within a week, Esher twice lunched with Kennedy Jones, introducing him to Fisher – he described them as 'kindred spirits' – and dined with Northcliffe, 'talking for two hours on the navy'.[82] Not all, however, went smoothly to plan. There were temporary but potentially very embarrassing hiccoughs.

Grey complained to Fisher. He had been told that Garvin admitted it had been on Fisher's authority that in his editorial of 21 March he had stated the eight Dreadnoughts in the estimates were secured by the Foreign Secretary threatening he would resign. This was nothing less than the truth. Garvin's mistake had been to tell Chirol and Northcliffe. Fisher passed Grey's complaint to Garvin who, with typical belligerence and more impertinence than veracity, wrote to Grey claiming that he had been misrepresented. What he had written had been based not on any information given him by the First Sea Lord but upon his own deductions from the circumstances together with his knowledge of the Foreign Secretary's character. Grey had no alternative but to swallow Garvin's brazen falsehood and make his peace.

> Please do not let this make mischief between you and anyone else. What it was reported to me that you had said did not come direct and the error may not have been with the original informant.
>
> For the rest I would only say this – all that a man in a position of responsibility says in public is obvious matter for free comment: his unexpressed opinions are matter for fair speculation in the press: if he himself talks indiscreetly in private he must bear the responsibility for his views appearing in public: but what is intolerable is that others who are in official and confidential relations should make statements about his individual views, upon which statements can be founded in the press whether correct or incorrect contrasting his position with that of his colleagues.
>
> If that rule breaks down the safe conduct of public opinion by the men entrusted with them becomes impossible. That is why I wanted to clear the matter up at once as between Fisher and me; and it could only be done by his clearing it up as between you and himself.[83]

The sentiment and sense of Grey's response to Garvin's 'real back-hander', as Fisher had described the editor's letter, was noble and unimpeachable. It was not in Garvin's temperament to share Grey's nobility of demeanour and he wrote a carping note to Northcliffe to say that he was 'distressed beyond measure by the insidious and I think somewhat ignoble dexterity with which my most private words to you & Chirol have been paraphrased to Grey'. As he was 'absolutely certain' he had not been betrayed by Northcliffe, he knew that his letter would be shown to Chirol.[84] The response Northcliffe received from Chirol might have been anticipated.

> I had better return Garvin's letter to you. I have heard nothing from him though one might have expected him to let me know exactly what the charges are which he brings against me before denouncing me to third parties. I went to see Maxse and told him all about it. He is of the opinion that the best thing is to do nothing, though in his present overwrought condition one has to reckon with the possibility of his starting in next Sunday's Observer some wild story of a conspiracy to damage Fisher and perhaps naming me as the arch-conspirator! . . . I am really distressed about this wretched business because I think he is really irresponsible.[85]

Chirol's was not an entirely candid disclaimer. He and Moberly Bell were not as convinced as was Garvin of Fisher's towering genius. It was Bell who probably told Grey of Garvin's indiscreet admission with the intention of damaging Fisher rather than Garvin. At Printing House Square attitudes to the naval building programme were dictated by the imperatives of the European diplomatic scene and were not inspired primarily by the Admiralty. Both Chirol and Bell believed that it was a great weakness that Garvin seemed incapable of perceiving any fault in Fisher and so based his case on too narrow a ground. Chirol had said as much to Garvin on occasion without any response, and repeated his doubts and criticism to Northcliffe. Now it was Northcliffe's turn to tax Garvin with being too much in the Admiral's pocket to recognise that he was not pluperfect. 'With regard to Fisher,' Garvin responded, 'don't think for a moment that I am losing my patient head. Nothing of the kind. . . . On every issue *since we began to work together* there has been no difficulty nor is there ever likely to be.'[86] Northcliffe seemed suitably reassured.[87] The degree to which Northcliffe allowed himself to be influenced on naval matters by Garvin was most clearly reflected in the columns of the *Daily Mail*. H. W. Wilson's support for Beresford was snuffed out by a direct fiat from Northcliffe, while Maxwell's scathing criticisms of Lord Charles were encouraged. Wilson was not slow to recognise the need to bow his head and acquiesce to Northcliffe's wishes. He so adapted his arguments in his letters to the Chief that his opinions were soon scarcely distinguishable from those of Garvin.[88]

The incident of Grey's letter together with the opening of another, even more acrimonious stage in the battle between Fisher and Beresford prompted the First Sea Lord to show an increased concern for the welfare of his most powerful and faithful press lieutenant.

> I am glad you're right with Northcliffe! *Cling to him I entreat you!* . . . Forget me. . . .
> I know for certain . . . that Thursfield, Hurd, Arnold White, Fiennes, Appleyard . . . even old Stead have one and all suffered by helping me and it is so important to you at this prosperous time of your flowing tide not to get set back – *It really does not* matter about me![89]

Fisher's concern did him credit. A warm-hearted man given to generous impulses, undoubtedly he was genuinely anxious that Garvin should not join the formidable list of journalist luminaries whose lamps had been temporarily or permanently put out by their over-close association with him. But there was calculation as well as sentiment in his insistent instruction. Stead also observed, when writing to Garvin to pass on a hint from Esher, it might be as well for the moment if 'pious Aeneas' sought another 'fidus Achates' to do his will; 'some other organ than the Observer for using his material ... might be useful'.[90] Garvin in a swift response concurred. While the inquiry prompted by Beresford's complaints against Fisher proceeded, 'it would be inadvisable for me to start what they would hold to be a mere campaign of personal attack started by Fisher himself for the purpose of injuring his rival.... As soon as the Inquiry is over I shall hold myself free to act. It is always an instant brake upon me when other persons are likely to be prejudiced by an action of mine.... As regards abuse of me personally I never care one straw. Those who know me do not misunderstand. The others do not matter....'[91] There followed a temporary lull in the correspondence between journalist and Admiral.

In the wake of the announcement of Italian and Austrian Dreadnought building programmes, and the mounting crisis over Lloyd George's budget, on 21 July 1909 the Cabinet, without dissension, approved the laying down of the four contingent Dreadnoughts. Just before this Cabinet decision Fisher resumed his letters to Garvin. Using information supplied by the Admiral, Garvin prepared public opinion for McKenna's announcement of the government's decision. For once, Fisher was cautious. 'Have I sent too much?' he anxiously inquired. 'It is so important that you should not be tripped up in your facts.'[92] Fisher was well aware that the case for the contingent Dreadnoughts was rather thin, especially as Grey on 29 March had told the Commons the government now accepted German assurances about their naval building plans. In May McKenna had the true facts of Germany's building rate confirmed, as Garvin had learned from Fisher.

> This is *very, very* secret ... *so burn this letter at once* – the Germans to mislead us have set back their building! *no doubt of it* and our attaché taken round purposely to verify this – We haven't yet fathomed it all – but it's a bomb! However, we shall fight on as before for the 8.... No other human being but you outside McKenna self and the Controller know this.[93]

In his statement to the Commons, McKenna did not attempt to deny the assurances given earlier by Grey and consequently was torn to shreds by the reductionists led by Murray Macdonald and John Dillon. He was obliged to resort to vague and shifting platitudes, but changing the ground of his argument from moment to moment did not make for a convincing defence of the government's decision to build the contingent four. 'That plan', *Labour Leader* declared, 'was a fake too thin and transparent to impose upon any sane or ordinarily observant person.' The country had been misled. The government had intended, come what may, that eight Dreadnoughts should be built or begun in 1909. Now, 'with solemn and measured eloquence', McKenna had admitted it had all been a 'confidence trick'.[94]

The Tory contribution to the debate had been far from inspired and, according to Fisher, altogether missed the point. More pertinently, the Opposition had been anxious not to exacerbate the problems the Liberal front bench suffered at the hands of its own nominal supporters. The consequence was that not until the 1910 estimates were published was it finally certain that the 'phantom four', as the contingent Dreadnoughts had been felicitously dubbed by Arthur Lee, had been part of the 1909 programme. When reality finally overtook prediction in 1912, the Germans had built not twenty-one Dreadnoughts but nine – less than their published programme! Asquith and McKenna were pilloried by their own backbenchers as the major culprits who had engineered an unnecessary panic. Yet both men in the spring of 1909 had been utterly convinced that Germany was outbuilding Britain. If anything, their public statements had not revealed the true measure of their concern and anxiety.

A naval scare had been worked, but if culprits had to be designated then it was Fisher and Garvin rather than Asquith and McKenna who deserved to be arraigned. The Admiral had primed a gun which the editor had been only too pleased to fire with devastating effect. Their motives were not disinterested, inspired only in part by a genuine concern for national safety. Despite the fervent and frequent assurances that defence was a matter above politics, the campaign injured the Liberals as was intended, and promoted a spurious image of the Tories as a party that put the nation's interest before its own. For this reason, the navalist press, guided in large part by Garvin, created the unholy fear that the 'socialist measures' of Lloyd George's budget were a deliberate wasting of the nation's competence by weakening the navy in the face of a threatening and ever-mightier Germany. In H. W. Wilson's words written to Northcliffe in May 1909, 'To lay heavy taxes for the navy and national defence has much to be said for it. As it is, it is the distribution of soup–tickets provided by super taxes to the Government supporters. I fear it will profoundly damage the prosperity of the nation and put us more behind Germany than ever.'[95] No one better exploited this theme than James Louis Garvin. The variations he conjured upon it were sweetly tuned to profit and publicise his *Observer*, enhance his own prestige, and, far from incidentally, to improve the chances of the Tories replacing the Liberals in government. The navy was 'a dominating issue' that 'divides the other side and rall[ies] considerable numbers who otherwise would not support us'. It 'breathes new life into our party'.[96] Stead, who shared Garvin's insatiable appetite for Dreadnoughts, was right when he described Garvin as 'the only leader of the Opposition worthy of the name'.[97]

Nobody would deny that Garvin was a genius among journalists, but he was also not a little mad and bad. The long-term significance of the 1909 naval scare was that, leading a group of journalists only too pleased to follow him, he persuaded a gullible public that the complex pattern of international relations with its innumerable rivalries, its thousand cross-currents and divergences, could be reduced to one simple thesis. Britain's navy stood alone between Germany and that country's dream of international hegemony. Whatever the cost, Britain's naval supremacy should never be placed in jeopardy. After the alarums of 1909 that very simple idea was indelibly etched upon the mind of the British public.

The sinking of Admiral Fisher

It would not surprise me if Beresford were to break openly with the
Admiralty. He is, I suppose, aet 63 or 64, and cannot expect to do much
more afloat but he probably looks forward to a brilliant spell of notoriety
at home. He has very intimate relations with the Press . . . I should,
however, not like to have him as an ally.

Lansdowne to Balfour

I hope things will soon become straighter in our Service and the Naval
Lords return to the honourable plan of trusting the Press instead of
squaring it.

Hedworth Lambton to Sandars

How the evils arising from quarrels between Admirals, and between
Admirals and the Admiralty are to be cured by such methods as Charlie
proposes to adopt, puzzles me beyond words! If he carries out his intentions,
I cannot see how we are to avoid a great – and, I should have supposed,
a quite unnecessary scandal, which may hurt Fisher and possibly the
Government but certainly cannot benefit the Fleet.

Balfour to Cawdor

The spark that lit the fuse for the next public phase of Fisher's quarrel with
Beresford was an altercation between Lord Charles and one of the most senior
officers in his command, Rear-Admiral Percy Scott, a gunnery fanatic and a
particularly close friend of the First Sea Lord. The incident – 'the paint-work
affair' as it was called by the press – arose out of an intended inspection of
the Channel fleet by the Kaiser. Scott was obliged to cancel gunnery exercises
after receiving a message from Beresford that ships were to be put in best
order for the forthcoming imperial inspection. Scott signalled to the captain
of the *Roxborough*, a cruiser in his squadron, 'Paintwork appears to be more
in demand than gunnery so you had better come in and make yourself pretty.'
When Beresford learned of this message he summoned Scott to his flagship.
There, in the presence of Admirals Custance and Foley, the Rear-Admiral was
administered an almighty dressing-down by Beresford before being summarily
dismissed. Apparently not satisfied, Beresford completed Scott's humiliation
by recapitulating all the circumstances in a general signal to the fleet. He then
reported the incident to the Admiralty and demanded that Scott should be
removed from his command of the First Cruiser Squadron for his signal to

the *Roxborough* had been intended as a public insult to the authority of his commander-in-chief. When the Admiralty refused his request, Beresford assumed that Fisher had influenced the decision to protect his friend. To exorcise his anger and frustration with Fisher, Beresford insisted that Scott should be treated as a social pariah by the other senior officers in his fleet.

The incident was very soon taken up by the press but generally their comments were less than friendly towards Beresford. This did not surprise Lord Charles. Fisher, as usual, had been getting at the newspapers. This time, however, he would once for all end the First Sea Lord's game. He would sue the press for libel. He wrote to Cawdor:

> I shall subpoena the Editors of papers who have not been got hold of by the Admiralty and who I find are prepared to swear that they were shewn State Papers of most confidential and secret nature in order to bias them to write up the Admiralty and Admiralty methods. I hope when I start the libel case to be able to shew up the criminally wicked, treacherous, mean and cowardly action that has been taken with regard to several officers of the Service by the inspired Press. Also proof that official secrets have been given to the Press in order to make them support the Admiralty methods for the last two or three years.[1]

'What do you advise me to say in reply to this extraordinary letter?' Cawdor asked Balfour. 'I do not feel at all disposed . . . to mix myself up at all in CB's manoeuvres. Fisher is, I think, unwise in the way he sends about confidential documents, but nothing can justify CB's disloyalty.'[2] Generally the popular press seemed inclined to share Cawdor's sentiments. How could Beresford complain of insubordination when there were so many recent examples of him behaving similarly towards Fisher and the other Lords of the Admiralty? On 18 January 1908 the scurrilous weekly journal, *John Bull*, entered the arena with an article entitled 'The Truth about the Matter'. Beresford was dismissed by the author, Horatio Bottomley, as suffering from a 'swelled head'. It was not simply that Lord Charles did 'not see eye to eye with Sir John . . . but that he wishes to succeed him as First Sea Lord'. Though Beresford was prepared to 'please the Government if he could secure the reversion of Sir John's post . . . it will hardly be questioned that he has proved himself unfit for this great position'.[3]

By this time Beresford had come ashore and was hove to in a suite at Claridges Hotel. There, according to Esher, he was 'shamming illness in order to inveigle Cabinet Ministers and others to his bedside. . . . Imagine interviewing Beresford in a night-cap with Lady Charles holding his hand on the far side of the bed! What a picture of naval efficiency and domestic bliss!'[4] The article in *John Bull* was the last straw as far as Beresford was concerned. He did not doubt that although Bottomley was the nominal author, 'the true inspiration for this latest, most determined, audacious, treacherous and cowardly attack . . . was Fisher . . . the gentleman from Ceylon.'[5] This fulmination was despatched by Beresford to his fellow Irishman, Sir Edward Carson, his legal adviser and also chosen parliamentary champion. A deluge of letters descended upon Carson. 'I wish that I was free and that this was not a personal question. I could so thoroughly swab the floor of the House of Commons with

Fisher & Co.' One of these tirades ended with a sharp, untypically brief critique of Fisher's rule at the Admiralty. The immediate inspiration for this letter was 'a strong article' in the *Observer* by Garvin, 'trying to resuscitate our dangerous lunatic'.

> We are in for an immense expenditure of money during the next two or three years, most of which might have been avoided by common sense administration, less advertisement and the absence of false economies. The advertisement of the 'Dreadnought' has set all countries going, and we start at scratch with that class of ship. . . . If we went to war this year we should be hung up for stores. The whole state of the Navy is shocking. . . . Added to all I have told you, the grand old morale of the Navy is gone.[6]

Beresford's fury alienated many powerful men. Nevertheless Fisher seemed to have overstepped the mark this time and there was reason to fear Beresford's charges. Even the King, who was one of Sir John's staunchest supporters, was shocked when he received a communication purporting to have been sent by Percy Scott asking that several thousand copies of the *John Bull* article should be distributed to the fleet. Edward told Beresford not to bother himself any more as the matter was now in his hands.[7] The King was not alone in his regret that the quarrel between the two Admirals could not be conducted in a more dignified and gentlemanly manner out of the sight and sound of the general public. Balfour, without any great confidence, asked Cawdor whether he thought there was 'the smallest chance of keeping things quiet by "peaceful persuasion" '?[8] The proper place for these matters to be discussed was, as Lansdowne had said, 'before the Defence Committee'.[9] The public trumpetings of Beresford were quite bad enough, but now Fisher, engaged upon all fronts with the CID invasion inquiry and quarrels over the naval estimates, was acting and talking in a manner even more violent than usual, claiming, 'he had enough of magnanimous actions and was going to keep his enemies under in the future'.[10]

While Fisher raged and Beresford thundered, Thursfield, who ought to have known better, tried 'to assuage the quarrel between Lord C and Sir J through the lady confidants of the former, Lady Londonderry and Lady St Austel'. This ploy, to recruit the soothing charms of the gentler sex, foundered for 'when Beresford gets home he falls under the influence of Lady C . . . and then is as bad as ever.'[11] Lansdowne always referred to Lady Charles as 'that poisonous woman'.

Before a delighted public gaze, February brought the sensation of the Kaiser Tweedmouth correspondence. Nothing tickled its palate more deliciously than to be privy to a brouhaha among its social 'betters'. The king, always inordinately sensitive about any overt breach of social propriety, was furious with his favourite Esher who had started the whole thing with his letter to *The Times*.[12] George Clarke had thought that Esher's suggestion, that the Germans were anxious to see Fisher dethroned as First Sea Lord, had been 'shockingly bad form', but perhaps more to the point had told Chirol the claim was 'obviously absurd. If the Kaiser and his Admirals know anything about the British Navy they must desire above all things that JF should remain First Sea Lord with plenary powers for the next ten years.'[13] Chirol did not appreciate Clarke's joking innuendo, but members of the Imperial Maritime League would have happily concurred with the judgment. Encouraged by Beresford, the IML broke away from its parent body, the British Navy League, with the declared intention not to rest until Fisher had been kicked out of office.[14] This had prompted an unwonted *jeu d'ésprit* from the normally sober pacifist monthly, *Concord.* 'There may be hope yet that the naval alarmists, like the Kilkenny cats, will end by exterminating each other.... Naval jingoism is a kind of rabies, and having united to bite the public these gentlemen are now breaking up into droves and rending one another.'[15]

The IML pressed for an independent inquiry into the state of the navy. Similar requests had been made since 1906 but, supported by the leaders of both political parties, Fisher had so far successfully resisted. That he was not altogether unaffected by the criticisms of the IML and other like spirits was apparent in his sudden interest in strategic problems. When Esher brought Arthur Pearson to the Admiralty, supposing the owner of the *Daily Express* and *Standard* was about to purchase *The Times*, and anxious that 'under the new management [it] should take the right line about naval affairs', Fisher talked to the newspaper proprietor for an hour and three quarters on 'naval peace strategy'. Esher pronounced the lecture 'quite admirable'. Surely, he thought, 'only old-fashioned fogeys . . . personal foes or political wreckers [would] want to destroy' the First Sea Lord.[16] If, as had then seemed likely, Pearson was about to add *The Times* to his empire, it was essential that paper should not be captured for the Beresfordians. Repington was already making things hot enough for *The Times*'s 'blue water' men, without having the new owner encouraging the military correspondent in his campaign. Even Sir William White, who was certainly no friend of Fisher, had written to Strachey when he read *The Times*'s leader supporting Repington's 'revelation' of the Kaiser Tweedmouth letters, 'My first thought was has Pearson already taken charge?'[17] Esher recognised only too well that in the stormy days ahead Fisher would need every scrap of help he could get from the press. To have the 'Thunderer' as his ally was a prize he could not afford to despise.

Tweedmouth's replacement by Reginald McKenna as First Lord made no difference to the Fisher Beresford contretemps, for McKenna soon established himself as a doughty and more politically astute friend of Fisher than his predecessor had ever been. This, however, did not for a moment stifle Beresford, nor did Sir John behave with any greater degree of discretion. In April, Beresford requested minelayers and submarines for the Channel fleet. Fisher's reply was so peremptory and rude that even he on reflection was frightened by what he had said. 'The result can only be conjectured,' Slade wrote in his diary, 'but [Beresford] will not sit down under the rebuff.'[18] They did not have to wait long for the *dénouement*. Attending a *levée* on 11 May, Slade, like all present, witnessed 'a very unpleasant occurrence . . . between Sir J and Lord C.' Fisher 'was standing against the wall talking to Winston Churchill with Lloyd George when Lord C passed after having made his bow. He shook hands with Lloyd George and Winston Churchill, but when Sir J put out his hand he turned his back on him. He behaves just like a naughty schoolboy.'[19]

Beresford's studied insult immediately became public property. Then, almost at once, followed two other damaging incidents. On 1 July, while on manoeuvres with the Channel fleet, Percy Scott overruled a signal made by Beresford. Scott maintained that had he adhered to Beresford's command there would have been a collision between the cruisers *Good Hope* and *Argyll*. When Lord Charles demanded Scott's court martial, this was refused. Sensation followed sensation for on 6 July, *The Times* printed a long letter from the Tory naval spokesman Arthur Lee who, 'without consulting anyone', determined that it was for him 'to grasp the nettle and bring the Beresford Fisher quarrel into the public domain where the damaging feud could be thoroughly ventilated and settled once and for all'.

> The Commander in Chief of the Channel Fleet (who is presumably the Admiralissimo designate in the event of war) is not on speaking terms with the Admiral commanding his cruiser squadron on the one hand, or with the First Sea Lord of the Admiralty on the other. What hope is there of that close and constant communion which can alone produce the highest efficiency in the time of peace and ensure loyalty and effective cooperation in the day of battle? . . . I venture to ask what steps the First Lord of the Admiralty, or the Cabinet, propose to take in order to put an end to a grave scandal which is not only sapping the foundations of good discipline and good feeling throughout the Service, but constitutes a serious menace to our national security.[20]

Lee's letter provoked a flood of comment in the press. Thursfield, in *The Times* insisted that Beresford should be

> confronted with the historic alternative, *se soumettre ou se démettre*. . . . So long as he holds his present responsible position he is not free to let it be known whether by his action or by his demeanour, either to his Fleet or to the world at large, that his attitude towards the Board of Admiralty is one of scant respect for its authority and avowed dissent from its policy.[21]

This editorial entitled 'Disunion in the Navy', together with another article which appeared the following day, 'Strange Occurrences in the Fleet', caused Beresford to see red.

It was not enough for Lord Charles that he was stoutly supported by the *Standard, Morning Post* and *Daily Express*. The other newspapers were being 'deliberately misled' by Fisher's miserable minion, Thursfield. He wrote to tell Blumenfeld how,

> On Monday 6th July, Thursfield and Fisher were closeted in a room at the Admiralty for three hours that afternoon. This is very well known to every underling at the Admiralty. On the following day appeared the article in the TIMES and on the 8th July there was another disgraceful article in the TIMES against my reputation. The whole thing is worthy of the time of the assassins of the Doges of Venice.[22]

Beresford was not slow to bruit abroad that *The Times*'s articles had been 'inspired', even 'dictated' by Fisher. Thursfield, a gentle man and sensible of his honour and good reputation, protested to McKenna that there was 'not a word of truth' in the 'allegations which might have reached your ears and might in that case easily prejudice me in your estimation'. It was true he had met Fisher at the Admiralty, but their meeting was 'purely accidental'. When he had mentioned the ramming incident 'Sir John assured me he had not even heard of it.' This was an extraordinary claim and must have been 'cooked-up' some time after their meeting as Thursfield's letter arrived the same day as one from Fisher making exactly the same absurd profession.[23] Was McKenna supposed to be so naive as to swallow Thursfield's final disclaimer that in a three-hour conversation 'Fisher to the best of my recollection expressed no opinion whatever'?[24] If McKenna did believe this unlikely story then, as far as the Beresfordians were concerned, this was further proof that the First Lord was in Fisher's pocket. This would also explain McKenna 'failing to punish Scott (who by the way is a bounder) in a critical and disgraceful breach of discipline'. One did not need to be particularly perceptive to see that McKenna and Fisher were working together 'to hound Beresford out of the active service of the Navy'.[25] The deeper purpose that lay behind Beresford's victimisation was a matter for debate. Sir William White, with a permanent bee in his bonnet about Dreadnoughts, supposed it 'extremely probable' that this was 'Fisher's latest move . . . to divert attention if he can from the big ship question'. At least Beresford deserved 'fair play'. The behaviour of *The Times* had 'been beyond contempt'.[26] Strachey agreed with this part at least of Sir William's hypothesis. 'I have spoken out very strongly about it in the Spectator,' he told White. But Strachey believed things had come to such a pass that now only a clean sweep could possibly cleanse the Augean stables of the Admiralty.

> If I were McKenna I should show that I mean to be real master of the Navy by dismissing Fisher, Charles Beresford and Scott at once, and appointing a new First [Sea] Lord and a new Admiral of the Channel Fleet. Such action would no doubt be not quite fair to Charles Beresford but it would certainly give McKenna a tremendous position and would I believe in the end be good for the Government.[27]

It happened that McKenna was intent upon removing from power certain key naval personnel. Fisher did not figure in his calculations but Beresford certainly did. All that July he vainly struggled with his Cabinet colleagues to persuade them Beresford's command should end when the Channel and home fleets combined in 1909. Fisher accurately claimed that the ministers 'funked' the opportunity, too frightened by the storms that Beresford might raise in the country. In August, when Percy Scott was moved out of harm's way by giving him a command in the South Atlantic, the King railed against his ministers accusing them of being too cowardly to rid themselves of Beresford as well. It took McKenna six months of constant cajolery before he triumphed and Beresford was told that he would have to strike his flag and come ashore in March 1909, a year short of the normal term of command. Now both the king and the Prince of Wales questioned whether the right decision had been made. What hornets' nest of public anger might Charlie not stir, Prince George wondered anxiously? 'He will probably agitate for a Parliamentary enquiry into the Navy and God knows what.'[28]

As Fisher struggled for more generous naval estimates, Beresford carefully orchestrated a series of violent attacks upon his enemy in the press. Fisher told Garvin not a day went by at the Admiralty that he did not receive 'conclusive proof of Beresford pursuing a path of *Absalomic* cunning in feasting journalists and parliamentarians to make him king – (not that I compare myself to Solomon except seeing Lady Londonderry as the Queen of Sheba)'.[29] Of his press lieutenants, none was keener to do Beresford's bidding than Blumenfeld. A few days before Lord Charles surrendered his command of the Channel fleet, the *Daily Express* proclaimed to the world, 'We arraign Sir John Fisher at the bar of public opinion and with the imminent possibility of national disaster before the country we say again to him "Thou art the man"!' Beresford could not have been more pleased.[30] In this particular, where the *Daily Express* led, the *Standard, Morning Post* and *Daily Graphic* needed no urging to follow. H W Wilson would very much have liked to join in the chorus of vilification in the *Daily Mail* had not Northcliffe warned his editor, Thomas Marlowe, to restrain the naval expert.[31] The charges rehearsed by the anti-Fisher press were stale and familiar. The only thing that added piquancy to this latest of many outbursts – for the principals at least – was the delusion that this time not only might they tip Fisher from power but also the Liberals as well. Beresford was absolutely convinced that the Liberal government would be defeated when the naval estimates were debated. This illusion did not survive a meeting with Balfour. The Tory leader did not share Lord Charles's conviction of the government's imminent demise and therefore unfortunately could not avail himself of the Admiral's most generous offer to become First Lord in return for hushing up the true state of naval affairs![32]

When, at Portsmouth on 24 March 1909, Charles Beresford hauled down his flag as commander of the Channel fleet, the *Standard* bellowed, 'He has been dismissed because he has so fearlessly told the truth.' Fisher knew now that his enemy was free even of the notional restraints imposed by active service, he could expect Beresford to be more energetic and persistent in promoting his calumnies, more vitriolic, more scurrilous, more determined in his attacks than ever. It was not a prospect to delight the First Sea Lord or his friends, none of whom was more concerned for the Admiral's future prospects than Esher. He morbidly recalled a story told him by Margot Asquith. A threat from the Prime Minister's formidable spouse, implied or otherwise, was not to be taken lightly. She had told Stead that 'Fisher has shown great feebleness in dealing with Beresford: when two servants quarrel you get rid of one or both.'[33] With Lord Charles gone was it now to be Sir John's turn? It must have been a tempting thought to the government, with the Radicals screaming for disarmament, to slaughter Fisher as a suitable sacrificial lamb. He was, after all, the chief protagonist of the policy its own supporters condemned. Beresford's 'kept' press was unrestrainedly on the rampage designating its chosen victim in banner headlines. Would it happen, as Esher feared, that the hapless Fisher would be ground between the upper and nether millstones of patriotic publicists and radical reductionists?[34] The darkness thickened about Sir John on 22 March when he received two letters. The first, from Edward Grey, complained that Garvin was boasting that what he had said about the Foreign Secretary's attitude in Cabinet and printed in the *Observer* had been supplied to him by Sir John.[35] The second letter was from the king, usually a staunch supporter. He angrily demanded to know why it was the Admiralty under Fisher had allowed Britain's position in the arms race with Germany to deteriorate to the sad and dangerous level indicated by the estimate debates in the Commons.[36]

During his interview with Balfour at the end of March, Beresford had asked whether the Tory leader had any objection to him raising Cain about the navy in public – as though he had been doing anything else for the past several years! Balfour temporised and suggested that Asquith ought to be informed if there was to be a public campaign. A meeting was subsequently arranged between the Prime Minister and Beresford on 30 March followed three days later by a long, detailed and surprisingly sober letter setting out the Admiral's reasons for his disquiet about the Admiralty. After consultation with various colleagues, Asquith wrote to tell Beresford that his charges 'clearly call[ed] for prompt and thorough examination'. He therefore proposed to institute an inquiry by the Committee of Imperial Defence and that he would take the chair. This was a considerable triumph for Lord Charles and such was his confidence that he was prompted to object, successfully, to Esher being a member of the inquiry as he was notoriously biased in favour of Fisher.[37]

When told the news, Fisher was beside himself with rage. What a humiliation for him and the Board of Admiralty! Effectively they were being put on trial at the say-so of an undisciplined subordinate. 'The Young Turks are not in it,' he fumed to Esher. 'The country must indeed be in a bad way if so governed!'[38] Not for the first time Fisher contemplated the possibility of retirement rather than fight another round with the execrable Beresford and his gang of ruffians. After all, Esher had been urging him to go on his fifth anniversary in office in October 1908. He now decided, however, after a long talk with Esher, that honour dictated that since an inquiry had been called, he should face out his critics and detractors. He would not resign and 'nothing but a "file of marines" should get him out of the Admiralty'.[39] Another letter from the king cheered Fisher enormously. It appeared he had been entirely forgiven and discharged of any responsibility for the apparently parlous state of England's navy. He was commanded to retain office 'in spite of all'.[40] It was certain that he would not resign now and he advertised his rediscovered pugnacity by complaining furiously to anyone who would listen that the fault was Asquith's. The Prime Minister's pusillanimity had made him concede unnecessarily to Beresford. Esher did not say as much to his friends, but he was still haunted by the thought that the government might well decide to sacrifice Fisher in an attempt to divert the criticisms of its opponents both within and outside the Liberal party.[41]

Before the sub-committee met, Fisher suffered yet another hard and humiliating knock from one of his most bitter and vengeful enemies. Sir George Armstrong had entered the navy in 1878 but had been obliged to resign the Service in 1891 for making imprudent remarks about Fisher for which he had to apologise publicly. He had then joined the staff of the *Globe,* a newspaper owned by his father, and for twelve years was its editor. He was also part proprietor of the *People.* First in a speech at the Constitutional Club and then in a letter to *The Times*[42] Armstrong revealed that in 1906 Fisher had charged one of his supporters, Captain R. H. Bacon, then serving in the Mediterranean under Beresford's command, to send him private reports. At a later date, with a view to discrediting Beresford, Fisher had these letters printed and circulated among chosen officers. It had been neither a wise nor an honest course to follow and now here was positive proof made public of that 'crime' with which the First Sea Lord had long been charged by his enemies. It appeared incontrovertible that he had employed a system of 'espionage' in the fleet. Fisher's enemies made the most of this opportunity, both in the press and parliament. Within a month Esher was the first to tell Fisher there was a possibility that Beresford and his friends were about to publish further incriminating letters. 'Every base artifice is being employed to drive me out,' Fisher complained to Garvin. 'The lad Armstrong is going to bring out some more letters – goodness knows what he may have purloined or even got himself from me as I have no idea at all what passed 3 or 4 years ago when I was fighting day and night.'[43]

In the Commons, McKenna pleaded with members that they ought not to allow themselves to be misled by these 'trumpery matters into censuring in the slightest degree a man who has given the very best service to the public that any man could'. Such an appeal was not likely to stifle Fisher's critics. Spender, in the *Westminster Gazette* noted their conduct suggested that their interest was neither the welfare of the navy nor the maintenance of proper relations between serving officers, but the pursuit of a vendetta against one man.[44] Esher, for once, was not too alarmed. He thought that the Armstrong letters would not do much harm to Fisher as rumours of their existence had been circulating since 1907. This short and unpleasant campaign did, however, cost Sir John the friendship of Prince George.[45]

The inquiry began on 27 April and in the next four months the committee met fifteen times. The report, which did not include the evidence upon which the findings were made, was issued on 12 August.[46] Throughout the proceedings, for his own good Fisher was kept very much in the background. McKenna conducted the case for the Admiralty while Beresford appeared for himself. The essentials of Lord Charles's case were; first, that to divide the fleet in home waters under separate commands was dangerous as necessary withdrawals for repairs and refit had meant that the Channel fleet was constantly vulnerable to sudden enemy action. Second, there were grave deficiencies in home waters in the numbers and quality of small craft, destroyers and cruisers. Third, when he assumed his command there had been no strategic scheme or plan of war for the disposal of his forces. Thus, if the Admiralty did have a war plan, at the beginning of hostilities – and all the 'experts' agreed this was the most vital period – it would be impossible to execute it immediately.

When presenting his evidence, Beresford was given 'every possible indulgence'. Should McKenna, when cross-examining, attempt to discredit Beresford on personal or meticulous detail, he was restrained by Asquith. Sandars concluded that Beresford had 'failed badly'.

> He could have been made to fail worse ... one never knew what he was
> driving at, save the eternal repetition of generalities. ... Had he been
> before an ordinary court of law, the cross-examination would have broken
> him down in one afternoon. ... I am not sure whether Asquith and
> Haldane were wise in fooling him into the belief that he was doing well
> before the Committee: that they did fool him is plain from the conversation
> which he has held with outsiders like myself.[47]

It was not entirely because he had been 'fooled' by Asquith and Haldane that Beresford was inspired to send a circular letter to the press in which he stated 'in the main' his charges had been justified. The conclusion of the report, especially the last paragraph which spoke of the need for 'further development of a Naval War Staff', was a direct slap at Fisher. Sir John recognised this and was very sore. The inquiry should have 'smashed' Beresford on the evidence as a 'blatant liar. He would have been so discredited that no newspaper would have noticed him ever again.'[48] But throughout the inquiry Fisher had insisted to his friends though he was 'winning a complete victory ... whether we are to reap the fruits is another matter! That's a matter of political expediency!'[49]

Sandars told Esher that had he been in Fisher's position he would have been very angry. Yet, for someone who was supposed to be Fisher's friend, he added a malevolent postscript: 'I would gladly write to him, but will he print or circulate my letter?' What puzzled Sandars was the fuss Fisher was making. Why did he continue to storm to his friends that the Cabinet was terrified of Beresford?

> Jackie in his prime ... would set these issues on right lines. ... I feel he
> is struggling with more than a man of his age can tackle and that his
> hand is losing its cunning. He smarts under censure to which he was once
> accustomed; his press is no longer faithful; his work, no matter how
> good it may be, is spoilt by the malignity of many enemies for whom he
> cared not in the heyday of his success, and now comes this report: the
> neutral tinted report.
>
> It is all very, very sad and I wish for his own sake that we could see
> our old friend making his bow, honoured in any way that he would wish at
> the hands of the King.[50]

There was more than a grain of truth in what Sandars said. Whether for reason of his increasing age, or because he was so hard pressed by many enemies, Fisher had certainly lost something of his former fine touch in dealing with the press. Once, when countering his foes, he had picked his targets with discrimination, known the value of ignoring the lesser fry and concentrated for his sport upon the bigger fish. The years of unrelenting warfare seemed at last to have taken their toll and increasingly Fisher revealed an unpleasant streak of petty-minded vindictiveness that was to have most unfortunate consequences when he was recalled to the Admiralty in 1914. Old wounds remained sore; there was no capacity to forgive and forget. Yet for those with eyes to see, that same malign disposition had been evident in the last two years of his initial period as First Sea Lord. Fisher had been fighting for so long that he was no longer able to understand that others might champion different causes from his for good, sincere and not necessarily perverse reasons. He was convinced that his enemies were anxious only to pay off old scores and were animated by nothing save spite and petty animosity.

There was a certain justification for his attitude. Much mud had been slung by Beresford's less scrupulous supporters during their campaign against the First Sea Lord. Sometimes their excesses, in their enthusiasm to recruit others to their cause, had misfired. Henry Chalmers Roberts, the American editor of *World's Work*, told Esher how he had been 'twice approached with all manner of attacks in the dark . . . regular fish-wife slanders emanating from the highest quarters. The manner of these communications aroused in me almost as much opposition as the matter.' He refused to pillory Fisher.[51] Arnold White and W. T. Stead, 'full of blood and fury on my behalf', had begged Fisher to answer Beresford in kind. Though sorely tempted, Fisher had not succumbed. He told Garvin,

> They are throwing a lot of mud at me just now and dear Maxse calls me the 'Mud Admiral' as opposed to Beresford, the 'Sea Admiral'. I should like to publish Beresford's dossier which I have! When he hoisted his flag as Admiral he had less sea time than many of the Lieutenants in the Fleet and most of his service in Royal Yachts and Royal Cruises and on shore & I think all included he had only 8 years service. N'importe . . . but *it is* galling. . . . Hurd told me the day before yesterday of endless machinations to force me out, but, 'J'y suis. J'y reste!' Don't say anything about the dossier. I don't want to 'mud' back!![52]

Unfortunately the constant attacks of the Beresfordians undermined Fisher's better judgment to ignore if not to forget.

The rumours that Fisher was about to retire stirred Beresford's campaigners to even greater efforts, and none more than Leo Maxse. He went so far as to suggest in his *National Review* that if it came to hanging for his 'catalogue of high crimes and misdemeanours', then the First Sea Lord was 'entitled to the nearest lamp post'. At last, prepared to accept the inevitable, Fisher agreed that he would go on his sixty-ninth birthday in January 1910. In the king's birthday honours' list in November, Fisher was made a baron. He had hoped for a viscountcy. Even the least step in the peerage for Fisher caused Maxse acute pain. 'How could the king, of all people,' he asked Esher, 'have been so misled into conferring a peerage on our principal betrayer . . . now that the scales have fallen from blinded eyes?'

> The very few who for the last three or four years have been fighting against Fisherism . . . for a long time were regarded as simple maniacs, but now it seems to be generally acknowledged that the strongest thing ever said in the National Review on the subject, pales beside the actual reality. He has betrayed our most sacred trust as it has never been betrayed

in English history by any sailor. One is prepared for that sort of thing from politicians, but from a British Admiral![53]

More serious than Maxse's vituperative censures was Repington's claim, in a letter to Esher, that 'putting aside the personal and wranglesome part', there had been 'no better statement of our naval needs . . . than in Beresford's letter' that had sparked off the final crisis. 'If Beresford's principles are followed, we should be all right as far as we can be without the initiative.' In the margin of this letter Esher wrote, 'How silly! But he hates Fisher.'[54]

Esher's easy dismissal missed altogether the point of Repington's observation. A letter the military correspondent wrote to his editor in January 1912 deserves quotation in this context, for it illustrates exactly what lay at the root of so much damaging strife that divided those who should have been natural allies. As a consequence, Britain was less well prepared to face the Kaiser's Germany in August 1914 than she might otherwise have been.

> My idea always has been, and is, that both Services should be directed by instructed statesmanship . . . an object which is gradually being attained by the Defence Committee . . . [It was necessary] to bring the Admiralty to the heel of statesmanship, and this has been secured by the Invasion and Beresford Inquiries. . . . The Navy desired not to follow policy but to direct it.[55]

This was undoubtedly a correct charge. Politicians for years had known that Fisher's attitude was extraordinarily independent and high-handed. They had 'funked' doing anything about it until it could no longer be ignored. Pride in the navy had degenerated into myopic departmental selfishness. At enormous expense of money and efficiency, narrow territorial imperatives, dictated not by national priorities but the selfish temporary advantage of a supposed enhancement of the prestige of one Service, one ministry, or one cabal over another, wasted much of Britain's competence. Inter-Service rivalry was poisonous enough, but the self-inflicted wounds of constant internecine warfare within the navy were even more debilitating. Fisher was not alone in his attitudes; Beresford was every bit as blinkered. His cooperation with Roberts and Repington had been inspired not by any far-sighted vision that recognised the need for an end to inter-Service rivalry and the planning of joint strategy, but solely by his enmity towards Fisher. It was no good looking to admirals and generals for a sensible strategy based upon the nation's needs and capacity. Such vision apparently was vouchsafed only to more junior officers, like Slade and Ewart. Their careers suffered as a consequence of their prescience.[56] When Repington had offered Fisher a sensible, beneficial and honourable compromise that would have better served the interest of army, navy and nation than the constant squabbling, Fisher refused. He supposed that Repington must be Judas for he was an army man. 'I wonder when Haldane is going to pay him his thirty pieces of silver?' he asked McKenna.[57] He could only think that any suggestion from Repington would necessarily be prompted by an enmity for the navy. For the same reason, he failed to recognise that Haldane was one of the very few ministers who appreciated the need for a strong army *and* navy.

The trouble with Beresford was that he never knew when to leave well alone. It should have been enough for him that Fisher had been forced to resign. The inquiry report seemed to heighten Beresford's insufferably smug sense of self-righteousness and further prompted his crusading spirit. Sandars had not been the only one wrongly to suppose that once it was known Fisher was to resign 'there would be an immediate slump in CB's stocks'.[58] Charlie thought of only one thing – to rub in his supposed advantage. He wrote to tell Balfour, 'Now I have begun to fight for my brother officers; all disgusting intimidation must come out that has been practised for the last five years.'[59] From April to October he addressed a series of letters to Asquith that ostensibly instanced examples of 'intimidation on the one hand and favouritism on the other for which the Admiralty has of late years been notorious'. Beresford's charges were reckless and inaccurate; his tone bullying and hectoring. Asquith anxiously referred the indictment to McKenna who had no difficulty in rebutting it. As a final fling, Beresford published the correspondence in *The Times* and Asquith responded by publishing the last, most complete and damaging retort to Charlie's wild accusations. Quite unabashed, Beresford insisted that the validity of his case was unaffected. 'I say again, as I have said before, that a system of espionage, favouritism and intimidation exists at the Admiralty.'[60] Fisher had to admit to Archibald Hurd, 'Beresford is unsquashable. When convicted of a lie he simply tells another! and then people say "Oh! it's only the Celtic temperament!" and pass it over.'[61]

When Fisher's retirement was made public Beresford did not attempt to hide his glee and satisfaction that 'We have got rid of the Mulatto at last.' He suggested that a suitable celebratory toast should be: 'To the death of fraud, espionage, intimidation, corruption, tyranny and self-interest which have been a nightmare over the finest Service in the world for the last four years'.[62] It must have been a sore temptation for Fisher to answer Beresford in kind, but he manfully resisted the entreaties of those like Arnold White that he should, when leaving office, make a great speech that would crush his tormentor. 'Facta non verba,' Fisher responded. 'Let deeds set forth what has been done these last five years.' But to Garvin he could not resist a careful rehearsal of his achievements as First Sea Lord. 'We shall be *certainly* "2 keels to 1" in March 1912. ABSOLUTELY SURE. . . . The German navy will have only *11* but I never contradict the 13 given out.' He quoted his successor, Arthur Wilson's, estimate after 'a close and critical three week examination'.

The Admiralty policy has been excellent. You have kept well ahead of the Germans and you did most wisely to hold back these last years for you are getting immeasurably finer ships by the delay and yet preserving an unassailable supremacy! *Yes it's true!* Do you know that the Lion and Orion are as far superior to the Dreadnought as the Dreadnought to all before her? Imagine 70,000 Horse Power the Dreadnought only 21,000!!! Imagine the new 13½ inch guns as superior to the Dreadnought's armaments as the Dreadnought to all before her. *The German guns rank as pea shooters in comparison.* Wait till the Germans wake-up to these super-Dreadnoughts! Wait till the d-d rabble again cry out 'that cursed pestiferous late First Lord at it again!' A fresh era of ship-building!! D- -N HIM![63]

Fisher had clearly convinced himself that his earlier economies – which he supposed more than any other action had cost him so many of his friends in the press – had been a carefully rehearsed Machiavellian design to insure the technical superiority of British over German capital ships. This was a sad and dangerous delusion. Fisher had made economies because he had been obliged to. As to the technical superiority of British capital ship design, that was a comforting thought to which key politicians and naval personnel alike clung tenaciously until it was given the lie at the Battle of Jutland.[64]

The Beresford Fisher quarrel had provided the press over a long period with excellent copy. Was commercial enterprise the only or the most important consideration of the popular newspapers when they took sides and advertised the rift in the navy's lute? Northcliffe, for example, was notoriously open to the charge that he put commercial gain before all else. When his *Daily Mail* ran its Blatchford scaremongering series about Germany,[65] the immediate reaction of one Fleet Street reader was to ask himself, 'What is Northcliffe's game? . . . The mechanism by which the series was introduced was thin – even to emaciation. What *is* the game? Is it mere newspaper commerce?'[66] It had not been the merits of the case he argued but its commercial implications that prompted a delighted letter from Northcliffe to Garvin for championing Fisher against the claims of the *Morning Post.*

> If you would only keep the 'Morning Post' advertising us like this it will save us a great deal of money. I hope you will return to the charge next Sunday. Their advertising rates are £20 a column for display, and about double that for reading notices. I reckon this morning's mention was therefore worth at least £40 to the 'Observer'.[67]

But in this as much else, Northcliffe was hardly typical. Those journalists who wrote the stories concerning Beresford and Fisher often withheld opinions or information that if published would ideally have served an immediate polemical purpose. They may have been wrong, frequently they were, but their intentions were most often shaped by what they perceived to be the national interest. If we consider someone as overtly partisan as Gwynne who so resolutely championed Beresford; even he could sometimes cry 'enough is enough'. He wrote to Arnold White about the 'paint-work' incident: 'Do you not think with me that it is the duty of everybody who takes an interest in the Navy, whether they be critics or approvers of the present Admiralty policy, to drop this subject? . . . It seems to me that it is bound to react to the detriment of the Service generally if quarrels between high officials are discussed in the Press.'[68]

The important point is not whether Gwynne was pleading a special case or even being purposely disingenuous; his last observation was undoubtedly true. The popular press, whatever Fisher's initial publicity successes, soon proved itself to be an inappropriate venue for reasoned debate. It was suited only to be an amphitheatre where brutal blows were most loudly applauded. More than once it became a theatre of the absurd. The play was the thing – but only so long as the groundlings were amused. Rhetoric displaced reasoned debate, personality, not policy, consumed all interest and energy. The losers in the long term were the nation and the navy. Yet Strachey had been the only editor who suggested and approved a radical 'solution' to the navy's woes. It would have been better had both Admirals been removed from their posts.

•••••••••• **PART 3** ••••••••••

For national security and party advantage: the politicians

Naval scaremongering: Garvin's election cannon-ball

Mr Blatchford is a nobody. His stylistic outpourings would amount to nothing if they did not appear in the Daily Mail. They become important political documents the moment a great political party identifies itself with them. . . . Germanophobia and preparations for war against Germany thereby become an essential part of the programme with which the Unionists hope to attain power, and which must be carried out if they win.

Kreuz Zeitung

The two-keels-to-one standard. . . . would inspire enthusiasm in the party. . . . It would be intelligible to the dullest elector. . . . It would put the other side in a fix. We could carry the country clean out in my opinion.

Garvin to Sandars

Our opponents have made a variety of efforts to obscure the issue . . . in the hope that, by bringing the Navy onto the scene public attention might be diverted from the House of Lords. A well-known Socialist writer has been pressed into the service of a Tory newspaper, in order to make your blood creep with horrible imaginings as to the designs of a great friendly foreign Power.

Speech to constituents by McKenna

Lloyd George's opposition to any increase in the naval estimates had prompted Northcliffe to predict to *The Times*'s staff that 'the emptiness of the Chancellor's head will soon become painfully apparent to the country'. His notoriously poor opinion of Lloyd George was confirmed when, on holiday in Germany, he learned the details of the 1909 budget. He wrote to tell Garvin how he hoped it might induce an early election that would remove the Liberals, 'men . . . drugged into some mysterious inactivity' who were obviously unsuited for the task of making adequate naval provision for the protection and safety of the country. Northcliffe's visit to the fatherland had once more impressed him with the Germans' organised prosperity and their violent antipathy towards the English. Even his German relations, 'who ought to know better', he told Garvin, 'at a family party yesterday expressed extreme anti-English views'.[1] The many letters Northcliffe despatched to England on that visit emphasised 'the vast industrial strides made in practically every town. Every one of these new factory chimneys', he wrote to H. W. Wilson 'is a gun pointed at England.' Wilson could only echo the chief's sentiments and ask what should be done. He told Northcliffe that Marlowe, the *Mail*'s editor, proposed 'to make the Budget issue a naval one, ie put out the view that the Budget does not make sufficient provision for the Navy and therefore it should be rejected'.[2] Garvin was already set upon the same path. During the next two months, in a series of brilliant articles in the *Observer*, he argued that it was nothing less than his 'patriotic duty' to attack the budget because Lloyd George was intent on bribing the electorate at the price of effectively crippling Britain's sea power. If the navy was given insufficient funding then Britain would be vulnerable to attack by Germany, a claim that the *Daily Chronicle* dismissed as 'a thumping lie'.

It was not Garvin who was pilloried by the Liberal press, particularly the *Daily News*, for the opinions he expressed in the *Observer*, but Northcliffe. He was a wealthy man conducting a campaign to serve his own selfish ends. He was not really concerned about the navy's welfare so much as the depredations he supposed the Chancellor planned to make to his pocket. The *Daily News* perceived this design in the 'confused efforts' of the *Daily Mail* which were scorned. But it did not underestimate the siren influence of 'the emotional person who pens the leading articles of the *Observer*'.[3] Nothing was said about the treatment of the budget by *The Times*, Northcliffe's other, more recently acquired newspaper property. At Printing House Square, editorial opinion was divided and confused. Wilson had informed Northcliffe that in his absence it had been 'distinctly weaker in policy . . . ha[d] said little of the Navy and not much on the Budget'.[4] Buckle was prepared to go wherever Balfour chose, but the master had not yet pointed the way. Chirol's concern was that if as a consequence of the budget there was an election, the Radical element in the Liberal party might well be strengthened with disastrous results for Grey's sensible conduct of foreign policy. Most of the Unionist press, like the parliamentary party, seemed undecided about what should be done. The ever impatient Maxse wrote to Garvin.

> I feel sure that you are equally concerned as I with the mess into which things are being allowed to drift through the ineptitude of our friends in the House and the want of grit in the Unionist press. . . . I have remained silent for a considerable time in spite of much provocation . . . but when I see the entire position being compromised I realise the folly of such acquiescence.[5]

On domestic political issues, Northcliffe had a disconcerting disposition to be less blinkeredly partisan than his more rabid Tory colleagues would have wished.[6] He was a purveyor of news, not a party ideologue. That was Garvin's *métier*. For Northcliffe, creating news, 'scooping' his adversaries – whatever their political loyalties – remained an abiding passion, long after he had abandoned writing regularly for his journals. It was a wayward propensity that always spelled danger in the context of party political strife and was to betray him on a chance, unaccustomed visit that he made to Westminster in August 1909.

It was Henry Dalzeil, Liberal MP and newspaper proprietor, who spotted Northcliffe sitting in the peers' gallery, and was quick to seize the opportunity to introduce him to Lloyd George. Together with his brother Cecil, the Liberal MP for Droitwich, Northcliffe was spirited off to the Chancellor's room for an hour's *tête-à-tête*. Cecil Harmsworth later recorded in his diary how 'Ll.G devoted all his powers to capturing Northcliffe. It was a dazzling performance.' But for all the Chancellor's efforts Northcliffe showed no particular sign of enthusiasm until Lloyd George took from his desk a draft of a Bill on road development, handed it to his visitor and told him that he might make what use of it he pleased. Though the ploy was obvious Northcliffe could not resist the lure.

> Northcliffe was taken aback as they say. . . . 'What, in tomorrow's Daily Mail?' he asked incredulously. 'Before the House itself has heard it?' . . . Ll.G waved objections aside. Northcliffe put the precious draft in his inner pocket and left.[7]

The day after this unexpected meeting, in its 'Political Notes' *The Times* perceived a change of opinion in favour of the budget, 'comparable to the turning of the tide'. Garvin hastily dictated a seventeen-page screed to Northcliffe. His 'sixth sense' warned him of a probable Tory surrender to the budget, 'the gravest situation that any of us has yet known'. Indulging his unrivalled gift for the histrionic Garvin predicted an England set upon the path to become 'a Socialistic Republic in everything but name'.[8] The next day, 5 August, in a special article by a 'Parliamentary Correspondent', the *Daily Mail* admitted that the budget might well win much popular support and that it was an attractive basis for an election programme. The article featured prominently the proposed Development of Roads Bill. On the same day, there was a report in the *Daily News* suggesting that as a consequence of his visit to the Commons, Northcliffe had modified his views on the budget. It was a rather obvious attempt to create discord and despondency among Tory supporters, but Garvin was palpably alarmed at the direction events seemed to be taking. In great consternation he wrote to Northcliffe enclosing the report clipped from the *Daily News*.

> The whole tone of the Times and the Daily Mail seems to me utterly disastrous . . . I am *right, right, right* in entreating you not to encourage by indirect means in your papers thoughts of a surrender on the Budget which would ruin the Empire. . . . Oh, believe me, half England will not sit down to be despoiled without fighting; and if your papers won't fight their battle they will turn to the papers that will.[9]

Northcliffe was not impressed by Garvin's hysterical bluster. He did not like threats, implied or expressed, and he did not need telling his duty by one of his editors. His article on 5 August in the *Mail* had been an indulgence, an irresistible journalistic *jeu d'ésprit*, but he had already written to Balfour enclosing Garvin's earlier, inordinately lengthy missive, asked the Opposition leader for an interview, and generally admitted that as matters had 'gone against us rather badly recently' there was need for the party to mount a concerted campaign.[10] Nine months later Garvin claimed to Sandars that he had 'risked [his] professional life and nothing less pulling the Daily Mail round last August.'[11] That was a gross exaggeration although he must have suffered a momentary qualm when he heard nothing from Northcliffe for six days, and then received a studied inquiry about the state of his health. This, he well knew, was Northcliffe's usual overture before dismissing an employee!

For some months it had been agreed that Garvin would accompany Northcliffe on a holiday to North America. Now he insisted that he must stay in England to fight the budget. When he had told Balfour this, the Tory leader implied it was unnecessary and precipitate. 'As far as I can forecast, you may spend a month on the sea and in the Rockies, and find us still at work on your return.'[12] Garvin would not be dissuaded, and Northcliffe accepted the decision. He had other things on his mind beside the budget and the nervous, undoubtedly exaggerated apprehensions of the *Observer*'s editor. A particular, immediate and pressing concern was the economic future of *The Times*. Moberly Bell was unwillingly commandeered as the new travelling companion – a convenient ploy that would allow Northcliffe's trusted henchmen, Pryor, Kennedy Jones and Nicholson, in Bell's absence, to tighten his proprietorial grip on the Bashaws of Printing House Square. As a manager, Moberly Bell was proving insufficiently cost-conscious and rather too intractable for Northcliffe's taste. Removed from the scene he could be 'jumped on' as and when required. 'When he sees you are in earnest,' Northcliffe wrote with supreme confidence and arrogance to Kennedy Jones, 'he becomes duly obedient.'[13] So Garvin was left behind in London nervously fulminating about the iniquities of the Liberals while assuring Northcliffe that his nervous tension was physical and not mental!

Like a lover parted from the object of his desire, so with each day's absence in America, Northcliffe's heart grew fonder towards his brilliant if wayward Garvin. Not only distance lent enchantment. Garvin told in his letters of how he had persuaded Balfour to adopt the tactics for fighting the budget that he had prescribed in the *Observer*. At once Northcliffe telegraphed the *Daily Mail* to borrow freely from the *Observer*'s editorial columns. Throughout the Unionist press, the unadulterated gospel of tariff reform held sway.[14] Northcliffe was certainly no 'whole-hogger', as was Garvin, on the issue of protection, but for the moment he seemed content to let the *Observer*'s editor make the pace for his other newspapers. He wrote from America of how he saw that 'The Times ... has been doing its best. ... The Daily Mail has been doing its work well. ... The Observer simply splendid.'[15] He could not, however, altogether resist the opportunity to poke fun both at his friend's passionate crusading spirit and execrable handwriting.[16] 'So when the Budget and the Germans have captured England we must all come and live here,' he wrote from Newfoundland. 'We will give you a nice free homestead, and you can turn your pen into a ploughshare. I only hope your furrows will be more distinct than your writing.'[17]

Northcliffe's reference to Germany was not accidental. Even before his arrival he had been pilloried in certain American and Canadian newspapers as 'a leader of the growing war party in Great Britain'. On a visit to Canada the previous year, Northcliffe had been surprised and concerned about the degree of influence German sympathisers exercised in the North American press. As a consequence he determined 'to create a press cable service of news satisfactory to patriotic Britons on both sides of the Atlantic'. Earl Grey, the Governor-General of Canada, had described Northcliffe's influence on that visit as 'volcanic, a light on the mountain tops'. He told his friend Milner, 'This man is a Napoleon, full of ideas and energy . . . genuinely possessed by the religion of Empire.'[18] Interviewed by the press in 1909, Northcliffe insisted it was not war with Germany that he sought but British preparedness should hostilities ever break out. Why trust Germany when she had a record of 'making unprovoked attacks on other nations'? Germany's refusal to discuss the true nature of her naval armaments was 'more than significant – it [was] threatening'.

About this time, while still in Canada, Northcliffe agreed that Robert Blatchford should be commissioned to go to Germany, to view and write about the army manoeuvres for the *Daily Mail*. The choice was inspired. When Blatchford accepted his commission he would have known exactly what was required of him. On the subject of Germany, the editorial disposition of newspapers was as notorious as the sympathies of certain well-known journalists. Writers confined their comments to that which they wished to notice and newspapers published what they supposed their readers ought to see. They did not seek to modify or qualify opinion but to fortify popular prejudice. This immutable rule applied to every journal and every journalist on Fleet Street, whether Radical or Tory.[19]

It would be wrong to suppose that every Unionist, even within the tariff reform camp, was pleased by the exaggerated attention the press paid to the protection issue. Milner was extremely angry on this score with the *Morning Post*. Its editor, Fabian Ware, was an enthusiastic admirer and disciple of Milner, but his greater loyalty to the unadulterated orthodoxies of the Birmingham School's gospel meant that questions of defence were now virtually ignored. 'I always hammer away at defence when speaking in the country,' Milner complained to Roberts, 'but in the hubbub one gets little attention for anything except Tariff. The Liberals shout "Budget" and we shout "Tariff" and the question is who shouts the loudest. It is horrid.'[20] Balfour's political secretary, Jack Sandars, took a somewhat different view. What concerned him was that the apparent unanimity affected by the Tory press in late August, by the end of September was once more beginning to show dangerous signs of breaking up into the too-familiar pattern of factional voices pronouncing different remedies with discordant emphases. He complained to Balfour. On several occasions, and at a time when party tactics were supposed to have been agreed, their press was ineffectual because it did not speak with one predetermined voice. He asked Balfour to consider his account of a typical evening he had recently spent with Tory journalists and editors.

First Buckle arrived. . . . After he had gone I saw representatives of the 'Telegraph', 'Daily Mail', 'Daily Express' and 'Standard'. They kept me until a late hour, but I was glad I saw them for they were hopelessly on the wrong track. Altogether I think without conceit I can say I did something towards keeping them on reasonable lines.[21]

To Esher, Sandars was prepared to admit that whatever efforts he made to understand them, Northcliffe's newspapers remained a source of perplexity. 'Northcliffe is no politician – he is a man of business . . . he exhibits complete ignorance of political mankind.' Of all Northcliffe's newspaper properties, it was *The Times* that proved Sandars' greatest headache. 'Where is the power lodged?' he asked despairingly. 'I see the editorial people in the old gang – they talk as if their hand alone held the rudder: then I am told that K[ennedy] J[ones] is the power; but it is difficult to detect it in the undecided tones of our leading paper.'[22]

When Sandars compared the Tory with the Liberal press he recognised that its major weakness was the lack of an efficient link between the party organisation and its newspaper allies. Under the tutelage of Sir Henry Norman, Liberal newspapers were working hand-in-glove with their party organisation. It was a nice paradox that Norman, Liberal MP for Wolverhampton and Secretary of the Budget League, as an active journalist writing in the *Pall Mall Gazette* and the *Daily Chronicle* had promoted divisions in his party by his unequivocal support of Rosebery. Now he had wooed and won the major news agencies for the Liberals and their press sang in rare unison. 'Our opponents have gained much by cultivating their own press,' wrote Sandars, ascribing this advantage entirely to the efforts of Norman.[23] Speeches, even by distinguished Tory leaders, were not adequately reported. Fabian Ware was particularly distraught that Austen Chamberlain was not receiving sufficient publicity. 'It is a real scandal', he told the politician, 'that the Press Association should not have reported [your speeches].' On the other hand, Winston Churchill's words were reported in full. Admittedly, that worthy left nothing to chance, supplying the agency with 'verbatim reports . . . with applause and everything else inserted by the author'.[24] Chamberlain had grumbled to Garvin of how his neglect by *The Times* was the fault of Northcliffe. Garvin rejected the idea. 'He is not responsible for the "Times" where he is much hampered. . . . I spoke to him about the treatment of Unionist speeches, yours especially, and I said that it reminded me of the impartiality of the Irish historian who was so impartial he was invariably unfair to his friends.'[25]

It was due to the efforts of Jack Sandars, 'Balfour's other-self', that by the late summer of 1909 Garvin was established in a particularly intimate and influential position within the private counsels of the Tory party leader. In the name of party unity, he was prepared to temper somewhat his enthusiasm for the full, unadulterated tariff reform doctrine, and did not hesitate to criticise vehemently other journalists not so quick as he to set aside their prejudices for the common cause. He thought Fabian Ware and Richard Jebb of the *Morning Post* a pair of 'querulous asses . . . devoid of an atom of practical political facility' because they oscillated between 'surrender to the Liberals' and 'pushing their policy of vendetta against AJB B[alfour] under the name of "straight forward" politics'.[26] Garvin was now meeting with Sandars almost every day at Carlton Gardens and they constantly exchanged letters. Soon to dictate even the minutiae of party tactics, Garvin had immediately established his authority in all matters of party publicity. Almost one of the first things he did was to produce a scathing seven-page typed report on Tory campaign literature.

> The inferiority of our party literature . . . is the most serious disadvantage, and indeed, a very real danger . . . To seize the imagination, which our present dead stuff can't do, we, like the other side must have two things.
> A. A Dream
> B. A Bogey.
> Our dream Imperial Strength and Industrial Security based upon Tariff Reform; and our bogey must be the freely importing foreigner. . . . The country responds very strongly to every form of the appeal 'Britons HOLD YOUR OWN.' For this reason it wants the Fleet to be placed upon a footing of unassailable superiority.[27]

Sandars readily acknowledged Garvin's genius as a publicist, but was aware that there might be risks involved in taking the editor so wholeheartedly on board. 'You know him and know the value to be attached to any opinion of his,' Sandars wrote to Balfour.

> Garvin is an enthusiast, but is I think not one of violent prejudice. Certainly he is not prejudiced as Maxse, Wilkinson and others of that School. . . .
> I beg that you will not consider that I am anything more than a Post Office in transmitting to you G's opinions. I do not trouble you with comments on them one way or another. I merely record them as being held by a man who is an enthusiastic lover of his country and a keen observer of the public mind and a journalist possessing influence.[28]

Sandars might have tempered this extraordinarily enthusiastic recommendation had it been possible for him to have read the particular views Garvin had earlier confided to Northcliffe on who should be dominant in any partnership between the press and politicians. 'Until the newspapers command and cease to follow the opinion of conventional parliamentary people, always years behind their age, nothing will be well with this nation.'[29]
Arthur Balfour hardly came into the category of a 'conventional parliamentary personage', but this did not stop Garvin in the *Observer* prompting the Tory leader to 'go to Birmingham . . . and there declare the triple policy of Tariff Reform, Social Reform and Naval Security', a challenge Balfour duly accepted a week later with his speech at Bingley Hall. 'Your advice on this point has not been thrown away,' Balfour wrote to flatter and reassure his powerful journalist ally.[30] Knowledge of Garvin's 'influence', both with the party leader and at Central Office, was not slow in reaching W. T. Stead. In two letters written to Garvin in October and December 1909, he described the *Observer*'s editor as 'Director in chief of the Tory party . . . Balfour's master . . . Master of the House of Lords and leader of the Leader of the Opposition. . . . I have certainly done my best to acknowledge the mightiness of your position.'[31]
Powerful though he knew his voice to be in the press, Garvin, like Sandars,

recognised the overwhelming advantage of winning Northcliffe's total adhesion to their chosen course and tactics. Secure that allegiance, and Northcliffe's 'sense of pervading vitality and suggestiveness [would] help everything'.[32] The two prepared for Northcliffe's imminent return. Sandars dutifully reported to Balfour, 'I have seen Garvin at length - mostly on the subject of Northcliffe. We have both determined to keep him well disposed to us, and to save him from the embraces of Winston who flatters him and toadies him in a sickening way, and then laughs behind his back.'[33]

Feeling tired and jaded after his exhausting tour, Northcliffe prescribed for himself a favoured tonic – a short holiday in Paris. But first he responded to the urgent pleas of Sandars and Garvin to examine the way Tory Central Office was conducting relations with the press. The staff of Central Office regarded the popular press more as an enemy than a potential ally. They had a particular loathing for Northcliffe as they supposed he intended to take them over and install Kennedy Jones as principal agent. This distrust never diminished, but a new, more professional attitude towards party propaganda and publicity was reflected in the quintupling of the running costs of the press bureau within two years of its establishment.[34]

Northcliffe's immediate proposal had been that Sandars should talk with S. J. Pryor.[35] Sandars was impressed with Pryor who, if his manner was 'rather dominant', was 'clearly a master of his subject. I made plain the difficulties of our situation,' Sandars wrote to Northcliffe, 'and of my own desire to do all that I could to attach to our Central Office some machinery which would establish both an intimate and general communication with the higher authorities of the friendly newspapers.'[36] Within a few days Sandars wrote again declaring his delight that 'Already you would think better of our press relations – that is entirely due to you and to the services of Mr Pryor.'[37] Convinced that a newspaper magnate was best treated in the same manner as Disraeli courted the favours of Queen Victoria, Sandars was unstinting in his flattery of Northcliffe and his favoured child, the *Daily Mail*. 'Let me say how admirably the party is served by the "Daily Mail". It is a most potent auxiliary. . . . Its arguments, its facts, its criticisms supply the best and most modern ammunition. I told Mr Balfour of its leading articles last week, and he said he would read them.'[38]

When he returned from his Paris holiday, Northcliffe had a long interview with Sandars. Though he 'warmly approved' of all that had been done he warned there was much still to be accomplished, sentiments with which Sandars very much agreed, particularly the idea that there should be a press bureau attached permanently to Central Office.[39] The advantage of having Northcliffe to cast his seasoned eye over the party's press arrangements was undeniable, but he still showed a distinct reluctance to abandon his view that tariff reform, and more particularly the higher cost of food – in his words 'stomach taxes' – placed the party at an electoral disadvantage. In the columns of the Carmelite House press, protection was constantly demoted to make way for the more familiar, rumbustious, scare campaigning against Germany and constant talk of the perils faced by an insufficiently funded British navy. 'I only wish Northcliffe knew as much about politics as he does about business,' Sandars complained.[40]

That the navy should play a part in the election campaign had been inevitable from the moment when the octogenarian senior Liberal member for Portsmouth, Sir John Baker, died in November 1909, and Lord Charles Beresford, who for several months had been seeking a convenient constituency, was adopted as the Tory candidate. Immediately, alarm bells had begun to ring at the Admiralty. According to Fisher, Beresford had already announced that 'he was PROMISED to be First Lord of the Admiralty "to keep WILSON RIGHT"!!!' Beresford was certain 'to float the Navy Scare which will cost the Radicals the Election. Serves them d-d well right!'[41] Fisher's malevolent electoral forecast was prompted by his disgust with Asquith and Haldane. Had they not 'watered-down' the Inquiry Report, then Beresford would have been 'pulverized out of existence'. Instead, with every prospect of a Tory victory, Fisher and his friends feared Beresford would go to the Admiralty, either as First Lord or First Sea Lord under Walter Long. Either way, Admiral Wilson's power would effectively be curbed. Whatever the cost Fisher determined Charlie would have to be kept out of the limelight otherwise he might 'create an obligation that would force Balfour and Cawdor into his arms'.

Fisher's first step was an attempt to postpone the issue of an electoral writ. He wondered whether the First Lord's wife could not 'prevail upon [her] friend Mr Pease [Liberal Chief Whip] or whoever runs the Elections to defer the writ'?[42] That impossible tactic was frustrated by Asquith calling a general election. Garvin was now recruited by Fisher to tackle Jack Sandars. Could not Tory Central Office refuse to recognise Beresford as a candidate? With a sweet reasonableness that did not altogether disguise his anxiety that Garvin or Fisher might do something foolish, Sandars outlined why Garvin's suggestion was impossible.

> If the Local Association agree upon C. Beresford, we cannot dispute its right to run him; and whether he is the man we ourselves would have liked or not, is wholly outside our province in this aspect of things. . . . You won't, I know, disorder *our* machine . . . supposing the Association sticks to its present form and insists on having CB.
>
> We have had so many troubles over this 'vexeta questio' of recognition. . . . DON'T make our headquarters position difficult. Remember where the decision as to candidate really rests and our party grounds do not make CB impossible.
>
> After all, JF goes to one House of Parliament. Let CB go to the other.[43]

Garvin was obliged to relieve his frustration in a series of letters exchanged with like-minded friends. To accept Beresford on grounds of party loyalty – and he knew that with Beresford as candidate, the Portsmouth constituency was eminently winnable – remained a very high price to pay. 'I am rather sick of our too smart, jocose, party managers,' F. S. Oliver told Garvin. 'Sending the egregious Charlie to Portsmouth was, I agree with you, not entirely creditable. It is like the score that a small, sharp grocer or draper would have been pleased to make. We want dignity now and "high seriousness".'[44] Another of

Garvin's intimates, 'Paddy' Goulding, reluctantly accepting the *fait accompli*, suggested it would be wise 'to arm ourselves with ammunition in case CB attacks F when in the Commons'.[45] For his part, Beresford had already decided the lines upon which he would fight his campaign. There would be no tariff reform nonsense for him. 'Our position is very serious. Germany is going on by leaps and bounds, but our people are obsessed with nothing but internal legislation, paying no regard to national defence whatever.'[46]

The naval question had been debated *ad nauseam* in March and apparently had finally been laid to rest in July with the announcement of the Cabinet's decision to build the four contingent Dreadnoughts. Therefore, it was not unreasonable to suppose that the navy would make little appeal to the electorate as an issue in December. However, this was to ignore the residual disquiet, even fear, about German intentions that had been carefully fostered in the popular press by the invasionist lobby. At the turn of the year, Mulliner, who had played some part in promoting the naval panic of the previous March, suddenly re-emerged with the publication in *The Times* of letters and extracts from his diary.[47] Mulliner had reason to be a bitter man. The information about Germany's increased capacity for building armaments which he had supplied to the Admiralty, the War Office and leading politicians of both parties had not led, as he might reasonably have expected, to increased orders for his ordnance factory, but to pressure for his resignation to which he had finally succumbed in July. His letters and the extracts from his diary appeared to confirm the Opposition's earlier charge that the Liberal government had been guilty of 'criminally neglecting' the navy.

The trouble with Mulliner as an electoral asset was that, like Beresford, his motives were highly suspect; Mulliner because of his enforced resignation, and Beresford because it was soon apparent that while, like any other party hack, he dutifully attacked the Liberals, most of his eloquence and spleen was reserved for a constant, detailed and venomous personal critique of Fisher and the First Sea Lord's conduct of affairs at the Admiralty. In a thoroughly alarmist and dishonest speech at Grimsby, Beresford claimed that the navy was short of 19,000 sailors. He also conjured with the excited imaginations of his audience by picturing the fearful consequences of the liner, *Mauretania*, being sunk by German trampships in the North Sea. This speech was too much for Fisher who wrote to Mrs Garvin: '*Secret*. Sir Arthur Wilson having gone himself over every requirement for war has satisfied himself only 1,500 men are wanted of which 1,200 have already been provided by McKenna - & Beresford today says 19,000 are wanted! It's *ludicrous*!! and still more ludicrous the German tramps with 6 pounders killing the Mauretania!!! It is all too funny. *But leave it all alone*.'[48] This last injunction was, after Fisher's usual style, intended to produce the opposite effect. As for Mulliner, Garvin informed Northcliffe, his letters were 'full of inaccurate rubbish [which] makes me thoroughly distrust him.' What Garvin did not say was that he had received a peremptory command from Fisher – 'Do not touch Mulliner – pitch. He "let in" Balfour.'[49] Garvin was concerned that the 're-examination of questionable detail' would serve only to confuse the electorate. What was required was 'a broad impression', and this could best be achieved by 'sticking to comparative battleship strengths and comparative expenditure'. Garvin concluded his letter of warning to Northcliffe, 'Unless we are careful, Mulliner will spoil Blatchford.'[50]

At the end of the second week in December, the first of a series of ten daily articles by Robert Blatchford appeared in the *Mail*. His scaremongering raised the efforts of Mulliner and Beresford on to a completely different plain. 'What a trio to engineer a scare!' Fisher commented. 'A discredited Socialist, a shady company promotor and a blatant Admiral. What a Trinity!'[51] Blatchford was a talented writer and his simple, graphic style was ideally suited to popular journalism.[52] Initially his association with Northcliffe cost him dearly,[53] but when his ten articles were reissued as a pamphlet they sold like hot cakes to the tune of more than a million and a half. The reason for this was quite simple. People were eager to read the message that Blatchford so eloquently yet simply delivered.

> I write these articles because I believe that Germany is deliberately
> preparing to destroy the British Empire; and because I know that we are
> not ready or able to defend ourselves against a sudden and formidable
> attack. . . . At the present moment the whole country is in a ferment about
> the Budget and the Peers and the Election. It seems sheer criminal lunacy
> to waste time and strength in chasing such political bubbles when the
> existence of the Empire is threatened.[54]

The words could as well have been written by Northcliffe. A very large piece of salt needs to be taken with the sentiments expressed by the *Daily Mail* in its editorial accompanying Blatchford's final article, that it had been persuaded to publish only 'after the most careful consideration'. Marlowe, Wilson and the other key figures at Carmelite House, all recognised that Blatchford's contributions were sensational journalism – and very attractive commercially.

> Nothing that has appeared in the 'Daily Mail' in recent years has attracted
> more attention, has aroused more discussion or has been followed by
> our readers with closer interest. . . . His articles have been denounced in
> measured terms. . . . It has been said that they have been published to
> influence the elections. . . . They ought to influence the elections [for
> they] . . . point to a neglect by Ministers of national defence. Ministers
> would have nothing to fear if they had not reduced the British Navy and
> replied to Germany's immense naval preparations with half-measures, or
> something worse. In Blatchford's own words, the 'craven politicians of the
> Cabinet . . . realise our unreadiness but lack the moral courage to confess
> it'.[55]

From sympathisers and opponents alike, Blatchford's articles won a positive response. The *Manchester Guardian*, like most Liberal newspapers, dismissed them as a too-obvious yet typically sordid pre-election party manoeuvre by the Tories to drum up popular alarm for votes. 'Last April they were all anti-Germans and patriots, presently Dukes; then . . . beer as being more popular, then Protection, and now it is patriotism again. . . . Deliberate raking of the fires of hell for votes is an act of political depravity and no party extremity can excuse such behaviour.'[56] The king let it be known that he 'lamented Blatch-ford's violence', and Esher, as always taking his cue from his royal master, when he wrote to his son enclosed a copy of the *Daily Mail*, 'to show you the unscrupulousness of these people.... I don't think political crime can go much lower.' He had conveniently forgotten his own enthusiastic support for scare tactics nine months earlier. He could only suppose that Blatchford, 'a Socialist and self-advertising fellow', had been exploited by Northcliffe unwittingly.[57] But a letter from Charles Ottley pointed out that Blatchford's real appeal did not rest on any partisan, political basis. He had expressly said the country did not want Liberal or Unionist governments but a MAN.[58] 'His strength is that he knows what he wants and is not afraid to ask for it in plain language.... The burthen of the song is – compulsory service, a strong navy and a general raising of the standard of education and living of the masses of the British people.'[59]

Whatever reservations some might have entertained, Leo Maxse was abso-lutely delighted with the articles, particularly their condemnation of the government's policy of 'conciliation' towards Germany as 'FUNK', and Blatch-ford's description of Germany's policy as 'a bludgeon that fits the hand of a foot-pad'. His challenging solution to dissentients had been perfection – 'Arm or surrender . . . no middle course is open to us.' Maxse told Northcliffe how he had 'freely plundered' Blatchford's writings for the next issue of the *National Review*. 'They are so admirable and express views which I have been trying to express for the last ten years with such terseness and force that I could not resist borrowing freely.'[60]

From Berlin, Wile cabled Northcliffe: 'In a long experience . . . I do not recall a foreign journalistic event which so focussed the attention of the German press and public.'[61] German newspapers, great and small, metropolitan and provincial, of every political and religious persuasion, were as one in condemning Blatchford and questioning his sanity.[62] The Social Democratic *Vorwärts*, the Catholic, *Volks Zeitung* and the implacably Pan-German, *Taegliche Rundschau*, pronounced in unaccustomed unison that the *Daily Mail* had pub-lished Blatchford's call for naval and military armaments as 'an aid to Conserv-ative election demagogy'. When the German Chancellor made his anger with the anti-German tone adopted in the British election very evident to Ambas-sador Goschen, Grey suggested it would be best to explain the articles and speeches as 'not really anti-German but alarmist . . . to create a scare. . . . For this purpose it is essential to magnify the aspect of danger.' The Foreign Secretary avowed that he 'would not be driven off course by the "Daily Mail" . . . but for me or any one of us to attempt to moderate their writings and speeches would only lead to a redoubling of their efforts'.[63] The election campaign had taken the exact path that Lloyd George had predicted in October. 'Another concerted effort will be made to rouse a fresh naval and military panic to rush the Government into the criminal extravagance of unnecessary armaments by land and sea. There will be the usual crop of rumours about German plans and preparations.'[64]

In mid-December, with more than half Blatchford's 'Menace' articles pub-lished, Garvin suddenly produced a slashing leader in the *Observer* on Anglo-

German naval rivalry. Next day he wrote to Sandars: 'The Americans talk of an electioneering final as a "cannon-ball campaign!" Now, what's our cannon-ball? ... *The two-keels-to-one standard* ... would inspire enthusiasm in the party and would take the country.'[65] Here, Garvin claimed, was an issue that could be understood by 'the dullest elector'! In a word, he was advocating, specifically for purposes of party gain, the deliberate exploitation of the issue that was most likely to stampede the electorate into the Tory corral. Sandars was excited by Garvin's 'admirable' suggestion. 'If I were responsible I should not hesitate to use your 12 inch gun as the final shot when the enemy are sighted in the opening week of January, but I propose and others dispose. At all events, your view shall be well displayed before the only man who can adopt it with effect.'[66]

As good as his word, Sandars passed on Garvin's 'instruction' to Balfour, then temporarily recouping his energies in Scotland before a final bout of speech-making in the provinces. Garvin was not the only one forwarding advice to the Tory leader. Northcliffe had instructed H. W. Wilson to prepare a set of 'Notes on the Navy' that might be used by Balfour in his forthcoming speeches. On 3 January Northcliffe duly received a note of thanks for 'information admirably done'. Balfour, however, added a caveat. 'The difficulty I feel in dealing with the Navy on the platform is that it is hard to make the public understand the danger of the position without saying things about Germany which hardly seem discreet in the mouth of an ex-Prime Minister.'[67] What an admirable sense of moral propriety, responsibility and restraint Balfour's words suggest, yet they were as flatly contradicted by the speech he made the next day at Hanley as they were contrary to the spirit of the sly letter he posted to Garvin on 30 December which implied that the Liberals were involved in 'a little game with the Germans to come to an arrangement over naval armaments', so that they might retain office and 'undermine our criticisms on naval policy. I have no proofs', Balfour admitted, 'only suspicions: but you ... may be able to say something either to confirm or explode them.'[68]

As overture to a repeat performance of the naval scare campaign, the words of Balfour's Hanley speech could not have been more carefully calculated. He was sufficiently impudent to disclaim any intention, either by himself or his party, to use the navy as a vote catcher. He assured his audience that he spoke to them now on that subject only because it was an absolute necessity. With beguiling reluctance he admitted that the Liberals seemed to have squandered that naval supremacy they had been bequeathed by their responsible, patriotic, Unionist predecessors. Then followed a thirty-five minute harangue condemning the government's foreign and defence policies that ended upon a sensational high note.

> Go about at this moment if you will and consult the statesmen and
> diplomats of the lesser Powers and I am perfectly confident that you will
> find among them an absolute unanimity of opinion that a struggle sooner
> or later between this country and Germany is inevitable ... and ... we
> are predestined to succumb.

By any standards – even those set by Blatchford and Maxse – given the authority of his position and experience, Balfour's speech was a blatant piece of scaremongering.

For the remainder of the election campaign the whole of the Tory press concentrated upon the issue of the navy giving particular emphasis to the 'predestined' national débâcle *unless* more ships were built. Northcliffe's popular newspapers,[69] the *Daily Mail,* the *Evening News* and the *Sunday Despatch,* had always been disposed to give more attention to the navy and scaremongering stories about Germany than Pearson's newspapers, the *Daily Express,* the *Standard* and the *Evening Standard.* They, until mid-December, had unwaiveringly maintained protection as the key electoral issue. The *Express* was the first to break ranks, closely followed by the *Standard.* The naval issue soon dominated their news and opinion columns. In the country, Tory spokesmen demonstrated the same overwhelming interest in naval matters. If keen to demonstrate their patriotism – a quality that Cromer proudly and publicly asserted he shared with Blatchford – when stoking the fires of panic they were always at pains to assure their audiences, as had Balfour at Hanley, that they were not being alarmist simply to catch extra votes. There was not a single major Tory speech in January 1910 that was complete without some extended reference to the German menace and the need to increase the size of the navy. This metamorphosis did not impress Maxse. To Esher, he expressed his contempt for 'our chronically insouciant parliamentarians' who had done nothing until the last possible moment about 'the supreme question of National Defence'.[70] Fisher, recognising to whom credit was really due for the naval campaign, complimented Garvin, 'You have done great work for the Navy.'[71]

To counter the scaremongering, Liberal ministers reproved the Tories for 'plucking the feathers of the German's eagle's tail with war alarms . . . the last resort of men who see their game is lost'. In their attempts to disprove the claim that they had neglected the navy, their statements about the preparedness of the British battle fleet became increasingly provocative. 'There is not a German', Lloyd George boasted to a Grimsby audience, 'who does not know that if the German fleet in a moment of madness ever attempted to take us, that German Fleet would be at the bottom of the German Ocean in a very few hours.'[72] So much for the pacifist inclinations of the chief 'little navy' spokesman in the Cabinet. It seemed to underline the reason for Fisher's satisfaction that 'all and every naval agitation keeps the screw on Lloyd George'. He told Garvin that McKenna believed that the scare campaign had 'effectively crippled Lloyd George and Co as regards the Navy'.[73] The National Peace Council was right to claim that the final stage of the Tory election campaign was 'a base attempt to confuse judgment by exciting fear and jealousy of a friendly Power . . . and appeal to ignoble prejudice by an odious agitation'.[74]

Towards the end of the campaign, Garvin allowed his almost daily correspondence with Sandars of the previous four months to lapse. 'Do not misunderstand my silence this last great fortnight,' he wrote in reply to an anxious inquiry. 'Every bit of me was occupied by our business and by newspapers and by Northcliffe in one way or another . . . Northcliffe grows in my affections . . . if he is well and cheerful and assured of more enjoyment of life, he will do priceless things for us.'[75] The last shots in the election locker were to be exchanged between Northcliffe's *Times* and the German Ambassador. At a celebration of the Kaiser's birthday Metternich admitted that it was 'not easy to reply to the hallucinations of timorous souls. The mind that can conceive that we are only waiting the opportunity to fall upon any weaker Power is not open to reasonable argument.' Germany's conscience, he asserted, was clear. She had kept the peace of forty years. Nor did her *Weltpolitik* have any sinister connotation for it implied only 'the peaceful acquisition of new markets'. Germany did not aspire to becoming 'the strongest Power on the sea'. Her fleet, 'fixed by Act of Parliament', was designed to protect 'commercial and colonial interests only'. *The Times* questioned both Metternich's facts and his sincerity, but was promptly slapped down by the *Manchester Guardian. The Time*'s interpretation of the 1900 German Naval Law was 'garbled, demonstrably false and historically impossible. But why answer? Why not simply accept the word of a man of honour?'[76] By implication, the *Guardian* charged the Tory press and party with besmirching their honour by drumming up an unnecessary scare merely to capture votes.

Despite all, the Liberals retained their hold on government, though with a greatly reduced majority. Had the naval scare been an important determinant of voting behaviour? This is a difficult question to answer with any certainty. In a naval and dockyard constituency like Portsmouth, it was bound to have some effect, and there was a 20 per cent swing in favour of Beresford and his colleague, B. G. Falle, who were both returned to Parliament. But Portsmouth was a very particular constituency and, save in 1895, in the six previous general elections the swing there had always gone against the government. The southern English counties in January 1910 recorded the biggest rejection of Liberal members of any area, but the 'patriotic' appeal upon which the scaremongering campaign was built is difficult to separate from the immediate, parochial concern about unemployment in dockyards and arsenals. This might well have been a more potent factor in bringing back voters to the Tory fold after the exceptional triumph of the Liberals in 1906. Certainly the Tory *Western Morning News*, on the morning of the poll, bluntly warned its readers in Devonport and Plymouth that their prosperity would decline, 'unless there is a strong government determined to maintain our Navy . . . to repel aggression'. They were pointedly reminded of the dockyard discharges, 'immediately after the election of the Radicals . . . in 1906'.[77] But whatever influence the naval scare did or did not have in the constituencies, it undoubtedly affected thinking in the Cabinet. Nor did its influence end with the summoning of the new Parliament.

Eighteen months earlier, in July 1908, H. A. Gwynne had written to the leader of the Canadian Conservative party, R. L. Borden, to give him the views, 'not of the extremists on the war side . . . but . . . of moderate men' concerning Anglo-German relations and the naval rivalry between the two Great Powers.

Five years ago the more thoughtful and reasonable of our politicians . . . did not pay attention to the somewhat extravagant talk of publicists on both sides as to the possibility of a conflict. Within the last year, the increase of the German Fleet and the feeling that there is a *National* movement in Germany towards greater expansion has caused us all . . . to look upon the German danger as something which is at least within the realms of practical politics. . . . [The moderate man] is inclined to believe that the German danger is one that every month becomes more menacing. . . . The German Government and Nation believe that a strong Navy is absolutely necessary. . . . This strong Navy she is obtaining with phenomenal rapidity and we here feel that a crisis is not very far distant. At any rate, whether right or wrong, the thoughtful man in England, of whatever political complexion, feels that Germany is a great and growing danger to England.

In the City . . . the feeling is much accentuated. . . . They look upon the possibility of a conflict between England and Germany as something certain.[78]

Gwynne, earlier than others, had perceived the possibilities of manipulating the naval question to the electoral advantage of the Tories. At the Croydon by-election in March 1909, caused by Arnold-Forster's death, Col. Sir Robert Trotter Hermon-Hodge, a candidate who in the past had enjoyed very mixed fortunes as member for Accrington and then Henley, added more than three and a half thousand to the Tory vote campaigning on the slogan, 'We want eight and we won't wait.' Gwynne had written to Sandars the day after the declaration of the poll that if Balfour chose to take up the naval issue, not only would he 'save the country from a great danger', but also, '*secure for many years the supremacy of the party*'.[79] The naval scare that spring did nothing to diminish public apprehension about Germany – the deliberate intention of some at least of its fomenters. In public they justified their campaign on the ground of national interest, but clearly they saw the issue in terms of party calculation and advantage.

The German Chancellor, Bülow, in August 1909 was replaced by Bethmann-Hollweg. Hatzfeldt compared the new Chancellor with his predecessor. 'Bülow, though probably very pleasant with you,' he told the British Ambassador, 'was always a bitter enemy of England. You couldn't trust him an inch. . . . You will find Bethmann the exact contrary; he is fond of England, and he is as honest and single-minded a man as is to be found in Germany.'[80] Even the notoriously anti-German Tyrrell told the German chargé d'affaires in London that with Bülow out of the way he hoped for a certain détente between their two countries.[81] Almost immediately after coming into office, Germany's new Chancellor sought a renewal of the previous year's naval negotiations between the two countries that had earlier proved abortive. The conversations begun in August 1909 had been temporarily abandoned when the Lords rejected Lloyd George's budget in November. Grey then instructed Goschen that further negotiations would have to wait until after the election in January.[82]

In his annual report on Germany for 1909, Goschen concisely summarised the state of German opinion in the pre-election period.

[From Bethmann-Hollweg's appointment] till the publication of Mr Blatchford's articles in the 'Daily Mail' there was generally speaking considerable improvement in the relations between the two countries. . . . During the last half of the year there was a strong desire, both on the part of the Imperial Government and a not inconsiderable portion of the public to come to an understanding with Great Britain. . . . Mr Blatchford's articles . . . and it must be added, some of the political speeches founded upon them, caused the greatest indignation. . . . [83]

On New Year's Day, 1910, the Kaiser told Goschen how very angry his Chancellor was with the anti-German tone of many election speeches. Blatchford's articles he described as 'very mischievous and singularly ill-timed', and expressed the hope that after the election 'the wave of anti-German feeling would subside and no more be heard of it'.[84] Three months later, William was still talking about 'the election naval scare'. He maintained that 'Nothing approaching [it] had taken place in England since the years immediately following the Crimean War.' The scare 'seemed to extend from "the Dukes to the lowest in the land"'. He instanced a speech made by Cawdor in Leeds which had linked Home Rule with the German threat! Not without reason, the Kaiser professed himself to be puzzled by the state of mind that could 'contemplate the possible conversion of Belfast into a German naval base'.[85]

It was only with the greatest reluctance and when urgently pressed by ministers that the Foreign Office responded in July 1910 to another German initiative to push on with the naval discussions. A half-hearted memorandum on the subject was eventually delivered by Goschen to Bethmann-Hollweg on 14 August. The eighteen months of intermittent negotiations, not surprisingly, ended without achieving anything.[86] It proved impossible to recapture the earlier mood that hinted at possible compromise. The atmosphere had been totally poisoned by the naval scare. The general disposition of key personnel among the permanent staff of the Foreign Office had always been distrustful. Eyre Crowe, fearing a trap in anything the Germans suggested, must have been delighted with the attitude displayed by Arthur Nicolson, Charles Hardinge's successor as Permanent Under Secretary. Privately Sir Arthur rejoiced at the government's decision to lay down yet more Dreadnoughts, and insisted vehemently to a dinner companion in June 1911 that so long as he was head of the Foreign Office, England would *never* be friends with Germany.[87]

In November 1909, the Admiralty Board had considered that four Dreadnoughts would be sufficient for the 1910–11 estimates. A month later this had been increased to six. A Cabinet crisis was successfully avoided by everyone agreeing to a programme of five capital ships for 1910 and the same for 1911. For the first time, the naval estimates were more than forty million pounds. The *Daily News* complained of how, 'The appetite of this monster of armaments grows by what it feeds on. It is the creation of irrational hates and craven fears.' That same day, the *Daily Mail,* though it considered the estimates as 'far from ideal' accepted they were 'as much as we can expect from a Radical Government'.[88] Generally the Tory press, like the party in the Commons, showed little of its usual belligerent spirit. There was even some confusion in the Tory ranks when Arthur Lee rejected the idea of 'two-keels-to-one' as a notion of 'wild men'. His outburst made Esher extremely angry.[89] Lord Charles

Beresford proved a very tame warrior once inside the House, and those contributions he did make to debates were incoherent. It was as though all passion for the navy had at last been spent. 'After the election merely the pale wraith of the Spring scare and its successors remained.'[90]

With the great constitutional issue of the fate of the House of Lords dominating everything else, only Northcliffe's newspapers attempted with any consistent purpose to keep the naval issue alive in 1910. In an earlier exchange of letters with Arthur Mee, Northcliffe had delineated the German character as 'envious and suspicious'. He argued that wars 'nearly all begin by suspicions, and suspicions are best allayed by saying nothing', sentiments one would expect more naturally from a civil servant than a newspaper man.[91] That he did not heed his own advice was probably due as much as anything to the constant efforts of H. W. Wilson, described by the *Daily Mail*'s editor, Marlowe, as 'the mental back-bone' of the *Mail*. Scarcely a letter from Wilson to Northcliffe or Lady Northcliffe did not allude to some aspect of the navy. While other commentators seemed preoccupied with domestic politics, he pursued the Dreadnought question with as much alarmist energy as in the previous year. In April 1910 he wrote:

> There are now ten Dreadnoughts building in the Mediterranean for
> Austria and Italy, and if the Germans bait their trap well, they may on
> the great day have all these ten ships on their side. . . . The French
> Admiral, Fournier, has just written a most excellent book on our position.
> He warns us of something which we are apt to forget; that the Triple
> Alliance is angling for Turkey, and with Turkey on its side, will be so
> strong as to paralyze Russia, and this of course means paralyzing France.
> The truth is that the only chance for England is to arm to the utmost with
> the utmost possible speed when the situation is saved. But she is not doing
> it and perhaps nothing but a tremendous disaster will awaken her. With the
> Radicals there is no hope of getting a strong army or the naval programme
> which we need. With the Unionists it will be difficult enough. . . .[92]

Throughout the summer Wilson provided a steady stream of feature articles in the *Daily Mail* on the general theme of 'Is Our Navy Ready for War?'[93] In July and October, A. T. Mahan published a series of essays which were subsequently republished as a pamphlet entitled 'Britain and the German Navy'. After a visit to Germany, William Maxwell, formerly the *Standard*'s Berlin correspondent, published five alarmist articles in the *Mail* in August and September. Wilson was still worried, and had worked himself into a lather of concern.

> The Ministerial statements in the House of Commons underestimate the
> advantage Germany has gained. Grey's statement however admits that
> the new German ships may be of a type completely to outmatch our own.
> Our best gunnery people say they are such, and the range tables of the new
> Krupp guns which have recently been secured by the Intelligence
> Department, staggered the Admiralty. This last is private. . . .[94]

With Northcliffe's agreement, Wilson promoted a campaign in the *Daily Mail*, supported by Maxse's *National Review*, which for the last six months of the year advocated a naval loan 'to finance a two-keel-to-one programme fixed for a term of years . . . that will maintain the supremacy of our fleet which must be regarded as a permanent feature in our national policy'.[95]

The little navy group of Radicals in the parliamentary Liberal party, now re-emerging, having first been crushed by the 1909 panic and then decimated by the election, because they sought cuts in armament expenditure were branded by the *Daily Mail* as, 'the friends of every country but their own' and told that they were 'directly responsible for the very existence of the evil which they profess to deplore'.[96] The *Mail* even gave prominence to the 'exploded gas bag' Beresford when he wrote to Asquith claiming that 'if steps are not taken . . . the naval defence of the Empire will be fraught with a danger whose gravity I believe to be difficult to exaggerate'. Asquith replied that the government was 'fully alive to the paramount importance of maintaining our naval supremacy', but the *Mail* still deplored the fact that the Prime Minister was hampered in his national duty by 'a coterie of Little Englanders in his Cabinet and his party'.[97]

In the period immediately before the second general election of 1910, the *Daily Mail* once more recruited Blatchford as 'a very present help in time of trouble', but his series of letters on 'The Greatest Issue of All' had nothing like the effect of his previous efforts, while his disclaimer to McKenna's charge that he had obviously been recruited to encourage Tory votes with his blatant scaremongering was more vigorous than persuasive.[98] If Blatchford's aim was, as he claimed, 'to challenge the ignorance and indifference of the public to matters of foreign policy and defence', his audience showed no sign of responding. In the second election of 1910, though Northcliffe and Garvin would have had it otherwise, defence was never an issue.

Garvin had urged Sandars that the question of sea power should once more be a powerful and important element in the Tory campaign. 'I entreat you to tell your chief how dominant I find to be in many typical minds this question of greater security for naval defence.'[99] This time Balfour did not respond. A month earlier, the Tory leader had attempted unsuccessfully to reignite the scare issue in a speech at Glasgow. This had been in response to pressure from Esher who was concerned by rumours that there was a plot afoot to push McKenna out of the Admiralty at a time when the Board, with Arthur Wilson as First Sea Lord, was a much less dynamic force than it had been under Fisher. 'There is much to be said', Esher had written to Balfour, 'for again rubbing in the navy.'[100] Unfortunately, the man whose bacon Esher thought to save, effectively quashed Balfour's claim that there remained 'a lamentable and dangerous margin' between British and German capital ship production.

The better relationship between the Tories and their press that had been so painstakingly constructed a year earlier collapsed during the second general election of 1910. In part, this was a consequence of a growing distrust by party officials of Garvin's influence.[101] There were also journalists who did not look too kindly upon Garvin's position within the party. Charles Graves, assistant editor of the *Spectator*, wrote to tell Maxse how he wished he would 'keep [his] friend in order. . . . I *always* distrusted Garvin's judgment while admitting his brilliancy. His advocacy of Jacky Fisher strengthened my distrust and now that he has returned to his vomit – Home Rule – he may be written down as a purple ass.'[102] Not every journalist would have agreed with Graves's cruel and particular comments. Wickham Steed wrote to tell Garvin:

> What pleasure it gives a working journalist like me to see a working journalist like you lead the political thought and inspire the soundest elements of the soundest party in the country.
> I, of course, can only judge things *en gros* and might differ from you on minor questions, but I am deeply thankful to you for vindicating the power of the press when it is served by a fearless pen and a clear brain. . . .
> May your courageous fight have its full reward.[103]

Wickham Steed's last comment referred to Garvin's 'die-hard' attitude over the constitutional wrangle with the House of Lords, and it was this issue rather than defence that prompted Kennedy Jones to tell Esher he thought that Garvin and Northcliffe had 'temporarily smashed the party'.[104] This claim Esher dismissed as 'an exaggeration', but he told Sandars he did not think Garvin's violence a source of strength. Three days later he again reported to Balfour's secretary on the same subject. 'Garvin (entre nous) is mad. . . . KJ whom I saw yesterday, thinks Garvin a lunatic although a genius.'[105]

Northcliffe, who never took kindly to his advice being ignored, was incensed with the Tory leaders for disregarding the electoral tactics he had so clearly delineated in his papers. Frustrated and angry he wrote to Andrew Bonar Law. If the Tories wanted to allot blame for not succeeding in the election, then they should look to the party and not to the press.

> During this election, some of my workers, though loyal and keen, have practically revolted; and from the newspaper standpoint, there are very serious personal issues at stake. The Unionist Party has been accustomed always to regard the newspapers as a sort of door-mat; but they have just awakened to the fact that the newspapers are of increasing importance as part of the machine.
> Speaking of the Press as a whole, not including my own, it is a most efficient part of the organisation. It is notorious that the Unionist Press is more efficient than the Liberal Press. It is equally true that our organisations are not as efficient as the Liberal organisations. It is depressing work criticising worthy, but incompetent people, who are doing their best, but I propose, with much respect, telling Mr Balfour what I know about this matter.[106]

A week elapsed before Northcliffe wrote to Balfour and his anger had then cooled. He contented himself with observing 'from a careful study of the German Press – of what is printing and also what is not printing – that our friends across the North Sea are in no wise slackening their preparations while we are amusing ourselves with an unnecessary General Election'. Wearily Balfour placed the responsibility upon the Liberal leadership who still held office as the election had made no significant change in the balance of power between the two great parties. 'A propos what you say about the Germans. I still trust that the Government will give us good Naval Estimates. It all turns, I suppose, on whether they are more afraid of the Germans or their own tail – an unhappy position for the rulers of a great country!'[107]

Whatever concerns were expressed in private,[108] in public debate the arsenal of political ill-will and strife was replete with domestic squabbles. William Heaford, in the December 1910 issue of *Concord*, found it 'amusing to reflect that the imperial fire-eaters who have been thinking in Dreadnoughts and pining for Conscription in order to defend the United Kingdom against a phantom foe from without, have largely superseded their German war scare by an English Civil War scare'.[109] Heaford was referring to Curzon's warning that the Belfast Unionists were raising funds for civil conflict.[110] It was all a very far cry from Cawdor's naval scaremongering of the previous December when he had warned that any minute Belfast might become a German port.

Conscription, or how to lose friends and votes

A British tariff would lead to a commercial war with Germany which could easily become . . . a military and naval war. I do not see how we can go in for protection without some form of compulsory service and that I suppose is impossible.

Tyrrell to Spring Rice

As for the *Army*, though I believe heart and soul in National Service, I have carefully confined myself to showing that Haldane's scheme can't work.

Garvin to Northcliffe

Admit compulsion and any fool can make an army. I am convinced that the time for compulsion has come, and that the National Service League plan is the right one, but please do not credit that it will help us on the Meuse at the first go off.

Repington to Maxse

The shock of the Boer war had dented national complacency and directed attention to the urgent need for army reform. There seemed to be a general determination at last to do something. In the early days of hostilities, Edward Lawson confidently asserted to Garvin that 'The general public . . . has made up its mind to con the actual lessons of this war, to improve our general organisation that all we have lacked will be made good and that in no detail of defence shall any European Power be allowed to surpass us.'[1] That was a large claim and unfortunately the various schemes that had been proposed, first by St John Brodrick and then by H. O. Arnold-Forster, had proved impracticable. Essentially, Brodrick's scheme had been over-ambitious in the face of the demands for economy combined with the arguments of the 'blue water' strategists; while Forster's scheme proved too niggardly as it would never produce sufficient long-service troops for India. When it seemed that every variety of combination, distribution and juxtaposition of regulars, reserves, militia and volunteers had been tried, it still remained that the army was incapable of fulfilling its required strategic role. This included, after 1905, in addition to the traditional task of securing the boundaries of empire and the homeland against invasion, the secret plan to fight alongside the French should Britain's entente partner be attacked by the Germans.

The 1903 Elgin Commission had bluntly insisted that 'no military system [could] be satisfactory which [did] not contain powers of expansion outside the limit of the regular forces of the Crown'.[2] Because public opinion seemed as firmly attached as ever to the voluntarist principle, the obvious answer to the continuing conundrum – to conscript any extra troops that might be required – was not really available to politicians. In any event, this 'solution' merely begged another and technically more difficult question. How *many* men would be needed? The answer to that question depended upon what exactly Britain was intent to defend, against which enemy and with what urgency. Was it to secure the north-west frontier of India against the Russians, Britain from invasion by the Germans, or perhaps, to support the French against a German attack in Europe? Any or all these possibilities, separately or in combination, suggested very different answers.[3]

The National Service League did not concern itself with such technical problems supposing that conscription was the specific to cure all ills. This was their panacea that would arrest the decline of Britain's international status as a Power as surely as it would help promote imperial unity. The league, however, was as much concerned with the quality of its potential recruits as their quantity. That, they supposed, was a worrying aspect that also needed urgent treatment.[4] Members never talked of conscription overtly in public, for it 'was the one word more than any other that aroused the loathing of John Bull'.[5] Thus, to reluctant politicians and public alike, the NSL spokesmen invariably prefaced their exhortations with the assurance that their advocacy of 'national service' or 'universal training' did *not* mean conscription. They defined conscription as 'long-term compulsory service based on the drawing of lots'.

After a meeting with Roberts, the NSL's President, Arnold-Forster wrote in his diary:

> The NSL have not really the courage of their opinions. They do mean conscription ie 'compulsory' service as well as 'compulsory' training, but they dare not say so for fear of becoming unpopular. Hence they advocate training without service, which is a farce. . . . They know that if they were to propose conscription for foreign service, which is the logical outcome of the whole business, they would utterly fail to move public opinion.[6]

Conscious of the hostility aroused in the public's mind even by mention of the dread word, in the second edition of George Shee's best-selling book, *The Briton's First Duty*, the sub-title was changed from 'the case for conscription' to 'the case for universal training', a semantic nicety that roused Col. E. C. Browne to rage against

> Any form of universal training for war taking the nature of compulsion is stigmatised as 'slavish', 'un-English', 'an attack on the liberty of the subject', 'militarism', 'compulsion' 'coercion' and so forth. Not one of these expressions is applicable to universal service to the State. . . .
> These cries are 'wind and fury' meaning nothing; and will not stand the test of examination.[7]

While the public was prepared to listen with a measure of respect and not a little affection to what Lord Roberts might have to say on the subject, it remained indifferent to NSL propaganda. 'I attribute little importance to these leagues, manifestos and so forth,' Repington told George Clarke in February 1906. 'They all vanish into the limbo of things forgotten once the government programme is before the country.'[8] Repington, and for that matter, Roberts, pinned their main hope for the future upon the efforts of Haldane, the newly appointed Liberal Minister for War.

When he formed his Cabinet, Campbell-Bannerman was under no illusion about the difficulties facing Haldane.[9] Malicious gossip even suggested that it had been these difficulties that had prompted Sir Henry to give Haldane the War Office as a suitable 'reward' for his part in the abortive Relugas compact. That plot had been designed by the three Liberal Imperialists, Asquith, Grey and Haldane, to banish Campbell-Bannerman to the Lords.[10] Somehow Haldane was obliged to find an answer to the perennial problem of the auxiliary forces that had defeated both his immediate Tory predecessors. The Prime Minister reminded him that 'the inevitable result of failure' would be an 'agitation for compulsion', a prospect that would immediately stir the volatile Radical element in the party into open revolt.

With his Territorial and Reserve Forces Bill introduced to the House in February 1907, Haldane proposed to reorganise the second line forces into a Territorial Army.[11] Many Liberals were afraid that Haldane's Bill was a covert design intended to lead to compulsion. The Tories claimed his scheme was no good as it would never attract sufficient recruits. It was due to Balfour's efforts – and the Tory leader was seeing much of Haldane at the time for they agreed on the approximate number of troops required for all reasonable contingencies – that the measure was eased in its passage through Parliament. It was this support by Balfour – so markedly contrasting with his own experience – that particularly aroused Arnold-Forster's wrath. In a series of letters and articles to the press, the ex-Minister for War poured out his criticisms of the Bill, while his friend, Maxse, railed at the Tory party in Parliament for 'supporting patriotism by proxy' and not exposing 'the great Haldane humbug'.

In his dealings with Haldane, Maxse revealed the worst side of his nature. He hunted the Minister of War, remorselessly, and after the outbreak of war, irrationally. Maxse's bitter vendetta reveals certain distinct prejudices he shared with other contemporary Tory critics. There is that strand of anti-intellectualism of which Haldane, dubbed by his own leader, Schopenhauer, was always the main butt. In countless cartoons, Haldane was portrayed as a fat don surrounded by or atop a pile of philosophical tomes one of which would inevitably be titled 'Cant'. Maxse also shared the general distrust and dislike of lawyers; casuists who for a fee would defend any cause; pedants, too entangled by precedent to protect the nation's interests. The Liberal Cabinet was stuffed with lawyers and when they dismissed Lord Roberts's case for invasion and the need for conscription, Maxse pictured them deprecating the landing of a German Army Corps in England while Haldane applied to Chancery for a writ of injunction to restrain the invading force. Maxse, on occasion, demonstrated anti-Semitism and railed against 'the Hebrew influence', though he did choose to distinguish between 'patriotic National Jews' and 'International Jews'. These last, he seems to have supposed, were particularly influential in the councils of the Liberal party and were 'the enemies of England and the more or less avowed agents of Germany'. If Maxse's prejudice against Jews seems a strange bias to rehearse in relation to Haldane, we have only to recall Northcliffe's favoured 'joke' when twigging that minister: 'I am sure you must be a Jew, you have such a Scotch name.' As a Scot, Haldane touched a common prejudice among Tory writers that the 'greatness' of Britain was synonymous with its Anglo-Saxonism, and had nothing to do with the 'Celtic fringe', again so well represented in the Liberal party. The price paid by the country for that party's indulgence towards the Irish, Welsh and Scots, Maxse insisted, was to deliver 'a once great imperial Power, trussed and helpless' into Germany's hands. The Liberal party had reduced Britain to 'an island in the German Ocean, governed by Scotsmen, kicked by Irishmen and plundered by Welshmen'.[12]

Though Haldane's Bill had successfully negotiated its parliamentary hurdle, the minister recognised his Territorial scheme would stand or fall by the number of recruits it attracted. Repington, who had loyally supported the measure in its passage through Parliament, warned Haldane that it was 'the last chance for voluntary service. Should it fail again, the country is not likely to ask another War Minister to devise a new scheme on the voluntary basis.'[13] It was to encourage recruitment that Haldane established a department at the War Office instructed to supply suitable items of information to any newspaper that demonstrated friendliness towards his scheme. This immediately attracted unfavourable comment from Arnold-Forster.[14] Haldane was cheeky enough to thank the *Daily Mail* in the Commons for popularising his scheme which did nothing for the minister's image of trustworthiness among his own backbenchers. Actually, Northcliffe's feelings towards the Territorials were equivocal. He admitted to Garvin:

> I was not at all keen on the Territorial boom, and only consented in order to show what an immense amount of pushing a paper would have to do to get a miserable eleven thousand men. I have no means of knowing Mr Haldane's secret mind on the subject, but his brain is one of the best balanced that I have encountered, and I dare say he knows as well as we that the inevitable break down of the Voluntary Territorial system will lead towards some form of compulsory service.[15]

Northcliffe insisted to Marlowe that he expected 'to get conscription through the comparative failure of the Territorials', and instructed the *Mail*'s editor to 'resist any inclination to urge us to aid recruiting outside the London Territorials'.[16] Northcliffe still remembered vividly the response of his readers to the *Daily Mail*'s first overt stand in favour of conscription in May 1904. In response to an editorial inquiry, 'Can a half-armed people survive when the whole of the rest of the world is trained to arms?', in a single week he had received more than five thousand letters of abuse. 'Conscription', he had then been obliged to admit, 'was opposed not merely by Pacifists and Little Englanders but the overwhelming majority of commercial men and of the working classes.' He had decided that caution was the more prudent part than valour when his newspapers dealt with a subject that aroused such violent and wide-spread opposition.[17]

Repington in *The Times* was Haldane's staunchest and most consistent ally in the press. So long as the military correspondent continued to advertise the Territorials as 'the best possible scheme in existing circumstances', Haldane did not resent the added assertion that eventually the country would have to accept conscription. As to Repington's further rider that the scheme 'left the door invitingly open for future progress',[18] Haldane recognised his organisation could, if required at some future date, receive and train conscripts. He was not above admitting in public that he sympathised with those who asked, 'Why don't you ask Parliament to impose an obligation on all to serve for Home Defence?'[19] It was typical of this supreme casuist that while his Territorial Army scheme was intended to reinforce the Expeditionary Force, he sold it to his Cabinet colleagues, to the Commons and the public as a Home Defence system.[20]

The change of government in November 1905 had not disturbed Roberts. He actually told Kitchener he supposed a Liberal administration 'far more likely to introduce a measure of compulsory training than the [Tories]'.[21] He informed Milner that he knew the minister was grateful for what the National Service League was doing and supposed any differences between the NSL and Haldane were of detail and emphasis only. Milner was prepared to go so far as to admit his uncertainty to Garvin, whether 'at heart Haldane does not believe in conscription'. It was for this reason that he declined to 'weigh in' with an article for *Outlook*. 'I am sure that for the cause we both have at heart, it is better for *me* not to join in the scrimmage over Haldane but to keep, for the present at least, in the somewhat stiller waters of theory. . . . I want to steer clear of seeming to attack him or to side with his fellow shirkers. . . . I am not criticizing your line, but the roles are somewhat necessarily distinct.'[22] Among Roberts's closest associates, the irascible General Henry Wilson never for a moment believed that Haldane was an ally of the conscriptionist cause in disguise. He never thought well of the minister and quoted Beresford's opinion of Haldane with relish – 'an oily customer . . . if you put a wick in his head he would burn for three years'. All Haldane's schemes, Wilson pronounced, were 'wild-cat', or 'quite the worst, the most impractical of any that I have ever heard'. Totally unsympathetic to Haldane's problems, and quite uncaring of the complexities of political manoeuvering, Wilson was convinced 'the only possible way of making any material change for the better is by compulsion. These miserable politicians won't face the problem and resort to any subterfuge except the truth.'[23]

It is true that Haldane had a remarkable capacity, at different times, to be all things to all men, but Roberts's confusion about the minister's intentions was because he had no intellectual grip of what exactly was going on. With unconscious humour, even his friend and admirer, F. S. Oliver, emphasised the Field Marshall's 'highest intellectual quality was his instinct . . . which he trusted with unshakeable confidence'.[24] When it came to understanding party politics, Newton told Strachey, 'The old boy knows as little about them as a

Patagonian.'[25] There was every reason, therefore, for Repington to suppose that with Roberts as its President the NSL would achieve nothing until such time as it could persuade a party leader – and it would have to be Arthur Balfour – to back its policy. Only reluctantly was Strachey won to this view. He had earlier insisted to Roberts, 'the very last thing we want is to make National Service a party matter'. He was, however, prepared to admit that as the feeling in favour of national training had grown so much in popularity, 'If Balfour, as head of the Unionist party, were to set himself against it, he would lose a great deal of support.' But it has always to be remembered that Strachey's early advocacy of conscription was based on its 'moral, physical and intellectual benefits to the nation ... quite apart from military considerations'. He was anxious that conscription should not be thought of as 'some kind of fad external to the essential life of the nation which party politicians may pass over as something below their notice like anti-vaccination or vegetarianism or so forth'. For Strachey, the case for conscription was moral as much as military or strategic – nothing less than the spiritual regeneration of the nation. This, he was at pains to explain to Roberts, was the true message of his book, *A New Way of Life*.[26]

Such different aims and emphases among sympathisers and members of the NSL caused considerable confusion which was reflected in the changing programme the league sponsored at different times. One proposal that maintained its favour with many league members was copied from the Swiss system of short-term conscription originally outlined by Camille Favre in his book, *A Model for a National Militia* (1904) and adapted by George Shee. Initially the demand had been that all men under the age of 40 should be trained for a year. The year was then whittled down to two months under canvas with fourteen days' training in each of three succeeding years. Two months became three and eventually four and then was coupled with military training in schools. The encouragement of rifle shooting as a sport remained the only constant factor. To limit the period of initial training to months rather than a year was a cause of considerable consternation to those who, like Lord Cardigan, from their Volunteer experience, considered so short a period 'would be no more good than a headache'. The league, he told Maxse, either should support 'a proper measure of conscription with compulsion for foreign service', or, 'much better accept Haldane'. Maxse was the last person on earth inclined to render any aid to the minister he had described as 'filling many gasometers with talk' to provide, 'not the Army of our ideals ... but the British Army of German ideals'. As for the Territorials, they were fit only for ridicule. 'If you disapprove so much of the auxiliary army, why didn't you advise their destruction long ago?' Cardigan asked Maxse pertinently. 'All Haldane has done is try and form an army out of them. You say that he has destroyed the Militia? They were not an army but 90,000 infantry who shot very badly and were recruited from the very lowest class. ... Even now, to keep the army up to its present size, we enlist a lot of riff-raff.'[27] Maxse would not have his wrath with Haldane assuaged by any rational argument. He attempted unavailingly to recruit Austen Chamberlain to join in his censures. 'I believe Haldane's scheme to be both bad and costly,' Chamberlain agreed, 'but I can stir no feeling against it.'[28] Quite undeterred, Maxse continued to rage in the *National Review* against 'Mr Haldane's Apologetics', and quoted *Temps* 'for a continental view of our so-called Territorial Army! "Great Britain is a comparatively useless ally as her military weakness renders her impotent to afford effectual assistance in keeping the dreaded German aggression at bay." ' Maxse also approvingly published the epitaph that Garvin had coined for Haldane's schemes: 'He saved a million, and lost an Empire.'[29]

Maxse campaigning against Haldane in the *National Review* was one thing: Garvin attacking the Secretary of State for War in his *Observer* was an altogether more formidable and dangerous proposition. Garvin never seems to have entertained a particularly good opinion of Haldane's capacities, a prejudice that was eagerly reinforced by Fisher who repeatedly asserted that the minister's schemes were bound to damage the navy. Less important, but as persistent, were the efforts of friends and fellow journalists like Maxse and H. W. Wilson, who retailed stories about the minister that did less than justice either to the merits of his schemes or his personal patriotism. Another important influence on Garvin's thinking about Haldane was Arnold-Forster. Haldane's most implacable parliamentary foe was frequently consulted by Garvin on military questions as an expert adviser, and the Tory ex-minister was not inclined to say anything complimentary about his successor if he could help it.

Milner had first brought Garvin into close touch with Roberts, arranging a meeting between them in October 1905. 'It is lamentable', he had written, 'that Roberts's propaganda has so far made little impression. He means well but he does not know how to make his advocacy effective. If you could show him how, and no one, I should think, could do it better, it would be a national service.'[30] Garvin was impressed both by Roberts's demeanour and his ideas. He became a sturdy public advocate for the earl, drafting detailed notes for many of his better speeches, writing many of the letters that appeared over Roberts's name in the press, and even being prepared to show an untypical patience when, from time to time, he received pedantic and turgid instructions from George Shee, the NSL's Secretary.[31]

Roberts was not slow to appreciate the advantage of having Garvin as an ally. For this if no other reason, he took considerable interest in his health and professional fortunes. Almost as often as he encouraged Garvin to give up smoking, he inquired anxiously about his future prospects. When Garvin left the *Outlook* in 1906, Roberts trusted that he would 'find a worthy berth ... one in which you can be of as great service to the Nation as you have been hitherto'. Garvin never wanted for work and there was always the *Daily Telegraph* where his opinions on the army were rather more welcome than his thoughts on Germany. When Roberts read his frequent articles on the need for compulsion, 'as always with the greatest delight', he admitted it made him regret all the more 'that you are not the head of an influential paper'.[32] With his appointment as editor of the *Observer*, Garvin had at last secured a platform in the national press that he was to make worthy of his outstanding talents as a journalist – even if Chirol's initial frosty observation when he heard the news was to write, 'I should scarcely have thought it a matter on which to congratulate *you*.'[33]

Garvin was aware of very serious disadvantages in championing Roberts's campaign for compulsory service in the *Observer*. It was a very different proposition from giving aid to Sir John Fisher's schemes. He did not make light of these difficulties in a letter to Roberts.

> From a business point of view, National Service is not yet a cause that
> arouses universal enthusiasm. But if you think the cause might on the
> whole be served in this way, I shall grapple with the whole question one
> of these weeks and do my best to arouse as much interest throughout
> the country on behalf of the Army as was excited a few weeks ago by the
> 'Observer' articles on the Navy. Altogether, apart from that, it will always
> be my pleasure to do what I can.[34]

Inevitably, in the first year of running his new property, many urgent and absorbing technical and business problems distracted Garvin. In November, he wrote to explain to Maxse how 'taking command of waterlogged newspapers always means a lot of dreary work. It takes months of sheer pumping before one can sail the ship neatly and fight her well.' The naval metaphor perhaps unconsciously betrayed where his first loyalty and priority lay. Nevertheless, he insisted that he 'hoped to wage a stronger battle henceforward' for the army.[35] Certainly there appeared to be no lack of will, for he had told Roberts that it was his wish to turn 'a searchlight of glaring clearness upon the actual condition of the Army.... I hope it may be possible to see you before taking action, and I shall do nothing without your approval, and, if you will allow me, will submit all matter in proof before it appears.'[36]

To have the wholehearted support of the *Observer*, which under Garvin's leadership was rapidly assuming a position of considerable political influence, was particularly appreciated by Roberts. He had not been impressed by recent comments in *The Times* on military matters. It 'ought to be leading opinion'. Instead it blew 'hot and cold in turn, at one time advocating one policy, and at another time, another'. He addressed his complaints to A. F. Walter who did not accept kindly the assertion that his newspaper was giving 'undue prominence to the simply disastrous views of a little party of extreme Blue Water doctrinaires'. Nor would he accept Roberts's claim that *The Times* had 'no settled defence policy'. Walter simply ignored Roberts's offer of 'assistance in the matter of defence', replying politely if frigidly that he considered it 'a compliment to be placed in possession of [Roberts's] views', but 'beg[ged] to say that [*The Times*] already ha[d] a settled defence policy ... which may be broadly stated thus:'

> First, the Two Power standard for the Navy: Second a strong and sufficient
> Army for Foreign Service: Third, a large Territorial Army, as well-
> trained, equipped and organized as maybe for Home Defence. Personally,
> I should like to see every man in the country brought up to discipline
> and trained in a certain measure to bear arms in defence of his country
> – But we cannot expect this just yet.[37]

Garvin shared Roberts's poor opinion of *The Times*. The newspaper was 'weak and tardy' when it 'ought to be a national organ doing moral sentry duty for the Empire'.[38] His confidence in the attitude of *The Times* on defence questions was further shaken when, a few days later, he received an unexpected letter from Repington. The letter began happily enough with a complimentary reference to Garvin's work on the *Observer*. 'I congratulate you upon the proof you have given of how one man can transform a paper in one day. Whether we like it or not, and whether we agree with you or not, we have to read you and you have made the British Sabbath almost bearable.' Then Repington turned abruptly to his main business.

> I am sorry to see you condemn the Territorial Army ... because I fear this may discount your views upon the subject of a more truly national Army hereafter. There are already serious signs of financial stringency and if your cry and Lord Roberts' is taken up, I fear we will not get our artillery material distributed over the country. I think it is wiser to wait a bit before starting a serious campaign for compulsory training, perhaps six months or a year, so that voluntary effort may have a fair field. Après nous verrons. We shall be in a much stronger position if we have the whole organization laid out, and money spent upon it than if we have to start from scratch. A little patience, that is my idea, and then we ought to bring about a dozen press people who count together, and all start together. Please weigh this.[39]

Of Repington arguments, the most persuasive was the financial. Among others, Arnold-Forster had reminded Garvin on several occasions that as there was insufficient money to go around, the Liberal government would necessarily test its defence programme against financial criteria rather than the needs of the Services.[40] Garvin, however, was stung by Repington's reproach that he had been too precipitate. He told him, 'You know that with regard to the Services and foreign affairs I take my responsibilities rather seriously and never write without great deliberation on these matters. ... I have come to the conclusion that Haldane's scheme will be a total failure. Right or wrong that is now my decisive feeling and we have all been far kinder to the Liberal Minister for War than we were to his Unionist predecessors.'[41] After this sharp rebuff, they did not correspond again for more than two years. Neither man was inclined to take his own opinions other than very seriously. Garvin told Roberts that Repington had written to him, 'deprecating a strong campaign now and urging six months or a year's delay. I do not agree. My mind is made up that something must be done. ... Of course I shall now keep the ball rolling and shall have a column next Sunday upon some military matters.' Roberts was reassured. 'A strong campaign now is essential,' he insisted. He thought Repington's attitude was easily explained. He 'has been got hold of by the Secretary of State, and if we delay six months or a year all the mischief will be done – the public must be enlightened now'.[42]

For the rest of 1908, Garvin hammered away at Haldane and the shortcomings of his Territorial scheme. He had Roberts's constant encouragement to censure in the strongest terms possible, 'Haldane's Tomfoolery'. In between requests for help with drafting letters to the press, or with notes for speeches, Roberts applauded Garvin, in particular for an article where he had stated: 'No War Minister ever had such powerful assistance as Mr Haldane has received notwithstanding which nothing will save the system and nothing ought to save it.'[43] Roberts remained unshaken in his belief that 'as soon as the fallacy of the Territorial Army is realised, we shall have another Army founded on Universal Military Training'.[44]

Despite the energy expended, the rolling phrases, the persuasive arguments, the splendid invective, there was to be no victory. When Garvin's critics suggested to Fisher that the editor's uncanny prescience and effectiveness as a campaigning journalist owed much if not all to the information he was given from official and secret sources, the Admiral countered that his friend's genius was explained by 'his careful sifting of the facts & alert common sense' that was as effective as 'listening behind the door!!!'[45] Garvin even employed this same argument himself against both Tweedmouth and Grey. But though he succeeded in his campaigns for Fisher and the navy, his campaigning for Roberts and compulsory service failed. It was much harder, he admitted, to work his alchemy upon opinion on a subject where the public was so antipathetic. More importantly, on military matters Garvin lost his fine touch because he never had access to anyone's door behind which it was worth his while to listen!

The intensification of hostility between European Powers in 1908 increased public interest in questions of defence. Despite constant internal wrangling and uncertainty about what programme exactly it did support, the National Service League's membership tripled. Roberts was anxious that Repington should discover whether the Tory party would now espouse the NSL programme. Repington's response was not optimistic: 'I wish to tell you confidentially', he wrote, 'that I felt the ground in this direction over a year ago believing that the time had come for a move, but I met with no encouragement.'[46] Repington constantly urged greater patience as a necessary virtue, but most league members, and not least their president, were impatient. 'The fruit ripens slowly and public opinion is not yet ripe,' Repington counselled the intemperate brethren in March. In June, before the annual general meeting of the NSL, he warned that they were unwise to condemn Haldane's schemes while reaffirming his own wish 'to secure the desirable object of national training'.[47] Only after 'very mature consideration', which was its own restrained but inaccurate public version of violent argument, did the NSL's executive 'agree to withhold all detailed criticism of Mr Haldane's scheme until after the date which Mr Haldane himself fixed as the time when it would be possible to judge whether it was likely to succeed or not'.[48] In a confused letter written late at night, Milner revealed the uncertainties and dissensions that plagued the NSL. For his own part he desired a gradualist approach, he told Midleton, but would not dare admit as much 'even to my associates, at least, not all of them'.

> If I thought like Maxse that a continental nation was going to jump on us in ten minutes, of course I should say, 'even at the risk of total

irretrievable defeat of your whole plan, I put the thing to the test at once'. . . . The process of conversion is going on very fast. But when you consider how immense a revolution it all is in our national habits of mind, you can't expect to go more than sixty miles an hour, at least you risk total shipwreck in doing it. . . . Is it not better to put the question in its final and authoritative form say two years hence with a 50% chance of getting an affirmative answer than today with only a 10% chance?[49]

A series of offhand remarks by Haldane provoked a paroxysm of rage in Maxse who avowed that compulsion would bury the Minister for War. Together with his friend Newton he challenged the Tory leadership to abandon its tacit support of Haldane and expose him for the imposter he really was.[50] Roberts wrote to compliment Maxse on his efforts in the *National Review*, the way in which he always coupled the issue of compulsion with dire warnings of the 'German Peril'. Roberts considered that it was 'most unfortunate that not a single man on the front Opposition bench seems to care one straw about Home Defence'.[51] Nevertheless, he did not seem disposed to recruit Tory support openly and, despite the promptings of friends, refused the opportunity to write anything on compulsory service in friendly journals. It was as though he had suddenly determined to withdraw altogether from the arena of public debate. His strange new mood caused consternation to several of his closest friends and supporters. They could offer no adequate explanation for his sudden decision to fall silent when they were intent on mounting a stiff campaign against Haldane. 'I am certain', wrote Blumenfeld to Gwynne, 'that if I had his name and undoubted influence to work with, we could soon rouse public opinion to a suitable pitch. But Lord Roberts has never given me the slightest hope in that direction; on the contrary, he has distinctly discouraged any efforts on my part to go ahead.'[52] It might have been that Roberts was reacting to the violence of the campaign against Haldane, or even the absurdity of some of the proposals made by newspapers like the *Standard* that for a time touted John Burns, of all people, as a candidate to replace Haldane at the War Office.[53] A more likely explanation, however, is that Milner had for the moment succeeded in impressing upon Roberts the wisdom of his gradualist arguments so that for once, the old warrior's activities were confined to an occasional encouragement of his troops, Duke of Plaza Toro fashion, 'from behind'. Roberts was certainly far from happy. He admitted to Cromer that his 'spirit was dampened', and that he 'despaired of anything being done until it is too late'. The public in their 'great apathy and ignorance' seemed to 'regard any word of warning which a soldier may address to them as mere jingoism'.[54] As Britain was 'committed to strict alliance with France . . . is not that the more reason for us to be prepared for what that alliance may bring forth?' he asked Rosebery who, in his usual fashion, made no direct reply. He would only express his admiration and sympathy for Roberts's 'efforts to awaken the country to the need of defence'. He did not comment upon Roberts's translation of the entente into an alliance, but deprecated 'the effects of the English and German Press . . . which I dread. If this goes on there will be such an inflammable state of feeling in both nations that war, felt to be inevitable will become inevitable.'[55] Yet for all his concern about the military implications of the entente, when Roberts spoke in the Lords in November, Esher considered that he struck a damaging blow against Anglo-French amity. He angrily noted in his journal, 'I never gave a vote with more satisfaction than against his motion.'[56]

One member of the executive of the NSL who despised Milner's Fabian tactics was the maverick Liberal MP for Stratford-upon-Avon, Captain Malcolm Kincaid-Smith. His victory in the 1906 election, where he added more than 50 per cent to any previous Liberal vote in the constituency, was one of the more amazing and unlikely wins of the Liberal landslide. Once at Westminster, Kincaid-Smith seemed to forget that he had been returned as a Liberal. He voted against his own government and campaigned vigorously in his constituency for compulsory service. By 1907, even the easy-going, local Liberal Association had suffered enough of their representative's 'independence' and, without success, attempted to force his resignation. Unperturbed, Kincaid-Smith intensified his local campaign for conscription and to the NSL proposed that it should endorse any parliamentary candidate, irrespective of the opinions he might hold on other questions, provided he made national service a major issue of his campaign. In July 1908 he voted with the Opposition in the naval debates and sought to amend Haldane's Territorial scheme to embrace national military training.

In April 1909, without consulting anyone, Kincaid-Smith announced in a letter to *The Times* that he proposed to resign his seat and would contest the by-election on the single issue of national service. 'It is my conviction that it is only in this way that the question of national military training can be brought without further loss of time to a practical issue.'[57] Like most of the Unionist press, *The Times* declared its strong sympathy for Kincaid-Smith's gallant decision, though everyone recognised it would be very embarrassing if the local Tories put up their own candidate to oppose him. The Liberal *Daily News* could only rub its hands in delighted anticipation of 'the Big Navy scaremongers engaged in internecine strife with their first cousins the Big Army advocates'.[58] The prospect horrified Milner. 'I have had a great "facer" in taking up my Times this morning,' he admitted to Balfour. 'If such a man were to lose his seat by Unionist votes, it would in any case produce a very bad effect. For a good many people like myself, who without perhaps being good party men are yet whole-hearted supporters of yours, it would create an almost impossible position.' Milner readily appreciated the difficulties that the Tories faced on the conscription issue, but his plea to Balfour was that the Stratford by-election presented them with a 'special' case.

> Much education of public opinion is required before any party can be expected, as a party, to commit itself to the advocacy of so great a change. Besides, it is fatal to overload party programmes and you already have so much 'hay on the cart'.
>
> But it is one thing to acquiesce, as I most readily do, in the fact that the Unionist party is not prepared to go in for National Service as a party at the present time. It is quite another to sit still, if, as a party, it's going

to throw its whole weight into the scale against National Service, *in a case where that is the only issue.*[59]

The next day Balfour received a letter from Roberts who admitted that he could not 'resist the temptation to appeal to [Balfour]. . . . to take advantage of this opportunity'. The trouble was that Roberts, unlike Milner, did not begin to realise the difficulties that Balfour faced. 'Bobs' claimed that though his personal wish had been to keep the question of national defence out of politics (sic!), he now felt that this pious hope was no longer possible. 'Like all other Great Questions it will have to be settled on Party lines.' He proposed to bring a Bill before the Lords after the Easter recess. Like Kincaid-Smith's earlier unsuccessful amendment, it would demand 'universal military training' in order to provide 'Haldane's admirable framework with the required number of adequately trained men'. Roberts asked – though it was couched more like an instruction – for Balfour to 'speak out fearlessly' in its support.[60] Roberts, for all his insensitivity and ignorance about the parliamentary political game, this time seemed to have anticipated a swelling tide of favourable opinion in the Tory party. The *Morning Post,* recovering from its first doubts about the wisdom of Kincaid-Smith's action, now demanded that the Tory party should 'stop trifling with the vital problem of national defence', and 'place the question of national military training in the forefront of its programme'.[61]

The problem that faced the Tory leadership was nothing like as simple as Roberts or the *Morning Post* supposed. Its solution would call for fine judgment. If Tory hearts favoured conscription, Tory heads rejected sentiment and recognised that so long as there was a national prejudice against national service, to support that policy could only cost votes – and this at a time when they had good reason to suppose that with the next appeal to the electorate they would reverse the 1906 decision. It would be irresponsibly quixotic to risk so much for the sake of supporting Kincaid-Smith at Stratford, There were, however, those who disagreed with this estimate. Rowland Hunt, Unionist member for Ludlow, thought there would be no disadvantage in the party backing Smith, 'distinctly a personality from an electioneering point of view', as he informed Acland Hood, the Tory whip. In any event, the party could not 'conduct a great patriotic agitation . . . and then for party purposes oppose an independent candidate whose purpose in standing was for that very thing alone'. Hunt pointed out that his own agent had been 'in a dreadful funk' and had begged him to stop telling his constituents that he supported Kincaid-Smith. But 'in travelling about the constituency he discovered to his astonishment that every man said I was right'.[62] Whatever the disposition of the hunting squires of the English shires, at Central Office the mood was hard-headed and not at all euphoric. Sandars, reporting his discussions with Acland Hood, told Balfour that although the party might be abused for opposing Smith, there was 'practically no alternative'. Apart from 'Universal training – a question which is not included in our official programme', they would be asking 'the party in Warwickshire to vote for a man who is against us on all the main principles of our case'. Sandars argued that there was no reason why the party as a whole need suffer for there was a way of escape conveniently available. The responsibility for the final decision would rest with the local constituency association. 'There is nothing to call for any special action on our part.'[63] Sandars knew that the South-West Warwickshire Association was determined to put forward its former member, P. S. Foster. A tariff reformer, Foster had already publicly declined to adopt universal training as part of his electoral platform.

Kincaid-Smith's peremptory action caused as much embarrassment to the leaders of the NSL as it did to the panjandrums of Tory Central Office. Milner had written angrily to Roberts that it was 'a very awkward business . . . raised in the clumsiest possible way by a weak advocate. Whatever course the League takes it is bound to fall foul of some of its supporters. . . . The only practicable course, as it seems to me, is for the League to remain officially neutral.'[64] After much heated wrangling, this was the solution accepted by the executive of the league. The ill tidings were passed on to Smith by Roberts with the less than helpful disclaimer, 'If I were not precluded, as a member of the House of Lords, from taking part in a contested election for the House of Commons, I personally should support your candidature.'[65] Though many members were unhappy about the official position of neutrality adopted by the NSL, they reserved their 'extreme disgust' for 'the way in which the election is being worked by our party. We ought to have supported Kincaid-Smith,' Newton insisted to Maxse. 'It would have been a magnificent opportunity to fight the question and one which is not likely to occur again.'[66]

The Stratford by-election deteriorated into farce. While Kincaid-Smith made blatant overtures to the Tory leadership, *The Times* called for Foster to stand down. Balfour and Chamberlain reluctantly endorsed Foster's candidature, but their letters studiously avoided any mention of defence issues. The publication of Lloyd George's budget proposals effectively buried the national service question under that of tariff reform to which gospel, Smith, at the last moment, proclaimed himself a convert. His economic apostasy made no difference for when the poll was declared Foster had been elected with more than five thousand votes while Kincaid-Smith trailed the rest of the field with less than five hundred. The Liberal press crowed its delight at what it described as 'the defeat of compulsion'. Milner admitted the result had been 'very disappointing', but comforted himself by supposing that the NSL had minimised the damage by remaining neutral. He told Strachey, 'Of course, if Kincaid-Smith had been a less absolutely hopeless person, the result would not have been quite so bad, but in any case the party candidate would have won.'[67]

The best measure of the desperation in the conscriptionist camp at this time was an untypically wild suggestion by Repington in an article he wrote on the Territorial Forces in *The Times*. While agreeing that 'in principle it is not a sound thing to disseminate effort by creating semi-military bodies outside the accepted military organization', he nevertheless suggested the government ought to subsidise, to the tune of a thousand pounds a year, the Legion of Frontiersmen. They, together with rifle clubs and Baden-Powell's boy scouts, could provide 'a national army of second line in Great Britain'.[68] He also wrote to Roberts to tell him how hopeless and thoroughly depressing the outlook seemed. 'We ought to be hurrying up National training and yet the Tories run

a man against Kincaid-Smith who stands on this platform. . . . I hope you will
castigate this miserable party move.'[69] Repington warned Maxse that he was
convinced that even if the Tories were to win the next general election and
form the government,

> Balfour will change nothing. I don't think he will ever restore the lost
> Regular battalions, and I fear he will not go for compulsion. It appears
> to me that the Tory leaders fear compulsion because they fear to arm the
> people and prefer the better class TF (better I mean than a conscript
> army) because the TF is a conservative force and will not paint the town
> red if there are riots or troubles. This is my idea, though not a word
> has been said about it.[70]

Garvin, more inclined to exaggerate than Repington, on this occasion remained
remarkably calm. 'You see the absurd state of theatrical convulsions into which
we are throwing ourselves,' he wrote to Dr E. J. Dillon, the distinguished
foreign correspondent. 'I think there is now no real doubt that the next
Government will introduce National Service. . . . But that is still far off.'[71]

Strangely Maxse did not respond to Repington's suggestion that Tory reluctance to accept conscription was dictated by fears of social revolution. Instead,
in a letter to Strachey he suggested that Balfour was 'disinclined to touch
compulsory service in any shape or form because the Unionist party already
has enough to carry'. He noted how, 'Our enemies are exploiting Kincaid-
Smith's insignificant poll as conclusive evidence of the unpopularity of our
cause, and with what are called practical politicians it is only popularity that
counts.'[72] It was the old and too familiar story of timorous politicians more
anxious for their own future and fortune than the nation's welfare. Since the
previous autumn, Strachey had earnestly advocated the Tory party's adoption
of compulsory service.[73] His arguments had not impressed Milner who insisted
that the NSL should 'stay out of elections', confine itself to being 'simply an
Educational Agency and *keep on preaching*'.[74] Strachey warned Milner that if
the league stuck to this course, then 'we might as well throw up the sponge'.

> We shall not be doing any real injury to the Unionist cause by insisting
> that Unionist candidates toe the line in regard to national service. . . .
> Unless we make ourselves a little disagreeable to the party hacks who
> greatly dislike the notion of what they call the unknown, we shall never get
> what we want.
>   Our business as a League must be to insist that the question shall be
> placed before the country at the next general election, no matter how
> much the Tapers and Tadpoles may scream.[75]

Milner remained unimpressed by Strachey's arguments, but Roberts promised
the *Spectator*'s editor that he would push his views at the next meeting of the
NSL's executive committee.

If Roberts supposed that Balfour and the other Tory leaders were likely to
change their minds he would have been sadly disappointed by the reception
they gave to the National Service Bill he introduced to the Lords in July 1909.
Following Lansdowne's lead, the Unionist front bench in the Lords turned

their back on the measure. 'The Mandarins played their usual pitiful part,' Maxse commented bitterly in the *National Review*. Any lingering doubts about their disposition must have been dispelled when Roberts, in December, was informed by H. M. Durand, a member of the NSL and one of the Tory candidates for the dual seat Plymouth constituency, that Lansdowne had advised him that 'to raise the question of national service at this moment might do harm to the Unionist cause'.[76] This injunction by the Tory leader in the Lords was given at the same time as Blatchford in the *Daily Mail* was asserting that 'half a million, perhaps even 300,000 British troops would turn the scale ... secure France from attack by Germany [and] save the downfall of the British Empire. We have not got them and we cannot have them without universal service.' If the Tories did not hesitate to exploit the navy as an electoral issue, why were they so reluctant to take the same course for the army? Walter Long was typical of many Tories when, on several occasions, he admitted to Blumenfeld that although he was 'strongly in favour of doing something in regard to Compulsory Training and Universal Service', he was 'not sure how far either of these objects commend themselves to the party as a whole.... There is a great divergence on the subject, many being afraid that if these questions were to be included in the Party Programme, they might bring us some trouble and difficulty.'[77]

The rapid increase in membership during 1908 had persuaded many in the National Service League that success was not only assured but imminent. 1909 proved a year of sad disillusionment. The Stratford-upon-Avon by-election had been an unmitigated disaster. Neither gradualist tactics nor direct appeals had succeeded in persuading the Tories to adopt the league's proposals as part of their party programme. Esher, so often in the opinions he expressed a reliable guide to what Balfour was thinking, had told Roberts in June that it would be 'odious' if the country adopted compulsory service, and he repeated his 'ethical judgment' later in a public speech he made at Callender. On that occasion he embroidered his argument with the claim that it would be a dangerous move likely to injure the future welfare of the navy and undermine the nation's offensive spirit, arguments that were to be employed against Roberts a few years later by both Ian Hamilton and J. E. B. Seely. To Haldane, Esher suggested the inevitable hiatus of several years while Britain changed from a voluntary to a compulsory system of recruitment would place the country in a vulnerable position that the German General Staff was not likely to ignore. Apparently Haldane thought this a convincing argument.[78] Roberts merely dismissed Esher's jeremiad as inspired by Fisher and comforted himself with the thought that although Esher was 'undoubtedly clever', he was 'very generally distrusted'. There was also the King's private secretary, Knollys, to be considered whenever Esher made a public pronouncement. The two men were very close and Knollys 'has always been sceptical about the German danger and voted against the Bill I brought in last July'.[79]

Roberts was inclined to blame others for his failures, but before the disastrous year was out he gave another conclusive demonstration of how he was often betrayed by his 'instinct'. In December he unsuccessfully attempted to recruit King Edward's support for the NSL. Yet, whatever his failings, Roberts, had the supreme ability to shrug off his misfortunes and on the very first day of the new year his resilience and optimism seemed at last to be about to be rewarded. To celebrate New Year's Day, 1910, Esher joined Roberts at Englemere and to the surprise and scarcely concealed delight of the assembled company announced that he had decided to resign as chairman of the London Territorial Association. He had spent 'large sums of private money with hardly any results'. There were insufficient recruits and those that had been secured were 'ill-officered, not trained, and quite incapable of defending the country'. Henry Wilson was, if possible, even more delighted with this news of Esher's change of mind than Roberts. 'So at last the bubble is going to be punctured,' he gloated in his diary.[80] Roberts seemed to take on a new lease of life. He wrote to tell Maxse that 'as soon as the election is over I hope there will be a general movement in aid of National Defence'. His account of the NSL's organisation and administration suggested increases in efficiency, numbers and influence, especially in the English shires.[81] Was there at last, real cause for optimism in the compulsionist camp?

One hundred and twenty-seven new members swelled the Unionist ranks in the Commons as a result of the January 1910 general election, and most were sympathetic to the idea of introducing compulsory service. It was also evident by that date that the Territorial Army's initial success in attracting volunteers to its ranks had waned. When the army estimates were debated in March, Opposition speakers adopted a harsher tone towards Haldane than ever before. When Arthur Lee suggested that Haldane would be 'remembered above all things by posterity as the War Minister who paved the way for compulsory service and made it inevitable by the reforms which he introduced', it was not intended as a compliment. In May came the remarkable party truce, or 'a truce of God' as Garvin promoted it in his *Observer*, occasioned by the sudden, unexpected death of King Edward. It was at this time that the possibility of a rare conjunction of journalistic talent that would have operated to the enormous advantage of the pro-conscriptionist camp, foundered because of the priggery and self-conceit of the two principles involved. Repington suddenly wrote to Garvin offering the editor his occasional services for the *Observer*. 'You don't seem to have anybody especially told off (to write upon the larger aspects of defence by sea and land) so I write to learn your views. You give people a good kick which lasts them through the week and I should like to bear a hand [*sic*] if it can be arranged.' The suggestion came to nothing, and the short correspondence ended abruptly and acrimoniously with Repington reminding Garvin, 'We are neither of us indispensable to the other and I think it silly to fall out at this stage when the big battle for military efficiency has still to be fought against considerable odds.'[82]

The party truce fired the imagination of the Chancellor of the Exchequer. 'Lloyd George, bored by mere constitution-mongering, and increasingly alarmed at the effect of unbridled partisanship upon the nation's capacity to tackle a whole range of desperately urgent problems, became convinced of the need for a coalition government with an agreed programme.'[83] On 17 August 1910, he submitted a 'memorandum on the formation of a Coalition'. This listed among those 'questions which call for immediate attention and could properly and effectively be dealt with by some combined effort', national defence.

> I am strongly of the opinion that even the question of compulsory training should not be shirked. No party dare touch it, because of the violent prejudices which would be excited even if it were suspected that a Government contemplated the possibility of establishing anything of the kind. For that reason it has never really been looked into by statesmen in this country. The Swiss Militia system might be considered and those liable to serve might be chosen by ballot. . . . We might aim at raising 500,000 armed militia to supplement our Regular Army to provide against contingencies.[84]

Haldane was one of the senior Liberal ministers who saw the memorandum in October, and his reaction was favourable. By November, however, the party truce had failed and normal partisan hostilities had been resumed. It remained that the document, and not least its proposals on compulsory military training, was an extraordinary initiative by the Liberal Cabinet minister who was popularly supposed to be a Radical extremist wedded to retrenchment in expenditure on both Services.

Although Esher had not, as he had earlier promised Roberts, resigned as Chairman of the London Territorial Association, he made a startling contribution to a Lords' debate in July on the strategic efficiency of the Territorials. He bluntly rejected the government's claim that the force could he expanded. 'In my opinion, in London as elsewhere in the country, the limit has been reached.' Roberts wrote immediately to Esher telling him what 'great pleasure' his speech had afforded. 'I hope in November we shall have another [debate] in which you will be able to take part in support of the Territorial Army having reached its limits under the voluntary system.'[85]

Between June and August 1910 a series of articles entitled 'The Cabal' appeared in a magazine called *The World*. Haldane, described as 'an amateur not even entitled to wear a volunteer uniform', was accused of undermining the defence interests of Britain. Esher, described accurately as 'a mysterious power and influence behind the scenes', was accused of abusing royal influence, manipulating the press, possessing monumental arrogance and not being subject to parliamentary scrutiny. Esher was not only furious with these charges, he was sufficiently stung – and self-complacently smug – to answer his critic with an article on the decline of the ideal of voluntary service. The unwritten but clearly implied personal message of this essay was the author's unrivalled claim to be seen as the supreme embodiment of the selfless virtue of dedicated, voluntary service to monarch and nation. Haldane, who had been sent an advance proof, did not wish the article to be published, but it appeared that September in Maxse's *National Review*. With sublime insensitivity, Esher told Haldane that he was sure Maxse would not misuse his essay to make a rod for the minister's back.[86] He told Spender his hope was 'that the article will only make people think and will not do any harm'.[87] What particularly upset Haldane were Esher's comments on enrolment for the Territorials. 'There is no sign that the 60,000 required annually will be forthcoming. . . .

There is no steady increase, no advance. There is in many cases retrogression. . . . It may be that the sirocco of democracy is withering in our people the spirit of sacrifice.' The inescapable, overall impression Esher's words gave was that the time had come for compulsory military service. 'This country can be saved only by imposing by law upon our children the duty to bear arms in defence.'

Naturally Haldane was upset. It was a gratuitous condemnation of much that he had attempted as Minister for War. Yet Esher smugly referred to Haldane's letter asking him not to publish as 'half pathetic, half petulant'. Haldane had every reason to feel angry and betrayed.

> He says that my having helped him to organise the Territorial Force practically disqualifies me from expressing doubts about the success of the scheme. In short I must pretend that it is a success, just as if I were a paid politician. . . . They care only for peace at any price. It shows how badly the country is governed . . . a system under which criticism is stifled and 'eyewash' prevails.[88]

Esher's protestations were as loud as they were transparently insincere. Many of Haldane's critics, though they had little love for Esher, were delighted with his article. R. J. Marker could only suppose that conscription must now be imminent. 'Why else should Esher have turned on Haldane? He is seldom behind the cat,' he observed to Blumenfeld.[89] Roberts wondered whether now was the time once more to exert pressure on the Tory leadership to adopt conscription. Leo Amery, a young but influential lieutenant, told Roberts that he did not think so.

> The more I consider the practical political aspects of the question, the more I realise the extreme difficulty, almost hopelessness, of carrying national service through as a party measure. . . . So I think all the work we can put in in getting hold of eminent Liberals during the next few months will be to the good, and in generally emphasising as much as possible the non party character of the League.[90]

Amery's was a realistic assessment. Esher's outburst was an exercise in simple pique and in no way implied that Balfour was about to welcome conscription as a plank in the Unionist party's platform.

Haldane did not feel he could entirely ignore Esher's damaging statement. His response was to ask General Sir Ian Hamilton to write a memorandum on compulsory service. 'Johnny' Hamilton, a dashing, very popular officer and a close friend of Roberts, was the second military member of the Army Council and had just been promoted GOC Mediterranean and Inspector General of Overseas Forces. When Hamilton had completed his memorandum, Haldane added a long introduction. Their joint literary venture was published by December 1910, entitled, *Compulsory Service: A Study of the Question in the Light of Experience.* Hamilton had many friends who were journalists and Strachey and Gwynne were particular intimates. When his book on compulsion was published, however, Hamilton soon discovered, as he later told Seely, 'the whole Compulsory Service Press machinery was set working on a carefully selected line to pulverise my humble self'. For all its 'engineered violence, lo and behold, I was still alive, only some of the dust and rust brushed off me! But I no longer had any personal friends among journalists.'[91] The enemies that Hamilton made in 1910 were not to take their real revenge until 1915. For the moment, one of Hamilton's most bitter critics, Kipling, assuaged his feelings of contempt with a doggerel squib he enclosed in a letter to his cousin, Stanley Baldwin.

When Haldane's Hound upon Haldane's hobbies
Writes a book which is full of lies
Then we find out what a first class job is
And how Inspector Generals rise.

Hamilton's contribution to the book had been in the form of an open letter pledging his continued support for the minister against the critics of the voluntary principle. It was written in his usual breezy, none too careful style.

Let the British workman undertake a duty of his own free will and no one will be at greater pains to execute it thoroughly. To the authoritative command 'Fall in!' his inclination (not always repressed) is to retort 'Fall in yourself, and be d-d to you!' . . . I deny and ever will deny, that to force food down a Briton's throat with a stomach-pump will give him an appetite for his dinner. . . . War searches the innermost part and the uttermost corner. It is on moral forces that we must stand or fall in battle. . . . Aren't these more likely to be found living and active amongst volunteers than amongst conscripts?[92]

The most unusual feature of the Hamilton Haldane book was that the major conclusions were stated in the lengthy introduction. Patriotism, it was insisted, would insure sufficient volunteers. A voluntary army best suited Britain's particular needs because, as an island, a non-professional, conscripted land force would be an unnecessary burden, 'a stone to hang around our necks while we struggle in the slough of insolvency'.

Hamilton had not rejected conscription at all times and in every circumstance. Time of war or national emergency, he argued, created conditions suitable for what he described as 'latent' compulsion. This, of course, provided a convenient gap in his argument through which the national service polemicists drove a coach and horses. Nevertheless, Haldane was very pleased with the book. Within a month a second edition appeared which included a memorandum by the First Sea Lord, Wilson, ridiculing the idea, so often employed by the compulsionists, that there was any risk of Britain being invaded by a hostile Power. Haldane wrote to tell his mother that the book had been 'a tremendous success', adding prematurely and with more optimism than the circumstances merited, that it had 'done its work in educating the public'.[93] It was true that there had been a plethora of reviews and articles in the press, generally favourable, but this, as much as anything, was due to the unremitting efforts of both authors to insure their work was well advertised and received. Strachey soon regretted the three-column review he had given the book in the *Spectator.* He explained to Roberts, 'I was . . . almost obliged to notice it as I was practically challenged to do so by Haldane and Hamilton who are both friends of mine.'[94] Not everyone had responded so eagerly to the complimentary copies Haldane and Hamilton showered upon likely targets. Henry Wilson dismissed the book as 'absolute rubbish'.[95]

Strachey advised that it would be best not to answer the book in kind: 'the more we combat it the more we shall keep it alive. It is a very futile performance even from their point of view.' His opinion was overborne by the general feeling in the Roberts camp. Milner was particularly insistent that a refutation should be published.

> Ian Hamilton must be answered. It is a great chance for us, for this is a
> very bad book, full of wrong history and transparent fallacies and self
> contradictions, and Haldane having welcomed it with both hands ... the
> system they are defending is exposed to a crushing reply. *But* it wouldn't
> do to muddle it. ... I am not so much impressed with the need of haste.
> Certainly the sooner the better – but infinitely more important ... it should
> be *complete and final.*[96]

Within four months, the conscriptionists' reply to Haldane and Hamilton was on sale to the public.

Roberts was named as the author of *Fallacies and Facts,* but part had been contributed by Professor J. A. Cramb, and much the longest section dashed off in a few weeks by the volatile L. S. Amery. No one admired Roberts more than Amery. He contrasted the old warrior's kindliness, gentleness, patriotism and selflessness with the character of the coldly calculating Kitchener who made no secret of his contempt for 'Poor old Roberts; just wasting his time. No one is going to listen to him. Nobody is going to organize the Army properly in peace.'[97]

As busily as Haldane and Hamilton, Roberts sought to recruit favourable reviews from friends in the press. Northcliffe lent his unrivalled aid. Repington was very much out of favour for having reviewed *Compulsory Service* generously in *The Times* which disqualified him, so Roberts thought, from reviewing his book. Repington was not the only problem at *The Times.* 'Buckle,' Roberts complained to Northcliffe, 'has never appeared interested in the Army.'[98] Nothing could be done about that, but a fairly convincing case was nevertheless made against Hamilton and Haldane. The main charge they faced was inconsistency and impracticability. A particular feature of the reviews was that they concentrated more upon the supposed errors of fact and judgment in *Compulsory Service* than in arguing the positive case for national service. Of course, the NSL's contribution was puffed. 'Far from interfering with ... the problem of recruitment,' as had been claimed, it offered 'material assistance with the solution'. Hamilton's argument that a large army of home defence would militate against the offensive spirit was summarily dismissed. 'The existence of such a force will not only give greater freedom to our attack in the first instance, but can only supply that in which we are at present most conspicuously lacking, the power of keeping up the attack by continuous reinforcements of trained men.' Both parties to the debate insisted they were the victors, but the fairest surmise would seem to be that neither made a significant number of converts by their literary efforts.

Roberts could not afford to remain too long preoccupied with this stalemate. His attentions were focused upon the debate due to take place the next month in the Lords. The House of Commons, he admitted to Northcliffe, was quite hopeless. 'No one of any stature seems to care about our military position. . . . Balfour believes in Haldane and all on his side of the House follow his lead. Believe me, we are no better prepared than we were in 1899. I will endeavour to point this out as forcibly as I can in the debate, but speaking in the House is of no value unless one is supported by the press.'[99] He used almost exactly the same words when addressing an identical appeal to Garvin for support the next day.[100] With *The Times* disabled as a really effective ally because Buckle was so attached to Balfour, Roberts needed every ounce of help Northcliffe could give him in the *Daily Mail.* He was not to be disappointed.

In early April, Roberts proposed the motion that the Lords, in the altered strategic conditions of Europe, viewed with growing concern the inadequate military arrangements of the empire. The compulsionist press that month made great play with talk of the Balance of Power and of the 'obligation' imposed by the entente with France, to place an adequate British force in the line against any German attack. The debate in the House of Lords was unusually acrimonious. Haldane, recently ennobled, was particularly scathing in his attacks on Roberts. When the House divided, the motion was approved by ninety-nine votes to forty. Curzon was not slow to claim that whereas two years earlier the conscriptionists had been in a minority of twenty, they were now a considerable majority in the Upper House. What Curzon conveniently ignored was the fact that Lansdowne and other leading Unionist peers who were most influential in their party had voted with the Liberals against the motion. Roberts bluntly declared that the majority of members in both Houses of Parliament were 'persuaded in their minds that compulsory service is not only advisable but essential . . . but they are restrained from giving utterance to these views not from lack of conviction but from party considerations'. The *Daily Mail* constantly emphasised that Roberts 'has no party axe to grind in his fight for military efficiency. . . . The War Office will drift and live in a world of make-believe till disaster overtakes British arms. It is to avert such a calamity that Lord Roberts has made his impressive appeal to his countrymen.' Such claims were familiar to the *Mail*'s readers, but the editorial concluded with an impressively cogent and persuasive definition of the strategic position that Britain now held in Europe.

> It was stated by Sir Edward Grey with perfect clarity two years ago: 'An
> attempt by any great Continental Power to dominate and dictate the
> policy of the Continent would certainly produce conflict.' If these words
> have any meaning at all, it is this: In the event of any Great Power attempting
> to dominate the policy of the Continent we must be prepared to resist. . . .
> But how are we to carry out that policy? Have we the great striking force
> which is required? No one believes it. . . . *Words alone will never save the*

British Empire. . . . Let it never be said that Britain lost her Empire on the battlefields of Lorraine.[101]

The *Daily Mail* argued that the fate of the army was a national problem above party politics, but it nevertheless concentrated its invective upon the Liberals. What distressed Roberts was that so long as Balfour remained the Tory leader there was little prospect of that party's support. He wrote to Lord Percy, a frequent contributor to the *National Review* on military topics. 'If national defence is to be a party question it is essential that the leader of the party should believe in it. But like Pitt and his immediate predecessor, Lord Salisbury, Balfour takes no practical interest in the Army. . . . As long as this continues, how can we feel sanguine of any change for the better being effected?'[102] Roberts had received a letter from Clemenceau which bitterly complained that Britain was not devoting a proper military effort to making the entente an effective restraint upon Germany's aggressive designs.[103] Roberts wrote to Curzon complaining that neither major political party 'seems to take a serious view of the change which is taking place in Europe and in the world – to our detriment. Both parties seem either blind to what is going on or desire to keep the public in ignorance.'[104]

Beresford chose this moment to make one of his blundering incursions into public debate with several speeches, the substance of which were published later in his book, *The Betrayal*. He attempted to develop Roberts's criticisms of the First Sea Lord's memorandum published in the second edition of *Compulsory Service*. According to Beresford, still fighting the old fight, Wilson's views on strategy were 'really an endeavour to confuse our own people in order to serve the ends of party politics'.[105] In the face of all the evidence to the contrary Beresford seemed convinced that the Tory party could be swept effortlessly into the conscriptionist camp. Roberts had been disillusioned upon that score once too often and had abandoned hopes of nailing the colours of the NSL to the Tory party's mast.

How could anyone any longer trust politicians to make wise choices for the security of the nation when, even after the frightful warning of the second Moroccan crisis at Agadir in the summer of 1911, Tories and Liberals continued to bicker and squabble endlessly over the constitution? Roberts addressed an open letter to the nation's press. 'Let us cease to blind ourselves by vain sophistries to the dangers which beset us. Let us face the reality. . . . It is necessary to have a reliable National Army. The question is not a party one; it is a question in which every man and woman in these islands ought to take an interest. . . . I therefore appeal to you to consider this subject from a patriotic point of view. The issue is nothing short of the future of this country and of this Empire.'[106] His absolute despair with politicians he made obvious in the private injunction he sent to editors like Blumenfeld that accompanied his open letter.

Neither Party will deal with the question and my hope rests in the press. If you and other editors will kindly do all you can to enlighten the public to the necessity for our having a proper National Army, all will go well; otherwise the country will get into serious trouble.[107]

Roberts was now pushed back to the position he had held in 1906, but without any of the optimistic illusions he had then entertained that Haldane was a conscriptionist in disguise or that the Tories would happily support conscription. Perhaps the next logical step would be 'to press for an enquiry . . . and see who is to blame'?[108] A letter he had written to Garvin almost two months earlier hinted at a question in Roberts's mind whether the National Service League and his close association with that body had been altogether a blessing and advantage in his crusade.[109]

Despite their bitter, frequent, often debilitating, internecine squabbles, the 'big navy' advocates won the wholehearted support of the Tory party in Parliament and the country. For a time they effectively dictated party tactics both in the House and in the first 1910 general election. This had been crucial in establishing the credibility and ultimate success of their scaremongering campaign for ever-increasing expenditure upon the navy in general and on large all-big-gun capital ships in particular. The advocates of conscription had been no less skilful and persistent in waging their propaganda campaign but never succeeded in winning the overt support of the Tory party leaders. Consequently, their scaremongering, while disconcerting, was never more than a series of disconnected interludes confined for the most part to the columns of the popular press or debated in the Upper House whose very future existence was questioned.[110] The conscriptionists were never able to command for sufficient time a dominant place at Westminster, the central stage of the Edwardian political drama.

It was largely due to Balfour that the Tories rejected the conscriptionists. His leadership was crucial on this issue.[111] In June 1912, he would write to Sir Edward Grey, 'Submarines and airships seem to me to be much more to the purpose of Home Defence than conscription and certainly are much cheaper and easier to obtain!'[112] The words could have been taken straight from the mouth of Admiral Fisher. Later that same year, 1912, Balfour wrote to Andrew Bonar Law who had then replaced him as party leader. 'If we must base our views upon those of experts, the experts that we should follow are sailors rather than soldiers.'[113] Throughout the 'Balfour must go' campaign, Bonar Law evinced a very decided enthusiasm for conscription. Once he became leader of his party, this enthusiasm waned.[114] Balfour's advice, would have earned Fisher's approval. It was the soundest party political tactic in peacetime for it encapsulated the general popular prejudice that always looked kindly upon the welfare of the navy while, at best, tolerating military matters.

'Big navy' supporters were forever asserting that their purpose was to serve not a party but a 'national' interest. This most conveniently vague and elastic of political concepts was waved as a banner of convenience, brandished as an unimpeachable slogan of legitimacy, advertised as a guarantee of public-spirited disinterestedness. It was the most useful auxiliary of all in the armament of political rhetoric. For the compulsionists, however, 'national interest' became for them not a convenient rhetorical device but the very marrow of the dialectic they were obliged to adopt because they failed to persuade the Tories to make 'universal compulsory service' a plank in their party programme. It did not matter that a significant number of Tory backbenchers, and not a few shadow ministers, in their hearts believed in conscription and wished the country would adopt it. Balfour and key colleagues in the party hierarchy rejected it, not so much on grounds of principle but of political expediency. What they feared was, should the party, rather than individual members, advocate conscription, this might well lose critical and precious votes in marginal constituencies. Nor was it the prospect of permanent Opposition that only paled enthusiasm for compulsion. There always remained the unspoken but permanent fear that because the most uncompromising tariff reformers were the most enthusiastic advocates of conscription, to adopt it as party policy might seriously disturb, even destroy, the delicate equilibrium upon which the party's unity was precariously created and maintained.[115]

•••••• PART 4 ••••••

'And he gathered them in a place called . . . Armageddon'

Collapse of the Triple Entente

This time the coup has been made more cleverly than at Tangier. . . .
Practically Bülow and Aehrenthal say to Isvolsky, 'Come to terms with
us on our basis with regard to the East; or stick to England and take the
consequence.'

H. W. Steed to The Times*'s office*

Grey's climb-down seems to have satisfied the German Government, and
now he has made another speech about disarmament. . . . The 'Temps'
calls his speech childish which is also true, inasmuch as it does not deal
with the reality, that in order to economize in war preparations you must
have a peace policy abroad. It is impossible to run high Imperialism on
the cheap.

W. S. Blunt's Diary

We doubt whether the poison of the Jingo newspapers for the last five or
six years can really have done as much damage among the people as is
commonly supposed. The chief aim of our foreign policy now should be
the pursuit of friendship with Germany . . . and everything seems to be
in good train to that end.

Manchester Guardian

Although at first most British Radicals had been enthusiastic supporters of the
entente with France, Grey's completion of the grand diplomatic design with
the signing of the Anglo-Russian Convention was not so happily received.
The Germans complained incessantly of their 'encirclement'; that the entente
Powers had drawn 'a ring of iron' about the Triple Alliance; that the British
were determined to isolate Germany. When the contract between France and
England was carefully re-examined, a bargain struck over French rights in
Morocco and British rights in Egypt seemed very much like a case of honour
among thieves. Events in Morocco gave particular cause for concern. The
French bombarded defenceless native villages and acted in a fashion that was
at best careless of and often contrary to the spirit and the term of the Algeçiras
Act. Germany, as a signatory of that agreement, could not for ever be expected
'to consent to France's adventures without exacting a heavy price'.[1]

The Unionist press continued to give its support unreservedly to French
action, but in private, individuals – even a sturdy Francophile like Rowland

Blennerhassett – frequently expressed their concern for the future of the entente. The Liberal government should put a curb upon its backbenchers, Blennerhassett told Garvin in July 1907. 'The Parisian Jews and cosmopolitan financiers were always unfriendly to the entente . . . and the present English ministry is playing into their hands. I hear from the most different quarters rumours of the fall of Clemenceau's government.'[2] Clemenceau had said often enough that war with Germany was inevitable. 'We must do nothing to provoke it, but we must be ready to wage it . . . it will be a life and death struggle.'[3] So long as the darling of the French chauvinists remained France's premier, French policies would be given an anti-German emphasis. But if France led by Clemenceau had the will, did she have the means to make her an effective and resolute ally? 'Alas, I fear that France is now in a bad way,' Sir Rowland wrote despairingly to Garvin.

> I believe you will find if you ask that our reports at the Admiralty on the condition of the French navy disclose a state of things indicating not merely hopeless indiscipline but signs of a rapidly decaying State. What is to become of Europe if France utterly fails to keep her position? . . . As a friend once said to me in Berlin, the complete fall of France means that European civilization must hop on one leg![4]

Maxse, a close friend of Clemenceau, was anxious to explain the French Prime Minister's attitude towards Germany so that it should not be misunderstood by the British government. Tyrrell, he insisted, should make it clear to Grey that:

> When a Frenchman says, 'Cela veut dire la guerre', he does not mean, 'I am going to war', but merely that the outlook is ominous. I don't think Englishmen in the least realise what it means to France to be next door to Germany, the bully of Europe. Their exposed position compels Frenchmen to follow every move in the international game far more closely than we do, and they are aware of a great many devious tricks played by German policy of which we are ignorant, or which we choose to ignore. Clemenceau said to me, 'In a war with Germany France stakes her existence; it would be very different for you.'[5]

Maxse need not have concerned himself. Grey shared the general disposition of his permanent officials at the Foreign Office. France was given unreserved support, even when she bombarded Casablanca. The Wilhelmstrasse remained amazingly unconcerned about these events. But when there were mutterings in the German press, this was enough for Eyre Crowe to minute a despatch: 'I think this development is of a kind to cause legitimate anxiety. . . . Prince Bülow may resort to another bullying campaign intended to frighten and cow France. . . . At least France will not this time be as conciliatory as was M. Rouvier's government when they dismissed Delcassé.'[6]

In May 1908, President Fallières visited England. At a Buckingham Palace banquet, English king and French President exchanged toasts to the *entente resserrée* and *entente permanente*. In *Le Temps*, a newspaper known to be very close to the thinking of the Quai d'Orsay, André Tardieu[7] argued that the entente should now become an alliance with all the necessary formal military and naval arrangements that status implied. He also insisted that as a necessary preliminary step the British should adopt universal military service. Clemenceau frequently repeated the same demand.[8] The *Daily Mail* gave prominent notice to this view, emphasising that the entente implied reciprocal sacrifices from both partners. The French should strengthen their naval power, and England ought 'immediately to effect a profound reform of her land forces'.[9] Maxse used Tardieu's outburst as yet another opportunity to strike at Haldane. 'German diplomacy is not backward in exploiting Haldanism to our detriment and suggesting that Frenchmen have put their money on the wrong horse.'[10] *The Times*, however, had not welcomed Tardieu's admonitions while the Liberal press, unanimously and spiritedly, renounced the idea of compulsory military service. The *Manchester Guardian* was concerned that Tardieu's injunction had exposed 'the dilemma of conscience' that was an inevitable part of closer diplomatic ties with a chauvinistic France. 'What demands might France make and Britain acquiesce in as an ally?' It seemed as though a Liberal British government was 'accepting the lead of its "patriotic" press and giving unlimited support to a Power whose enterprises in Morocco are morally the equivalent of buccaneering'.[11] From his conversations with Metternich, Spender assumed Germany's official view was that Britain had allowed herself to be dragged along behind the chariot wheels of Clemenceau's France. The German Ambassador had asserted that

> he could not think of advising his Government to abate their precautions. He had been told ... by two successive Foreign Secretaries that if Germany attacked France, England would be on the side of France. Neither of them could have supposed that Germany had the slightest intention of attacking France and therefore, both must have meant that England would for all purposes be with France against Germany.[12]

There was sufficient reason for Metternich's pessimistic view of future Anglo-German relations. That spring, against the background of the naval debates in Parliament and the incident of the Kaiser's letter to Tweedmouth, George Prothero, editor of the *Quarterly Review*, had written to his friend since boyhood, Cecil Spring Rice. Prothero wanted the diplomat to write an article on 'the present state of the German mind'. Spring Rice declined, but instead provided Prothero with a detailed set of notes on the subject. These the editor successfully persuaded Garvin to use as the basis for a long article, 'The German Peril', that appeared in the spring number of the *Quarterly*. Prothero described Spring Rice's notes to Garvin as both 'very interesting and valuable'. Yet they lacked 'the most important thing of all – the *proofs* of German hostility and their intention to attack us if they get the chance.'

> That is why the B[ritish] P[ublic] refuses to believe at present, and so long as it disbelieves no amount of argument will mend matters. ... Ententes and alliances are worthless as a means of salvation. The BP seems to think now that they will do instead of an army and navy – the fools. It is only when you are well armed that an alliance is any use at all.[13]

Garvin required no 'proofs' of what he had known in every fibre of his being for more than a decade. His article was unsparing of the Germans, caustic about 'the Liberal pro-German press', and bitterly censured 'the bulk of the British public still somnolent and blind with respect to the German peril'.

> Nothing can be more certain than that the German Government and the whole German people . . . the least satisfied of all the Great Powers, regard the strength of England and the existence of her maritime supremacy as the first and the chief obstacle to the realisation of their ambitions by land and sea. . . . It must be admitted that any realistic estimate of the future relations between England and Germany will come as near to a theory of antagonisms clenched and predestined as the history of the world has ever known.[14]

Garvin's outburst was taken sufficiently seriously in Germany for Bülow, in an interview with Sidney Whitman published in the *Standard*, to try to blunt his censures with soft words. Garvin refused to be placated. He returned to the fray in a second, even more furious article that prompted Sydney Brooks to send him his 'envious congratulations on your superhuman rejoinder . . . most damnably without any mercy of any sort'.[15]

Garvin's polemic never needed reinforcement, but its effect was sharpened by a minor diplomatic contretemps, subsequently dignified by the grandiloquent title, the Casablanca Incident. Initially, the striking of a junior German consular official in a brawl involving three German deserters from the French Foreign Legion was treated with restraint by the German authorities. The Kaiser, particularly anxious that nothing should damage Franco-German relations, unwittingly exacerbated the problem with his *Daily Telegraph* interview. In an attempt to distract German public opinion, Bülow instructed Radolin to seek unconditional satisfaction for the insult to the dragoman. The French refused. Immediately the chauvinist press in both countries clamoured for war. This sudden turn of events generated considerable anxiety at the British Foreign Office and Eyre Crowe compared German attitudes with those of 1875 and 1886, 'when Bismarck tried to provoke war with France and took care to rouse public opinion for the purpose'. Grey's response was immediately to inform McKenna, 'I think the Admiralty should keep in readiness and make preparations in case Germany sent France an ultimatum and the Cabinet decided that we must assist France. . . . I do not like the way in which the Germans have revived the Casablanca difficulty with France. A fortnight ago Bülow himself said it was practically settled.'[16] Garvin, who seems to have been informed of every move, considered Grey's 'splendid firmness' very reassuring.[17] Another much impressed by the Foreign Secretary's response was Esher. He described the day Grey sent his message to McKenna as the most anxious he had ever known. The French should be told that they could count upon British support, for this 'would strengthen the entente and the chances of peace'. A week later, the crisis had subsided. Esher commented:

> The French were firm and determined and as I suspected the Germans drew back. They are bullies. . . . The French have behaved perfectly and with great distinction. Grey was touched by their self-restraint. They

never asked whether we were going to their assistance. In point of fact, Asquith, Grey and Haldane had decided to do so. Haldane told Asquith that if we failed France he would not give ten years purchase for the British Empire. This was very straight and courageous. Grey never wavered or doubted. . . . This attitude and language make the perfecting of our Navy and Army more imperative than ever.[18]

The public announcement of a reciprocal statement of regret by France and Germany, and the reference of their dispute to arbitration, was greeted with much pleasure by the Liberal press, although the *Nation* claimed that it was 'quite superfluous' to make any comment on the sensible solution of what had been a 'trivial controversy'. At the same time it emphasised how 'certain newspapers, confessedly in touch with official sources of information, had talked as though it might have led to a European war'.[19] The utter worthlessness of the scaremongering tactics of the jingo press that had insisted Germany and France were irreconcilably at odds over Morocco seemed irrefutably demonstrated when *The Times* announced that Edward had arrived in Berlin to pay a visit to his nephew the Kaiser on the same day, 10 February 1909, as the Germans signed an accord with the French over Morocco. *The Times*'s description of this as 'a happy coincidence', was very much out of tune with the way in which, for weeks past, it had insisted that it was 'no good disguising the truth that for long the feelings of Germany and France have not been as friendly as we would desire them to be'. Its admission of 'cautious optimism' was not allowed to pass without the rather damning caveat, 'The rapprochement between ourselves and Germany, depending as it does upon the rapprochement between Germany and France, will be all the more enduring if we do not hope too much from it at once.'[20] *The Times* had good reason for adopting so grudging a tone.

Charles Towers, an experienced foreign correspondent who, although he wrote for a 'Potsdamised newspaper', took a rather jaundiced view of German diplomatic intentions, wrote to tell Strachey of a recent long interview with an official at the Wilhelmstrasse. 'He made it clear that Germany only let the French off the ropes for purposes of international and domestic prestige.' Towers warned that Germany's 'true' attitude remained 'one of patent hostility'.[21] The editorial disposition of *The Times* had been determined by a stormy interview between Clemenceau and George Saunders which suggested that growing Franco-German accord was being purchased at the price of undermining the Anglo-French entente. Chirol reacted by asserting, as Blennerhassett had earlier, that especially among the moneyed interests, there had always been a disposition in Paris to put an entirely undeserved evil construction upon British actions. However, the sting in the Saunders/Clemenceau interview had been in the Frenchman's parting shot. 'There is a cleft in the entente and care must be taken that it does not widen.'[22]

One group in Britain had received news of the Franco-German accord with unreserved delight; the Radical politicians and journalists who constantly criticised Grey's conduct of foreign affairs. They believed that the ending of the Morocco squabble would 'make the task of bringing England and Germany together much easier'. It had been the disputes over Morocco that had 'given a recurring anti-German edge to the Anglo-French understanding'. What they did not say openly was that they no longer had any reason to suppose that the Anglo-French entente was specifically hostile towards Germany.[23]

If there was less reason for concern about France, the Franco-German accord did nothing to placate Radical doubts about the 'suitability' of tsarist Russia as England's partner. No one better recognised the sensitivity of elements in the Liberal party on this issue than Arthur Balfour. He made sport of them in the House for accepting the Anglo-Russian convention without protest. Balfour's words pricked and irritated the Radical conscience, but it took the announcement that Edward was to meet the Tsar at Reval to change their muted grumbles to clamorous denunciation. From his announcement in May of the Reval visit, Grey was constantly sniped at and ambushed by incensed Radical backbenchers at Question Time. Eventually, the government gave way and allowed a full debate on 4 June. Radical and Labour critics were prepared to admit that, 'They might unwisely have swallowed the gnat of an Anglo-Russian Agreement, but the Government and its Tory supporters should not be surprised when they strained at the thought of that agreement becoming a rapprochement and then by degrees an alliance.'[24] A. G. Gardiner's Daily News was particularly vociferous, constantly sounding a note of alarm about 'the forces of reaction' represented on the Treasury Bench by Asquith, Haldane and Grey, who 'seemed disposed to exaggerate relations with Russia from correctitude into affection'.[25] Even so, only with great reluctance did Grey acknowledge that he was obliged to answer his critics in open forum.[26]

Grey dealt sternly and unkindly with his tormentors. He mocked them as peace-lovers whose policies could only lead to war. His policy, he insisted, would lead to peace. Should it be rejected or its working made impossible, he would resign. He also warned that if the king's visit to Reval was cancelled 'you might as well tear up the Anglo-Russian Convention'. Grey made it abundantly clear that he did not intend to be dissuaded from closer relations with Russia by the ill-considered baying of back-bench critics. He would not decelerate, but rather intended to force the pace of Anglo-Russian rapprochement. Before this formidable assault and in the face of the Foreign Secretary's obvious intransigence, Radical opposition crumbled.[27]

Strachey, always a stout advocate of Grey and his conduct of Britain's affairs, wrote to the Foreign Secretary.

> I must congratulate you very heartily upon the success of the Reval meeting and upon the splendid way in which you met your detractors in the House of Commons. The action of the 'Daily News' has really been monstrous. The attitude of the German Press towards the Reval meeting is very significant and shows what would happen if we did not take these precautions against fire.[28]

In his reply, as in all his letters of this period, Grey made no attempt to conceal his anger and contempt, for his opponents. 'The difficulty with emotional people of the Daily News type', he told Strachey, 'is that they cannot believe any fact which does not make for their own view; and they are so pervaded by the consciousness of their own good intentions that they sometimes dispense with the precautions which are necessary to find out what is true.' Such was the passion Anglo-Russian relations stirred in Grey's breast that he could stray so far from his usual correct and reserved demeanour as to call Gardiner, who was a distinguished, thoughtful and responsible Liberal editor, a liar. What was more, this charge he laid at the feet of a Unionist editor.[29] Grey's anger had scarce cooled a month later when he characterised his critics to the king's secretary, Knollys, as 'extreme and violent men whose intransigence makes it impossible for the Government . . . to bring out the merits of the case'.[30]

Grey's Radical opponents would not have been surprised to learn that he sought balm for his wounded feelings and support for his policies from his nominal political foes. During the Reval debate in the Commons, the Labour member for East Leeds, James O'Grady, had made a palpable hit, warmly cheered on the government back benches, when he had pointed to Grey flanked by Asquith and Haldane and said, 'We heard nothing like this when the late Premier was in his place.' The as yet unspoken but generally shared assumption among the Foreign Secretary's critics was that so long as Campbell-Bannerman lived he had kept a firm grip upon the Liberal Imperialist triumvirate. Now they asked themselves whether a government, led by Asquith, boasting such ministers as the Secretaries of State for Foreign Affairs and War, was truly entitled to be called 'Liberal'? Why also, in matters of foreign affairs, was there this constant demand for and emphasis upon secrecy? 'England is prepared to trust a Liberal Cabinet,' avowed *New Age*, 'but only so long as a Liberal Cabinet trusts England. Is the present plan in foreign affairs one of general amicability or one of defensive and offensive alliances? Ententes we can understand and support – but alliances are a horse of another colour.'[31]

Looking back over the pre-1914 period, Archibald Hurd, leader writer and naval expert of the *Daily Telegraph*, counted it 'a providential ordering of affairs that the Asquith government and not the Conservative party was in control. . . . In those fateful years, the Conservative party would have been harried by the left wing section of the Liberals and it is unlikely that the Liberal Imperialists, lacking inside information of what Germany was doing, would have given it support.'[32] These were recollections made in the far from tranquil circumstances of a second great war with Germany. But Hurd was an informed commentator on the navy. Britain's naval preparations were the leitmotif that ran through the debates of those years, connected Britain's attitude to both France and Russia and dictated the deep suspicion of Germany. Germany's pursuit of *Weltpolitik* made rivalry with a world Power like Britain inevitable. The Imperial Navy was the necessary instrument forged to effect Germany's new policy. It could not be reduced, as the Germans repeatedly made plain to British politicians and officials. As the Kaiser, in his inimitable manner, told Charles Hardinge, Germany would rather go to war than discuss naval limitation. In part this intransigence is explained by the German view of British attitudes on the subject. They supposed that British talk of naval arms limitation was hypocritical, designed to maintain at the least possible cost the substantial advantage Britain already enjoyed over all other nations. The naval strength,

258   *'And he gathered them in a place called . . . Armageddon'*

actual and potential, of the two Powers was a constant factor in any diplomatic move. The other significant consequence of Germany's pursuit of *Weltpolitik* was that she became more dependent than in the past upon Austro-Hungarian friendship in Europe. This, in turn, had important consequences for the new diplomatic alignment of Russia with England. All these considerations were part of Grey's calculations. That is why he deplored what seemed to him to be the simplistic, blinkered and compartmentalised thinking of so many of his critics.

Whatever the original intentions of the Russian and British governments when they signed their convention, the result of their handiwork was certain to operate to Germany's disadvantage. The Russians took pains to emphasise to the Germans that they were not biased against them, but a combination of inept German diplomacy and the growing strength and influence of the pan-Slav movement within Russia slowly pushed Russia out of the orbit of the Central Powers. Renewed Russian interest in the Balkans coincided with another violent spasm of instability in that frequently volatile area. Austria-Hungary, under Aehrenthal's tutelage, had determined to reassert its own authority. Though Russia proved to be a difficult partner, particularly in Persia, the Anglo-Russian Convention laid the last great imperial bogy for Britain – a Russian attack upon India. This, in turn, powerfully concentrated British attention upon questions of the Balance of Power in Europe and the increasingly obvious threat to British security posed by a modern, powerfully armed German navy across the North Sea. The political and strategic implications of the Anglo-Russian agreement were as enormous as they were difficult for contemporary commentators and politicians to comprehend immediately. The simplistic imperatives dictated by loyalty to outdated traditions, the short-sighted priorities of political debate, like the complacent shorthand of so much popular journalism, hid rather than illuminated the inherent complexities. From the moment King Edward met Tsar Nicholas at Reval, the expression 'Triple Entente', signifying the network of understandings between Britain, France and Russia, became common currency.[33]

The presence of Admiral Fisher and General French as members of King Edward's suite on his Reval visit meant one thing only to continental observers: the two Powers were obviously engaged in military and naval conversations. Here also – had it been required – was 'proof' of the true European significance of the agreement between the two imperial powers. This was certainly the popular view in Germany to which the Kaiser gave expression when reviewing his troops at Döberitz. 'It appears as though they want to encircle us. We will know how to bear that. . . . Just let them attack. We are ready.'[34] Bülow, however, insisted that it was fanciful to suppose that Britain was intent upon isolating Germany in Europe, and told George Saunders that the Emperor had not used the word *einkreisen* in his speech at Döberitz. Bülow was 'sick of the word and hoped never to hear it again'.[35]

In the *National Review*, Maxse was happily and busily asserting that the duty of every patriotic Englishman was to form as faithful and firm a friendship with Russia as with France. He offered his wholehearted support to Grey whose wisdom as Foreign Secretary was confirmed by the manner in which

he was being pilloried by his left-wing critics. They charged Grey with ignoring
Liberal principles and adopting 'an ignoble policy of alliance and intrigue to
forestall German ambitions'.[36] When *The Times* asserted that 'understandings
readily become the parents of alliances should unjustifiable aggression by
others ever render alliances necessary', this confirmed the belief of many of
Grey's critics that the one remaining safe policy was for Britain to withdraw
into isolation. *Nation* was not prepared to go as far as some and believe that
Grey entertained aggressive designs towards Germany, but would not deny
that his demeanour suggested he supposed war with Germany was inevitable.
'He sees the risk to European peace from German ambitions and he raises
against that danger barrier behind barrier, and after insurance,
reinsurance. . . . Such preparations against the "inevitable" war . . . tend to
realise the fear that has become an obsession.'[37]

Patriotic editors did not share the same concerns as Massingham and Gardiner. 'I am profoundly convinced myself of the danger of being unprepared in
the case of Germany,' Strachey unnecessarily prefaced a letter to Grey with
which he enclosed a note that he proposed to send to a German publisher,
Tauchnitz, who had complained of the *Spectator*'s 'anti-German bias'. Did
Grey think that he had stated the case fairly?

> Our weakness is indeed, to my mind, an unfair temptation to the ambitious
> and aggressive party in Germany. I always to some extent sympathised
> with the Irishman who excused his friends in a certain village for having
> shot the local landlord in these terms: 'What right had he to tempt poor
> people on his estate by goin' about quite unarmed and unprotected?' I do
> not want to tempt the ruling oligarchy in Germany into doing something
> wrong and something which may cause the greatest misery in the world
> by going about unprotected and unarmed.

Grey replied, 'I think your letter puts the facts of the case very well. Our
attitude towards the Germans is not unfriendly but they have forced us to
make it defensive.'[38]

With relations between the Powers so volatile that a nudge rather than a
heave might fatally disturb the delicate equipoise, the replacement of George
Saunders as Berlin correspondent of *The Times* was as much a subject of
anxious comment among British Foreign Office staff as it was the cause of
much heart-searching at Printing House Square. Moberly Bell and Chirol at
first decided to transfer Henry Wickham Steed from Vienna to Berlin. Steed
had agreed but with considerable reluctance. His hostile reports from Vienna
had prompted a stream of complaints from Mensdorff, the Austrian Ambassador, to Tyrrell. Attempts by Tyrrell to have Steed muzzled had been unsuccessful, but by July 1908, Bell was having second thoughts about the wisdom
of sending Steed to Berlin as Saunders's replacement. He therefore wrote to
Steed admitting that:

> The suggestion you should go to Berlin raised such an outcry that I had
> to enquire its reason and find that while nobody doubts your ability you
> are regarded as a firebrand of the most dangerous type. Saunders who

was not loved in Berlin – was regarded as an angel of peace compared
to you – I was warned by the highest authorities that sending you to Berlin
would place us wholly in the wrong and that if you were even in Paris the
Entente would not last 12 months. I think that you should know this and
endeavour to acquire a better reputation for sobriety of judgment.[39]

Steed was not inclined to accept Bell's reproof quietly. He responded with
an immediate, spirited counter-charge, insisting that Bell owed it to him 'to
read patiently what I have to say'.

I do not know what the quarters are in which you say I have established
positive distrust in my discretion; but diplomatic and other friends have
frequently repeated to me similar expressions as having been used with
regard to me by my colleagues Lavino and Saunders. 'Clever, yes
certainly; but deplorably little judgment and no discretion,' was a kind
remark repeated to me only a fortnight ago by a diplomatist who heard
it from Saunders in Berlin. . . . The warning that 'even if I were in Paris
the Entente would not last twelve months' is new to me. . . . To attribute
to me such a responsibility (if the Entente should go smash) would be as
ludicrous as it is to believe that the Entente was created by Lavino.

Steed next turned to savage Lavino. Had it not been for Walter's refusal,
Lavino had proposed that an émigré Hungarian musician in Paris, rather than
Steed, should be employed as the most reliable source of information on
Austria. The man had subsequently been revealed as an ex-agent of the
Austrian Foreign Office dismissed by his employers as unreliable.

Bell was reminded that Steed, in a letter of 10 May, had asked *not* to be
sent to Berlin.

Unless you appointed Maxse you could hardly find an Englishman,
certainly no member of our staff, whose appointment to Berlin would
be so obnoxious as mine to the German Government. Saunders is not
liked but I am hated in Berlin. I have the strongest reason to believe
that the German Government . . . would regard my appointment as a
provocation. . . . They regard me as having helped to spread distrust of
Berlin in this country [Austria] and in Italy, and as having worked against
German leadership in the Triple Alliance and the extension of German
influence in and around the Adriatic. . . . I believe that if I went to Berlin,
I should be expelled at the first moment of tension. . . . The German
Government, through the Ambassador at Rome and here, repeatedly tried
to use me as a tool, against Saunders – and failed. It then tried to set me
up against the Anglo-French policy in Morocco – and failed. Having
learned at the Austro-Hungarian FO that the whole Austrian press was
by contract in servitude to Germany in matters like the Morocco question,
the attacks on Lord Lansdowne and on King Edward, I revealed the fact
in the paper and by degrees spiked the biggest international Pan-German
gun, the Neue Freie Presse. You may not know[40] that Vienna, not Berlin,
has been the centre of German intrigues against England for the last three
years and that I, not Saunders, have had to bear the brunt of the attack.

The eight pages of typescript ended with Steed's insistence that he bore no grudge against either Lavino or Saunders. Nevertheless, he doubted their ability to judge the true nature of Austro-Hungarian affairs and thus to comment upon his competence. He seems to have assumed that reservations about his suitability as a correspondent were limited to the jealousies of newspaper rivals. Outside the charmed circle of *The Times*'s foreign correspondents, he gave examples of how he had been unjustly attacked and misrepresented by a correspondent of the *Daily Mail* and by Julius Andrassy, the Hungarian Minister of the Interior. He assured Bell he was not particularly disturbed about having to stay in Vienna, but had he been posted to Berlin he would have understood the reluctance of the Germans to accept him.

> The German Government dreams of controlling the international press to prevent criticism of its schemes. . . . It does not want – just when they have got rid of Saunders – to have in Berlin a man like me who, through his former intimacy with Germans in high positions knows so much of the workings of the German secret service. . . . You insisted that I should go and in order not to add to your difficulties, I regretfully acquiesced; but I made up my mind that, as soon as my appointment should be definitive, I would go to Berlin, see my old friends, Jagow or Flotow who now hold high positions at the Wilhelm Strasse, and say that. . . . I should try to find a common denominator between the interests of my own country and those of the country I lived in, and that, if they gave me fair play, they would have no reason to complain of any lack of reciprocity.[41]

Steed was not appointed to Berlin. Tyrrell supposed that it had been his words to Chirol that had decided the Vienna correspondent's fate. 'He would have been a disastrous appointment both for the Times and us,' Tyrrell wrote to Spring Rice who, together with Lascelles, had also argued against Steed's appointment. 'Steed in Berlin,' Spring Rice had informed his friend Chirol, would have been 'like a red rag to the Teutonic bull'.[42]

Lavino's sudden, unexpected death in August, and the equally unexpected appointment of Saunders as Paris correspondent, deeply offended Steed. He coveted that appointment and had confidently expected to be Lavino's successor. Nevertheless, it was the treatment of his close friend, James David Bourchier, *The Times*'s Balkan correspondent, that determined he would resign when he reached the age of 40 in 1910. Nothing Chirol said could persuade Steed otherwise, and he confirmed his intention in a letter to Bell of 19 October. Thus, for several months, the foreign department of *The Times* was in sad disarray. It was not to enjoy a measure of harmony and unity of purpose until the spring of 1909 - a crucial six-month period during which there was intense diplomatic activity occasioned by Austria's annexation of Bosnia-Herzegovina. The real source of debility at Printing House Square was not so much the clash between incompatible personalities and the petty professional jealousies of foreign correspondents, but the continued ill-health of Chirol, which meant frequent and long absences, and Moberly Bell's exhaustion from overwork as the direct consequence of Northcliffe's purchase and reorganis-ation of *The Times*.

In August 1908 King Edward, having met the Kaiser at Cronberg, travelled to Ischl to meet the Emperor Franz Joseph. Charles Hardinge had told Steed of the Kaiser's angry reaction when the diplomat had dared to 'take the bull by the horns' and mentioned the naval question. William had avowed that Germany would rather go to war than accept dictation from Britain either about the speed of construction or the size of her naval building programme that had been increased that April.[43] The meeting at Ischl promised to be an altogether more friendly gathering, and Steed wrote to tell Bell of how 'the King and F. J. are like two old chums.' Nevertheless, he warned that Aehren-thal, 'a very slippery customer', was more than likely 'to play us another dirty trick as soon as he wishes to please himself or procure a personal success'.[44]

At the beginning of August, Steed had been sounded out by Friedrich Gaertner about Britain's likely reaction to an Austrian annexation of Bosnia-Herzegovina. When Steed told King Edward this and that Austria was preparing for annexation, Edward dismissed the idea as incredible. His mind was filled with thoughts of the need to cultivate better relations with Germany, while a conversation with Clemenceau had convinced him that Britain needed to strengthen her existing diplomatic ties with France and effect a thorough reform of her army based upon some form of compulsion.[45] On 25 August, Steed had a conversation with Isvolsky, the Russian Foreign Minister. He had been assured that the Anglo-Russian Convention was now one of the settled bases of Russia's foreign policy. While Isvolsky did not consider Austrian annexation of Bosnia a likely contingency, he insisted it would be viewed by Russia as a clear infraction of the Berlin Treaty.[46] A fortnight later, Steed learned the Austrian and Russian Foreign Ministers had reached an agreement over the Balkans. Isvolsky was to procure French and British compliance with the annexation of Bosnia-Herzegovina. But when Isvolsky reached Paris on the first stage of his mission, he discovered a note awaiting him from Aehren-thal. Austria was not prepared to wait for Anglo-French concurrence; the annexation would be announced immediately. Isvolsky had been tricked. Aehrenthal was behaving exactly as Steed had warned. Austria's Foreign Minister even had sufficient gall to outface a very angry British Ambassador, Goschen, who called him a liar for denying, on previous occasions, any know-ledge of the annexation or the proclamation of Bulgarian independence.[47]

In London, Grey's immediate reaction to the news was to protest vigorously. All British political parties and the press joined in rare unanimity to condemn Austria. Bell approached Mensdorff directly but learned nothing new that might have explained Austria's action. When told this, Steed could not resist pointing out that in an article written two years earlier which *The Times* had chosen not to publish, he had stated that everything had been prepared for annexation in September 1906. On that occasion, only the unwillingness of the populace had forestalled the scheme. Steed was uncertain in his mind whether Isvolsky had been a willing victim or whether he had been swindled by Aehrenthal. What he was certain of, beyond any doubt, was that 'The annexation scheme, the proclamation of Bulgarian independence and the whole business was the realisation of a pre-conceived plan between Aehrenthal and Germany and that its main object was, as before – to drive a wedge between England and Russia and if possible between England and France.' The excuse given by Aehrenthal and Mensdorff, that Austria had been obliged to act as she did because of the constitutional movement in Turkey, was nothing but 'hocus pocus'.[48]

One of the fruits of Chirol's tour that autumn from St Petersburg to Vienna via Belgrade, to see and, if possible, soothe the various disgruntled and discontented *Times* foreign correspondents, was a series of six articles that appeared between 1 November and 5 December on 'The Situation in the Near East'. The series was remarkably fair-minded in its comments on Austria, but Forgách, Austria's minister in Belgrade, first suggested that Chirol's visit had been planned to organise a press campaign against Austria, and then denounced *The Times*'s foreign editor for stirring up war fever in Serbia. All the while, in London, the Austrian Ambassador complained constantly to the Foreign Office about the tone of the British press and the behaviour of British journalists whom he charged with 'fomenting trouble'. In particular Mensdorff complained about the *Daily Telegraph* and the work of D. D. Braham to whom Steed wrote in late December in the most pessimistic tones, 'As regards the European situation in general, I am inclined to share the opinion expressed by Clemenceau to Cartwright – that Europe is drifting to war.'[49]

Months passed and the crisis continued to drag on with no sign of resolution, a constant reminder of the dangerously uneasy relations between the Great Powers. The British Radical press that at first had rushed in concert with its patriotic contemporaries to compliment Grey upon his principled stand against Austria's action in Bosnia was obliged to reassess the position. Perhaps, upon reflection, it would have been wiser had Grey taken a wider, less juridical view of the problem and accepted Austria's *de jure* sovereignty in an area which had long been hers *de facto*. The *Manchester Guardian*, as befitted a stern proponent of international law, had praised Grey in October as its 'guardian spirit'. In December, it was claiming that to lecture Austria on her wickedness was 'a form of cant being very much overdone'.[50] In January 1909, the *Nation* was prepared to admit that Austria's action had been 'understandable' in the light of 'the pronounced anti-German flavour of British foreign policy'. By February, it had decided the 'most deplorable feature' of the whole crisis was not Austria's initial action, but 'the marked isolation of Germany'. That matters had not gone from bad to worse owed nothing to Grey's handling of the problem but was due to 'the reticence and self-suppression of German diplomacy'.[51]

The change of heart in the Radical press between October 1908 and February 1909 was prompted by two important considerations. It was reluctantly but eventually recognised that Grey, in censuring Austria, had effectively widened the divide between the Central Powers and the Triple Entente. This fear was confirmed by Asquith's solemn warning made to a Guildhall audience on 9 November. 'We shall stand by our friends, and we mean to keep ourselves furnished with the means to serve them to good purpose should such service on our part become needful.' The Prime Minister's speech was acclaimed by the Tory press. Worrying as were both its content and sentiment, the major concern of Radical journalists was their difficulty in continuing to condemn Austria while the patriotic newspapers were doing the same thing in order to justify an enormous increase in naval armaments and to arouse fear and hatred of Germany to fever pitch.

A letter Garvin wrote to George Prothero in mid-November 1908 contained sentiments that were typical of the attitude adopted by Tory journalists. 'If the German scare helps us to get an extra Dreadnought, as seems most likely, then the work of the last few months will have done the best it could.'[52] Depending upon the predilections of the writer and the domestic political contingencies of the moment, for the next eighteen months the strength of the navy or the army was the major focus of concern among Tory journalists. It was for this reason that they insisted upon interpreting every move in the diplomatic game as evidence of German hostility towards England, and always, the same conclusion was drawn. 'The Power which has not force at its back to defend its rights will, in time, be brushed or roughly pushed aside.'[53] The final dénouement of the crisis, with Germany's appearance in 'shining armour' at Austria's side obliging Russia to accept the annexation and to back down, was instanced by the patriotic propagandists as a case that proved their point. At the same time, and setting aside the question of Anglo-Russian relations, many commentators, like Percy in the *National Review*, argued there had been a weakening of the Anglo-French entente because England was incapable of offering France worthwhile military aid should the Germans attack. Commenting with approval on Percy's articles, Milner wrote to Roberts, 'I believe Clemenceau was a sincere friend to this country and I have no reason to suspect the present French Ministry, but how long will they be able to hold the nation if the impression of our military weakness and inability to help them gains ground, is very much more doubtful.'[54]

Writing in *The Times* immediately after Russia's surrender to Germany's *coup de main*, Chirol excused the Russian action in the circumstances as a case of 'sheer necessity'. He added, the leading Slav Power 'would not forget or forgive'. By a naked act of aggression Germany had overthrown the Balance of Power in Europe, and Chirol was not slow in pointing out the lesson to English readers.

> The course which Germany has chosen to adopt . . . cannot make for permanent peace. For no Power which in the course of history has arrogated to itself the right to dominate Europe and to impose its own will by sheer force has ever ensured or secured peace. . . . There is one moral at any rate which Englishmen should lose no time in drawing from these startling developments. The British Navy has stood more than once between Europe and the claim of some great Continental Power to be the sole and supreme arbiter of its destinies. . . . The British Navy is the real bulwark of European freedom.[55]

What afforded Chirol particular comfort, so he told Northcliffe, was that for the first time that he could ever remember, 'the "Times" on the German danger was quoted by the "Westminster Gazette" . . . practically endorsing it and paraphrasing it. It is these little things that make one hope after all that one is not merely a voice crying in the wilderness.'[56]

It was significant that the level-headed Spender should have agreed with Chirol's chilling analysis, but the Radicals merely shrugged their shoulders and reminded themselves that the editor of the *Westminster Gazette* had long been very close to Grey and had always been a sympathetic interpreter of his policies. Where they had argued for a Liberal foreign policy, distinctive in tone and content from that pursued by Unionist governments, Spender had urged the primacy of 'continuity' in the conduct of British foreign affairs. But there was no hiding the fact that the Radicals were, for the moment, uncertain and undoubtedly shaken by Germany's brutal resolution of the Bosnian crisis. Their first reaction was not to seek a strengthening of the Triple Entente as insurance of British security, but rather to advocate isolation. The 'progress' of Radical thinking during the next three months can easily be measured in the columns of the *Manchester Guardian*. In May it advocated isolation. By June it was asking: 'If our statesmen had the wit to make friendship with France and even with Russia with whom our political quarrels were far older and more difficult of adjustment, then why not have Germany as a friend rather than an enemy?' In July, confidence somewhat restored, the *Guardian* was asserting that as Germany was the leading European Power it was better and wiser that she should be on Britain's side rather than 'to coquette with the idea . . . of forming European combinations against her'.[57]

As Grey had been given the credit for creating the apparent solidarity of the Triple Entente, he now suffered the most acute embarrassment at its collapse and the obvious futility of conventional guarantees in the face of German determination and Austrian intransigence. Arthur Nicolson, who was extremely pro-Russian and had for long constantly and staunchly advocated the conversion of the ententes into alliances, could not have been more pessimistic in his assessment of the diplomatic scene. France had dragged her feet throughout choosing to settle her Moroccan difficulties with Germany in the middle of the crisis. This did not bode well for the future of Anglo-French relations. The hegemony of the Central Powers in Europe seemed confirmed by their Bosnian triumph. Once more England was virtually isolated. 'The Franco-Russian alliance had not borne the test: the Anglo-Russian entente [was] not sufficiently deep-rooted to have any appreciable influence.'[58] Not as emotionally involved as Nicolson with the fate of Anglo-Russian agreement, yet a sympathetic critic of Grey's policies and one of the best informed of commentators on European affairs, Dr E. J. Dillon concluded from recent events that 'the notion of a union of Slav, Anglo-Saxon and Gaul has been exploded and the conduct of France and Russia during the crisis suggests that the concept of the Triple Entente has been a prodigious and perilous mistake'.[59] There was disillusion and confusion on both sides of the domestic political divide as Tory and Radical alike sought to discover the best path forward after the shock of the annexation crisis. Nor did Rosebery do anything for clarity of thought or national confidence when, rousing himself from retirement, in a speech he made to the Imperial Press Conference in June he talked of *tacens bellum* – silent war – and the calm before the storm. Europe, he claimed, for the past forty years had been nothing but an armed camp and was now bloated with armaments. Yet he called not for retrenchment but the building of even more Dreadnoughts and the introduction of 'a kind of National Service' – demands that were eagerly headlined by papers like the *Daily Mail*.[60] The Radical press could maintain only a rather bemused silence in the face of the earl's strange and confusing response to 'bloated armaments'.

Of Britain's two entente partners, undoubtedly Russia seemed the more paradoxical and difficult to support. The Tsar's visit to Cowes in August 1909, just as the continuing problem of Persia, merely emphasised the frailty and the problems inherent in the Anglo-Russian association. Most of the Liberal press sought every opportunity to denigrate Grey as the architect of an abhorrent connection with a reactionary régime, while the patriotic press gave aid and comfort to Sir Edward and supported the convention. Radical disgust with this 'unnatural coalition' of Liberal Foreign Secretary and jingo press was epitomised by *New Age*'s despairing outburst. 'The *Daily Mail* is more competent than Sir Edward Grey to pursue a foreign policy – and that is the most offensive remark we can make.'[61] On foreign affairs, 1909 ended as it had begun, with a slanging match between Tory and Radical critics. Nevertheless, there was no gainsaying the truth of the assessment of the year made by the pacifist monthly, *Concord*. Although 'there ha[d] been plenty of explosive material at hand', and, 'despite the mishandling of many issues', the comforting distinction of 1909 was 'for all the efforts of Jingoes there has been no great war'.[62]

It was a disquieting thought for those who shared Leo Maxse's vision of Europe, that in England, 'the voice of the pedlars of peace potions' was much too loud and influential in the land. The nation's security was at risk, undermined by the soft words and muddled thinking of 'cranks' and 'Potsdam-loving lunatics'. Norman Angell's book, first published in November 1909 as *Europe's Optical Illusion*, soon to reappear, greatly enlarged and revised, under its more familiar title, *The Great Illusion*, was a huge popular success. It appeared to challenge and controvert thinking that hitherto had been considered axiomatic and unassailable by every civilised European Power. Not just the usual faddists, but an ever-increasing number of influential and thoughtful people were attracted by Angell's thesis that war in the twentieth century could never again be a source of profit to the victor. H. W. Wilson was outraged by the 'apostasy' of one of the 'Chief's' employees. ' "Norman" is very clever,' he admitted to Northcliffe, 'and it would be difficult to write a better book in defence of his particular thesis than his; let us hope that he will succeed better in fooling the Germans than in convincing me.'[63]

But it was not only Norman Angell about whom Maxse and his friends had cause to complain. The Anglo-German Friendship Committee, the World Peace Congress, the Interparliamentary Union, the Associated Council of Churches of the British and German Empires, were some among many diverse groups that were amazingly active, promoting the ideals of peace, arbitration and armament retrenchment in general, and Anglo-German friendship in particular. They exchanged visits, made speeches, published papers and with rare unanimity asserted confidently, in Alfred Fried's words, that 'the sunshine of civilisation and of true human fellowship will destroy the germs and spur us on to international jealousies and internecine strife'. Adolf Richter, President of the German Peace Society, in a New Year's message to the International Peace and Arbitration Society in London, commended 'the energetic manner with which you have replied to those who have been trying by misrepresentation and distrust to disturb the steadily growing agreement between our two countries'.[64] The death in May 1910 of the king – 'Edward the Peacemaker' - and the tearful behaviour of the Kaiser at the funeral, was all grist to the mill of those who now *demanded* an end of hostility towards Germany. Who now could doubt, the Liberal press demanded in chorus, the Kaiser's sincerity or his goodwill towards Britain? Even 'the most nervously distrustful politician' should 'be convinced of the baselessness of the fears they have sought to plant in our minds'.[65]

Maxse, beside himself with frustrated rage and disgust at the growing strength of the peacemakers' campaign, determined that he would challenge the Quaker owner of the *Daily News*. He was encouraged and delighted, he told Sandars, that Balfour had awakened to the dangers of the peacelovers' campaign and was advising the Tory party to get off the defensive. 'I much prefer permanent aggression upon the other side,' he added unnecessarily. 'In this spirit I have drafted an article which will be a tremendous blow to the enemy if successful.' When Sandars replied cautiously, mentioning the risks of libel, Maxse cheerfully affirmed, 'Of course it is a defamatory article ... but it is more than improbable that the Cocoa Kings [the Cadburys] will care to face the music. ... I want to deal a blow at the anarchists who are trying to wreck this country.'[66] Henry Wilson told Mary Northcliffe he hoped that Leo would 'get plenty of scalps without any libel actions. It is perilous this head-hunting, but he at least is ready to kill or be killed.'[67] The Cadburys, as Maxse had anticipated, refused to rise to his bait, even when he produced another, more damaging attack. He received the effusive congratulations of John Walter for this second onslaught, 'but the adversary seems to prefer that the case should go by default rather than that the public interest in the matter should be unduly stimulated by argument. "Least said, soonest mended." ' [68] The Cadburys had always been a source of intense irritation to right-wing polemicists. Maxse was following a well-trodden and familiar path where he had ventured before in the company of, among others, Bottomley's *John Bull*, *The World* and the *Standard*. The *Daily News* pressed the case for disarmament more ardently than any other daily newspaper save the *Manchester Guardian*, propagated the pacifist message assiduously and constantly advocated and agitated for a rapprochement with Germany. It was best to ignore Maxse for that merely irritated him the more.[69]

Despite his personal humiliation over the Bosnian annexation, and the obvious German desire that he should be removed from office, Isvolsky did not retire as Russian Foreign Secretary until September 1910, when he assumed his country's ambassadorship in Paris. His replacement, Sazonov, was a man of very different temper. He, together with the Tsar, hastened to meet the Kaiser, accompanied by Kiderlen, at Potsdam. There the Germans sought a written pledge from the Russians that they did not favour Britain's anti-German policy. In return they offered assurance that they were neither obliged nor prepared to side with Austria. When Sazonov refused, this did not confound the resources of German diplomacy. With the aid of Tardieu, whose compliance was purchased by a suitable bribe, and possibly Isvolsky, news of a 'Potsdam Agreement' between Russia and Germany was leaked to the press.[70] The lie was then given official confirmation by Bethmann-Hollweg when, on 10 December, he assured the Reichstag that agreement had been secured and that in future neither Power would enter into any hostile combination against the other.

The *Daily News* joyously concluded that the Triple Entente was now well and truly dead and buried. If the *Manchester Guardian* was rather more sceptical about the German claim, it nevertheless supposed that there no longer existed any danger of the entente system being converted into a series of military and naval alliances.[71] The Conservative press was thoroughly roused by what it considered was an entirely perverse interpretation of the European diplomatic scene. Maxse raged against 'our Cocoa contemporaries who are intent upon throwing the whole of Europe into Germany's arms'.[72] Garvin's attempts 'to awaken Englishmen to the real significance of the Potsdam meeting' brought him congratulations from Fred Wile, but also a warning.

> You have, as usual, hit the nail on the head, squarely in my judgment, and I attempted to say as much in a despatch to the 'Mail' last night. . . . When I was in London . . . I neglected no opportunity to impress people with the profound importance of the Russo-German deal but except for the Chief [Northcliffe] I was chagrined to find that my words seemed to fall on deaf ears. Nobody seemed to take the thing seriously. Upon one gentleman in particular, who enjoys some fame as a foreign 'authority', I managed to create the impression of a loon.[73]

Foreign Office staff were concerned that Grey might be obliged to concede to the Radicals in his party. Now they were not only a vociferous and troublesome group on the back benches but a force to be reckoned with inside the Cabinet. Would Grey, they wondered, be obliged to make concessions to the Germans in order to maintain party unity? Arthur Nicolson gloomily noted the growing popularity of the Society for Anglo-German Friendship, spurred on by the vigorous patronage of Britain's former Ambassador in Berlin, Lascelles. In Parliament, the Tories were fractious and dispirited after two failures within a year to unseat the Liberals from government. Nicolson would not have forgotten Hardinge's letter of the previous year that had discussed the chances of converting the ententes into alliances. 'It is impossible', Hardinge had written, 'to hope for a step forward by this Government. . . . When Balfour comes into office it may be different, but we must hope that it may not be too late.'[74] With the Tory failure at successive general elections to remove the Liberals, Esher admitted to Sandars he feared that politicians would so absorb themselves in domestic squabbles that inevitably Britain's international position would be undermined.

It is too long a story to write, but the entente with France is weakening

in the City and in commercial circles and this will one of these days
react on the action of the Ministers. We shall have to go carefully over
the whole strategical position which will become very grave in a few
years time unless we can fix up a Treaty with the United States. The *Jews*
– a powerful influence - loathe the Russian entente, and the great
financiers think the French use the entente to injure them and their
concerns.[75]

Gloomy prognoses about the Anglo-French entente became commonplace
when, in March 1911, taking advantage of French preoccupation with whether
or not they should send troops to Casablanca to punish the rebel Zaers, the
Germans raised money on the French market to finance the completion of the
Baghdad railway. Valentine Williams, then the *Daily Mail*'s Paris correspondent, informed Northcliffe that Cruppi, who had replaced Pichon at the Quai
d'Orsay, was nothing like as strong a supporter of the entente as his predecessor. In France there was 'a general feeling and fear that the Liberal Government is not quite *firm* on the entente'. As a consequence, the French were
'apprehensive and touchy'. Williams could only suggest that 'we should make
much of them at the Coronation'. Apparently the French were even disturbed
by King George's poor command of their language, and compared his regard
for their country very unfavourably with that of his late father.[76]

Later that same month, in a debate in the Commons, Grey, responding to
a reductionist amendment moved by Radical backbenchers, totally undermined
their criticisms by talk of arbitration and the need to decrease expenditure
upon armaments at some future, uncertain date. The Radical opposition
collapsed before Grey's blandishments and was reduced to 'a quivering jelly
of sentiment'.[77] What had particularly moved the Foreign Secretary's critics
was not only his talk of 'the progressive removal of all possible causes of
dispute' between the great European Powers, but the unaccustomed warmth
of his tone when referring to 'the excellent relations between the British and
German Government'.[78] Leo Maxse was furious. If the morale of the Radical
Liberals was high, his was correspondingly low. The Triple Entente appeared
to be in ruins. Grey apparently had 'absorbed the propaganda carried on by
sentimental Radicals and disloyal Jews, ostensibly in the interests of Anglo-
German "friendship" but actually aimed at the Triple Entente . . . the mainstay
of European peace and the only serious barrier to Teutonic aggression'. Now
the British Foreign Secretary seemed to think that his principal duty was 'to
gush about arbitration and weaken relations with our friends with a view to
conciliating our enemies'. Grey's latest and most tragic speech had 'opened
the flood gates of fatuity' so that 'every flatulent fool [was] on the peace path'.[79]

A domestic interlude: Lord Northcliffe asserts himself

I regard my position as that of a public trustee, with immense responsibilities.

Northcliffe to J. Compton-Rickett

So far as I am concerned the 'Observer' is nothing. It is everything to Garvin. . . . Under no circumstances will I continue in the 'Observer' with him. I am extremely fond of him, but I think he acted with great unwisdom.

Northcliffe to Max Aitken

Buckle wrote to me about the 'independence' of 'The Times'. I have learned a great deal of the 'independence' of 'The Times' during the last three years, and I know something of its 'independence' since the Jameson Raid, and I am ready for that sort of nonsense if required. Would indeed that 'The Times' were independent. It has about as much independence on certain matters as the hall porter at the Foreign Office or a Bond Street picture dealer's assistant.

Northcliffe to Reginald Nicholson

I have determined to make 1911 see 'The Times' in its old position, and am reorganizing it from cavern to cupola. . . . The quacks insist on the golf, and after three long years of Times' muddlers, it is essential that I smite them as vigorously as I try to the golf balls.

Northcliffe to Charles Whibley

'I am not very well,' Northcliffe plaintively informed George Sutton in February 1910, addressing his letter as from 'The Asylum, Manchester Street'. Confined for a month to a nursing home for 'complete rest' by Bernard Dawson, his latest medical consultant, Northcliffe likened the experience to being in prison. As inordinately concerned with the state of his own health as he was eager to diagnose and offer advice on the ailments of friends, employees and acquaintances, the newspaper proprietor was never a good patient. He was restless, disobedient, rude to his doctors and rarely followed their expensive advice. Philip Seymour Price, chosen from among 730 applicants as Northcliffe's personal medical adviser, was told that he was 'slow in the uptake' and was obliged to promise that he would mend his ways. Dr Price's advice was heeded only when he managed to discover some evidence of cardio-vascular damage in his petulant patient.

Constantly on the move; from house to house, from nursing home to hotel, from London to Paris to North America; frequently bewailing his 'weakness' yet filling his waking hours with interviews, telephone calls, dictation of notes to his secretaries on this, that and everything; perpetually scrawling pencilled notes with peremptory instructions to others; Northcliffe, supposedly suffering from nervous exhaustion, certainly induced it in others. Physically easily fatigued, he was by turns irritable, peevish, petulant and irascible with everyone save his 'Darling Mums' who was frequently if inaccurately assured that he was 'sticking closely to [his] cure'.

There were occasions when his behaviour, often agitated, was quite bizarre. The editors of his many juvenile papers were suddenly accused of depraving the tastes of their young readers. Evelyn Wrench, then sales manager of the Amalgamated Press, was severely wigged for allowing 'hundreds of vulgarities and indecencies in my papers . . . *Merry and Bright,* No 3. The front page is occupied by a fat man and an over-developed young woman . . . vulgar. On Page 6 there is a man holding a revolver. I never allow revolvers in the paper at all.' There did not seem to be a moment when either Northcliffe's tongue or his pen was idle. 'Such mental energy,' Garvin noted. 'But you need to relax. You should be kept chloroformed for six weeks.' The frequent holidays were not rest cures. Northcliffe's chosen travelling companions usually returned in a pitiable state of exhaustion. Moberly Bell painfully recalled how, on their trip to North America, Northcliffe changed his plans hourly, discussed the fortunes of *The Times* from early morning until late at night, while his sudden inspirations would involve others in endless correspondence.

> An hour ago he said to me: 'Now I am going to have three days of absolute peace, nothing to read, no one to abuse, I'm going to store my batteries!' Ten minutes ago he hammered at my door, 'Just look at this,' showing a local paper with some figures about immigration. 'We're not taking this seriously enough. Wire to Cook. Write to Buckle, leave letters for Grigg, and try to get hold of Amery, etc, etc . . .[1]

Northcliffe's erratic behaviour justified the persistent rumours circulating in London that he must be suffering from an incurable disease. But in November, Lady Northcliffe, who had been disturbed by her wayward husband's strange, frenetic antics, told Sutton, 'The Chief looks to be better than he has done for ten years – younger, firmer – better altogether. He eats well and sleeps perfectly. *But* he is rather nervous about himself.' Northcliffe promised Sutton that from now on he would rest more and follow Seymour Price's advice. 'I don't propose to resume really active work for a long time. . . . I fear I have been worrying everybody. Forgive me, dear Sutkin, if I have been cross.' It seemed that Northcliffe had made a complete and sudden recovery from the malaise that had dogged him throughout 1910, a recovery that was aided by his once more taking up golf at the instruction of Price, this time, however, with an almost religious fanaticism. 'Nothing ever did me so much good,' he was insisting a year later to Garvin. 'Steal one working day a week for this game.'[2]

To all outward appearances, at the beginning of 1911 the Garvin-Northcliffe partnership was closer and more amicable than ever. Yet there remained certain underlying tensions in this business and personal relationship of two self-willed Titans. Garvin admired Northcliffe but he still retained certain doubts about the 'Chief'; what he had described earlier to Maxse as 'a terrible reluctance . . . Northcliffe is sound about Germany but I might find myself at any moment up to my eyebrows in dirt about some other questions.'[3] For his part, Northcliffe was genuinely fond of Garvin and unstintingly admired his editorial and journalistic skills. Nevertheless, he found it increasingly difficult to support their constant petty squabbles over the *Observer*'s finances. From the beginning of their business relationship Northcliffe had made it abundantly clear that he regarded the *Observer*'s financial success as 'insurance' for the Garvin family. He had wanted to own a journal of opinion that counted in the nation's affairs, and Garvin had given him this. Northcliffe expected the *Observer* to pay its way like any other of his properties, but he was convinced the paper could achieve profitability in time, and that once established, the profits would increase. 'This has been my universal experience with newspapers,' he assured Garvin in August 1909, while congratulating him on the paper 'more and more becoming a journal of opinion which it ought to be'.[4] Northcliffe's confident prediction was realised in 1910, but instead of inducing greater harmony it led to a further series of scrapes about the interpretation of the original agreement between them and what proportion of the profit was due to the editor. It was Garvin who prompted this unnecessary friction, and he was being as difficult as only he knew how to be. For Northcliffe, distracted and debilitated as much by his innumerable and complex business affairs as by his illnesses, real and imaginary, and anxious to concentrate his attention upon reforming *The Times*, Garvin's carping placed an intolerable strain upon their friendship. 'Do not think me cavalier,' he wrote to Garvin in August 1910, 'but I literally cannot continue on the directorate of "The Observer" if it is to be a perpetual source of work. I am not the least interested in it financially and only care that it affords the Empire a peep at your great vision, only please do keep the country informed about Germany that unknown quantity.'[5]

Northcliffe's personal affection for his temperamental but brilliant friend remained undiminished, and he was never jealous of Garvin as others were later, unkindly and inaccurately, to suggest.[6] He was intrigued by the authority that Garvin had established with the Tory leadership; how he alone among journalists was privy to the secrets of the Constitutional Conference otherwise jealously guarded from prying eyes by the politicians; and grateful to share these secrets divulged by Garvin in long, fascinating, detailed, personal letters. When, in October, Garvin threatened once more to jeopardise their friendship with yet another ill-judged spat over his remuneration, Northcliffe's generous response was to insist, 'Do what you like about "The Observer". . . . The finance of "The Observer" is immaterial to me.' His only cautionary note was a warning that Garvin ought to 'concentrate upon that paper and do less outside work'.[7] Just when it seemed that all cause of discord between them had at last been removed, a political disagreement permanently sundered their working relationship.

Since September, the *Daily Mail* had been telling its readers that the imperial bond would be irreparably weakened should Canada grant special economic concessions to the United States, warnings prompted by the opening of discussions between the Canadian and American governments for possible mutual tariff reductions between their two countries. The previous year, Canada's Governor-General, Earl Grey, had complained to his friend Milner that Canadians regarded as insulting 'suggestions in the Observer, the Times and the Daily Mail that imperial sentiment is weakening', or that if Britain did not adopt protection giving tariff preference to Canada, that the Canadians would 'haul down the Canadian flag and run up the "Stars and Stripes" '.[8] Northcliffe was convinced that if Canada and America reached an agreement, this would mean the end of tariff reform and imperial preference. At best a reluctant tariff reformer, Northcliffe's dislike of food taxes – 'stomach taxes' as he preferred to call them – had been set aside only by Garvin's persistent siren persuasion. On Canada, with reason, he considered himself the better informed judge.[9]

Rallying now to his earlier loyalty to the Chamberlain clan (recently under suspicion because of his dealings with Balfour), Garvin proposed a scheme, greater both in vision and implication than an imperial unity based upon economic arguments. In the negotiations between Canada and the United States he perceived a seed that might grow into a mighty 'English-speaking alliance'. His vision was encouraged by the knowledge that the Germans were all too anxious to see Anglo-American relations ruptured, and was fortified by the enthusiastic descriptions of America and the American way of life provided by his old friend, Fisher, recently returned from a visit to the New World. 'Those who know', Fisher had written, 'proved to me the population would reach 250 million! Where are your Germans, Teutons, Slavs – Hebrews &c – compared to that concentrated figure. . . . The *language* is *English* – the literature is *English* – the traditions *English* & quite unknown to themselves their aspirations are *English!*'[10]

When the first details of the Canadian American Reciprocity Agreement became available in January 1911, the *Daily Mail*'s response was to insist that there could no longer be any hope of a commercial union between Canada and Britain based upon preferential tariffs. In a series of four leading articles the newspaper argued that the Chamberlainite gospel was now irrelevant to British domestic and imperial politics.[11] Though he must have known that his request would be unavailing, Northcliffe expressed the hope that the *Observer* would follow the lead of the *Daily Mail.* Garvin's response – although he was at pains to reaffirm his personal affection for Northcliffe – was uncompromisingly hostile. ' "God Help the Empire". . . . For the "Daily Mail" to appear to be the advocate of the "banged, barred and bolted door" seems to me as bad as bad can be. . . . I stick to my whole political faith. Like Luther: *Ich kann kein anders.*'[12] Northcliffe appealed to Garvin. Come to *Elmwood* and discuss everything 'before anything definite is done – it is a matter I thoroughly understand and feel strongly about'. Garvin remained obdurate despite this and other telegraphed messages, insisting that it was impossible for him to leave London. More honestly, he admitted that a meeting would only be a 'miserable and futile ordeal for us both. . . . You are not to be influenced by me . . . nothing can confuse my convictions. . . . If I could not express them according to my mind and conscience my public usefulness would be at an end. . . . I can't be silent and I will not lie by concealing or weakening my view.'[13]

Northcliffe's attitude on the issue was clear and he retained, as Garvin was well aware, a specific legal right of veto over any political article in the *Observer*. Nevertheless, in the next issue of that newspaper, 5 February 1911, Garvin slated the views of the *Daily Mail* arguing that imperial preference could 'perfectly well be combined with Anglo-American reciprocity'. He insisted that his and Chamberlain's vision was not redundant, as the *Mail* had claimed, but remained 'the master-key of policy, more living, more urgent, more powerful, more inspiring than ever'. The *Daily Mail*'s opinion – and by implication Northcliffe's – he likened to 'the mumblings of King Lear in his dotage', and 'staking the fate of the Empire on a hope, like Mr Micawber, that something will turn up'. These editorial views accompanied a prominently displayed and detailed account of a speech on reciprocity that Austen Chamberlain had made the previous evening in Birmingham. Austen's immediate response was to confirm that Garvin was firmly enfolded in the bosom of the protectionist elect: 'Your admirable Notes in today's Observer . . . most timely. What is the secret of the Daily Mail's desertion?'[14]

Northcliffe had sought and found consolation in a new ally, Max Aitken, recently elected member for Ashton-under-Lyme. Aitken, described by Northcliffe as 'the only man in England who knows the Canadian situation', arranged a meeting with Andrew Bonar Law, soon to replace Balfour as leader of the Unionist party but then nursing a recent electoral defeat at North West Manchester. The three men agreed that they would work together to rid the Unionist party of its attachment to food taxes, 'the Liberal sword of never-ceasing sharpness against which the Unionists have no shield'.[15] While the Liberal press, and the *Daily News* in particular, gloated over the trouncing the *Observer* had administered to the *Daily Mail*'s campaign, seeing this as clear evidence that their opponents had no intelligible policy, Northcliffe instructed G. F. Cornford, secretary of the Observer Company, to remove his name from the list of directors. Garvin was advised he had three weeks in which to find a purchaser for the *Observer*.[16]

The sudden breach between Northcliffe and his most able press lieutenant naturally caused both consternation and speculation among their mutual friends. H. W. Wilson wrote to tell Garvin that he could not 'understand what Alfred is about: it is all an enigma to me. I had hoped that you had attained a commanding influence over him, and that the Radical attacks on you, which would to me instantly commend you and show that the enemy feared you more than any other man, would have strengthened your position. But it is now clear to me that some subterranean power is working against you.' Wilson and Maxse had racked their brains to discover who this 'unknown force' was, but to no avail. Northcliffe was 'studiously avoiding discussing the business . . . though he referred to you in terms which left no doubt in my mind of his respect and affection for you'.[17]

Garvin's immediate future was secured when W. W. Astor, multi-millionaire owner of the *Pall Mall Gazette,* bought the *Observer.* It was popularly supposed that Garvin's success in finding a purchaser for the *Observer* was a setback for Northcliffe. 'I am truly glad you are out of a tight place,' wrote Henry Lucy. 'I, as an old journalist, would have regarded it as something like a crime if after triumphantly recreating the paper you had been chucked aside as if you were the hall-porter or the office boy.'[18] In fact, Northcliffe had behaved very honourably and with considerable magnanimity towards his difficult if brilliant editor. In a very real sense their rupture over the Reciprocity Agreement and their subsequent behaviour reflected to both their credits.[19] Northcliffe was certainly more generous in his dealings with Garvin than towards the senior members of *The Times*'s staff. Now that he had lost the *Observer* he was more determined than ever that his will should be done at Printing House Square. Even as he sundered his connection with the *Observer,* he was engaged in a pitched battle with the 'Grey beards' of *The Times.* The immediate source of conflict was the ratification of the Declaration of London, but the underlying problem was an old one. Who was to be master at PHS?

Moberly Bell as manager, Buckle as editor and Valentine Chirol as foreign editor, saw themselves as the protectors and guarantors of the integrity, traditions and spirit of *The Times.* Northcliffe contemptuously referred to them as the 'Old Guard'. He did not dislike them as individuals, but for him they personified that unfortunate general attitude at Printing House Square, ignorant, resentful and suspicious of the best modern ideas of efficient business practice. They seemed uncaring that *The Times* should be a viable, commercial venture. Increasingly Northcliffe displayed his impatience and displeasure with the attitudes of the 'Black Friars', and as early as March 1909 had suggested, only half-jokingly, to Bell, that a suitable motto to be displayed 'over the portals of this mid-Victorian barrack' would be 'Abandon scope all ye who enter here.' His introduction of Pryor, Kennedy Jones and Nicholson had been at best, a qualified success. There was obvious need for changes at Printing House Square in method, attitude and personnel.[20] Nicholson was repeatedly instructed to 'get it into Bell's head that there is to be one master at PHS'. Yet, try as he might, Northcliffe's intentions were frustrated. To effect any change or reorganisation there, he claimed, was 'like boring a feather bed. Perhaps we shall see some results', he told his wife, 'in ten or twenty years.'[21] Once, in total exasperation, Northcliffe had snapped at poor, long-suffering, Bell, 'There you go again ... saying can't, can't can't. It runs through this office, a steady, deadly opposition to every new idea. It won't do, it really won't do. You must break yourself of the habit or we shall quarrel.'[22]

Although the death in February 1910 of A. F. Walter, Chairman of The Times Publishing Company, had no immediate effect upon the constitution of *The Times,* it had afforded Northcliffe the opportunity to discuss and clarify his business relationship with the new chairman, John Walter IV. The younger generation of the Walter family, while they respected the traditions of *The Times* and recognised the ties of loyalty and sentiment between them and their long-serving editor, Buckle, naturally were not indifferent to the possibility of at last receiving a handsome financial return on their property. Thus they were generally disposed to be sympathetic to Northcliffe's enterprise.

Using Carmelite House as his base, Northcliffe flooded *The Times* with messages and letters of admonition, criticism and instruction. For the first time he was seen at Printing House Square interviewing employees, overheard hectoring, badgering and bullying senior editorial staff. This sudden emergence at the forefront of affairs was in marked contrast with that distant anonymity that he had previously affected. Pro and anti-Northcliffe lobbies formed within *The Times*'s office. If the 'Old Guard' were reluctant to bend their necks before this barnstorming style of autocratic rule, the sympathy and loyalty of a powerful and distinguished trio of foreign correspondents, Bourchier, Morrison and Wickham Steed, who at various times had all quarrelled with Chirol, were being carefully cultivated by Northcliffe.

Moberly Bell, at great cost to his health and nervous energy, shielded Buckle and Chirol from the worst of Northcliffe's intemperate behaviour. Both editor and foreign editor had been incensed when, in January 1910, without reference to *The Times*'s Board, Northcliffe put a new editor in charge of the weekly edition. Bell pointed out that when Northcliffe purchased *The Times*, it had never been part of the bargain that he should not involve himself with financial and business matters.

> The one thing I attached importance to was that there should be no interference with the political line of the paper. . . . Two years ago we were in a desperate position and we clutched at a means of escape for the sake of preserving the independence of The Times. . . . If we divide among ourselves that independence will certainly disappear – so long as we hold together we can maintain it until we are all rejected! The time may come when we shall have to make a united stand against an attack on the independent political attitude of the paper.[23]

Though reluctantly, the distinction that Bell drew between 'political' and 'financial and business' independence was accepted by Buckle and Chirol.[24] However, this did not alter their conviction that, if only as a matter of courtesy, Northcliffe *ought* to have discussed any proposed changes with the Board.[25] By 1910, Moberly Bell could hardly have supposed that the time was far distant when Northcliffe would insist on imposing his view on a matter of political judgment. Bell talked of 'guarantees' given by X (Northcliffe) when he purchased *The Times* in March 1908. Either he had forgotten or, more likely, he chose to ignore the letter he had been obliged to write at Sutton's dictation in February 1908. He had then agreed that if Northcliffe acquired *The Times*, 'I shall act as your Managing Director for 5 years *& carry out your absolute instructions.*'[26] Buckle and Chirol frequently spoke of resigning, but Bell persuaded them that if they persisted and stuck together, they would better be able to withstand Northcliffe's incursions and possibly wear him down by a policy of attrition. On the last day of the year Northcliffe wrote to Buckle a letter which although it spoke in terms of sweet reasonableness also had an unmistakable threatening note for the future.

This very anxious year of 1911 will be a great weight on my shoulders, for on me will fall the responsibility if our venture fails. . . . The situation is difficult and delicate. A number of men of very different origins, training, and experience; all of them with the defects of their qualities, have been brought together to repair the errors. . . . The process is one demanding great mutual forebearance.[27]

At the opening of the New Year Northcliffe admitted to George Saunders that because *The Times* was 'so eaten up with old personal antagonisms and jealousies with which I have no concern and mismanagement has gone so deep', had he not been restored to health, 'I should be obliged to pass my burden on to another.'[28] As immediate evidence of his reviviscence, there was a stormy six-hour visit to Printing House Square. The 'Old Guard' were asked to address their attention not to the past but to the future of the paper. When Buckle yet again offered his resignation, Northcliffe made comforting noises, but instructed Bell in private that it was time to seek a successor for the editorial chair. The choice was the 37 year-old Geoffrey Dawson, recently returned from South Africa.[29] He was attached to the Imperial and Foreign Department but doubled as a kind of informal secretary or assistant to Buckle. No definite promises were made to Dawson and for once both the 'Old Gang' and Northcliffe seemed equally pleased. Dawson took up his new appointment on 14 February. His accession to Buckle's chair was still more than a year and a half distant. What Northcliffe did not reveal was that he had kept his eye on Dawson as a potential editor of *The Times* since 1908.[30] Chirol's suspicions, usually so easily aroused, were quite disarmed. There would be time enough to weigh Clarke's later warning: 'I think that when Northcliffe provides his man he counts on his doing what he wishes.'[31]

Beginning the third week of January 1911, the *Daily Mail* had mounted a furious campaign against the ratification of the Declaration of London. Many Liberals believed that private property carried by sea during wartime should be immune from capture or, destruction by belligerents. To appease neutral opinion at the Paris Peace Conference, at the end of the Crimean War Britain had abandoned the right she had previously claimed (though had waived as not relevant in her war with Russia) to seize enemy goods carried by neutral ships. This had been embodied in the Declaration of Paris (1856). The Declaration had not defined the term 'enemy contraband' and as the right of 'effective blockade' of an enemy's coast remained, it had no immediate or real consequence for the British navy's offensive capability. As far as naval defensive strategy was concerned, the *Royal Commission on Supply of Food and Raw Material in Time of War*, which had reported in 1905, clearly stated, 'We look mainly for security to the strength of our Navy: but we rely in only a less degree upon the widespread resources of our mercantile fleet, and its power to carry on our trade and reach all possible sources of supply wherever they exist. . . .'[32]

George Clarke, as Secretary of the Committee of Imperial Defence, in May 1906 had presented a long memorandum on the capture of private property of belligerents at sea which concluded that Britain had 'nothing to gain and much to lose by abandoning the right'. Lord Chancellor Loreburn, as might have been expected,[33] and Asquith, vehemently rejected this advice. At a later date, Grey intimated to Clarke that he agreed with it, and in June 1907, Charles Hardinge had assured Clarke that the Foreign Office would be 'quite firm about private property at sea'.[34] In an attempt to salvage something from what promised to be the total débâcle of The Hague Peace Conference, the Liberal party's Radicals fixed upon the 'right of capture' as the token of the sincerity of British professions that her naval power was a defensive and unaggressive force.[35] Grey rejected the contention that there was any connection between disarmament and the 'right of capture'. The Radicals insisted, correctly, that it would limit British naval offensive strategy and thus strengthen the repeated official assertion that the British navy was essentially a defensive, peace-keeping force. Further it would undermine the German argument that they needed a large navy to protect their growing mercantile marine.[36]

At The Hague Conference, a series of conventions on the laws of war were drafted, one of which established an international prize court to act as a court of appeal from national prize courts. It was to deal with this issue in particular that the British government proposed an international naval conference which met in London from December 1908 to February 1909. Its labours produced a Declaration which closed the loophole left by the earlier Paris Declaration on the definition of contraband, while on blockade it affirmed the old ruling that it should be 'close' to the enemy coastline.

An Admiralty committee, chaired by Captain G. A. Ballard, had agreed three years earlier that improvements in naval defensive armaments – the mine, torpedo and submarine in particular – made 'close' blockade of the enemy coast impracticable. Ballard had also chaired the three-man committee at the War College which prepared contingent war plans. A consistent feature of all Admiralty war plans before 1914 was their emphasis upon the primacy of the effective commercial blockade of all German ports. 'It is believed that the prolongation of a *distant* [my emphasis] blockade will inflict injury upon German interests, credit and prestige sufficient to cause serious economic consequences to Germany.' More than this, it was hoped that the Germans, in order to break this stranglehold, would be obliged to undertake a general fleet action, the one event most devoutly desired by everyone within the British navy, from the lowliest 'snotty' to the First Sea Lord.

Writing to the First Lord, McKenna, on 5 December 1908, Ottley had insisted that the problem of blockade had been

> constantly under investigation during the whole three years I was DNI, and Admiral Slade tells me he has given particular attention to it since he succeeded me. . . . The geographical position of this country and her preponderant sea power combine to give us a certain and simple means of strangling Germany at sea. . . . The mills of our sea power (though they would grind the German industrial population slowly perhaps) would grind them 'exceedingly small' – grass would sooner or later grow in the streets of Hamburg and widespread death and ruin would be inflicted.[37]

Given the Admiralty's attitude, it is difficult to understand why Ottley and Slade, its representatives at the London conference, agreed to the Declaration which not only hindered defensive strategy but disabled the navy's most effective offensive weapon against Germany. Ottley was then Secretary to the CID and that body had already agreed the key general principles of British strategy in the event of war with Germany. First and most important, was to secure command of the world's oceans and most particularly the North Atlantic and North Sea. The United Kingdom would thus be made safe from invasion and an unhindered flow of necessary commerce and supplies would be guaranteed. Offensively, it would allow the transfer of troops to the continent and at least hinder the supply of manufactured goods and raw materials to Germany. The Declaration of London was never placed before the Committee of Imperial Defence.

After a short though sharp exchange in the Commons on 6 April 1909, Grey had promised that at the earliest opportunity time would be provided for a full discussion of the Declaration.[38] Pressure of other parliamentary business crowded the issue out of the 1909 session and, as the matter was not raised in 1910, it seemed the Declaration had been quietly dropped. Outside Westminster, however, a lively debate continued. Grey received a letter from Gibson Bowles who was considered an authority on naval matters. 'I do most sincerely hold', he wrote, 'that in this matter you have been misled, and it is one of such vast importance to me in which I have always taken so great an interest that at last I felt I must at all events make a humble pronouncement.' The 'humble pronouncement' was a very long and detailed article published the next month in *Nineteenth Century* followed closely by the publication of his book, *Sea Law and Sea Power* (1910). Eyre Crowe, who had been a delegate at the London conference, immediately wrote a long, ponderously detailed refutation of the Bowles article. His most interesting and revealing argument was that belligerent rights had not been weakened by the Declaration. If Britain's enemies sank neutrals then so would Britain![39] Despite the grumbles and hostility of informed and interested bodies, the Foreign Office remained unshaken in its opinion that the Declaration should be ratified. In November 1910, a detailed protest by the Glasgow and Edinburgh Chambers of Commerce coincided with a letter from A. T. Mahan to the editor of *The Times* which emphasised that, 'As a matter of European politics, the right of maritime capture is the principal if not the only strong weapon of offence possessed by Great Britain against the nations in arms of the Continent.'[40]

At Printing House Square, Thursfield, following the Admiralty's lead, and Chirol, adopting the equally strange line of the Foreign Office, supported ratification. Bell and Buckle saw no reason to disagree. Northcliffe, however, was adamant that *The Times* should join with his other newspapers in condemning ratification. He could only suppose the 'Old Guard' had not considered the case on its merits but were merely 'bowing their heads down to officials'. He told Marlowe, 'I have a natural horror of that sort of journalism ... from which I suffer a great deal at Printing House Square.'[41] He telephoned Bell to tell him how strongly he disapproved of *The Times*'s attitude. When this achieved nothing, he sent him an explicit letter. 'As far as the

Declaration of London is concerned I have made up my mind what I am going to do about it and I shall act very definitely. I do not propose to allow one farthing of my fortune to be used in connection with that which would injure this country. I trust these words to the wise will be sufficient.'[42] That same day Northcliffe instructed Nicholson, 'I have heard nothing from The Times in regard to the Declaration of London. If resignations are offered, accept them.'[43]

Buckle and Chirol did not respond kindly to Northcliffe's bullying. His threat was 'intolerable', his interference 'flagrant'. To Bell fell the unenviable task of determining how they should respond to Northcliffe's incursion. After three anxious days of discussion, he wrote to Chirol.

> I should like to put on record the points on which I agree with you and the reasons that make me take a somewhat different attitude in this crisis.
>
> I entirely agree with you in thinking that N's action in this matter is in distinct contravention of our agreement with him. . . . [We] have a perfect right . . . to take any action we may think expedient on the ground that that agreement has been broken.
>
> I further agree with you in saying that the matter is one of principle and not directly one as to the advantages or disadvantages of the Declaration of London. . . .
>
> We entered into the agreement with N in order to save the independence of The Times. We admit that on one, two or possibly three occasions he has infringed that agreement. Is that sufficient reason to say, 'We will abandon the fight and give you the whole of it'? . . .
>
> I think that if the time comes at last when we have to admit that the position has become untenable we shall strengthen our position by being able to show that we did not at once throw up the sponge at the first attack on a very controversial subject – that we exacted terms of surrender even upon that and adopted neutrality upon a point practically already decided. Compare that with what we have to say if we force a quarrel now and get ejected. Imagine a shareholder asking us the reason. 'Because the independence of The Times was threatened' – 'But have you secured the independence?' – 'No, but the principle was infringed.' – 'Did you thereby obtain the ratification of the Declaration of London?' – 'No, because it was certain beforehand.' – 'What have you saved?' – 'Our dignity!'
>
> Don't think, however, that I do not thoroughly sympathize with your view.[44]

With considerable reluctance Buckle and Chirol allowed themselves to be persuaded by Bell's arguments. The Times adopted an editorial position that was neither for nor against the Declaration. Slowly but surely the resistance to Northcliffe was crumbling and within a few weeks his power and influence at Printing House Square were greatly increased when Bell, 'from overwork combined with the strain, slavery and scruple of recent crises',[45] suddenly collapsed and died. Nicholson was immediately promoted to take his place as manager. The pressure upon Chirol and Buckle intensified.

Northcliffe, who had frequently impressed Chirol with his desire that *The Times*'s foreign department should be 'changed', 'reorganised' and 'improved', now became even more insistent. Chirol's health, uncertain at the best of times, necessitated ever more frequent and prolonged absences from the office. That May, Wickham Steed was welcomed as a guest to *Sutton Place*. The Vienna correspondent's future with *The Times* was still uncertain for his resignation, postponed a year at Bell's request, was soon to take effect. Northcliffe spoke to Steed of Chirol's desire to 'retire from the treadmill'. Would Steed be prepared to take charge of a new European division in the foreign department? Steed assumed that Northcliffe was making a definite offer rather than a simple inquiry. He returned to Vienna and from there wrote frequently and at length to Northcliffe. That autumn, at Northcliffe's request, he wrote a review of European affairs for the *Daily Mail Year Book* to be published in December 1911. Steed described his article, 'Is it War?', as 'a stone to throw into the pond of quacking ducks ... in some English Radical newspapers who were crying "Grey must go"', and as 'a chance of telling approximately the truth'.

> The shadow of war lies over Europe, a shadow cast ... by the conflicting aims of European Powers.... The goal of German policy is unchanged – to break, by menace or persuasion, the Anglo-French Entente that has, for seven full years, curtailed German power to reap, with unsheathed sword, the fruits of armed victory.... The aim of German policy has not changed, will not change, cannot change until Germany puts her own affairs in order and lives, manufactures, trades and arms within her own means. Until then it behoves England to take counsel of France and to keep her store of powder not only dry but large.[46]

Steed boasted of how his anonymous article caused the 'pro-German ducks in London, financial and diplomatic', to quack 'lamentably'. Northcliffe was pleased by its tone and content, so much in tune with his own beliefs and disposition, and was impressed when the German and Austrian Ambassadors, eagerly but unavailingly, sought the author's name. His delight was complete when Garvin wrote to tell him that when given the article, Bonar Law 'read it again and again and mastered every word'.[47] It was clear to Northcliffe that Steed's abilities would repay cultivation. A correspondent who shared his distrust of Germany and who was possessed of a profound knowledge of European affairs was a man whose opinions deserved to carry weight. Steed could provide the voice in the 'Thunderer' whose accents he would approve. Steed's capacity to exercise influence within and beyond England's shores was undeniable. Yet, when Chirol finally announced his resignation Northcliffe's instruction to Nicholson was no more precise than 'Don't forget Steed.'[48]

The differences between *The Times*'s senior staff and Northcliffe, highlighted by the question of ratifying the Declaration of London, could never be erased even less resolved, by an editorial decision to adopt a neutral attitude. Buckle, deprived now of Moberly Bell's support and with Chirol seldom in the office, found the pressures upon him intolerable. When, on Northcliffe's behalf, Nicholson complained that the editor had allowed a paragraph in the *Law Journal* favouring ratification to be reproduced in *The Times,* Buckle protested vehemently.

> Northcliffe's treatment of the Editor and the Paper in regard to [the Declaration] is not reasonable. . . . I cannot remain Editor with loss of my self-respect and it is sorely tried over this business. Even before this interference, not merely with editorial independence, but with the settled policy of the Paper, I had told Northcliffe that I felt doubtful whether, in the new conditions, it would not be better that I should retire and make way to a younger man of his choice. He was good enough at the time to protest against the suggestion. But it has never been long out of my mind since, though Bell's death has naturally made me more reluctant, in the interests of the Paper, to take a step which would involve a further serious breach in its continuity.[49]

Northcliffe genuinely and sincerely believed that to ratify the Declaration would be 'to accept sea-laws made in Germany'. When the *Daily Mail* organised a meeting in the City designed to bring together all the various agencies that unavailingly had conducted their separate campaigns of protest, he wrote to Balfour, 'I do not know whether you have had the time to study the provisions of the Declaration of London, but I hope you will not think it presumptuous, or lacking in sense of proportion, when I say that I believe the matter to be much more vital than any of the measures now being discussed. . . . I am, therefore, most anxious to enlist your help.' Balfour replied that he would do his best.[50] As good as his word, the Tory leader, who previously had admitted little knowledge or interest in the subject, sacrificed a weekend to discuss the issue with Lord Desborough and Tommy Gibson Bowles. Subsequently he appeared on the platform of the Cannon Street Hotel meeting organised by the *Mail* to attack the ratification and repeated the same case two days later in a debate on the Naval Prize Bill in the Commons.[51] The Prize Bill passed the Commons but was decisively rejected by the Lords. Thus Bell's earlier confident prediction that the Declaration would become law proved incorrect. By the end of the year Bell was dead, Chirol had finally handed in his resignation, and Buckle was soon to relax his already tenuous hold upon *The Times's* editorship. Northcliffe's triumph over the 'Old Guard' at Printing House Square was apparently complete.

To Evelyn Wrench, Northcliffe had described 1908 as 'my Times' year'. Before the Great War the true *annus mirabilis* in his relations with that news-paper was 1911. It was as though the physical lassitude and debility that had plagued him throughout 1910 had been but an opportunity to store his extraordinary energies which now erupted in a mighty torrent that, if part exhausted by the summer, by autumn were again in full spate. By 1912, most of Northcliffe's hopes and plans had been achieved or seemed within comfortable distance of final realisation. Nor had his superabundance of nervous and physical energy been confined simply to his struggles with the

'barnacle-covered whale' of Printing House Square. 'This business is a Frank-
enstein,' he had admitted once to Sutton. 'It gives me no peace whatever.'[52]
The complex affairs of the Amalgamated Press, which handled Northcliffe's
many magazines, were satisfactorily resolved and all operations centralised in
the newly built Fleetway House, thus releasing much wanted space at the
previously hopelessly overcrowded *Daily Mail* headquarters.

Northcliffe had not ignored the *Daily Mail*, constantly, in his own words,
'tightening up things' at Carmelite House. Industrial disputes had curtailed
the *Mail*'s profits and his personal income for the year dipped to £118,000.
Not for the first or last time, John Brainerd Capper, Buckle's editorial assistant,
was reminded that the prosperity of the *Daily Mail* supported *The Times*. Not
quantity but quality was the subject to which Northcliffe addressed himself in
telegram, letter and memorandum to the long-suffering but invariably patient
Marlowe. 'For all the *Daily Mail*'s vast circulation,' Northcliffe wrote, 'I am
reminded every day, and I entirely believe those who say so, our leading articles
carry no weight.' The *Mail* had become 'a machine-made paper' that depended
far too much upon its editor. The individuality of writers' copy was being
destroyed by 'interfering sub-editors'. All the sub-editing required 'sharpen-
ing-up'. There was need also for 'new blood. Most of us are drifting towards
middle-age, apparently without knowing it.' There was disagreeable evidence
of a disposition among certain staff to be 'too pliable – wanting to bow down
to officials. A newspaper is meant to publish news and not to please highly
placed people.' But Northcliffe's constant preoccupation was the degree of
influence exerted by editorial opinion in the *Mail*.

> I want you to consider the question of the reform of our leading articles.
> We have got into a groove. Not enough time is spent on considering
> them. . . . Our paper ought to carry more weight of opinion. . . . It is
> hardly ever quoted for its opinions in the French papers. The reason is
> obvious: we ourselves do not treat the matter seriously enough.[53]

Three years Northcliffe's junior, Marlowe suffered proprietorial interference
with a stoicism that the 'Black Friars' of *The Times* could not possibly match.
He recognised that the true 'revolution' in the press had been the swing of
the balance of power to the commercial side with the inevitable consequence–
proprietorial usurpation of the editorial throne. At Carmelite House they were
used to deferring to Northcliffe's whims. Northcliffe, more than any other
owner, possessed an incorrigible itch to interfere with minor details as much
as big, important issues. This constant concern in 1911 with the 'quality' and
'weight' of the *Mail*'s opinion was the public manifestation of a growing private
belief that he did not trouble to hide from certain close subordinates, that he
and the *Daily Mail* were largely running the country. Wrench records a revealing statement made that year by Northcliffe. 'He thought the best thing that
could happen to Great Britain was to increase the power and influence of the
Daily Mail.'[54]

Northcliffe's megalomania was growing but most of the time was still held
in rein. It is important not to judge his actions in 1911 by his subsequent

behaviour during and after the Great War as his illness moved towards its inevitable tragic conclusion. His parting company with Garvin over the *Observer* made it even more imperative not only that *The Times* should be bent more closely to his will but that it should become a much more effective and influential journal of opinion. He sought to secure younger and more vigorous men of ideas. There could be a clean break with the past only when Nicholson, Dawson and Steed occupied the positions held by Bell, Buckle and Chirol. The complacency at Printing House Square was unwarranted; it required a severe shake-out, and Northcliffe, in his pose as 'Lord Vigour and Venom' had good reason to hustle and bustle his property into the twentieth century. A stern warning administered to Alexander Kenealy, editor of the *Daily Mirror*, concerning the 'ignorance and bad taste' of certain recent items in that newspaper, won a response that must have caused Northcliffe to reflect darkly on the real merits of certain *Times* personnel whom he so often criticised for treating news as though it were vintage wine that would improve with keeping. 'Highly educated men', Kenealy wrote, 'as a rule have no sense of news. They always want to write about Rome or what happened to Jupiter. Anything recent is regarded as unimportant. We have Oxford men here and Eton men ... they are woefully ignorant of anything that has happened since 42 BC.'[55]

The Times's historian has claimed that Northcliffe found 'the formal special articles, the solid foreign dispatches and measured leading articles' all alike unendurable. 'Anything that had the length necessary to a convincing piece of exposition or reasoning must be "dull". His health, no less than his taste, forbade close reading. All he demanded from the printed page was news. His genius fell short of understanding how necessary it was for *The Times* to print not only news but a view of what the news meant.'[56] This judgment suffers from the shadow cast by Northcliffe's later behaviour when his mind was quite unhinged. In adapting the arguments of the 'Old Guard' it comes perilously close to being no more than an apologia for their behaviour. Northcliffe admired and coveted the influence that *The Times* possessed. He did not seek to trivialise what he recognised was an 'institution' by a mad pursuit of profit by popularisation. He scornfully rejected such advice as 'wanting to put a Punch and Judy Show on in Westminster Abbey'. It was never part of his plan to adopt for *The Times* the same magazine techniques that had been so successful with the *Daily Mail*. Yet although the *Mail* served a very different constituency of readers from *The Times*, he fully endorsed Marlowe's insistence that there should be 'no attempt to appeal to a lower class of reader ... by aiming high we can always command the attention of the lowest, whereas by aiming low we should lose everything'.[57] As this was Northcliffe's clear disposition at Carmelite House, he was hardly likely to wish to reduce *The Times* to nothing but a superior news-sheet. He required that *The Times* should remain respected as a journal of record and opinion, but that its influence should be strengthened and its essential character secured by seeking inspiration in the twentieth and not the nineteenth century.[58] For all the hauteur affected by certain worthies at Printing House Square, Northcliffe had already rescued the dignity of *The Times* and its independence by removing the need for its involvement in the kind of ugly, dubious, and eventually unfortunate financial and advertising expedients to which it had been driven in order to make ends meet. Yet the desperate concern of the 'Old Guard' remained that should they once relax their control, then Northcliffe would turn *their* newspaper into the de luxe edition of the *Daily Mail*. This was the burden of Buckle's message when he finally relinquished the editorial chair to Dawson. 'What *ought The Times* with its history and traditions to say about this? has always been in my mind.' Buckle's emphasis was a moral as much as an empirical imperative. 'I know you agree with me', he concluded, 'on the extreme importance of giving the lie to the taunt about a "twopenny halfpenny Daily Mail".'[59]

Northcliffe had already warned Dawson about the perils of too-close contact with the 'superabundance of obstructive and destructive criticism at Printing House Square mostly proceeding from ignorance and the cloistered life'. He insisted Dawson should 'ignore existing prejudices'.[60] It was insufferable that Buckle should actually have supposed that *The Times*, 'for sake of continuity', would benefit from a prolongation of his tenure of the editorial chair. Buckle's loyalty was not the least of his many virtues, but his attitude to the newspaper had been shaped and his values dictated by the assumptions of an earlier century now dead, and to Northcliffe's way of thinking, best forgotten. *The Times*'s 'tradition' to him appeared to be no more than according precedence to the satisfaction of the interests and demands of a very narrowly conceived and exclusive group. In 1908, as he had told Steed, he did not intend nor did he suppose it would ever be necessary to act as 'Chief' of *The Times*, as he was 'Chief' of the *Daily Mail*. 'The Times is conducted entirely by Messrs Walter, Buckle, Bell, Chirol and Monypenny who understand the task better than I ever could.'[61] But, the 'Old Guard' had been found wanting. Northcliffe therefore had no alternative but to break them to his will and purpose. The attitude they had demonstrated over the ratification of the Declaration of London showed they were determined not only to frustrate his will, but were prepared to ignore, at the nation's peril, larger imperatives for no better reason than a selfish sense of outraged and offended parochial propriety. *The Times* should have realised that neutrality was both an unworthy and impossible expedient to adopt on a vital national issue. One could not be 'neutral' about 'German made sea laws' when 'from 1908', he had been 'convinced that an Anglo-German conflict was a certainty'.[62] The mistake the 'Old Guard' made was to confuse what was no more than a tender regard for their own *gravitas* with the security and maintenance of the dignity and influence of *The Times*.

1911: *Annus mirabilis*

What Germany wants is the hegemony of Europe. The French game in
Morocco has been stupid and dishonest but it is a vital interest for us
to support her on this occasion in the same way in which the Germans
supported the Austrian policy of 1908 in Bosnia.

Tyrrell to Hardinge

The solution of the Morocco crisis is not to be found in Fez but among
the pines of the Vosges. What is afoot in Morocco makes sense only if
we are prepared to fight in the Vosges.

Charles Maurras, in Action Française

The European situations have been (and still are) *very* much more critical
than any of us knew. I had a talk this afternoon with a distinguished
General at the War Office and tho' the best opinion now is that there *won't*
be war, the most tremendous preparations have been made for it.

Geoffrey Dawson to his aunts

We must save Grey from his natural weakness and from the cranks who
are continually attacking him in the interests of Germany. . . . Grey's
hands must be strengthened.

Maxse to Bonar Law

Choosing to ignore their recently signed accord with Germany, the French
behaved as if they supposed their supremacy in Morocco was part of the
natural order. Both the tone and the content of speeches made by French
political leaders implied that France would continue to behave in North Africa
just as she liked for she had nothing to fear from Germany.[1] The reopening
of the Moroccan question was 'inevitable', claimed *New Age,* from the moment
Delcassé was appointed to the Monis Cabinet, for he was 'determined upon
a bold forward policy as the best means of reaffirming the prestige of France
in Europe. . . . He feels sure that Germany won't think it worthwhile to fight
over Morocco, and if she does, why, let Germany fight and be damned to her
says the French Government.'[2] The British Radical press, with good reason,
censured France's contemptible and irresponsible behaviour. When, ostensibly
to protect Europeans, the French sent a military expedition to Fez, *Nation*
dismissed the claim as 'a pretext as mendacious as the legends by which Dr
Jameson sought to excuse his rush to Johannesburg'.[3] Self-righteous avowals

of 'ideals' and claims about 'peaceful penetration' were worthless. Everyone knew that in Morocco France was 'engaged in a sordid, imperialistic venture'.[4]

For the sake of the entente, the Unionist press said as little as possible. 'Patriotic' editors and commentators might deplore French recklessness in private, especially at a time when Germany's diplomatic strength had been so considerably enhanced. But as Chirol reminded Steed, 'We are not in a position to bite and there is therefore not much use in barking.'[5] They could only put the best possible public face upon French behaviour. Thus, when France declared her intention of sending troops to Fez, *The Times* congratulated her for 'laying her plans so frankly before the world, confident in their honesty and without fear that they can give rise to any rational misgivings of her purposes'. Readers were assured that French troops would stay only so long as was 'absolutely necessary'. This, *The Times* knew, was humbug, as was its confident insistence that the French could continue to rely upon 'the loyal support of Russia and England'.[6] Was it politic to give such assurances when Bethmann's advice not to send the expedition had received a dismissive reply? France claimed that her actions did not concern Germany for they were justified by international practice. When Kiderlen had indicated that for suitable territorial compensation Germany was prepared to overlook the matter, the French government had said nothing.

Although afforded no editorial support, Repington, in a series of articles, emphasised the need not only for a unity of strategy that embraced both Services, but, as significantly, both partners to the entente.[7] From his examination of the German army, Repington was convinced that the future peace of Europe depended upon Franco-British military and naval cooperation. To him, it was inconceivable that the Germans would respect the neutrality of smaller countries bordering Germany and France. From this he argued that an acute responsibility was placed upon the entente partners to determine *immediately* the various parts they would be obliged to play in a war against Germany on land and sea. The Committee of Imperial Defence should have a 'cut and dried' solution available. The Kaiser was quick to point out to the British military attaché in Berlin, Col. Russell, that work for an understanding with Britain was not helped by *The Times*'s military correspondent 'saying that you ought to practise the same tactics as the French so that you can fight side by side against the Germans'. William could not resist adding that, in any event, 'the few divisions that [Britain] could put into the field could not make any appreciable difference,' an observation with which the editor, the naval correspondents of *The Times* and most members of the Admiralty would happily have agreed.[8] Though obliged to admit, 'in England there is no general recognition of the fact,' Repington insisted that 'the preservation of France from a German attack ... *is absolutely vital for Britain's subsequent security.* ... We should be able and ready to send a thoroughly efficient force to aid France.'[9]

Unlike Buckle, Northcliffe was impressed by Repington's arguments. When it came to Germany's intentions and British involvement, those personal qualities both men shared – an abundance of vanity and supreme confidence in the rightness of their own opinions – for once promoted mutual understanding. But when Repington accepted the editorship of the new quarterly *Army Review,*

Northcliffe's confidence was shaken. How could Repington's new post possibly be properly combined with his work for *The Times?* He told Buckle that it would be 'quite impossible for Col. Repington to criticise the War Office and take payment from them'.[10] There was a further complication. Might not foreign readers suppose that the views Repington expressed in *The Times* were 'official' rather than his own? Typically, Repington responded that he had accepted his new post so that he might 'retrieve the £500 a year by which my pay and expenses were cut some two years ago'! In the face of the correspondent's insistence that it could only be to the advantage of *The Times* that he should hold both positions simultaneously, Northcliffe reluctantly abandoned his opposition.[11] The regular editorials that Repington contributed to the *Army Review*, 'Imperial Defence', for the most part reiterated opinions with which his *Times* readers would have been familiar. He made no secret of his appointment. In July 1911, he twice puffed the contents of the *Review* in *The Times*, and his own estimable qualities as its editor.[12] The first of these shameless self-advertisements was published the same day as the French government was advised by the Germans that they had sent a small warship, the *Panther*, to Agadir. She was to stay there so long as there was any danger to German merchants.

For months, the permanent staff of the British Foreign Office had worried about the truculence of French behaviour in Morocco. On occasion, Eyre Crowe's mind had been exercised by an unhappy suspicion that perhaps France was playing fast and loose with Germany and maybe making a deal behind Britain's back. The arrival of the *Panther* at Agadir changed everything. He immediately assumed that this intervention had nothing to do with the old, familiar game that the European Powers had played for several decades in Africa, bargaining over new colonial territory and economic rights.[13] It was a direct assault upon the entente. 'Germany is playing for the highest stakes,' he confidently pronounced, 'the subjection of France.' Should Germany succeed, then the whole Balance of Power in Europe would be overthrown. It was 'a trial of strength. Concessions mean not loss of interests or loss of prestige', he insisted to Grey, but 'defeat with all its inevitable consequences'.[14] Both he and Nicolson agreed that a proper British response would be to send their own warship to Agadir. Grey resisted. Several of the editorial staff at *The Times* thought the idea sound, not least Repington. He also pointed out to Buckle, who as usual took no notice, that 'it would be as well to look after ourselves nearer home'. The editor rejected an article on the threat of invasion, and Repington wrote of his worries to Geoffrey Dawson.

> I have been looking at our Home Fleet at Portland by day and night and
> see that not only are no precautions whatsoever taken, but that hundreds
> of men are leaving Weymouth on furlough for all parts of the country.
> My view is that a period of diplomatic tension has begun and that owing
> to German action already taken and owing also to new men who inspire
> German action, we must expect acts of vigour if German ambitions
> cannot be satisfied by a French (or a British) surrender. With our military
> system we have no right to run these risks.[15]

The general disposition at Printing House Square had been to accept Crowe's estimate of Germany's intentions. The one important exception was Edward Grigg. He viewed Agadir as but one more incident in a purely African clash. As far as he was concerned Germany might 'bag the whole of Equatorial Africa if she wants it. She will only be buying trouble.'[16] Grigg's analysis was overborne because his editorial colleagues were convinced that colonial bargaining was a subsidiary factor. What Germany was determined to bag was not a slice of Africa but the hegemony of Europe. Nevertheless, Grigg's influence was sufficient for the initial reports on the German move to be reserved. The headlines spoke of 'A Strained Situation'.[17]

The one British newspaper that might have been expected to comment in exaggerated tones about Germany's dramatic act was the *Daily Mail.* Instead, the *Panther's* arrival at Agadir inspired two comparatively mild leading articles. A private letter to Northcliffe from the newspaper's Paris correspondent, Valentine Williams, emphasised that the French saw the *Panther* as 'no more than Germany putting in the brokers men to make sure France does not overlook her claim for compensation'. Williams admitted that the French were apprehensive that the Radicals in the British Cabinet might hinder Grey in giving support to France. Otherwise, Williams had 'the feeling that this Morocco business is going to adjust itself amicably'.[18] His letter confirmed Northcliffe's initial reaction that there was no immediate or particular cause for concern. This judgment was reinforced by a cable from Steed in Vienna. Austria was showing little interest and even less enthusiasm for her ally's African enterprise.

Domestic, social, political and constitutional crises engaged the immediate attention of the British public. Metternich noted, with evident satisfaction, general public disinterest in foreign affairs and the relatively reserved tone adopted by the usual firebrands of the British patriotic press. On 6 July, the Prime Minister in a short statement to the House asserted that the *Panther's* arrival at Agadir involved British interests in Morocco.[19] *The Times* amplified this claim insisting that Germany's action was specifically designed to test the entente. The *Daily Mail* and the *Standard* argued that there were naval and strategic reasons why Britain should be concerned about the future of Agadir. 'We cannot wait until the time comes that gives an appearance of permanency to the German occupation of a port which commands the narrowest part of the Atlantic and the most important trade routes in the world.'[20] The article was patently designed to stir the Admiralty from its remarkable apathy, into some sort of action. For once, the *Manchester Guardian* became the voice of the Senior Service, pointing out that to secure Agadir, which in any event could not be easily fortified, would be a source of weakness rather than strength to the Germans. To maintain the port they would need to detach an element from their High Seas Fleet.[21] The Admiralty was then stirred sufficiently from its complacent somnolence to observe that it would be concerned only if the Germans took a port on the Mediterranean coast of Morocco.[22] Public attention was not arrested by these rather far-fetched hints of a naval threat. Those who took any interest at all in the events would most likely have shared the private view of *The Times*'s Berlin correspondent. Germany's action had been rather clumsy and provocative, but the French had only themselves to blame because their own behaviour had been disgraceful.

Most members of the Liberal government shared the public's preoccupation with domestic problems. For the next fortnight they refused to respond to the Foreign Secretary's growing agitation. On 19 July Grey complained to Asquith that if the Cabinet continued behaving so passively, 'Irreparable harm may be done.'[23] The immediate cause of his concern was his learning that day of the enormous claim for territorial compensation demanded by the Germans. Five days later, *The Times* published this information for its readers together with a long editorial that said Germany's demands were 'impossible and extravagant'. Here was 'proof' of Germany's intention to humiliate France and thus the more readily to be able to sunder the entente. As these assertions were prefaced with the familiar formula, 'We understand', the impression was created that the account was officially inspired. *Le Matin* quoted *The Times*'s spirited editorial as evidence that the British government would support France with all energy. It remained for the next day's issue of the *Kölnische Zeitung* to deny that the report and editorial came from an official source, suggesting instead that it had been prompted by the anti-German, big-business, press interests of which *The Times* had so long been the English centre.[24] Whatever its true source, the editorial proved to be a remarkably fitting overture for the unexpected, uncharacteristically jingoistic intervention made next day by, of all politicians, the Chancellor of the Exchequer.

If it had been necessary to add sauce to the prospect of that piquant dish, *The Times*'s 21 July edition carried a story that must have given a perverse delight to every advocate of the 'bolt from the blue' school for it seemed there was a distinct possibility that their frequent warnings in the past might well be about to be realised. At a time when the various elements of the British fleet were scattered in a dozen different ports in various states of unpreparedness, the whole of the German High Seas Fleet was at sea. It was supposed to be upon its way to Norway, but what if it should suddenly emerge out of the mists before Portland? The Admiralty could do nothing. The navy that so frequently and for so long had boasted that it was Britain's one sure, certain and complete shield against invasion had been betrayed by its own apathy. Subsequent efforts in August and September to repair the Admiralty's tarnished image became an excuse for the German naval propagandists to beat the drum for increased expenditure and to work up a scare.

As each day passed and the Cabinet did nothing, Grey's position had grown more delicate and difficult. Obliged to resist the extreme promptings of his officials – particularly Nicolson, Crowe and the British Ambassador in Paris, Bertie – somehow he had to push a number of influential yet reluctant Cabinet colleagues who were more absorbed with the problems posed by the House of Lords and industrial and social unrest than an inconvenient, distasteful squabble over territorial rights in Africa, to agree to a stern affirmation of *Britain's right* to be consulted and involved in the settlement of the Moroccan problem. His suggestion, that there should be a conference on Morocco and that a strong hint should be given to the Germans that if they refused, Britain would take the necessary steps to protect her interests, immediately aroused the suspicions and the hostile opposition of the Little Englander group led by Loreburn. All the old, long-harboured, tribal fears about the untrustworthiness of a 'Liberal-League' government seemed confirmed by Grey's request. 'Take care that we don't get into war with Germany,' Loreburn warned the editor of the *Manchester Guardian*.[25] The Cabinet would agree to do no more than to ask the French to submit counter-proposals to the Germans with the warning that should they be tempted to resist German territorial gains Britain would not consider it sufficient cause to wage war. If Grey was disappointed, Crowe was outraged. It was not enough that the Cabinet should run away but it was giving hints to the French that they should let Germany into Morocco.[26] Grey was left with the unpleasant if not impossible prospect of having to rely upon ambiguous hints in his conversation with the German Ambassador when the interests of the entente would better have been served by a stiff note.[27] It was at this moment of painful quandary and embarrassment that Lloyd George offered Grey what, at the time, seemed the exact measure required.

After the unsatisfactory Cabinet meeting on 21 July, the Chancellor of the Exchequer showed Grey the draft of a speech that he was to make that evening at the Mansion House. Grey 'cordially agreed' to the wording of the passage which, although vague, would be recognised by Germany as an unmistakeable warning. Britain would not allow herself to be treated 'as if she were of no account in the Cabinet of Nations . . . peace at that price would be a humiliation intolerable for a great country like ours to endure. National honour is no party question.' What made this format particularly appropriate was that although there was no specific reference to Germany, the implication would be clearly understood by the Wilhelmstrasse. At the same time it gave no obvious cause for offence and therefore was not likely to provoke a belligerent response from the German press. However, the Unionist press took it upon its more than willing shoulders to spell out the implication of Lloyd George's message, most baldly in the *Observer*'s blunt assertion that 'We must stand with France at any cost against unreasonable demands, no matter of what nature.' *The Times* declared that Lloyd George's 'clear, decisive, statesmanlike reference to the European situation created by German demands . . . will be endorsed without distinction of party by his countrymen'. France and Britain would not allow themselves to be 'overborne by German power'. Subsequent editorial comment, in particular in *The Times*, *Daily Chronicle* and *Daily Mail*, implied that Lloyd George's speech had been an expression of 'the considered judgment of the Cabinet', and 'an official announcement of Government support for France'.

The British Radical press was bemused and confounded by what had seemed remarkably like a contingent declaration of war. The particular reason for its discomfort was duly emphasised by *Le Temps*. 'The well known opinions of M. Lloyd George, his liberalism, his pacifistic tendencies, his sentiments towards Germany, underline the importance of his declaration.' A few days later Asquith found himself attempting to explain away Lloyd George's words to a very worried John Morley as 'no more than *bona verba*'. In November, Grey was to tell the Commons that the Chancellor's words had been 'merely a platitude on the lips of a minister of a Great Power'.[28] The attitude adopted by the *Manchester Guardian* would be judged as a public indication of the state of Radical thinking. Its editor, however, had already been persuaded by Lloyd George to desist from making any specific critical comment. Thus the impression left after the Mansion House speech was that newspapers of every political opinion had closed ranks at a time of national emergency. The reality of a threat to the nation's safety seemed confirmed by the speeches made later in the Commons by Balfour for the Tories, and more significantly, Ramsay MacDonald for Labour.[29] The *Manchester Guardian* was only to break ranks several days later after a conversation between Grey and C. P. Scott. The editor was then obliged to conclude that Britain's options were no longer open and that whatever the price, the Foreign Secretary had determined that Britain would support France.[30]

Grey's meeting with Metternich on 24 July had been stormy. The German Ambassador bitterly complained that Lloyd George's words had been unnecessarily provocative. By employing a public declaration and ignoring the usual diplomatic channels, the British government appeared to be intent not only upon encouraging its entente partner but also on urging British opinion to adopt a chauvinist pose. Grey petulantly responded that Britain had a right to be treated as a Great Power. If Lloyd George's speech had occasioned surprise in Germany then they must have supposed that they could ignore Britain.[31] That same day, Grey told McKenna that naval precautions should be taken. 'We are dealing with a people who recognise no law except that of force between nations.'[32]

On 27 July, when the Foreign Office vote was debated in the Commons, Asquith made a designedly soothing speech. Little more than platitudes were exchanged between Opposition and Government front benches on the subject of Morocco. In November, Grey was to claim that after the Commons debate there were 'no further difficulties between the German government and ourselves about the Moroccan negotiations'.[33] Nicolson interpreted the tame exchange in the Commons as mirroring 'a perfect unanimity in Britain to stand by France', although he admitted, 'not much has been said in our Press'.[34] How could it have been otherwise? Public attention was focused upon, not the possibility of imminent war with Germany over a supposed infringement of British rights in Morocco, but the reality of a bitter and bloody social struggle in its own backyard. When the secretary of the Railwaymen's Union said that 'War has begun,' there was no danger that his meaning would be misunderstood. He spoke of class, not international conflict. Foreign affairs were a pale, distant, inconsequential background to the imminent threat of industrial and economic anarchy. Even at Westminster what little interest could be conjured for foreign affairs was reserved for the deterioration of Anglo-Russian relations in Persia. For one day only Morocco attracted attention when it was rumoured that a rupture of the Franco-German negotiations was likely. That day, the Official Secrets Act was rushed through Parliament with scarcely a dissenting voice.[35] Frustrated in his attempts to bring order to the industrial scene, the Prime Minister recruited Lloyd George in his more familiar role as industrial pacifier rather than international incendiarist. The Chancellor won the compliance of the workers by appealing to their patriotism. At a time when there was not even the breath of a hint of any international crisis in the press, he asked the men's representatives whether the unions sought to imperil the national interest when the country stood upon the verge of war with Germany. Surely they were not so myopic or self-destructive as to disrupt necessary troop movements that depended upon rail transportation? The strikers meekly gave way. If there was a national danger, then Parliament, with the threat of a general strike removed, showed an almost indecent haste in proroguing for its summer recess. Grey's own backbenchers, who might have forced the Moroccan issue into the glare of public scrutiny, remained quiescent.

As Lloyd George could appeal so easily and effectively to the patriotism of railway workers, one might have expected someone like Leo Maxse to have been foaming at the mouth at the prospect of war with Germany. Instead, the day after Lloyd George's Mansion House speech, he was happily agreeing to the suggestion of H. W. Wilson, another journalist normally ultra-sensitive to the least sign of German aggressive intent, that it would be better to 'tone down' an article on Morocco for the next issue of the *National Review.* This was not simply because both men supposed 'the government mean to be firm', but they had good reason to doubt Germany's ability 'to fight just yet'. War would come, but 'not for two or three years . . . when they have drawn much closer to us. Today they have nine Dreadnoughts ready to our fourteen, odds which ought not to give them much chance.' They were aware that 'The Foreign Office regard the position as serious but not alarming.'[36] Their estimate could not have been more different from that of Repington. His concern was that Britain's numerical advantage in Dreadnoughts would be more than outweighed by poor strategy. His letters of complaint and warning to Buckle went unheeded and he was obliged to confide in Geoffrey Dawson.

> Please note that everything in Germany that can float and fight is now at sea. . . . I am not allowed to say anything about our naval dispositions but I consider them perfectly damnable. . . . Get Grigg to have news from Berlin of the strength and disposition of the German Fleet from day to day. The Foreign Office will not move until it is too late unless it is pushed, and with our present First Lord I hope for nothing from Admiralty initiative.[37]

While Repington worried, fumed and fussed in vain, Maxse, in uncharacteristically phlegmatic mood, was already turning his mind to an examination of the reasons why Germany had been *encouraged* to interfere once more in Morocco, 'whose problems had been settled once in 1904 . . . a second time by the Algeçiras Agreement in 1906 . . . and a third time by the Franco-German understanding of 1909.' He supposed it could only have been because in the previous year the British government had talked of arbitration and disarmament and had appeared to have 'swallowed the preposterous doctrine that Europe had entered a new moral age where policy not armed strength was the real preventive of war', where '*coups de main* were deeds that belonged to a dark past that had been eliminated by progress'. Consequently, the lesson of Agadir was simple. European peace would never be assured 'by the fetiches of our Pacifist Radical Ministers'. The only way of guaranteeing a curb upon Germany was 'armed force, confidence and the unity of the Triple Entente'. So much of Maxse's analysis was all too familiar. But, significantly, on this occasion he chose not to spare the Opposition, condemning them for being 'at best half-hearted'.[38] The reason for the dangerous compliance of the Unionists, Maxse was not alone among Tories in believing, was 'Foozles' style of leadership.[39] The time had come to challenge what Garvin described as 'the Byzantine theory of Unionist leadership – the theory of speechless loyalty to an hereditary succession'.[40] Maxse now became the noisiest, the most vigorous partisan, in a crusade designed to oust A. J. Balfour from the Tory leadership.

Although it would be incorrect to wrench the 'Balfour Must Go' campaign entirely from its familiar context of domestic politics and the particular problems of the power struggle between the two Houses of Parliament and two kinds of Tory, its conception, conduct and final successful outcome had a vital bearing upon issues of foreign and defence policy. Esher was quick to recognise this by claiming that to betray Balfour was tantamount to betraying the national interest.

> When we survey the position of affairs on the Continent and the difficulties which hem us in from so many quarters, the feelings of those who, like myself, look upon [Balfour] as the only statesman to whom the destinies of this country can be safely entrusted, may be imagined. Even in Opposition he acted as a bulwark.[41]

No one shared Esher's concern for the dangers that faced England from Germany more than Maxse, but he entirely disagreed with Esher's estimate of Balfour's contribution to national security and preparedness. To Sandars he had described the Tory leader as 'a spent force', influenced by 'craven counsellors'.[42] Maxse coined the slogan, 'Balfour Must Go', but, for the rest, as Balfour's biographers have demonstrated, his influence in the campaign was minimal.[43] Yet what is significant was not the extent or the degree of Maxse's influence but what he perceived would be the likely consequences if his campaign succeeded. His priorities were as much national as they were narrowly partisan. His first letter after the *coup*, addressed to his friend Bonar Law, Balfour's successor, did not emphasise domestic political problems, rather, 'the urgency and primacy of the German question'. He pleaded with Bonar Law 'to play a more dynamic role in the matters of safety and defence' than had his predecessor.

> Of late years the Opposition has had no policy whatsoever as regards National Defence, and this at one of the most critical times in our history. . . . We have quietly looked on. . . . His Majesty's Opposition have hardly less serious responsibilities than His Majesty's Government and can do far more than has yet been done to strengthen the hands of the few men in the Cabinet who are abandoning their ostrich-like attitude.

This last reference was to the so-called 'Radical twins', Churchill and Lloyd George. They, so Maxse assured Law, were now 'complete converts to the gravity of the German danger . . . even speaking the language of the National Review'![44]

Maxse had his own, very particular view of the Liberal Cabinet. He was convinced that it contained a significant proportion of 'German-loving ministers' who made up the Potsdam Party – 'a group of Little Englanders who are anti-Empire, anti-Entente and anti-Grey'. The significance of the recent schism between Lloyd George and Churchill and the rest of the Radical group needed little emphasis. Where formerly the two ministers had been notorious as economists, advocates of armament retrenchment, scorners of the notion that Germany menaced or threatened British security, Winston and Lloyd George now had so much changed their opinions that they had eagerly leapt to occupy the foremost position in the martial van. Grey was later to recall how he found young Winston, 'his high-metalled spirit exhilarated by events', keeping him constant company 'for love of the crisis'.[45] Nor was Churchill's metamorphosis to go unnoticed or unrewarded by Northcliffe. In November, he dismissed Churchill's thanks for printing his speeches so prominently in his newspapers with the friendly disclaimer, 'I have not been the least kind to you. I judge public men on their public form and I believe that your inquiring, industrious mind is alive to our national danger.'[46] Lloyd George's 'conversion' was even more dramatic than Winston's. He was now the darling of the hardline, anti-German, Foreign Office staff. For partisan reasons, *The Times* would later suggest that his intervention had been designed to draw attention away from domestic political problems,[47] but at the time, Nicolson had no doubt that the Mansion House speech was 'no sudden inspiration but carefully thought out' to comfort the French. Later, in conversation with Almeric Fitzroy, Nicolson applauded the Chancellor's patriotism and insisted that 'no one could have done better . . . such a stand-by throughout our recent difficulties.'[48] Certainly it was Lloyd George's speech that, more than any other British action that summer, was to lodge and fester in German minds. Writing from America to Northcliffe, Fred Wile retailed a recent talk with the German Ambassador in Washington.

> Bernstorff told me that when he was dining with the Kaiser the other night, the speech of Lloyd George was the topic of conversation, and the consensus of opinion was that the speech was as provocative an affront to German honour as was the telegram of Napoleon III which precipitated the Franco-German War. Others of the personages at the table expressed the view that Germany ought to have gone to war with England to avenge Lloyd George's insult. Not having done so, the consequent humiliation will leave its sting for many a year.[49]

With Parliament in recess, those British politicians concerned to improve Anglo-German understanding busily occupied their vacation by sounding German opinion. They were left in no doubt that the key incident of the Moroccan tension was Lloyd George's speech. They were convinced it had been both unnecessary and dangerous.[50] They, like the Germans were mystified as to what exactly were the 'vitally affected' British interests to which the Chancellor had referred. One baffled Radical MP wrote to his wife, 'What business had [Lloyd George] taking on the Kaiser when he already had enough on his hands with the Lords?' The whole episode might have been dismissed as mere mid-summer madness had it not been for the occasional eruption of disconcerting hints and rumours. In the space of a fortnight Charles Trevelyan received two letters from his closest friend in the Cabinet, Walter Runciman. In late August he was told, 'the situation is very explosive . . . we may easily be involved if France and Germany come to blows.' Then silence, until another letter confidently pronounced, 'Events in Morocco likely to be more tedious than dangerous.'[51] What sense could be made of these sudden oscillations from imminent danger of war at one moment to peace at the next?

In Germany it was clear it had been decided that not France but Britain was the villain of the piece. In early August, the Kaiser told Sir John French that the only way Germany and France would ever come to blows was if Britain and her press encouraged the French to do so. He instanced the *Daily Mail* and *The Times* as 'most hostile' and 'doing the most harm'.[52] Just the tip of the iceberg of German resentment and anger with Britain was revealed by the diatribes in the Pan-German and militarist press. The *Kölnische Zeitung* insisted that German determination would not be affected by the thought of any risk incurred in a trial of strength with the entente partners, and like *Die Post* and the *Hamburger Nachrichten*, it claimed that Germany would not tolerate any diminution of her world power. *Deutsche Armee Blatt* boasted that one of the fifty army corps Germany could fling at France would be enough to obliterate the English clay colossus. If there was war, England and not Germany faced the greater risk. But this was so much whistling in the dark to keep up badly dented spirits. The *Deutsche Tageszeitung* might talk of following the Kaiser 'with joyous enthusiasm to the grave, or if God so willeth to a new Sedan',[53] but the actions of the soberer of the German population made nonsense of these vaunting claims. In September, rumours of British naval and military preparations were sufficient to cause a panic on the stock exchange and a run on the savings banks. The *Daily Mail* commented patronisingly, 'Germany has a right to a place in the sun; her trouble is she is always striving unnecessarily to put her neighbours in the shade.'[54]

Despite what the Kaiser had said to General French, *The Times* adopted a studiously neutral and unsensational attitude when reporting events and opinion in Germany and the continuing Franco-German negotiations over Morocco. This was due primarily to the influence of Gordon Browne in the newspaper's Berlin office. Chirol's continued absence meant that D. D. Braham was temporarily in charge of the foreign department. He was content to accept as true Browne's estimate of the temper of Germany's feelings and intentions. It was a blessing that the French would not allow themselves to be bullied into submission by the Germans, although Braham was less happy about the unfortunate and provocative way the French were inclined to express their newfound determination. He did not for a moment question the British *obligation* to give 'hearty support' to France 'on general political grounds', but admitted that his feelings of partisanship had been weakened rather than strengthened by the Moroccan incident.[55] Repington, however, seemed to harbour no such reservations about the French.

In October, he attended the annual German army manoeuvres. His reports to *The Times* recognised German strengths, but he compared their army very unfavourably with the French.[56] Admittedly the Germans were well drilled and disciplined, but they lacked individuality, initiative and freshness. These comments attracted much attention in Germany although more important and pertinent had been Repington's observations concerning likely German military tactics. He was confirmed in his earlier opinion that Germany would employ its favoured tactic of envelopment against France. This necessarily meant ignoring the restrictions imposed by the frontiers of neutral states.[57] Some of the German militarist press accused Repington of 'inciting the French to resistance *à outrance,* by holding out the prospect of military success and weakening German diplomacy abroad'. They also accused 'the crafty penman of Printing House Square' of 'hoping to arrest naval expansion because German naval competition is so irksome to Great Britain', by attributing military faults to an over-lavish expenditure on the imperial navy. This last was merely the echo of their own immediate propaganda concern. There were other German newspapers that claimed the articles had been written not by Repington but the British military attaché in Berlin. They had been 'inspired' by the British government's wish to bolster French morale as part of its policy of encirclement. Col. Russell was instructed by the War Office to establish whether this view was held in German official circles and also whether it was supposed that Repington's views were necessarily shared by the General Staff. Russell was able to confirm this was not so, but both Kiderlen and Bethmann complained bitterly to the British Ambassador about the damage caused by Repington's pen.[58]

Directly inspired by recent events in Morocco, in both the *Army Review* and *The Times,* Repington argued that the Anglo-French entente ought to be converted into a precise naval and military alliance. Such arguments were not necessarily pleasing to many of his readers as there was still much reluctance, as Repington freely acknowledged, to forfeit what was euphemistically referred to as Britain's 'free hand' for the sake of formalising the continental commitment.[59] Such feelings were still widely held in Printing House Square where Thursfield was encouraged by Buckle to oppose Repington. The 'blue water' lobby readily accepted the challenge for it was seen as yet another instalment in the now familiar struggle between War Office and Admiralty for dominance in determining Britain's strategic role in any future war with Germany. Eventually, his patience tried quite beyond endurance, Repington addressed a very sharp remonstrance to Buckle about Thursfield's work, particularly the leader writer's unwillingness, in any forseeable circumstance, to accept the sending of a British Expeditionary Force to France.

> I shall not reply to Thursfield at present ... but Clemenceau, Cambon and every other French statesman will tell you that the only help of real service to them is the military force which we can place in the line in 14 days. Thursfield's article has fortunately not been noticed yet in France, but if it is it will do serious harm. The whole argument, which bristles with controversial points, is designed to lead up to Thursfield's Radical view that no military force should be sent to the Continent. This means the end of the Entente and you must not make any mistake on the

subject. . . . If an act of aggression is committed against France it is vitally important for us to stand by her. It is not a military advantage to us, but a vital necessity of our existence. So, for Heaven's sake, do not publish any more advice not to prepare for this act in advance for it can only make England distrusted abroad and the Times ridiculous at home.

Repington made it plain to Buckle that in his view *The Times*'s opinion on defence problems no longer deserved serious consideration. At one time the paper had led opinion; now it paid court to the outdated and impracticable prejudices of the Admiralty. A meeting 'to thresh out these problems' was 'long overdue'.[60] Although Repington declared he had recently discussed the problem at length and in great detail with the Minister of War and the new First Lord, Buckle still resisted. The editor insisted that, as yet, there was insufficient reason to warrant changing the entente into an alliance.[61] The entente promised British diplomatic support for France. This had been delivered in both Moroccan crises. With negotiations in progress for a naval agreement with Germany, it would be inconsistent and impolitic to embark upon a military alliance with France. This, however, was not the only reason for Buckle's aversion to Repington's ideas. Buckle was convinced that any war with Germany would primarily be the concern not of the army but the navy. For him, despite the alarms of July when the navy had been so obviously unprepared, the Senior Service remained Britain's guarantee of security. He was not persuaded that to send an expeditionary force to France (an insignificant number when compared with the French and German armies that would be deployed), could ever be a 'vital necessity' for Britain's safety. He simply ignored Repington's reminder that 'the two last First Sea Lords agreed that the despatch of troops to France could proceed safely'.

The bargaining between France and Germany reached its climax in mid-September. As yet unknown to the public, for not even a hint appeared in the national press,[62] for three weeks Britain was in a state of what passed for high military preparedness. Nicolson's very optimistic account, sent to Hardinge on 14 September, of the superiority of the French to the German army and of the thoroughness of British preparations, was more a case of wishful thinking than an accurate estimate.[63] Tension relaxed only when Kiderlen modified his demands to the point where France was asked to make territorial concessions she could easily afford. On 11 October, the Germans agreed to recognise France's position in Morocco. On 3 November the crisis was finally resolved with the signing of a convention. But there were other European concerns in Africa that were not settled by this arrangement.

On 28 September the Italians declared war on the Turks. A week later, Italian troops landed at Tripoli and Benghazi. Throughout the Agadir episode, the difficulty had been to persuade those who saw it as no more than a colonial confrontation between two equally greedy European Powers bent upon aggrandisement, that British rights or interests were in any way involved. To make such an assessment required a view to be taken, not so much upon the particular circumstances of the case, but upon imperatives dictated by a particular judgment of the general European diplomatic climate. Italy's invasion of Tripoli and the subsequent barbarous behaviour of her troops laid bare the expediency that dictated, in certain British minds, loyalty to the entente at any cost, and the spirit of opportunism that sought to seize and exploit any possibility of weakening Germany's own diplomatic arrangements.

There was nothing to commend Italy's action. The immediate response of the British public was to condemn, and this was reflected in the editorial comment of Unionist and Liberal press alike. There were exceptions. Leo Maxse took a hard-headed view of the war from the beginning, insisting that to condemn Italy was nothing but 'scandalous and hysterical twaddle'. If Britain supported Italy, he foresaw an opportunity to detach the Italians from the embrace of the Triple Alliance and thus perhaps eventually add another component to the entente.[64] For Grey, the war was an unlooked-for, unwanted and dangerous embarrassment. He did not find Maxse's arguments convincing. It would be better 'to refrain from any temptation to exploit the situation to bring Italy into the entente camp, lest the cure prove worse than the disease'.[65] The apparent indifference the Foreign Secretary felt obliged to affect in the face of Italy's brutal and greedy act brought down upon his head the full wrath and pent-up frustration of the British Radical press. For Grey to do nothing, they argued, amounted to an overt repudiation of those same principles that he had so recently maintained in his criticism of Austria's annexation of Bosnia. Now he revealed that his fine sentiments had been 'no more than sticks with which to beat the Germans'.[66] Moreover, the Italians claimed that Britain had known in advance of their intentions, a claim that seemed confirmed by a report filed by Lucien Wolf for the *Daily Graphic.* The campaign against Grey gathered momentum. To claim that Britain was neutral was a patent fabrication when the government sanctioned loans to pay for the fighting. To remain silent was tantamount to condoning the atrocities perpetrated by the Italian troops. The measure of the passion felt by Grey's critics, and their contempt for the revealed moral bankruptcy of a *Liberal* administration, was caught exactly in W. T. Stead's ringing appeal in the November issue of his *Review of Reviews* for a 'Gladstone to cry out against this injustice'.[67]

So hard pressed was Grey that he took what was for him a most unusual step. He directly approached Braham to seek *The Times*'s support for the government's action, or rather, inaction. This was before Nicolson, who with Louis Mallet was a strong supporter of Italy, while deprecating 'the deplorable line taken by the English press', had suggested the possibility of inducing 'some of the less unreasonable Editors to maintain a decent neutrality'. They might also be reminded at the same time that 'their hysterical outburst against Austria ... did not improve matters'. A week later and the Foreign Office staff noted with satisfaction that 'The Press seems to be becoming more sensible although the "Daily Mail", which has a large circulation in Italy, still distinguishes itself by the fatuity of its leading articles.'[68] They need not have concerned themselves overmuch about the Carmelite House maverick. Northcliffe was about to exert his overweening influence in the direction that they sought. An exchange of letters between Northcliffe and Steed reveals how a section of the Unionist press, after an initial bout of conscience, managed successfully to hide its scruples and support Italy. Steed, a growing influence at Printing House Square, like Northcliffe, chose to support Italy for the same reason as Churchill, who, while recognising that 'all the strongest elements in Liberal opinion [are] anti-Italian', could argue, 'clearly we must prefer Italy to Turkey on all grounds – moral and unmoral'![69] Ethical scruples simply could not be afforded. The criterion against which all actions and reactions had to be measured was the likely effect upon the European Balance of Power. Thus, like Grey, they were obliged to admit themselves trapped in a game where the rules were now inflexible.

Admitting his pleasure that *The Times* had recovered from an unhealthy tendency 'to wobble at the beginning of the atrocities agitation', Steed told Northcliffe how,

> Just before the ultimatum was presented, the office asked me for suggestions as to policy and I urged the expediency . . . of remembering that in future Italy will count her friends and enemies according to their present attitude. . . . I added that *from the point of view of practical politics*, it would not be disadvantageous to us and France if Italy, a member of the Triple Alliance, were engaged elsewhere when Germany was following an aggressive policy towards the Anglo-French entente. [my emphasis]

'My views are entirely yours in regard to Italy,' Northcliffe replied, 'and I went out of my way to write a leading article in the "Daily Mail" . . . but between ourselves, the Italians have behaved extremely badly. . . . It has been very difficult work to support them.' The true context of the eventual response of the 'patriotic' press to the Turco-Italian war was concern about the status of the Anglo-French entente in the event of war with Germany. The question that was foremost in their minds was, when will Germany attack France? Steed did not believe that there would be war as early as the spring of 1912. This, so he gathered from the Countess de Castellane, was the expectation of the French General Staff. The same conclusion might have been inferred from the French Ambassador in Vienna during the last three months constantly repeating, 'Nous allons vers la guerre.' The best estimate that Steed could make suggested that peace might be maintained for perhaps a year, but not much longer.

> The precarious position of German industry and the determination of the Prussian Junker class to force on if possible some foreign complication in order to prevent the destruction of Junker privileges by internal reform are, to my mind, the main elements in the situation. In different ways both of them make for war. Our interest is to see that we are not enticed into offending France by concluding a dupe's bargain with Germany and that we do not, by a show of ill-will towards Italy, consolidate the rickety Triple Alliance. Above all, we must get our Army into order and see that our reserves of weapons and ammunition are sufficient for all possible emergencies.[70]

To Steed's manifesto, Northcliffe responded shortly. 'La Countess Jean de Castellane . . . need not worry herself as to the Entente, because I am a firm

adherent and am always working privately and publicly for it.'[71] Northcliffe
had determined that henceforth in his newspapers the invariable wary eye
kept upon Germany should be complemented by 'Faithfulness to existing
Friendships'. Loyalty to France and the entente would be their unvarying
watchword, a concentration of vision that exactly matched the advice he had
recently given Maxse. 'The only possible thing for a strong newspaper to do
is to take up one of two main lines of attack and stick with them; the other
course gives the impression of nagging, wearies the public and loses
readers. . . . A nagging paper is like a nagging wife.' Lest Maxse should
suppose mere business practice rather than national imperatives dictated so
single-minded an attention to the fortune and health of the entente, or that
his was a sudden infatuation as soon to be abandoned as taken up, Northcliffe
was at pains to send Leo even 'a rather bad report of a speech I made some
months ago on the subject of France. On France and the entente,' he assured
Maxse, 'we are in entire agreement.'[72]

It was as well that all elements of the Unionist press should join in supporting
the entente, and more immediately and particularly, Grey's conduct of foreign
affairs, for an insistent crescendo of complaint against the minister and his
policy arose from the Liberal back benches and in the columns of the Radical
newspapers. Even the problem of Persia, that had seemed satisfactorily resolved
with the Shah's banishment to Odessa, suddenly became a live issue. The
Shah's release was swiftly followed by an outbreak of civil strife encouraged
by Russian funds. The Russians had taken the opportunity afforded by British
involvement in Moroccan affairs to renege on their promise under the Anglo-
Russian convention not to interfere in Persia, confident that they would not
be confounded in their treachery because of the insurance provided them by
the Germans with the Potsdam agreement. There was little that Grey could
do. In George Buchanan's words, 'The Foreign Office cannot risk giving
umbrage to Russia, though the steps she has taken are quite inconsistent with
our mutual engagements, and in the end we shall probably have to acquiesce
in proceedings we altogether condemn. Such is the risky game of European
combinations.'[73] Russian action in Persia was, if possible, more an embarrassment to Grey than the Italian invasion of Tripoli. He temporarily forfeited the
support of even J. A. Spender,[74] while the Radical press was louder and more
persistent than ever in its complaints and censures.[75] There was, however, a
most interesting indication of the way the wind was blowing concerning Persian
affairs from the 'patriotic' side of Fleet Street. The *Morning Post* refused to
recognise that a Tory cabal, led by Curzon, had joined with Radicals to censure
Grey. The *Post* lectured its contemporaries on the merits of 'Refrain[ing] from
all gossip on foreign policy. The impression should not get abroad that Grey
does not enjoy the support of the nation as a whole.'[76]

The sad trail of events in Persia, Tripoli and Morocco suggested to Grey's
critics that his conduct of the nation's foreign policy was both immoral and
inept. The immediacy and terrifying reality of the dangers inherent in his
playing the game of Balance of Power politics was suddenly highlighted by the
startling revelation that a few months earlier Germany and Britain had apparently stood upon the very brink of war. With considerable accuracy, in

September, *New Age* published in outline the military preparations made by Britain at the height of the Moroccan crisis. 'In spite of all official technical denials', the author insisted the account he gave was 'absolutely accurate, even if this information may seem strange to those who have constantly denied that we are under any agreement or compulsion to aid France'.[77] There were also indiscreet 'hints' along similar lines in an article by A. W. A. Pollock in the October issue of the *Nineteenth Century*.[78] The same intelligence given by Arthur Ponsonby, the Radical MP, finally attracted widespread attention when headlined in the usually pro-Grey *Daily Chronicle* as 'An Alarming Statement'.[79] In the *Contemporary Review*, another Radical MP, Noel Buxton, told his readers that 'In the month of September both sides were prepared to attack. Horses were bought. English officers were recalled from leave. In Germany, even the Reservist got his equipment ready . . . In England the secret was well kept; in Germany the rumours were sufficient to produce a panic on the Berlin Bourse.'[80] The gloomiest forebodings of the Radicals seemed confirmed. Though 'there was no ground of quarrel between England and Germany . . . no question susceptible of arrangement by negotiation . . . certainly none that would justify war', the two countries had 'stood upon the brink of the greatest of calamities which could befall the world. If the present tendencies continue unchecked the disaster to European civilisation of war between England and Germany will certainly come.'[81]

Though with considerable reluctance,[82] Sir Edward Grey, as the focus of this discontent and distrust, was obliged to meet the charges of his critics in open debate in the Commons. Not for the first or the last time, Esher supposed the entente 'decidedly imperilled . . . Edward Grey is to speak on Monday and Europe is awaiting his speech with some anxiety.'[83] The immediate fear was not that Grey might be obliged to resign to satisfy the carping of his party's malcontents, but that he would trim his policies to their prejudices as he had appeared to do at the beginning of the year. Were the outraged sensibilities of the Liberal party's Teutophiles and pacifists once again to be soothed with talk of disarmament and treating the Anglo-French entente as though it were of little consequence?

Esher was the major source of information to the Opposition as to what exactly had happened at the height of the Moroccan crisis and, in particular, the true significance and the likely political consequences of an extraordinary meeting of the Committee of Imperial Defence summoned by Asquith on 23 August where, apparently by design, leading Radical members of the Cabinet had been excluded. At the meeting, General Sir Henry Wilson, the DMO, had given a brilliant exposition of the General Staff's plans to send six divisions to France immediately war was declared with Germany. The First Sea Lord had then outlined the Admiralty's war plans. They effectively had not changed from when Fisher had charge – close blockade, capture of advance bases and the familiar invasion idea. In comparison with General Wilson, Admiral Wilson cut a poor figure, and all the subsequent political changes, particularly McKenna's removal from the Admiralty and his replacement by Winston Churchill, indicated the likelihood that the General Staff's view of strategy had triumphed.[84]

Esher's version of the schism within the Liberal Cabinet was that an inner group was 'working behind the backs of the minor mandarins'. Balfour thought that Asquith had 'managed the whole business badly in that he concealed his policy from such an intriguer as Loulou Harcourt and so vain and touchy an individual as Morley'.[85] In a memorandum that Jack Sandars wrote after a lunchtime conversation with Esher on 24 November, he thought it likely that the Liberal government would 'break up in the debate on foreign policy'.

> It is believed that the Government will retire from its policy to afford
> military aid to France, and that for the future the continental undertaking
> of 1904 will be announced to be little more than the amicable assurance
> of this country to continue peaceful relations with her neighbours across
> the Channel. . . . Grey has to manage a retreat in good order saving what
> he can from the wreck of his August policy.
>   Morley on the other hand, with Harcourt and the remaining nonenties
> in the Cabinet, has to avoid anything like a triumphant assertion of their
> own opposition to the forward policy of their militant colleagues and at
> the same time to reduce the French Entente to the language of mere
> polite friendliness.

It is easy to imagine what effect this version of the likely progress of the foreign policy debate would have upon a Tory hothead like Maxse. Perhaps even more sinister, Esher supposed that Steed had been 'got at' by the Little Englander group in the Cabinet and was to write articles for *The Times* 'representing the policy of those members of the Cabinet who have been in opposition to the Inner Ring'.[86]

A week before Grey's speech in the Commons defending his conduct of foreign policy, 'Taffy' Gwynne wrote to the new Tory leader, Andrew Bonar Law.

> I have just come from the Foreign Office where I have had a long talk
> with Tyrrell, Grey's private secretary, and an old friend of mine and a
> coming man. It occurred to me that it would not be a bad thing if you
> could have a quiet talk with him if possible before the debate on Foreign
> Affairs next Monday. What do you say? . . . Of course he is a vigorous
> defender of Grey, *but I imagine that we all are* especially as the extreme
> left are going for him like pick-pockets.[87]

Although in the past the apparent unanimity of the two front benches on foreign policy had caused grave offence to his own backbenchers, Grey nevertheless valued the knowledgeable support of Balfour. Now he provided Bonar Law in advance with an outline of his projected speech, an arrangement that emphasises how well stage-managed was the approaching 'confrontation'.[88] Attitudes were determined, the opposing forces carefully calculated and arraigned, long before Grey had uttered a single syllable in defence of his conduct of affairs. Thus it was of no real substantive significance that Grey, 'choosing his words with a precision and felicity . . . judgment, temper and lucidity that . . . nothing could have exceeded', provided 'a great performance in every way characteristic'.[89] He did not, as Asquith triumphantly claimed, 'torpedo his critics'.[90] As much in sorrow as anger, shortly afterwards A. G. Gardiner wrote in the Daily News,'Sir Edward Grey as Foreign Secretary is impossible.'[91] Grey's Radical critics understood only too well the deadly implication of his own defence, nor had it required a postscript from Asquith which, even more clearly than Grey's advance insistence to Bonar Law – 'We must not lose our old friends'[92] – baldly asserted, 'We are influenced in our conduct outside the strict letter of Treaty obligations by the desire to maintain in their full strength the friendships we have formed; and the understandings that we have entered into.'[93] For this reason, Gardiner's Daily News chose to headline its account of the debate, 'No secret arrangements, but we must support France.' What a country to have to support, Gardiner would have reflected, and for the same reasons that prompted Maxse in the contrary spirit to write excitedly to Northcliffe of his most recent experience of the temper of that nation.

> Our people haven't the smallest idea of the great change that has taken place [there] under German pressure. I only wish that we had made as much progress on patriotic lines during these past years as the French have. . . . The morale of the nation has received a splendid tonic from the perpetual German bullying and when, one of these fine days, the French bite, our German friends will be astounded by the consequences.[94]

Maxse and like-minded friends had a very simple explanation for the 'anti-British' attitude of 'international faddists' like Gardiner, or Leonard Courtney who, the day after Grey's speech, had delivered a withering attack upon the Foreign Secretary in the Lords.[95] It was that 'the peculiar susceptibilities of their Radical fanaticism had been skillfully fomented by German misrepresentation and intrigue'.[96] Any Briton prepared to put nation before party, fact before sentiment, would surely have responded to Grey's words with acceptance and approval. But the real source of right-wing satisfaction was that the fears they had entertained less than a year earlier that the Triple Entente had collapsed had been proved exaggerated and unreal so that when H. W. Massingham cried out in the Nation that in Persia, as in Morocco, British independence of action had been sacrificed for the 'foul idol of the Balance of Power', Maxse and his friends could only rejoice that Grey was an acolyte who served at the same altar as themselves. 'Grey was splendid,' Garvin gloated to Maxse, 'and has realised the highest expectations I ever had of him, which is saying a great deal.'[97] To Jack Sandars, Esher correctly listed the priorities of the Radical repulse. It had been enough that Bonar Law had been 'quite good', and the debate 'good', the really important consideration was that Grey had been 'first rate'.[98] And Grey had been 'first rate' because, in Mahan's words, 'Things will now go smoother. He has smothered the ignorant optimists.'[99] This was Garvin's exact meaning when he admitted to Henry Lucy that the Foreign Secretary had 'fulfilled all my expectations of him . . . Henceforth I will back him through thick and thin so deeply is my faith in his strength and judgment deepened.'[100]

With Grey lying on the bosom of the patriotic press it was not to be expected that the Radicals would condescend to remain silent. With chapter and verse they denounced the evils of secret diplomacy, imperialism, international finance, the wickedness of the armament manufacturers and, above everything else, the dangers inherent in the pursuit of Balance of Power notions. They recognised the symptoms of Europe's sickness but, for a variety of reasons, were disabled from treating its causes. This fatal frailty was recognised, gloated over and exploited by Grey's Unionist apologists in the press. Nothing would seem to dent the optimism shared by Radicals, socialists and pacifists. Their view of international politics enshrined hopes that were proof against everything. Not reason but faith dictated their passionate belief that 'Caesarism and nationalism which today we crown with laurels will cease to be a standing menace to the world and pass away. Have faith and rejoice.'[101] Some, with a weariness induced by age and long, sad experience, were at least obliged to recognise the temptation of giving up a struggle that year by year seemed ever more useless. Wilfrid Blunt recorded how Churchill, though he did not like the Italians, clung to them 'because we cannot afford to make for ourselves another enemy'. The First Lord's Radical conscience, Blunt diagnosed, had been stilled by 'the bite of Grey's anti-German policy'.[102] There were those radicals, like E. D. Morel, who either from naivety or vanity could suppose it was enough that 'none of the facts had been contested' in the book that he published on the antecedents of the Agadir crisis, *Morocco in Diplomacy.* This did not mean, however, that the validity of his thesis and arguments had been generally accepted.[103] Thus Grey's opponents shouted loud and long, and were even not above borrowing the shabby methods employed by their arch-enemies – as in the ill-fated 'Grey Must Go' campaign. All was to no avail for in the end they made the fatal mistake of grasping at easy cures that were no less easily revealed by their enemies as hopeless remedies.

It was foolish for them to suppose, and an even greater mistake to advertise their belief, that Socialist victories in the Reichstag elections would hasten Anglo-German rapprochement. 'Travel in Germany and you will soon realise that nobody cares a — how many victories they win,' Northcliffe instructed Marlowe. 'Socialist victories have no importance in international affairs. Please emphasise the correct point thoroughly. The English peace party have a foolish and misleading theory that if Socialists are returned there will be less likelihood of war.'[104] *New Age* cruelly compared the pacifists among the German Socialists with Liberalism's Nonconformists – 'voices that are heard in a manner out of all proportion to their numbers and weight. . . . The whole nation is unanimous in its desire to secure for Germany a place in the sun. . . . There are no parties in Germany but all for the State.'[105] Fred Wile assured Northcliffe: 'As far as armaments and relations with England are concerned . . . the non Anglophobe party is still a hopeless minority. The big army and navy element still predominate in the Reichstag.'[106] It was left to Frank Chilvers, *The Times*'s assistant correspondent in Berlin, to emphasise to Maxse that whether she would or no, Germany was 'incapable of abandoning her ambitions', and the Socialists were 'not the sort of people to make her do it'.

The spirit [in Germany] is just the same as it was in 1884. The peasant has become a 'Socialist' merely to spite the local Squire, or the Parson, or the official . . . but he raves about the Navy just as I remember his father raving about the Army. He is proud of it and has oleograph prints of all the new ships hanging on the walls of his kitchen.

This sort of 'Socialism' . . . is so artificial that it can safely be neglected. . . . I cannot see any way out. We must keep an unbroken front to the world because of the possibilities latent in Germany. . . . We are too generous (once our interests are secure), too handsome, and we think others are the same.[107]

Maxse did not need persuading that Germany would not change her tune simply because she had four million so-called socialists in a population of sixty-five million. They would not change the spirit of the régime. As well expect a tiger to change its stripes. Germany was ambitious and would continue to pursue its policy of *Weltpolitik*. Thus Britain's problems remained unchanged. How best to sustain the entente secure at whatever the cost against all trials? How to ensure the maintenance of the doctrine of continuity in the conduct of the nation's foreign affairs? How best to frustrate any appeal for disarmament? How best to crush any sentimental appeal for Anglo-German rapprochement? It was not sufficient that this time they had saved Grey; 'His hands must be constantly strengthened against his own natural weakness and from the cranks who are continually attacking him in the interests of Germany.' As Maxse told Bonar Law,

We trust that the Foreign Minister will keep foreign affairs in his own hands (and) resolutely adhere to broad lines of policy, national and imperial in conception, national and imperial in object, so that the Government may in this department continue to enjoy the support and confidence of all who place country before Party.[108]

In February 1912, a good friend of Edward Grey, Mrs Mandell Creighton, asked the Foreign Secretary whether he had minded the attacks made upon him. 'Well really,' he replied, 'I haven't had time to read the papers except *Times, Westminster Gazette* and *Spectator* and I have seen very little of the abuse.'[109] It was a significant measure of the turmoil of 1911 that a Liberal Foreign Secretary should find his best comfort among those who, excluding Spender, only months earlier had fretted and fumed because they supposed he had sold the nation's interests to assuage the criticisms of the Radicals in his party who, as all patriots knew, put every other country's interest before their own!

Priming the magazine

The parlous condition of the Mediterranean continues to occupy our attention and the attention of the Press. The Times is stupid to a degree, and the Westminster is disgraceful.

General Sir Henry Wilson's Diary

The Territorial Force is at the moment the finest educative moral force in England. No wonder the volume of criticism against it grows. . . . The blind and the half-witted are alas always in the majority with us.

Ian Hamilton to J. E. B. Seely

Out of the tangle of races and religions which complicate the problem of confusion in the Near East, some mighty volcanic eruption of miscellaneous national hatreds would almost seem fated to arise, if not from the unbridled passions of Turk and Christian at any rate from the jealousies and ambitions of the Great Powers.

H. S. Perris in 'Concord'

Early in 1912, Repington published some information in *The Times* on the strength of the British regular army that he had abstracted from the army's *General Annual Report*. The report had not been seen by members of the Commons, and immediately questions were tabled about the exact status *The Times*'s military correspondent enjoyed at the War Office. Northcliffe anxiously informed Haldane that he had warned Repington when he accepted the editorship of the *Army Review* that sooner or later there would be trouble. The present contretemps was 'causing acute unpleasantness in The Times' office and . . . odious suggestions in the lobbies and places where people talk.'[1] In the Lords, Haldane, and in the Commons, J. E. B. Seely, the Under Secretary of State for War, stoutly defended Repington against the attacks of Liberal and Tory members. Arthur Lee claimed that Repington's joint appointment was 'incompatible with public interest, an administrative scandal, an anomalous and extremely objectionable position'. Seely responded that he, on the contrary, thought it 'a very good arrangement. If you want to get the very best man to edit the *Army Review* I do frankly say I am convinced that Col. Repington is the very best man.'[2]

When Repington had been adviser to the group of backbenchers that had made Brodrick's life at the War Office so difficult, he and Seely had been close friends. But the qualities that made Repington such an effective ally also made him a very dangerous enemy. Seely knew that Repington was not enthusiastic about his appointment. What was more, Repington maintained very close contact with Haldane and did not hesitate to tell the Lord Chancellor that he thought Seely's promotion had brought a dramatic fall in the general efficiency of the War Office. 'I like Seely personally and get on with him,' Repington wrote to Haldane, 'but he does nothing and carries no guns. As Harris says, it is useless to look behind a screen when there is nothing there. Seely's jealousy of you leads him to accept placidly criticisms of your work.'[3]

Repington's wish to resign the editorship of the *Army Review* became the focus for a discussion between him and the new minister about their relationship. Repington argued that he was 'overdone by the editorial business [and] preferred work as a freelance to life in official harness'. Seely refused to accept Repington's resignation as he had recently rejected complaints by the newly appointed German Ambassador, Marschall, about his attacks on the German army. To resign after that would seem too much like trucking to German wishes. The argument sounded plausible. Among journalists there had been considerable nervous apprehension that Marschall's arrival in London heralded a determined German attack on the entente. George Saunders was one who, recalling his earlier experience at the Second Hague Peace Conference, warned that the German Ambassador was 'one of the most seductive managers of the Press that ever engaged in diplomacy'.[4]

Repington agreed to postpone his resignation until January 1913. He told Dawson, with whom he had swiftly established both a closer and happier working relationship than Buckle,[5] that he did not think Seely had revealed the true reason why he wanted him to remain editor of the *Army Review*.

> I got out of him that he thought I was going to attack him; and his real fear to my mind is that the dog may get off the chain and bite him. I told him that he had not played the game by me; that Haldane had always told me everything and had consulted me before taking any steps, whereas, he, Seely, had not even answered my letters and that I had no intention of serving at the War Office when a policy might be sprung upon us of which I knew nothing. He was apologetic and promised amendment. . . . I told him that I thought he would be wise in his own interest to tell me things that were happening before they occurred because in 9 cases out of 10 I usually supported the official view when I had all the evidence before me and that I did him no harm when I occasionally differed from his official advisers. . . . He then opened up a new project . . . that he should have the exclusive use of my services. . . . He practically asked me what I wanted . . . I was not impressed. It will be amusing to see the offer, but I told him I was more use where I am.[6]

Seely's concern either to have Repington on his side, or effectively muzzled as a critic by an official appointment to the War Office, was understandable. The Unionist Opposition was making life very difficult for him. Like his predecessor, he was adept at making fudging responses about the function and purpose of the Expeditionary Force, even in the face of astute and pointed questioning by Arthur Lee and L. S. Amery.[7] It was not so easy, however, to answer the growing volume of complaint both in the Commons and outside Westminster that maintained that the Territorial Force was wholly inadequate, ineffectual and impractical.

The general atmosphere among conscriptionists at the beginning of 1912 was more than a little hysterical. Roberts's genuine fears were being played upon with some effect and evident relish by Henry Wilson. The general retailed alarmist news that he had garnered on several recent visits to the Foreign Office. In the space of five days he had spoken to Tyrrell, Arthur Nicolson and Eyre Crowe. All three were utterly convinced that war with Germany was likely by spring. With war apparently imminent, nothing should be left undone to prepare both army and navy.[8]

Roberts addressed himself, not, as might have been expected, to the Minister of War but to Churchill at the Admiralty. He pointed out how, during the previous summer, 'our regular Army, small as it was, was unprepared for war, whilst our Territorial Force was wholly unfit to take the field. . . . The continued existence of our Empire cannot rest on the voluntary efforts of a few of the best of our citizens. . . . We must adopt compulsion as the bedrock of our military system.' Churchill made no secret of his private sympathy for compulsory service, 'But I am far less certain that it is necessary or *that it would be convenient.*'[9] Although the minister's opinion had changed, his party's had not. Equally, the greater part of opinion in the country remained either indifferent or bitterly opposed to conscription. In any event, it was argued there could be no place for compulsion so long as Haldane's scheme was successful.[10] The first and obvious step was, therefore, for the conscriptionists to demonstrate that Haldane's Territorials were a failure. There were those who, for a variety of reasons, were only too eager to harry Haldane, not least his most vehement public critic, Leo Maxse. It was no accident that in the pages of the *National Review*, the 'Balfour Must Go' campaign having achieved its purpose, the next slogan Maxse advertised was 'Haldane Must Go.'

Two years earlier, Haldane, in conversation with the Clerk to the Privy Council had claimed that his work at the War Office was 'complete'. He would be 'glad to hand the system he had created over to the Opposition which . . . in combination with the County Associations could at this stage do more to develop the Territorial organisation'. Almeric Fitzroy noted particularly how Haldane 'spoke with great gratitude of the assistance he had received from his political foes'.[11] This was neither the first nor the last time that the Liberal Minister for War suggested that on military reforms he owed more to the Opposition, and Balfour in particular, than to his own party.[12] Maxse emphasised this 'unnatural partnership'; how Balfour had 'given his sanction to the Territorial sham of his friend Viscount Haldane, and has protected that humbug from attack in the House of Commons'. Leo's insidious poison worked. Arthur Lee seriously proposed to Bonar Law that Balfour had been 'bamboozled' by Haldane and that the Opposition's leader had been 'perhaps too intimate with him socially'.[13] There would be no question of Bonar Law aiding and abetting Haldane. He was too anxious to secure the loyalty of the extreme right of his party. In a speech at the Albert Hall he made a swingeing attack on the Liberals in general, and poor, undeserving Haldane in particular, charging him with having reduced both Regular and Territorial Forces by twenty and thirty thousand men respectively, and arming those that remained with inferior weapons.[14] The charge was incorrect but it stuck.[15]

In February 1912, Haldane visited Berlin. A week earlier the *Nation* had confidently stated that the time had come to strike a bargain with Germany.[16] This was the culmination of its own campaign, begun in October 1911, for an 'Ambassador of Peace' who, given that he was 'a capable and unprejudiced negotiator', might solve Anglo-German difficulties 'by a few months of patient work'.[17] Such were the hopes of the Radicals. Having failed to disturb Grey they were convinced that the time had come 'to strike a psychological blow for peace'. Any number of Radical and pacifist groups within the general Liberal embrace, including the National Liberal Federation, had been exerting constant pressure upon the Foreign Secretary to come to a friendly understanding with Germany. It was known that a new navy law was about to be presented to the Reichstag. In a speech at the Guildhall in November, Churchill had attempted to head off the possibility of increased building programmes by asserting that if the Germans made no new move then the British naval estimates would be reduced. Ernest Cassel and Albert Ballin, fearing that continued naval expansion would lead inevitably to an Anglo-German clash – something to be avoided as not at all to their commercial and financial advantage – proposed to alleviate the tension by direct conversations between British and German statesmen. A leading pacifist, William Fox, reporting a conversation with Grey on 8 January, told Leonard Courtney that he had been assured that the Foreign Secretary was 'favourably disposed to the suggestion that Lord Haldane should be sent to Berlin . . . on a special mission to open up negotiations'.[18]

The truth of the matter was that Asquith and Grey were in an awkward and unenviable position. They were obliged to make some sort of response to the mounting pressure for action within their own party. Also, it would be politic to attempt to appease German pride that had been so sadly dented by the Moroccan settlement. At the same time, they could neither undermine British naval supremacy nor endanger the Anglo-French entente. Asquith was all too conscious of the delicate balance of forces within the Cabinet. The entente strategy which he and Grey supported was secured within the administration by the uncertain loyalties of Churchill and Lloyd George, volatile and ambitious men of infinite resource. What guarantee was there that this mercurial pair who now blew hot for war where earlier they had extolled with equal passion and conviction peace and retrenchment, might not turn their coats again in formidable alliance with the pro-German cabal led by Harcourt and Morley? In Parliament as in the country, the Liberal party was everywhere beset by problems – social unrest, violence and the unmistakeable rumblings of revolt in Ireland. A small parliamentary majority bolstered by uncertain political bargainings put an enormous premium and strain on the loyalty of the Liberal party's Radical tail. Without enthusiasm the suggestion was put to and agreed by Cabinet that as Grey could not and Winston would not, that Haldane might talk to the Germans. From the first Repington perceived the exact measure of Haldane's task. He wrote to tell Buckle:

The truth seems to be that the tension between us and Germany has become serious and that something had to be done (1) to see whether any arrangement of an amicable character was open to us, and, (2) to satisfy the Radical Tail that all possible had been done to come to such an arrangement, so that, if it failed the party might stomach the natural consequences, namely increased estimates as promised by McKenna. . . . I do not think Haldane will give any points away. . . . I know that he desires and intends to meet the German increase with a reply which will satisfy the most combative of us. Winston is similarly inclined, and so are the rest of the inner circle of the Cabinet (A, G & LLG), but of course they have to humour their followers, and I suppose this mission is as good a way of setting about the matter as can be suggested.[19]

Esher also wrote to *The Times*'s editor. There was no danger in the mission as Britain's entente partners, Russia and France, were being 'kept informed of every move on the board'; no danger that was so long as Britain continued 'to build stolidly two vessels to every German one' and if Haldane was not 'too clever in this matter'.[20]

Grey, preoccupied with the coal strike, left the preparations for the mission and the subsequent negotiations to the unwilling Nicolson, who had made his prejudice clear to Bertie. 'I do not see why we should abandon the excellent position in which we have been placed and step down to be involved in endeavours to entangle us in some so-called "understandings" which would undoubtedly, if not actually impair our relations with France and Russia, in any case render the latter countries somewhat suspicious of us.'[21] Nicolson saw his part as ensuring that the formula presented to the Germans was as meaningless as possible. Germany responded to Britain's patent prevarication by introducing the Novelle, a new law to increase her warship building programme, and concluding the abortive attempt at reconciliation. Nicolson basked in the sunshine of his friends' approval convinced that he had extricated Britain from 'a quagmire . . . into which we have been led by our unscrupulous adversaries and our singularly naive and feeble negotiators'.[22]

Maxse had been enraged by the Haldane mission supposing that it indicated the 'Potsdam party' now enjoyed a dominant position within the Cabinet. To Maxse's jaundiced eye, Richard Haldane was the key figure in that group he described as a 'miscellaneous assortment . . . at the beck and call of German diplomats, soft-headed sentimentalists, snobs hypnotised by Hohenzollern blandishments, cranks convinced that their own country is always wrong'. The Minister of War had set himself up as an 'authority on Germany on the strength of his having been annually bamboozled by German professors in his earlier days'.[23] As recently as May of the previous year, Haldane had lent credence to Maxse's absurd theory by giving a private luncheon party for the Kaiser at his Queen Anne's Gate rooms. In August, this 'convinced admirer of all things German', as he was described by the *Daily Mail*, gave an 'appreciation' of Germany to the University of Oxford.

Mutual suspicions are largely due to mutual misunderstandings. English politicians must learn that vague and sentimental appeals to German statesmen provoke distrust. . . . Germany is penetrating everywhere and to the profit of mankind. Nothing is likely to keep her back, and nothing is so likely to smooth her path as really frank and easy relations in commerce, in politics and in society with this country.[24]

Maxse believed that such sentiments 'proved' that Haldane supported a policy of sell-out to the Germans. Knowing that Grey was unenthusiastic about the Berlin visit, Maxse made the unwarranted assumption that Haldane was acting contrary to the Foreign Secretary's wishes. Maxse was not alone in this misapprehension which was elaborated into the thesis that there were two competing foreign policies. That which Grey espoused was correct and healthily pro-French. The other was mistaken, perverse and insidiously pro-German promoted by the Cabinet's 'Potsdam group', supported by assorted peace-lovers and Teutophiles within the Liberal party, 'cranks . . . continually attacking Grey in the interests of Germany'. If Grey was ever to triumph over this group, then Maxse supposed that Bonar Law ought to take a hand and 'tell the country the kind of thing which requires saying in some shape or form at the present'.

> The people of this country are getting somewhat weary of futilities and earnestly hope to see the end of the seriocomic operations of the amateur diplomatist . . . A term should be put to all this craven whining to Germany . . . we shall not allow ourselves to be entangled in any negotiations inimical to our vital national interests.[25]

Some small excuse for Maxse's hysterical outburst might be found in the way that the government sought to pretend Haldane's visit to Germany was a private affair concerned with educational matters, having nothing to do with the navy or foreign policy. This patent fabrication revealed how low the government rated the public's intelligence. Wile told his *Daily Mail* readers that 'the fiction' of a private visit 'has never been seriously entertained in any intelligent quarter'.[26] The government was reluctant to give any worthwhile information about the visit even to prominent members of the Opposition. Consequently the Opposition was obliged to rely upon 'leaks' that were often partially accurate only.[27] Although Maxse's claim that Grey had been thrust unwillingly aside 'by his intimate and treacherous friend' was nonsense, the mystery surrounding Haldane's visit gave credence to even the wildest rumours, the most popular being that Haldane and Grey were pursuing different policies. When Grey received the Garter in February, the *Daily Mail* claimed this was a sign that the King approved Grey's policy that 'has no relation to Haldane's "conversations" '.[28]

Haldane made matters worse for himself than they need have been, choosing to keep silent for what at the time seemed to him good and honourable reasons. 'I leave all speaking to others,' he told his mother. Despite the difficulties and although it was 'premature to be certain', he still believed that 'good results' might come from his visit.[29] After this fashion Haldane became the willing victim of the way in which the Foreign Office chose to conduct its business. Prepared to pay lip service to democratic ideals when it suited its own devious purposes, the Foreign Office never attempted to persuade or convince the public by providing accurate information. Because everything was wrapped in mystery, no minister could ever seek informed support from the public. Although it would have defeated his elaborate conspiracy theory of how Haldane was promoting a different policy from Grey, Maxse addressed himself to this vital problem in a letter to Tyrrell in early March.

> You must be aware that the Germans are exploiting the Cassell-Haldane Mission to our detriment everywhere, and their agents are circulating positive legends in the Continental Press, especially in Russia and France, upon the unfortunate episode. It is really no answer to say that we did not take the initiative and we shall do nothing without consulting our partners. That may be good enough for the *Governments*. . . . But we want to keep right with the *Peoples* as well as the governments . . . To spade-workers like myself, who are prepared to take any amount of trouble for the policy we believe in, the Haldane 'Mission' was worse than a crime – it was a blunder.[30]

Haldane's status in the patriotic press as the best friend Germany had in the Liberal Cabinet grew by increments. Sadly his own actions contributed materially to this unfortunate and false image. The *Daily Express* made a point of reminding its readers how the Kaiser had called Haldane 'my friend'. A series of speeches the minister made on behalf of Anglo-German friendship suggested that his consuming anxiety was to demonstrate his affection and admiration for William. These speeches culminated with a fervent eulogy made at the Savoy Hotel in June before an audience that included the Ambassadors of Germany, Austria, Hungary and Italy.

> The German Emperor is a great man. He is gifted by the gods with the highest gift that they can give . . . *Geist*. He has *Geist* in the highest degree. He has been a true leader of his people – a leader in spirit as well as in deed. He has guided them through nearly a quarter of a century and preserved unbroken peace. I know no record of which a monarch has better cause to be proud. In every direction his activities have been remarkable. He has given his country that splendid fleet that we, who know about fleets, admire.

Could this be the same fleet that Churchill had earlier dismissed as a '*luxus Flotte*'? 'An astounding speech . . . one of many the Lord Chancellor has recently made,' the *Daily Mail* commented, noting how strangely it compared with the words of Balfour in the most recent issue of the Berlin monthly, *Nord und Sud* that it had quoted extensively and with approval. Writing of the German fleet, Balfour had emphasised that 'the mere instinct of self-preservation obliges Englishmen not merely to take account of the growth of foreign navies but anxiously to weigh the motives of those who build them'.[31]

As he was distrusted by so many in his own party, Haldane was more vulnerable to the attacks of the Tory press than any other minister in the Asquith Cabinet. Because he was wedded to a tradition that viewed government as an instrument designed to restrain rather than enhance public passion and prejudice, he naively supposed that if German and British politicians were allowed to negotiate in a calm atmosphere there was every possibility that, as in the earlier case with France, the causes of friction might eventually be removed. His inclination was therefore to say as little as possible in his own defence against the wilder accusations of extremist critics. He supposed to act otherwise might well provoke a vindictive atmosphere. This would force politicians to adopt intractable positions that would not only render peaceful compromise impossible but provide ammunition both for the Anglophobes in Germany and the Teutophobes in Britain. Subsequently he was charged during the war with being a dissimulator who had for selfish party reasons denied the army's need for more recruits and munitions.[32]

In May 1912 there had been rumours that Haldane was to replace Edward Goschen as Ambassador in Berlin. A visit by John Morley to that city in the middle of the month was popularly supposed to be a follow-up to Haldane's February visit. Northcliffe was worried by 'the number of staff on my papers being invited to the German Embassy. . . . There is a lot of bungling spade-work going on. I cannot, of course, control the private lives of my staff,' he told Maxse, with obvious regret and pain, 'but a list of the journalists who have been wined and dined would be instructive. I could reprint any remarks you might make about such a list. . . . I do not like Morley's visit and I do not know what they are up to.'[33] When, in June, Haldane returned to Germany for his annual holiday, there was widespread speculation in the press that he was finishing his mission. Everywhere he went he was pursued by the German press which was under the impression that he was about to sign a treaty. His brother John, who accompanied him, was mistaken for Asquith. Maxse, as ever in the van of the wild men of the Radical Right, continued to publish a stream of calumnies against Haldane in the *National Review*, more than ade-quately abetted by the young Lord Percy who wrote of 'Haldane's crooked ways and thoughts'.[34] Willoughby de Broke, like Haldane holidaying in Germany, more wise in the ways of horses and hunting than the intricacies of international politics, on the basis of a conversation with his masseur boldly informed Maxse that 'the mass of public opinion' in Germany 'wants an alliance between England and Germany to keep the peace. . . . [It] hates any entente of any kind between England and France, and hates France with a deadly hatred. . . . Did you say something about an Entente Committee? If the Radicals send their envoys to Berlin why should we not send ours to Paris?'[35]

Throughout 1912 'Roberts and his Rabble', as Fisher designated the National Service League, continued to press for compulsory service. In the early months of the year there had not been as much comment in the press as they would have wished. Notable allies were for the moment disabled from commenting, but not because they wished to drop the question. 'The more I go into it,' Garvin told Bonar Law, 'the more serious appears our military position and that of the Government with regard to it.' Party leader and editor agreed they were 'compelled by the pressure of other topics to postpone resumption of the question'.[36] Haldane's appointment as Lord Chancellor in June became the signal for an intensification of the campaign for compulsion. A twin attack was mounted; on the hopelessness of the Territorial Force and against the character of its creator. Roberts, who planned to 'hammer away on the anvil of the electorate' with three set-piece speeches at the Mansion House in July, Norwich in September and Manchester in October, was greatly cheered when, on the tenth anniversary of the Peace of Vereeniging, Garvin wrote a powerful leader in the *Pall Mall Gazette.*

> The cardinal weakness of our military position – the divorce of the people itself from the whole system of national defence – remains as complete as it was before the disasters of Natal and the 'hope deferred' upon the veldt shook us out of our self-complacency. One can only shiver at the fatuous spirit which plumes itself upon LORD HALDANE'S 'reforms'. . . . The military power of our great rivals has increased while we have been losing and throwing away numbers. They have added another generation of men to the roll of effective patriotism; we have allowed another generation to grow up useless and inept in danger. The Royal Commission of 1904 told us that a system of national training was vital to our security. LORD ROBERTS after a lifetime's service to the Empire with arms and brain, has made the last sacrifice of a veteran's privilege of leisure to bear the same witness. And our response, our sincerity, our achievement are summed up in the word – nothing.[37]

Roberts could not have been more pleased with Garvin's timely intervention. 'We are in anxious times, and it behoves all who realize the danger of being unprepared to bring it home to our apathetic countrymen.' Roberts was convinced that Britain's 'present difficulties are mainly due to the want of . . . a sufficiently large land force to be of any use' both to the entente and to the navy. His interest in the fortunes of the navy had been sparked by Churchill's decision, without any reference to the CID, to reorganise the British fleets. Roberts's main objection to the planned withdrawal from the Mediterranean was not strategic. He agreed with the need 'to be strong in Home Waters to cope with the German Navy'. What he feared was that the decision would 'lower Great Britain's prestige in India, in the Colonies, and in the eyes of all the nations of the world'. He supposed there was an easy solution to the problem. There should be 'a great increase in the Navy' and its 'required freedom of action' could be guaranteed 'by having a sufficient number of trained men in the country'.[38] Thus Churchill's decision had very important implications for the future of any successful campaign for conscription.

Since his appointment as First Lord of the Admiralty in October 1911, Winston had introduced a series of sweeping and significant changes. His pugnacious personality was very evident in the way that he presented his first estimates to the Commons. There was, for example, a convention that the name of Britain's chief naval rival should not be spoken, or if mentioned, the reference should be suitably apologetic. Churchill would not be a party to such flummery. 'The time has come', he told the House, 'when both nations ought to understand without ill-temper or disguise what will be the conditions under which the naval competition will be carried on during the next few years.' Britain would not surrender her naval supremacy. If Germany increased her number of Dreadnoughts then so would Britain, and whatever the cost she would always retain her 60 per cent superiority.[39] This element of Churchill's speech was widely acclaimed by the Conservative press. *The Times* insisted that it was 'the best exposition of naval policy . . . since Lord George Hamilton's famous statement in 1889'.[40]

Admiral Fisher, still overseas in self-imposed exile, was fond of likening himself to Holland – '*Because I lie low and am damned all round!*'[41] Nevertheless, it was generally recognised that Winston had installed him as his 'unofficial adviser and uncrowned First Sea Lord'.[42] Initially, Fisher had not been too happy about 'condoning the d – d dirty trick played on McKenna',[43] replacing him as First Lord with Churchill. But he soon recognised Winston's strengths, and was even quicker to appreciate the opportunity once more to occupy a position of power and influence. The familiar connection with Garvin, now editor of the *Pall Mall Gazette* as well as the *Observer* – 'What a splendid prospect to outshine John Morley' – was quickly re-established. 'Trust me to send you *every d – d secret I know* of. . . .'[44] The Admiral told Churchill 'he might rely upon [Garvin] as a Patriot before Party as regards the Navy. . . . I hope he will seize an early opportunity of fore-gathering with you.' Fisher made it clear to Garvin how much he enjoyed working with Winston whose wisdom was beyond question for he shared so many of Sir John's own prejudices!

> Winston sees that only damn fools like Repington and the 'Morning Post' think that Land and Sea strategy are alike. I've always told you that any bloody fool can be a General and they mostly are! . . . Winston is now saturated and is diabolically clever at exposition so I am happy and look forward to bigger and better things. . . . Winston is weak on the 2 Keels to 1, but perhaps I am also to blame there in *putting forward less to gain more*! So the 'Islanders', the Navy League, you and Stead and Alan Burgoyne and Fiennes are alright in hammering away at the 2 keels to 1, as it strengthens and backs up Winston in his own camp![45]

By a stream of letters and, whenever possible, supplementing the written word by long conversations aboard the Admiralty yacht, *Enchantress*, Fisher advised, encouraged and inspired the young minister. At the beginning of March he asked Winston, 'What on earth is the use of our risking our existence for France if we get no return? Let the French take care of the Mediterranean, and a hot time they'll have of it with submarines poking about in that lake. We are well out of it.'[46] A fortnight later Churchill told the Commons that he proposed to reorganise the various British fleets and squadrons as from 1 May. To counteract the increased German building programme, the Home Fleet in the North Sea would be strengthened but at the cost of weakening the British position in the Mediterranean. As in his demand for Supplementary Estimates in July, Churchill argued that he was responding to 'the brute force of facts'.[47] In effect, he was accepting Fisher's dictum that 'We cannot have everything and be strong everywhere. It is futile to be strong in the subsidiary theatre of war and not overwhelmingly supreme in the decisive theatre.'[48]

There were three possible solutions to the problem facing the Liberal Government. First, it could enter a definite and binding alliance with France and trust its ally to look after British interests in the Mediterranean, thus releasing British battleships for the North Sea station and protection of the French coast. Alternatively, it could provide funds to build enough ships to be sufficiently strong in both the North Sea and the Mediterranean. Churchill had adopted the third solution. Because it was the cheapest, the simplest, and did not involve the 'perilous leap in the dark' of alliance with France – which would mean abandoning Britain's 'free hand' and the certainty that the French would insist upon conscription – initially the Radical press, much to its surprise, found itself supporting Churchill.[49]

The First Lord's bold pronouncement had put the cat amongst the pigeons. At the War Office, Haldane was not in the least reassured by Churchill's arguments, but then only succeeded in adding to his distress by sending for Henry Wilson who immediately 'advocated an Alliance with France for the specific cause of German aggression'. Haldane, naturally, would not wear this proposal 'because he sees it would probably mean conscription'. The minister admitted that the proposed naval withdrawal from the Mediterranean 'frightened him'.[50] At the Foreign Office, Nicolson took every opportunity to advertise his opinion that there should be an alliance with France. Grey would not countenance the idea recognising that it would lead inevitably to the break-up of the Cabinet.[51] The General Staff were appalled by Winston's scheme. As far as they were concerned it was just another example of the navy's irresponsible behaviour, placing an unbearable strain upon military resources and strengths which were already insufficient and overstretched. A misalliance of convenience began to emerge between those normally at daggers drawn with each other. Though they pursued very different ends, the Radicals in the Cabinet – usefully supported by McKenna, anxious to get his own back on Churchill for his dismissal from the Admiralty – joined with what might be described as the 'Establishment', whose views were best expressed by the arch-intriguer, Esher, busy writing to one and all. The confusion this unlikely congeries of interests caused was reflected in the Conservative press, and not least *The Times*. Dawson visited Henry Wilson 'to ask what attitude the Times should take with regard to the Mediterranean evacuation'. Wilson supplied his answer only to find next day in *The Times* 'a preposterous letter by Thursfield ... and an equally ridiculous leader [which] annoyed me much especially in view of my conversation with [Dawson] last night'. Nor had things improved the next day. 'The Times', wrote Wilson, 'is stupid to a degree.'[52] Esher, meanwhile, was trying to persuade Repington to 'father' a memorandum he had drafted as the basis for an article in *The Times*.

The choice lies between such an increase in Naval Power as will ensure sea command in the Mediterranean, or the substitution of a conscript for a voluntary army, or the abandonment of Egypt and Malta and a complete reversal of the traditional policy of Great Britain in regard to her trade routes and military highways to the East.

There is no other alternative. Any attempt to rely upon 'alliances' or the Naval Forces of friendly Powers is bound to prove illusory. Britain either is or is not one of the Great Powers of the World. Her position in this respect depends solely upon sea command and sea command in the Mediterranean.[53]

The attitude adopted by *The Times* caused Beresford typically to assume that it was dictated primarily by Fisher's old compatriots, Thursfield and Robinson, trying to score off him. The only other alternative he could think of was that Northcliffe was trying 'to fog the public and mystify the situation'. But why should the 'Black Man' try to do that when his *Daily Mail* had come into line and he must have been aware that the German newspapers were advertising the 'abandonment' of the Mediterranean as 'the first great victory for their Fleet'? Being Beresford, as he wrote to tell Maxse, he felt obliged to face Northcliffe with the problem.

> I said to Northcliffe, 'Why did you put that extraordinary article in the "Times" making out everything was alright, although the Mediterranean was evacuated?' He got quite red and said, 'They don't do such a thing as that again. I gave it to them well for putting in such an article at all.'[54]

To his surprise Churchill discovered that the opposition ranged against his proposal was too strong for him and he was obliged to acknowledge, after a meeting of the CID on 4 July, that his wings had been clipped. On 10 July Grey with some relief announced to the Commons that the Mediterranean would not be 'abandoned'.[55] Esher was delighted: 'Whatever the cost may be it is cheaper than a conscript army and entangling alliances.'[56] It took time for him and others to recognise the illogicality of the position they had assumed. Not so the Radicals inside the Cabinet who, as soon as they had to devise the means to implement their policy decision, discovered that they had been hoist by their own petard. Churchill quietly pointed out that economies in shipbuilding meant numerical weaknesses that could only be compensated for by dependence on France. As they were not prepared to rely on France, then he must ask for more money for more ships. The Cabinet had to give way.

In his speech to the Commons asking for more funds for building, Churchill concentrated upon the North Sea.[57] By the end of 1913 he claimed that Germany would have twenty-five battleships in her High Seas Fleet and four in reserve making twenty-nine in all. At the same date, and including the eight ships with the Fourth Battle Squadron at Gibraltar, Britain would have thirty-three battleships in the Home Fleet. The immediate response of the Tories in the House was to suggest that this margin was much too narrow. The superpatriots outside Parliament who day in day out in their press had been demanding more ships, more soldiers, more everything, immediately made great play with the four-ship margin as 'disastrously' less than the 60 per cent superiority the First Lord had promised but months earlier. Arthur Lee and Bonar Law, in much less judicious tones than Balfour had employed and with Beresford bumbling and threatening in the wings, demanded a crash naval construction programme. Fisher was delighted by the agitation. While he emphasised to Bonar Law that strategically the aim was to be 'overwhelmingly supreme in the *decisive* theatre in Home Waters' and that it was 'futile to be strong in the subsidiary theatre of the Mediterranean', nevertheless, 'As an apostle of numbers! *Only numbers can annihilate*', the campaign for more ships could only bear good fruit. 'We are very much stronger than anyone supposes, but we are not too strong, for as Nelson said – *we never can be!* – and the surprises of war are terrible.'[58] With the 'Commons submerged in a welter of war talk', the *Nation,* with sad thoughts of 1909, wrote of 'Panic made Permanent'.[59] As the Radicals hastily mounted another reductionist campaign[60] and the *Westminster Gazette,* due to Spender, argued that if Britain's superiority in pre-Dreadnought vessels was taken into account then thirty-three to twenty-nine was a sufficient margin, the patriotic press divided its time between insulting Churchill as 'a treacherous windbag', and playing the game of naval arithmetic.[61]

While each editor or contributor seemed to have his own idea of what exactly the 60 per cent margin of superiority meant and published it with a degree of certainty that suggested it had been vouchsafed from on high engraved on tablets of stone, there was a constant exchange of opinion behind the scenes that was to continue until the next year's debate on the naval estimates. Grigg, more concerned than most with the problems of imperial defence and the contribution that the Dominions should make to the navy by way of Dread-noughts, declared himself 'horrified' to see Garvin 'supporting Alan Burgoyne's two keels to one standard including Dominion ships in today's *Observer.* . . . That is a lower account of this country's responsibilities than has yet been put forward anywhere – outside the Daily News!' On the other hand he thought Garvin's 'own standard of two keels to one excluding Dominion ships' at best 'arguable' and probably 'far too much'. Nevertheless, it was 'better to go on and more power to your elbow! But don't, failing your own standard, suddenly sink to Burgoyne's which asks too little and asks it in the worst possible way.'[62]

In June, in answer to Churchill's importuning, Fisher returned to England to chair a commission on oil supplies. 'The liquid fuel problem has got to be solved. . . . No one else can do it so well. Perhaps no one else can do it at all. . . . Yr gifts, yr force, yr hopes belong to the Navy . . . as yr most sincere admirer & as the head of the naval service I claim them now.'[63] How could Fisher resist such an appeal? His return stirred his old enemy Beresford into a whole series of gratuitous insults and slanders poured into the ear of Blumen-feld to be suitably displayed in treacherous paragraphs in the *Express.* 'We are in tremendous danger. . . . It would be interesting to know who made money over Vickers and Armstrong having a monopoly. . . . The public is certain to be again defrauded over the new effort to get oil fuel into the Navy.'[64] Garvin rushed to the defence of his friend which gave Churchill the opportunity in several long letters to explain his policy. As to Beresford:

He is evidently very much upset at Fisher's appointment, and quite regardless of truth or discretion. . . . The harm he does in Germany is very great and the party advantage here quite negligible. . . . He has injured his profession and disgraced himself.[65]

Thus Beresford's tatty campaign was summarily dismissed. What Churchill wished to demonstrate was that the policy he was pursuing at the Admiralty was 'very little short of the two keels to one' that Garvin was demanding in the *Pall Mall Gazette* and *Observer*.

> There really is no need for anxiety so far as the relative strength of the German and British fleets is concerned. A steady overhauling process has now begun and will operate from 1915 onwards. In this and the next five programmes, Germany proposes to build 14 capital ships and we 25. . . . You must remember also that the power of the unit is continually increasing, and that the great fleet of Dreadnoughts which the Germans have already built will soon be outclassed by the preponderance of later British ships over later German ships.

There followed page after page of technical details concerning the size, number and weight of fire power in the new British ships being built.

> Our estimates are double the German estimates, and will be more than double next year. Our reserves of ammunition, in torpedoes, in guns, show almost at every point a considerable surplus over the prescribed amount, and all the provisions for future needs have been greatly accelerated.
>
> This letter is for your private eyes *alone*, and I write it because you are a patriot and deserve to be reassured. As long as we do not relax our exertions, and proceed on the sober lines I have laid down, we shall – in the absence of any new development – break these fellows hearts in peace, or their necks in war.[66]

The tone as much as the content of the First Lord's private letters must have been cheering to Garvin. The editor's excessive patriotic energies, however, were not limited to his campaign for 'Two Keels to One'. His two newspapers, in tandem with Northcliffe's *Daily Mail*, gave constant support to Roberts's continuing campaign for universal compulsory service which he combined with vitriolic criticism of Haldane's Territorial Force. Roberts told Garvin, 'If the Territorials are to be of any use they must be plainly informed that they must work for the adoption of a system of Compulsory Service.'[67] The outbreak of the First Balkan War was important to Roberts only in so far as it provided more convenient grist for his particular mill to grind. The 'wonderful success' of the Balkan allies against their Turkish masters 'ought to be a lesson to us. No war can be carried on successfully unless the NATION takes part in it.'[68] Convinced despite all his earlier disappointments that at last 'the psychological moment for success' had arrived, Roberts promised his journalist friends that he would 'work harder than ever'.[69] Certainly his speech at the Free Trade Hall in Manchester on 22 October caused a sensation; not for his familiar and expected appeal for compulsory service but because of Roberts's unvarnished comments upon Germany.

> In the year 1912, our German friends, I am well aware, do not – at least in sensible circles – assert dogmatically that war with Great Britain will take place this year or next; but just as in 1866 and just as in 1870, war will take place the instant the German forces by land and sea are, by

their superiority at every point, as certain of victory as anything in human calculation can be made certain. *Germany strikes when Germany's hour has struck.* That is the time-honoured policy of her Foreign Office. That was the policy relentlessly pursued by Bismarck and Moltke in 1866 and 1870. It has been her policy decade by decade since that date. It is her policy at the present hour. It is an excellent policy. It is or should be the policy of every nation prepared to play a great part in history.[70]

There was the immediate, inevitable uproar in the Radical press, led by the *Nation*, untypically adopting *ad hominem* arguments. 'Lord Roberts is a mere Jingo in opinion and character, and he interprets the life and the interests of this nation and this Empire by the crude lusts and fears which haunt his unimaginative soldier's brain.'[71] Though eschewing personalities, the attacks of the *Manchester Guardian* and a few days later of the *Daily News* were no less powerful.[72] More interestingly, the Conservative press was not as one in defending Roberts. The *Evening Standard* criticised him as a 'wanton mischief maker'.[73]

Letters printed in several leading Tory newspapers, like that from the former Financial Secretary to the War Office, Bromley Davenport, in the *Morning Post*, gave the game away. Professional politicians considered it was as well to 'cry for the moon' as ask for compulsion.[74] The party mandarins saw compulsory service as a sure-fire vote loser. Yet, the 'million-man standard' espoused by Garvin's and Roberts's supporters was rooted in the idea that if the British working man was not misled by the professional politicians, his patriotism could be relied upon to answer to the 'national' need. Maxse was another dedicated to this proposition but inclined by the passion of the moment to claim conscription as a Unionist virtue. Roberts, who valued Maxse's powers as an orator, had been at pains to emphasise he was 'not to speak as if the NSL were a Unionist body'.[75] Naturally, Haldane would 'oppose Compulsory Service as long as he possibly can', but, in the end, compulsion would be 'introduced by a Liberal Government supported by the Opposition'.[76] Not a wit abashed or disconcerted by the opposition of the Tory mandarins, the compulsionist lobby increased its efforts in the press. The *Daily Mail* insisted, 'Our politicians must give a clear lead in a matter which is vital to the nation. Not one of them but feels in his heart that Lord Roberts speaks the truth. Not one of them but is aware of the grave weakness of the Territorial Force. . . . Is there no man in the Ministry with courage to stand out, tell the nation the truth, and call upon it to give its answer before reform is too late?'[77]

In addition to the *Express*,[78] *Pall Mall Gazette*, *Observer* and *Daily Mail*, the *Nineteenth Century* almost assumed the status of a 'house magazine' for the compulsionists. The *National Review*, as ever, was foremost in any fight to discredit Haldane. General Wilson, together with certain friends – Fred Oliver, Hugh Dawnay, Arthur Lee and Milner – planned his own newspaper campaign to be led by 'Taffy' Gwynne in the *Morning Post*. The editor was, in Wilson's words, 'full seized with the necessity of killing the Territorials during the life of the present Government so as to force the Government to go to the Opposition about Compulsory Service'.[79] Gwynne, in his turn, pressed Strachey to play a more vigorous part for the cause in the *Spectator* rather than confine his efforts to touting for the National Reserve. Roberts had declined Strachey's request to push the National Reserve. He admitted his fear that 'it might be taken hold of by politicians as an efficient substitute for universal military training'.[80] Strachey gave way to Roberts's gentle wooing, and started his own *Spectator* campaign in early December.[81]

The one notable absentee among this group of Unionist publications drumming up support for conscription was *The Times*. This was all the more remarkable since Northcliffe was giving Roberts and Wilson every support in the *Daily Mail*, and Geoffrey Dawson was known to be a keen conscriptionist. F. S. Oliver was detailed to seek action from his friend. 'Our present position from the military point of view . . . is thoroughly unsatisfactory. . . . It is quite certain that voluntary enlistment will have to be supplemented or superseded by some form of compulsion. Therefore Lord Roberts' campaign is thoroughly safe, sound, laudable and opportune.' Oliver appealed to Dawson. 'Roberts . . . needs all the assistance he can get. . . . Help him all you can.'[82] Dawson wanted to help, but had discussed the issues involved with Repington and was conscious that the problem was not as simple as the Roberts camp maintained. 'Let me know when you have excogitated your policy,' Repington wrote to his editor on 7 December. 'The question is whether we do not want a different sort of army for Imperial purposes than we do for fighting Germany in a fortnight. This is really a question of *policy*, and you must decide it for yourself. Do not be in a hurry for we must stick to our line once we take it. You cannot please everybody.'[83]

It was not that Repington was against conscription, but he was sickened by the way his old enemy Wilson was encouraging Roberts and his newspaper allies to attack the Territorials. Repington wrote of these worries to Haldane suggesting ways in which the worst aspects of the campaign could be stifled.

> [Wilson] is in serious danger, now that his constant intrigues threaten the existence of the TF. . . . Wilson ought to go and be replaced by Robertson who would give you the ballast now wholly lacking. . . . An Army Order should be published warning officers deprecating our armed forces in the Press in very firm Wellingtonian terms. In no other country is the licence permitted that we allow – *vide* the 'Daily Mail' and 'Standard'. It is all part of a game to destroy the voluntary system and it is more than high time that a stop was put to it. . . . The situation is so serious that I think you should ask the Prime Minister to intervene with a firm hand and put matters to rights.[84]

Repington had claimed that Seely was quite useless. Haldane agreed. He told J. A. Spender how ineffectual his successor at the War Office was, accusing him and the Liberal party generally of giving too much away to the Unionists in the Commons.[85] Haldane was extremely worried by Roberts's campaign. He admitted to his mother it might 'do a great deal of damage'.[86]

By 10 December 1912 Dawson felt sufficiently certain of his own mind on the conscription issue to write a long leader on the subject in *The Times*. 'I don't know what you thought about it,' he wrote to Repington, 'but it expressed my very strong belief that – apart from military necessities altogether, of which I am no judge – we must have universal and compulsory service if we are to become a solid nation at all.'[87] Repington approved of the leader's 'vigour and brilliancy', but took exception to Dawson's description of the Territorials as a 'sham'.

> That phrase will be, I fear, the only part of the article which will be repeated. It is not true. It is a feather-brained observation worthy of Garvin & Co but unworthy of The Times. . . . It is not much good for me to continue to take an interest in a Force which my Editor calls a sham, following the fatheads who know nothing of the Force. . . . I have no taste for the destructive line in military criticism; but all the critics of the TF are alike: they cannot build. This tone will lead to a steady depletion of the Force by natural discouragement, and you have nothing to suggest to put in its place except unexceptionable phrases and high principles which are beautiful in their way but butter no parsnips.

With the bit between his teeth, Repington read Dawson a lesson on 'how much we have built up in five years from pure chaos'. In order to improve the army, to make advances, it was 'not the least necessary to crab the TF' as Wilson and his minions were doing. He hoped that Dawson would persuade the Tory party to accept conscription. 'It is the noblest flag to fly and I would like to see the Party committed to Opposition until they carry it to victory.' He concluded his letter by restating that he would not mount his own campaign until he was certain of Dawson's 'wishes and policy and know that I can agree with them'.[88] Dawson accepted this rating from his military correspondent, even rushing off a reply by return although he had urgent personal business to attend to. He apologised for using the word 'sham' of the Territorials. The Force was 'a first-class foundation to be built upon, and not an impediment to be swept away'. As to conscription, it should be adopted 'whatever its effect on the Unionist party may be'.

> I feel we have a real mission to convince the working classes of England that the present moment, in which they have no direct interest in the making or stopping of war, and feel no appreciable taxation, is essentially a system of capitalism and militarism, whereas universal national training is essentially democratic and an instrument of peace.[89]

Repington was cheered by Dawson's response. They could now mount an effective campaign, editor and military correspondent in tandem. However, Repington was obliged to wait while other, more immediate events attracted attention and in effect 'crabbed' the whole conscription programme. The Unionists turned to rend one another, not about the virtues or otherwise of the Territorial Force, but on the old question, tariff reform.

On 14 November at the Albert Hall, Lansdowne, supported by Bonar Law, had told a meeting of the Conservative National Union that in April the Shadow Cabinet had decided that food taxes would remain as an element in the tariff reform programme, but that the referendum pledge given by Balfour in 1910 would be dropped. Unionist free fooders, like Strachey, loyally accepted this decision as the only way to create an united party to oppose Liberal plans for Home Rule in Ireland. But the tariff reform group suddenly divided, many asserting that the party would never gain power unless food taxes were dropped. Northcliffe, seizing his chance to divest the Tory party once and for all of the hated 'stomach taxes', mounted a stern campaign in the *Daily Mail* in which *The Times*, under Dawson's guidance, joined. Garvin immediately jumped to the defence of the unadulterated Chamberlainite doctrine. Full-scale war was declared between the Astor and Northcliffe newspaper empires.[90] The conscription campaign was swept out of sight. Bonar Law, in a vain attempt to bring unity to his party and heal the rift, made an unwise speech at Ashton-under-Lyne reaffirming the decision to drop the referendum but claiming food taxes would not be imposed unless the colonies said that was what they wished. The effect was only to make matters worse. Garvin, completely losing control, turned upon Northcliffe, calling him 'Uncle Five Heads', issuing 'Chinese Edicts' from his 'Dragon Throne' at Carmelite House and Printing House Square. The Radicals were naturally delighted by the spectacle of the Opposition tearing itself apart. Massingham forecast that the Unionist party's chances of forming a government had probably 'disappeared for a generation if not always'.[91] L. S. Amery admitted to Gwynne the damage done to the Tory party. He had been sadly disappointed with the line taken by *The Times*, but assured Gwynne this had nothing to do with Northcliffe. 'It is rather that Grigg and Robinson [Dawson], holding very strong Round Table views,[92] are inclined to minimise the importance of the economic side and seem to have been annoyed by the Ashton speech which undoubtedly was clumsily worded.'[93]

By January 1913 the fracas was over. Northcliffe and those opposed to food taxes had won. Garvin was obliged to recognise this, though he did so with an ill grace.[94] Dawson wrote to Chirol explaining that he had become involved in the controversy against his will. Unlike Grigg he preferred to 'keep the millstone around our necks' rather than 'prejudice the Unionist party while we are still in Opposition and quite unable to carry out any projects.' It was Lansdowne and Bonar Law who had 'put the fat in the fire'.

> I had no conception that the feeling against food taxes was so strong, and from the moment that it showed itself I have been perfectly clear that the only possible course was to drop these duties altogether. . . . We have been vilified and besmirched in every possible way by Garvin in the *Pall Mall Gazette* and *Observer*.[95]

An undoubted consequence of Garvin's unbridled attacks upon *The Times* was that Dawson was drawn even closer to Repington who had consistently criticised the *Observer*'s editor for his intemperate comments on military, naval and foreign policy issues.[96] This was to have important consequences in the near future.

Dawson had occupied the editorial chair at *The Times* a matter of months. His days, as he admitted to Chirol, had been passed 'in a state of most frightful rush and pressure'. The outbreak of the First Balkan War in October 1912 added an enormous increment to his already formidable burden. He had not only to determine the newspaper's policy towards the war but also advise and control several senior and temperamentally difficult members of his staff. The first immediate result of the Balkan League's attack on the Turks was to reveal an uncomfortable frailty in the entente partnership. As might have been anticipated, there was a campaign in certain German newspapers, led by *Die Post*. They argued that 'the secret threads of the Balkan crisis [had] been spun in London', for the sake of 'British interests in the Near East'.[97] What had not been expected was *Le Matin*'s claim that the war was Britain's responsibility. Saunders reported this and similar comments in *Le Temps* inspired by André Tardieu. There swiftly followed disconcerting news from Steed in Vienna that there was 'a strong impression' in the Austrian capital that France and Germany were drawing closer together.[98] Dawson was concerned that Steed was questioning the wisdom of the British government's policy towards the Balkan War which *The Times* had supported. 'I will not go into the arguments for and against that policy or whether it is right or wrong,' Dawson informed Steed, 'my point is that it is fatal that the paper should print leading articles taking opposite sides in different parts of the paper. . . . Readers seeing these conflicting opinions would come to the conclusion that the paper has no policy at all.'[99] Lovat Fraser, who Dawson had insisted should write the main leaders while the fighting was going on, told Garvin that the editor was 'bowdlerizing' Steed's telegrams and that he was 'unduly influenced by Repington's theories'. The result, he believed, was 'the "Times" is made to look silly'.[100]

Events in the Balkans moved with an alacrity that amazed everyone. The Turkish army enjoyed a fine reputation but apparently with little difficulty the Serbians took Kumanovo and Monastir, the Greeks entered Elassona and Salonica, while in Thrace the Bulgars won an overwhelming victory at the battle of Kirk-Kilisse. By early December Adrianople was invested and the armies of the Balkan League stood before the lines at Chataldja. The Turkish empire in Europe that had lasted half a millennium had almost ceased to exist in less than three months.[101] While these dramatic military blows followed close upon each other, Steed and Saunders speculated upon the likely diplomatic consequences for the Great Powers. As circumstances changed so swiftly their prognoses of the consequences, particularly Steed's, changed with equal speed. Dawson decided to take his foreign correspondents to task. He instructed Steed, 'A simple message of definite exclusive news . . . is worth columns of speculation and quotation when the business has not progressed at all. I am writing in the same sense to Saunders and Mackenzie because I am really nervous lest we should cater too exclusively for a comparatively small section of our readers.'[102] In subsequent letters, Dawson spelled out the style of reporting he required. He was concerned that the newspaper lost

> strength and directness . . . by using too exclusively the language of diplomatists. . . . The function of *The Times* as I understand it, is not to take part in diplomatic conversations but to expound them in such a way as to guide a great body of lay opinion outside the diplomatic circle. . . . I have long felt that *The Times* has wasted its knowledge and

strength in times of diplomatic crisis by not being sufficiently short, simple and direct.[103]

The correspondents, not least Steed, who could be inordinately sensitive, took the editor's rating in good part. Nor did Dawson neglect to compliment them when they satisfied the criteria he had laid down. 'I have several admirable letters to thank you for,' he wrote to Steed in mid-December. 'To me they seem to contain in a nutshell the true doctrine of British policy in Europe.'[104]

Printing House Square shared the general relief in England, common to men of all political opinions, that the Balkan League had so swiftly conquered the Turk. When Asquith pronounced 'the victors are not to be robbed of their spoils which cost them so much', the sentiment was heartily endorsed in a *Times* editorial.[105] Within a few days there was a cheering first speech by Lichnowsky, the new German Ambassador. He told the Royal Society, 'Never has there been more intimate and more sincere relations between England and Germany than at present.'[106] Dawson, though under continual stress at Printing House Square where he likened the atmosphere to that of a 'lunatic asylum', was in constant touch with Nicolson and Grey.[107] The optimism he felt as 1912 drew to its close was to prove short-lived.

January 1913 brought disconcerting rumours to *The Times* from its Berlin and Vienna correspondents. Mackenzie spoke of 'significant dissatisfaction' among Germans with their government for pursuing a peaceful, cooperative policy.[108] Steed, reviewing the prospects facing Austro-Hungary, concluded that if it was to have a future then it must choose one of two policies. The first – slow and careful internal reconstruction – would require painstaking patience. The other – to restore former imperial glories by a series of military victories – was superficially easier and more attractive. The country's military party under von Hoetzendorf, increasingly powerful and influential, seemed convinced that the Austrian army could defeat a combined Russian and Serbian force.[109] Steed's words must have reminded Dawson of his earlier uncomfortable forecast made in November: 'We have tended to encourage Austria to go too far. . . . We should not plunge into Armageddon blindly.'[110]

On 23 January the negotiators at the London Peace Conference were interrupted in their work by the news that in Constantinople, Enver Bey had denounced the proposal that Turkey should surrender Adrianople. With his followers he had forced his way into the Council Chamber and murdered Nazim Pasha, the Turkish Commander-in-Chief. Negotiations were immediately suspended and the conference broke up. Within three weeks the First Balkan War had been resumed. The same day as hostilities were declared, the London press announced that the Germans proposed to raise the peacetime strength of their army to 850,000.[111] At this single stroke was swept away the hope that Anglo-German relations might at last be showing signs of mending. These hopes had been inspired not only by the two Powers' amicable cooperation over the Balkan problem, but also the reasonable tone of speeches made by Lichnowsky, Jagow, Kiderlen's successor, and Tirpitz. The best interpretation *The Times* could put on the measure was that it did not *necessarily* imply that Germany's spirit was warlike and aggressive. The *Kölnische Zeitung*, with a series of articles, did its best to disabuse *The Times*.[112] Without any equivocation, Northcliffe instructed Dawson, 'Europe is getting onto a war-footing.' He had gained the unfortunate impression that *The Times* recently had not been 'sufficiently alive to that fact'.[113]

Military matters: Repington fights real and imagined foes

I seem to see the gleam in the near distance of the weapons and accoutrements of this army of the future – the Citizen Army, the warder of these Islands, and the pledge of the peace and of the continued greatness of this Empire.

Lord Roberts to NSL Meeting in Glasgow

In his speech at the Union Jack Club, Admiral Prince Louis of Battenberg administered the *coup de grâce* to those critics of Lord Roberts who tell us that invasion is impossible because the Fleet will prevent it. 'There could', said Prince Louis, 'be no more foolish and mischievous statement. The Fleet alone cannot do it, and the presence of a sufficiently trained professional army in this island kingdom at all times is quite as necessary.' ... Prince Louis' speech hoists for the nation the signal of danger.

Daily Mail

If a Territorial Force of 313,000 men was required in 1907, when the armies of Europe were 40 per cent weaker than today, when our naval preponderance as against Germany's was twice as great as it is at this hour, can it be pretended for a moment that we are safe with a Territorial Force of 240,000 men? That is the question which the British Government have to answer.

Daily Mail

Why is the Territorial Force unequal to the task of repelling raids? Presumably:
(a) Because a Government would not be likely to embody them till war was declared.
(b) Because the opposition in Parliament; or public opinion as voiced by the *Daily Mail*, does not consider them fit to fight at all. ...
Personally, I question both (a) and (b), and (b) commonly held though it appears to be makes me feel very angry – makes my boils blood as was once remarked by a well known noble orator.

General Ian Hamilton to the Minister for War

There was no reason for Dawson to be either defensive or apologetic in his response to Northcliffe's claim that in recent months *The Times* had insufficiently concerned itself with the growing mood of unrest in Europe and the massive military preparations. The editor's thoughts and time had been more than usually occupied by military and strategic matters. He referred Northcliffe to 'all our articles of the last ten days – 3 or 4 leaders, long messages from Paris and Berlin, articles by Repington on the French and German armies – I think that you would agree, we have dealt with it pretty thoroughly and I will not let it go.' Dawson made one reservation only. The subject was 'very difficult to handle without inflaming popular excitement & passion & frustrating all our efforts to set our military defences here in order'.[1]

From mid-December 1912, Dawson and Repington had been planning a series of articles and leaders in support of compulsion for the Territorials. Roberts was aware of this and on 21 January he lunched with the editor to discuss, among other topics, the decision made by the Executive Committee of the National Service League on 3 January to mount their own campaign to attempt to gain Liberal and Labour support for national service. Roberts had agreed to make a number of key speeches at Bristol, Leeds, Wolverhampton and Glasgow beginning the next month.[2] Also, early in February 1913, a debate was planned for the Lords, ostensibly on the unfitness of the Territorials to repulse any invader but in reality intended as a plea for compulsory service. Dawson described Roberts as being 'in very good form and extraordinarily sensible about his campaign'. Roberts said that he did not intend to speak himself in the Lords' debate 'for he could only be partisan', and he 'disclaimed all idea of discouraging the Territorial Force or any other useful agency'.[3] That evening, Dawson dined with F. S. Oliver and Repington. The military correspondent was in the final stages of preparing his articles for publication and wrote next day to Dawson, 'You will find, I hope, that all your criticisms have been fully met. . . . Look at the corrected proof and tell me whether you are now quite satisfied.'[4] But before the first of these articles could appear in *The Times,* an old, familiar problem once more raised its head.

On 1 February Repington wrote to tell Dawson that he had just learned that the Committee of Imperial Defence was about to re-examine the question of invasion.

> In principle I agree, but I recall that some months ago one of the lesser members of the Government confessed to me that they were terribly hampered by the last decision of the Committee about the 70,000 men invasion argument. My fear is that they will upset our standard to salve their political consciences and that they will be helped thereto by our GS [General Staff] which is lamentably weak. . . . All they care for is the war on the Meuse and they will pass any folly regarding the 'impossibility' of invasion in order to get their head about the continental war. The Radicals will win all along the line for they will say that invasion is now no danger and so the deficit of the Territorial Force does not matter and they will take d-d good care our army does not go to France. Great watchfulness is necessary.[5]

Repington immediately bearded Esher to warn him that the General Staff were 'ready to sacrifice everything' so that the whole of the Expeditionary Force would be free to go to the continent.[6] It has been suggested that the inquiry was inspired by Repington's determination to limit Wilson's full-blown continental strategy,[7] but a much more likely explanation is that the inquiry was brought about by Churchill's lobbying as a consequence of the 1912 naval manoeuvres, and the First Lord's apprehensions about recent developments in naval armaments. What is certain is that there had been a radical change in thinking about invasion at the Admiralty since Churchill's appointment as First Lord, sparked primarily by his unconventional thinking and because he was not a diehard 'blue water' advocate.

At the beginning of 1912, citing the Italian invasion of Tripoli, 'blue water' supporters were crowing in the press that the British provision for home defence vastly exceeded the actual need. 'If it takes 35,000 troops almost three weeks to carry out an overseas attack with no opposition . . . how long would 70,000 take in the face of very dangerous opposition even if the bulk of the defending fleet is out of the way?' The 'bolt from the blue' school was quick to respond that the invasion of Tripoli was not an 'appropriate analogy'.[8] That summer's naval manoeuvres provided important and pertinent evidence that seemed to support the invasionist case. Designed to test the fleet's ability to prevent a raid, the Red (German) fleet was judged to have landed at least 12,000 men. The exercise was theoretical, but, as Churchill wrote in a memorandum to Asquith,

> Nothing obviates the possibility of a determined enemy . . . making a series of simultaneous or successive descents upon different portions of the British coast and landing men in bodies of from 5,000 to 10,000 strong. Such forces would not . . . be formidable so long as we had on shore a compact force of Regulars with good artillery which would strike swiftly and vigorously at the detached heads of invasion and destroy them before they could combine.[9]

Churchill's claim could not have been more different from Fisher's earlier assertion that the best that the Germans might manage to land in England was a dinghy with five soldiers! Nor would Winston's memorandum have pleased Henry Wilson because the General wanted *all* the Regular Army in France, not some employed on home defence as Churchill suggested.

On 6 and 7 February Repington's first two articles appeared in *The Times* strongly supported by editorials written by Dawson. They asserted quite bluntly that the voluntary principle had failed. The Territorials were 50,000 short of their establishment which in any case ought to be doubled to 600,000 because the naval manoeuvres of 1912 had revealed the figure set by the 1908 invasion inquiry to be woefully inadequate. Only conscription would bring in sufficient men. Wilson considered the articles were 'rotten'. But what had really upset him was Repington's assertion that unlimited continental interference (the General Staff's plan) was 'out of the question', and that the navy was 'worth 500,000 bayonets to the French, a decisive point'. Wilson rated the navy as not worth 500 bayonets, and supposed the French did not value it 'at one bayonet! Except from the moral point.'[10]

February 1913 was a month dominated by military matters. On 11 February there was an acrimonious nine-hour debate in the Lords. Statements made earlier by Seely in the Commons, and an hour-long diatribe in the Lords by Haldane, prompted Repington to write that both ministers had 'completely evaded the point at issue'. The 'absence of any serious plan for completing the TF is simply deplorable. I hate to oppose you and the Chancellor after all these years,' he told Seely, 'but the time has come when . . . my patriotic duty conflicts with the claims of private friendship.' The next day, in a long article on the public announcement of the invasion inquiry, he described the government's policy towards the Territorials as 'procrastination', and suggested the inquiry was designed as a 'cover-up'.[11] Within the space of a week, Roberts began his crusade for conscription with a wildly successful public meeting in Bristol, the Balkan War resumed, and the German decision to raise its peace-time army to 850,000 men was announced. Repington, in an important article published on 20 February, pointed out that Germany, with twice France's population, now had 300,000 more men in arms than her neighbour. Good officers and sound spirit counted for much in military success, but the inescapable logic of this arithmetic quite outweighed the advantages of sound leadership and élan. An editorial in *The Times* the same day was directed at the armament retrenchment campaign of the Radical 'Suicide Club'.[12] It argued that it was wiser to determine the size of an army by comparison with the military capability of its potential enemy rather than to demand retrenchment on the basis of a few friendly speeches by politicians and the German Ambassador.[13] While direct comparison with the German navy was accepted as sensible by everyone, the same rule was not applied to the army.

The recent tone of editorials in *The Times* was causing concern to George Saunders in Paris. He feared that *The Times*'s sudden preoccupation with military matters might be interpreted by the French government as British support and encouragement for the pursuit of an aggressive policy. Saunders's suggestion alarmed Dawson. He had not given his support to conscription in order to place a conscript British army on the Belgian frontier 'but for Home Defence . . . to release our Navy at all times, and if necessary our Expeditionary Force'.[14] Repington persuaded Dawson that it might be useful for him to pay a visit to Paris to discuss military details with the French authorities. Repington also supposed that he might use this visit to resolve the quarrel between Saunders and Tardieu. Dawson agreed to Repington's suggestion. Suddenly France was a popular place to visit. Roberts was there making a series of speeches on why Britain required national service,[15] while Northcliffe was studying possible future developments in military aviation. He reassured Dawson that there was no need to concern himself about French chauvinism. 'I do not see any signs of it . . . but, no more squeezing, no more knife to the throat.'[16]

The problem of Britain's foreign and defence policy was discussed against a threatening and gloomy domestic background. The political parties were bitterly divided, especially by the Ulster question. Consequently genuine attempts on both sides of the political divide to offer serious and disinterested advice on complex issues were ignored, ridiculed and, with increasing frequency, twisted to serve sectarian purposes. The *Daily News* denounced the *Daily Mail* for scaremongering: the *Daily Mail* denounced the *Daily News* as pro-German and anti-entente. Midleton was convinced that Haldane's attitude on military matters was determined not by the nation's need but by the petty dictates of party advantage.[17] These sectarian suspicions even embraced membership of the invasion inquiry committee. A feature of the twelve major articles Repington wrote on the subject of invasion between mid-April and mid-May was the repeated implication, first publicly referred to by him in an article published on 12 February, that the inquiry was the result of an intrigue designed to serve the interests of the Radicals in the Liberal party.[18] In the June issue of the *National Review* this same charge was repeated in a more extreme form in an essay, significantly entitled 'A Marconi Enquiry on Invasion'.[19] It was claimed that a majority of the committee's members were 'Radical politicians with no knowledge of strategy'. Esher, who had told Repington in April that he also thought the inquiry was the result of political intrigue, was described as the only 'independent' member.[20] The inclusion of Balfour was explained as 'an attempt to forestall the Opposition'. This was to repeat a charge made privately by Bonar Law anxious to ingratiate himself with the extremists in his party and to distance himself from the former leader. As Repington had told Dawson, Law had made clear his opposition to 'Balfour serving on the Inquiry [and gave] the impression that he would try to induce AJB to abandon the idea of taking part, [claiming] that AJB is not entirely sound on the invasion question and that if he consents to some plan which the Committee may adopt to mislead the public, the Unionist party will be more or less committed to it.'[21] The article argued that the inquiry ought to concentrate its attentions upon the abject weaknesses of the Territorials, described as a 'mob of men with rifles and antiquated guns, without cohesion, without trained officers'. The solution offered was, naturally, compulsory service.

General Wilson also had his reservations about the committee. Despite Repington's fears, Wilson had not been anxious to serve as a member of the inquiry. When, very reluctantly, he had been dragooned into membership, he concentrated his efforts in an attempt to get the committee to examine the nation's overall strategic requirements.[22] Wilson thought that with twenty members the committee was much too large and cumbersome. Meetings became rambling and discursive affairs. After attending one he wrote, 'As usual, an immense amount of talk and nothing decided. I told Haldane I could not understand anyone going to a pantomime so long as the CID was sitting. He seemed hurt! But I have never seen so incompetent a committee. *Far* too large.' Asquith's failings as a chairman did not help matters, and Wilson approvingly recorded Simon Lovat's tart observation that the Prime Minister, 'what with drink, bridge and holding girls' hands, is now incapable of doing anything except drift'.[23]

In the early spring of 1913 the case for compulsion seemed to be enjoying a greater degree of success than ever before. In the country, Roberts's speeches were heard by huge, wildly enthusiastic public meetings. In the Commons, with increasing confidence and truculence the Opposition hunted the Minister for War. In the Debate on the Address, the Army Estimates and at Question Time, Seely fought a less than convincing rearguard action against the compulsionist lobby. Bonar Law had admitted privately on a number of occasions that he personally wanted national service and that practically all the members of his party favoured it, but that he would not adopt it as part of the Unionist programme.[24] Repington had given the Tory leader a copy of the memorandum that he had prepared on behalf of Roberts, Lovat, Scott and himself which had been submitted to the inquiry. Repington described Law's attitude as 'admirable. We have told him everything and he will be of great value to us.' He had even asked Repington to coach him for the defence debates.[25] Perhaps the best measure of the growing coherence of the compulsionist lobby was that Lovat successfully prevailed upon Wilson and Repington to dine together.[26] On 13 March G. J. Sandys, Tory MP for Wells, supported by the usual gaggle of Unionist MPs and a solitary Liberal, Sir Charles Rose,[27] introduced a Private Member's National Service (Territorial Forces) Bill which was talked out without a vote on its second reading on 11 April. The fatal division of purpose among the conscriptionists over the General Staff's full continental policy was revealed by Seely's suggestion (in response to Wilson's coaching) that the Expeditionary Force could go abroad confident that the Territorials would cope with an invasion force of 70,000. Seely twice repeated this claim when pressed by Bonar Law. Repington's immediate response was to write an article for *The Times* taking the General Staff to task.[28] Wilson was also very angry with Seely because he had claimed the General Staff were against compulsion. He was so offended by this claim that he persuaded Sir John French to threaten the minister with their resignations unless he withdrew his statement. Seely went some way to meet this pressure but the threat was defused by French's promotion to Field Marshal.[29]

The invasion inquiry had begun its meetings. As Seely for the War Office and Churchill for the Admiralty submitted their evidence, it became increasingly obvious that since the previous inquiry, thinking on invasion at the two departments of state had reversed. Whereas in 1908 the army had stressed the dangers of invasion in order to expand the home defence forces, now they played it down, and claimed the Territorials were a more than adequate defence force. Their purpose was to free *all* divisions of the regular army for service in the Expeditionary Force. In 1908 the navy had argued unsuccessfully that invasion was a question that concerned them alone. In 1913 they no longer claimed that serious invasion was impossible and sought to increase the army's responsibility for home defence.

When Seely argued that the Territorials had the numbers, strength and efficiency to have sole responsibility to repel any invasion, and that to retain two divisions of regulars in the United Kingdom was not only unnecessary but would have a deleterious effect upon the morale of the Territorials,[30] it was Esher who took the minister to task. In a series of sharp exchanges with Seely, who attempted to dismiss him and his arguments as 'the counsel of despair', Esher listed the faults of the Territorials on the basis of his experience with the London Territorial Force. He insisted that the inquiry's main concern should be to determine whether the Territorials were sufficient in numbers, training and quality for the task they had been assigned. In a letter to Asquith he summarised the progress made by the inquiry, reiterated his concern and suggested a possible course of future action.

The War Office seem to be anxious to prove that a raid of 20,000 men is the maximum hostile force against which it is necessary to prepare resistance, and that against such a force the TF and the Flying Column are ample provision. Their object is apparently to free the *whole* of the Expeditionary Force for immediate service oversea.

They fail to realise that if the CID accept this conclusion a powerful section of public opinion will question the right of the War Office to maintain the Army Estimates at their present figure.

The Admy, on the other hand, seem desirous of showing that two regular Divisions should always be kept in this country, and yet they are reluctant to admit that even a raid of 20,000 men can pierce the naval guard.

Their object seems to be a double one.

(a) to keep two Divisions at home,

(b) not to make admissions that would prevent *them*, the Admy, from using these 2 Divisions oversea, for *naval strategical purposes*.

I asked Hankey yesterday whether he would not suggest to you the advisability of summoning Lord Roberts *as soon as possible*, so that the case of invasion in its most aggressive form – can be laid before the Committee by its real protagonist, instead of by means of hypothetical cases framed (one is forced to conclude) in the interest of departmental proclivities.[31]

Esher's suggestion that the Roberts group should be called to give evidence was acted upon. The first meeting was not a success. 'We are not allowed by the PM to ask the CIGS questions which go to the root of the matter under investigation,' Repington complained to Dawson. Their morning had been 'wasted on tittle-tattle'[32] and Repington had written to Roberts telling him he did not propose to attend any more meetings 'unless we are permitted to ask the questions which we have handed in'.[33] Things, however, improved after this unpropitious start, and Repington was in high good humour when he wrote to his editor on 17 July. At that morning's meeting, 'They all listened very kindly and I made all my points. Had an amusing lunch with Seely afterwards and told him I had only come to plot with him the details of my next attack on the WO.'[34] The quartet enlarged upon the arguments in the memorandum placed before the inquiry in March.[35] Since 1908 the situation had deteriorated in five important particulars, but the essential argument, which Churchill naturally supported, was that the Territorials were not sufficiently strong in their present form to look after home defence and would be particularly vulnerable at the most dangerous period – the outbreak of war – when many would not be sufficiently trained.

There was no doubt that some members of the inquiry had been impressed by the evidence, particularly the arguments of Repington and Roberts. Seely's credibility had been seriously eroded by the constant attacks made upon him in the Commons and in the press. Urged by the Tories to guarantee the safety of the country if the Expeditionary Force was absent, Seely reluctantly complied only to be accused by Repington in *The Times* of prejudging the results of the inquiry.[36] On 5 June, in the Army Estimates debate, attempting to silence the compulsionists Seely quoted Nelson's adage that 'one volunteer is worth ten pressed men', adding, 'If that were true in the old days, it is much more true today because of the strain of modern war.' He was severely taken to task by Percy in an article in the *National Review*. Percy in an earlier article had already torn to shreds Seely's comparison of universal service with the press gang system.[37] Now, helped by Wilson of the *Daily Mail* and Roberts, he wrote another article which he hoped would once for all 'stop Seely talking rot'.

It is fallacious to say, 'Whatever the defects of the Voluntary System it has enabled us to create the Empire'. . . . Our utterly insignificant military history shows the system has broken down in every emergency. In fact it has had nothing to do with the creation of our Empire.[38]

Percy likened any anti-conscription argument to the 'Chinese slavery' issue of 1905. The Radicals were 'running it for all it's worth' presumably as a pre-election stunt.[39] Maxse, while encouraging his eager, young, compulsionist lieutenant, had, like Garvin, lifted his eyes on to a higher plain and was contemplating without much satisfaction the future of the entente. Garvin in the *Observer* had been emphasising the need to retain Russia's friendship. 'I rejoice at what you say,' wrote Roberts. 'Now that railways are approaching nearer to India, it is more than ever necessary we should not break with Russia.'[40] Maxse told Northcliffe that the Germans were 'working overtime to detach us from France and Russia'. He would not be the least surprised if they achieved success for 'this country is full of first class idiots [and] as the world must know that we have long been under Panama Government, there is less confidence in us than ever'.[41]

Throughout 1913 the *Daily Mail*, as though intent upon confirming the frequent assertions in the Radical press that it had become little more than the 'mouthpiece for the armaments industry', left contemplation of the fate of the ententes to others while concentrating almost exclusively upon matters military, naval and strategic. With frequent references to 'Germany's Remorseless Preparations' on land, sea and in the air – 'the day is at hand when the Power which controls the air will be able to obtain access to every part of these islands'[42] – it sounded the invasion alarm, invariably combining this with the demand for 'a well-trained military force behind the Fleet'.

This force must be provided whatever the cost. If Ministers will not adopt national service, it is their business and duty to tell us what other plan they have in view to provide it. The danger of the present policy of drift in the face of increasing perils and responsibilities, grows every day.[43]

In April, prompted by the admission of the First Sea Lord that the fleet alone could not guarantee the safety of Britain from invasion, the *Mail* made great play with its own version of the 1912 naval manoeuvres. Despite odds of two to one against and 'the unrivalled experience and extraordinary success in manoeuvres' of Battenberg, 'a fleet representing the German Navy was able

... to land 28,000 men on the Yorkshire coast.'[44] The next year's manoeuvres were to provide even richer pickings for their case.

More than a fortnight before the 1913 manoeuvres were due to begin, Repington was able to reveal in *The Times* that their object, as in the previous year, would be to establish whether a hostile raiding party could be landed in the face of naval opposition. Although the Territorials would not be mobilised or the shore defences tested, an actual landing force would be used to provide more realistic conditions.[45] Such information was supposed to be highly confidential and Churchill was to complain to the inquiry about 'press conjectures'. As usual, the Admiralty was leaking its secrets like a sieve. The actual source of Repington's information is uncertain,[46] but the former First Sea Lord, Bridgeman, was certainly providing much useful material to a number of friends, including Sandars.[47]

Francis Bridgeman had been appointed Wilson's successor as First Sea Lord although Churchill had wanted to recall Fisher and Asquith had suggested Louis Battenberg.[48] Bridgeman found Churchill an extremely difficult master because the First Lord interfered in many matters which were not his concern. Churchill sought the first possible opportunity to ask Bridgeman for his resignation, and, after a year, the First Sea Lord's uncertain health provided a suitable excuse. Battenberg was promoted from Second to First Sea Lord. Bridgeman made his discontent at being 'forced out of the Service' clear to a number of friends. While the *Morning Post* and the *National Review* in particular had a field day pillorying Churchill, the Opposition seized on the opportunity to attack the First Lord in the Commons. Beresford and Bonar Law were Bridgeman's parliamentary champions. The debate was extremely acrimonious. The whole sad business left Bridgeman more than ever convinced he had been dismissed because Churchill had feared his opposition. It was 'damnable, undignified and extremely bad for the Service'.[49]

Bridgeman attended the naval manoeuvres sailing with the Red (German) fleet commanded by Jellicoe. On 28 July he wrote to tell Sandars that they had been stopped – 'perhaps wise from a political point of view, for if Red Fleet had continued with successes in matter of landing troops, the country would I expect become excited'.[50] The next day, the Admiral was able to tell Sandars the whole story.

> The success of the invading force was complete. They landed in all 60,000 men and could have landed 100,000.
>
> At dawn [Jellicoe] pushed forward a strong force of oldish battleships, TBD's and submarines, blew up the forts and overwhelmed the defending naval force and then let in the big transports.
>
> Behind the transports was a screen of the biggest and best ships under J to protect his transports. The landing was completed – docks seized – railway stations and railway junctions broken up. . . . At Blyth another landing was effected both on the North and South side of the place and with good success.
>
> The manoeuvres were stopped. Jellicoe called onto *Enchantress*. Greeted

by Winston. 'Well Jellicoe you have made history. The PM will be frightened out of his life. But we must stop these manoeuvres.'

The scheme has therefore been interrupted at a most interesting juncture. J and his officers grievously disappointed. J's next plan, which he had indeed begun, was to go round by the North and seize the defences and land men on the Clyde – but this is not to be.[51]

Repington's comments on the 1913 manoeuvres, supposedly written by Col. Von Donner und Blitzen, and supported by letters to *The Times* signed as though they had been written by a German infantry officer who was a friend of the Colonel's, gave a remarkably accurate account of what had gone on. The only answer to the problem was a national army, British command of the air and adequate coastal defences.[52] Repington did not have the field to himself in *The Times*. There was a prolonged exchange of correspondence, and George Clarke was prominent among those who attacked Repington's pessimistic assertion that a real enemy could have landed three times the force that had disembarked.[53] In his private report to Asquith, Churchill, though his tone was more pessimistic than in 1912, concluded that the paralysis induced in British admirals by the thought that they alone were responsible for Britain's defence against invasion could be alleviated, provided that they could count upon a proper armed force – by which Churchill clearly implied a contingent from the regular army – kept at home to swallow up any invading troops that might get through.[54] The manoeuvres were not discussed by the invasion inquiry until November when Churchill admitted that the Admiralty's reluctance to make information readily available was because it had not been its wish 'to create a situation which would have been used in certain quarters to create a panic in the country .... We did not wish to make an alarmist case.'[55] The First Lord's gloss was intended to highlight the 'reasonableness' of Admiralty demands, but it also paid a kind of compliment to the past successes of the invasion publicists in attracting widespread interest for their campaign. In 1913 the invasion issue was not drummed anything like as hard in the press as it had been on earlier occasions. The length and thoroughness of the committee's proceedings made it difficult for popular newspapers to sustain readers' interests in a story that never reached a conclusion.

Sir John French and particularly Henry Wilson for months had prated at and lectured, bullied and hectored the unfortunate Seely to provide a more effective defence of the General Staff's strategic view. Naturally they were upset and not a little frustrated that after the apparent triumph of military strategic thinking in August 1911, when it seemed the politicians were successfully won over to the 'continental' view, they now discovered the Admiralty, under the devious tutelage of Winston aided by the ill-informed and narrow-sighted vision of publicists like Repington, threatening their plans for the Expeditionary Force. Seely had found in Ian Hamilton a better ally than the bullying Wilson, more sympathetic to the difficulties he faced as a minister. Wilson, having insisted that the Territorials were a broken, useless force, was now equally adamant that they were capable in numbers and ability of countering any raid by an enemy. At least Hamilton had never doubted the capacity of the Territorials.

> I should consider it the day of my life if I could lead the South Midlands Division against a brigade of sea-sick Germans. A brigade of Territorials led boldly into attack against a division of invaders would, I'll be bound, kill so many of them as to give quite a Pyrrhic air to their victory, and cause them to think with longing of their long-since torpedoed transports!

However, as Hamilton was obliged to admit, the Government was

> face to face with a skillfully engineered prejudice against all non-professional voluntary service troops. Lord Northcliffe's 'Territorial Farce' headings have poisoned public confidence for the time being and it may therefore be politic, necessary perhaps (because distrust quickly realises itself in untrustworthiness) to stiffen up the Territorial Force and the Special Reserve with a professional element during the early stages of war.[56]

Thus Hamilton recognised that the General Staff had lost the argument. Although Hamilton blamed Northcliffe, Wilson might have reflected, had he been the sort of man who could find fault in himself, that he had actively worked with and encouraged Northcliffe to despise and disparage the Territorials. He had continued with that campaign despite the clear, public warning that Haldane had given in the Lords in April. 'The only result of the agitation which is going on . . . [will be] to hamper [the nation] in the use of its Expeditionary Force and compel it to keep part at least of that Force at home.'[57]

The invasion inquiry spawned related examinations of home defence and invasion problems so that the report was not completed and printed until April 1914. It asserted that the Territorials were not an inept but an 'improving' force. Nevertheless, at the outbreak of war and until all danger of invasion was past, two divisions of regular soldiers should be kept in Britain to support the force in its home defence duties. Wilson when he read this was beside himself with rage and frustration. It was 'rubbish'. Yet he failed to press his view successfully in an interview with Asquith.[58] In Parliament, the Opposition repeatedly demanded that the Prime Minister should announce the inquiry's findings. However, so successful was Asquith at prevarication that war was declared with Germany before he could fulfil the pledge he had given the House of a detailed statement and the opportunity for a general debate.[59]

It could hardly be said that Repington had succeeded except in frustrating the General Staff. The establishment of the Territorials was not increased and there had been no mention of compulsory service to fill the cadres of the home defence forces. A campaign which had started so propitiously with every promise of success had foundered and run into the sands with 'the scientific soldiers', as Percy called them, quarrelling with their former allies. What rescued the situation was the response of the 'Voluntarists' to the NSL campaign. 'We must be making progress,' Percy avowed to Maxse, because 'the "Peace at any price" people have been getting so angry.'[60] When Repington and Dawson had begun their conscription campaign in *The Times* in February, their intention had been 'to influence debate so that it might lead to something in the nature of a compromise on the question . . . between the two parties'.[61] That intention, never publicly expressed, had soon been perverted to serve sectarian purposes. Some of the expressions that creep into Repington's private letters of the period – as in his reference to the Liberals as 'the bribery party'[62] – suggest an unfortunate and too close association with Maxse and his prejudices. But it was his suspicion that the Radicals for party advantage had promoted the invasion inquiry to thwart the conscriptionist case as compared with Bonar Law's enthusiasm that really turned Repington into a Tory partisan. When the conscription campaign foundered because of the confusion induced by quarrels among former allies, it was revived by the Radicals mounting their own determined anti-conscription campaign, and Haldane, as usual being too clever by half, trying to capitalise on the divisions within the conscriptionist camp by forming his Voluntary Service Committee in November 1913.[63] All that was needed to heal the schism in the conscriptionist ranks was for Haldane to attempt to drive a wedge between Sir John French and Roberts. Wilson soon put a stop to that little plan. 'He put French in a car the other day and took him down to Englemere and made him swear eternal friendship with Lord Roberts.'[64]

In the first half of 1913, George Wyndham had been an important influence prompting increased attention to army matters on the Opposition benches. Anxious to resuscitate his damaged political fortunes and hoping for a future appointment as Tory Minister for War, with the active support of Leo Amery he had been prominent in debates demanding a British army capable of dealing with what he and his associates were convinced was not only a growing but imminent German threat. The measure of their pessimistic estimate of Britain's military preparedness was starkly outlined by General Wilson when briefing Bonar Law before the Army Debates.

> In ten years of profound peace we ha[ve] lost the command of every sea in the world except the North Sea, and that [is] in dispute; that in consequence all our overseas garrisons and defended ports and even India herself [are] in danger. At the same time as we [have] lost command of the Sea, our Regular Army, Special Reserve and Territorial Force [are] getting weaker, and at the same time as all this, all other countries are strengthening themselves at an appalling rate.[65]

Wyndham and Amery's close collaboration as members of the reactivated Defence Committee of the Halsbury Club was suddenly cut short by Wyndham's death in June 1913. Selborne now asked Amery to complete the work the two men had begun on a series of memoranda for the Tory leadership. In September, from Australia, which he was visiting during Parliament's adjournment in order to study their system of national training,[66] Amery submitted a detailed memorandum to Bonar Law. There was one problem to which he drew the Opposition leader's particular attention: 'The great difficulty of initiating any system of national training is to find the officers who can train, and when we come in we ought to concentrate at once on really dealing with the officer problem.'[67] Questions of quality as much as quantity were exercising many though not all minds in the conscriptionist camp. Roberts drew Garvin's attention to a deputation of members of the Territorial County Association to the Prime Minister asking for more money to help swell the ranks of the Territorials. Such efforts filled Roberts with despair.

> These men, many of them Unionists of standing are foolishly led to believe that members alone are necessary and that if the establishment of 315,000 is reached all will be well! Whereas the truth is that if the force were double or treble its establishment it would be of no use in war unless it were properly trained and commanded by Officers that knew their duty.
>   We cannot expect that the Citizen Army can be given the same amount or the same continuous training as Regular Soldiers. All the more reason then for it including in its ranks the most intelligent and best educated men in the country. It is the inclusion of such men in the Ulster Citizen Force that makes it so formidable.[68]

The problem of Ulster's future completely divided the country and demoralised the army. Many senior officers convinced that 'Ulster will fight and Ulster will be right' supported the arming and drilling of volunteers to resist separation from Britain. Bonar Law had repeatedly declared that his party would go to any lengths to stop the coercion of Ulster, and it had been to give substance to this outrageously irresponsible verbal threat that a League was formed – the League for the Defence of Ulster and the Union. The League already boasted more than 10,000 members pledged to join the Ulster Volunteers and fight for the Union. The egregious Willoughby de Broke was Chairman and Roberts and Henry Wilson were actively engaged in the enterprise. Possibly because the mixture of violence and intrigue was too much for de Broke's simple mind, he became convinced that he could solve the conscription problem by introducing his own measure in the Lords, The Territorial Forces (Amendment) Bill. It has been claimed that de Broke 'advanced his Bill with no hope and little seriousness',[69] but there can be no question about the sincerity and earnestness of his intent. His measure was designed to conscript 'gentlemen', their status determined by income,[70] education or membership of a higher profession.

De Broke lobbied hard in preparation for the debate on his Bill. Seeking R. D. Blumenfeld's support in the *Daily Express,* he argued that if the 'comfortable classes' guaranteed their good faith by accepting conscription then 'the sound elements in the Nation' would assuredly follow their example.

> The question that is asked in the Bill will put all the slackers and rotters in a very awkward position. How can Ramsay MacDonald and Philip Snowden say that they will not do their duty, but also will try to prevent anybody else doing it?

He concluded his plea to Blumenfeld with a claim that reflected a constant strand in the thinking of certain members of the ultra right, not least Leo Maxse and other diehards who had been so opposed to the Tory party's surrender over the House of Lords. The idea was not original,[71] but had been given a new impetus, stimulated by the resentment felt for the influence of parvenu wealth in the nation's affairs. In de Broke's ideal world there would have been no industrial revolution and Britain would have remained perpetually a 'green and pleasant land' ruled by its 'natural', hereditary leaders, bound to their people, not by any cash nexus but the chivalrous dues of an idealised feudal morality. This was what he meant by the preposterous claim that his Bill was 'the first step towards transferring power into the hands of the competent, the willing and the patriotic, and taking it away from the Little Englanders and demagogues'.[72] When de Broke demanded Haldane's support, the Lord Chancellor poked kindly fun at the confusion of his thinking. 'The idea of *noblesse oblige* I like very much – the scheme of the Bill I think unworkable. . . . I can only say that your bold conceptions attract quite as much as they repel me. But the result of attraction and repulsion at the same time is immobility.'[73]

The most interesting feature of the three-day debate on the second reading before the Bill's defeat was the revelation of certain fears about the temper of the industrial urbanised workers that are more usually associated with nine-teenth-century concern about violence and revolution. Roberts, for example, claimed that de Broke's proposal would rouse the workers' suspicions that the wealthier classes were attempting to gain full possession of military power. Sydenham had made his own fears quite explicit in a letter to de Broke when refusing to support the Bill.

> I fear that the training of the 'comfortable' classes would be widely
> regarded as an attempt to enable these classes to deal with such situations
> as have arisen in S. Africa, and would therefore be bitterly resented. . . .
> The present unrest among the so-called working classes is a grave symptom
> and one of my objections to the proposals of the N. S. League is that, if
> acted upon, they would produce a very large force the greater part of which
> might and I fear would be used someday to overthrow the State.
> I believe that before long some organized effort will have to be made
> to resist militant socialism which is the real enemy.[74]

By 53 votes to 34, the last and most singular measure for conscription discussed by Parliament before the outbreak of war was dismissed to limbo. The confusion induced in the minds of conscriptionists by the introduction of the question of class also caused considerable consternation among the voluntarists. Much of the effect of a pamphlet written by C. P. Trevelyan in 1913, *Democracy and the Public Service*, described by Walter Runciman as 'quite the best statement of the Liberal view on compulsion yet written',[75] was dissipated by a rebuttal published by another Liberal, C. G. Coulton, in January 1914, *True Liberalism and Compulsory Service: An Appeal to the British Working Man*. Coulton became an active conscriptionist during the war; Trevelyan, a founder member of the Union of Democratic Control and a staunch supporter of the No Conscription Fellowship. What was most interesting about Trevelyan's squib was that he exactly anticipated the kind of thinking that inspired de Broke's abortive measure.

All men that live in our democracy are not democrats. There survives a powerful old opinion in England which wants subservient workers, and to them the discipline of compulsory service makes a strong appeal. They deplore labour unrest. They resist the idea of equality between an employer and his men. They are certain the landlord system is both economic and beneficial. They want some moral tonic for a nation they suppose is decaying, collapsing in every direction.[76]

There had been something faintly ridiculous about the de Broke Bill so that most of the Tory press commented upon it with an embarrassed cursoriness, although the *Standard* could not resist the opportunity to make amusing copy out of de Broke's absurdly romantic and anachronistic conception.[77] There was, however, nothing even remotely romantic about the Zabern Incident that brought a sinister and threatening end to a year that had been more than usually concerned with military problems.

After the finalisation of the German Army Bills in July, with Dawson's full support Repington had written a series of four powerful articles on 'Europe's Armed Camp'. Examining the French and German armies, Repington argued that naval and military preparations had provided Germany's diplomats with the ideal weapon with which to pursue an offensive policy. The French army, for all its many excellent qualities, could not compete in terms of size and required military aid from its entente partner to resist possible German aggression. Britain should build up her army and the entente should be converted into an alliance. Only in this fashion could the Balance of Power be maintained and peace in Europe sustained. The Balance of Power was already in jeopardy as a consequence of the Balkan wars.[78] Events at Zabern in Alsace – one of the two provinces forfeited to Germany after the Franco-Prussian War of 1870 – chillingly highlighted both the strength and immediacy of the threat to European peace posed by the German militarist lobby. So gross had been the behaviour of certain German officers towards the civilian population of the village of Saberne that horror had been expressed throughout Europe, even in Germany itself. Horror turned to sensation and apprehension when the officers were acquitted by a military court. The French were outraged and even the German Reichstag passed a vote of censure against the Chancellor. He, however, could afford to ignore it. Among foreign correspondents in Berlin reporting these events, Fred Wile alone, in his immediate[79] response and comments, pointed out to the readers of the two American papers that retained his services, the *New York Times* and *Chicago Tribune*, that the unique place enjoyed in German hearts by their army was strengthened by Germany's political and geographical circumstances in Europe. The Germans recognised they owed their existence and their continuing safety to the army which secured them against the barbarous Slav in the East and the revengeful, chauvinist French in the West. Wile's accounts of the Zabern Incident were 'mangled beyond recognition', cut down 'lamentably' and 'heart-breakingly', by the sub-editors at Carmelite House. His outraged complaints he passed to H. G. Price from whom they found their way to Northcliffe who was only too pleased to receive ammunition to help him in the assault he planned for 1914 upon his various newspaper properties.[80]

Henry Wickham Steed, having at last abandoned Vienna for an appointment at Printing House Square, happened to be in Alsace at the time of the Zabern trial. He managed to get into the courtroom and sent detailed daily accounts back to London, though via *The Times*'s Berlin office to protect his anonymity.[81] On his return to London, Steed wrote a leader for his paper designed to emphasise the 'two lessons' of Zabern. The first was that events had demonstrated beyond any question that in Germany the army ruled. Behind the façade of civilian constitutionalism, the really dominant force in Germany's government was the military. His second lesson was based upon a hypothetical question. What if, as at one time appeared probable, the German soldiers turned their machine guns upon the totally innocent and helpless villagers? 'How French public opinion would have taken a massacre of Alsatians is a delicate question not to be answered off-hand,' Steed wrote, while clearly implying it would have led to war. Conflict between France and Germany would necessarily have involved Britain.[82]

Steed, who had just taken permanent charge of the Foreign Department at Printing House Square, was delighted to receive a congratulatory note from Northcliffe. 'How pleased I was about Zabern ... I have heard about it continually, both here and in France. I wish you would seek out other opportunities of the same kind to distinguish "The Times" and yourself.' Steed's response was to write an ingratiating note to 'the ablest journalist in the world' from one who 'though less experienced is anxious to learn and do his best. . . . I communicate all your letters to Mr Pryor and the Editor, and keep all the men in my Department informed of the suggestions and criticisms they contain.'[83] With Northcliffe vowing that he was absolutely determined to 'wake-up the Black Friars' it was as well, thought Steed, that he should curry favour. He had discharged his national duty by warning his readers of Germany's clear intentions: it was only politic that he should prepare his own emplacements for another kind of warfare that was equally imminent, inevitable and likely to be very damaging.

•••• 22 ••••

Over the brink

Sometimes one cannot help thinking that people are right who say 'War
Must come'!

Edward Goschen's Diary

Vague sense of danger all day, without any definite reason.

Henry Nevinson's Diary

In spite of your 'liberty of the Press', at a hint from your Government,
your whole national Press becomes unanimous on questions outside your
domestic politics – it is the best handled Press in the world. . . . Anglo-
German relations would undoubtedly be sweetened if the British Press
would leave Germany alone for a bit.

Tirpitz to the British Naval Attaché, Berlin

3 August 1914: A queer kind of holiday! I was at work all day and far
into the night . . . I went to the H[ouse] of C[ommons] after [luncheon]
to hear Grey – a very impressive and also very skilful speech which
completely united the House. It was a remarkable scene wh[ich] I sh[ould]
be sorry to have missed. Later the Government, being by this time well in
it, demanded Germany's intentions w[ith] regard to Belgian neutrality.
4 August 1914: A curt reply from Germany led to our Declaration of War
as from 11pm tonight – a difficult business to disentangle things moved
so quick at the last . . . W[inston] in v[ery] good form – a cheering crowd
outside the Adm[iralty]. Flanagan rising to the occasion with magnificent
leaders.

Geoffrey Dawson's Diary

'All sorts of things are *discussed*,' Northcliffe fumed in a letter to Howard
Corbett, the new assistant manager of *The Times*, 'but nothing ever happens.'[1]
His patience was exhausted, and in January 1914 the long threatened storm
was about to break in full fury upon Printing House Square. For almost a year
one question in particular had been exercising Northcliffe's mind. Without
sacrificing its character, could the price of *The Times* be reduced from three-
pence a copy to increase its stagnant circulation? Sales stuck stubbornly at
around 40,000 copies a day. When the price was reduced to twopence in May
1913 the resulting 15 per cent increase in readership was a bitter disappointment to Northcliffe. He shared the feelings of many of the staff at Carmelite

House, that at Printing House Square it was insufficiently recognised that their 'coffers were being replenished with the hard won fruits of the *Daily Mail*'s success'.[2] Northcliffe was unhappy about *The Times*'s make-up as well as its circulation. He protested his faith in Dawson but required wholesale changes in the editorial department. In June 1913, Hugh Chisholm, a former editor of the *St James's Gazette*, was appointed day editor with specific instructions 'to instil a spirit of connected and united vitality into each department'. Northcliffe discerned that 'a priggish slackness' continued to permeate Printing House Square. He had 'thrown men, energy, ideas and fortune into *The Times*' with negligible results. He admitted to Dawson that 'in six, ineffective years we have not much more than marked time'.[3] If matters did not improve, if the dullards continued to sustain their stranglehold, he warned the editor, there would be no alternative but to change *The Times* into 'a popular, illustrated penny journal'. This threat was not taken seriously by senior staff, but it was certain that Northcliffe was entirely serious about his declared determination to earn a dividend on *The Times*'s ordinary shares. The proprietor's efforts 'to galvanize into a semblance of life the giant sloth PHS' at last achieved a limited measure of success. When he returned from a visit to Newfoundland in October 1913, he learned that sales of *The Times* had increased marginally. Ironic congratulations were despatched to Dawson. 'I hear that the old lady of Printing House Square gathered up her skirts and shrieked as at the sight of a man under the bed in the face of a real increase in demand for *The Times* for the first time since her middle age.' But Northcliffe recognised at the end of another year he was still nowhere near a real solution to the problem of *The Times*'s limited circulation.

January 1914 brought a spate of new appointments to Printing House Square, designed 'to ginger up the news services and reporting and to get some of the Carmelite House dash into them'. Among others, George Beer, the *Daily Mail*'s night news editor was transferred to *The Times* as news editor.[4] In his diary, Dawson bewailed Northcliffe's frenetic interference. 'Fearful worry and chaos in the office. Northcliffe raging about and giving contradictory orders. . . . Lunatic raging and nagging. . . . Another diabolical day.'[5] Dawson felt that matters had reached so intolerable a pitch that he must unburden himself to John Walter.

> Things are not going very well with The Times and there is a serious risk
> of their going very much worse . . . because we are losing people with
> the knowledge which is at least as great an asset of The Times as rapidity
> in getting and translating news. . . . To take the Foreign News
> Department alone – we are now losing Saunders and Braham
> simultaneously,[6] the two men who know most and have the best judgment
> of foreign affairs. Both of them have defects of which I am perfectly aware,
> and in any case, I am not arguing about them here. That chapter is
> closed. But remember the foreign page every night is now in the hands
> of MacGregor, a most capable sub-editor, but a man who does not and
> does not pretend to have, the slightest knowledge of foreign countries,
> languages and affairs. . . . Steed, of course, is invaluable when he is here,

but it is not intended, I gather, that he should be here at night, and in any case it is desirable that he should be a great deal abroad. The essential thing now is that we should lose no more people with well-filled minds and trained judgment – such men, I mean, as Richmond, Repington, Chisholm, Shadwell, and one or two others of that calibre. It is not very difficult to find good sub-editors and reporters, but people of the type I have named cannot be abandoned without serious damage to the paper, and I feel that there is a danger at the present moment of losing everyone who gives distinction to The Times.[7]

As was intended, John Walter passed the letter to Northcliffe then in Paris to consult a specialist about his eyes but also to settle the final details in his own mind of the stratagem that would finally 'save' *The Times*. He accepted, demurely enough, the reasonable case Dawson had made. To Pryor, with whom he had consulted about staff changes and appointments, he wrote, 'I want the whole office to get into the best spirits for the immense task that they have before them.'[8] The exact nature of that task he revealed to Dawson whom he had summoned to Paris. The price of *The Times* was soon to be reduced to a penny. The exact date had not been fixed but in the event, Northcliffe's hand was forced by a report in the *Daily Chronicle* anticipating his move. At first the report was vehemently denied, but a fortnight later the change was announced to take effect as from Monday 16 March 1914. 'The Times at One Penny' was puffed for all it was worth by Northcliffe's newspapers, but in all the press there was a general welcome given the revolutionary move. Despite the dire warnings of the 'Old Guard', it was soon apparent that the essential character and quality of *The Times* was unaffected by its drop in price.

The decision had been Northcliffe's alone. To him belonged the triumph and the satisfaction of seeing his highest hopes vindicated as sales immediately more than tripled to 145,000. With the outbreak of war in August 1914 – *not* part of Northcliffe's calculation – circulation again rose dramatically to 280,000 copies a day. The mould had been shattered. Such a massive increase in readership was bound to enhance the assumed influence of *The Times*. Liberated at last from its narrow constituency of purchasers, it now reached out to an entirely new class of reader whose prejudices, as well as cultural, intellectual and political disposition, Northcliffe presumed he understood.

The treatment of foreign news by *The Times* remained an abiding concern with Northcliffe. The loss of the experienced 'Europeanist', Paris correspondent George Saunders, and leader writer, David Braham, he believed was more than compensated by the advancement of Steed to lead the foreign department. Steed was now firmly re-established in Northcliffe's affections. Dawson's increased reponsibilities, largely the result of Northcliffe's new appointments and his unsettling reorganisation of the editorial department, combined with the editor's absorption with the mounting Ulster crisis, which also engaged much of Northcliffe's attention and energies, meant an enormous enhancement of Steed's position as the major influence in interpreting European events at Printing House Square. Northcliffe's good opinion of Steed was helped by the foreign editor affecting the Carmelite House genuflection by addressing the proprietor as 'Chief'. Steed was compared, to his advantage, with his predecessor. Valentine Chirol's experience, his subtle and informed comprehension of diplomatic complexities, was forgotten. All Northcliffe chose to remember was that Chirol was one of the awkward triumvirate, the 'Old Guard', 'an arch muddler . . . who, I believe, cost the paper some scores of thousands of pounds'.[9] Northcliffe did not choose to notice Steed's inordinate egotism, his over excitable character, or his readiness 'to believe in plots and conspiracies', an inclination 'to see "hidden hands" and "sinister influences" where more balanced men would only see stupidity or lack of imagination'.[10] Northcliffe saw only a foreign editor who appeared to share not only his dislike of Jews[11] but also his general view of European affairs. Northcliffe's simple apprehensions were encapsulated in the *Daily Mail*'s constant campaigning for national service, a reorganised army and ever larger naval estimates. The *Mail*'s inability to comprehend the 'true inwardness' of European affairs was the subject of increasingly frequent and strident complaints from its Berlin correspondent, Wile. Of the Russian war scare in early March 1914, which, due to J. E. Mackenzie's reports from Berlin had been blazoned in *The Times*, Wile wrote unavailingly to Northcliffe:

> I told all about these things, succinctly and briefly. . . . What happened in Carmelite House? With that unfailing lack of appreciation of the value of German political events the Russian war scare – since grown to the most important Continental political incident of recent times – was dismissed with a four line paragraph.[12]

Wile's reports were not, this time, the victim of an insensitive or ill-informed sub-editor. At Carmelite House it was well understood both by the editor, Marlowe and the chief leader writer, Wilson, that the only German influences which currently preoccupied Northcliffe were those that he supposed were operating in Ireland. The 'war' for which the 'Chief' was preparing his *Daily Mail* staff was to be in Ulster. On 21 March 1914, Northcliffe despatched Andrew Caird to Belfast as *generalissimo* of the *Daily Mail*'s war staff in Ireland with James Dunn as his right-hand man. Northcliffe's explicit instructions were that nothing was to be spared in the way of reporters, money or effort. A special courier service had been devised and a steamer chartered to stand by to take copy to Liverpool should other means fail.[13] So intensely was Northcliffe involved in the fortunes of Ulster that it even temporarily banished from the headlines of the *Daily Mail* its perennial exaggerated interest in the recently presented naval estimates.

When, in March the previous year, the First Lord had presented his naval estimates to the Commons, like the rest of the Tory press the *Daily Mail* initially concentrated upon the number of Dreadnoughts in the programme. Winston had made provision for five. The reductionists argued that four were more than enough. The *Mail*, like all its patriotic contemporaries, insisted upon six as the minimum. The sole original contribution made by the *Mail* to the all-too-familiar pattern of the estimates' debate in 1913 was a series of three articles on modern warfare written by H. G. Wells. The author was bold enough to scorn those 'hypnotised by the Dreadnought idea'.[14]

There seems to have been a complete arrest of the British imagination in naval and military matters. That declining faculty, never a very active or well-exercised one, staggered up to the conception of a Dreadnought and seems now to have sat down for good. Its reply to every demand upon it has been 'more Dreadnoughts'. The future, as we British seem to see it, is an avenue of Dreadnoughts, and super-Dreadnoughts, and super-super-Dreadnoughts, getting bigger and bigger in a kind of inverted perspective. But the ascendancy of fleets of great battleships in naval warfare . . . draws to its close.

There was the clear warning that the nation was spending vast sums of money upon 'the things of yesterday when the money is sorely needed for the things of tomorrow. With our eyes averted obstinately from the future we are backing towards disaster.' Wells insisted that the emphasis should be upon aeroplanes, airships and submarines.[15] His belief in the superiority of air over the naval Service was shared in part by Northcliffe. There was a lively debate in *The Times* during October 1913 on warship design, but most of those, like Admiral Bridge, who questioned the Dreadnought policy had their eyes turned to the quarrels of the past rather than the realities of the future. It was clear, however, that there was a growing body of opinion that believed if submarines could accomplish part only of what was claimed for them, then the Dreadnought policy might well prove a disastrous failure.[16] It remained that Churchill shared the general disposition. He concentrated his efforts upon securing a big capital ship building programme, so much so that he was prepared to sacrifice eight light cruisers in a single year's programme and allowed a dangerously low margin of oil reserves. Both decisions were to have serious consequences during the war.[17]

The other feature of Churchill's 1913 estimates that attracted attention was his 'naval holiday' proposal. Winston's suggestion that there should be no fresh building of capital ships for twelve months either by Britain or Germany was attacked by the 'big navy' press in both countries. Apart from the technical difficulties, indeed impossibilities of the proposal, *The Times* insisted that while they like everyone else deplored the competition in armaments, it was 'vain in a practical argument to overlook the fact that armaments are, in the present condition of the world, the touchstone of national character and organizing power'.[18] There were elements in the German press that employed exactly the same argument, and generally Churchill's proposal was dismissed as 'insincere, grotesque, swaggering, absurd bluff'. Reventlow, in the *Deutsche Tageszeitung,* accused the First Lord of 'a felonious attempt to influence that section of German public opinion which has been opposed to German naval expansion in the past and which he hopes will keep on doing so'. An editorial in the *Taegliche Rundschau* claimed that all Churchill wanted was 'to make "Rule Britannia" cheap. If we let him, there is a place awaiting us in the fool's gallery of the world's history.'[19]

Whatever others might have thought, Churchill took his own proposal seriously. In a letter to Grey immediately after recommending his plan to a Manchester audience, he wrote, 'Surely reflecting men should see the profound advantage to us of procuring a cessation. . . . It is a profound British interest to procure a halt, and worth running serious risks for. . . . I *do* think this is right. I am sure of it.'[20] But again, the proposal received a very dusty answer from the German press. *Die Post* was typical when characterising the First Lord's offer as 'the generosity of the burglar who places his revolver in his left pocket and takes another from his right pocket'.[21] In March, without in any way suggesting official endorsement, Bethmann had made complimentary, even flattering noises about Churchill's proposal. By the autumn, through a speech by Tirpitz and privately by somewhat ambiguous hints from Jagow to the British Ambassador, it was made clear that Churchill's initiative could not be the basis for serious negotiations between the two governments. In the Reichstag, support for the idea had come only from 'the extreme wing of the Liberals'.[22]

In England, only the Radical press treated Winston's proposal seriously. Even Hardie's *Labour Leader* dismissed it as 'nothing more than a pious preamble to naval estimates that are likely to be sensational'. It was designed to be 'a sop to the political conscience of British Radicals',[23] a conclusion shared by Esher who put the whole episode down to 'Winston playing to the Radical gallery again'.[24] Most of the Tory press echoed the sentiments of the *Morning Post*. The holiday the nation most required was for the First Lord to take a year off from speechmaking. He should not be dabbling with disarmament. Garvin supported Winston in the *Pall Mall Gazette*, but only because he thought the idea of a naval holiday 'a smart proposal that would allow time to clear up the back-log of work in the naval yards'.[25]

At Manchester in October 1913, Churchill had hinted that if his naval holiday initiative was rejected then there would have to be an increase in the naval estimates. The next month, in a speech at the Guildhall, Churchill made his threat explicit. The next naval estimates would show a large increase and so long as he was in charge of the Admiralty they could expect nothing less. Lloyd George, apparently quite recovered from his Agadir apostasy and once more determined to lead in the reductionist van, derided Churchill's threats as madness. The public would not tolerate such claims by a Liberal minister. Even Asquith, less bland than usual about the indiscretions of the Cabinet's *enfant terrible*, admitted to senior colleagues that he was 'furious' with Winston.

When Churchill presented his estimates to the Cabinet in December they were summarily rejected. Some minor reductions which brought the figures marginally under fifty millions were similarly dismissed. If major economies were to be effected then the number of Dreadnoughts would have to be reduced. There was total impasse in the Cabinet. However, the number of Dreadnoughts to be laid down for the new programme – Churchill and the Sea Lords wanted four, their opponents two – was not the actual determinant of ministerial responses. They were based upon political and personal calculations. In the end the reductionists' case was not bested by any of Churchill's technical arguments but by a combination of Asquith's patience, his remarkable, unfailing ability to reconcile the irreconcilable, and the reluctant recognition by Liberal ministers that there was no way of escaping the logic of the total political circumstances in which the administration found itself in the last year of peace.

As the struggle went on within the Cabinet, Churchill was promoted as the darling of the Tory press.[26] This was because of stirring if desperate and finally unavailing efforts by the Radical press in support of a campaign for retrenchment by the National Liberal Federation led by its President, Sir John Brunner and with Francis Hirst, editor of the *Economist*,, as its ringmaster.[27] The cause of economy was powerfully reinforced by an interview with Lloyd George published by the *Daily Chronicle* on 1 January 1914. The Chancellor of the Exchequer reviewed and reviled 'the organized insanity of the overwhelming extravagance of our expenditure on armaments'. Such statements by Liberal ministers were nothing new. In October, even Winston had told a Dundee audience that he thought the time was ripe for an Anglo-German initiative to tackle the armaments problem. But Lloyd George's interview was of a different order. It appeared to be nothing less than a direct appeal to the public to support the cause which he championed in a divided Cabinet. Certainly this was how it was interpreted by politicians of both major parties.[28] In a long, astute letter to Selborne, Balfour analysed the position.

> I think the move on Lloyd George's part is purely political. I do not mean to say that, as Chancellor of the Exchequer and a tax payer, he is not seriously alarmed at the growth of expenditure. I have no doubt that he is; at all events I am. What I do suppose is that he wants an Election cry which will rally what remains of the old Radical Nonconformist Party, the new semi-Socialist Radical and the Labour Party. A campaign against armaments is admirably suited for the purpose. He also, of course, wants the public mind to be, as far as possible, distracted from the question of Ulster, and he perhaps doubts whether this Land campaign[29] will be sufficient to attain this end.
>
> On the other hand, I think he may be moved by political considerations other than those connected with the electoral welfare of the Radical Party. There may be, and probably are, private and personal ambitions which would be served by pressing these divisions to breaking point over a subject like military and naval retrenchment. . . .
>
> What I do *not* believe is that Lloyd George, or any of his colleagues, have thought out a scheme by which our existing expenditure can be safely diminished on any large scale – perhaps on any scale whatever. Certainly nothing that has come under my notice at the Defence Committee suggests such a possibility.
>
> What then, if you were in Churchill's place, would you wish the Opposition to do? This is a hard question to answer; but I am very much inclined to doubt whether at this stage Churchill's party in the Cabinet, if he has one, would think themselves strengthened by a Unionist agitation against reduction. . . . There is much to be said for waiting till we have more definite information.[30]

The Tory press was not prepared to take the long view of Lloyd George's speech that Balfour advocated. *The Times* in particular, imagining that an intransigent attitude on armaments best reflected the determination and commitment of the nation, denounced the Chancellor's speech as 'remarkable and reprehensible'. He might talk as he wished but 'the nation is resolved to maintain its naval supremacy. We know that this supremacy is vital not only to our greatness but to our existence and our liberty.' Worried about French opinion, in two further editorials the newspaper emphasised that there was no reason for French alarm. 'The views of the pacifists are no more those of England than the ideas of M. Jaurès represent the real mind of France.'[31]

Asquith meanwhile adopted those same methods that he had tried and found successful in the past. He temporised, playing the arguments along in Cabinet as slowly as possible until other events overtook present difficulties. He appealed for unity, suggested a measure of sympathy for Churchill's position and made cautionary noises about a possible appeal to the country. By the beginning of February the reductionists knew that their case was doomed. McKenna, who had long disliked and distrusted Lloyd George, told C. P. Scott that the Chancellor was now 'a Churchill man' and was 'acting as a bell-wether to bring the stalwarts into the Churchill fold'.[32] More appeals mixed with warnings by the Prime Minister and on 11 February 1914, the naval estimates were finally accepted. The agreed amount was fifty-one and a half millions sterling, an unprecedented total. The single sop offered to the outraged Radical economists was the promise that next year's estimates would show a substantial reduction. They had heard that story often enough before. In the account of these events that he later published, Churchill paid tribute to the 'solid, silent support' he had received from Asquith.[33] But the real source of the First Lord's strength in Cabinet was the knowledge, shared by every reductionist minister, that if Churchill resigned then so also would Grey. That would mean the collapse of the government.[34] The Tory press recognised that the most significant feature of the estimates crisis in the Cabinet had been the formidable conjunction of power represented by the alliance of First Lord and Foreign Secretary. Thus, in the final crisis of August 1914, patriotic editors considered the opinions and actions of these two ministers the most important indicators of likely government action.

Churchill presented his estimates to the House in a speech described by the *Daily Telegraph* as 'most weighty and eloquent'. Addressing his arguments to two opposed groups – the reductionists in his own party and the 'big navy' Tories – he succeeded in satisfying neither. To the First Lord's assurance that the estimates had been reduced to their irreducible minimum, *Concord* replied, 'We say without hesitation that these Naval Votes, in time of complete peace, are exorbitant in wholesale and retail, in policy and administration. It is a very grievous thing that they were not more seriously challenged.'[35] The *Daily News* described Churchill as 'the fount of profligate extravagance and wasteful administration' and suggested that his conception of a 60 per cent advantage over Germany 'every day looks more like the old Two Power standard'.[36] *The Times,* to the contrary, concluded that Churchill's estimates had 'reduced British naval strength'. Like the *Daily News, The Times* questioned the First Lord's arithmetic claiming that he had made insufficient provision because he had taken no account of the loss of the promised three Canadian Dreadnoughts for the Mediterranean.[37]

The problem of the naval defence of the Mediterranean had been exacerbated in September 1913 by the Italians' announcement of a four super-Dreadnought building programme. *The Times*'s attitude on the subject of dominion contributions to imperial defence was always strained. The 'Europeanists' at Printing House Square deprecated the 'disloyalty' of the Canadians. The 'imperialist' faction, led by Grigg, excused the dominion's response as understandable. When Westminster took a more informed imperial view of strategy then the problem would resolve itself. But when this had been said, there was still an uncomfortable awareness of unresolved economic difficulties concerning preferential trading with the dominions that threatened the tenuous unity of the Tory party. Dawson, temperamentally and intellectually sympathetic to the imperialists' arguments, nevertheless placed himself between the two factions, exercising restraint upon both. He was also curbing the more esoteric naval strategic thoughts of *The Times*'s military correspondent. Repington, inspired by the Italian Dreadnought programme, was engaged in calculating the consequences of a war between an isolated Britain and the Triple Alliance Powers. Dawson was particularly sceptical of the idea that the Italians and the Austrians could cooperate effectively as a naval unit in the Mediterranean.

> They are probably building their ships against each other quite as much as for any other purpose and to assume them working as a single fleet at sea requires a great effort of imagination. . . . I doubt the wisdom of assuming publicly a naval alliance between Italy and Austria-Hungary without pointing out its inherent improbability . . . I should prefer you on the whole to alter your article in this sense. On the other hand, you are absolutely entitled to your own view, and I am prepared to publish the article as it stands. But in that case I must to some extent 'turn it down' in a leader, and on the whole I prefer that we should shew no division of opinion.[38]

Repington deferred to Dawson's wish.

There had been little time for Dawson to reflect upon the extraordinary success of the decision to reduce the price of *The Times* to one penny before his attentions and energies, like Northcliffe's, had been fully engaged by the long smouldering Irish question which, in the third week of March, suddenly threatened to explode with the prospect of an attempt by the government to use the army to coerce Ulster. First news of resignations by officers at the Curragh did not begin to come into *The Times*'s office until late Friday evening, 20 March. The next day Dawson learned from Milner and General Henry Wilson what exactly had happened: that General Arthur Paget, GOC Ireland, meeting with his senior officers had given them the option of resigning rather than enforce the government's policy. Following the lead of General Gough, almost sixty officers had tendered their resignations. During the next few days, in his diary Dawson admitted that he was 'distracted and driven to death . . . desperate nights at the office'.[39] The immediate crisis was resolved by an ambiguous pledge by the Cabinet concerning the use of the army, and Asquith taking Seely's place as Minister for War. Sir John French also resigned. Dawson's fear was that the Liberals would misrepresent the attitude adopted by the Tory party over Ulster and employ this as a powerful and persuasive argument in the general election that he was convinced would be called that summer.[40] There was the further nagging worry over the effectiveness of the army. Nothing would ever be resolved so long as Asquith held the War Minister's portfolio in addition to the premiership. In mid-June, after a day spent talking with friends at the War Office, Repington informed Dawson that 'the PM means to do nothing ... and is merely playing out time. He is rarely there, does nothing, and does it extremely well.'[41]

Wickham Steed was less concerned about Ulster than he was with information given him by the London correspondent of *Le Figaro* that, without the knowledge of the French, the British and German governments had been engaged in secret talks over colonial holdings in central Africa. April marked the tenth anniversary of the signing of the Anglo-French entente, and in May, King George and Queen Mary were due to visit Paris. These two events afforded the ideal opportunity for a public campaign to reassure the French of British *bona fides* and to tighten the diplomatic, military and naval bonds between all three entente Powers. Although these remained comparatively unimpaired, relations had not been over-cordial of late. France had shown a distinct disposition at the conclusion of the Balkan Wars to pursue a policy towards Turkey independent of that of Britain. As Russia was pursuing a different policy it would soon be apparent that Britain could not support the policy of both her partners in the Near East. With *The Times* wedded to the notion that peace in Europe depended upon an equilibrium between the Triple Entente and Triple Alliance, there was obvious cause for concern at Printing House Square that not only was the unity of the entente in grave danger but also the prospect of maintaining peace. Consequently, the anniversary of the Anglo-French entente, 8 April 1914, was marked by a *Times* leader emphasising that the balance of power between Triple Entente and Triple Alliance was the guarantee of peace in the world. It also stressed 'the sense of responsibility which chastens and restrains the boldest and most reckless. . . . Any Power or Powers which may meditate recourse to arms must first satisfy those other members that the quarrel is necessary and just. They are no longer unfettered judges in their own cause, answerable to none but themselves.'[42]

Steed, having sounded opinion at the Foreign Office, had been encouraged to ask the eminent French historian, Ernest Lavisse, to write a letter for *The Times* to mark the anniversary of the entente. The letter was based on a draft agreed between the foreign editor, Lavisse, and assented to by the French President, Poincaré. Lavisse's letter was published on 16 April. It avoided the direct question of transforming the entente into an alliance but clearly implied that the French thought the doctrine of balance, or equilibrium, was in itself not enough without a balance of armaments. Steed, in his later, published account of this episode, claimed that the letter 'had its effect and, by the discussion it caused in the French and British press, contributed noticeably to warm the atmosphere for the visit of the King and Queen to Paris in May'.[43]

Certainly the royal visitors with their diplomatic entourage, which most notably included the British Foreign Secretary, Sir Edward Grey, were warmly welcomed by the French. Frequent public assurances, applauded by *The Times*, that, in Poincaré's words, 'the entente is a pillar of European equilibrium', caused considerable distress in the British Radical press. 'All good Liberals have strenuously resisted this notion of equilibrium,' wrote the *Daily News*. 'The conception of the entente as designed to guarantee the balance of power contradicts violently the conception of the entente as only the first and the model of a series of understandings to embrace all the other Great Powers.'[44] *New Age*, anticipating Maxse's response in the *National Review*, derided 'the flatulent organs of the Cocoa trade talking their usual twaddle, the Radicals as usual deluding themselves'.[45] What the Radicals most feared was a tightening of the bonds that embraced autocratic Russia. It was for this reason that the *Manchester Guardian* sought to devalue the Triple Entente as 'little more than a slovenly piece of diplomatic jargon'.[46] There would have been cause for real concern had they known that Grey, on a visit to the Quai d'Orsay with Bertie, had agreed, at the request of Cambon and Doumergue, to accommodate the Russian desire for naval talks.[47] The Russians could hardly believe their good fortune.[48] It was not long before the Wilhelmstrasse knew about the talks, informed by a leak from the Russian embassy in London to Theodor Wolff, editor of the *Berliner Tageblatt*. Ten days after the Cabinet had approved the talks, Wolff published his first article emphasising that the conversations could only be aimed at Germany. They imperilled Anglo-German relations and would be used by German chauvinists as a powerful argument to demand an increase in Germany's naval strength. Wolff appealed to British Liberals to thwart this possibility. Neither his accurate exposé nor his appeal went unnoticed.[49] Grey's response to questions in the Commons about the naval talks was more than ambiguous; he did not answer the questions he was asked. 'We do not feel satisfied,' wrote the *Manchester Guardian*. 'These answers do not allay uneasiness. . . . The secret, in so far as there is one, is a secret from the British Parliament and people, not from any possible enemy.'[50] *Nation*, which in May was asking, 'Why are we always left in doubt to guess the precise nature of the Triple Entente?', a month later surmised on the basis of Grey's statements that the provisions of the entente 'are really as good as most alliances and rather better than some . . . Our responsibility and our share is direct and heavy in the rivalries which are in progress and in the conflict which they might by mischance unchain.'[51] The Tory press stood firmly by Grey stoutly supported by J. A. Spender in the *Westminster Gazette*.[52] Only eight days later, the Archduke Franz Ferdinand and his consort were murdered at Sarajevo. A few short weeks of peace remained separating Europe from the fatal plunge into the maelstrom of war.

On the morning of 28 June 1914, a little before noon, Gavrilo Princip, a Bosnian who lived in Serbia, shot down the heir to the Austro-Hungarian throne who was visiting Sarajevo, capital of the Austrian province of Bosnia Herzegovina. Most Englishmen learned of the event next day when they opened their Monday morning papers. The general disgust of the British public with the archduke's murderer was probably best captured by an article in *John Bull* that claimed because Serbia was a party to the murder that country ought to be annihilated.[53] The Serbs were not popular with the English and almost without exception,[54] the British press claimed the Austrians would be perfectly justified in requiring the Serbs to take whatever steps were necessary to prevent any recurrence of a similar outrage. In most British newspapers the political implication of the murder was worthy of little more than cursory attention. While news from Vienna, Budapest, Belgrade and Sarajevo and rumours of Serbian complicity in the assassination filled the main news pages of the German press, relations between Austria and Serbia were soon dismissed to the comparative anonymity of the inside pages by the British press. The headlines were occupied with social and sporting stories; the death of Joseph Chamberlain and the continuing crisis in Ireland. In the period immediately before Austria's ultimatum to Serbia the two stories that vied for attention in English newspapers were the trial of Madame Caillaux for the murder of the editor of *Le Figaro* and accounts of gun-running in Ulster.[55] If, in the light of subsequent events, this might seem strange, it should be noted that there was no undue concern shown by the professional diplomats at the Foreign Office. Nicolson had written to the British Ambassador in Vienna on 6 July that, Albania apart, there were 'no very urgent and pressing questions to preoccupy us in the rest of Europe'.[56] As for the politicians, at the Guildhall on 17 July Lloyd George was telling his audience that a quarter of a million men under arms in Ireland and an implacable revolutionary ferment which threatened the total disruption of British industry posed a more direct and immediate threat to Britain than any foreseeable diplomatic contretemps in Europe. The assassination at Sarajevo he dismissed as 'no more than a very small cloud on the horizon . . . and you never get a perfectly blue sky in foreign affairs.' Elaborating on this forecast, the Chancellor assured the House six days later that relations between Germany and Britain were better than they had been for years past. Next day Austria delivered her ultimatum to Serbia.

Most Englishmen knew nothing and, if it was possible, cared less for the Balkans. One man who was knowledgeable about that part of the world was Steed. From the first he suspected that there was more behind the murder than met the eye, and warned his colleagues at Printing House Square that it would be prudent to restrain expression of horror about the assassination and wholesale denunciation of the Serbs, as the war party in Austria could well make capital out of such statements.[57] Substance was given to Steed's suspicions by rumours coming from Vienna that caused a growing unease that the Austrians proposed an action against Serbia out of all proportion to that suitable in the circumstances. Suspicions were alerted in minds much less prone to seeing plots than Steed's by memories of the earlier Agram and Friedjung trials that had revealed how Austria had not hesitated in the past to pursue political ends by employing trumped up evidence.[58] The warnings of the British Ambassador in Vienna that wholesale denunciations of the Serbs by Austria should not be accepted without evidence were echoed by British newspapers of every political persuasion. By about 9 July, however, as nothing definite had developed, and lulled by a comforting speech that day by Count

Tisza to the Chamber of Deputies at Budapest, the press bent its attention to apparently more urgent domestic concerns.

The German government decided the time had come to try to influence the British press in Austria's favour. Berchtold, acting upon information sent him by the Austrian Ambassador in Berlin after a conversation with Jagow, instructed Mensdorff in London 'to conduct a press campaign on our lines during the coming weeks'. Lichnowsky, who accepted his brief with great reluctance and pessimism, was similarly instructed by Jagow to do his best to influence the press. 'Your Excellency knows how important for us the attitude of Britain will be in the event of any further consequences of the conflict.'[59] Mensdorff first tackled the problem of *The Times*, choosing to make his approach through the Tory ex-Foreign Secretary Lansdowne. After a friendly conversation, Lansdowne was given extracts from the Belgrade press together with a note summing up the Austrian view. Thus armed, Lansdowne wrote to Dawson who replied that he hoped soon to draw attention to Serbian attitudes and the dangers arising therefrom. Mensdorff also spoke to Rosebery, 'the best friend of the Dual Monarchy in England'. Rosebery seemed understanding and promised he would do what he could.[60] The other newspaper Mensdorff sought to influence directly was the *Westminster Gazette*. Baron Franckenstein was instructed to see J. A. Spender. The two men had a rather inconclusive conversation and Spender might have thought no more of the matter had he not received a visit three days later from von Schubert of the German embassy who begged him to tell the Serbs they could not expect British support if they refused the Austrians satisfaction for their crime. Spender told Grey of his two visitors only to learn that the Foreign Secretary had spoken to Mensdorff in much the same terms as Spender had used with Schubert and Franckenstein. Spender decided he must write an article on the subject which appeared on 17 July, the day after *The Times*'s article 'inspired' by Lansdowne's letter to Dawson.[61]

The Times's leader, written by Flanagan, advised Serbia to undertake an inquiry into all the circumstances of the assassination and to lay the full report before the Powers. If this was done 'openly and fairly, without fear or favour, she will do much to put herself right with outside opinion'. Austria was complimented for having 'acted with self-possession and with restraint . . . We earnestly hope she will continue so to act until the end.'[62] Mensdorff was pleased with the article supposing its tone reflected his activities. The odd note of admonition of which he did not approve he put down to Steed's notorious bias against Austria.[63] Spender's *Westminster Gazette* article was markedly more pro-Austrian and anti-Serbian in tone. Both articles were noticed by diplomats and commented upon. The status of *The Times* as an 'official' paper was rarely questioned on the continent, and the *Westminster* also enjoyed a semi-official status because of the known close connection between Grey and Spender.[64] A report in the *Daily Telegraph* published on 13 July, written by E. J. Dillon with much special pleading for the Austrian position, was not similarly noted.[65]

Flushed with his apparent success, Mensdorff now sought to attempt the more ambitious task of bringing Steed within the fold.[66] On the afternoon of

16 July Steed accepted an invitation to supper the next evening from Max Goldschieder, London correspondent of *Neues Wiener Tageblatt.* When he arrived at Goldschieder's modest lodgings, Steed was surprised to see preparations for an elaborate dinner and an unexpectedly grand list of guests including all the senior members of the Austrian embassy other than the Ambassador, together with Sidney Low, leader writer of the *Daily Telegraph* and Condurier de Chassaigne, President of the Foreign Press Association in London.[67] In the after-dinner conversation which concentrated upon the Sarajevo assassination, Steed challenged the views expressed by the diplomats but they remained unruffled. The next day Steed received an invitation to lunch with Mensdorff at the embassy. The journalist could not have been more amazed.[68] Despite his reluctance to accept he was finally persuaded to meet Mensdorff on Tuesday 21 July. After luncheon Mensdorff told Steed, 'I wish to appeal to you as a friend of Austria to use your influence in the British Press to make the position of Austria-Hungary in this crisis rightly understood. . . . Serbia must be punished: but if The Times will give the lead the rest of the press will follow, British public opinion will remain friendly to us, and the conflict may be localized.' Steed refused to help and insisted that Britain would be bound to intervene. 'You do not know the strength of English public feeling,' he informed the Ambassador who, carried away by the passion of their exchange, made the fatal admission that he had 'assurances' that Britain would not intervene.

Convinced that Austria intended to attack Serbia, Steed rushed round to the Foreign Office to see Grey but instead was obliged to tell Willie Tyrrell that he had 'conclusive proof' that Austria was bent upon war with Serbia, that Germany was backing her, and that Mensdorff believed that Britain would not intervene. Grey should be told to speak out and make Britain's position clear. From the Foreign Office, with urgency and a due sense of his own importance, Steed hurried to a conference with Northcliffe and Dawson. Overwhelmed by Steed's passionate account it was decided the time had come for *The Times* to speak out on the true state of affairs – carefully and cautiously, but very firmly. Flanagan wrote the leader, 'A Danger to Europe', which appeared next day. Austria was warned that unless, 'to the reasonable satisfaction of European opinion', it could be proved that the Serbian government had been involved in a conspiracy over the Sarajevo assassination, if Austria went to war she would be branded as an unjustified aggressor needlessly endangering the peace of Europe. Austria should not delude herself that the conflict could be localised.

The bulk of the British press, between 21 July and the publication of the Austrian ultimatum, seemed more conscious than the Foreign Office of the direction that events were taking. Warned in a telegram by their Ambassador in Vienna on 21 July that there was good reason to suppose the Austrians might launch a sudden attack, Eyre Crowe was dismissive and Nicolson very doubtful.[69] However, when the ultimatum was published, it was significant that newspapers like Garvin's *Pall Mall Gazette* and the *Observer*, Blumenfeld's *Express*, 'Taffy' Gwynne's *Morning Post* and the *Daily Mail*, all supposed it justified, if excessive, and condemned the Serbians.[70] *The Times* remained consistent to the line dictated by its leading article of 22 July. The unnecessarily offensive tone of the ultimatum was criticised and, more interestingly, foreign Powers were warned not to count upon the effect of Britain's domestic problems! By 27 July, Serbia having accepted all but one of Austria's prepost-erous demands, though there had been no evidence provided of Serbian complicity in the archduke's murder, the whole of the Conservative press seemed to swing into line with *The Times* This shift was important as it suggested to Radical journalists like Gardiner, Hirst and Nevinson that it was Northcliffe's *Times* and 'its attendant satellites' which were dragging the nation towards war.[71] Nor was this interpretation discouraged by certain Cabinet ministers in conversation with their journalist allies.[72]

On 28 July Austria broke off diplomatic relations with Serbia. Editorial comment in the next day's *Times* spoke in somewhat ambiguous terms of 'the people of England knowing what the Serbian war would mean to the whole world'. However, the uncomfortable thought that the people of England, or more particularly the British government, might not choose the 'correct and honourable' course, was reflected in the tone of the leading article for 30 July. Attention was focused, not on the Balkans, but on France and Belgium. 'If France is menaced, or the safety of the Belgian frontier . . . we shall know how to act.' The distinguished, elderly politician, Leonard Courtney, was perturbed that neither Asquith nor Grey, while trying to get the Powers to join in offering mediation, had not stated unequivocally that Britain would remain neutral, 'especially as "The Times" is dwelling on our "alliance" and the balance as binding us to action under possible circumstances – the circumstances being France joining in the war'.[73] Nevertheless, when A. G. Gardiner invited Courtney to declare his concern in the *Daily News*, he declined. 'I must choose the moment for speech or writing even at the risk of being too late,' he told the editor.[74] Politicians might hesitate, but the press was obliged to proffer an opinion.

The Tory press was united in demanding that the government should support Britain's entente partners but the Liberal press was divided. Spender was prepared to condemn the violent campaign for intervention, but the *Westminster*, like the *Daily Chronicle* would not take a positive stand either for or against neutrality. Later, Spender was to justify his stance by claiming the situation was 'beyond journalism'.[75] The *Chronicle* at the time suggested 'the crew of the ship' should wait upon 'the orders of their appointed captain'.[76] The disposition of Scott's *Manchester Guardian* and Gardiner's *Daily News* was that they simply could not afford to stand idly by while 'the Harmsworth press was shrieking for war'.[77] The two newspapers became the leading public protagonists for neutrality, absolutely opposed to 'the participation of this country in the greatest crime of our time'.[78] Gardiner provided 'masterpieces of polemical journalism'[79] countering the interventionist arguments, while the *Manchester Guardian* argued the case for neutrality in cool, dispassionate detail. But as the odds multiplied against them, an hysterical note betrayed a mounting anxiety. On 1 August the *Manchester Guardian* spoke of 'an organised conspiracy to drag us into war'.[80] The general consensus of Radical opinion was that this conspiracy was being led from Printing House Square. Lord Fitzmaurice, twice Under Secretary at the Foreign Office and a Liberal Chancellor of the Duchy of Lancaster, wrote to Spender,

> I am more alarmed than I can say by the articles in the 'Mail' and 'The Times' this morning. They are evidently the commencement of a campaign to drive this country into joining in the war, if it is to be localized; and bearing in mind the close connection there has been for many years between Grey and 'The Times' . . . they are doubly alarming.[81]

Matters were not quite so straightforward at Printing House Square as the Radicals supposed. There was cause for concern not only with the Liberal government but also with the apparent nonchalance affected by the Opposition leadership. As the first reports of German and Russian mobilisation began to trickle into the Foreign Office, a young Tory MP, George Lloyd, suddenly presented himself in Steed's room and dramatically announced that the government was about to 'rat' and back down to Germany. This information had been vouchsafed him by General Henry Wilson. 'What are the Opposition leaders doing?' Steed inquired. 'They are going into the country to play lawn tennis,' was the bitter response. 'Balfour, Bonar Law, and the whole lot of them. You forget that Monday is a Bank Holiday!'[82] Bonar Law had gone to the country for the weekend, but to discuss the prospect of coalition prompted by a communication from Churchill. The Tory leader's cool demeanour was in marked contrast to that of Lloyd, Henry Wilson and Maxse. Leo had been telephoned by Wilson and told, 'We are in the soup.'

The Tory leaders returned to London and consulted. Their talks continued into the Sunday morning, 2 August, when Bonar Law agreed to send a note to Asquith offering the Opposition's 'unhesitating support . . . in any measures they may consider necessary'. The nature of those 'measures' was implied by the assertion that 'it would be fatal to the honour and security of the United Kingdom to hesitate in supporting France and Russia'. The most interesting feature of this letter, which Asquith received before attending a morning Cabinet, was the absence of any mention of Belgium.[83]

The uncertainty and concern felt at Printing House Square during that momentous Bank Holiday weekend was understandable. Apart from the apparently lackadaisical attitude of Opposition politicians, there were hints of panic in the City. Dawson, returning to Printing House Square after a day in the country, found the office 'considerably confused and excited with Steed in particular pouring out volumes of incoherent "Europeanism" '. Dawson's immediate reaction was to recruit Grigg to restore balance with an article on the Empire. He was aware of 'a deep schism in the Cabinet. Grey struggling for peace – Winston making every disposition for war.'[84] The last editorial he had written had been three days earlier – 'a peace-making leader on Ireland'. Not until 1 August would he write to his friend Maurice Headlam and admit at last the Irish situation was 'entirely eclipsed' by European events.[85] Dawson's return to the office added a much needed measure of calm to the frenetic atmosphere that had largely been engendered by Steed. For once, Northcliffe was comparatively calm, certainly not bellicose. He was even roused to caution Repington for a contribution published on 31 July. 'It is the nature of a political declaration coming from a soldier and as such is likely to be seized on by the anti-war party here, who are only too prone to suggest that military men are urging us to war.'[86] Repington said nothing. He had employed neither argument nor language different from that he had used for many years in *The Times*.

For *The Times* no less than the country, the moment of crisis was almost at hand. Lord Rothschild summoned Hugh Chisholm to his office. He wanted *The Times* to stop printing editorial articles that were leading the country into war. Britain should remain neutral. Chisholm retailed the banker's instruction to an editorial conference on the afternoon of 31 July. Northcliffe asked Steed for his opinion. 'It is a dirty German-Jewish international financial attempt to bully us into advocating neutrality and the proper answer would be a still stiffer leading article tomorrow.' Northcliffe concurred. 'Let us go ahead,' he told those present.[87] The main leading article next day used as its peg the news of general mobilisation by the Russians. 'The dominant feeling is that the whole religious and national basis of the Russian Empire is involved and challenged by the precipitate attack of Austria-Hungary upon a small Slav state. . . . Should we remain passive, should the future war go against those whose interests march with our own, we know full well that it would be our turn next.' But to judge from other parts of the newspaper it did not seem that many *Times* readers shared this editorial view. Typical was a manifesto signed by many eminent Cambridge dons. This claimed to make war on Germany in the interests of Serbia and Russia would be a sin against civilisation. The Liberal press was loud with lamentations and criticisms by the just and the famous, bewailing and berating *The Times* in particular, but all the Tory press in general, as 'the organs of an insignificant and beaten minority. Yet they have the effrontery and impertinence', wrote the Radical MP, Roden Buxton, in the *Manchester Guardian*, 'to speak as if they are the voice of England.' They were 'anti-democratic' and the doctrine of the Balance of Power they preached was 'the doctrine of a small aristocratic clique which dominates the Foreign Office'.[88]

Northcliffe hesitated. These were powerful voices calling for neutrality. Perhaps a naval demonstration would be enough? He called Dawson, Steed and Marlowe to an editorial conference at Printing House Square for four o'clock that afternoon. It proved inconclusive. Steed argued that there was no alternative but to continue pushing the policy of intervention even if, as Northcliffe claimed, he had good reason to believe the government would go for neutrality. Marlowe was not prepared to oppose the government at a time of national emergency. Dawson pronounced that there was much to be said for both points of view. He was inclined to wait and see.[89] At this point Northcliffe received a telephone call from Rothschild. Arrangements were made for a meeting and the editorial conference was adjourned until the next day. Northcliffe met Rothschild and his brother Leopold, who repeated their request that *The Times* should support neutrality. Was Northcliffe unaware of Germany's overwhelming strength? The Empire would last no more than a few weeks. Steed later wrote, 'How Lord Northcliffe treated them he did not tell me; but I gathered from another quarter that their interview with him was very brief indeed.'[90] At the time Steed had not known how Northcliffe might react to the Rothschilds' assault. He had left Printing House Square in a depressed and wretched mood.

The resolution of Britain's quandary, as Dawson had recognised, lay in the hands of certain key Cabinet ministers, not in the decisions of editorial conferences. He had heard enough from Beauchamp over luncheon at the Travellers 'to know that a large part of the Cabinet was for leaving France (now plainly to be attacked by Germany) in the lurch'.[91] Dawson decided that the key minister to see was Churchill and managed a short conversation with him at the Admiralty before dining at the Beefsteak where he was further depressed by another meeting with the 'utterly unsound' Beauchamp. The editor of the *Morning Post*, 'Taffy' Gwynne, inspired by the same thoughts as Dawson, preferred to concentrate his efforts upon Grey but was obliged to confine his worries and advice instead to a letter to Grey's secretary, Willie Tyrrell. If England did not act in full accord with France against Germany, Gwynne argued, then surely she deserved the title *Perfide Albion*.

> We have been led by the Foreign Office under your chief's guidance to be prepared for cooperation with France. . . . We have worked hard to prepare public opinion for it, and now when we get to the jump, as it were, we are refusing it. . . . Let Sir Edward remember he holds the *honour* of England in his hands, that eighty per cent of Englishmen are behind him and that he has enormous personal power if he likes to use it with which he could force his views on the Cabinet and the country.
>
> We want a lead, a strong manly lead. We have always expected it from Sir Edward. Surely now we are not to be disappointed?[92]

Early the next morning, 2 August, Dawson walked across to McKenna's house. He was pleased to discover that the minister was 'at least on the fence'. McKenna claimed that the government was powerless, 'unless the people are behind them and the people are against war'.

An inconclusive morning Cabinet was followed by another meeting. Dawson spent most of that afternoon at the Admiralty waiting unavailingly for Winston. The editor gathered from members of the First Lord's entourage that he was engaged in a final struggle to carry his colleagues in the Cabinet with him for intervention. Grey, Haldane and Samuel were on Winston's side; Asquith's concern, as always, was to hold his government together. Lloyd George was leading the other faction which included Harcourt, Morley, Burns, Beauchamp, Simon and others. Dawson left for a full editorial meeting at Printing House Square, presided over by Northcliffe with John Walter in attendance. Walter had recently returned from the Kiel regatta where he had been the guest of Albert Ballin. Walter's host had sent him a letter received that morning. It was offered for publication and read to the conference. It accused Russia of forcing war on Europe by dragging in her allies and rejected any idea that the Kaiser or Germany had organised an aggressive war. The decision not to publish the letter was based upon the assumption that it might hamper Grey.[93] Dawson advised his colleagues, as at their previous meeting, not to be precipitate. His instructions to the leader writer before he left the office indicate that he clearly expected the matter to be resolved within hours. He interpreted the decision to call up the Naval Reserves as clearly implying the government *had* accepted the principle that Britain was involved. He anticipated the resignation of certain Cabinet members.[94]

When the Cabinet broke up, Dawson was able to snatch a moment's conversation with Winston and Grey. 'They were both obviously cheered by its results which had been clarified by the German invasion of Luxembourg; and Grey told me that he had given Cambon a written pledge of British support.' Grey, together with Tyrrell and F. E. Smith, went off to Admiralty House with Winston. Dawson repaired to Brooks where Lansdowne, Devonshire and other Tory grandees were dining. During the course of the evening Balfour told Dawson how Churchill had been involved in talk of coalition. Balfour described Winston as 'splendid'.[95]

The Times on 3 August headlined the news that the Germans had violated French territory at four points without actually declaring war. Despite all the pressures on his time, that afternoon Dawson went to the House of Commons to hear Grey's historic speech. 'Later the Government, being by this time well in it, demanded Germany's intentions with regard to Belgian neutrality.'[96] The invasion of Belgium clinched *The Times*'s argument for British intervention. It was now not only a matter of self-preservation but also international obligation. On 4 August *The Times* could declare, 'It is no less our duty than our interest to protect Belgium.' The Fleet was at war stations, the army was being mobilised. 'Things move very quick at the last – a difficult business to disentangle,' Dawson admitted in his diary. He was pleased to accept an invitation that evening 'to snatch a little dinner with Winston, his wife, mother and [Jack] Churchill'. The First Lord was in 'very good form' and a happy if hurried meal was accompanied by the sounds of cheering from a crowd that hung about the Admiralty. Dawson did not doubt that Winston deserved the acclaim. The First Lord and Grey were the two real heroes of the day. Yet Dawson was a good enough editor to remember at that moment the debt he and his newspaper owed to J. W. Flanagan who had risen to the challenge of the crisis and matched the occasion with a series of magnificent leaders.[97]

On 5 August 1914, *The Times*, like every other British newspaper, told its readers what many already knew. Britain and Germany were at war.

·····EPILOGUE·····

Account rendered:
the rewards of excess

If the Government promised to declare war for an object which did not
commend itself to public opinion, the promise would be repudiated and
the Government turned out.

Memorandum, May 1901, Lord Salisbury

Kommt der Krieg ins Land
Gibt Lügen wie Sand.

Epigraph introducing A. Ponsonby, 'Falsehood in War-Time'

4 August 1914: War is declared. Lord Northcliffe has his teeth
sharpened.

'War Diary' of E. V. Lucas

War came with an incredible and terrible swiftness in August 1914. The
ignominious collapse of the neutrality campaign seemed to confirm the claim
that war between Britain and Germany had been inevitable. Norman Angell
was not convinced. He believed that the neutralist case had failed because
'there seemed to be no realisation on the peace side that the danger was
desperate, that we were on the edge of a volcano. There was thus created a
situation in which all the psychological momentum, which goes for so much
in these things, was on the side of war.'[1]

Before the Battle of the Marne in September 1914, the Germans advanced
towards Paris and the Channel coast with alarming speed. There were widespread rumours – apparently officially authenticated – of atrocities perpetrated
by the German army on hapless civilians. At such times and in such circumstances it was easy to generate loathing and hatred of Germany. To feel
anything else seemed to be a denial of natural instinct. The pitifully few who
were nevertheless prepared to voice their opposition to war huddled together
for mutual comfort. 'What an insignificant minority we were,' Bertrand Russell
later recalled.[2] The patriotic press on the side of the big battalions could safely
indulge in jingo excess, safely gloat and preen itself on its prescience. With
this public display of bravado it was almost possible to forget the desperate
fear, never stronger than in the last few days of peace, that Britain might not
join with her entente partners, France and Russia, to fight the Hun. In a single
line of the letter he wrote to Milner on 5 August, F. S. Oliver summed up
the true feelings of many Fleet Street warriors of the Radical Right. 'What a
relief Monday evening was!'[3]

From their singular conception of history, the super-patriots of the British Radical Right in the two decades before 1914 fashioned and publicised a particular view of world politics. They emphasised European primacy and the superiority of the white over other races. The war was first to shake then shatter general acceptance of this view. By 1919, it was no longer popular to suppose that the war had been the inevitable outcome of natural and historical forces that had placed the Great European Powers in opposition for a final shooting-match to determine the future leaders of the world. A growing number of people were convinced by their personal experience of war that they had been, not the actors in a great Darwinian drama to determine the survival of the fittest, but the unwitting victims of the avarice of rulers who had abused their powers and privileges. After Armageddon, new explanations for man's destiny were sought. The innocence and naivety of the pre-war generation did not survive the holocaust. A dreadful empiricism tempered by cynicism and scepticism turned most of the familiar assumptions of the recent past upon their heads. In the post-war world, the emotional and intellectual atmosphere was unsympathetic to most of the orthodoxies of pre-war thinking.

Old wounds still ached; old scores remained unsettled; the wicked still paraded their truculence before the meek and the righteous; the peacemakers had not inherited the earth. Despite the fine talk of 'the war to end all wars', of democracy triumphing over autocracy, those who in 1914 had opposed the war perceived that victory brought only a vindictive peace settlement. The victors demonstrated not magnanimity towards the vanquished but moral and political turpitude. It seemed that what A. G. Gardiner had prophesied in 1914 when he had attacked Northcliffe had now materialised. Those same elements that for so many years had howled for war now, in peace, encouraged the basest passions of the populace. Their irresponsible rhetoric also informed and reinforced the blind prejudices of the nation's leaders. Even as before the war, so in peace, the guns of the Radical and patriotic press remained trimmed to aim and fire at each other.

The Radicals determined to discredit the patriotic press once and for all. Their design was based upon an idea that had existed in embryo before 1914. Likewise, its motivation was coloured by a perception of events that belonged as much to the now-distant political battles of the Edwardian years as to present events and concerns. The Radical thesis was founded upon an assumption and a proposition. The assumption was that the press could and did shape public opinion. The proposition, that the patriotic press had abused this power, deliberately falsifying and exaggerating the evidence presented to their readers. The examples cited in the indictment were intended to convict, out of their own mouths, the proprietors, editors and journalists of the patriotic press. Had not newspapers, like Northcliffe's *Daily Mail*, gladly accepted the charge of Teutophobia and scaremongering? Had not the excesses of the war years, the exaggerated xenophobia, the unreasoning hatred, the deliberate encouragement of the inherent capacity for barbarism and pugnacity in the people by falsehood and lying innuendo been nothing but an extension of the methods employed before the war; the campaigns for unnecessary armaments, the naval scares, the demand for conscription, the support for Germany's deliberate alienation and encirclement? The rhetoric of the Fleet Street warriors was shaken out of dusty newspaper files and presented to a post-war audience who were asked to accept it at its face value. Before accepting the indictment there is a need to look more closely at the assumed power of the press to shape opinion.

It is comparatively easy to understand why journalists should attach enormous significance to the influence of the press. It is less obvious why others should subscribe to the same belief. Then as now, politicians, whatever their party allegiances, though in public they might affect indifference to the press, in private courted its favour assiduously. Balfour, fond of claiming that he never read a newspaper, maintained very close contacts with all the leading Tory journals and journalists through Jack Sandars. At the least it was thought unwise unnecessarily to antagonise the friendly press. There was a convention to which, however reluctantly, politicians subscribed, that the press would have an increasingly important part to play in modern 'democratised' politics. There was then no other popular medium than the printed word capable of communicating with huge audiences. This monopoly not only enhanced the attractions of the press but also tended to exaggerate its importance. The rapidly burgeoning number of ennobled press men seemed to imply a tangible acknowledgment of press power. It was not quite as simple as it seemed. A peerage was as often reward for a fortunate coincidence of political views or gratitude for a generous donation to party funds drawn from the profits of successful commercial enterprise as it was an acknowledgment of the ability of the press to shape opinion. In June 1912 Bonar Law was advised before lunching with the elder Astor at the Ritz that the owner of the *Observer* and the *Pall Mall Gazette* thought that he had been 'neglected by the Party and that his efforts had not been recognised'. Law's 'principal object' should be to soothe Astor's injured feelings. 'He thinks Balfour might have put forward his name for a Peerage. . . . Recognise what he has done for the Party by Pall Mall, Observer and great financial assistance.'[4]

Following the earlier and successful example of the Liberals, the Tory party in the last years of peace had sought to reorganise, formalise and improve relations with its press allies. Balfour and Sandars gratefully accepted and implemented the professional advice of Northcliffe and Garvin. The reforms they introduced left a bitter legacy of distrust among personnel at Central Office. They were convinced that Northcliffe's real intention had been to make Central Office a mere annex of Carmelite House. When Bonar Law became the party's leader, Garvin's influence with the party organisation rapidly diminished. However, because Law's promotion to and maintenance of supreme power rested upon the support afforded him by the Radical Right, he could not afford to be less than polite to men like Maxse, Gwynne and Northcliffe. On Ireland, as on military and naval questions, Bonar Law required favourable publicity for his ideas, and this he was afforded by the right-wing publicists.

Because so many politicians appeared to share with journalists an exaggerated belief in the abilities of the press both to understand and shape public opinion, it was possible for H. A. Gwynne, without blushing and with a barely disguised hint of menace, to instruct Asquith in the early months of the war, 'My views are not merely held by myself, but by the vast majority of the public.

An Editor is always and has to be in touch with the trend of public feeling.'[5] *The Times*, as ever conscious of its own distinction, supposed that it enjoyed a particular and privileged position when it came to understanding and influencing *demos*. 'We are The Times,' wrote H. W. Steed to Valentine Chirol in June 1907. 'We mould today and shape tomorrow. . . . We are where the real power lies, understanding its nature, controlling its workings, never allowing it to ignore its responsibilities. . . . We are an expensive paper and cannot go direct to the masses but we can get the ear of and influence those who have the ears of the masses.'[6] The popular press did not altogether despair of influence among the nation's great, but laid most emphasis upon its 'intimate relationship with and understanding' of the general public.

What attitude informed the proprietors' end of this special relationship? If Lady Bathurst's *obiter dictum* to Gwynne is any indication, it was most certainly not based upon respect. 'The public', she blithely informed the *Morning Post's* editor, 'are marvellously ignorant and will swallow anything.'[7] Whatever was said in public, in private it was sometimes admitted that 'special relationships' were based upon convenient fictions. Chirol, in a letter to Strachey describing a meeting with Morley, cut through the usual cant about why a journalist might support one politician's ideas and denigrate another's. 'I found him most interesting and wise – which means, you will say, that I found him in very close agreement with me on most things! That is so.'[8] As for the frequent claim that one newspaper showed 'an intelligent impartiality' while another was 'either a fool or a canting hypocrite', Moberly Bell bluntly described this as 'nothing but humbug. What is often regarded as impartiality is only coincidence of views and what is called partiality is difference of views.'[9] It remained that few journalists, and then only to their friends, were prepared to admit that the press was better at pluming and preening its prejudices than informing and reforming men's ideas. Newspapers were generally engaged in preaching to the converted. Such a view cut across a well-established Liberal principle. Those who had fought against the newspaper duties as 'a tax on knowledge', believed the job of a newspaper was to help its readers reach conclusions in the light of sustained, informed commentary based on objectively realised facts. Ostrogorski might question this claim,[10] but the Radical-Liberal press never doubted that it fulfilled this duty.

The role of the press as an educator of public opinion was a theme taken up with enthusiasm by Edward Grey – but *after* the war.[11] While a Radical newspaper, like the *Manchester Guardian*, was quick to censure its popular Tory contemporaries for falling short of the standards it supposed *ought* to be adopted by the press, it utterly failed to acknowledge the particularities of its own methods and the pose that it consistently adopted towards its own readers. A certain nonconformist minister is said to have once begun an extemporary prayer, 'O Lord, thou hast doubtless seen it reported in the *Manchester Guardian*. . . .' Here the *Manchester Guardian's* place in the history of opinion (and we might add Massingham's *Nation* and to a lesser extent Gardiner's *Daily News*) is pointed to a nicety. For more than half its life the *Guardian* was the chosen vehicle wherein the Radical, dissenting establishment revealed their 'truth' with solemnity and certitude. The mistake is to suppose that the public voice of the Radical conscience was ever as certain and consistent as it would have had its readers believe. The message purveyed to the faithful, for all its high moral tone and cool prose, was as often as not an apocalyptic celebration rather than the exposition of a point of view.

There was a tendency among journalists to take themselves, their newspapers and their profession so seriously as on occasion to undervalue the mutual benefits bestowed by their close relationship with politicians. They sometimes thought they could do the politician's job better than the politician. Northcliffe, for example, was prepared to rate Bonar Law for the Tory party's 'mistake' in not adopting the tactics that the *Daily Mail* and *Observer* had espoused for the second election of 1910. He also censured the party's organisational arrangements for not matching either in efficiency or enthusiasm those of its press auxiliaries. Arnold White, as became his more humble position in the world of journalism, confined his complaints to his private correspondence with a friend. He did not think that the party mandarins sufficiently appreciated the efforts of R. D. Blumenfeld and the *Daily Express* – 'the only Tory paper that is read by working men'.[12] W. T. Stead asserted that the journalist's task was to act as society's watchdog. This implied a degree of independence of judgment that his colleagues were quick to agree with and applaud, forgetting that a dog is wise not to bite the hand that feeds it. However, only occasionally were the elaborate rules governing loyalty between a group of politicians and their press acolytes overtly sundered. A lack of ambition, frustration combined with outrage, insensitivity or simple stupidity were the usual reasons for a politician breaking the rules. Similarly, a small journal with a particular and loyal clientele could afford to be careless of the conventions and proprieties. But the time and the targets were carefully chosen, even by someone like Leo Maxse. The monthly *World* was once unkind enough to print that 'Viscount Esher's claim to possess marvellous abilities' rested upon them being 'constantly ascribed to him by his many press friends'. This was hitting below the belt, a practice generally confined to the lucubrations of the German emperor.

Esher had a profound personal belief in the power of the press. His faith was not shaken by the *World*'s vulgar assertion. In February 1913[13] he suggested that the best way of solving the Irish question, which for so long had defeated the wit of men, was 'to concentrate the great power of the Amalgamated Press and the Harmsworth family upon upsetting the Government'. When writing to newspaper proprietors or editors to solicit their support, politicians always demonstrated a profound respect. Their correspondence displayed a careful deference and was often larded with hyperbole. Rosebery favoured a more restrained approach when he wrote to Strachey in 1905, 'The Spectator has often differed from me but that has all the more made me recognise the extraordinary weight of its influence.'[14] Such subtlety did not feature in Sandars's correspondence with Northcliffe. The press baron was assured that he enjoyed the respect and gratitude of all Tories, not least their leader, for the influence exerted on their behalf by the estimable *Daily Mail.* While a politician was free to attack the newspaper allies of his political opponents he would trespass at his peril upon the carefully cultivated susceptibilities of journalism's collective professional pride. Lloyd George earned himself a very bad press for daring to suggest that Strachey might have changed his opinions in order to boost the sales of the *Spectator*.[15]

Before the Great War, politicians generally behaved towards the press as though the necessary price they paid for public credibility was never to offend and at every opportunity to truckle to the 'fourth estate'. Such attitudes were naturally exaggerated the mightier and more powerful the press representative. Not until after the declaration of war did a major Tory politician attack Northcliffe in public. In November 1914 Strachey wrote to congratulate Edward Carson on his courage. 'You are the first public man who has ever dared to defy Northcliffe openly!!! Hitherto it has been abuse in private and flattery or silence in public.'[16]

No one believed more in the influence of the press than Northcliffe. He became increasingly convinced not only that he and his newspapers were better fitted to rule the country than a group of self-seeking politicians chosen by the vagaries of popular election, but that such a design was feasible. The major flaw in this scheme was his own manifest incapacity. Esher, in his first meeting with the Napoleon of Fleet Street, caught almost the exact measure of the man: 'clever, vain, not very intelligent about anything except organisation and money-making, yet full of aspirations for power'.[17] He might have added that Northcliffe could demonstrate amazing generosity, sentimentality and deviousness and that at heart he was a bully who lacked the moral courage to match his overweening ambition. On serious political issues Northcliffe again and again demonstrated that he did not possess the courage of his convictions. He complained of others 'licking Ministers' boots', of 'bowing down to officials . . . being too pliable'. He insisted to his editors that 'Newspapers are meant to publish news and not to please highly placed people,' but his own actions did not square with his instructions. If his opinions caused offence to someone when published and he was taxed about them face to face, he would bluster and equivocate or more usually blame another for misrepresenting him. 'If he had the courage of his opinions he would speak out,' Strachey claimed, 'but for some odd reason the last thing that this up-to-date journalist likes to do is to give a strong lead on his own account. He is always looking for somebody else to take the responsibility.'[18]

This was undoubtedly a true charge, so why should the Radicals have chosen Northcliffe as their particular *bête noir*? The reason is comparatively simple. Fond of assuming all the credit for a popular idea, in 1914 Northcliffe gladly assumed responsibility as the prime agent of Teutophobia and pre-war scare-mongering. To have been prescient about Germany's ambitions for world hegemony was creditworthy in 1914. Being Northcliffe he sought to take *all* the credit for himself and his newspapers. Circumstances favoured this outrageous exercise in self-conceit. For a few days before the outbreak of war, Northcliffe's greatest newspaper property, *The Times*, was watched with inordinate care and concern by men of all political persuasions. Its semi-official status was invariably enhanced and exaggerated at times of crisis. For a few days – more due to Steed's influence than Northcliffe's – it led the Tory side of Fleet Street against the neutralist Liberal press. Seeking excuses for the collapse of their own campaign for neutrality, the Radical press chose as its symbolic enemy *The Times*. In a sense this action was both censure and accolade. The censure was for betraying the supposed 'proper' duty of a newspaper – to inform objectively. The accolade was the assumption by one group of newspapers that another newspaper had the power to move the minds and shape the purposes of men. The true measure of press ability to influence events at that critical juncture was best represented by the fears of Steed that he and *The Times* were powerless, and Dawson's actions in seeking to divine the way matters would develop by keeping a careful watch upon and contact with two ministers – Churchill and Edward Grey. Spender was not trying to avoid his responsibilities but was making an honest estimate when he claimed that events in the last days of peace were 'beyond journalism'.

The scale and the success of Northcliffe's newspaper empire dwarfed that of contemporaries and this also made him a convenient symbol to represent the Tory press. The way in which Northcliffe constantly interfered with his editors' prerogatives, quite out-distancing similar efforts by other proprietors,[19] made it a kind of poetic justice that he should in the end have attracted most of the opprobrium of post-war Radical censure.[20] It is normally the editor's duty to make judgments on the wisdom or otherwise of the men, events and ideas that his paper comments upon, praises or derides. No one suffered more than Thomas Marlowe, editor of the *Daily Mail*, from Northcliffe's never requited itch to interfere as much with small as large issues. Northcliffe's relationship with Marlowe epitomised the revolution in the newspaper world that swung the balance of power from the editorial to the commercial side. At Carmelite House, Marlowe was constantly obliged to yield to the dictates of his 'Chief'. Among his journalist colleagues Marlowe was respected. It was supposed that because of the quiet masterfulness of his demeanour, he resisted Northcliffe's incursions. But Marlowe was, above all else, a prudent man. He knew that if he was to remain editor of the *Daily Mail* then he must constantly acknowledge Northcliffe's status as 'the supreme disposer of the paper's fortunes and reputation'. When he advertised his own opinions to Northcliffe it was always, in his own words, 'with great deference'.[21] Northcliffe required that all his editors should recognise their will was to be bent to his. Those who refused were either dismissed, like Garvin, or like Buckle, eventually broken by a policy of attrition. Although he was Northcliffe's own appointee as Buckle's successor, even Geoffrey Dawson eventually fell victim to the owner's uncontrolled megalomania.

This having been said, it would be wrong to suppose that Northcliffe's tyranny knew no curb. Inevitably the size and complexity of his newspaper empire imposed restrictions and presented peculiarly intractable problems from time to time. The status enjoyed by *The Times* as a national institution provided him with much credit, but also certain difficulties that could not always be resolved to his immediate satisfaction. He failed, for example, to bring that newspaper into line with his other properties during the July 1911 crisis over the House of Lords. 'A newspaper proprietor has difficulties which critics overlook,' wrote H. W. Wilson on that occasion, unavailingly attempting to defuse the wrath of his diehard, Tory friend, Leo Maxse.

On the Mail we have perforce at such a time to follow the policy of The Times, or at least, not diverge greatly from it. The Times had made up its mind to scuttle and we had to scuttle with it greatly to our chagrin. Otherwise Alfred would have been accused of sheer treachery. It could have been said that in one of his papers he counseled surrender . . . and that in the other he advises fight. Remembering the unjust manner in which he is attacked and blamed, I cannot find fault with him for deciding that both his papers should say the same thing . . . Alfred was against scuttle but The Times carried the day.[22]

As Northcliffe was the giant among Tory newspaper proprietors, so Garvin was the colossus of Tory editors and journalists. His genius as a publicist was freely recognised by his contemporaries of all political persuasions and cannot be doubted. Garvin was not only the most influential, he was the most partisan of Tory journalists. The ancient cross-bench traditions of the *Observer* did not survive a week of his dynamic editorship. On matters of defence he flew the national interest as the flag at the *Observer*'s masthead but it was a patent fabrication. It was conventional that every Tory publicist when addressing himself to military or naval affairs should dress his arguments in that convenient garb. Garvin's career before the war most clearly illustrates the intimate connection forged between party and press. It was perhaps as much a measure of Balfour's desperation about the divided forces of Toryism as Garvin's undoubted powers of persuasion, that a fundamentally decent if occasionally weak political leader adopted the editor's unscrupulous tactics in the first 1910 general election and was persuaded not to employ them a second time only after it had been demonstrated that a naval scare was unlikely to succeed in its purpose. This is not to say that Garvin's ploy failed altogether. On the contrary, the 1909 naval scare and the subsequent electioneering of 1910 indelibly printed on the minds of the British public a simple 'truth' that patriotic publicists had been pushing with limited success for years. Garvin succeeded in reducing the complex pattern of international relationships and rivalries to a single, simple thesis easily comprehended by the least sophisticated mind. First, that Germany's political aims and ambitions were incompatible with the future security of Britain and her empire. Second, that Germany's ambition was manifest in her naval challenge. Third, that only the British navy could frustrate Germany's design for world hegemony. Fourth, that *nothing* should ever be allowed to jeopardise British naval supremacy as it was the nation's sole worthwhile guarantee of security.

Garvin's success as a naval as opposed to party publicist (though the two functions were rarely mutually exclusive as the success of the 'We want eight and we won't wait' cry demonstrated at the Croydon by-election), owed as much to his close relationship with Admiral Fisher as to his skill as a journalist. While senior naval personnel sought to use the press for their own purposes, none compared with the scale and success of Jack Fisher's enterprise. The intrusion of his quarrel with Charlie Beresford, the determination of the Senior Service to retain a monopoly over the nation's affections, the manner in which the pre-war navalist campaign was fought, as much in Westminster as in Fleet

Street, meant that in 1914, when the British fleet put out to sea to fight the Germans, it suffered from a number of grave material and strategic faults. The navy's vulnerability was neither properly recognised nor acknowledged until the shock of battle revealed it to a wondering, bemused public and professional gaze. Lest undue emphasis be placed upon the navalist press for this state of affairs it should be noted that successive First Lords of the Admiralty promoted an emphasis upon Dreadnoughts at the expense of other craft; that Radical reductionists in Parliament as much as their 'big navy' opponents conducted the debates on the estimates in terms of less or more capital ships; that at different times politicians of both parties encouraged an unwarranted independence of political control in the navy; that strategy was rarely if ever discussed outside specialist Service journals. If part of the success of the eight Dreadnought naval scare campaign in 1909 can be attributed to the navalist press and the Tories exaggerating public fears, it has to be remembered that the ultimate triumph of that campaign depended upon three key Liberal ministers – Asquith, Grey and McKenna. It was because they were persuaded of the reality of the danger, on the basis of information provided by their professional advisers, that the eight Dreadnoughts were built.

No one ever exceeded Fisher's ability at buttering press parsnips, but soldiers were as anxious as sailors to employ the influence of the press to their advantage. General Ian Hamilton when writing to St Loe Strachey was neither so impolitic nor insensitive to that power as to admit to 'feeling bored at receiving valuable assistance from a General like yourself who commands the minds and therefore the bodies of readers of at least, I suppose, the strength of a Division; perhaps, for all I know, the strength of an Army Corps'.[23] To J. E. B. Seely, Hamilton suggested the main reason for the failure of the Territorial Force was because Northcliffe had so often represented it as a 'farce'. Hamilton, Roberts, Wilson, Nicholson – like Wolseley before them – never questioned the influence the press exercised, and, like their naval counterparts, never doubted the advantage to be gained from ready, familiar and sympathetic access to their Fleet Street auxiliaries.

If, like party politicians, Senior Service personnel did not question the value of the press to achieve the ends they sought, the 'official' attitude adopted by the various departments of state was reluctant and disapproving of this unhealthy disposition to involve the 'fourth estate'. The disapproval was based upon the engrained prejudice that the art of government was a mystery whose secrets were best understood by experts and that its smooth processes were not matters suitable for discussion and debate in newspapers. If the newspapers had to be involved in the process at all, then the information supplied to them should be limited and distributed only through officially approved channels. The War Office and Admiralty shared this prejudice and were particularly concerned about the indiscretions of Service personnel, leaking information, subsequently blazoned in the press, that could be useful to a potential enemy. Their paranoia on this score was accurately reflected in their stupidly restrictive treatment of war correspondents. The unnecessary restrictions they sought to place upon journalists only promoted a determination to thwart the system. For years, the Committee of Imperial Defence sought a voluntary agreement with the press

– the precursor of the 'D Notice' system – which amounted to the journalists agreeing that they would print nothing 'in time of emergency or war' that had not been officially approved. The Official Secrets Act of 1911, and the way in which that statute was subsequently employed and interpreted, accurately reflected what was and has remained the suspicious and disapproving official attitude of governments of every political persuasion towards the press. George Clarke, who as an ex-journalist and also former secretary of the CID was well placed to make an objective assessment, described these attitudes as 'unnecessarily secretive . . . stupid and impolitic. When hard up they try to use the press. Ordinarily they try to keep you at a distance and wrap themselves in a cloud of silly mystery.' Any information, even the most innocuous, unless supplied through the regulation, official peep-holes was thought of as 'contraband'. As Clarke told Chirol, a well-disposed and cooperative press would have been an enormous advantage to any government, but officials persisted in their unnecessary alienation of a potential ally by maintaining a stubborn silence when it would have been better had 'the accredited representatives of the press [been told] frankly all that can be made public. Most things can.'[24] Government departments wanted their relationship with the press to be that of patron and client. Further, they supposed that any patronage they afforded implied an obligation by the press to accept it in a spirit of uncritical servility.

Relations between the Foreign Office and the press demonstrate the tensions and the misrepresentations that could arise as a consequence of these attitudes. The disposition of the Foreign Office was crucial because its professional concern was with relations between the Powers and its policy decisions implied certain strategic responses and material requests by the War Office and Admiralty. Further, it was claimed by Radical critics not only that Grey was unduly influenced by his permanent officials but that they surreptitiously encouraged the jaundiced view of Germany provided by the patriotic press.

Although there was no formal, institutionalised contact between the Foreign Office and the press – a press bureau – Foreign Secretaries, just like other politicians and their permanent officials, whatever was said to the contrary in public, never despised the usefulness of the press. On an individual basis, by letter, conversation, interview or calculated leak, contacts with journalists were primed and maintained with the clear intention of creating a particular appreciation of policy either by a foreign Power or the public. Kennedy Jones claimed that the Fashoda incident in the autumn of 1898 'marked the breaking down of the barriers of Downing Street'. This was an exaggerated estimate of Sanderson's interpretation of an initiative first suggested by Bertie to Salisbury, that there ought to be a degree of formalisation of contacts between the Foreign Office and the press to replace the existing chaos.[25]

Just as in other departments of state, the Foreign Office kept an official list of newspapers. To these, diplomatic intelligence was regularly circulated. From time to time, certain newspapers were temporarily excluded as a punishment for fancied or real breaches of confidence or etiquette. By a 'gentleman's agreement', some newspapers enjoyed favoured access to highly placed Foreign Office personnel, even to the Foreign Secretary himself. Such arrangements were either the accidents of history or more usually reflected personal friendships between individuals. As an example of the latter, Mudford and Austin enjoyed privileged access to Salisbury and Iwan Müller to Balfour. Mackenzie Wallace and Chirol, both former members of the service, were frequent visitors to the Foreign Office. Though Wallace was close to Salisbury, the premier and Foreign Secretary distrusted Chirol as he did Moberly Bell. Because it was known to be constantly in touch with the Foreign Office, *The Times* enjoyed a semi-official status in the eyes of foreign Powers. They always tended to exaggerate the intimacy of the connection because they underestimated the independence of *The Times* personnel, particularly Chirol. Similar status, at various times, for different, usually mistaken reasons, the Germans afforded other British papers. *The Standard,* for example, retained that distinction long after Salisbury had left the Foreign Office and Mudford had retired. With better reason, during Grey's tenure of office, the editorial opinion of the *Westminster Gazette* on foreign affairs was noted carefully. J. A. Spender was known to be a close and valued friend of the Foreign Secretary.

The special status afforded *The Times* never implied to its staff that their newspaper should be the compliant mouthpiece of official policy. Though politically sympathetic to the Unionists, *The Times* was both closer to and less critical of Grey than his immediate Tory predecessors in office. For a number of reasons they shared Grey's distrust of German intentions, and like him, advocated adherence to the theory of the Balance of Power as the best guarantee of European peace. This coincidence of disposition between them was strengthened by the dominance of the 'Europeanist' over the 'imperialist' faction at *The Times* which was, if anything, stronger under Northcliffe's proprietorship than Walter's.

The Times possessed an unrivalled team of foreign correspondents and provided a more extensive and detailed coverage of foreign affairs than any other newspaper. Its foreign correspondents were not distinguished from those of other British newspapers by the sources of their information. As Steed told Moberly Bell, in Vienna, 'four correspondents have arrangements with *Tageblatt,*[26] three with members of the *Neue Freie Presse* staff, some with both.' It was almost impossible for a correspondent to divulge exclusive news without betraying the confidence of his source. Another problem with confidential news was that the correspondent was generally bound to secrecy until it became public property. Steed concluded, 'The chief difference between the value of one correspondent and another nowadays lies in the degree of culture, experience, coup d'oeil and in power of literary presentation of facts within the reach of all.'[27]

In an earlier letter to Bell, Steed emphasised one other important consideration. 'If foreign correspondents were condemned to please everybody then the paper would soon cease to be worth reading.'[28] In the two decades before the Great War, if *The Times*'s sense of independence was an occasional irritant to the British Foreign Office, the newspaper's foreign correspondents were a frequent source of frustration and anger to foreign Powers. At different times Lavino suffered attacks from the French, German and Italian press, all 'inspired' by their governments. Saunders and Chirol, as *The Times*'s Berlin correspondents, were frequently vilified in the 'kept' German press. Saunders, even in Paris, was subject to the inspired barbs of André Tardieu in *Le Temps*. Morrison, during his career, was expelled from Peking, loathed by the Russians, despised by the Germans, vilified by the Italians, and, like Saunders, served a term as Tardieu's victim. Hubbard was denounced by the Italians as Italy's enemy and a clerical intriguer. Bourchier, for his criticism of the Greeks, was credited with single-handed having turned them into Britain's bitterest enemies. Braham was expelled from St Petersburg while Steed was denounced by the Hungarians, thoroughly distrusted by the Germans, his books banned by the Austrians and he was traduced on different occasions by almost everyone.

The Times was generally assumed to be a powerful ally and a dangerous enemy. Relations with the Foreign Office were sometimes difficult, but the peccadilloes and tantrums were accepted not least because the Foreign Office recognised the value of *The Times*'s foreign news and comment. Ambassadors frequently culled most of the information for their reports from *The Times*'s local representative. The opinions of men like Saunders, Wallace, Harris and Steed were always worth careful weighing for, as Curzon once admitted about G. E. Morrison, because of their special knowledge, *The Times*'s foreign correspondents were often able to anticipate facts before they occurred.[29]

On the subject of Anglo-German relations, while Lascelles constantly bewailed the damage done by the 'patriotic fire-eaters' in the press, Charles Hardinge, Arthur Nicolson, Cecil Spring Rice, and Grey's secretary, Willie Tyrrell, maintained and cultivated their contacts with a group of journalists who were foremost in advertising their suspicions of Germany. These embraced not only friends that worked for *The Times*, but owners and editors like Maxse, Strachey, Prothero and Gwynne. Eyre Crowe was the one important permanent official at the Foreign Office who disdained currying the affections of British journalists. He was scathingly dismissive of the idea that they could exercise any material influence on the conduct of foreign affairs. Even on the Venezuelan and Baghdad Railway crises, Crowe was not inclined to give much credit to the press campaign initiated and orchestrated by Maxse and Strachey that had frustrated Lansdowne's declared policy. Despite Crowe's disclaimer, these two incidents clearly demonstrated the capacity of the press to create pressures that, at the least, could be said to complicate the diplomatic process.

The official attitude of the Foreign Office to the press was an amalgam of three disparate considerations; its particular conception of what exactly 'public opinion' was, its perception that diplomacy was the exclusive concern of experts, and its uncomfortable awareness that new-fangled democratic notions could not altogether be resisted. The particular circumstances surrounding the conduct of foreign affairs strengthened the official predilection to hide as much as possible from ill-informed prying eyes, not only those of journalists ostensibly acting on behalf of the public, but also politicians. The need for secrecy could conveniently be extolled and emphasised on the grounds of national interest and security. Further, even if the public, press and politicians could not altogether be excluded from discussing the diplomatic process, at least their function was carefully delineated as essentially negative. Their task was to respond by praise or blame to the initiatives of the professionals. Frontbench spokesmen of both major political parties constantly emphasised that foreign policy was a national and not a party concern – a view opposed only by those Radicals who denied the validity of the concept of 'continuity' in the conduct of foreign affairs. Critical comment was therefore further distanced and muted than it might otherwise have been, both at Westminster and in Fleet Street.

It was only *after* the war that Grey became an enthusiastic convert and advocate of the idea that public opinion should be educated on the subject of foreign affairs. He designated the press as the most suitable instrument. In office he had often been before his permanent officials in wishing to stifle any kind of debate both in Parliament and the press. He successfully negotiated the hurdle of changes in parliamentary procedure designed to make the Foreign Secretary more accountable to the House.[30] His disposition to limit any discussion of foreign affairs to a small, intimate coterie of experts was reinforced by a distinction that by the turn of the century had clearly emerged in Fleet Street between 'serious' newspapers which catered for an informed educated minority, and 'popular' newspapers primarily designed to entertain the rest of the reading population. *The Times*, as the leading 'serious' newspaper, had a circulation for most of the years before the war of about 40,000. Small as this was, a much smaller, exclusive group formed its opinions on the conduct of Britain's foreign affairs by reference to that newspaper's detailed reports and analyses. These reports were designed to be read and understood only by those familiar with the language and technicalities of professional diplomacy. In the popular dailies, readers were not provided with detailed information and analysis but were given instead a set of general assumptions which, by constant reiteration, became elevated to the status of unquestioned truths.

Reiterated general assumptions are ideally suited to create and reinforce a public mood or disposition. While Grey slated his Radical parliamentary and press critics, he made no effort to emancipate them from their assumed ignorance either by education – his post-war panacea - or by making his conduct of foreign affairs more accessible by providing better information than that supplied in Blue Books,[31] or by explaining himself more frequently either in the country or at Westminster. He denigrated his Radical critics as the promoters of simplistic solutions for complex problems, emotional dram-drinkers, and ill-informed sentimentalists prone to gush. The Radical critique of Grey was, on the contrary, based upon a sound if different ideological perception of what *ought* to constitute a Liberal foreign policy. It espoused the Concert of Europe rather than the equilibrium or the Balance of Power, disarmament instead of increasing armaments, publicity instead of secrecy, arbitration instead of war. Perhaps more significantly, while Grey savaged critics within his own party as simpletons, he rarely challenged the prejudices that informed so much of the support given him by the popular, patriotic press.

Like his Tory predecessors and his permanent officials, Grey, whenever he deployed the notion of public opinion professionally, did so as a useful prayer in aid to be wheeled out at convenient times to serve his own purposes. He used it, for example, to fend off the impatient, inconvenient importuning of Cambon, the French Ambassador. Similarly, in the last week of the final crisis, Nicolson wrote to the British Ambassador in St Petersburg that 'No

Government practically can take any decided line without feeling that public opinion amply supports them.' He then added, 'The tone of our press . . . has come around to the fact that it would be difficult, if not impossible, for us to stand outside a general European conflagration.'[32] Nicolson's can only be described as a very particular view of public opinion as it was of the British press. What he described to Buchanan as 'the voice of public opinion' was those Tory newspapers who were following a lead given by *The Times*. He entirely ignored most of the Liberal press which was demanding British neutrality.

Nicolson's letter had been written in response to two earlier messages from the Ambassador to Grey which asserted that German embassy officials in St Petersburg were seeking to persuade the Russian foreign office that Britain would remain neutral in a European war because 'with the exception of *The Times* nearly the whole English press was on the side of Austria'. The Germans were also plausibly suggesting, given that Britain had a Liberal government, that 'opinions in certain Liberal papers represented the view of HMG and of British public opinion'.[33] Thus, in the last ten days of peace, both German and British Foreign Office personnel were quoting selectively from the British press to support their own particular view of the British government's likely response to public opinion.

In part because of its own tradition of a 'kept' press, the Wilhelmstrasse constantly exaggerated the British government's influence over British newspapers. Frequent disavowals on the part of the British government did not change this disposition. The importance that the Wilhelmstrasse attached to newspapers is confirmed by its attempts over many years, by direct and indirect means, to influence the proprietors, editors and journalists of British newspapers. Its avowed intention was to influence public opinion and thus bring pressure to bear upon the British government. The last campaign of this kind by the German and Austrian embassies in London and by the Rothschilds and Ballin was orchestrated and inspired by Berlin. Just as with most of its earlier efforts, most notably by Bülow's agent, Bernstorff, the campaign ended in failure although initially there was some degree of success in getting pro-Austrian leaders published in both *The Times* and the *Westminster Gazette*. British journalists were inclined to take the threat of German interference more seriously than the Foreign Office. Thus the appointment of Marschall as Ambassador to the Court of St James caused enormous consternation at Printing House Square when it was recalled how successful he had been in manipulating the press during The Hague Peace Conference in 1907.

The Kaiser and some German diplomats shared a delusion that Russian agents were an active element in determining the anti-German tone of certain British journals. Some of Garvin's pro-entente, anti-German polemical squibs, under a variety of pseudonyms, were ascribed to the pens of Russians. Strachey was for long embarrassed by the widespread but incorrect rumour that his campaign against the Baghdad Railway scheme was prompted by the Russians, even that the *Spectator* was owned by the Russian government. Similarly, the Wilhelmstrasse's 'kept' press frequently asserted that Printing House Square was the international centre of a Russo-Franco-British press conspiracy against

Germany. Such thoughts were the product of febrile imaginations, an over-fondness for conspiracy theories and the Kaiser's persecution mania. Russian agents were certainly active in the French press, but so also were the Germans who kept a number of distinguished correspondents in their pay.

The Quai d'Orsay, by leaking advanced information to certain journalists, sought to employ British newspapers to exert pressure upon Westminster. Thus *The Times* was given a detailed list of German military concentrations upon the French frontier in excess of French defensive preparations. The list was published the next day with the clear implication that Germany intended to cross the frontier with her armies. But the compliance of *The Times* did not have to be won either by bribery or subterfuge. Printing House Square was every bit as anxious as the Quai d'Orsay to secure a positive response from the British government, an acknowledgment of its 'duty' as much as the need to give military as well as diplomatic support to its entente partner.

It is clear that the assumption that the press could influence public opinion was held not merely by journalists but also by the politicians, government officials and Service personnel of every major European country. Similarly it is apparent that what was supposed to constitute public opinion depended upon who was defining the term and for what purpose. Both formal and informal arrangements between the press and various governmental agencies and individuals were designed to deploy the influence of the press to the advantage of the different parties engaged in the exercise. A convenient single issue large enough for it to be possible to test the assumption and examine the methods employed by the patriotic press is the question of invasion.

'For the pre-war generation, the possibility of invasion was nothing less than a national obsession.'[34] Interest in the subject was not confined merely to Service experts or to the narrow coterie of the British governing elite. It became the catalyst of the activities and interests of many groups: naval and military staff, supporters of the voluntary principle and conscriptionists, the leaders and backbenchers of the major political parties, the Committee of Imperial Defence, War Office, Foreign Office and Admiralty officials, and publicists from every kind of newspaper and specialist journal. It is one of the very few clear examples of an issue where official policy makers undoubtedly responded to public pressure. There is a direct correlation between public scares and subsequent exhaustive government inquiries.[35]

On the subject of invasion there was a considerable degree of agreement between the Liberal and Unionist leadership at Westminster. This was reflected in cross-party support for the 'blue water' theory and personified by Balfour maintaining an important and influential voice in the CID during the years of Liberal rule. Consequently, the advocates of the 'bolt from the blue' theory were obliged to plan, and to a large extent conduct their campaigns outside Westminster. As they had easy and privileged access to the press they sought to attract interest, stimulate support and gain influence for their ideas through that agency. A sufficient public brouhaha would lead to discussion and debate in Parliament and subsequent government inquiry. Most 'patriotic' editors, owners and journalists fought on the side of the invasionists. Without wishing to detract from the direct pressure that could be exerted through personal contacts and friendships by editor owners like Leo Maxse and St Loe Strachey, undoubtedly the leading press advocate of the 'bolt from the blue' theory was Charles à Court Repington. This claim does not rest simply upon Repington's known close relationship with Haldane, his contacts at the War Office, his deep knowledge of all aspects of defence and strategic policy, or the excellence and persuasiveness of his writing on the subject of invasion which was invariably detailed and informed. Repington's campaigns not only prompted debate at Westminster and detailed examination by the CID, but also lengthy and contentious exchanges of correspondence in *The Times* which confirmed that newspaper's claim to be the primary platform for the informed public debate of the invasion issue.

It is true that the same debate also featured in the popular half-penny dailies before a larger if certainly less well-informed audience. Northcliffe's *Daily Mail* publicised the invasion issue, on occasion *ad nauseam*, but there was a distinct difference of purpose and method that divided Repington and Northcliffe. This can be illustrated by an exchange of letters between the two men in August 1913. Northcliffe demanded that the military correspondent should provide more 'indiscretions' in his writing. He made the usual obligatory reference to Delane and talked of 'pride and priority' but Repington recognised the proprietor's real intent.

> It has been my practice hitherto to reserve indiscretions for important occasions. . . . However, I am sending a batch of indiscretions to Freeman tonight to meet your wishes. Personally I consider that the chief value of your military correspondent lies in expert criticism of home and foreign military affairs and not in the divulgation of secrets which infuriates the authorities and especially the Crown.[36]

Northcliffe wanted news that attracted the attention of his readers. That was a commercial necessity because more interested readers meant more advertising revenue. He did recognise, on national as opposed to private criteria, the need to create a public opinion to exert pressure upon the politicians that would insure Britain's safety. He did not doubt that invasion was a serious topic worthy of his newspapers' attentions. Nevertheless, news and views should be presented in such a way as to stimulate and sustain interest primarily in the newspaper. Opinion making and winning were important, but first and last Northcliffe's major preoccupation was improving circulation figures. A very good example of this was the way that he exploited Le Queux's story, *The Invasion of 1910*, to boost interest in the *Daily Mail*. Repington never despised the power of money, but as a journalist he was committed to a conception of himself as the instructor of a critical and intelligent readership, one who deployed his specialist knowledge in a detailed examination of those complex strategic and logistic naval and military problems that had to be resolved if the nation was to secure its future safety. The Radicals hated the man they called 'the gorgeous Wreckington', but his philosophy as a journalist was very much in the Liberal tradition. He, after all, began his regular journalistic career on Spender's *Westminster,* and even after the Kaiser/Tweedmouth incident, retained that editor's grudging respect.

Life was never easy for Repington. Until the summer of 1912, he was almost permanently at odds with his editor and had to overcome the influence at Printing House Square of 'blue water' advocates like Capper and Thursfield whose Admiralty-inspired strategic views dominated thinking at *The Times*. His credit with Buckle and Moberly Bell was constantly undermined by Valentine Chirol whose own animosity and distrust was fuelled by the jealous and spiteful insinuations of George Clarke. So long as Jack Fisher ruled the roost, the Admiralty harboured Repington's most bitter and vengeful foe. The First Sea Lord, immensely powerful and influential, autocratic, departmentally myopic, his love for the navy inspired and sustained as much by his contempt for the army as anything else, viewed Repington's activities – whether or not in tandem with Charlie Beresford – as a direct threat to the Senior Service. Repington was a dangerous apostate, a Judas who had sold himself to the 'bolt from the blue' school for Haldane's thirty pieces of War Office silver. Sir John loathed Repington because he supposed he sought to destroy him and the navy. The two were, in Fisher's mind, inseparable.

At the War Office, things were only marginally better for Repington than at the Admiralty. There he had as many enemies as friends. Most notable among his military foes was the influential General Henry Wilson. His enmity was inspired by envy, personal ill-will and jealousy. Repington's support of Haldane was as much a source of criticism and animosity as it was of strength and influence. Because he refused to join forces with that minister's critics whose campaign was inspired by personal spite, party jealousy and ill-judged and ill-informed contempt for the Territorial Force, Repington was sometimes opposed by those who otherwise would have been his allies. To add to these difficulties, a great snob himself he was frequently the victim of the same miserable prejudice.

Despite formidable odds, Repington fought a brave and constant campaign in support of Haldane whom he correctly discerned was much the most able, thoughtful and unprejudiced as he was the most maligned Minister for War. Repington supported the Committee of Imperial Defence even though many of his friends despised it as anti-constitutional, cutting as it did across departments and concentrating power in the hands of the Prime Minister. He pleaded for inter-Service cooperation in strategic planning, sought to curb the dangerous independence of the Admiralty, questioned Fisher's too-great reliance upon the Dreadnought, revealed the First Sea Lord's limitations as a strategist, supported conscription and questioned, criticised and saw the overthrow of the dominant 'blue water' theorists. Paradoxically, as his hand was strengthened at *The Times* by Dawson's appointment as editor, so Repington's writing began to take on a more strident, less balanced, more partisan tone. Convinced of a plot by the Radicals where earlier he would have dismissed them as an impotent political force, and with his vanity undoubtedly tickled by Bonar Law's apparent conversion to his views, Repington's sectarian prejudices intensified. His loathing of Radical politicians began to assume the same paranoid proportions one associates with Leo Maxse. His 1913 campaign with Dawson for conscription, begun on a lofty, supra-party note, degenerated into a sectarian squawk.

Did Repington's work on invasion have any substantive effect? By 1914, the Admiralty and the War Office had completely reversed their thinking on the subject. In part, this can be explained by the failure of the 1912 and 1913 naval manoeuvres, Churchill's open-mindedness, the General Staff's commitment to a continental strategy which they assumed had been accepted after the extraordinary CID meeting in August 1911, and their wish to despatch all divisions of the Expeditionary Force to France at the outbreak of hostilities. Though all these factors were undoubtedly important it remains that the questioning and final overthrow of the previously unchallenged orthodoxy of the 'blue water' strategists owed much to the efforts of Repington and his fellow 'bolt from the blue' campaigners.

The invasion scares were quoted by Radicals as classic examples of scare-mongering,[37] yet Repington's usual *modus operandi* – the making of a case by the assiduous collection of data – plus his belief in his role as an educator of opinion, would not seem to be the attributes usually associated with scaremongering. He did, however descend to that ploy when he sought to manipulate the Kaiser's indiscreet letter to Tweedmouth. This was a last, desperate but calculated throw when the tide of official opinion seemed to have set against the invasionist case in the CID. Repington was supported in the Tory press only by Maxse. The intention had been to create a public furore which the malleable politicians could not ignore. It failed, not so much from lack of publicity but because the Tory leadership at Westminster did not choose to avail themselves of the opportunity Repington had given them to exploit. Within a few months the 'blue water' men at *The Times* were once more firmly in the saddle and Repington had to begin his fight all over again. The crucial feature to recognise in this failure of Repington's scaremongering was his inability to win the overt support of the politicians. The success or failure of a scaremong-ering campaign whether it concerned the army, navy or Anglo-German relations depended on its premises being adopted or exploited by politicians.

If we examine the classic pre-war scares of Radical mythology this pattern becomes apparent. In the comparatively minor Casablanca incident of the autumn of 1908, Grey supposed England to be on the verge of war yet he never wavered in his determination that Britain would support France against Germany.[38] Had they known this at the time, the majority of Grey's party would have been horrified. Grey was supported by the Prime Minister, the Minister for War and the First Lord of the Admiralty. The most morbidly rabid Teutophobe publicist could not have faulted the attitude of these key *Liberal* ministers. During the Agadir crisis, Grey, supported somewhat incon-gruously by Churchill and more importantly by Lloyd George, former Radical champions, took the German threat seriously enough to deploy the Mansion House speech as a public, contingent declaration of war. In the final crisis of 1914, Grey, supported eventually by almost the whole Liberal Cabinet, never doubted that Britain should honour her entente commitment. The invasion of Belgium merely obscures the issue, for once more the key Cabinet ministers had already made up their minds to support France. The strategic disposition of the British navy in advance of the ultimatum to Germany confirms this. Britain's diplomatic 'free hand' was not abandoned in response to the pleas of the jingo press – it had long been a fiction to placate Radical Liberal sensibilities. Thus, if the patriotic press thought they were influencing the key ministers in the Liberal Administration they were entirely mistaken because they were pushing against a door that was not only unbarred but flung wide open. The 1909 naval scare succeeded because the majority of the Liberal Cabinet were convinced eight Dreadnoughts were required and, however reluctantly, the minority opposed to building eight acquiesced in this decision. The invasion scare succeeded only in so far as the arguments used by the invasionist lobby were accepted by the appropriate ministers not as jingo fictions and febrile exaggerations but as hard facts that had to be recognised. Even the often absurd associated spy and sabotage scare was accepted and acted upon by government, not merely because of the efforts of wild polemicists in the press but because it had been a subject of government inquiry for a number of years and the Admiralty, War Office and Foreign Office believed in it.

Perhaps even more clearly than the apparent 'successes' of scaremongering campaigns, a failure illustrates the powerlessness of the patriotic press when not afforded the support of politicians at Westminster. The campaign for conscription, although waged with enthusiasm and enormous energy over a decade, failed hopelessly. Its success could have been assured in peacetime only if the Tory party in Parliament had accepted it as a plank in their electoral programme and demonstrated that it was not a vote loser. Balfour rejected it out of hand; Bonar Law was personally convinced of the need for conscription but like most of the party mandarins was not prepared to put the issue to the test. The fact that conscription formed part of a possible coalition programme indicates that in pre-war Britain the prejudice could only be overcome if the traditional mould of politics was shattered.

The Radical Liberals, most of whom by 1920 had joined the Labour party, developed a more than somewhat ambiguous attitude towards the senior ministers in pre-war Liberal administrations and admitted, more or less reluctantly, that perhaps, all along, they had been duped. But if it was conceded that certain Liberal ministers had sold the pass, it could not be doubted that they had been encouraged in their infamy by the pre-war 'militarisation of the nation'. Conveniently forgetting their own voluntarist campaigns they cited as evidence to support this claim the campaign for conscription, the birth of the boy scout movement and other 'para-military' youth organisations, and the high hopes and dreams of glory of those who volunteered to go to France, best represented in the poetry of Rupert Brooke. A recent detailed study of Edwardian militarism concludes,

> The verdict on Edwardian militarism must be a mixed one. . . . It is
> perfectly true that the New Army's 'spring-tide of faith and joyous
> illusion' had its roots in pre-war Britain, but the outbreak of war triggered
> latent emotions which had not dominated that society. . . . There had been
> important counter voices to the exhortations of the patriotic militarists and
> a considerable reaction from the business and commercial classes and from
> Radicals and Labour MP's. Only some sections of the working class were

affected by new patriotic slogans and the cult of the rifle; the majority remained apathetic if not hostile.[39]

Until the second year of the war, the nation in arms remained the unrealised dream of Tory publicists, professional soldiers, poetic visionaries like Kipling who had written in 1904 of *The Army of a Dream*, a few academics like Professor Cramb of King's College, London,[40] the warriors of the National Service League led by their venerable President, Lord Roberts, and some maverick, disowned socialists like Hyndman and Blatchford. The general sentiment of the British public towards the army and the profession of arms, for all the beating of the patriotic drum, had changed little from that expressed by Mrs Robertson when she learned that her beloved only son had gone to be a soldier. 'The Army is a refuge for all Idle people,' she wrote in obvious anguish and bemusement. 'I shall name it to no one for I am ashamed to think of it. . . . I would rather Bury you than see you in a red-coat.'[41] The recipient of this letter was appointed Chief of the Imperial General Staff in January 1916. The only Field Marshall in the British Army to rise from the ranks, Willie Robertson was the exception that proves the rule!

The Radical indictment against the scaremongers of the patriotic press begins to appear more and more fragile until we look again at what the publicists actually wrote, puffed up as it undoubtedly was with bold belligerency and reckless intransigence. Nevertheless, before the war, much of the patriotic ranting of the warriors of Fleet Street was a mere façade behind which lurked a fatalistic pessimism that the authors carefully kept for their private converse and letters. Their public nationalism and jingoism appeared to reflect an aggressive offensive spirit, but it was most often inspired by fear: fear that the country's leaders were effete, fear that the country's institutions were inefficient, fear that politicians were corrupt and self-seeking, fear that the country had lost its sense of greatness and purpose, fear that the middle classes were declining having been persuaded to adopt the unnatural practice of contraception, fear that the working classes were physically degenerate. Patriotic publicists took an inordinate interest in military and naval affairs because they were all too aware that the Boer War, like an earlier, more famous engagement, had been 'a damn close run thing'. If the army had stumbled before the challenge of a few recklessly bold farmers on the veldt, how much less likely was it to succeed in holding back the armed might of an efficient Germany? It was no accident that conscription was advertised by many for home defence; that Northcliffe's first action on 5 August 1914 was to insist that a sufficient force of regular troops should remain in Britain until all fear of invasion had disappeared; that the navalist demand for an ever-stronger navy was first and foremost to protect England's shores; that the constant argument to support France in arms against Germany, before honour, conscience or contractual obligation, was self-interest. These patriots saw a British army fighting on the Marne with the French as not so much defending Paris as London and the future existence of the British Empire. Behind the deliberately bold and defiant assertions of jingo braggadocio lurked the constant fear that Britain and her empire were dreadfully vulnerable to an aggressive and determined enemy. These fears, widespread in the jingo camp before January 1906, after the Liberal electoral victory intensified. 'Either the country must destroy the Asquith Government, or the Asquith Government will destroy the country,' Maxse trumpeted in the July 1914 issue of *National Review*. Yet it was not 'Boozle' and his fellow ministers that Maxse and his friends feared so much as the pernicious influence of the Radicals in the Liberal camp. They, as much as Germany, were Britain's enemy. Beware the enemy within the citadel, the Radical Right exhorted the public, for they are dedicated to undermine the spirit and the preparedness of the nation with their foul litany of 'Peace, Retrenchment and Reform'.

People invariably seek to increase the stature of the evil that they wish to denigrate and stamp out. The Radical Liberals and the Radical Right both fell into this trap. Both were weaker and less influential than either could afford to admit for the sake of their own credibility. They took each other's rhetoric seriously because the major political objective of each was the destruction of the other. A brief examination of the strengths and weaknesses of the Radical Liberals will help to explain the true nature and rationale of much scaremongering by the Radical Right.

Before 1914, the Radicals provided the only coherent and consistent critique of the Liberal government's conduct of foreign, military and naval policy. After their apparently overwhelming electoral triumph in January 1906, the Radicals rapidly became an increasingly ineffectual political force at Westminster. John Morley recognised their fatal flaw. They were 'of all sorts of temperament . . . capable of agreeing on few things in concert . . . dissipating their energies upon any number of different projects'. To a determined, single-minded minister like Grey, they never presented a serious difficulty.[42] The Radical search for a leader to hide their crisis of identity and purpose was frustrated or disappointed. Death removed Campbell-Bannerman, vanity Morley, incompetence John Burns, while circumstance and personal ambition laid Lloyd George low. One lesson the Radicals took from this sad experience was that office corrupted idealism. The Radical Right agreed.

The Radicals wanted the Liberal government to walk in *their* ways. However, they could not afford to be seen too frequently demonstrating their dissatisfaction or disloyalty by pressing their disapproval of the Liberal leadership's conduct of foreign affairs. Domestic policy, which was always the Radical priority, was conducted much more acceptably. If by voting against their government it was defeated, the alternative was a Tory administration. If a misguided Liberal Cabinet sought to build too many Dreadnoughts or alienate Germany unnecessarily, the actions a Unionist government might propose did not bear contemplation. After the 1910 general elections, the Radical group in Parliament was smaller and its loyalty even more at a premium to defend the eroded government majority. The *Nation* recognised the Radicals' dilemma. 'When they go into the Government lobby to vote reluctantly on the handling of Anglo-German relations or the increase of armaments they are in fact voting for Free Trade, Home Rule and Social reform.'[43] In Parliament the Radicals were made impotent by their own innate failings and the operation of the two-party system to which they subscribed. The Radical Right would 'die in the ditch' to defend the anachronistic powers of the Lords, or arm revolutionaries in Ireland in the name of defending the constitution. The Radical Liberal disposition was to seek change by persuasion and resolution not revolution.[44]

Outside Westminster, Radical influence appeared immensely strong. Radical policies were advocated by publicists, theorists and apologists of the greatest distinction. A galaxy of literary luminaries in a plethora of quarterlies, monthlies, weeklies and dailies, persistently broadcast Radical nostrums for Britain's domestic and foreign ailments. But if the voice of Radicalism was loud in the land, it remained the voice of disagreement, the voice of a self-conscious minority that never doubted its influence or questioned its import-ance. Among the elite, Massingham's *Nation*, in 1910, designated Scott's *Manchester Guardian* 'the supreme voice of Radicalism'. Massingham also described Lancashire as 'the natural rallying ground of British democracy'. This judgment unconsciously confirmed that Radicalism was associated with an area whose influence was rapidly declining. A linotype operator on the *Guardian*, more accurately than Massingham, assessed the true position of the newspaper when he told his editor that it was an illusion to believe that it enjoyed much influence with the electorate. 'They do not read the *MG*.'[45]

The *Manchester Guardian*, like Radicalism, suffered from a crippling handicap – provincialism. The political influence of the great northern and midland cities was fatally undermined by the 1885 Redistribution Act. Thereafter, they never again spoke with the same weight and authority either in the country or at Westminster. The incubus of provincialism is clearly demonstrated by the emasculation of the National Liberal Federation's influence. The Radical press suffered a double blow because 'public opinion' increasingly became a synonym for 'metropolitan opinion'. The popular press revolution was born and based in London. Its products, rapidly and widely distributed by rail, reinforced and accelerated this tendency. These changes were not immediately apparent to contemporaries and, in any event, journalists were the least inclined to recog-nise any ailment, even in a rival newspaper, lest the infection spread. It was in the general interest of the press of whatever political complexion never to doubt its power to shape and direct opinion.

Because the Radical Liberals and their press shared a number of strengths and weaknesses with the Radical Right, that in part explains the virulence of their mutual antipathy. What passed for the Radical Right's perception of political realities embraced not only the most extraordinarily naive expectations – only matched by the Radical Liberals in the first flush of their electoral victory in January 1906 – but also diametrically opposed ideas. The first may be demonstrated by their hopelessly romanticised view that compulsory service would reveal the latent patriotism of the British worker and be the means of achieving national unity by breaking down social barriers. As an example of them holding opposed ideas, we might cite the different attitudes adopted to the prospect of coalition in 1910, or to a federalist solution of the Irish problem. Though most were fervent protectionists, not all were. The blatant contradictions in the thinking of the Radical Right suggest a need to modify the convenient but rather too neat categorisation of them before 1914 as a homogeneous, anti-modernist group.[46] Incoherences and contradictions in their thinking about domestic political issues could always be conveniently disguised by exaggerating the supposed baleful and ubiquitous influence of the Radicals with the Liberal Cabinet while at the same time emphasising the hostility that Ultras shared towards German ambitions. They submerged 'their own uncertainties about the sort of society they wished to construct in an emotional campaign against the enemy that threatened the Empire – the Germans and their dupes and sympathisers within Britain itself. The great triumph of the Diehards came in August 1914.'[47] Only after the war was it possible for the Radicals to seek to punish the Radical Right for that triumph. By then the scaremongers of the patriotic press had enjoyed a field day, and the Radicals had suffered far worse indignities at their hands than they had ever experienced before the war.

In the face of a national crisis, the Tory editors presumed that patriotism overbore the limits formerly imposed by the laws of libel. The poison of invective was not to be diluted by a too-scrupulous exactitude. Methods rehearsed before the war were now 'improved', made more damaging by innuendo, slander or malicious lie. When there were no dramatic, decisive British military victories, no latter-day Trafalgar as the mighty ironclads skulked in the mists of the North Sea and refused to come to blows, the British public sought suitable and convenient scapegoats for the war's unsatisfactory lack of progress. The easiest targets were delineated first; the barbarous behaviour of the Huns and the criminal nature of the Kaiser who deserved hanging for his infamy. Soon those who opposed the war in Britain were also seen as suitable victims for the lynch-mob mentality. Fear and uncertainty bred paranoia which the press fed and excited. Enemy agents were supposed to exist where in reality there were only hapless foreign refugees or Englishmen with foreign sounding names or appearance. 'Intern them all,' was the cry of the *Morning Post* and the public clamoured its agreement.

The pattern followed by the trumpet majors of the patriotic press in the first winter of the war was an exaggeration of behaviour that they had indulged in for almost two decades, as part of the domestic party political conflict. By the mid-1890s, the newly aggressive Unionism personified by Joseph Chamberlain and his press lieutenants,[48] in its struggle with the Liberals established as an accepted party tactic an appeal to the nationalism and patriotism of the newly enfranchised electorate. The 1900 'Khaki' election was a determined attempt not only to capture the patriotism of the electorate for the Tory party, but also to deride the patriotism and imperialist fervour of their political opponents. A popular and widespread piece of Unionist election propaganda was a poster with the legend, 'A vote [for the Liberal candidate] is a pat on the back for Kruger.'[49] Particularly in London, jingo prejudice was deliberately excited by the popular Tory press. Rowdies were successfully encouraged to break up Liberal meetings. When the base passions of the mob had not been worked upon in this fashion it was possible to hold anti-war meetings.[50] Exactly the same methods were repeated during the 1914–18 war with the *Daily Express* again in the van.[51] Where Blumenfeld and Arnold White led, Maxse, Gwynne, Bottomley and Cecil Chesterton were never far behind, insisting that any opposition to war was the work of 'German-loving', 'Treason mongers' and

'Traitors' who were being 'financed by German money'. Their campaign, which began with obvious targets like Ramsay MacDonald and Radical members of the Union of Democratic Control, like Ponsonby, Trevelyan and Morel, by degrees embraced first long-hated Liberal ministers like Haldane, and eventually the whole Liberal Cabinet.[52]

The Radicals had not been slow in recognising the effectiveness of the new Tory electoral method of attracting votes. In the 1906 general election the Tories were hoist in part by a version of the petard they had designed. 'Chinese slavery' was the Radical equivalent of Tory 'Khaki' tactics. Garvin, unconscious of the irony of his words, complained bitterly in *Outlook* about the 'triumph of yellow politics'. The lesson of 1906 was not forgotten. By late 1909, Garvin effectively was dictating Tory party propaganda and publicity as the electorate prepared for a year of elections. Garvin sought to counter the 'Socialistic' appeal of Lloyd George's budget by a Tory appeal to patriotic sentiment. Garvin 'used' the navy by claiming the Liberal government had purposely jeopardised national security by eroding the British navy's numerical advantage in Dreadnoughts over the German navy, in order 'to provide doles and soup tickets for their supporters'.

In the last years before the outbreak of the Great War, scaremongering established itself as a significant weapon in the armoury of domestic political tactics. Warnings about Germany's political ambitions and warlike preparations were employed to demonstrate that in an increasingly hostile and dangerous world, the Asquith government – an administration in thrall to pacifists, Germanophiles, internationalists, Radicals, socialists and other assorted unpatriotic cranks – was incapable of securing the future best interests of the nation and its empire. The political style of the Radical Right's wildest publicists embracing the intransigence of the diehard, the energy and blind enthusiasms of the Ultra, the xenophobia and the reckless rhetoric of the super-patriot, was annexed to serve the ambitions and hopes of the whole Tory party. It was sincerely believed that there was no better way to frustrate the knavish schemes of the Kaiser's Germany. But far from incidentally, it was also designed to encompass the downfall and destruction of the Liberal government.

Sources and notes

Prologue

1 W. M. Pope, *Twenty Shilling in the Pound* (London, 1948), p. 398.
2 H. Fyfe, *The Making of an Optimist* (London, 1921), pp. 27–8.
3 See *Labour Leader*, 30 July and 6 August 1914.
4 *Nation*, 'The war of fear', 8 August 1914.
5 *New Age*, 13 August 1914.
6 Balfour's description of Grey's Radical and Labour critics after the Foreign Secretary's 3 August 1914 speech. See *Hansard*, v:65:1810–84 for complete debate.
7 See on treatment of anti-war critics, Keith Robbins, *The Abolition of War* (Cardiff, 1976); M. Ceadel, *Pacifism in Britain, 1914–45* (Oxford, 1980), Part I; Catherine Cline, *E. D. Morel* (Belfast, 1980), ch. VII; M. Swartz, *The Union of Democratic Control* (Oxford, 1971), ch. 6; A. J. A. Morris, *C. P. Trevelyan: Portrait of a Radical* (Belfast, 1977), ch. 7.
8 The quotations are taken from J. A. Farrer, *England Under Edward VII* (London, 1913), pp. 104 and 187–9; N. Angell, *The Public Mind* (London, 1927), p. 162; Caroline Playne, *The Pre-War Mind in Britain* (London, 1928), p. 114ff.
9 *Concord*, vol. II, no. 2, February 1906, p. 27.
10 J. A. Spender, *Fifty Years of Europe* (London, 1930), p. 239.
11 Undated typescript, Carson MSS, D 1507/5/80.
12 Quoted in S. E. Koss, *Fleet Street Radical: A. G. Gardiner and the Daily News* (London, 1973), p. 160.
13 See Lovat Fraser to Northcliffe and Northcliffe to Fraser, 5 and 15 December 1914, Northcliffe Dep 4890/XCIX.
14 J. A. Spender, *Life, Journalism and Politics* (London, 1927), vol. II, p. 167.
15 Max Pemberton, *Northcliffe: A Memoir* (London, n.d.), p. 87.
16 See Chapter VII, below.
17 Northcliffe to Repington, 20 January 1916, Dep. 4890/CI.
18 J. L. Garvin to Northcliffe, 1 December 1906, *ibid./LXXXV.*
19 See E. T. Cook, *Delane of The Times* (London, 1915), pp. 69 and 262.
20 Northcliffe to Rosebery, 8 November 1898, Rosebery MS, 1011, ff. 129–30.
21 J. L. Garvin to Northcliffe, 20 August 1909, Dep. 4890/LXXXV.
22 A. P. Ryan, *Lord Northcliffe* (London, 1953), p. 103.
23 For the story of *Our German Cousins* and how Northcliffe turned it into a best-seller, see, Pound and Harmsworth, *Northcliffe* (London, 1959), pp. 389–90. See also Wile to Northcliffe, 6 and 13 January 1910 and 1 October 1912 (enclosing copy of Goldschmidt letter), Northcliffe Dep. 4890/LV.
   There is a complete collection of Wile's *Daily Mail* articles as Berlin correspondent in bound volumes in his papers. Even allowing for the interference of sub-editors, about which Wile constantly complained to Northcliffe, Wile's published

writings in the pre-war period are nothing like as anti-German in tone as he later suggested by his entry in *Who's Who*, and in his later books.

24 Tom Clarke, *Northcliffe in History* (London, 1950), p. 153.
25 Northcliffe, *The Rise of the Daily Mail* (London, 1916), pp. 33–4.
26 Memorandum dated 24 November 1899. Translated in E. T. S. Dugdale, *German Diplomatic Documents* (reprint, New York, 1969), vol. III, p. 114.

PART I: MAKING FRIENDS AND CHOOSING ENEMIES: THE DIPLOMATS

Chapter 1: The Kaiser sends a telegram and Chirol is aggrieved

1 Quoted in Zara Steiner, *Britain and the Origins of the First World War* (London, 1977), p. 23.
2 Quoted in C. H. D. Howard, *Splendid Isolation* (London, 1967), p. 29.
3 G. E. Buckle to A. F. Walter, 21 July 1895, Times Archive.
4 *History of The Times* (London, 1947), vol. III, p. 125. (Hereafter this work is cited as *HoT*.)
5 E. T. S. Dugdale, *German Diplomatic Documents* (reprint, New York, 1969), vol. I, p. 193.
6 Sanderson to Lascelles, 21 March 1900, FO 800/9.
7 Amery writes of Chirol, 'wrecking his finances in youthful exuberance', which, if true, was at odds with his later character. See L. S. Amery, *My Political Life* (London, 1953), vol. I, p. 93.
8 *Standard*, 26 April 1895.
9 Spring Rice to F. Villiers, 17 January 1896, FO 800/9.
10 Dugdale, *op. cit.*, vol. II, p. 349.
11 The editors of the *Morning Post* were kept in leading reins by the owner, Baron Glenesk, of whom Salisbury had a poor opinion. See R. Lucas, *Lord Glenesk and the Morning Post* (London, 1910).

During this period, what the *Standard* had to say on foreign policy was generally approved in the Foreign Office. The credit for this was given to W. H. Mudford, the newspaper's editor and manager. See Sanderson to Lascelles, 5 December 1896, FO 800/9. Mudford, formidable, haughty, independently minded yet fair in his treatment of political opponents, retired because of increasing ill-health in 1900. He 'enjoyed' a strange triangular relationship with Salisbury and Austin. On occasion, when Salisbury had reworked one of Austin's leaders, Mudford would strike out the premier's additions and corrections.

Long after its purchase by Pearson, the Germans still considered the *Standard* a powerful and influential paper close to the government. Northcliffe commented upon the dangers of this belief in a note to Garvin complaining of the activities of H. A. White, Berlin correspondent of both the *Standard* and the *Daily Express*. 'White ... is dangerous and a firebrand. The Germans do not know that the "Standard" is no longer the paper it was and are much misled. Apparently White sends one message and it is rewritten in London for the two Papers and what he says is dangerous.' Northcliffe to Garvin, 22 May 1909, Garvin MSS.
12 Dugdale, *op. cit.*, vol. II, p. 368.
13 Quoted in J. A. S. Grenville, *Lord Salisbury and Foreign Policy* (London, 1964), p. 102.
14 See *The Times*, 1 January 1896; *HoT*, *op. cit.*, vol. III, ch. IX *passim*.
15 *Ibid.*, 3 January 1896.

16 Dugdale, *op. cit.*, vol. II, p. 387.

17 Chirol to Wallace, 4 January 1896, Wallace Add 7341/15, ff. 69–72; Wallace to Chirol, 6 January 1896, Times Archive.

18 Dugdale, *op. cit.*, vol. II, p. 394.

19 Chirol to Wallace, 25 January 1896, enclosing copy of his letter to Lascelles of the same date, Wallace Add 7341/15, ff. 97–9.

20 Quoted in H. W. Steed, *Through Thirty Years* (London, 1924), vol. II, p. 70.

21 Sanderson to Lascelles, 15 January 1896, FO 800/9.

22 Spring Rice to Villiers, 17 January 1896, FO 800/23.

23 Chirol to Wallace, 14 March 1896, Wallace Add 7341/15, ff. 118–20.

24 See the letter Chirol drafted to Holstein, showed to Lascelles, but was not sent on Wallace's instructions as he thought it might aggravate already sufficiently strained relations. Chirol to Holstein, n.d. (copy of draft), Wallace Add 7341/15, ff. 122–3.

25 Chirol to Wallace, 9 March 1896, Wallace Add 7341/15, ff. 116–17.

26 Chirol to Wallace, 2 March 1896, *ibid.*, ff. 113–14.

27 Spring Rice to Villiers, 2 May 1896, FO 800/23.

28 Wallace to Chirol, 11 March 1896, Times Archive.

29 Chirol to Wallace, 4 April 1896, Wallace Add 7341/15, f. 127.

30 Dugdale, *op. cit.*, vol. II, p. 369.

31 *The Times,* 7 January 1896.

32 Quoted in N. Rich, *Friedrich von Holstein* (Cambridge, 1965), vol. II, p. 472.

33 See W. S. Blunt, *My Diaries, 1888–1914* (single vol. edn, London, 1932) pp. 212 and 214; Dugdale, *op. cit.*, vol. II, p. 404.

34 E. H. C. Moberly Bell, *Life and Letters of C. F. Moberly Bell* (London, 1927), p. 212.

35 For example, on 14 January it published an article, 'Germans in England', drawing attention to 'the preponderance of swindlers, gamblers, and members of the unspeakable *souteneur* class', contrasting them with the English in Germany who were said to be 'persons of means and birds of passage, not settlers'. Quoted in A. J. Ll. Morris, 'Diplomacy and publicity, 1896–1904', in *Moirae,* vol. VI, p. 21. Compare with Hugh Chisolm's remark when refuting Crook's assertion that the *St James's Gazette* was in the pay of Berlin and conducted in the German interest because its proprietor, Edward Steinkopff, was a German. 'My proprietor . . . is German by birth but he is for that reason (as is the case with so many Germans resident in Great Britain) more hostile to Germany and German policy than a good many Britons.' Quoted in S. E. Koss, *The Rise and Fall of the Political Press in Britain* (London, 1981), vol. I, p. 377.

36 See Chirol to Moberly Bell, 10 January 1896, Times Archive.

37 *The Letters of Queen Victoria: Third Series, 1886–1901,* edited in 3 volumes by G. E. Buckle (London, 1930), vol. II, pp. 12–14.

38 Baron von Eckardstein, *Ten Years at the Court of St James* (London, 1921), pp. 85–6.

39 Sanderson to Lascelles, 15 January 1896, FO 800/9.

40 Even the best efforts of J. L. Bashford, the *Daily Telegraph*'s Berlin correspondent, who indefatigably represented the views of the Wilhelmstrasse, were, for once, blithely ignored or dismissed as 'an ingenious explanation . . . but the facts seem to indicate the contrary'. See O. J. Hale, *Publicity and Diplomacy* (New York, 1940), pp. 115, fn. 36.

41 The comment was made originally by Eric Barrington, then Salisbury's private secretary. Quoted in J. A. S. Grenville, *op. cit.*, p. 365.

Chapter 2: The new tenant at 66 Dorotheenstrasse

1 H. W. Steed, *Through Thirty Years* (London, 1924), vol. I, ch. 3.
2 *Fortnightly Review*, April 1901, p. 674.
3 G. Saunders to D. H. Saunders, 15 November 1898, Saunders Papers, SAUN 2/GS/1/132.
4 Same to his parents, 20 March 1889, SAUN 1/GS/2/53.
5 G. Saunders, *The Last of the Huns* (London, 1915), Preface.
6 G. Saunders to D. H. Saunders, 14 January 1900, SAUN 2/GS/1/141.
7 Quoted in *History of the Times* (London, 1947), (hereafter referred to as *HoT*), vol. III, p. 369.
8 G. Saunders to Margaret, 29 August 1914, SAUN 3/GS/2/51.
9 *Morning Post*, 4 January 1896.
10 See Wilfrid Hindle, *The Morning Post 1772–1937, Portrait of a Newspaper* (Edinburgh, 1937), pp. 220–34.
11 *Morning Post*, 9 and 11 January 1896.
12 Sanderson to Lascelles, 5 December 1896, FO 800/9.
13 G. Saunders to Wallace, 10 February 1897, Times Archive.
14 G. Saunders to D. H. Saunders, 4 November 1896, SAUN 2/GS/1/114.
15 Quoted in *HoT*, vol. III, p. 300.
16 See N. Rich, *Holstein*, vol. II, pp. 478–9 and 527.
17 See Saunders to Moberly Bell, 8 March 1897 and 23 February 1901; Saunders to Wallace, 8 March 1897, Times Archive.
18 Saunders to D. H. Saunders, 9 October 1899, SAUN 2/GS/1/134.
19 Gooch and Temperley (eds), *British Documents on the Origins of the War, 1898–1914* (London, 1927), vol. I, pp. 42–3 (hereafter cited as *BD*).
20 Lascelles to Salisbury, 1 February 1898, *ibid.*, vol. I, pp. 43–4.
21 Lascelles to Balfour, 23 August 1898, *ibid.*, vol. I, pp. 100–1.
22 Lascelles to Lansdowne, 6 February 1903, FO 800/18. The Kaiser's reference was to that occasion in January 1898 when Sir Theodore Martin, as the queen's representative, had interviewed certain editors about critical and facetious remarks concerning the Kaiser. Martin told the queen that the temper of 'our principal journalists' was 'conciliatory', although Buckle when he was interviewed had said that the very general feeling of bitterness towards the Germans throughout the country ought to be recognised. Despite the editor's grumbles, a message was despatched to Saunders: 'We think it advisable not to say at present anything unnecessarily irritating to the Germans.' See *Letters of Queen Victoria: Third Series, 1886–1901*, edited in 3 volumes by G. E. Buckle (London, 1930), vol. III, pp. 224–5.
23 Chirol to Saunders, 4 September 1899; Saunders to Chirol, 15 September 1899, Times Archive.
24 Saunders to D. H. Saunders, 9 October 1899, SAUN 2/GS/1/134.
25 *The Times*, 30 October 1899.
26 Saunders to Chirol, 8 December 1899, Times Archive.
27 Saunders to Chirol, 10 November 1899, *ibid.*
28 This paragraph is based on material in A. J. Ll. Morris, 'George Saunders, *The Times*' Berlin correspondent: a case study in diplomacy and publicity, 1896–1904', in, *Moirae*, Trinity 1981, vol. VI, pp. 30–1.
29 E. T. S. Dugdale, *German Diplomatic Documents* (reprint, New York, 1969), vol. III, p. 108.
30 *Ibid.*, vol. III, p. 110.
31 Baron von Eckardstein, *Ten Years at the Court of St James* (London, 1921), p. 130.

32 Saunders to Chirol, 8 December 1899, Times Archive.
33 Chirol to Hardinge, 14 June 1904, Hardinge MSS, vol. VII, ff. 89–96.
34 For example, *BD*, vol. I, pp. 43–4.
35 See Dugdale, *op. cit.*, vol. II, p. 474 and pp. 420–21; *BD*, vol. I, p. 255. For dealing with the press, Salisbury used Schomberg McDonnell, for fourteen years his principal private secretary. Henry Lucy, in his diary, wrote of McDonnell, he 'has a breezy manner and a volubility that comforts the unaccustomed caller with the impression that he is quite off his guard, and that ministerial secrets will be cheap today. When he leaves at the conclusion of the interview, he will find his stock of information has not been appreciably augmented.' Sir Henry Lucy, *The Diary of a Journalist* (London, 1920), p. 205.
36 When Glenesk protested that *The Times* was given exclusive information by the government denied to other newspapers and press agencies, McDonnell agreed and instructions were given officials at Foreign Office, Colonial Office and Admiralty to make amends. In April 1896, *The Times* brought an action against the Central News Agency for providing 'fabricated and untrustworthy information' contradicted by 'confidential information' given to *The Times* by the Foreign Office. Northcliffe (or Harmsworth as he then was) was given favoured treatment by McDonnell as 'a really good friend' to the party. See S. Koss, *The Rise and Fall of the Political Press in Britain* (London, 1981), vol. I, pp. 366–7, 370–1.
37 Sanderson to Lascelles, 28 March 1900, FO 800/9.
38 Chirol to Sanderson, 29 May 1902, FO 800/11.
39 On military and naval matters in particular, *The Times* had on occasion achieved almost the status of an 'official' publication for advance information. As Koss points out (*ante*, p. 367), 'To *The Times*, the question was not one of privilege but of accuracy.'
40 For example, Chirol in a letter to J. L. Garvin, where he admitted his regret at the asperity of some of Steed's comments, wrote that he had informed the correspondent that it was his desire 'that the Paper should steer more of a middle course. . . . I hate putting too much pressure upon our correspondents to make them, as it were, write to order. In this matter again I try to steer a middle course, but it is difficult.' Chirol to Garvin, 10 October 1905, Garvin Papers. See also, A. F. Walter in answer to Roberts's charge that *The Times* had 'no settled defence policy', wrote, 'You must remember . . . we consider it desirable to allow a good deal of licence individually to our correspondents. These writers often hold conflicting opinions and belong to different schools of thought.' Walter to Roberts, 6 February 1908, Roberts Papers, R46/147.
41 Sanderson to Lascelles, 14 and 21 March 1900, FO 800/9.
42 In this second letter to Lascelles, Sanderson suggested that Chirol's inordinate sensitivity might still be colouring his attitude years after he had suffered a slight. 'I don't think he has ever forgiven the lectures he received when he was in Berlin.' Sanderson concluded his letter, however, with a reflection that reveals Chirol was not altogether impervious to personal appeals. 'If I have to go at him again,' wrote Sanderson, 'I shall say he is causing you [Lascelles] personal inconvenience. I believe that argument would have more effect on him than most.'
43 See *BD*, vol. I, p. 247, and *HoT*, vol. III, p. 314.
44 Chirol to Saunders, 5 March 1900, Times Archive.
45 Saunders to D. H. Saunders, 14 January 1900, SAUN 2/GS/1/141.
46 See von Eckardstein, *op. cit.*, pp. 140–1 and 144; Dugdale, *op. cit.*, vol. III, p. 124; and, *BD*, vol. I, pp. 254–5.
47 Saunders to D. H. Saunders, 14 and 29 January 1900, SAUN 2/GS/1/141–42.

48   S. Gwynn (ed.), *The Letters and Friendships of Sir Cecil Spring Rice* (London, 1929), vol. I, p. 261.
49   Quoted in *HoT*, vol, III, p. 319.
50   Chirol to Lascelles, 6 March 1900, Spring Rice Papers, CASR 1/14/39–41.
51   Quoted in M. Balfour, *The Kaiser and His Times* (Pelican edn, London, 1975), pp. 226–7.
52   Saunders to L. S. Amery, 22 September 1900, Times Archive.
53   Saunders to L. J. Maxse, 20 September 1900, Maxse MSS, 477, ff. 783–4.

Chapter 3: Leo Maxse's ABC of better relations with Russia

1   Lady Milner's article on L. J. Maxse, in L. G. Wickham Legg (ed.), *The Dictionary of National Biography, 1931–40* (London, 1949), p. 607. At the time, the retiring editor of the *Cape Times*, Edmund Garrett, supposed that Maxse was reluctant to give up the *National Review* 'just when it is beginning to reward all your trouble, certainly when it is becoming known as an uncommonly well done thing and *sui generis*'. It was also not certain whether Maxse might 'sooner or later drift into politics at home'. E. F. Garrett to Maxse, 2 August 1900, Maxse MSS, 447, ff. 758–9.
2   L. J. Maxse, *Germany on the Brain* (London, 1915). The quotations are from the 'Introduction', pp. 6–9.
3   A. T. Mahan to Admiral Bouverie F. Clark, 23 July 1909, Mahan Papers, Box 4.
4   Quoted in S. E. Koss, *Lord Haldane: Scapegoat for Liberalism* (New York, 1969), p. 174.
5   Roberts to Maxse, 2 September 1908, Maxse MSS, 485, f. 746.
6   Maxse was a very effective speaker though the effort involved made great demands upon his frail constitution. 'You know what immense pains Maxse takes, as a public man should, to speak well, and how brilliantly he does it. He is looking very harrassed, worn and thin.' Garvin to Northcliffe, 1 November 1907 (copy), Garvin Papers.
7   Repington to Maxse, 17 February 1906, Maxse MSS, 455, f. 264.
8   The quotations are taken from Stephen Koss's *Lord Haldane, passim*.
9   Maxse to Northcliffe, 7 February 1908, Northcliffe Dep 4890/XXIII.
10   Garvin to Maxse, 29 October 1901, Maxse MSS, 466, f. 434.
11   Garvin to Maxse, 20 February 1912, *ibid.*, 476, f. 37.
12   Chirol to Maxse, 5 February 1908, *ibid.*, 458, ff. 647–8.
13   See Chirol's long letters to Maxse of this period, and particularly, Chirol to Maxse, 31 January 1908, *ibid.*, 458, f. 638.
14   Lovat Fraser to Maxse, 11 May 1910, *ibid.*, 458, ff. 647–8. During this period and particularly after the change of editorship, Fraser is not always reliable as a commentator on *The Times* because of his own quarrels and dissatisfaction. See, for example, Fraser to Garvin, 29 September 1912, Garvin Papers.
15   Quoted in Birkenhead, *Rudyard Kipling* (New York, 1978), pp. 183–4.
16   L. J. Maxse, *op. cit.*, p. 8.
17   D. C. Lathbury's entry on Blennerhassett in S. Lee (ed.), *The Twentieth Century DNB, 1901–1911 Supplement* (London, 1920), p. 181. Lathbury's statement concerning the 'inevitable' consequences of Germany's ambitions was, of course, written during the war.
18   L. J. Maxse, *op. cit.*, p. 8; Saunders to Maxse, 15 July 1900, Maxse MSS, 447, ff. 746–7.
19   *National Review*, 'Episodes of the month', January 1900.

20 Saunders to Maxse, 15 July 1900, *ante.*
21 R. Blennerhassett, 'Great Britain and the European powers', in, *National Review*, March 1900.
22 See, for example, Chirol to Lascelles, 6 March 1900, Cecil Spring Rice MSS, CASR 1/14/39–41.
23 Chamberlain to Strachey, 10 December 1899, Strachey Papers, S/4/6/9.
24 See Saunders to Maxse, 20 September 1900, Maxse MSS, 447, ff. 783–4.
25 Grey to Maxse, 22 October 1901, *ibid.*, 448, f. 430.
26 Maxse to Northcliffe, 23 December 1911. See also Northcliffe to Maxse, 26 December 1911 (copy), Northcliffe Dep. 4890/XXIII.
27 Maxse to Strachey, 15 January 1907, S/10/9/8.
28 It is impossible to ascertain the degree to which Maxse used material supplied by Blennerhassett in his article as the original drafts no longer exist. I am grateful to Professor Paul Kennedy who pointed out to me Blennerhassett's involvement, and first drew my attention to the Blennerhassett letters cited below. To this extent, I have modified the views I expressed on the authorship of the article in an essay I wrote earlier, 'Leo Maxse and the "German peril": scaremonger, crank or patriot?', in *Moirae*, vol. IV, Michaelmas 1979, pp. 8–31.
29 Blennerhassett to Maxse, 13 October 1901, Maxse MSS, 448, f. 416.
30 Grey to Maxse, 24 May 1901, *ibid.*, f. 450.
31 E. T. Cook to Maxse, 8 October 1901, *ibid.*, 448, f. 411.
32 See Blennerhassett to Maxse, 10 October 1901, *ibid.*, f. 413.
33 Grey to Maxse, 9 October 1901, *ibid.*, f. 412.
34 Saunders to Maxse, 23 October 1901, *ibid.*, ff. 431–2.
35 Compare these statements and sentiments concerning France with those of George Saunders in his letter to Moberly Bell, 14 June 1902, quoted in Chapter IV.
36 *National Review*, November 1901, vol. XXXVIII, pp. 343–58.
37 A. T. Mahan, USN (1840–1914), had retired from active service in 1896. In 1899, he was a delegate for his country at The Hague Peace Conference where he met Jack Fisher. His writings were syndicated throughout the United States and from 1901 he contributed articles to the *National Review*. Through Maxse, Mahan later contributed to Northcliffe's *Daily Mail* and *Observer*. In 1890, Mahan had published *Influence of Sea Power upon History* which, more than any other of his books on naval history, had an enormous influence on British and German naval strategical thinking. Of this book, Esher wrote to Sir William Harcourt, 'Fisher, who is perhaps the best of our seamen, thinks the book a classical work. So it has the approval of an expert.' M. V. Brett (ed.), vol. I, p. 312.
38 Maxse to A. T. Mahan, 7 February and 15 March 1902, Mahan Papers, Box 4.
39 Blennerhassett had suggested there should be 'reference to myself with a view of throwing people off'. To Maxse, 10 October 1901, Maxse MSS, 448, f. 413. So many drafts were in circulation to so many people, it is amazing that the Germans remained puzzled as to the name of the true author(s).
40 See E. T. S. Dugdale, *German Diplomatic Documents* (reprint, New York, 1969), vol. III, p. 157.
41 Chirol to Maxse, 24 November 1901, Maxse MSS, 448, f. 449.
42 Chirol to Hardinge, 11 October 1901, Hardinge Papers, vol. 3, ff. 191–2.
43 Hardinge to Maxse, 16 October 1901, Maxse MSS, 448, ff. 419–20; Maxse to Hardinge, 31 October 1901, Hardinge Papers, vol. 3, ff. 199–200.
44 Saunders to Maxse, 14 and 23 October 1901, Maxse MSS, 448, ff. 418 and 431.
45 Chamberlain to Maxse, 31 October 1901, *ibid.*, f. 440.
46 See *British Documents on the Origins of the War, 1898–1914* (London, 1927), vol.

II, pp. 84–6; N. Rich and M. H. Fisher (eds), *The Holstein Papers* (Cambridge, 1957), vol. IV, pp. 239–41 and 244–6; N. Rich, *Friedrich von Holstein* (Cambridge, 1965), vol. II, pp. 668ff.
47 J. L. Garvin, *Chamberlain* (London, 1932–4), vol. III, p. 511.
48 W. S. Blunt, *My Diaries, 1888–1914* (single vol. edn, London 1932), p. 417. On other articles by Garvin using the pseudonyms 'X' and 'Ignotus', see A. M. Gollin, *The Observer and J. L. Garvin* (London, 1960), p. 13, n. 2.
49 Garvin to Maxse, 29 October 1901, Maxse MSS, 448, f. 434.
50 O. J. Hale, *Publicity and Diplomacy* (New York, 1940), p. 265.

Chapter 4: To league with the shameless Hun

1 S. Gwynn (ed.), *The Letters and Friendships of Cecil Spring Rice* (London, 1929), vol. I, pp. 328–9.
2 *British Documents on the Origins of the War, 1898–1914* (London, 1927), vol. II, p. 66.
3 Sanderson to Lascelles, 5 March 1902, FO 800/9.
4 E. T. S. Dugdale, *German Diplomatic Documents* (reprint, New York, 1969), vol. III, p. 141.
5 Quoted in *History of the Times* (London, 1947) (hereafter referred to as *HoT*), vol. III, p. 334.
6 See, for example, Sanderson to Lascelles, 21 and 28 March 1900, FO 800/9.
7 See N. Rich, *Friedrich von Holstein* (Cambridge, 1965), vol. II, pp. 663–5; *HoT*, *op. cit.*, vol. III, pp. 323–34; V. Chirol, *Fifty Years in a Changing World* (London, 1927), pp. 291–6; and *Dugdale, op. cit.*, vol. III, pp. 146–51.
8 See Chirol to Steed, 12 November 1901, Times Archive.
9 N. Rich and M. H. Fisher (eds), *The Holstein Papers* (Cambridge, 1957), vol. IV, pp. 236–7.
10 *The Times*, 20 November 1901.
11 See Rich, *Holstein*, vol. II, pp. 666–8; Rich and Fisher (eds), *Holstein Papers*, vol. IV, pp. 237–43.
12 See, *HoT, op. cit.*, vol. III, pp. 341–3. For Bülow's instructions to Metternich, see Dugdale, *op. cit.*, vol. III, pp. 151–2.
13 *BD, op. cit.*, vol. II, pp. 87–8.
14 *Daily Mail*, 9 January 1902.
15 Lascelles to Sanderson, 30 May 1902, FO 800/18.
16 Bell to Saunders, 12 June 1902, Times Archive.
17 Saunders to Bell, 14 June 1902, *ibid.* There is a fuller version of the centre part of this long letter in *HoT*, vol. III, pp. 365–70. The manuscript letter clearly reveals the speed and passion with which it was written by Saunders.
18 S. Gwynn (ed.), *op. cit.*, vol. I, p. 351.
19 Balfour to Strachey, 22 July 1898, Strachey MSS, S/2/4/3.
20 Maxse to Mahan, 29 May 1902, Mahan Papers, Box 5.
21 Maxse to Mahan, 25 June 1902, *ibid.*
22 Conversation reported in Lascelles to Sanderson, 27 September 1902, FO 800/18.
23 Chirol to Strachey, 12 October 1903, Strachey MSS, S/4/9/5.
24 See *Daily Mail*, 17 December 1902. Lord Burnham's *Telegraph* was generally sympathetic towards Germany. J. L. Bashford, its Berlin correspondent, was favoured by Bülow, but on this occasion it is likely that the most significant factor was the close friendship between Balfour and E. B. Iwan-Müller, the paper's foreign editor. Milner, a contemporary of Iwan-Müller's at Oxford and a close

friend, had described him when he worked on the *Manchester Courier* as 'the Government's chief journalistic support outside London'. He had joined the *Daily Telegraph* in 1896 after a short period as editorial assistant to Henry Cust on the *Pall Mall Gazette*. See Milner's article on Iwan-Müller, in S. Lee (ed.), *Dictionary of National Biography, 1901–11* (London, 1912), pp. 354–5.

25 Lascelles to Sanderson, 27 December 1902, FO 800/18.

26 See Dugdale, *op. cit.*, vol. III, p. 165, and G. W. Monger, *The End of Isolation* (London, 1963), pp. 106–7.

27 Maxse to Mahan, 6 March 1903, Mahan Papers, Box 5.

28 Mahan to Maxse, 14 July 1902, *ibid.*

29 S. Gwynn (ed.), *op. cit.*, vol. I, p. 350.

30 Goschen informed Milner, 'Venezuela was bad. . . . It has robbed Lansdowne of the credit he had gained and made the Foreign Office very unpopular.' 6 February 1903, Milner Ad MSS c. 688, ff. 194–6.

31 See *BD*, vol. II, pp. 178–9.

32 The questioner was Tommy Gibson Bowles, the founder and editor of *Vanity Fair*. Bowles's independent attitude in politics caused him to gravitate through the whole spectrum of available parties and he conducted his last unsuccessful election campaign in 1916 for the Harborough Division of Leicestershire as 'Candidate for Leicestershire Attested Married Men's Protest Society'. At the hustings he invariably advertised his independence by referring to this episode in 1903. He supposed he was a major influence in deciding the fate of the Baghdad Railway scheme. There is a slim but entertaining biography of Bowles by L. E. Naylor, *The Irrepressible Victorian* (London, 1965).

33 'Episodes of the Month', April 1903.

34 W. B. Thomas, *The Story of The Spectator, 1828–1928* (London, 1928), p. 87. Since R. H. Hutton's death in 1897, closely followed by Meredith Townsend's retirement from active editorship, Strachey had been the sole editor and proprietor of the *Spectator*. Under his energetic leadership the paper doubled its revenue and readership. In the tradition of the paper's founder, R. S. Rentoul, Strachey preached free trade and the *Spectator* became the leading organ of the Free Trade Unionists, opponents of Chamberlain and the tariff reform group in the Tory party. See also W. V. Cooper's article in J. R. H. Weaver (ed.), *Dictionary of National Biography, 1922–30* (London, 1937), pp. 816–18.

35 The Wilhelmstrasse, because of the 'ABC' article in the *National Review*, supposed that Maxse was in the pay of the Russians. They were persuaded by a story, told them by Gwinner, one of the German bankers involved in the project, who said he was told it by Dawkins, that the Russian embassy in Paris had opened negotiations with Maxse who straightway scampered over to France where he was given all the details.

    There was a variation of this story that suggested it had been Strachey who was summoned to Paris by the Russians. Strachey was strangely sensitive about this story and for years afterwards was haunted by rumours that the *Spectator* was owned by the Russian government. As late as June 1909, he was earnestly assuring Milner '*in strictest confidence* that I have never seen a Russian diplomatist of any kind in my life. . . . Dawkins could hardly call Spring Rice and Louis Mallet Russian agents.' See Strachey to Milner, 10 June 1909, and Lyall to Milner, 14 June 1909, Milner MSS, Dep. 36, ff. 17–21. See also Spring Rice to Strachey, Easter Day 1903, and Strachey to Butler, 18 June 1909 (copy), Strachey Papers, S/13/4/3 and S/3/4/5.

36 Maxse to Strachey, 20 April 1903, S/10/9/6.

37 M. V. Brett (ed.), *Journals and Letters of Viscount Esher* (London, 1934–8), vol. I, pp. 396–8.
38 Chirol to Strachey, 12 October 1903, Strachey Papers S/4/9/5.
39 Quoted in Lord Newton, *Lord Lansdowne* (London, 1929), p. 254.
40 Curzon to Selborne, 21 May 1903, Selborne MSS, 10, ff. 95–100.
41 See Lansdowne to Balfour, 12 and 17 April 1903, Balfour Ad MSS 49728, ff. 41–8.
42 Maxse to Garvin, 30 June 1904, Garvin Papers.
43 Spender to Strachey, 21 October 1905, Strachey Papers, S/13/13/6.
44 See *BD*, vol, III, p. 429.

Chapter 5: New friends and old enemies

1 M. V. Brett (ed.), *Journals and Letters of Viscount Esher* (London, 1934–8), vol. I, p. 417.
2 E. T. S. Dugdale, *German Diplomatic Documents* (reprint, New York, 1969), vol. III, p. 176.
3 See S. Lee, *King Edward VII*, vol. II, pp. 236, 242 and 245–6.
4 Hardinge to Chirol, 3 June 1904, FO 800/2; Chirol to Hardinge, 14 June 1904, Hardinge MSS, vol. 7, ff. 89–96.
5 Chirol to Spring Rice, 22 February 1904, Spring Rice MSS, CASR 1/10/25–26.
6 *Daily Mail*, 14 May 1904.
7 Northcliffe to Strachey, 18 November 1904, Strachey MSS, S/11/4/16.
8 Maxse to Spring Rice, 15 November 1904, CASR 1/50.
9 Chirol to Strachey, 9 May 1904, S/4/9/6.
10 Strachey to Mallet, 4 March 1904 (copy), S/15/4/3.
11 *The Times*, 22 April 1904.
12 Mallet to Sandars, 1 June 1904, Balfour Ad MSS 49747, ff. 101–4.
13 Strachey to Mallet, 4 March 1904 (copy), S/15/4/3.
14 Goschen to Milner, 11 November 1904, Milner Ad MSS c. 687, ff. 267–8.
15 Chirol to Spring Rice, 1 November 1904, CASR 1/10/47–9.
16 Same to Lascelles, 26 October 1904, FO 800/12.
17 Mallet to Sandars, 11 November 1904, Balfour Ad MSS 49747, ff. 101–4.
18 Chirol to Spring Rice, 1 November 1904, CASR 1/10/47–49.
19 Hermann, Baron von Eckardstein, resigned his post as First Secretary in the London embassy because he considered it was 'useless to go on struggling against the flood of English bitterness'. However, he implied the Kaiser was largely the cause of the problem. The straw which eventually had broken Eckardstein's back was an indiscreet speech made by the Kaiser on a yachting trip. See Holstein's diary entry for 7 November 1902, in, N. Rich and M. H. Fisher (eds), *The Holstein Papers* (Cambridge, 1957), vol. IV, p. 270.
20 Bernstorff, *Memoirs* (London, 1936), pp. 66–7.
21 Bernstorff to H. A. Gwynne, 10 December 1905, Gwynne MSS 23.
22 *British Documents on the Origins of the War, 1898–1914* (London, 1927) (hereafter referred to as *BD*), vol. III, pp. 80–3.
23 Balfour sometimes excused himself by complaining that eye strain or pressure of work made reading the newspapers impossible. Hedworth Lambton told Jack Sandars that he did not believe Balfour read anything, 'not even the books he writes himself!' In fact, Balfour took an informed interest in the antics of the 'friendly' Unionist press, and his friend Iwan-Müller supplied him with précis of what was being said by the Liberal press. Especially in the later years of his

leadership of the party, Balfour had close and extremely important contacts with certain key Tory journalists – particularly J. L. Garvin. See Lambton to Sandars, 6 January 1908, Sandars MSS 756, ff. 33–4; S. E. Koss, *The Rise and Fall of the Political Press in Britain* (London, 1981), vol. I, p. 347, and fn. 2; Chapter XV below *passim.*

24 Balfour to Lascelles, n.d. (copy), Balfour Ad MSS 49747, ff. 155–62.
25 Wolf to Bernstorff, 20 February 1904 (copy), enclosed with Mallet to Sandars, 24 February 1904, Balfour Ad MSS 49747, ff. 73–5.
26 Schwabach to Rothschild, 16 July 1904 (copy), Balfour Ad MSS 49747, ff. 1–5.
27 See, for example, Holstein to Bülow, 29 July; Bülow to Holstein, 1 August 1902, in, N. Rich and M. H. Fisher (eds), *The Holstein Papers* (Cambridge, 1957), vol. IV, pp. 257–61.
28 See Saunders's account of this conversation with Schwabach in his letter to J. Walter, 1 December 1905, Maxse MSS, 453, ff. 162–7.
29 Dugdale, *op. cit.*, vol. III, pp. 224–5.
30 *Ibid.*, p. 223.
31 See *History of the Times* (London, 1947) vol. III, p. 409ff.
32 *The Times*, 6 April 1905.
33 George Monger, *The End of Isolation* (London, 1963), p. 190.
34 Translated and quoted in O. J. Hale, *Publicity and Diplomacy* (New York, 1940), p. 273.
35 Chirol to Maxse, 15 July 1905, Maxse MSS 453, f. 81. Seckendorff was an ardent Anglophile and had hoped to be appointed as German Ambassador to London. For Bülow's estimate of Seckendorff, see, *BD*, vol. III, p. 168. Albert Ballin was Chairman of the Hamburg-America Steamship Company.
36 Lansdowne to Bertie, 3 August 1905, FO 800/170.
37 Dugdale, *op. cit.*, vol. III, p. 223.
38 Quoted in S. R. Williamson Jnr, *The Politics of Grand Strategy* (Cambridge, Mass, 1969), p. 36.
39 See *BD*, vol. III, pp. 79 and 81–2.
40 Midleton to Selborne, 27 July 1905, Selborne MSS, 2, ff. 78–85.
41 Wilson to Northcliffe, 15 October 1905, Dep. 4890/XLIX.
42 *The Times* never faltered in its support of the entente, but frequently observed it wished that the entente signified something more than just a diplomatic agreement. See, for example, *The Times*, 12 July 1905. See also O. J. Hale, *Germany and the Diplomatic Revolution* (Philadelphia, 1931), pp. 170ff.
43 Not least in Austria, the third component of the *Bund*. See Solomon Wank, 'Varieties of political despair', in, S. J. Winters and J. Held (eds), *Intellectual and Social Developments in the Habsburg Empire From Maria Teresa to World War I* (New York, 1975), pp. 203–39.
44 Spring Rice to Strachey, 27 September 1905, S/13/14/13.
45 It was surprising not only because *The Times* was on particularly poor terms with the Russian government, but Chirol, because of his Indian interests and connection with Curzon, was always suspicious of Russia.
46 Chirol to Hardinge, 1 November 1904, Hardinge MSS, vol. 7, ff. 212–17.
47 Chirol to Hardinge, 24 July 1905, *ibid.*, ff. 474–7. On C. P. Trevelyan's attitude to questions of foreign policy prior to 1914, see A. J. A. Morris, 'The Odyssey of an antiwar Liberal', in S. Wank (ed.), *Doves and Diplomats* (Connecticut, 1978), pp. 85–108.
48 See Bernstorff to Spender, 3 January 1906, Spender Ad MSS 46391, ff. 128–9.
49 Spender to Strachey, 21 October 1905, S/13/13/6.

50 Grey to Spender, 23 August 1908, Spender Ad MSS 46389, ff. 11–12.
51 Spring Rice to Spender, 11 August 1905, *ibid.*, 46391, ff. 142–9.
52 Grey to Spender, 19 October 1905, *ibid.*, 46389, ff. 8–9.
53 Mallet to Strachey, 19 October and 24 November 1905, S/15/4/8–9.
54 So called after the name of Grey's fishing lodge where the conspirators met.
55 See A. J. A. Morris, *Radicalism Against War, 1906–14* (London, 1972), pp. 14–18.
56 Hardinge to Maxse, 8 December 1905, Maxse MSS, 453, f. 173.
57 See Stead's *Review of Reviews*, January 1906; *Manchester Guardian*, 11 December 1905; *National Review*, 'Episodes of the month', January 1906; Margot Asquith, *Autobiography* (Penguin edn, London, 1936), vol. II, p. 63; D. Lloyd George, *War Memoirs* (London, 1934), vol. I, p. 56.
58 See *HoT*, vol. III, pp. 460–2; M. V. Brett (ed.), *op. cit.*, vol. II, pp. 136–9 for Esher's memorandum for King on conversation with Beit re. Kaiser's comments.

Chapter 6: *Einkreisungspolitik* – encirclement

1 See M. V. Brett (ed.), *Journals and Letters of Viscount Esher* (London, 1934–8), vol. II, pp. 136–9.
2 Saunders to Walter, 1 December 1905, Maxse MSS, 453, ff. 162–7.
3 Repington to Marker, 9 July 1906, Kitchener-Marker Ad MSS 52277B, ff. 78–85.
4 Saunders to Maxse, 11 February 1906, Maxse MSS, 455, ff. 255–55a.
5 Grey to Nicolson, 21 December 1905, FO 800/336.
6 Mallet to Nicolson, 25 December 1905, *ibid.*
7 See H. Nicolson, *Lord Carnock* (London, 1930), pp. 170ff. The Kaiser described Wallace as 'very intelligent; a friend of King Edward's; a Jew naturally'. He supposed his influence over Nicolson to be benign and to Germany's advantage. When Nicolson became 'more accommodating', the Kaiser ascribed this to 'Wallace ... making himself felt'. See Dugdale, *German Diplomatic Documents* (reprint, New York, 1969), vol. III, pp. 234–49.
8 Saunders to Maxse, 1 December 1905, Maxse MSS, 453, f. 168. Saunders described Revoil, the French delegate, as a 'lamb compared with German wolves'.
9 *Speaker*, 31 March 1906.
10 Bernstorff to Spender, 3 January 1906, Spender Ad MSS 46391, ff. 128–9.
11 Article on 'The German grievance' by 'Diplomaticus' in the *Pall Mall Gazette*, 6 March 1906. For Tyrrell's long note, see *British Documents on the Origins of the War, 1898–1914* (London, 1927), (hereafter referred to as *BD*) vol. III, pp. 347–9.
12 See Dugdale, *op. cit.*, vol. III, p. 237.
13 *Concord*, vol. XXII, no. 4, April/May 1906, p. 58.
14 *The Times*, 20 April 1906.
15 *BD*, vol. III, p. 334. See also N. Rich, *Friedrich von Holstein* (Cambridge, 1965), vol. II, pp. 746–53, and *History of the Times* (London, 1947), (hereafter referred to as *HoT*) vol. III, pp. 470–1.
16 See F. W. Wile Papers, vol. IV. Wile was contracted by Northcliffe for the *Daily Mail*, initially for three years at a salary of £1000 per annum. Northcliffe to Watney, 1 December 1906, Northcliffe Dep. 4890/LV. Wile continued to work as a correspondent for the *New York Times* and *Chicago Tribune*. See O. J. Hale, *op. cit.*, p. 29 and fn. 28.
17 Lascelles to Hardinge, 25 January 1907, FO 800/19.
18 Hardinge to Lascelles, 24 December 1906, *ibid.*
19 Northcliffe to Kennedy Jones, 24 May 1909, Dep. 4890/XLIV.
20 Wile to Northcliffe, 29 and 30 April 1907. Wile constantly emphasised to

Northcliffe 'the value the highest quarters in Germany put upon the power and influence of the "Daily Mail".' See Wile to Northcliffe, 1 June 1908, Dep. 4890/LV.

21 See *Hansard*, iv:160:318.
22 Chirol to Strachey, 3 July 1906, Strachey Papers S/4/9/9.
23 See *The Times*, 24 June 1906; and Chirol's letter to Strachey, *supra*.
24 *BD*, vol. III, p. 360.
25 In his important memorandum, 1 January 1907, *BD*, vol. III, pp. 397–420, he quoted extensively from Wilkinson but without acknowledgment.
26 *BD*, vol. III, pp. 413–14.
27 Crowe to Dilke, 15 October 1907, FO 800/243.
28 Hardinge to Nicolson, 5 March 1907, FO 800/339.
29 Saunders to Walter, 1 December 1905, Maxse MSS, 453, ff. 162–7.
30 *National Review*, 'Episodes of the month', June 1907.
31 Stead to Strachey, 25 March; Strachey to Stead, 27 March 1907 (copy), S/13/16/8.
32 See Spender's account of the visit in his, *Life, Journalism and Politics* (London, 1927), vol. I, pp. 201–11.
33 Charles Towers to Strachey, 16 June 1907, S/16/1/10.
34 *Ibid*. On the Eulenberg Affair, see N. Rich, *Holstein*, vol. II, pp. 757–97.
35 Fitzmaurice to Lascelles, 31 May 1906, FO 800/13.
36 Blennerhassett to Grey, 31 August 1907, FO 800/105.
37 *Nation*, 2 March 1907.
38 *National Review*, 'Episodes of the month', April 1907; *Albany Review*, April 1907, p. 5; *Daily Mail*, 6 March 1907.
39 Almeric Fitzroy, *Memoirs* (London, 1927), vol. I, pp. 317–18.
40 H. W. Nevinson, *Fire of Life* (London, 1935), p. 219.
41 *Le Matin*, 8 January 1907, and *BD*, vol. VIII, p. 200.
42 Crowe to Dilke, 15 October 1907, FO 800/243.
43 *BD*, vol. VIII, p. 288. For Saunders's view, see Saunders to Maxse, 16 May 1912, Maxse MSS, 466, ff. 76–8. The problem about press relations at the conference stemmed from the character of the chief British delegate, Sir Edward Fry. Fry had informed the British press 'with frigid courtesy that he had nothing to say to them. The journalists accepted their fate and did not trouble Sir Edward again – resorting instead to Marschall von Bieberstein.' See obituary of Fry in *Nation*, and article, 20 October 1908. See also Agnes Fry, *A Memoir of Sir Edward Fry* (Oxford, 1921), ch. XIII.
44 *New Age*, 20 June 1907.
45 F. Whyte, *Life of Stead* (London, 1925), vol. II, p. 291.
46 H. W. Nevinson, *op. cit.*, pp. 219–20.
47 Quoted in Steiner, *Foreign Office and Foreign Policy* (Cambridge, 1969), p. 115.
48 Summary and translation in *Daily Mail*, 1 May 1907.
49 *Observer*, 12 and 19 May 1907.
50 *Daily Mail*, 18 September 1907.
51 For Balfour's argument see *Hansard*, iv:156:410ff; for Grey's instructions see *BD*, vol. VIII, p. 242ff.
52 See *BD*, vol. IV, pp. 227–8; Grey to Knollys, 28 March 1906, quoted in G. M. Trevelyan, *Grey of Fallodon* (London, 1936), p. 183.
53 H. Nicolson, *op. cit.*, p. 206.

54   See *BD*, vol. IV, p. 580; Z. Steiner, *op. cit.*, p. 94; R. P. Churchill, *The Anglo-Russian Convention* (New York, 1939), p. 344.
55   Hardinge to Nicolson, 21 August 1906, FO 800/338; H. Nicolson, *op. cit.*, p. 222.
56   *Speaker*, 23 June 1906.
57   *Concord*, vol. XXII, no. 6, June 1906, p. 77.
58   *The Times*, 23 July 1906. See also *The Times*, 1 February and 10 April 1906.
59   See *HoT*, vol. III, pp. 486 and 491.
60   In 1903, because of a series of articles written on the Russian pogroms.
61   Sanderson to Spring Rice, 21 October 1903, FO 800/241.
62   Chirol to Nicolson, 19 March 1907, FO 800/339.
63   See, for example, *Albany Review*, August 1907, pp. 515–16. 'It appears to be impossible to excite even a sporting interest in the national tragedy of Russia.' See also *Concord*'s summary in vol. XXIV, no. 1, January 1908, p. 3.
64   Wallace to Nicolson, 10 July 1907, FO 800/339.
65   *Nation*, 3 August 1907.
66   'Calchas' in *Fortnightly Review*, October 1907.
67   Strachey to Stead, 24 December 1907, S/13/16/9; *Spectator*, 'Sir Edward Grey', 21 December 1907, pp. 1038–9. Strachey had been working for an understanding with Russia since 1905. See Strachey to Spring Rice, 2 October 1905, Spring Rice MSS, CASR 1/62.
68   Strachey to Grey, 30 September 1907, S/7/8/4.
69   *Nation*, 7 September 1907.
70   *National Review*, 'Episodes of the month', August 1907.
71   Wallace to Nicolson, 4 September 1907, FO 800/339.
72   While Chirol feared German intrigues, because of his connections with Curzon and his particular interest in India and the Far East, he was much more suspicious of Russia than Saunders or Lavino. His suspicions remained long after the agreement was signed as revealed, for example, by his attitude to Bethmann's talk of rapprochement with Russia in November 1910. See *HoT*, vol. III, p. 692. His letter to G. E. Morrison, 2 September 1907, noted how strong German influence remained in Russia.
73   *The Times*, 2 September 1907.
74   *Westminster Gazette*, 2 September 1907.
75   *Nation*, 22 February 1908.
76   *The Times*, 10 September 1907.
77   *National Review*, 'Episodes of the month', October 1907.
78   See Luigi Albertini, *Origins of the 1914 War* (Oxford, 1952), vol. I, p. 189.

PART 2: ALARUMS AND EXCURSIONS: THE ADMIRALS AND THE GENERALS

Chapter 7: *Dies irae, dies illa*

1   Quoted in J. L. Garvin, *Life of Joseph Chamberlain* (London, 1933), vol. II, p. 644.
2   W. S. Blunt, *My Diaries, 1888–1914* (single vol. edn, London, 1932), p. 212.
3   Quoted in Birkenhead, *Kipling* (New York, 1978), p. 235.
4   Kipling to L. Cope-Cornford, 18 May 1909, Cornford MSS, CPC/6.
5   Lawson to Garvin, 24 January 1900, Garvin MSS. Lawson was created Baron Burnham in 1903.
6   S. Gwynn (ed.), *The Letters and Friendships of Cecil Spring Rice* (London, 1929), vol. I, p. 303.

7 'Army Reform', November 1900, Ardagh MSS, PRO 30/40/13. Unfinished original manuscript ff. 151–226, typescript, ff. 757–67.
8 Best captured in Kipling's poem, 'Tommy'.

> O it's Tommy this, an' Tommy that, an' 'Tommy go away';
> But it's 'Thank you Mister Atkins', when the band begins to play.

9 S. Gwynn (ed.), *op. cit.*, p. 301.
10 W. S. Blunt, *op. cit.*, pp. 285, 289 and 296.
11 *Hansard*, iv:129:552.
12 *Spectator*, 31 December 1904, p. 1071.
13 Brodrick to Roberts, January 1901, Roberts MSS, R7101/23/13/26. See also Ardagh, *op. cit.*, 'The intuitive proclivity of the Treasury is to refuse all applications for sanction of additional expenditure . . . and the people love to have it so.'
14 Spenser Wilkinson, born in 1853, had intended to practise as a lawyer, but a part-time involvement with the Manchester Volunteers soon became an all-absorbing interest that led directly to a new and his true vocation, military journalism. From his first account of a great Volunteer review at Windsor Park in 1881, he became the country's principal advocate of that body, first organised to meet a threat of invasion in 1859. For Wilkinson, see Jay Luvaas, *The Education of an Army* (London, 1965), pp. 253–90, and Spenser Wilkinson, *Thirty Five Years* (London, 1933), *passim*.
15 Quotations from Luvaas's essay, *op cit*.
16 Sir Almeric Fitzroy, *Memoirs*, vol. I, p. 26.
17 *Daily Mail*, 19 September 1899.
18 J. W. Mckail and G. Wyndham (eds), *Life and Letters of George Wyndham* (London, 1926), vol. I, p. 361.
19 Wolseley, as Commander-in-Chief, had set the example others followed, by his personal campaign in the press over twenty years to get the reforms he wanted but which were stubbornly refused by his political masters.
20 Paras 1, 4 and 9 of the 'Revised rules for newspaper correspondents at the seat of war', 1 June 1889, WO 32/7138.
21 Buller to Wyndham, 1 October 1899, WO 32/7137.
22 Lawson to Garvin, 28 February 1900, Garvin MSS.
23 Arnold-Forster to Adj. Gen., 8 November 1904, WO 32/7140. Repington considered the whole question of war correspondents thoroughly unsatisfactory from the newspaper's point of view. He advised the manager of *The Times* that 'if our object is to secure whether before war breaks out or afterwards, good information, *The Times* should resort to a secret service on a system which I have applied with success abroad when working under the FO. . . . This system will produce results.' See Repington to Bell, 19 November 1908, Times Archive.
24 Unsigned minute dated 15 November 1904, WO 32/7140.
25 Northcliffe to Roberts, 19 June 1909, Roberts MSS, R46/162.
26 R. D. Blumenfeld, *RDB's Diary* (London, 1930), p. 71.
27 See *Daily Mail*, 30 July 1901; Watney to Brodrick and Brodrick to Watney, 23 and 27 July 1901; memorandum dated 29 July 1901; Harmsworth to Brodrick, 30 July 1901; notice to press agencies, 31 July and 1 August 1901; Balfour to Brodrick, 14 August 1901; copy of a memorandum by Brodrick, 20 June 1903. All in Midleton MSS, PRO 30/67/11. See also F. A. McKenzie, *The Mystery of the Daily Mail, 1896–1921* (London, 1921), pp. 28–32.
28 See Brodrick to Watney, 3 May 1904; and Watney to Brodrick, 13, 18 and 20 May 1904, PRO 30/67/20.

29 C. Headlam (ed.), *The Milner Papers* (London, 1933), vol. II, pp. 43–4.
30 G. Arthur (ed.), *Letters of Lord and Lady Wolseley, 1870–1911* (London, 1922), p. 380.
31 *Hansard*, iv:78:30.
32 Edward Levy-Lawson to Garvin, 31 January 1900, Garvin MSS.
33 See J. A. S. Grenville, *Lord Salisbury and Foreign Policy* (London, 1964), p. 323.
34 See 'Episodes of the month', *National Review*, November and December 1900, pp. 331 and 462; and February 1901, p. 839.
35 S. Gwynn (ed.), *op. cit.*, vol. I, pp. 324–5.
36 Spenser Wilkinson, *Thirty Five Years* (London, 1933), p. 282.
37 S. Gwynn (ed.), *op. cit.*, vol. I, p. 301.
38 Milner to Maxse, 7 June 1905, Maxse MSS, 453, ff. 64–6.
39 Milner to Bertha Synge, 19 December 1901, Milner Ad MSS c. 687, ff. 293–5.

Chapter 8: Is the Kaiser coming for tea?

1   Hyndman to Maxse, 1 February 1908, Maxse MSS, 458, f. 642.
2   Fitzgerald to Maxse, 18 November 1905, Maxse MSS, 453, ff. 151–2.
3   See E. T. S. Dugdale, *German Diplomatic Documents* (reprint, New York, 1969), vol. III, pp. 284–8.
4   Spring Rice to Maxse, 3 June 1908, Maxse MSS, 458, ff. 699–704. For Spring Rice's ubiquitous influence on journalists concerning the German 'threat' during this period, see *inter alia*, the exchanges between George Prothero, editor of the *Quarterly*, and J. L. Garvin, 3 and 12 June and 12 November 1908, Garvin MSS.
5   H. W. Wilson, for example, using information given him by 'reliable contacts in Stettin, Kiel and Hamburg and the US Naval attaché in Berlin,' pointed out many 'mistakes' made by Dumas to Arnold White. Most of Dumas's mistakes were made because he relied upon the German press for his information. See Wilson to White, 17 January 1906 and 18 January and 1 April 1907, Arnold White MSS, WHI/200.
6   There is an excellent, comprehensive summary of these ideas of a sudden invasion of Britain over a period of a hundred years in John Gooch, *The Prospect of War: Studies in British Defence Policy 1847–1942* (London, 1981), pp. 1–34.
7   *Hansard*, iv:86;1469.
8   See W. S. Blunt, *My Diaries, 1888–1914* (single vol. edn, London, 1932), pp. 335 and 417.
9   *National Review*, September 1900.
10 *Spectator*, 23 December 1899.
11 *Daily Mail*, 20 April 1900; *Public Opinion*, 6 April 1900, p. 427.
12 *St James's Gazette*, 24 March and 2 April 1900.
13 Reported in *The Times*, 10 May 1900.
14 *National Review*, June 1900, p. 532.
15 *Ibid.*, 'Episodes of the month', January 1901; *Spectator*, 12 May 1900, p. 656; *Daily Mail*, 10 May and 6 September 1900, 18, 20 and 21 June 1901. Salisbury's proposed 'national network of rifle clubs' was resurrected unsuccessfully by Roberts in June 1905. On rifle clubs, see M. J. Allison, 'The national service issue, 1899–1914', unpublished PhD, London, 1975, pp. 69–73.
16 Dawkins to Milner, 20 February 1903, Milner MSS Dep. 3, f. 201.
17 *Parliamentary Papers*, Cd 2061, May 1904, p. 16.
18 See Clarke to Esher, 15 April, 17 June and 31 August 1904, Esher MSS, ESHR 10/33–34.

19 H. O. Arnold-Forster to Balfour, 13 January 1905, Balfour Ad MSS 49723, ff. 68–9.

20 See Peter Fraser, *Lord Esher: A Political Biography* (London, 1973), pp. 119–21. The clearest, most comprehensive short account of Arnold-Forster and the Volunteers is in Ian Beckett's essay in I. Beckett and J. Gooch (eds), *Policies and Defence* (Manchester, 1981), pp. 47–68. See also I. W. F. Beckett, 'The English Rifle Volunteer Movement, 1859–1908', unpublished PhD, London, 1975.

21 See Chirol to Spring Rice, 6 October 1903, Spring Rice MSS, CASR 1/10/20.

22 Arnold-Forster's diary, 22 April 1904, Ad MSS 50337.

23 See Sandars to Balfour, 11 August 1905, Ad MSS 49763, ff. 133–6.

24 Fisher to Sandars, 29 July 1904, Ad MSS, 49710 f. 150.

25 Reported in *The Times*, 15 May 1905. On Colomb, see further D. M. Schurman, *The Education of a Navy* (London, 1965).

26 Esher to Repington, 14 May 1905. See also Esher's draft letter, 19 May 1905, ESHR 10/25.

27 Clarke to Esher, 16 May 1906, ESHR 10/39. Clarke deeply disliked Wilkinson. Esher supposed 'Wilkinson's effusions do not count as they are dictated partly by personal malice and jealousy', but Clarke maintained 'if sufficiently persistent they do count.' See Clarke to Sandars, 25 September 1905, Balfour Ad MSS 49702, ff. 59–61.

28 Dawkins to Maxse, 15 May 1905, Maxse MSS, 453, ff. 54–5.

29 Milner to Maxse, 7 June 1905, *ibid.*, ff. 64–5.

30 Repington to Maxse, 27 February 1906, *ibid.*, 455, ff. 272–3.

31 Clarke to Maxse, 12 July 1905, *ibid.*, 456, ff. 320–1.

32 Clarke and Balfour, 25 March 1905, Balfour Ad MSS 49701, f. 109.

33 Clarke to Chirol, 4 April 1905, enclosing Ottley to Clarke, 25 March 1905, Sydenham Ad MSS 50832, ff. 15–19.

34 Clarke to Sandars, 25 September 1905, Balfour Ad MSS 49702, ff. 59–61.

35 Clarke to Balfour, 8 December 1905, *ibid.*, ff. 189–92.

36 Ottley to Esher, 6 January 1912, *ibid.*, 49719, ff. 207–11.

37 Clarke to Chirol, 7 May 1908, Sydenham Ad MSS 50832, ff. 171–9.

38 Gwynne to Marker, 16 May 1905, Kitchener-Marker Ad MSS 52277B, ff. 164–7.

39 Arnold-Forster's diary, 10 November 1905, Ad MSS 50352. The dinner party was given by Kitty and Leo Maxse and Arnold-Forster's 'accuser' was Mrs Herbert Chamberlain.

40 Clarke to Balfour, 16 December 1905, Balfour Ad MSS 49702, ff. 193–8.

41 Both Childers and Le Queux were founder members of the Legion of Frontiersmen, a paramilitary society dedicated to being 'the eyes and ears of the Empire'. See Chapter XII below.

42 For more detail, see, *inter alia*, I. F. Clarke, *Voices Prophesying War* (London, 1966), pp. 145ff; and J. Steinberg, 'The Copenhagen complex', in *Journal of Contemporary History*, 1966, vol. I, no. 3, p. 40.

43 Strachey to Roberts, 10 June; and Roberts to Strachey, 12 June 1907 Strachey MSS, S/12/3/33.

44 Roberts to Probyn, 9 November 1905, Roberts MSS, R 7101/23/122.

45 M. J. Allison's thesis, *op. cit.*, covers the subject of the National Service League in great detail.

46 *National Service Journal*, September 1905, p. 425.

47 Milner to Roberts, 22 July 1905 (copy), Milner MSS, Dep. 16, f. 122.

48 See Arnold-Forster's diary, 2 and 3 August 1905, Ad MSS 50350.

49 Roberts to Strachey, 12 August 1905, Strachey MSS, S/12/3/30.

50 Brodrick to Selborne, 10 November 1905, Selborne MSS, vol. 2, ff. 108–12.
51 Roberts to Probyn, 9 November 1905, Roberts MSS, R 7101/23/122.
52 Arnold-Forster's diary, 2 August 1905, Ad MSS 50350.

Chapter 9: Enter 'the gorgeous Wreckington'

1 Repington assumed the name à Court under the terms of an old will when he succeeded to the Amington Hall Estate in Warwickshire on the death of his father in 1903. See Colonel Repington, *Vestigia* (London, 1919), ch. I. Also Laetitia Stapleton, 'Lt. Col. Charles à Court Repington CMG', in *Army Quarterly*, vol. 105, no. 2, p. 159.
2 Mary Repington, *Thanks for the Memory* (London, 1938), pp. 154–91, where there is a detailed account of the personal circumstances of the scandal. Repington's brother officer, Henry Wilson, circulated the written agreement undertaken by Repington which obliged the Army Council to call for his resignation. The two men thereafter were bitter enemies. See Jay Luvaas, *The Education of an Army*, pp. 297–8. See also on the Wilson incident and for a bitter critique of Wilson, Edmonds's unpublished 'Memoirs', ch. XX, p. 28ff., Edmonds MSS, III/5. But cf. Edmonds's dismissive entry on Repington in J. R. H. Weaver (ed.), *Dictionary of National Biography, 1922–30* (Oxford, 1937), pp. 717–18.
3 Quoted in *History of the Times* (London, 1947), (hereafter referred to as *HoT*) vol. III, p. 463. Many leading staff members of *The Times*, particularly Valentine Chirol, had been bitterly opposed to the appointment of Repington.
4 Money was a subject upon which Repington frequently and eloquently corresponded with Bell and Buckle. On one occasion, he told Bell that eight men on the staff of the *Daily Mail* were paid more than £2,000 a year. The implication was obvious, but he added, 'I think I should want all that to write for the Daily Mail!' Repington to Bell, 23 November 1906, Times Archive.
5 See, for example, his letter to Raymond Marker, 23 October 1904, Kitchener-Marker Ad MSS 52277B, ff. 10–11. His optimism was dented only by the numbing experience of the Great War. See *Vestigia*, p. 299. There is much useful information on Repington as a writer in W. M. Ryan, 'Repington, a study in the interaction of personality, the press and the power', unpublished PhD, University of Cincinnati, 1976.
6 Arnold-Forster's diary, 5 December 1907, Ad MSS 50353.
7 Clarke to Chirol, 11 November 1907, Sydenham MSS, Ad MSS 50832, ff. 62–3.
8 Clarke to Chirol, 7 May 1908, *ibid.*, ff. 171–9.
9 See Repington to Esher, 12 and 18 July 1905, Esher MSS, ESHR 10/25.
10 For example, *The Times*, 3 February, 10 and 29 November 1905.
11 Forster to Balfour, 28 May 1908, Balfour Ad MSS 49723, ff. 252–7.
12 Arnold-Forster's diary, 10 November 1905, Ad MSS 50352; Forster to Maxse, 27 December 1905, Maxse MSS, 453, ff. 191–4.
13 Repington to Esher, 27 October 1909 and 6 March 1910, ESHR 5/32–33.
14 Repington to Marker, 17 April 1905, Ad MSS 52277B, ff. 17–21.
15 Repington to Marker, 15 August and 9 July 1906, *ibid.*, ff. 78–85 and 111–14.
16 Repington to Marker, 26 January 1906, *ibid*, ff. 35–9.
17 This following section is based, unless otherwise cited, on Repington's account in *The First World War, 1914–18* (London, 1920), vol. I, pp. 1–16. There is a full précis of the 27 December article in *Vestigia*, pp. 262–3.
18 Repington to Esher, 14 January 1906, ESHR 10/26.
19 Haldane to Grey, 17 to 19 January 1906, FO 800/102.

20 Gwynne to Marker, 18 July and 23 August 1906, Kitchener-Marker Ad MSS 52277B, ff. 171–81.

21 Repington to Marker, 14 December 1906, *ibid.*, ff. 127–30.

22 Repington to Esher, 5 October 1906, ESHR 10/27.

23 Repington to Mrs Haldane, 27 February 1908, Haldane MSS, 6080, ff. 5–6.

24 See, for example, Haldane to his mother, 21 June 1907, 6 July 1908 and 1 June 1909, *ibid.*, 5977, ff. 181–2; 5980, ff. 51–2; 5981, ff. 223–4.

25 See Haldane to Esher, 4 September 1906 (copy), *ibid.* 5907, f. 91. During the 1913 invasion scare, Haldane advised Esher that it would be 'disastrous' to refute Repington in public. 'The press always gets the last word. But the silent man in authority always wins in the end.' See *ibid.*, 5910, f. 137.

26 Repington to Esher, 5 October 1906, ESHR 10/27.

27 Ewart's diary, 21 June 1908, Ewart MSS, RH/4/84/4. The talks – to place British troops to fight with the French in the event of a German attack through Belgium on France – were known as the 'WF Scheme'.

28 Ewart considered all Radicals to be 'permanently in alliance with everything that is disloyal, anti-English and unpatriotic'. He described Churchill as 'a little, wretched, half-baked, half-bred American politician', and his Radical mentor in the Cabinet, Lloyd George, as 'a silly, sentimental Celt with the horizon of a small Welsh attorney's office and an evil record of Little Englandism and want of patriotism'. See Ewart's diary, 9 February and 6 June 1909, Ewart MSS, RH/4/84/4.

29 Repington to Esher, 5 October 1906, ESHR 10/27.

30 Ewart, unpublished 'Autobiography', incorporating diary entry for 14 January 1907, Ewart MSS, RH/4/84.

31 Repington to Marker, 14 April 1907, Ad MSS 52277B, ff. 133–4. Repington was very concerned about the Tories returning to power, 'a stupid and dead party in a military sense, but d-d fools, even front-bench Tories, could make a scheme that works with compulsion'.

32 A. J. Marder (ed.), *Fear God and Dread Nought* (London, 1952–9), vol. II, p. 146.

33 Forster to Balfour, 28 May 1905, Balfour Ad MSS 49723, ff. 252–7.

34 Repington to Maxse, 17 October 1907, Maxse MSS, 457, f. 588.

35 Repington to Marker, 16 June 1905, Ad MSS 52277B, ff. 23–4.

36 Repington to Esher, 18 May 1905, Balfour Ad MSS 49718.

37 Repington to Marker, 29 June 1906, Ad MSS 52277B, ff. 66–71. Strachey and Northcliffe were founder members of the NDA, and H. A. Gwynne and Arthur Pearson were members of the executive committee.

38 Repington to Marker, 2 January 1906, Ad MSS 52277B, ff. 29–34.

39 *The Times*, 12 March 1906.

40 Repington to Marker, 6 August 1906, Ad MSS 52277B, ff. 103–10.

41 Repington to Marker, 5 July 1906, *ibid.*, ff. 72–7.

42 Repington to Marker, 26 January 1906, *ibid.*, ff. 35–9.

43 *Ibid.*, ff. 72–7.

44 Clarke to Balfour, 20 September 1906, Balfour Ad MSS 49702, ff. 217–20.

45 Clarke to Balfour, 18 November 1906, *ibid.*, ff. 224–5.

46 Repington to Esher, 22 November 1906, ESHR 10/27.

47 Repington to Roberts, 22 November 1906, Roberts MSS R62/9.

48 Repington to Roberts, 28 November 1906, *ibid.*, R62/10.

49 Repington to Milner, 17 July 1906, Milner MSS, Dep. 132, ff. 104–7.

50 Repington to Bell, 21 April 1907, Times Archive. See also Ewart's diary, entries for 14 and 31 January, 26 April and 7 May 1907, Ewart MSS, RH/84. This was

not the first time that Repington had offered the services of *The Times*'s intelligence department to a soldier. In June and again in December 1905, he made the same offer to Huguet should there be a war with Germany. See S. R. Williamson Jnr, *The Politics of Grand Strategy* (Cambridge, Mas., 1969), p. 67, fn. 22.

51 See M. V. Brett (ed.), *The Journals and Letters of Viscount Esher* (London, 1934–8), vol. II, p. 357.

52 See the letters between Repington and Roberts between July and November 1906, Roberts MSS, R 7101/23/62.

53 Balfour to Clarke, 20 July 1907, Balfour Ad MSS 49702, ff. 249–55; Clarke to Balfour, 23 July 1907, *ibid.*, f. 256. See Balfour and Clarke's formal letters, together with notes on invasion supplied by Repington and his friends in CAB 3/2/42A.

54 Repington to Maxse, 15 October 1907, Maxse MSS, 457, f. 587. On Maxse's attitude towards Balfour, see Newton, a close friend and contributor to the *National Review*, in his autobiography, *Retrospection* (London, 1941), p. 117.

55 See Repington to Esher, 14, 18, 22 and 31 October 1907, ESHR 5/23.

Chapter 10: A discordant band of brothers

1 See *The Times*, 2 January 1907. For the views on Fisher and his reforms that are quoted, see Strachey to Bullen, 3 September 1907, Strachey MSS, S/16/1/17; Gwynne to Beresford, 28 May 1907, Gwynne MSS 16.

2 See Fitzgerald to Maxse, 18 February 1905, Maxse MSS, 453, ff. 11–12; Custance to Bridge, 17 October 1901, 3 January and 11 May 1902, Bridge MSS, BRI/15; Noel to Selborne, 14 July 1912 (copy), Noel MSS, NOE/5.

3 See Edmond Slade's diary, 11 April and 21 January 1908, Slade MSS.

4 As late as July 1908, Northcliffe wrote to Garvin, 'As this abominable Fisher and Beresford controversy is becoming so important, would you write for the "Daily Mail" a 1200 word sketch of Fisher. The country is beginning to take sides and almost everybody is on the side of Beresford simply because *his* personality is known to the public while Sir John, having worked quietly [sic] is almost unknown.' Northcliffe to Garvin, 8 July 1908, Garvin MSS.

5 White to Strachey, 8 July 1908, Strachey MSS, S/16/2/32.

6 Midleton (Brodrick) to Selborne, 9 July 1908, Selborne MSS, vol. 3, ff. 58–61.

7 Chirol to Spring Rice, 18 October 1904, Spring Rice MSS, CASR 1/10 45–46.

8 See Almeric Fitzroy, *Memoirs* (London, 1927), vol. I, p. 272.

9 Beresford to Tweedmouth, 30 October 1906, Tweedmouth MSS, A 179.

10 *Daily Express*, 28 December 1906.

11 A. J. Marder (ed.), *Fear God and Dread Nought* (London, 1952–9), vol. II, p. 117, n. 1.

12 A. J. Marder (ed.), *op. cit.*, vol. II, p. 88.

13 Thursfield to Buckle, 30 December 1906 (copy), Thursfield MSS, THU/1.

14 A. J. Marder (ed.), *op. cit.*, vol. II, p. 109.

15 H. W. Wilson to A. White, 17 January 1907. See also letters of 18 January, 1 April and 6 May 1907, Arnold White MSS, WHI/200.

16 See Admiral Kerr, *Prince Louis of Battenburg* (London, 1934), pp. 225–6.

17 Beresford to Blumenfeld, 12 August 1907, Blumenfeld MSS, BERE 2.

18 Fisher to Thursfield, 25 December 1906, THU/1.

19 Thursfield to Buckle, 30 December 1906, *ibid.*

20 See A. J. Marder (ed.), *op. cit.*, vol. II, p. 108, n.2; p. 113 and n.1.

21 Selborne to Midleton, 2 August 1905, Selborne MSS, vol. 2, ff. 86–7.

22 Fitzgerald to Maxse, 18 February 1905, Maxse MSS, 453, ff. 11–12.
23 Forster's diary, 21 November 1905, Ad MSS 50352; Forster to Maxse, 27 July 1907, Maxse MSS, 457, ff. 552–6.
24 Midleton to Selborne, 18 December 1907, Selborne MSS, vol. 2, ff. 205–7.
25 Forster to Balfour, 28 November 1907, Balfour Ad MSS 49723, ff. 237–8.
26 A. Chamberlain to Maxse, 5 February 1908, Maxse MSS, 458, ff. 649–50.
27 Esher's 'Journal', 19 January 1908, ESHR 2/11.
28 Beresford to Gwynne, 29 June 1907, Gwynne MSS 16.
29 W. White to Strachey, 2 and 7 December 1908, Strachey MSS, S/16/2/45.
30 R. Bacon, *The Life of Lord Fisher of Kilverstone* (London, 1929), vol. II, pp. 180–2.
31 Letter by Admiral Bridge, published by *The Times*, 19 February 1907.
32 R. Bacon, *op. cit.*, vol. II, p. 120.
33 J. A. Spender, *Life, Journalism and Politics* (London, 1927), vol. II, p. 67.
34 See A. M. Gollin, *The Observer and J. L. Garvin, 1908–14* (London, 1960), pp. 35–6, 41–2, and chs II and III.
35 Fisher to Garvin, 6 March 1905, Garvin MSS.
36 Arnold-Forster to Balfour, 28 November 1907, Balfour Ad MSS 49723, ff. 237–8.
37 Forster's diary, 5 December 1907, Ad MSS 50357.
38 Fisher to Thursfield, 27 January 1903, THU/1; Fisher to Thursfield, 31 May 1903, *ibid.*
39 Fisher to Hurd, 2 April and 8 August 1910, Hurd MSS, HURD 1/14.
40 Fisher to Spender, 25 September 1904, Spender Ad MSS 46390, ff. 1–2.
41 Fisher to Hurd, 1 August 1906, HURD 1/13.
42 See Gwynne to Beresford, 23 May 1907, Gwynne MSS 16.
43 Beresford to Blumenfeld, 22 July 1915, Blumenfeld MSS, BERE 21.
44 Beresford to Blumenfeld, 29 July 1908, *ibid.*, BERE 6.
45 See Sandars to Balfour, 3 December 1904, Balfour Ad MSS 49762, ff. 182–6.
46 See S. Dark, *The Life of Sir Arthur Pearson* (London, n.d.), p. 119.
47 Fisher to Gwynne, 4 December 1905, Gwynne MSS 19.
48 Fisher to Gwynne, 21 January 1906, Cope-Cornford MSS, CPC/1. Later Fisher seems to have thought Gwynne's defection was largely Cornford's fault. 'A pity Gwynne went in for "Copious" Cornford. These lame men are always bitter.' Fisher to Garvin, 13 March 1908, Garvin MSS.
49 Beresford to Gwynne, 19 February 1907, Gwynne MSS 16.
50 Gwynne to Beresford, 23 May 1907, *ibid.*
51 Clarke to Esher, 27 June 1907, ESHR 10/40.
52 Repington to Esher, 14 January 1906, ESHR 10/26.
53 Repington to Esher, 14 October 1907, ESHR 5/23.
54 Quoted in A. J. Marder (ed.), *op. cit.*, vol. II, p. 186.
55 Repington to Esher, 5 November 1907, ESHR 5/24.
56 Repington to Esher, 15 February 1907, ESHR 5/22.
57 Gwynne to Beresford, 28 May 1907, Gwynne MSS 16.
58 Arnold-Forster, for example, was only interested in striking a blow against Esher, while Maxse was most concerned that the Committee of Imperial Defence be disbanded. Repington supported both the CID and Esher and was not too concerned about Balfour. His target was Fisher alone, and he had little faith in Gwynne's scheme anyway.
59 See M. V. Brett (ed.), *The Journals and Letters of Viscount Esher* (London, 1934–8), vol. II, p. 222.
60 Chamberlain to Maxse, 5 February 1908 and 24 January 1907, Maxse 458, ff. 649–50; and 457, ff. 475–6.

61 Beresford to Blumenfeld, 12 and 17 August 1907, Blumenfeld MSS, BERE 2/4.
62 Strachey to R. Bullen, 3 September 1907, Strachey MSS, S/16/1/17.
63 Beresford to Blumenfeld, 12 August 1907, BERE 2.
64 See Beresford to Balfour, 7 March 1908, Balfour Ad MSS 49713, ff. 177–83.
65 A. J. Marder (ed.), *op. cit.*, vol. II, p. 151.
66 *Ibid.*
67 Repington to Esher, 22 October 1907, ESHR 5/23.

Chapter 11: The Committee of Imperial Defence investigates

1 Repington to Esher, 22 October and 5 November 1907, ESHR 5/23–24.
2 See, for example, Esher to Roberts, 28 August 1907, R29/15.
3 M. V. Brett (ed.), *The Journals and Letters of Viscount Esher* (London, 1934–8), vol. II, pp. 246–9.
4 Repington to Bell, 4 December 1907, Times Archive.
5 Repington to Maxse, 15 and 17 October 1907, Maxse MSS, 457, ff. 587 and 588.
6 See Midleton to Balfour, 16 December 1907 (copy) enclosed with Midleton to Selborne, 18 December 1907, Selborne MSS, vol. 2, ff. 205–13.
7 Balfour to Arnold-Forster, 4 December 1907, Forster Ad MSS 50353, f. 122.
8 Beresford to Repington, 17 November 1907, Roberts MSS, R62/23.
9 Repington to Roberts, 30 October and 5 November 1907, R62/14 and 16.
10 M. V. Brett (ed.), *op. cit.*, vol. II, p. 257.
11 Forster's diary, 5 December 1907, Ad MSS 50353.
12 A. J. Marder (ed.), *Fear God and Dread Nought* (London, 1952–9), vol. II, p. 150, fn. 1.
13 See Edward 'Paddy' Goulding to Garvin, 17 November 1907; and Fisher to Garvin, 14 November 1907, Garvin MSS.
14 *The Times*, 12 November 1907.
15 Membership of committee and all direct quotations are taken from CAB 3/2/42A.
16 There is some evidence to suggest that Garvin might also have been involved. See Roberts to Garvin, 30 June 1908, Garvin MSS: 'The enquiry, you will remember, was brought about by the paper you so kindly helped me with last November.' However, in Roberts to Garvin, 10 November 1907, Roberts talks only of 'help with notes for a speech say by the middle of December'. This presumably would have been for his speech to the Lords in the new session.
17 Between 1908 and 1909 the German navy did consider offensive operations in the Firth of Forth but not invasion. Thereafter their strategy became defensive. See P. M. Kennedy, 'The development of German naval operation plans against England, 1896–1914', in *English Historical Review*, vol. LXXXIX, 1974, pp. 48–76. This essay is reprinted in P. Kennedy (ed.), *The War Plans of the Great Powers, 1880–1914* (London, 1979), pp. 171–98. On the blockade strategy, see Chapter XVIII. The strategic views of the German Admirals' Friedrich von Baudissin and his successor as Chief of Admiralty Staff, Max von Fischel, are discussed in H. H. Herwig, *Luxury Fleet* (London, 1980), *passim*.
18 Esher's 'Journal', 21 and 28 November 1907, ESHR 2/10.
19 Repington to Roberts, 27 November 1907, Roberts MSS, R62/27.
20 See F. Lindley, *Lord Lovat, 1871–1933* (London, 1935), p. 117.
21 Esher's 'Journal', 3 December 1907, ESHR 2/10; and Brett (ed.), *op. cit.*, vol. II, p. 263.
22 Fisher to Balfour, 29 November 1907, Balfour Ad MSS, 49712, f. 20.

23 Fisher to Balfour, 23 December 1907, *ibid.*, ff. 23–4.

24 Repington to Roberts, 12 December 1907, Roberts MSS, R62/32.

25 Repington to Roberts, 22 December 1907, R62/33.

26 Repington to Roberts, 2 January 1908, R62/35.

27 Quoted by H. R. Moon, whose thesis, 'The invasion of the United Kingdom, 1888–1914', unpublished PhD, London, 1970, is much the fullest and best account of the invasion issue available.

28 A. J. Marder (ed.), *op. cit.*, vol. II, p. 137.

29 Slade quoting Fisher in H. R. Moon, *op. cit.*, p. 361.

30 M. V. Brett (ed.), *op. cit.*, vol, II, p. 263.

31 Edmond Slade's diary, 29 January 1908, Slade MSS.

32 See, for example, Roberts to Garvin, 20 February 1908, Garvin MSS.

33 The British Navy League, a powerful pressure group designed to publicise and encourage public interest in the British navy, was founded in 1895. Similar organisations were set up by the Germans – the Flotenverein (1898) – and the French – La Ligue Maritime (1899). The league established thriving provincial and imperial branches and published its own journal edited by H. W. Wilson. Among active journalist members were the Harmsworth brothers, Leo Maxse, Arnold White, Spenser Wilkinson, Fred Jane, Conan Doyle and Rudyard Kipling. The league became divided in its loyalties between supporters of Fisher and Beresford and eventually a splinter group supporting Beresford, the Imperial Maritime League, was formed. There is much useful information on this subject in W. Mark Hamilton, 'The nation and the navy', unpublished PhD, London, 1977.

34 The Reichstag had that month approved a Supplementary Naval Law that provided for an increased battleship building programme for the next decade.

35 The Kaiser, created a British Admiral in 1889 by Victoria, was inordinately enthusiastic about the navy and showered British admirals and ministers with memoranda on guns, tactics, navigation, even naval architecture. Passing on one such imperial missive to the First Lord the worldly-wise Salisbury wrote, 'You will probably have a tendency to imprecate when you read this. It rather looks to me as if he was not "all there".' See G. Cecil, *Life of Salisbury* (London, 1921–32), vol. IV, p. 367.

36 There is a copy of the letter in Asquith MSS, vol. 19, ff. 249–51. See also *British Documents on the Origins of the War, 1898–1914* (London, 1927), vol. VI, pp. 132ff.

37 Midleton to Selborne, 15 May 1908, Selborne MSS, vol. 3, ff. 26–30.

38 Forster to Maxse, 27 July 1907, Maxse MSS, 457, ff. 552–6.

39 For example, he had complained to Campbell-Bannerman with some justification, 'I am unfortunately the person primarily responsible for the Admiralty and feel very keenly that important matters can be treated without my knowledge and concurrence.' Copy in Asquith MSS, vol. 21.

40 See Keith Robbins, *Sir Edward Grey* (London, 1971), p. 177, where the best though not entirely convincing explanation for Grey's extraordinary conduct is offered.

41 See, for example, Blennerhassett to Garvin, 7 March 1908, Garvin MSS: 'I fear Tweedmouth has been talking about the letter all over London, evidently proud of having received such a communication from a sovereign so illustrious.'

42 Esher's 'Journal', 4 March 1908, ESHR 2/11.

43 See *ibid.*, 9 March 1908, where it appears that Repington showed a draft to Churchill who made him promise 'in his own interests' not to publish; but that same evening Winston received a note from Repington 'saying that he had changed his mind'.

44 See *The Times*, 6 March 1908.

45 Repington to Esher, 5 March 1908, ESHR 10/53, f. 11.
46 According to an entry in Esher's journal dated 9 March 1908, Asquith had been told by the same informant as Repington – 'a lady who was there', that is, at the Rothschild's Tring house where Tweedmouth had read the letter and talked of it endlessly to his fellow weekend guests.
47 Spender to Tweedmouth, 6 March 1908, Tweedmouth MSS, B/126.
48 E. T. S. Dugdale, *German Diplomatic Documents* (reprint, New York, 1969), vol. III, p. 275.
49 Repington had told Roberts, 'I fancy he may regret his [Tweedmouth's] impertinence to you and his description of our little party as a "ring of wild and self-convinced alarmists".'
50 Repington to Roberts, 7 March 1908, R62/47.
51 Maxse to Northcliffe, 16 March 1908, Northcliffe Dep 4890/XXIII.
52 Northcliffe to Maxse, n.d. (March 1908), Maxse MSS, 458, f. 669.
53 Northcliffe to Garvin, 11 March 1908, Garvin MSS.
54 Fisher to Garvin, 26 January 1908, Garvin MSS. The actions of those directly involved – Esher, Fisher and Knollys – suggest that the letter to the Imperial Maritime League was designed to win a response from a wider circle than Wyatt, Horton-Smith and their associates, though they could hardly have expected the Kaiser's reaction.
55 Repington to Maxse, 11 March 1908, Maxse MSS, 458, ff. 663–4.
56 Sandars to Maxse, 21 March 1908, *ibid.*, f. 671.
57 Repington to Maxse, 11 March 1908, *supra.*
58 See Sandars to Maxse, 21 March 1908, *supra.*; Villiers to Maxse, 16 March 1908, *ibid.*, f. 666.
59 Repington to Maxse, 17 March, *ibid.*, f. 667.
60 See Asquith to Tweedmouth, 8 April 1908; Elgin to Tweedmouth, 20 April 1908, Tweedmouth MSS, B/22 and B/135.
61 M. V. Brett (ed.), *op. cit.*, vol. II, pp. 317–18. For Balfour's speech, see CAB 3/2/43A.
62 See Ewart's diary, 22 October 1908. Fisher was largely to blame for the contretemps with Nicholson. He was never a respector of senior army officers. As he later told Garvin, 'Any bloody fool can be a General and they usually are!' Fisher to Garvin, 9 January 1912, Garvin MSS.
63 See Hyndman to Maxse, 25 June, 18 and 22 August and 7 September 1908, Maxse MSS, 458, ff. 731–42 and 748. The paradox of Maxse making kindly references to Hyndman and Blatchford to 'protect' them from Radical and Labour critics was more apparent than real. H. A. Gwynne also boasted, though in private not public, that Hyndman 'the arch Socialist is by way of being a pal of mine'. Gwynne to Tyrrell, 31 October 1912, FO 800/107.
64 See W. S. Blunt, *My Diaries, 1888–1914* (single vol. edn, London, 1932), 7 August 1908, p. 624.
65 Conclusions 3 and 4 of the report (CAB 3/2/44A) were vital for the invasionist case. 'That our army for Home defence ought to be sufficient in numbers and organization . . . to deal with an invading force of 70,000 men.'
66 Milner had written to Roberts on this subject while the inquiry had still been in session. 'The futility of all this official argumentation that we cannot be taken by surprise is extraordinary. They never seem to think that we might be attacked *when we already have our hands full* with our small army all abroad . . . or our navy engaged in keeping *distant* seas open for our communications. . . . However great the need of our fleet abroad, *we must always keep* more than half of it "tethered

like a goat" to home waters *because* we should be helpless as no other nation would be in case of invasion. Where then is our "Sea Power"? We are not and cannot be supreme *on the ocean* if we must under all circumstances, be able to block the North Sea.' Milner to Roberts, 10 January 1908 (copy), Milner MSS, Dep. 16, ff. 145–6.

67 Repington to Haldane, 18 November 1908, Haldane MSS 5908, f. 75.
68 Repington to Haldane, 20 November 1908, *ibid.*, f. 76.
69 See M. V. Brett (ed.), *op. cit.*, vol. II, p. 361.
70 Garvin claimed that it was he who first suggested the 'million man standard' to Roberts. See Garvin to Northcliffe, 16 March 1909, Northcliffe Dep. 4890/LXXXV.
71 The vote was 74 to 32. For debate, see *Hansard*, iv:196:1679ff.
72 Dugdale, *op. cit.*, vol. II, pp. 329–30.
73 For report and comment on Rosebery's speech, see *The Times*, 5 and 12 December 1908.

Chapter 12: Of secrets, spies and saboteurs

1 *Daily Mail*, 12 August 1898.
2 *Ibid.*, 4 January 1900.
3 R. D. Blumenfeld, *RDB's Diary* (London, 1930), p. 223.
4 C. Lowe, 'About German spies', in *Contemporary Review*, 1910, vol. XCVII, pp. 49–51.
5 See Almeric Fitzroy, *Memoirs* (London, 1927), vol. I, p. 137.
6 Clarke to Balfour, 12 January 1905, Sydenham Ad MSS 50836, ff. 56–8.
7 See E. T. S. Dugdale, *German Diplomatic Documents* (reprint, New York, 1969), vol. III, p. 281.
8 See W. Nicolai (translated by G. Renwick), *The German Secret Service* (London, 1924), pp. 28–53.
9 CAB 4/1/CID Misc. 39B, pp. 2–3. I have had the advantage of reading Alistair Palmer's unpublished essay. 'The origins of the D Notice Committee' (1980), which first drew my attention to some of this material.
10 Brooks to G. Clarke, 23 October 1905, CAB 17/91.
11 Brooks to Garvin, 31 October 1905, Garvin MSS.
12 R. J. Walling to Brooks, 27 November 1905, CAB 17/91. This file contains many of the letters Brooks received and also a list he drew up summarising the responses for the information of the CID. Comparison of Brooks's lists with the replies shows how he misrepresented the editors, and misled the CID.
13 Leng to A. R. Byles, 19 June 1906, CAB 17/91.
14 See summary of these events in W. G. Greene to W. S. Churchill, 1 January 1912, ADM 116/4082.
15 *Dundee Advertiser*, 20 July 1906.
16 See Clarke (on behalf of Campbell-Bannerman) to J. Leng, 2 August 1906, and Leng to Clarke, 6 August 1906, CAB 17/91.
17 See A. H. Millar's article on Leng, in Sidney Lee (ed.), *Dictionary of National Biography: 1901–1911*, pp. 454–5.
18 Cornish to Tweedmouth, 6 November 1907, CAB 17/91.
19 There was also the problem of a journalist publishing material derived from a number of sources. The problem could also arise where a journalist had quoted from an official handbook available to the general public. This last is well illustrated by Archibald Hurd's confrontation with Churchill when he had just been appointed

First Lord. He insisted that Hurd had broken a confidence and that the information he had published was known to only three men. Hurd refused to give the name of his informant. See A. Hurd, *Who Goes There?* (London, 1941), ch. V *passim.*

20 See Cornish to Campbell-Bannerman, 21 October 1907, enclosing copy of resolution of Annual Conference, 16 and 18 October 1907.

21 See, for example, Brooks to Garvin, 22 January 1908, Garvin Papers.

22 See Greene to Churchill, 1 January 1912, *ante.*

23 See, for example, King's Regulations, para 423 and Army Order 69 (1907).

24 See Ewart to Ward, 15 August 1907; Ewart to Lyttleton, 8 July 1907, WO 32/6466. See also *The Times,* 26 June 1907.

25 *Hansard,* iv:109:1258–9. Not everyone shared Beresford's complacency. Edmund Robertson thought the influence of the press 'ought to be diminished'. *Hansard,* iv:96:722. In 1883, the War Office admitted that information was often given to *The Times* before the House because members did not give as serious attention to military subjects as the newspaper. See *Hansard,* iii:279:760ff.

26 Beresford to Arnold White, 27 June 1901, WHI/19.

27 Fawkes to McKenna, 18 and 24 July 1908, McKenna MSS, MCKN 3/8/8.

28 This, in part, explains the joyful outburst of Fisher to Garvin, 'You are Jove now and the Times will take a back seat. Heaven prosper you and increase the circulation of the Observer.' Quoted in A. M. Gollin, *The Observer and J. L. Garvin, 1908–14* (London, 1960), pp. 41–2.

29 Thursfield to Selborne, 15 August 1901, Selborne MSS, vol. 29, ff. 103–4. See also Buckle to Selborne, 11 December 1902, vol. 33, ff. 77–8.

30 30 January 1908, ADM 1/8030.

31 See 'Defenceless Dover', in *Morning Post,* 21 March 1908; Daniell to DNI, 21 March 1908; Liddell to Greene, 25 March 1908, and various memoranda dated 24 to 26 March 1908, ADM 1/8030.

32 See CAB 16/8, p. 11.

33 Northcliffe to Roberts, 19 June 1909, Roberts MSS, R46/162.

34 This statement is taken from Chapter XX of Edmonds's unpublished *Memoirs.* Compare the different version in the Appendix to the Report on Espionage by the CID, CAB 16/8, p. 16. 'Headwaiter suspected of being an officer. Admitted he was an NCO in a fortress artillery regiment.'

35 J. Edmonds, *Memoirs,* ch. XX, pp. 1–2, Edmonds MSS III/5.

36 Pocock supplied Battenberg with plans and photographs of a Russian naval base, gun emplacements and warships in 1905. When Pocock founded his Legion that year, Battenberg became a member. He persuaded Pocock that the Frontiersmen were better sending their information to naval rather than military intelligence. The War Office, though initially impressed by 'the very many well-known names' among the Legion's membership, by 1910 was firmly convinced it was 'a harmful and essentially unmilitary organisation'. By 1908, the Legion had approximately 3,500 members. Le Queux was a founder member of the Legion and his ideas exercised an enormous influence on that impressionable group of super-patriots.

I am much indebted to Geoff Pocock for giving me information on the Legion, and providing me with a transcript of Roger Pocock's pocket diary, a transcript of material on the Legion from War Office files, and allowing me to read his unpublished typescript biography of Pocock, *The Road for the Rest.* See also R. Pocock, *Chorus to Adventurers* (London, 1931); R. Pocock (ed.), *Frontierman's Pocket Book* (London, 1909).

37 *Weekly News* was owned by D. C. Thomson. Le Queux stated that Thomson commissioned the work after being persuaded by 'evidence' supplied by Le Queux and one of Thomson's editors, G. B. Duncan, after the two men had 'investigated

espionage activity by the Germans in Scotland'. See W. Le Queux, *Things I Know* (London, 1923), p. 237.

38 Le Queux later insisted that his informer was a 'Herr N. under-director of the Kaiser's Spy Bureau', *Things I Know*, p. 235.

39 Including the DMO and I. See General Ewart's diary, May 1908. See also General Henry Wilson's diary, January 1910.

40 R. Baden-Powell, *My Adventures as a Spy* (London, 1915), pp. 52–7. I am grateful to Dr Chris Andrew for drawing my attention to this work.

41 See N. S. B. Sladen, *The Real Le Queux* (London, 1938), ch. 18, *passim*.

42 *Punch*, 17 March 1909.

43 *Quarterly Review*, vol. CCIX, July 1908, pp. 295–6.

44 *The Times*, 21 August 1908.

45 See *British Documents on the Origins of the War, 1898–1914* (London, 1927), vol. VI, pp. 117 and 131–2.

46 Ewart, *Autobiography*, 29 May 1908, RH4/84/4/128.

47 But see G. Steinhauer and B. T. Felstead, *The Kaiser's Master Spy* (London, 1930), pp. 48–50. Steinhauer confessed after the war, 'I had forty agents in England but the sum total of their remuneration was hardly worth worrying about.'

48 Secret War Office memorandum with Ewart's covering note dated 1 February 1908, quoted in C. M. Andrew, 'The mobilization of British intelligence for the two world wars', in, N. F. Drieziger (ed.), *Mobilization for Total War* (Ontario, 1981), p. 83.

49 Ewart's diary, summary of 1908, RH4/84/3/125.

50 *Ibid.*, 14 February 1908.

51 *Ibid.*, 30 March 1909.

52 Clarke to Chirol 28 August 1908, Sydenham Ad MSS 50832, ff. 222–3.

53 See Maxse to Sandars, 28 September 1914, Sandars MSS 766, ff. 171–2.

54 Maxse to Northcliffe, 26 May 1909, Northcliffe Dep. 4890/XXIII.

55 See R. D. Purefry to Maxse, 12 September 1908, Maxse 458, f. 750.

56 Maxse to Northcliffe, 20 August 1908. Northcliffe Dep. 4890/XXIII.

57 Of Guy du Maurier's play, *An Englishman's Home*, he wrote to his sister Elizabeth that it had 'created an extraordinary agitation' in favour of his Territorials. 'I have not yet dared to appear in the audience – but I think I must do so.' Haldane to Elizabeth Haldane, 2 February 1909, Haldane MSS, 6011, ff. 82–3. For other views, by Esher and Milner, on this play, and the unexpected consequences that could arise from 'using' the play to promote other schemes, see, M. V. Brett (ed.), *The Journals and Letters of Viscount Esher* (London, 1934–8), vol. II, pp. 367–9, and H. Harmsworth to Esher, 5 February 1909, ESHR 12/9; Milner to McIver, 13 March 1909, Milner Dep. 35, ff. 159–60.

58 See CAB 16/8, p. 10.

59 Edmonds, *Memoirs*, p. 5, ch. XX, Edmonds MSS, III/5.

60 M. V. Brett (ed.), *op. cit.*, vol. II, p. 379.

61 CAB 16/8, p. 4.

62 Appendix 2, Cases 19 and 26, pp. 16–17.

63 How perfectly innocent behaviour could easily be misinterpreted is well illustrated by a letter from Lovat Fraser to Garvin, 7 March 1908, Garvin MSS. Fraser, taking a short holiday at Lulworth Cove, Dorset, became the object of 'the local coast-guard's intense suspicion because I spent sometime looking at the Fleet off Portland early this morning with a pair of powerful binoculars. I am apparently, the only visitor in this unfrequented nook.'

64 Driscoll probably was supplied his figures by J. T. Sturgeon, head of the Intelli-

gence Department of the Legion of Frontiersmen of which Driscoll was a leading member. He joined in 1907. Among their claimed counter-espionage successes reported to the War Office was the discovery of machine guns and 5,000 rifles and ammunition in City Road, London; and a cache of arms under a hotel in Bournemouth.

65 See C. Lowe, *op. cit.*, pp. 53–4.
66 See C. M. Andrew, *op. cit.*, p. 93. But compare Fisher's claim to Garvin; 'British Naval Intelligence has incomparable agents and money flowing like water.' Fisher to Garvin, 26 May 1909, Garvin MSS.
67 Dated 22 June 1912, in J. E. B. Seely MSS, S/19, f. 145.
68 See CAB 16/8 and CAB 17/91.
69 Ewart's diary, 17 September 1908 and 12 July 1909, Ewart RH4/84/3/125.
70 *The Times*, 30 July 1909.

Chapter 13: *Hysteria navalis*

1 Fisher to Hurd, 10 July 1910, Hurd MSS, HURD 1/14.
2 After Fisher's appointment as First Sea Lord, the relationship between the two men was never again as close as it had been. In February 1909, Hurd argued that the *Spectator* had turned traitor to Fisher's cause after a period of being a 'navalist whole-hogger'. He cited a 'priggish leader in the *Spectator* on "The Admiralty and the press" written by Strachey'. Therefore, among Fisher's strongest supporters, Strachey was seen as an apostate and worthy of contempt. See Hurd to Garvin, 12 February 1909, Garvin MSS. For earlier correspondence between Strachey and Fisher, see Strachey Papers, S/6/2/1.
3 Brassey to Tweedmouth, 6 January 1908, Tweedmouth MSS, B/107.
4 Arnold-Forster to Garvin, 20 July 1908, Garvin MSS. Cf. Selborne to Midleton, 28 June 1905, Selborne MSS, vol. 2. ff. 57–8.
5 Custance to Bridge, 3 June 1902, Bridge MSS, BRI/15. The leading technical critics of Fisher in the navy were Admirals Bridge, Custance and Noel. Mahan was a powerful and influential critic of the Dreadnought. See his 'Reflections historic and other suggested by the Battle of the Japan Sea', in *Proceedings of the US Naval Institute*, June 1906. Arthur Marder, *From the Dreadnought to Scapa Flow: the Royal Navy in the Fisher Era, 1904–1919* (5 vols), vol. 1, *The Road to War, 1904–1914* (Oxford, 1961), p. 60, n. 20, considered White's article in *Nineteenth Century*, June 1908, 'The cult of the monster warship', 'perhaps the best all round critique of the dreadnought policy'.
6 Beresford to Cawdor, 5 January 1908 (copy), Sandars MSS, 756, ff. 44–7.
7 Bridge to Strachey, 9 March 1908, S/16/2/24.
8 Clarke to Balfour, 8 December 1905, Balfour Ad MSS 49702, ff. 189–92.
9 Salisbury to Selborne, 27 February 1901, Selborne MSS, vol. 26, ff. 119–20.
10 Bridge to Strachey, 9 March 1908, *supra.*
11 Garvin to Rosebery, 27 February 1908, Rosebery MSS, 10121, ff. 89–90.
12 Strachey to White, 3 December 1908, S/16/2/45.
13 See White to Strachey, 13 July 1908, and Strachey to White, 10 July 1908, S/16/2/32.
14 Maxse to Garvin, 10, 13 and 31 January, 8 February 1908, Garvin MSS.
15 Fisher to his son, Cecil, quoted in Ruddock Mackay, *Fisher of Kilverstone* (Oxford, 1973), p. 286.
16 Fisher to McKenna, 24 May 1908, McKenna MSS, MCKN 3/4/9.

17 Even his appointment as First Sea Lord Fisher had reason to suppose had been offered him because it was 'simply unavoidable' and that Selborne had then made other appointments 'to anticipate anything I might be up to . . . to checkmate me'. See Fisher to Esher, n.d. (May 1904), ESHR 10/41.
18 Memorandum dated 28 April 1904, in A. Chamberlain MSS, AC17/59.
19 Bruce K. Murray, *The People's Budget, 1909/10* (Oxford, 1980), p. 1.
20 *The Times,* 22 March 1909.
21 *New Age,* 25 March 1909, p. 437.
22 Fisher to Garvin, 7 February 1908, Garvin MSS.
23 For the details of these transactions, see A. J. A. Morris, *Radicalism Against War, 1906–14,* pp. 126ff.
24 See comments in *Nation,* 8 February 1908.
25 See *Daily Mail,* 7 and 25 February 1908.
26 See A. M. Gollin, *The Observer and J. L. Garvin* (London, 1960), p. 40.
27 Arnold-Forster to Garvin, 13 February 1908, Garvin MSS.
28 Spenser Wilkinson to Grey, 14/18 January 1908, FO 800/12.
29 *Hansard,* iv:185:1372.
30 *Ibid.,* Column 586.
31 Cope-Cornford to Gwynne, 12 August 1907, Gwynne 16.
32 *Hansard,* iv:185:1372.
33 The Liberal press also accepted Asquith's assurance passively, with the exception of Massingham in the *Nation* (14 March 1908), who castigated the Prime Minister for allowing himself to become the victim of Balfour's 'hypothetical scaremongering'. Was Asquith not aware that his Tory opponent was 'intent upon heading straight for war with Germany'?
34 M. V. Brett (ed.), *The Journals and Letters of Viscount Esher* (London, 1934–8), vol. II, p. 295.
35 *Concord,* April 1908, vol. XXIV, no. 4, p. 44.
36 See M. V. Brett (ed.), vol. II, pp. 329–30 and 370; Tom Jones, *Lloyd George* (London, 1951), p. 37.
37 *Daily Mail,* 18 April 1908.
38 See Lloyd George to McKenna, 11 September 1908; McKenna to Lloyd George, 13 September 1908, Asquith MSS, vol. 20, ff. 83 and 85.
39 M. V. Brett (ed.), *op. cit.,* vol. II, p. 309.
40 Reported in *The Times,* 2, 17 and 30 October and 10 November 1908.
41 *Hansard,* iv:196:560 and 1768.
42 *The Times,* 13 November 1908.
43 *British Documents on the Origins of the War, 1898–1914* (London, 1927), (hereafter referred to as *BD*), vol. VI, p. 226.
44 F. W. Wile to Northcliffe, 6 January 1910, Northcliffe Dep. 4890/LV.
45 F. W. Wile to Northcliffe, 13 January 1909, and 6 January 1910, *ibid.*
46 Enclosed with Boyd to Milner, 14 April 1909, Milner Dep. 35, ff. 180–3.
47 Haldane, in a letter to his mother, described the interview as 'an extraordinary performance. We know – this is private – that he corrected the proof for the Daily Telegraph himself.' 30 October 1908, Haldane MSS, 5980, ff. 154–5. See also Lord Hardinge, *Old Diplomacy,* p. 170. Alterations to the typescript were not made by the Kaiser. He did not see it as he was at Rominten at the time, his shooting box in East Prussia. The alterations were made by Klehmet of the political section of the Foreign Office. The original typescript is in the Bodleian Library, MS Eng, His, d256, f. 43. On the *Daily Telegraph* interview, see, L. Cecil *The German Diplomatic Service 1891–1914* (Princeton, 1976), p. 304; Alan Palmer, *The Kaiser*

(London, 1978), pp. 129ff.; C. H. D. Howard (ed.), *The Diary of Edward Goschen 1900–1914* (London, 1980), pp. 25, 27, 179, 293–97.

48　See, for example, *Labour Leader,* 6 November 1908.

49　See, for example, *Daily Mail,* 29 and 30 October 1908. Compare the remarkably mild tone of *The Times.* Was this a reaction to the earlier response of the press to *The Times*'s squib over the Kaiser/Tweedmouth correspondence? Extreme anti-German critics, like Leo Maxse, noted the 'significance' of the choice of the *Daily Telegraph* to publish the interview. Burnham's paper was considered 'soft' on Germany and had retained the services of the 'beastly Bashford' as its Berlin correspondent at the direct request of Bülow in 1902 when there had been talk of his replacement as he was too much under the influence of the Wilhelmstrasse. For the official reactions of the British Foreign Office to the Kaiser interview in the *Daily Telegraph,* see *BD,* vol. VI, pp. 201–26.

50　Bertie to Hardinge, 11 November 1908, Hardinge MSS, vol. 11, ff. 50–2.

51　The prevailing tone of the Kaiser's personal observations on England had been friendly and most of his indiscreet remarks were repeats of earlier statements already commented upon in the English press. For example, his comments on the Boer War and his claim to have advised on tactics had been discussed in the July issue of the *National Review* by André Mevil, and again in December 1907 by 'Ignotus' (H. W. Wilson). There had also been an article by J. L. Bashford in the January 1908 issue of the *Strand Magazine.*

52　Hale probably wrote two versions of the interview. The milder was submitted to *McClure's* who turned it down before it was accepted by *New Century* on the grounds of its 'novelty . . . and a near view of royalty'. In late August, Northcliffe had sent Tyrrell an account of the Kaiser's interview which he had received from the office of the *New York Times.* This was seen by Francis Bertie who questioned its authenticity. See minute dated 21 August 1908, FO 800/109. What were thought to be accurate records of the interview with Hale were secured by two British newspapers. When one considered publication, Grey prevented it. The Foreign Secretary was shown a copy of the banned article by the German Ambassador, Metternich. See Grey to Bertie, 18 December 1908, and Grey to Metternich, 21 December 1908, FO 800/61. But compare Gwynne to Maxse, 2 December 1908, Maxse MSS, 445, f. 178, where Gwynne claims, 'I got into hot water because I published as much of [the interview] as I could.' See also *BD,* vol. VI, p. 225.

53　Low to Maxse, 22 November 1908, Maxse MSS, 458, ff. 772–4.

54　See Stephen E. Koss, *Sir John Brunner* (Cambridge, 1970), p. 223; Francis Hirst, *The Six Panics* (London, 1913), pp. 51 and 91–2; *Nation,* 6 and 27 February 1909.

55　*The Times,* 15 October and 30 November 1908.

56　See Lord Riddell, *More Pages From My Diary, 1908–1914* (London, 1934), p. 17, and A. J. Marder (ed.), *Fear God and Dread Nought* (London, 1952–9), *op. cit.,* vol. II, pp. 235–6.

57　Memorandum, 15(?) January 1909, cited by A. J. Marder, *From Dreadnought to Scapa Flow,* pp. 155–6.

58　See A. J. Marder (ed.), *op. cit.,* vol. II, p. 203.

59　Lloyd George to Asquith, 2 February 1909, Asquith MSS, vol. 21.

60　*The Times,* 19 and 22 January 1909. See *History of the Times* (London, 1947), vol. III, p. 625.

61　Asquith to Lloyd George, 8 February 1909, Lloyd George MSS, C6/11/4. The Prime Minister was not obliged to make revelations to the press himself – he could always count upon the indiscretions of his wife Margot for that, though she could be a double-edged weapon. Asquith sent frequent notes of complaint to his colleagues full of high-sounding appeals to constitutional convention and the doctrine of collective ministerial responsibility, but they all fell upon deaf ears. For an example of one of these notes, see Asquith to All Cabinet Members, July 1910, in MCKN 3/17/9.

62 Lloyd George to Asquith, 8 February 1909, Lloyd George MSS, C6/11/5.
63 Garvin to Gerard Fiennes, 5 February 1909 (copy), Garvin MSS.
64 Record of a conversation with Fisher by Austen Chamberlain in his *Politics from Inside* (London, 1936), pp. 150–1.
65 Quoted in Gollin, *op. cit.*, p. 70.
66 See Lucy Masterman, *C. F. G. Masterman* (London, 1939), p. 124.
67 Verbatim report of meeting, 23 February 1909, Asquith MSS, vol. 21.
68 *Ibid.* In the notes Asquith made of the meeting, mostly doodles(!), the figure 54 is repeated and heavily circled.
69 The interesting feature of Asquith's compromise proposal is that in all its essentials it was the same ploy that Lloyd George had suggested a week earlier to J. A. Spender. Lloyd George was not a close associate of Spender's then and it seems likely that the Chancellor had been touting for the *Westminster Gazette*'s support for the little navy group. Spender was always closest to Grey. He rejected Lloyd George's proposal as 'unconstitutional' and a 'transparent shuffle' to which he could not see any government committing itself. See Wilson Harris, *J. A. Spender* (London, 1946), pp. 93–4.
70 See Gollin, *op. cit.*, p. 73.
71 Garvin to Northcliffe, n.d., 16(?) March 1909, Northcliffe Dep. 4890/LXXXV.
72 On their campaign and its failure, see A. J. A. Morris, *Radicalism Against War, 1906–14*, ch. VI *passim.*
73 For the debate, see, *Hansard*, v:2:930ff.
74 A. T. Bassett, *Life of John Edward Ellis* (London, 1914), p. 253. Asquith's 'admission' galvanised patriotic associations like the Navy League into redoubling their alarmist efforts, though they obviously thought the premier's words confirmed what they had long been claiming. The Secretary of the Navy League wrote to all members, 'Everyone who read the Debates on the Navy Estimates . . . must have received the impression of the seriousness of the position which will remain implanted in his mind during the remainder of his life. . . . The Two Power Standard has gone by the board and all patriots are now filled with anxiety as to whether in 1912 we shall possess even an equal number of Dreadnoughts with Germany.' Dated 26 April 1909, there is a copy in the Garvin MSS. Garvin was an executive member of the League.
75 Gollin, *op. cit.*, p. 75.
76 Garvin to Northcliffe, n.d. 17(?) March 1909, Northcliffe Dep. 4890/LXXXV.
77 A. Chamberlain, *op. cit.*, pp. 160–1.
78 M. V. Brett (ed.), *op. cit.*, vol. II, p. 377.
79 H. Wilson's diary. Entries for 18, 22 and 23 March 1909, Henry Wilson MSS, DS/MISC/80.
80 *Labour Leader*, 26 March 1909, p. 198.
81 See *Daily Mail*, 19, 23, 26 and 29 March 1909. On Higginbottom, see his autobiography, *The Vivid Life* (London, 1934), and J. W. Robertson Scott, *The Life and Death of a Newspaper* (London, 1952), pp. 392ff.
82 M. V. Brett (ed.), *op. cit.*, vol. II, pp. 377–8.
83 Grey to Garvin, 22 March 1909, Garvin MSS.
84 See Gollin, *op. cit.*, pp. 78–80.

85 Chirol to Northcliffe, 25 March 1909, Northcliffe Dep. 4890/XCIX.
86 Garvin to Northcliffe, 6 April 1909, *ibid.*/LXXXV.
87 This was the second time within a few months that Garvin's uncritical attitude towards Fisher had been raised in the context of *The Times*. In January and February, constant rumours had circulated in London that Northcliffe would replace Buckle as editor with Garvin. The whole complex story from Garvin's point of view is told in his letter to E. J. Dillon, 12 February 1909 (copy), Garvin MSS. The involvement of Fisher is explained in Gollin, *op. cit.*, pp. 161–7. It is possible that this *might* have been a consideration in the minds of Chirol and Bell, but it was Fisher who was undoubtedly their main target.
88 See, for example, Wilson to Northcliffe, 15 and 22 May 1909, Northcliffe Dep. 4890/XLIX.
89 Quoted Gollin, *op. cit.*, pp. 83 and 85–6.
90 *Ibid.*, pp. 86–7.
91 Garvin to Stead, 6 May 1909 (copy). See also Garvin to White, 4 and 6 May (copies), Garvin MSS.
92 Gollin, *op. cit.*, pp. 86–7.
93 Fisher to Garvin, 26 May 1909, Garvin MSS.
94 *Labour Leader*, 30 July 1909, p. 491. For Mahan in America, writing to his friend Admiral Bouverie Clark, distance dissolved the niceties of the problem to a simple assertion that 'the vacillating course of the Admiralty' was because 'the Cabinet is loaded down with socialistic promises'. Mahan sympathised with Clark's 'wrath and exasperation' and reflected that 'those who abuse armaments and war fail to see that both are the effects and not the cause of conditions'. Mahan to Adm. B. F. Clarke, 1 October 1909, Mahan MSS, Box 4.
95 Wilson to Northcliffe, 15 May 1909, Northcliffe Dep. 4890/XLIX.
96 Garvin to Northcliffe, 4 August 1909 (copy), Sandars MSS, 759, ff. 65–70.
97 See, W. T. Stead to Garvin, 14 October and 9 December 1909, Garvin MSS.

Chapter 14: The sinking of Admiral Fisher

1   Beresford to Cawdor, 5 January 1908 (copy), Sandars MSS, 756, ff. 44–7.
2   Cawdor to Balfour, 8 January 1908 (copy), *ibid.*, ff. 48–9.
3   *John Bull*, 18 January 1908, p. 55.
4   Esher's 'Journal', 19 January 1908, ESHR 2/11.
5   Beresford to Carson, 21 January 1908, Carson MSS, D 1507/5/9.
6   Beresford to Carson, 2 February 1908, *ibid.*
7   See S. Lee, *King Edward VII* (London, 1927), vol. II, p. 600.
8   Balfour to Cawdor, 9 January 1908 (copy), Sandars MSS, 756, ff. 50–1.
9   Lansdowne to Balfour, 18 December 1907, *ibid.*, 754, ff. 284–7.
10 Edmond Slade's diary, 21 January 1908.
11 *Ibid.*, 13 January 1908.
12 See M. V. Brett (ed.), *The Journals and Letters of Viscount Esher* (London, 1934–8), vol. II, p. 286.
13 Clarke to Chirol, 21 October 1908, Sydenham Ad MSS 50832, ff. 141–6.
14 The personal issue between Fisher and Beresford tends to obscure an important *political* consideration, and also a fundamental question about the *purpose* of the Navy League. In essence, the Beresfordians claimed that the League's executive, by standing on the principle of being above party, effectively supported the Liberals when it confined its activities to education and refused to attack Fisher. In its turn, the executive of the Navy League accused the Beresfordians of being the

cat's-paws of a section of the Tory press. See on this important subject Anne Summers, 'The character of Edwardian nationalism', in Paul Kennedy and Anthony Nicholls (eds), *Nationalist and Racialist Movements in Britain and Germany Before 1914* (London, 1981), pp. 78–80.

15 *Concord,* February 1908, vol. XXIV, no. 2, p. 20.
16 M. V. Brett (ed.), *op. cit.,* vol. II, p. 276.
17 W. White to Strachey, 12 March 1908, Strachey MSS, S/16/2/24.
18 Slade's diary, 24 April 1908.
19 *Ibid.,* 11 May 1908. See also Midleton to Selborne, 9 July 1908, Selborne MSS, vol. 3, ff. 58–61. 'Beresford cutting Fisher dead . . . of course put the King against him and the whole hierarchy are of course determined to have him out.'
20 *The Times,* 6 July, 1908. See also A. Clark (ed.), Viscount Lee of Fareham, *A Good Innings* (London, 1974), pp. 99–101.
21 *The Times,* 8 July 1908.
22 Beresford to Blumenfeld, 29 July 1908, Blumenfeld MSS, BERE 6.
23 See A. J. Marder (ed.), *Fear God and Dread Nought* (London, 1952–9), vol. II, pp. 184–5 and 189.
24 Thursfield to McKenna, 14 August 1908, McKenna MSS, MCKN 3/13/6.
25 W. White to Strachey, 8 July 1908, S/16/2/32.
26 *Ibid.*
27 Strachey to White, 10 July 1908, *ibid.*
28 Quoted in A. J. Marder, *From the Dreadnought to Scapa Flow: the Royal Navy in the Fisher Era, 1904–1919* (5 vols), vol. 1, *The Road to War, 1904–1914* (Oxford, 1961), p. 104.
29 Fisher to Garvin, 7 February 1908, Garvin MSS.
30 See Beresford to Blumenfeld, 28 March 1909, Blumenfeld MSS, BERE 7.
31 See Northcliffe to Marlowe, 16 February 1909, Northcliffe Dep. 4890/XLV.
32 A. J. Marder, *op. cit.,* p. 189.
33 Esher's 'Journal', 20 April 1908, ESHR 2/11.
34 M. V. Brett (ed.), *op. cit.,* vol. II, p. 380.
35 See A. M. Gollin, *The Observer and J. L. Garvin* (London, 1960) p. 78; and previous chapter.
36 S. Lee, *op. cit.,* vol II, pp. 680–1.
37 See G. Bennett, *Charlie B* (London, 1968), pp. 302ff.
38 A. J. Marder (ed.), *op. cit.,* vol. II, p. 211.
39 M. V. Brett (ed.), *op. cit.,* vol. II, pp. 382–3.
40 Quoted in Gollin, *op. cit.,* p. 77.
41 See M. V. Brett (ed.), *op. cit.,* vol. II, p. 383.
42 See *The Times,* 3 and 23 April 1909.
43 Fisher to Garvin, 26 May 1909, Garvin MSS.
44 See Fisher to Spender, 2 July 1909, Spender Ad MSS 46390, ff. 66–7; A. J. Marder, *op. cit.,* p. 191.
45 See *ibid.,* p. 192, fn. 10.
46 'Report . . . to inquire into certain questions of naval policy raised by Lord Charles Beresford', CAB 16/9.
47 Sandars to Esher, 15 August 1909, ESHR 5/31.
48 A. J. Marder (ed.), *op. cit.,* vol. II, p. 214. For the opinions of Fisher, Beresford, Esher and Sandars on report, see Esher to Balfour, 15 August 1909; Balfour to Esher, 16 August 1909; and Esher to Sandars, 24 August 1909, Balfour Ad MSS 49719, ff. 93–8.
49 Fisher to Garvin, 26 May 1909, Garvin MSS.

50   Sandars to Esher, 25 August 1909, ESHR 5/31.
51   H. C. Roberts to Esher, 7 February 1908, Garvin MSS.
52   Fisher to Garvin, 31 August 1908, *ibid.*
53   Maxse to Esher, 3 and 6 January 1910, ESHR 5/33.
54   Repington to Esher, 16 August 1909, *ibid.* 5/31.
55   Repington to Buckle, 7 January 1912, Times Archive.
56   See Ewart's diary, 4 January 1909, RH4/84/3/125. 'I can't help thinking, and I
     know Slade thinks it, that old Fisher is deliberately getting rid of him. Slade has
     shown himself to be a strong man, no fool, and perhaps he has been too friendly
     towards the Military.' Fisher sent Slade to the East Indies station while Ewart was
     effectively pensioned off as Commander-in-Chief Scotland! On Slade, see also
     Beresford's claim and McKenna's rebuttal, 29 June 1911 on second reading of
     Navy Prize Bill, *Hansard*, v:27:623.
57   Fisher to McKenna, 11 August 1908, MCKN 3/4/18.
58   Sandars to Esher, 16 September 1909, ESHR 5/31.
59   Beresford to Balfour, 29 October 1909.
60   See *The Times*, 25 October and 1 November 1909. Beresford's letters and also
     comment by Asquith and McKenna are available in the Asquith MSS.
61   Fisher to Hurd, 25 March 1910, HURD 1/14.
62   Quoted in G. Bennett, *op. cit.*, p. 310.
63   Fisher to Garvin, 22 January 1910, Garvin MSS.
64   The most recent account of this subject is in Stephen Roskill's *Earl Beatty* (London,
     1980), pp. 186ff. and the relevant footnotes which indicate some of the huge
     literature on the subject of Jutland and various opposing views. I find Captain
     Roskill's argument concerning armour plate quite convincing.
65   This series of articles and the political implications of naval scaremongering are
     discussed in Chapter XV.
66   R. Butler to A. White, 13 December 1909, WHI/77.
67   Quoted in Gollin, *op. cit.*, p. 60.
68   H. A. Gwynne to A. White, 1 April 1908, WHI/76.

PART 3: FOR NATIONAL SECURITY AND PARTY ADVANTAGE: THE POLITICIANS

Chapter 15: Naval scaremongering: Garvin's election cannon-ball

1   See Northcliffe to Garvin, 14 May 1909, Northcliffe Dep. 4890/LXXXV, and
    Northcliffe to Garvin, 22 May 1909, Garvin MSS.
2   Northcliffe to Wilson, 19 May, and Wilson to Northcliffe, 22 May 1909,
    Northcliffe Dep. 4890/XLIX.
3   See *Daily News* and *Daily Chronicle*, 3 May 1909.
4   Wilson to Northcliffe, 22 May 1909, *supra*.
5   Maxse to Garvin, 9 August 1909, Garvin MSS.
6   In an impromptu speech to the editorial staff of the *Daily Mail*, who were
    spending a day at 'Sutton Place' as Northcliffe's guests, he observed, 'One runs a
    newspaper, as one must do, with a number of men who have very strong feelings.
    I think we are rather more inclined to favour in reporting the party whose views
    we editorially support, and that, I think, to be wrong and unwise, a relic of the
    days when Dr Johnson said that in reporting the House of Commons he made
    the Whig dogs suffer. . . . I do ask our staff to try to make the paper as absolutely
    impartial as possible. . . . It is very important that so gigantic a power as ours

should be used fairly.' Quoted in R. Pound and G. Harmsworth, *Northcliffe* (London, 1959), p. 372.

7 Pound and Harmsworth, *op. cit.*, p. 377.
8 Garvin to Northcliffe, 4 August 1909, Northcliffe Dep. 4890/LXXXV.
9 Garvin to Northcliffe, 5 August 1909, *ibid.*
10 Northcliffe to Balfour, 4 August 1909, *ibid./*III.
11 Garvin to Sandars, 31 May 1910, Sandars MSS, 760, ff. 119–21.
12 Balfour to Garvin, 10 August 1909, Garvin MSS.
13 Northcliffe to Kennedy Jones, 27 September 1909, Northcliffe Dep. 4890/XLIV.
14 Even Strachey's *Spectator*, the main mouthpiece of the free trade Unionists, conformed, at least in the sense that it concentrated upon the demerits of the Liberals rather than the fallacies of the protectionist gospel. This change of tactic by Strachey points to the increasing difficulties of free trade Unionist sympathisers. A concern about overweening government interference had always been prominent in the thinking of this Whig remnant that was so uncomfortably folded within the Unionist flock. On that score alone, it was argued that the 1909 budget was a much more *immediate* threat than the possible imposition of protection at some uncertain future date. It was in this spirit that they joined their fellow Unionists, but they were utterly opposed to any idea that the Lords might reject the budget. They thought such a move not only politically unwise but totally unacceptable as contrary to established constitutional convention.
15 Northcliffe to Garvin, incorrectly dated 16 August 1909, Northcliffe Dep. 4890/LXXXV.
16 Garvin's spidery hand was made even more difficult to read by his habit of writing both sides of very thin paper. After this admonition, he made some effort to improve his handwriting. Many of his important letters were written at his dictation by his wife. Other letters to friends were usually typed by his secretary.
17 Postcard, Northcliffe to Garvin, 21 October 1909, Northcliffe Dep. 4890/LXXXV.
18 Grey to Milner, 4 December 1908, and 22 January 1909, Milner Dep. 35, ff. 54–60 and 129.
19 For this disposition on the Liberal side, see, Gardiner's attitude to Germany and German behaviour as discussed in S. E. Koss, *Fleet Street Radical* (London, 1973), pp. 82ff. See also Garvin to Amery, 1 July 1907 (copy), Garvin MSS.
20 Milner to Roberts, 24 November 1909 (copy), Milner Dep. 16, f. 188.
21 Sandars to Balfour, 14 October 1909, Balfour Ad MSS 49766, ff. 17–19.
22 Sandars to Esher, 16 September 1909, ESHR 5/31.
23 Sandars to Balfour, 22 December 1909, Balfour Ad MSS 49766, ff. 44–7.
24 Ware to Chamberlain, 21 December 1909, A. Chamberlain MSS, AC8/3/6.
25 See Garvin to Chamberlain, 15 December 1909, AC8/3/3. Three days later, Austen Chamberlain wrote to Garvin expressing his complete satisfaction with the arrangements that Northcliffe and Garvin had made for reporting and publicising his speeches. See Chamberlain to Garvin, 18 December 1909, Garvin MSS.
26 Garvin to Amery, 30 November 1909 (copy), Garvin MSS.
27 Typescript entitled, 'Campaign literature, 1909', in, 'Works', Garvin MSS.
28 Sandars to Balfour, 30 September 1909, Balfour Ad MSS 49766, ff. 9–13.
29 Garvin to Northcliffe, 1 December 1906, Northcliffe Dep. 4890/LXXXV.
30 *Observer,* 8 August 1909, and Balfour to Garvin, 10 August 1909, Garvin MSS.
31 W. T. Stead to Garvin, 14 October and 9 December 1909, *ibid.* The last

reference by Stead was to his description of Garvin in a magazine article as 'Io's gadfly'.

32 Garvin to Sandars, 14 February 1910, Balfour Ad MSS 49795, ff. 69–77.
33 Sandars to Balfour, 18 December 1909, *ibid.*, 49766, ff. 31–41.
34 See J. A. Ramsden, 'The Organisation of the Conservative and Unionist Party in Britain, 1910–30', unpublished DPhil, Oxford, 1975, pp. 232–3. The expenditure of the Press Bureau in its first year (1910–11) was £422. Two years later (1913–14), this had increased to £2,509.
35 On Pryor, see Pound and Harmsworth, *op. cit.*, pp. 210ff.
36 Sandars to Northcliffe, 18 December 1909, Northcliffe Dep 4890/I. See also a letter from the chief agent at Central Office (drafted by Sandars) to the editors 'of all friendly London newspapers for the arrangement of interviews wholly independent of the ordinary "channel of news" ', enclosed in Sandars to Garvin, 18 December 1909, Garvin MSS.
37 Sandars to Northcliffe, 22 December 1909, Northcliffe Dep. 4890/I.
38 Sandars to Northcliffe, 13 December 1909, *ibid.*
39 Sandars to Balfour, 24 January 1910, Balfour Ad MSS 49766, ff. 81–9.
40 Sandars to Balfour, 16 December 1909, *ibid.*, f. 29.
41 A. J. Marder (ed.), *op. cit.*, vol. II, pp. 277–8.
42 *Ibid.*, p. 279.
43 Sandars to Garvin, 5 November 1909, Garvin MSS. On the comparative powerlessness even of the Conservative leader in the matter of choosing a parliamentary candidate after the reorganisation of the party after the 1906 election, see Balfour to Selborne, 6 March 1908, Selborne MSS 1, ff. 68–79.
44 F. S. Oliver to Garvin, 28 November 1909, Garvin MSS.
45 Edward Goulding to Garvin, 20 November 1909, *ibid.*
46 Quoted in G. Bennett, *Charlie B.* (London 1968), p. 312.
47 See *The Times*, 3 August, 21 September, 14 and 17 December 1909 and 1, 3, 6, 7, 8, 12, 15 and 18 January 1910.
48 Fisher to Mrs Garvin, 1 January 1910, Garvin MSS.
49 *Ibid.*
50 Garvin to Northcliffe, 3 January 1910, Dep. 4890/LXXXV.
51 A. J. Marder (ed.), *op. cit.*, vol. II, p. 288.
52 Blatchford had been born to most humble circumstances in 1851. He joined the army as a better alternative to starving. He served six years in the colours rising to the rank of sergeant. When he married he supplemented his meagre earnings as a brush-maker by free-lance writing. His friendship with A. M. Thompson led to full-time employment as a journalist. In 1891, with Thompson and E. F. Fay, he established the *Clarion*, the first English socialist weekly. Blatchford popularised his own version of socialism – something akin to that of William Morris with strong patriotic overtones – in a best-selling penny booklet, *Merrie England* (1893). The *Clarion* retained its position as the most popular organ of English socialism until 1900 when Blatchford's ardent support of the Boer War alienated many of his former friends. In the following years, his support of conscription and warnings of Germany's aggressive designs against England led Blatchford to be as frequently pilloried in the Radical/Labour press as a jingo hot-head as H. M. Hyndman. In a letter to Maxse (7 September 1908, Maxse MSS, 458, f. 748), Hyndman wrote, 'They go for us all the time but Blatchford and I have already almost done what we set out to do. We have brought the whole discussion down into the street, and it will not die yet awhile, we'll take care of that.'

53 See, Northcliffe to Maxse, 29 December 1909, Maxse MSS, 460, f. 503. 'The man is a noble fellow because it has almost killed his "Clarion". The circulation has already gone down by half I believe.'

54 'The Menace'. The ten articles appeared in the *Daily Mail* between 12 and 23 December.

55 *Daily Mail*, 23 December 1909.

56 *Manchester Guardian*, 20 December 1909.

57 M. V. Brett (ed.), *op. cit.*, vol. II, pp. 422 and 426.

58 The Kaiser obviously read Blatchford's articles with care and apparently a sense of personal identification. This explains his cryptic comment to Goschen which the Ambassador admitted to Hardinge left him 'in a maze'. The Kaiser told Goschen, ' "*I* am not the strong man; you must look elsewhere for him!" This remark made with great emphasis tapping me on the breast to enforce it. . . .' See *British Documents on the Origins of the War, 1898–1914* (London, 1927), (hereafter refered to as *BD*), vol. VI, p. 437.

59 Ottley to Esher, 4 January 1910, ESHR 5/33.

60 Maxse to Northcliffe, 24 December 1909, Northcliffe Dep. 4890/XXIII.

61 Wile to Northcliffe, 15 December 1909, *ibid.*/LV.

62 The Kaiser did not consider Blatchford any different from other Englishmen. He told Goschen, 'They are all mad in England, and people seem to think that I am standing here with my battle-axe behind my back ready to fall upon them at any moment.' *BD*, vol. VI, p. 434.

63 See *BD*, vol. VI, p. 319.

64 *Nation*, 30 October 1909.

65 Quoted A. M. Gollin, *The Observer and J. L. Garvin* (London, 1960), pp. 129–30.

66 Sandars to Garvin, 22 December 1909, Garvin MSS.

67 Balfour to Northcliffe, 3 January 1910, Northcliffe Dep. 4890/III.

68 Quoted in Gollin, *op. cit.*, p. 130.

69 Northcliffe claimed the credit for 'having succeeded in bringing the Election to where it should be – the Navy, in my opinion, at the most important moment in our history'. He assumed it was his privilege to occupy the centre of any stage upon which he chose to stride, and that lesser mortals would happily assume their accustomed place in his shadow. He was well aware of the crucial part played by Garvin in determining Tory electoral tactics, but was vain enough to suppose that because he was who he was and communicated directly with Balfour, while Garvin was a mere newspaper editor in communication with Balfour's secretary, that his influence with the Tory leader was the greater. See Northcliffe to Alfred Butes, 7 January 1910, Garvin MSS; Garvin to Sandars, 31 May 1910, Sandars MSS, 760, ff. 119–21.

70 Maxse to Esher, 6 January 1910, ESHR 5/33.

71 Fisher to Garvin, 22 January 1910, Garvin MSS. Fisher remained sufficiently mindful of his own vendetta to send Lionel Yexley to Portsmouth to scupper, if he could, Beresford's electoral campaign. 'Fight the good fight,' he told Yexley, 'and get Ananias carried out dead as the result of the Election.' But Yexley could do nothing. Fighting a naval constituency, Beresford was opposed by a candidate who was so unfamiliar with matters nautical that when asked if he would supply sailors with ladders for their hammocks, replied, 'I will see to it.' Not surprisingly, Beresford topped the Portsmouth poll. See A. J. Marder (ed.), *op. cit.*, vol. II, p. 290. Yexley, an ex-able seaman, became a successful journalist and was founder and editor of the *Fleet*.

72 For Lloyd George's speech, see Frank Owen, *Tempestuous Journey* (London, 1954), pp. 186–7.

73 Although McKenna loathed Lloyd George, by any standards his statement to Fisher was a monumental indiscretion for one minister to make about another. It appears that although Lloyd George had made insulting remarks about Fisher in Cabinet, he told McKenna in the presence of Sir George Murray, 'We've made a d-d mess of it, letting Fisher go,' to which McKenna rejoined, 'Oh! You believe me at last do you. Yes you'll miss him I promise you!' See Fisher to Garvin, 22 January 1910, Garvin MSS. Part of this long letter is quoted in Gollin, *op. cit.*, p. 131.

74 NPC Manifesto, January 1910, National Peace Council Archive.

75 Garvin to Sandars, 29 January 1910, Sandars MSS, 760, ff. 29–30.

76 Report in *The Times*, and comment, 29 January 1910; *Manchester Guardian* 31 January 1910.

77 Quoted in N. Blewett, *The Peers, the Parties and the People* (London, 1972), p. 410. See also pp. 126ff. Blewett's study of the two 1910 elections combines detailed scholarship with wit. Other texts helpful with electoral details are Vincent and Stenton (eds), *McCalmont's Parliamentary Poll Book, 1832–1918* (Brighton, 1971), see particularly Part II, p. 332; and, H. Pelling, *Social Geography of British Elections, 1885–1910* (London, 1967), particularly pp. 125–40.

78 Gwynne to Borden, 10 July 1908, Gwynne MSS 15. Gwynne's claim to be a 'moderate' stands up only in the sense of his own comparison with Maxse. His picture of City attitudes (and his letter details a particular German loan) is at variance with the picture we get of businessmen's attitudes in Germany and Britain from the reports of embassy staff printed in the *British Documents*, particularly vol. VI, which covers Anglo-German relations for this period. It is not the purpose of this book to discuss these fascinating economic considerations in relation to Anglo-German hostility, but the best, most recent comments on this subject are in P. Kennedy, *The Rise of Anglo-German Antagonism*, particularly pp. 291–305.

79 Gwynne to Sandars, 30 March 1909, Balfour Ad MSS 49797, ff. 89–90 (my emphasis).

80 *BD*, vol. VI, p. 437.

81 E. T. S. Dugdale, *German Diplomatic Documents* (reprint, New York, 1969), vol. III, p. 406.

82 *BD*, vol. VI, pp. 312–13.

83 *Ibid.*, p. 323.

84 *Ibid.*, p. 434.

85 *Ibid.*, p. 441.

86 For the Anglo-German naval negotiations, see *ibid.*, pp. 434–665.

87 See *BD*, vol. VI, p. 591; Lady Wester Wemyss, *Life and Letters of Lord Wester Wemyss* (London, 1935), p. 128.

88 *Daily Mail* and *Daily News*, 10 March 1910.

89 See M. V. Brett (ed.), *op. cit.*, vol. II. p. 452.

90 *Nation*, 5 March 1910.

91 Quoted in Pound and Harmsworth, *op. cit.*, p. 332.

92 H. W. Wilson to Lady Northcliffe, 26 April 1910, Northcliffe Dep. 4890/XLIX.

93 See, for example, *Daily Mail*, 8 July 1910.

94 Wilson to Northcliffe, 20 October 1910, Northcliffe Dep. 4890/XLIX.

95 *Daily Mail*, 29 July 1910.

96 *Ibid.*, 13 and 15 July 1910.

97   *Daily Mail,* 28 September and 4 October 1910.

98   *Ibid.,* 24 and 25 November 1910 and 2 January 1911.

99   Garvin to Sandars, 11 September and 6 November 1910, Sandars MSS, 761, f. 60; and, 762, ff. 14–18.

100 See M. V. Brett (ed.), *op. cit.,* vol. III, p. 25.

101 The appointment of Malcolm Fraser as honorary press adviser to the Tory party in December 1910 marks the beginning of an attempt by the party itself more actively to intervene and influence the press. Garvin's influence waned until by 1913 it had become negligible. In response to considerable pressure, Balfour early in 1911 appointed the Unionist Organisation Committee which reported in June 1911, making a whole series of recommendations on, *inter alia,* 'Press/party relations'. See J. A. Ramsden's thesis, *op. cit.,* pp. 215–16 and 231–5; *Report of Unionist Organisation Committee,* June 1911, Sec. E, pp. 19–22 (incl), CCO/500/1/2. Arthur Steel-Maitland wanted a newspaper 'entirely under Central Office control – I really think it would mean a *very great deal* to us.' He was very keen to purchase the *Daily Express:* 'the "Express" does and can exert very considerable influence. We need the support of a half-penny paper in order to keep the "Daily Mail" within bounds.' See Steel-Maitland to Sandars, and, Steel-Maitland to Alexander Henderson, 20 September 1911, Sandars MSS, 764, ff. 51–4.

102 C. L. Graves to Maxse, 5 November 1910, Maxse MSS, 462, f. 749.

103 Wickham Steed to Garvin, 30 November 1910, Garvin MSS.

104 Esher to Sandars, 27 December 1910, Sandars MSS, 762, ff. 238–40.

105 Esher to Sandars, 30 December 1910, *ibid.,* ff. 266–7.

106 Northcliffe to Bonar Law, 6 December 1910, Bonar Law MSS, 18/6/139.

107 Northcliffe to Balfour, 13 December, and Balfour to Northcliffe 17 December 1910, Northcliffe Dep. 4890/III.

108 Esher made no secret of his anxiety 'about the outlook abroad: the absorption in domestic quarrels is going to lead indirectly to troubles beyond these islands.' Esher to Sandars, 27 December 1910, Sandars MSS, 762, ff. 238–40.

109 *Concord,* vol. XXVI, no. 11, December 1910, p. 135.

110 Curzon's speech, reported in *The Times,* 4 December 1910.

Chapter 16: Conscription, or how to lose friends and votes

1 E. Lawson to J. L. Garvin, 28 February 1900, Garvin MSS.

2 *Report . . . on the War in South Africa* (1903), Cd. 1789, p. 83.

3 On these considerations, see, *inter alia,* Ian Beckett and J. Gooch (eds), *Politicians and Defence* (Manchester, 1981), p. 82; J. Gooch, *The Plans of War, c1900–1916* (London, 1974), and *The Prospect of War* (London, 1980), pp. 110–11; S. R. Williamson, Jnr, *The Politics of Grand Strategy, 1904–14* (Cambridge, Mass., 1969), pp. 90–1. Gooch argues convincingly that Haldane did *not* fully accept that the BEF should be geared primarily to *speedy* intervention against Germany on the continent until 1909.

4 On the subject of the quality of recruits into the British army, see the articles by General Maurice, 'Where to get men', and 'National health: a soldier's story', in *Contemporary Review,* vols 81 and 83, January 1902 and 1903; Parliamentary Papers (1903) xxxviii, Cd. 1501; and (1904), xxxii, Cd. 2175; Almeric Fitzroy, *Memoirs,* (London, 1927), vol. I, pp. 162, 175–6, 179–82, 187–8, 195–7, 211 and 214. See also M. J. Allison, 'The national service issue, 1899–1914', unpublished PhD, London, 1975, ch. I, *passim.*

The quality of available recruits implied more than merely physique. Certainly as important if not more important, and always a significant factor in the volunteer-conscription debate, was the question of men's spirit or *élan*. While in the navy there was perhaps undue emphasis and reliance placed upon *matériel*, in the army, the man behind the gun was often considered as more significant than the gun itself. Hence the exaggerated respect for the offensive spirit in which the French army was inculcated. War tested a man's moral as much as his physical capabilities. On this important subject see, *inter alia*, D. G. Pryce, 'The military spirit and the doctrine of the offensive in Britain, 1901–14', unpublished MA, London, 1973; Michael Howard, *Studies in War and Peace* (London, 1971).

5 T. J. Miller, 'The imported pest', quoted in D. Hayes, *Conscription Conflict* (London, 1949), p. 37.

6 Diary, 21 May 1907, Arnold-Forster Ad MSS 50353, ff. 106–12.

7 E. C. Browne, *National Service* (Glasgow, 1904), p. 12.

8 Repington to Clarke, 20 February 1906, ESHR 10/26.

9 Campbell-Bannerman had been Financial Secretary to the War Office when Cardwell was Minister, and on two subsequent occasions was Minister for War himself, in 1886 and again from 1892 to 1895.

10 On the Relugas compact, see A. J. A. Morris, *Radicalism Against War 1906–14*, p. 14ff.

11 The fourteen divisions in England and Wales, together with the Highland and Lowland divisions in Scotland, were designed to fit into existing administrative areas and to secure adequate recruiting by appealing to local pride and loyalty.

12 The paragraph is based on material in S. E. Koss, *Lord Haldane: Scapegoat for Liberalism* (New York, 1969), *passim*.

13 *The Times*, 26 February 1907.

14 In Haldane's opinion, the ex-War Minister was not a little mentally unhinged by jealousy. Forster had never enjoyed much success with working the press to his own advantage as minister. In his last months in office he had become quite paranoid about his failure to win press support and even supposed he was abused by other government departments 'because they think they will be backed-up by the "Daily Mail", "Town Chats" and the rest of them.' See Forster's diary, 31 October 1905, Arnold-Forster Ad MSS 50351. For his comments in print on War Office relations with the press, see *Military Needs and Military Policy* (London, 1908), p. 32. For Haldane's view of his sanity, see Haldane to Mother, 20 June and 22 July 1907 and 29 January 1908, Haldane MSS, 5977, ff. 179–80, 5978, ff. 33–4, and, 5979, f. 39.

15 Northcliffe to Garvin, 9 March 1909, Northcliffe Dep. 4890/LXXXV.

16 Northcliffe to Marlowe, 13 and 16 February 1909, *ibid.*/XLVI.

17 See *Daily Mail*, 29 May 1904; F. A. Mackenzie, *The Mystery of the Daily Mail* (London, 1921) p. 66.

18 See *The Times*, 14 March 1908.

19 Quoted in Elie Halévy, *The Rule of Democracy* (paperback edn, 1961), p. 180, n. 1.

20 See A. J. A. Morris, 'Haldane's army reforms, 1906–08: the deception of the Radicals', in *History*, 1971, vol. LVI, pp. 17–34; C. Repington, *Vestigia*, p. 278.

21 Roberts to Kitchener, 2 August 1906 (copy), Roberts MSS, 7101/23/122, vol. 9, p. 255. See also S. Koss, *op. cit.*, p. 98.

22 Milner to Garvin, 25 July 1906, Garvin MSS.

23 Wilson's diary, 13 July, 2 August and 31 December 1906, Wilson MSS,

DS/MISC/80. The Beresford 'opinion' is from an entry dated 5 July 1912, 73/1/27.
24 F. S. Oliver, *Ordeal by Battle* (London, 1915), p. xxiii.
25 Newton to Strachey, 3 May 1909, Strachey Papers, S/11/1/2.
26 See Strachey to Roberts, 30 April 1907, S/13/3/32. Also Strachey to Roberts, 10 October 1906 and 1 June 1909, Roberts MSS, 7101/23/85/25 and 27.
27 Cardigan to Maxse, 14 and 17 April 1908, Maxse MSS, 458, ff. 680 and 681.
28 Austen Chamberlain to Maxse, 5 February 1908, Maxse MSS, 458, ff. 649–50.
29 'Episodes of the month', *National Review*, May 1908.
30 Milner to Garvin, 17 October 1905, Garvin MSS.
31 See, for example, Shee to Garvin, 29 November 1906, *ibid.*
32 Roberts to Garvin, 1 December 1906 and 10 November 1907, *ibid.* Roberts exercised some influence with the *Daily Telegraph* as he was very friendly with Harry Lawson, a Lt. Col. commanding the Royal Bucks Hussars and the eldest son of Lord Burnham, the *Telegraph*'s owner.
33 Chirol to Garvin, 1 February 1908, *ibid.*
34 Garvin to Roberts, 5 March 1908 (copy), *ibid.*
35 Garvin to Maxse, 12 November 1908 (copy), *ibid.*
36 Garvin to Roberts, 13 March 1908 (copy), *ibid.*
37 Roberts to Walter, 31 January 1908 (copy), and Walter to Roberts, 6 February 1908, Roberts MSS, 7101/23/122, vol. 10, p. 258 and R46/147.
38 Garvin to Roberts, 13 March 1908 (copy), Garvin MSS.
39 Repington to Garvin, 15 March 1908, *ibid.* Haldane's critics had strongly represented that the Territorial Army could not possibly be made fit to repel the regular troops of a continental army and therefore were useless either to maintain the Expeditionary Force, or repel invaders. One of Haldane's most revolutionary ideas was to equip Territorial batteries with the reconditioned field-guns of the South African war converted for quick firing. The regular army's batteries had been rearmed. Wilson and Roberts were certain the Territorial artillery was a joke, but there was considerable professional opinion in the army that believed the new batteries could be trained and made effective in much shorter time than was usual. Garvin was never convinced of this. For opinions of French, Douglas Haig and the king, see Sir F. Maurice, *Haldane* (London, 1937) vol. I, pp. 221ff.
40 See, for example, Arnold-Forster to Garvin, 20 July 1908, Garvin MSS.
41 Garvin to Roberts, 16 March 1908 (copy), *ibid.*
42 Roberts to Garvin, 17 March 1908, *ibid.*
43 'The machine and the man', in the *Observer*, 16 August 1908.
44 See Roberts to Garvin, 29 April, 30 June, 17 August and 30 November 1908, and Garvin to Roberts, 19 March and 30 April 1908 (copies), Garvin MSS.
45 Fisher to Garvin, 10 February 1908, *ibid.*
46 Repington to Roberts, 21 May 1908, Roberts MSS, 7101/23/62/49.
47 *The Times*, 6 June 1908. See also, 14 March 1908.
48 *The Nation in Arms*, July 1908, p. 156.
49 Milner to Midleton, 27 July 1908, Midleton MSS, PRO 30/67/24.
50 'Episodes of the month', *National Review*, July 1908.
51 Roberts to Maxse, 2 September 1908, Maxse MSS, 458, f. 746.
52 Quoted in Koss, *op. cit.*, pp. 100–1.
53 See *Standard*, 3 July 1908. If Burns was anything by this stage of his career, he was inclined to be anti-militarist.
54 Roberts to Cromer, 17 October 1908, Roberts MSS, 7101/23/122, vol. 11, p. 55.

55 See Roberts to Rosebery, n.d.; and Rosebery to Roberts, 14 and 20 November 1908, Roberts MSS, 7101/23/122, vol. 11, p. 75, and, 7101/23/64/10 and 11.

56 Esher's 'Journal', 26 November 1908, ESHR 2/11.

57 *The Times*, 6 April 1909.

58 *Daily News*, 17 April 1908. There is a detailed account of the by-election in D. Green, 'The Stratford by-election, May 1909: national defence and party politics', in *Moirae*, vol. V, Trinity 1980, pp. 92–110.

59 Milner to Balfour, 6 April 1909 (copy), Milner Dep. 35, ff. 169–70. The original reveals that the emphasis was Balfour's and not Milner's. See Balfour Ad MSS 49697, ff. 146–52.

60 Roberts to Balfour, 7 April 1909, Balfour Ad MSS 49725, ff. 288–90.

61 *Morning Post*, 14 April 1909. For its earlier reservations, even though the newspaper was usually a staunch supporter of compulsory service, see 6 April 1909.

62 Hunt to Maxse, 18 April 1909, Maxse MSS, 459, ff. 112–14.

63 Sandars to Balfour, 12 April 1909, Balfour Ad MSS 49765, ff. 217–20.

64 Milner to Roberts, 25 April 1909 (copy), Milner Dep. 16, ff. 166–9.

65 Roberts to Kincaid-Smith, n.d., Roberts MSS, 7101/23/122 vol. 11, p. 153.

66 Newton to Maxse, 17 April 1909, Maxse MSS, 459, f. 108.

67 Milner to Strachey, 8 May 1909, S/10/11/2.

68 *The Times*, 10 May 1909. A sum of £500 was made available to the Legion of Frontiersmen in 1909, the money apparently under the control of Esher which suggests the source was the king rather than the government. Roger Pocock deals with this in his 'imaginative' autobiographical account, but there are entries on the subject in his pocket diary which, as his biographer points out, was not a likely place where he would deliberately lie. See entries for 11 June, 14 and 28 July, 31 August, 1 and 20 September and 6 and 7 December 1909.

69 Repington to Roberts, n.d., Roberts MSS, R62/61.

70 Repington to Maxse, 19 May 1909, Maxse MSS, 459, ff. 188–92.

71 Garvin to E. J. Dillon, 12 May 1909 (copy), Garvin MSS.

72 Maxse to Strachey, 9 June 1909, Strachey MSS, S/10/9/10.

73 See Strachey quoted in *Nation in Arms*, November 1908.

74 Milner to Strachey, 8 May 1909, S/10/11/2.

75 Strachey to Milner, 3 May 1909, *ibid.*

76 Durand to Roberts, 27 December 1909, Roberts MSS, 7101/23/26/61. W. Waldorf Astor was Durand's fellow Unionist candidate. Both were defeated. Durand did not stand in December 1910 when Astor was returned top of the poll. Astor supported conscription, and his views on the consequences of conscription to society compare interestingly with Repington's earlier observation to Maxse about Tory fears of revolution if the workers were drilled and armed. Astor told Esher that he supported conscription, 'not so much for its direct benefit as for its humanizing effect upon the rough diamonds of the countryside and workshop. More than this, it is rare that a man who has learned the value of discipline and respect for authority inclines to Socialism.' Astor to Esher, 18 January 1910, ESHR 5/33.

77 See Long to Blumenfeld, 7 September 1910 and 11 March 1911, Blumenfeld MSS, LONG/W 5 and 7.

78 See Esher to Roberts, 6 June 1909, Roberts MSS, R29/17; and, S. E. Koss, *op. cit.*, p. 99.

79 Roberts to Probyn, 13 December 1909, 7101/23/122/vol. 11, p. 249.

80 General Wilson's diary, 18 January 1910, DS/MISC/80.

81 Roberts to Maxse, 1 January 1910, Maxse MSS, 461, f. 540.

82   See Repington to Garvin, 14 April and 24 May 1910, Garvin MSS.
83   John Grigg, *Lloyd George, the People's Champion: 1902–1911* (London, 1978), p. 264.
84   Quoted in *ibid.* The full text is given in Appendix A, pp. 362–8.
85   M. V. Brett (ed.), *The Journals and Letters of Viscount Esher* (London, 1934–8), vol. III, pp. 10–11.
86   See Esher to Haldane, 6 and 8 September 1910, and Haldane to Esher, 7 September 1910 (copy), Haldane MSS, 5909, ff. 45–54.
87   M. V. Brett (ed.), *op. cit.*, vol. III, p. 18.
88   *Ibid.*, p. 21.
89   Quoted in S. E. Koss, *op. cit.*, p. 102.
90   Amery to Roberts, 25 October 1910, Roberts MSS, 7101/23/1/22.
91   See Hamilton to Seely, 6 January 1913 and 9 January 1914, Seely MSS, S18, ff. 21–2 and 104–10.
92   *Compulsory Service* (London, 1910), pp. 89–90 and 106.
93   Haldane to Mother, 19 January 1911, Haldane MSS, 5985, ff. 11–12.
94   Strachey to Roberts, 27 December 1910 (copy), S/12/3/45.
95   Wilson's diary, 26 November 1910, DS/MISC/80.
96   Milner to Roberts, 26 December 1910 (copy), Milner Dep. 16, ff. 193–5.
97   See L. S. Amery, *My Political Life*, vol. I, pp. 216–17.
98   Roberts to Northcliffe, 19 March 1911, Northcliffe Dep. 4890/III.
99   *Ibid.*
100 Roberts to Garvin, 20 March 1911, Garvin MSS.
101 *Daily Mail*, 4 April 1911.
102 Roberts to Percy, 28 April 1911, Roberts MSS, letter book copy.
103 See D. James, *Lord Roberts* (London, 1954), pp. 449–50.
104 Roberts to Curzon, 6 June 1911, Roberts 7101/23/125/vol. I, p. 90.
105 C. Beresford, *The Betrayal* (London, 1912), p. 111.
106 *Daily Mail*, 15 December 1911.
107 Quoted in S. E. Koss, *op. cit.*, p. 105.
108 In notes on a speech made by Roberts, 27 November 1912, Repington did not spare Roberts. 'Lord Roberts himself allowed the best opportunity of our day to pass by. He was omnipotent in military affairs for 3 years and did nothing. He left the Volunteers without organisation, guns, engineers, medical and transport and supply services as well as very badly trained.' Repington to Dawson, 27 November 1912, Times Archive.
109 See Roberts to Garvin, 31 October 1911, Garvin MSS.
110 One of Augustine Birrell's, 'Birrellisms' reaches the heart of the matter. 'The House of Lords represent nobody but themselves, and they enjoy the full confidence of their constituents.' Quoted in Charles T. King, *The Asquith Parliament* (London, 1910), p. 125.
111 In the context of discussing Milner's suitability as a minister, Balfour wrote, 'I have never been able to accept this policy [national service] for a great many reasons, military and political; and if it ever fell to my lot to form a Government again, I certainly should not ask anybody to join it who, I thought, might subsequently break it upon this question.' Balfour to Sandars, 21 September 1911, Sandars 764, ff. 56–9.
112 Balfour to Grey, 12 June 1912 (copy), Balfour Ad MSS 49731, ff. 2–6.
113 Balfour to Bonar Law, 22 November 1912, Bonar Law MSS, 27/4/9.
114 Bonar Law claimed to Repington that he was not converted to conscription until 1913, and then on the issue of aerial warfare. 'He says practically all his party

favour it, but he will not adopt it as part of his programme.' See Repington to Dawson, 1 April 1913, Times Archive.

115 See Peter Yule, 'The tariff reform movement and Germany, 1900–1914', in *Moirae*, vol. VII, Trinity 1982, pp. 1–17.

PART 4: 'AND HE GATHERED THEM IN A PLACE CALLED ... ARMAGEDDON'

Chapter 17: Collapse of the Triple Entente

1 *Nation*, 14 September 1907.
2 Blennerhassett to Garvin, 25 July 1907, Garvin MSS.
3 Quoted in E. M. Carroll, *French Public Opinion and Foreign Affairs, 1870–1914* (New York, 1931), pp. 224–5.
4 Blennerhassett to Garvin, 30 January 1908, Garvin MSS.
5 Maxse to Tyrrell, 8 January 1908, FO 800/109.
6 *British Documents on the Origins of the War, 1898–1914* (London, 1927) (hereafter referred to as *BD*), vol. VII, p. 90.
7 Tardieu received £300 a year from the French Secret Service fund. When Briand struck him off the list, Tardieu suddenly developed an affection for the Germans which was encouraged by the civility shown the journalist by the German Ambassador in Paris. However, good manners did not pay bills, and as a result of 'a particularly expensive attachment' that he had acquired, Tardieu's creditors became increasingly pressing. The need to receive a subsidy from the French government persuaded the journalist of the merits of once more adopting an aggressive anti-German tone in his writings. See Bertie to Nicolson, 4 February 1911, FO 800/171.
8 For example, when meeting King Edward and Isvolsky at Marienbad later that year, Clemenceau insisted emphatically that 'England cannot maintain her position in Europe and in the world, nor can her friendship with France be secure against surprises unless she has an adequate army. "Ce n'est pas à Trafalgar, qui était une bien brillante victoire navale, mais à Waterloo, qui était une bien petite bataille, que l'Angleterre à cassé le cou à Napoléon."' See S. Lee, *King Edward VII* (London, 1927), vol. II, p. 629. See also the notes made by Steed of his conversation with Clemenceau, in his *Through Thirty Years*, (London, 1924), vol. I, pp. 286–7.
9 *Daily Mail*, 10 June 1908.
10 'Episodes of the month', *National Review*, May 1908.
11 See *Concord*, vol. XXIV, no. 6, June 1908, p. 67; *New Age*, 5 September 1908, p. 363; and *Manchester Guardian*, 9 September 1908.
12 Spender to Rosebery, 16 August 1908, Rosebery MSS, 10121, ff. 166–8.
13 See G. Prothero to Garvin, 3 and 12 June 1908, Garvin MSS. It is interesting that by October, Spring Rice was complaining particularly of *The Times* for pitching into the Germans. 'I think we should seize every possible opportunity (as the French are wisely doing) of showing friendship to Germany where this can be done without sacrificing our interests or rights. Politics should be like chess; one should have no prejudice in favour or against any piece in the game.' S. Gwynn (ed.), *The Letters and Friendships of Cecil Spring Rice* (London, 1929), vol. II, pp. 130–1.
14 *Quarterly Review*, June 1908, pp. 266–7.

15   Brooks to Garvin, 27 October 1908, Garvin MSS. See also *Standard,* 14 September 1908; *Quarterly Review,* Autumn 1908.
16   See *BD,* vol. VII, pp. 144 and 119–20.
17   Garvin to Prothero, 12 November 1908 (copy), Garvin MSS.
18   M. V. Brett (ed.), *The Journals and Letters of Viscount Esher* (London, 1934–8), vol. II, pp. 356 and 359–60. For Grey's estimate of the French, see *BD,* vol. VI, pp. 216–17.
19   *Nation,* 14 November 1908.
20   Cf. comment in *The Times,* 9 January and 13 February 1909.
21   C. Towers to Strachey, 27 January 1909, Strachey Papers, S/16/2/6.
22   See *BD,* vol. VII, pp. 133–4; Chirol to Saunders, 2 February 1909, Times Archive; *History of the Times* (London, 1947) (hereafter referred to as *HoT*), vol. III, pp. 676–8. George Saunders had become *The Times*'s Paris correspondent in September after Lavino's sudden death the previous month. Saunders had not long given up his Berlin appointment in order to return to Printing House Square. Although, in Chirol's words, 'the prince of correspondents', Saunders had not fitted in well in his new post. He had, however, not been at all enthusiastic about going to Paris, responding only reluctantly to Moberly Bell's plea, 'I ask you to do it as a service to the Nation,' and Chirol's more direct if less grand injunction, 'The one really important thing is Saunders – Paris.'
23   See *Nation,* 13 February 1909.
24   *New Age,* 13 June 1908, p. 122.
25   *Daily News,* 5 June 1908.
26   There are innumerable examples of Grey's reluctance to answer his critics in the House. Frequently he attempted to defuse their wrath by private interview when he would appeal to national security or party loyalty as a reason for extolling the virtues of silence. For examples of this on the Russian question, see A. J. A. Morris, *C. P. Trevelyan: Portrait of a Radical* (Belfast, 1977), pp. 103ff.
27   For the Reval debate, see *Hansard:* iv:190:211ff. There were only 59 votes cast against Grey: some Radicals, a handful of Irish members and all the Labour MPs. Social as well as political pressure was brought to bear upon one of the leading dissident Radical MPs, Arthur Ponsonby. For voting against Grey, Ponsonby was told by the Liberal Chief Whip that he would be required to keep his conscience in order in the future, and his name was subsequently omitted from the list of those invited to a garden party at Buckingham Palace. See Philip Magnus, *King Edward the Seventh* (London, 1964), pp. 405–6.
28   Strachey to Grey, 12 June 1908 (copy), S/7/8/5.
29   Grey to Strachey, 14 June 1908, *ibid.*
30   See Grey to Knollys, 25 July 1908, quoted in G. M. Trevelyan, *Grey of Fallodon* (London, 1936), p. 192.
31   *New Age,* 20 June 1908, pp. 141–2.
32   Sir Archibald Hurd, *Who Goes There?* (London, 1941), pp. 108–9.
33   See, for example, Ellis Barker, 'The Triple Entente and the Triple Alliance', in *Nineteenth Century,* July 1908.
34   Quoted in E. M. Carroll, *op. cit.,* p. 578 and n. 28.
35   *BD,* vol. VI, p. 155.
36   Cf. 'Episodes of the month', *National Review,* June 1908; and *New Age,* 18 July 1908, p. 224.
37   Cf. *The Times,* 11 June 1908; and *Nation,* 13 June 1908.
38   Strachey to Grey, 23 June 1908; Grey to Strachey, 30 June 1908 (copy) FO 800/111.

39 Bell to Steed, 10 July 1908 (copy), Times Archive.
40 Bell had admitted that he had 'never been able to get up an interest in Austrian politics', and that he had followed Steed's telegrams 'less carefully than those from other capitals'.
41 Steed to Bell, 14 July 1908, Times Archive.
42 See Tyrrell to Spring Rice, 16 July 1908, FO 800/241; and *HoT*, vol. III, pp. 646–7.
43 For different accounts by Hardinge and the Kaiser of their interview, see *BD*, vol. VI, pp. 184–90, especially pp. 188 and also 199.
44 Steed to Bell, 14 August 1908, Times Archive.
45 See Steed to Bell, 22 August 1908, Times Archive; *HoT*, vol. III, pp. 608–12.
46 Steed to Bell, 29 August 1908, Times Archive.
47 See *BD*, vol. IX, Part I, Appendix III, pp. 776ff. Compare the much fuller account of the Goschen – Aehrenthal altercation in H. W. Steed's, *Through Thirty Years*, vol. I, pp. 292–4, with Goschen's own account in his diary plus his meeting the next day with Aehrenthal, in, C. H. D. Howard (ed.), *Edward Goschen's Diary, 1900–1914* (London, 1980), pp. 176–7.
48 The complete letter from Steed to Bell, 19 October 1908, is quoted in *HoT*, vol. III, pp. 616–17. In July 1908, the Young Turk revolution had broken out in Constantinople. Grey had welcomed this. The Radicals in the Liberal party were delighted as this suggested there might be opportunities for reforms in Macedonia without having to depend upon the Russians. The Parliamentary Radical Balkan Committee strongly supported the Young Turk movement, even sending delegates to the opening session of Turkey's new democratic parliament. For Grey's speech welcoming the revolution, see *Hansard*, iv:193:965. See the reaction of *The Times* to these events, 9 and 28 October 1908. Radical enthusiasm is apparent in C. F. Buxton's contemporary polemic, *Turkey in Revolution* (London, 1909). The subject is dealt with sympathetically in V. de Bunsen's biography of *Charles Roden Buxton* (London, 1948), pp. 54ff.
49 See *HoT*, vol. III, pp. 620–1; and *BD*, vol. V, pp. 523 and 531–2.
50 Cf. *Manchester Guardian*, 6 and 10 October with 3 December 1908.
51 Cf. *Nation*, 9 January and 6 February 1909.
52 Garvin to Prothero, 12 November 1908 (copy), Garvin MSS.
53 *Daily Mail*, 15 May 1909.
54 Percy's article was published in the September 1909 issue of the *National Review*. Milner to Roberts, 3 September 1909 (copy), Milner Dep. 16, f. 185.
55 *The Times*, 27 March 1909.
56 Chirol to Northcliffe, 27 March 1909, Northcliffe Dep. 4890/XCIX.
57 See and cf., *Manchester Guardian*, 17 May, 7 June and 7 July 1909.
58 H. Nicolson, *Sir Arthur Nicolson Bart, First Lord Carnock: a study in the old diplomacy* (London, 1930), p. 305.
59 *Contemporary Review*, vol. XCV, May 1909, p. 619.
60 See report and comment, *Daily Mail* and *Daily News*, 6 June 1909.
61 *New Age*, 12 August 1909, p. 294. There was considerable muttering at this time that since its purchase by Northcliffe, *The Times* was little more than a grand megaphone for Carmelite House opinions. Northcliffe was very sensitive about such rumours. Wickham Steed thought it his duty to tell Northcliffe that King Edward's *aide de camp*, Colonel Ponsonby, had said to him after lunching with the king, 'Do you know what they call "The Times" now?' – and supplied his own answer. 'The *édition de luxe* of the "Daily Mail".' Steed to Northcliffe, 20 August 1909, Northcliffe Dep. 4890/XCIV.

62 *Concord,* vol. XXVI, no. 1, January 1910, p. 1.

63 Wilson to Northcliffe, 11 December 1909, Dep. 4890/XLIX.

64 *Concord,* vol. XXVI, no. 1, January 1910, p. 14. See also *ibid.,* vol. XXIV, no. 2, February 1908, p. 23.

65 See *Manchester Guardian* and *Daily News,* 20 May 1910. For a fuller account of the campaign for Anglo-German friendship, see A. J. A. Morris, *Radicalism Against War, 1906–14,* pp. 198–223. See also the perceptive article by H. S. Weinroth, 'The British Radicals and the balance of power, 1902–14', in *Historical Journal,* 1970, vol. XIII, pp. 653–82.

66 Maxse to Sandars, 14 and 18 April 1910, Sandars MSS, 760, ff. 96–7.

67 Wilson to Lady Northcliffe, 26 April 1910, Northcliffe Dep. 4890/XLIX.

68 J. Walter to Maxse, 6 July 1910, Maxse MSS, 462, f. 671. Lovat Fraser had suggested that Maxse ought to publish his attack on the Cadburys in pamphlet form. See *ibid.,* ff. 629–30.

69 It could have been that the Cadburys' decision was coloured by their earlier legal action against the *Standard* where, though successful, they had been awarded derisory damages of a farthing. See A. G. Gardiner, *Life of George Cadbury* (London, 1923), pp. 239–51. Maxse spent much time campaigning against the 'cocoa kings', the 'Cobden millionaires' or the 'Radical plutocrats', as he variously dubbed those in the Liberal party whom he accused of the hypocrisy of indulging in class politics while leading lives of self-indulgence. In October 1912 he actually set up a Radical Plutocrats Inquiry. Not all Tories, or Tory journalists, looked upon Leo's activities in this direction with unalloyed pleasure. See, for example, Lyttleton to Maxse, 21 October 1912, and Chirol to Maxse, 5 February 1908, quoted by Geoffrey Searle, 'The revolt from the Right', in P. Kennedy and A. Nicholls (eds), *Nationalist and Racialist Movements in Britain and Germany Before 1914* (London, 1981), pp. 25–6.

70 See A. J. P. Taylor, *The Struggle for Mastery in Europe* (Oxford, 1954), p. 464.

71 Cf. *Daily News* and *Manchester Guardian,* 11 January 1911.

72 *National Review,* 'Episodes of the month', February 1911.

73 Wile to Garvin, 16 January 1911, Garvin MSS.

74 Quoted in Zara Steiner, *The Foreign Office and Foreign Policy, 1898–1914* (Cambridge, 1969), p. 97.

75 Esher to Sandars, 27 December 1910, Sandars MSS, 762, ff. 238–40.

76 G. V. Williams to Northcliffe, 5 March 1911, Northcliffe Dep. 4890/LVIII.

77 *New Age,* 23 March 1911, p. 481.

78 For Grey's speech, see *Hansard,* v:22:1977–91.

79 *National Review,* 'Episodes of the month', April 1911.

Chapter 18: A domestic interlude: Lord Northcliffe asserts himself

1 *Life and Letters of C. F. Moberly Bell,* p. 306. The material on the health and behaviour of Northcliffe in 1910 is taken from R. Pound and G. Harmsworth, *Northcliffe* (London, 1959), pp. 403–30; Hamilton Fyfe, *Northcliffe: An Intimate Biography* (London, 1930); and Max Pemberton, *Lord Northcliffe: A Memoir* (London, n.d.), *passim.*

2 Northcliffe to Garvin, 25 December 1911, Garvin MSS. See also 'Lord Northcliffe as a golfer', in Pemberton, *op. cit.,* pp. 197–206.

3 Garvin to Maxse, n.d., 1908(?), Maxse MSS, 458, f. 813.

4 Northcliffe to Garvin, 27 August 1909, Northcliffe Dep. 4890/LXXXV.

5 Northcliffe to Garvin, 12 August 1910, *ibid.*

6 See Robertson Nicoll to Garvin, 8 March 1911, Garvin MSS.
7 Northcliffe to Garvin, 1 and 3 November 1910, *ibid.*
8 Grey to Milner, 22 January 1909, Milner Dep 35, f. 129.
9 One of the reasons Garvin was originally invited to accompany Northcliffe on his North American trip was for him to better inform himself about Canada. Canada held a special and important place in the thinking of all imperialists, but Northcliffe had a particular fondness and knowledge of the country.
10 Fisher to Garvin, 7 December 1910, Garvin MSS.
11 See *Daily Mail*, 28 January to 1 February 1911.
12 Garvin to Northcliffe, 1 February 1911, *ibid.*
13 Garvin to Northcliffe, 2 February 1911, *ibid.*
14 A. Chamberlain to Garvin, 5 February 1911, *ibid.*
15 *Daily Mail*, 4 February 1911; A. J. P. Taylor, *Beaverbrook* (Penguin edn, London, 1974), pp. 90–6. There is a detailed account of the Northcliffe-Garvin break in A. M. Gollin, *The Observer and J. L. Garvin* (London, 1960), ch. IX, where some of the letters I have cited are quoted in full.
16 Northcliffe to G. E. Cornford, 6 February 1911, Garvin MSS. Northcliffe used George Sutton as his agent for the sale of the *Observer* and was not personally involved.
17 Wilson to Garvin, 19 February 1911, Garvin MSS.
18 Henry Lucy to Garvin, 9 April 1911, *ibid.*
19 See also the extraordinarily generous way in which Northcliffe greeted Garvin's assumption of the editorship of the *Pall Mall Gazette* in his article in the *Daily Mail*, 29 January 1912. 'No greater journalistic writer and organiser has ever entered the field of evening newspaperdom.'
20 Northcliffe's concern was not confined merely to the business side of affairs at Printing House Square. He was as much concerned with the content and presentation of news and the general appearance of the paper. He took pride in the changes he had been able to make, particularly fuller coverage of foreign news. 'Few people realise how it is developing. *The "Times" was not what people think.* They forget the "Times" was usually an ill-printed 12 to 14 sheets, and that its foreign correspondence rarely ran to more than four columns a day.' Northcliffe to Strachey, 28 March 1909, Strachey Papers, S/11/4/19 (Northcliffe's emphasis).
    On attempts to reorganise the foreign news department, see Northcliffe to Chirol, 28 October 1910: 'The whole question emphasises what I mentioned two years ago, that everybody at PHS seems to be doing two or three entirely different tasks'; and, Chirol to Northcliffe, 4 November 1910: 'You must, however, bear in mind the difficulty of combining your spacious views concerning an adequate staff with the financial exigencies of our exchequer.' Northcliffe Dep. 4890/XCIX.
21 Retailed in Mary Northcliffe to Maxse, n.d., Maxse MSS, 462, f. 792.
22 Pound and Harmsworth, *op. cit.*, p. 408.
23 Quoted in *History of the Times* (London, 1947) (hereafter referred to as *HoT*), vol. III, pp. 672–4.
24 Valentine Chirol, in a letter to Leo Maxse (5 February 1908, Maxse MSS, 458, ff. 647–8) in defining what he meant by the 'Tradition of the Times', had specifically not separated financial independence from political and journalistic independence, in the same way as he had rejected the idea put forward by Maxse and Strachey that the foreign department was the only section of *The Times* whose independence was worth securing. Clarke had been quick to tell Chirol that Northcliffe was 'bound to grate on the susceptibilities of PHS, *but reorganization is absolutely essential and of course a man of his type is bound to insist upon it*' (my

emphasis). See Clarke to Chirol, 1 September 1909, Sydenham Ad MSS 50833, ff. 31–4. As Chirol had less than a good opinion of Strachey's views on the 'esse' of *The Times* and its place as a 'national institution' it is interesting that Northcliffe asked Strachey for his 'advice . . . as to the best way of establishing The Times . . . as a national institution'. Strachey to Northcliffe, 10 August 1908, printed in the *Spectator,* 22 September 1922.

25 Bell recognised that Northcliffe had 'never intended the Board . . . to be more than a device for the quietening of gossips like Lord Esher'. *HoT,* vol. III, p. 671. How successful Northcliffe had been in selling Esher an extraordinary 'milk-and-water' version of his intended role in relation to *The Times* may be judged from Esher's 'Journal' entry for 11 July 1908. See M. V. Brett (ed.), *The Journals and Letters of Viscount Esher* (London, 1934–8), vol. II, p. 327.

26 Bell to Northcliffe, 9 February 1908, (my emphasis), quoted in *HoT,* vol. III, p. 549.

27 Northcliffe to Buckle, 31 December 1910, Northcliffe Dep. 4890/1.

28 Quoted in Pound and Harmsworth, *op. cit.,* p. 408.

29 See Dawson's diary entries, 5 to 8 January 1911. 'Lord Northcliffe offered me a place in "The Times" and pressed me hard to try it – at any rate a trial. Rather nervous about it, but much too attractive to refuse.' MS Dawson 17, ff. 8–10. The talks went on until 22 January. See diary, and Dawson's summary of events in Times Archive.

30 See J. E. Wrench, *Geoffrey Dawson and Our Times* (London, 1955), pp. 66 and 78. George Geoffrey Robinson changed his name to the more familiar Dawson under the terms of a family will. Northcliffe, when in a good mood, always wrote to him as 'Robin'.

31 Clarke to Chirol, 6 September 1912, Sydenham Ad MSS 50834, ff. 165–8.

32 1905, Cd. 2643. Note, however, the reservation made by Edmund Robertson, p. 116ff.

33 See Loreburn's letter to *The Times,* 14 October 1905, and F. Hirst (ed.), *Commerce and Property in Naval Warfare* (London, 1906), *passim.*

34 See Sydenham of Combe, *My Working Life,* (London, 1927), pp. 203–4 and fn.

35 See *Nation,* 4 May 1907.

36 The same argument as Chirol had employed against Saunders in the late 1890s as the raison d'être for the imperial navy. See Chapter II *ante.*

37 Quoted in A. J. Marder, *From the Dreadnought to Scapa Flow: the Royal Navy in the Fisher Era, 1904–1919* (5 vols), vol. 1, *The Road to War, 1904–1914* (Oxford, 1961), p. 379. The best recent account of the difficult question of blockade in relation to the Declaration of London is in the early pages of Arthur Marsden's essay in F. H. Hinsley (ed.), *British Foreign Policy Under Sir Edward Grey* (Cambridge, 1977), pp. 488ff.

38 *Hansard,* v:3:1121ff.

39 See *British Documents on the Origins of the War, 1898–1914* (London, 1927), vol. VIII, pp. 352–66, where the *Nineteenth Century* article is also printed, note paragraph 15 of Crowe's critique; L. E. Naylor, *The Irrepressible Victorian* (London, 1965), pp. 163–5.

40 *The Times,* 4 November 1910. For Foreign Office responses, see *Parliamentary Papers,* 1910, Cd. 5418, LXXIV, pp. 133–60; and 1911, Cd. 5718, CIII, pp. 113–31. It is difficult to understand why the Foreign Office adopted the attitude it did. Grey must have been aware of the strategic implications. The fairest conclusion seems to be that it was primarily a public relations exercise. It implied a British concern for international law, while confirming the *bona fides* of the British claim that her navy was essentially a defensive force. It nodded acknowledgment

to a strong Liberal tradition but, in time, of war could readily be ignored. If this conclusion is considered too cynical, the remaining sensible explanation is that the Foreign Office believed England would be a neutral in the next war. This, given the disposition of Grey and the Foreign Office permanent staff, the repeated warnings and concern about Germany's hostile intent coupled with Grey's support of a big navy policy in Cabinet, is a most unlikely explanation.

41 Northcliffe to Marlowe, 10 February 1911, Northcliffe Dep. 4890/XLVI.

42 Northcliffe to Bell, 3 March 1911 (incorrectly cited as to Buckle in Pound and Harmsworth), quoted in *HoT*, vol, III, p. 749. Northcliffe's letter to Buckle of the same day stated, 'I thought Nicholson had made it plain that I will not devote a farthing of my fortune to supporting that which I know would be an injury to this country. This . . . is my final communication on this subject.' Northcliffe Dep. 4890/1. Northcliffe tried to use Dawson to exercise influence on this subject within Printing House Square. See Dawson's diary 9 March 1911, Dawson MS 17, f. 40.

43 Northcliffe to Nicholson, 3 March 1911, quoted *ibid.*, p. 748.

44 Bell to Chirol, 7 March 1911, quoted in *Life and Letters of Bell*, pp. 310–13.

45 Quoted in *HoT*, vol. III, p. 754.

46 See H. W. Steed, *Through Thirty Years*, vol. I, pp. 350–4.

47 See A. M. Gollin, *op. cit.*, p. 291.

48 There followed a long and complex hiatus before Steed eventually became head of *The Times*'s foreign department, a post that, had Chirol's view counted, would probably have gone to Saunders. See *HoT*, vol. III, pp. 759–65; and vol. IV, part I, p. 139. Northcliffe, for a time, modified his opinion of Steed because he supposed he was suffering from a 'swelled head'.

49 Quoted in *HoT*, vol. III, p. 756.

50 See Northcliffe to Balfour, 17 June 1911, and Balfour to Northcliffe, 20 June 1911, Northcliffe Dep. 4890/III.

51 The accounts of these events in Pound and Harmsworth, *op. cit.*, p. 411, and, F. A. McKenzie, *The Mystery of the Daily Mail*, p. 68, are not altogether accurate. The Commons debates on the Naval Prize Bill were, Second Reading, 28, 29 June and 3 July (Vote: 301–231); Third Reading, 3 and 7 December (Vote: 172–125). Balfour spoke on 3 July, *Hansard*, v:27:840ff.

Lord Hankey claimed in his *The Supreme Command* (London, 1961), vol. I, p. 100 and fn. 1. 'There is little doubt that in both Houses of Parliament the Conservative leaders based their speeches to some extent on my views.' Hankey's account of the Declaration is generally followed in S. R. Williamson Jnr's study, *The Politics of Grand Strategy* (Cambridge, Mass., 1969), pp. 240–2; and is accepted without comment or detail in Stephen Roskill's *Man of Secrets* (London, 1970), vol. I, pp. 105–6.

Considering his personal political sympathies, there is an interesting comment of approval on the Lords' rejection of ratification in R. C. K. Ensor, *England, 1870–1914* (Oxford, 1936), pp. 447–8. The balance of opinion on the wisdom or otherwise of ratifying the Declaration subsequently supported the views that Northcliffe consistently held. This is true even of Grey, *Twenty Five Years*, vol. II, p. 102.

52 Northcliffe to Sutton, quoted in Pound and Harmsworth, *op. cit.*, pp. 429–30.

53 See Northcliffe's letters to Marlowe, particularly 10 February, 15 March and 7 April 1911, and 16 January and 29 February 1912, Northcliffe Dep. 4890/XLVI.

54 E. Wrench, *Uphill* (London, 1934), p. 243.

55 Quoted in Pound and Harmsworth, *op. cit.*, p. 416. Kenealy, trained in America, valued sparkle and brevity in journalism. His efforts, and those of Hamilton Fyfe, had turned the *Mirror* into a paying proposition after its disastrous start as a

women's paper in 1903. See H. Cudlipp, *Publish and Be Damned!* (London, 1953), pp. 11 and 33.

56 *HoT*, vol. III, pp. 769–70.
57 Marlowe's undated summary of *Daily Mail* year (for 1911/12?), Northcliffe Dep. 4890/XLVI.
58 R. D. Blumenfeld tells a story that neatly illustrates how outdated attitudes were at Printing House Square. He showed Moberly Bell a copy of the *New York Herald* boasting a wood cut and predicted that one day *The Times* would not only print pictures but also have display advertisements and supplements. Bell's response was to hammer the desk and cry, 'Don't be a fool. *The Times* with pictures? *The Times* with supplements?' R. D. Blumenfeld, *The Press in my Time* (London, 1933), pp. 38–9.
59 Buckle to Dawson, 14 August 1912, E. Wrench, *Geoffrey Dawson and Our Time* (London, 1955), pp. 83–4.
60 Pound and Harmsworth, *op. cit.*, p. 419.
61 *HoT*, vol. III, p. 652.
62 E. Wrench, *op. cit.*, p. 198.

Chapter 19: 1911: *Annus mirabilis*

1 See the examples quoted by E. M. Carroll, *French Public Opinion and Foreign Affairs* (New York, 1931), pp. 237–8.
2 *New Age*, 4 May 1911, p. 3.
3 *Nation*, 6 May 1911.
4 *Concord*, vol. XXVIII, no. 6, June 1911, p. 69.
5 See *History of the Times* (London, 1947) (hereafter referred to as *HoT*), vol. III, p. 692.
6 *The Times*, 13 and 25 May 1911.
7 *Ibid.*, 23 and 30 January, 6 and 20 February 1911.
8 See *British Documents on the Origins of the War, 1898–1914* (London, 1927) (hereafter referred to as *BD*), vol. VI, pp. 594–5. Repington's main problem was that Buckle persisted in thinking that any British involvement in war would be confined largely to naval action. At *The Times*, the influence of the naval specialists, particularly Capper and Thursfield, was dominant. Naval questions were not considered a proper concern for Repington. So that he might trench upon these problems he invented the impossible character Colonel von Donner und Blitzen. Through him, Repington ridiculed the accepted orthodoxy that a strong navy alone was sufficient safeguard of British interests and security. See, for example, *The Times*, 4 February 1911. Generally, Repington confined himself to those areas where naval and military problems crossed, but his articles on purely naval issues, as for example his writing in *Blackwood's Magazine* on the subject of blockade, despite the unfavourable opinion of Arnold-Forster quoted *ante*, indicate not only his perspicacity as a naval critic but also the outdatedness of much naval thinking.
9 See 'The debate on defence', *The Times*, 7 April 1911 (my emphasis) Repington's attitude was shared by his enemy, General Sir Henry Wilson, whose own attitude was shaped largely by Foch. The French had little understanding of sea power. In their minds, British security depended upon the creation of a conscript army, and the role of the British navy should be to ferry British troops safely to France.
10 Northcliffe to Buckle, 27 May 1911, Northcliffe Dep. 4890/I. He blamed the Board for assenting to the arrangement and suggested, 'we strengthen our hands

by seeking a military adviser on military policy', in addition to Repington. Nothing came of this suggestion.

In *Vestigia*, p. 303, Repington claimed he was largely responsible for the idea of the new journal. F. J. Hudleston maintained that Repington had '*absolutely nothing* to do with it. The initiative was Lt. Gen. [then Col.] A. L. Haldane's. The first step was "Recent publications of military interest" which he and I concocted.' (Marginal annotation by Hudleston in the War Office Library's copy of *Vestigia*, n.d.)

Hudleston was War Office librarian from 1919–27. From 1902 he had been librarian of the General Staff section of the War Office Library. He had reason to resent Repington's appointment as after Haldane's departure in 1909, the *Review*'s predecessor had been largely Hudleston's responsibility. He therefore had sufficient reason to suppose that he and not Repington would be the new editor. Repington's claim, cited above, would seem to rest upon a letter he wrote to Esher suggesting a 'General Staff journal . . . to disseminate some notions on questions of Imperial Defence by land and sea'. Repington to Esher, 29 November 1906, ESHR 10/27. Edmonds hints in his *DNB* entry on Repington that the editorship was a move to get the correspondent back to the War Office permanently.

The Army Council letter (19 April 1911) stating that the *Review* would replace *Recent Publications etc.*, carried a clear disclaimer: 'Articles . . . are not to be considered as official or as carrying the approval of the Army Council . . . unless expressly stated.' Nicholson, the Chief of the Imperial Defence Staff, in his letter of introduction to the *Review* (dated 13 June, published 11 July, pp. 4–5), described the new quarterly as 'the natural outcome' of the creation of the General Staff. 'It will aim at amplifying and elucidating the general principles which it is the duty of a General Staff to formulate.'

I am most grateful to Mr. C. A. Potts who gave me the information on Hudleston and first drew my attention to his comments in *Vestigia*.

11   See Repington to Northcliffe, 29 June and 9 July 1911, and Northcliffe to Repington, 4 July 1911, Roberts Papers. For their very different attitudes to the material Repington could gain access to because of his contacts at the War Office, see the exchange of correspondence between them, 20 and 22 August 1913, Northcliffe Dep. 4890/CI.

12   *The Times*, 1 and 13 July 1911.

13   There was every reason to suppose that there was a sham conflict of interest because the exploitation of Morocco's iron ore was monopolised by a Franco-German combine, Schneider-Creusot, though their monopoly was being challenged by the German Moriesmann Brothers. See also Spring Rice's revelation about Caillaux and the German financiers and Goschen's comment, Goschen's diary, 16 January 1912, in, C. H. D. Howard (ed.) *Diary of Edward Goschen, 1900–1914* (London, 1980), p. 258.

14   *BD*, vol. VII, p. 372.

15   Repington to Dawson, 20 July 1911, Times Archive. This was not scaremongering by Repington. He was genuinely worried, and with good reason, about the strategic disposition of British naval forces. That he was convinced there was a high chance of an outbreak of hostilities is clear from his detailed notes, 'Suggestions for the organization of war news in case of war with Germany', 20 July 1911, addressed to Buckle, Times Archive. In these he wrote, 'a preliminary naval success by Germany will justify her in risking invasion'.

16   E. Grigg to G. Browne, 27 July 1911, Times Archive.

17   *The Times*, 3 July 1911.

18   G. Valentine Williams to Northcliffe, 4 July 1911, Northcliffe Dep. 4890/LVIII.

19   *Hansard* v.27.1341

20   See *The Times, Daily Mail,* 7 July 1911; *Standard,* 6 July 1911.

21   *Manchester Guardian,* 11 July 1911.

22   *BD* vol. VII, p. 358.

23   *Ibid.,* p. 378.

24   This subject is discussed in detail in *HoT,* vol III, pp. 699–700. However, the claim that the source of the information was *Le Matin* is questionable. The German demands were known at PHS on the same day as the Foreign Office received its information. See Dawson's diary, 19 July 1911, MS Dawson 17, f. 104. The British Foreign Office was the most likely source of the leak, and the most likely person was Nicolson.

25   T. Wilson (ed.), *The Political Diaries of C. P. Scott, 1911–1928* (London, 1970), p. 42.

26   See Crowe to Bertie, 20 July 1911, FO 800/160.

27   See *BD,* vol. VII, pp. 390–1.

28   *Le Temps,* 22 July 1911; Morley to Asquith, 27 July 1911, Asquith MSS, vol. 13; *Hansard,* v:32:50.

29   On Ramsay MacDonald's attitude, and that of Labour, see *Labour Leader,* 11 August 1911, and Lord Elton, *Life of Ramsay MacDonald* (London, 1939), pp. 201–31. See also A. J. A. Morris, *Radicalism Against War, 1906–14* (London, 1972), pp. 242–3; fn. 2 on p. 244, and fn. 5 on p. 250.

30   See T. Wilson (ed.), pp. 46–7; J. L. Hammond, *C. P. Scott* (London, 1934), pp. 153–64.

31   *BD,* vol. VII, pp. 397–9.

32   *Ibid.,* p. 625.

33   (Asquith), *Hansard,* v:28:1227–28; (Grey), *ibid.,* v:32:54.

34   *BD,* vol. VII, pp. 465–6.

35   See J. E. B. Seely, *Adventure* (London, 1930), pp. 144–6.

   One reason for the speedy passage of the Act through Parliament was the general understanding that it was directed in the main against spies and saboteurs. The question was soon to arise whether or not its provisions could be employed to muzzle the press. Although the Attorney General stated as his opinion that the government was 'bound in honour not to employ the Act against editors or other persons connected with the Press', R. H. Brade, chief War Office negotiator with the press, was quick to point out that there was 'no record to this effect in the official version of the debates'. Brade also inferred correctly from an opinion given to him by the DPP, that Section 1(c) of the Act *could* be applied to the press where information had been communicated that was directly or indirectly useful to the enemy. Subsequently, this sub-section of the 1911 Act was successfully used to prosecute journalists.

   A voluntary agreement on press control during time of war or emergency was effected by the autumn of 1912, due to the compliance of the proprietors. Brade described this arrangement as providing 'considerable support for the scheme of precautionary measures which form part of our system of military preparation'. And behind the voluntary agreement lay the Official Secrets Act which, as Seely was advised by Thring, 'can be used in a case of emergency rather more freely than it can in ordinary times.' See CAB 17/91, particularly pp. 11 and 24.

36   H. W. Wilson to Maxse, 22 July 1911, Maxse MSS, 463, f. 110.

37   Repington to Dawson, 13 August 1911, Times Archive.

38   'Our sentimentalists and our sea power', *National Review,* November 1911. Although the article was written by 'Ignotus', H. W. Wilson, the ideas that dominated were Maxse's, as Wilson later acknowledged. See Wilson to Maxse, 15 April 1912, Maxse MSS, 466, f. 64.

39 At the beginning of July, Maxse was referring to Balfour as 'Foozle', a term that he claimed he had 'invented in his bath'. Asquith, for obvious reasons, he called 'Boozle'. See Geoffrey Dawson's diary, 2 July 1911, MS Dawson 17, f. 89. It was a common theme of this period, both on the Right and the Left, that party politics had degenerated into a farce where collusion between the front benches effectively emasculated opposition. The classic text on this theme is Belloc and Chesterton's, *The Party System* (London, 1910).

40 Quoted in R. Blake, *The Unknown Prime Minister* (London, 1955), p. 71.

41 M. V. Brett (ed.), *The Journals and Letters of Viscount Esher* (London, 1934–8), vol. III, p. 69. See also Esher's letter of condolence to Balfour, 9 November 1911, Balfour Ad MSS 49719, ff. 199–200.

42 Maxse to Sandars, 22 July 1911, *ibid.*, 49861, f. 275.

43 See, for example, B. Dugdale, *Arthur James Balfour* (London, 1937).

44 Maxse to Bonar Law, 17 November 1911, Law MSS, 23/4/47.

45 Grey, *Twenty Five Years*, (London, 1925), vol. I, p. 238.

46 Quoted in R. Pound and G. Harmsworth, *Northcliffe* (London, 1959), p. 424.

47 See *The Times*, 21 November 1911.

48 Nicolson to Cartwright, *BD*, vol. VII, p. 396; Almeric Fitzroy, *Memoirs*, vol. II, p. 471. Tyrrell, who was very pleased with Lloyd George's general demeanour, reported to Goschen that the king had congratulated the Chancellor on his speech. Lloyd George spoke slightingly to Tyrrell about the attitudes of Morley, Harcourt and the other pro-Germans in the Cabinet: 'I only wish they would go.' See C. H. D. Howard (ed.), *op. cit.*, p. 244.

49 Wile to Northcliffe, 15 November 1911, Northcliffe Dep. 4890/LV. See also Goschen's account of a dinner at Friederichshof on 12 August 1911. 'The Emperor took me aside and gave me a good doing for ¾ of an hour. He was rampant about Lloyd George's speech and our interference.' C. H. D. Howard (ed.), *op. cit.*, p. 242.

50 See T. P. Conwell-Evans, *Foreign Policy From a Back-Bench, 1904–18* (Oxford, 1932), p. 58.

51 Charles to Molly Trevelyan, 31 August 1911; Trevelyan Papers, CPT Ex 16; Runciman to Trevelyan, 18 September 1911, *ibid.*, Ex 65; C. P. Trevelyan to Runciman, 17 September 1911, Runciman MSS, R18/11.

52 See *BD*, vol. VII, p. 463.

53 The quotations from the German press are taken from Twells Brex, *Scaremongerings from the 'Daily Mail', 1896–1914* (London, 1914), pp. 102–6.

54 *Daily Mail*, 3 September 1911. The direct reference was to a recent speech by the Kaiser.

55 Quoted in *HoT*, vol, III, p. 702.

56 In *Vestigia*, p. 303, Repington claimed that his intention was avowedly propagandist. 'Opinion is everything in war. There was a danger that the French and ourselves should think the German army invincible.' There was, however, personal pique also behind his remarks. He always intensely disliked the Germans and on this occasion was particularly resentful that their military authorities had not accorded him those 'special facilities' which he considered were his due.

57 See *The Times*, 12, 14, 17, 19, 24 and 28 October 1911.

58 See *BD*, vol. VII, pp. 645, 652–5 and 703–5. The British Ambassador in Berlin seems to have supposed that German irritation with Repington was 'justifiable'. However, he told Bethmann, when comparing German complaints about Repington's articles in *The Times*, and an article in the *Daily Graphic*, 25 October 1911, with German press reports on a recent speech by McKenna and the Cartwright

incident, that 'criticisms however unmerited and irritating were not in the same category as gross fabrications and abuse founded upon them'. See C. H. D. Howard (ed.), *op. cit.*, p. 248.

59 However, on 24 October, Haldane informed the German military attaché that during the Moroccan crisis Britain had taken certain military and naval precautions, though these had not been prompted by any *written* obligation to France. Germany was warned: attack France and Britain will intervene. The Kaiser concluded that, though an entente rather than alliance, with or without written agreement, 'We must now reckon upon it', i.e. British intervention. See S. R. Williamson Jnr, *op. cit.*, p. 202 and fn. 107.

60 Repington to Buckle, 7 January 1912, Times Archive.

61 Dawson had already outlined Repington's complaints to Buckle. The editor apparently knew nothing of 'coming naval developments'. See Dawson to Repington, 1 January 1912, Times Archive.

62 See E. Halévy, *The Rule of Democracy*, pp. 437–8, where he suggests it was 'a deliberate silence inspired by the patriotic wish not to embarrass the government. The country did not know because it refused to know. There is an ignorance whose true name is connivance.' S. Verdad in *New Age*, 28 September 1911, claimed that the information was not made available 'because of the cowardice of the English Non Conformists and their Press'. In Pound and Harmsworth, *op. cit.*, p. 423, the authors claim, 'Concerning "necessary precautions" on the British side, Northcliffe declared an unofficial censorship ordering his editors to "print nothing to fan the war spirit".' I have not been able to trace this document. Whatever the actual explanation, it is a fascinating commentary on the period, especially in the light of the continuing attempts by the Admiralty, War Office and CID to impose 'voluntary censorship in time of war' that, without any institutional aid like a Press Bureau, the government was able to bring all the significant agencies of opinion and communication together. The explanation probably lies in an appeal by a leading politician or politicians, probably to the newspaper proprietors, in the same terms as Lloyd George addressed the union leaders to avoid a general strike.

Earlier in the summer there had been some leaks of information about harbour defences and ship movements that caused concern in the War Office and Admiralty. See sub-committee report of the CID on relations with the press, p. 1, para. 5, CAB 17/91.

63 See H. Nicolson, *Lord Carnock*, (London, 1930), pp. 347–8. At the time the British military attaché in Paris, Col. Fairholme, was providing glowing reports of the French army's morale and the superior quality of its officers. See Balfour to Sandars, 21 September 1911, Sandars MSS, 764, ff. 56–9.

64 'Episodes of the month', *National Review*, October 1911; Maxse to Mrs Chamberlain, 20 November 1911, AC4/11/185.

65 C. J. Lowe, 'Grey and the Tripoli War, 1911–12', in F. H. Hinsley (ed.) *British Foreign Policy Under Sir Edward Grey* (Cambridge, 1977), p. 315.

66 See for example, comment in the *Manchester Guardian* between 26 September and 3 October 1911.

67 *Review of Reviews*, November 1911; *Concord*, vol. XXVIII, nos. 8 and 9, October and November 1911, pp. 96 and 102; *Manchester Guardian*, particularly issue of 5 October 1911.

68 See particularly the signed minutes in *BD*, vol. IX, part I, pp. 288–9, 291, 297–8 and 322–3. For a detailed analysis of an earlier alleged interference with the press at the direct instigation of Grey, see *HoT*, vol. III, pp. 840–2.

69   Churchill to Grey, 4 November 1911, FO 800/86; *BD*, vol. IX, part I, p. 278.
70   Steed to Northcliffe, 11 November 1911, Northcliffe Dep. 4890/XCIV.
71   Northcliffe to Steed, 16 November 1911 (copy), *ibid.*
72   See Northcliffe to Maxse, 11 March, 20 and 26 December 1911; and Maxse to Northcliffe, 23 December 1911, *ibid./XXIII.*
73   See Fitzroy, *Memoirs*, (London, 1927), vol. II, p. 470.
74   See for example, *Westminster Gazette*, 31 January 1912.
75   For example, Professor Browne's letters in the *Manchester Guardian* and Shuster's in *The Times*, 9 and 10 November 1911; *Contemporary Review*, vol. CI, pp. 642–51; *Nineteenth Century*, vol. LXXI, pp. 40–7; *Nation*, 23 December 1911.
76   *Morning Post*, 21 November 1911.
77   *New Age*, 28 September 1911, p. 509.
78   *Nineteenth Century*, October 1911, pp. 796–804. Pollock's article was really intended to strike at the complacency shown by the Admiralty during the summer crisis.
79   *Daily Chronicle*, 15 November 1911.
80   *Contemporary Review*, November 1911, p. 605.
81   See National Peace Council, *Minutes*, 15 October 1911; *Manchester Guardian*, 5 October 1911.
82   Grey suggested that they were stirring up unnecessary trouble after the crisis had passed, 'tapping the barometer of international relations every five minutes', and they would be better spending their time preparing for the Christmas festivities. See his speech at Plymouth, and *Hansard*, v:32:54:55.
83   M. V. Brett (ed.), *op. cit.*, vol. III, p. 74.
84   See S. R. Williamson Jnr, *op. cit.*, pp. 184–95. Edmonds, who deeply disliked General Henry Wilson, listed among his few gifts, 'a ready Irish wit, a striking capacity to appropriate and claim as his own the ideas and work of others, and a real ability to make military matters clear in simple language to civilians'. See his unpublished 'Memoirs', ch. XX, p. 28, Edmonds MSS, III/5.
85   Sandars to Lansdowne, 27 November 1911, Sandars MSS, 764, ff. 213–14.
86   Memorandum by Sandars, 24 November 1911, *ibid.*, ff. 206–7. Also copy, ff. 215–18.
87   Gwynne to Bonar Law, 20 November 1911, Bonar Law MSS, 24/3/63.
88   It was the constant complaint of Grey's critics that they were hampered by an institutional framework designed to make the questioning of foreign policy almost impossible. Concerning the uselessness of debates in the Commons, see *New Age*, 2 March 1911, p. 400. 'Parliamentary Debate . . . is as innocuous as bridge for love . . . the reports should be published not by Hansard but by de la Rue.' On control of foreign policy, see Arthur Ponsonby, *Democracy and Diplomacy* (London, 1915), pp. 48–54; *Select Committee on House of Commons Procedure* (1914), especially questions 1704–6, 2284–6 and 3002–3.
89   Account of John Morley's comment in Fitzroy, *op. cit.*, vol. II, p. 471.
90   Asquith to Crewe, 30 November 1911, Asquith MSS.
91   *Daily News*, 10 January 1912.
92   Grey to Bonar Law, 25 November 1911, Law MSS, 24/4/80.
93   *Hansard*, v:32:110.
94   Maxse to Northcliffe, 23 December 1911, Northcliffe Dep. 4890/XXIII.
95   See G. P. Gooch, *Life of Lord Courtney* (London, 1920), pp. 568–70.
96   F. S. Oliver, *Ordeal by Battle* (London, 1915), p. 299.
97   Garvin to Maxse, 29 November 1911 (copy), Garvin MSS.
98   Esher to Sandars, 30 November 1911, Sandars MSS. 764, ff. 221–2.

99 Mahan to B. F. Clarke, 15 December 1911, Mahan MSS, Box 4.
100 Garvin to Lucy, 28 November 1911 (copy), Garvin MSS. The good impression made by Grey upon Tory journalists was reinforced by the reactions of the German press. A few days later, in a speech Bethmann made in Silesia designed to placate the Conservatives in Germany, the Chancellor argued that better Anglo-German relations required not words but deeds from England. Stumm made a point of telling Goschen that there had been nothing in Grey's speech to efface the sad effect of Lloyd George's Mansion House outburst that still rankled all Germans. See C. H. D. Howard (ed.), *op. cit.*, p. 252.
101 Felix Moschelles in *Concord*, vol. XXVIII, no. 10, December 1911, pp. 112–13.
102 W. S. Blunt, *My Diaries, 1888–1914* (single vol. edn, London, 1932), pp. 791–2.
103 He was arguing thus as late as the autumn of 1913. See E. D. Morel to C. P. Trevelyan, 8 September 1913, Trevelyan MSS, CPT Ex 35.
104 Northcliffe to Marlowe, 13 January 1912, Northcliffe Dep. 4890/XLVI.
105 *New Age*, 22 February 1912, p. 389.
106 Wile to Northcliffe, 27 January 1912, Northcliffe Dep. 4890/LV.
107 Chilvers to Maxse, 18 February 1912, Maxse MSS, 466, ff. 34–6.
108 Maxse to Bonar Law, 20 May 1912, Bonar Law MSS, 26/3/32.
109 Quoted in K. G. Robbins, *Sir Edward Grey* (London, 1971), p. 254.

Chapter 20: Priming the magazine

1 Northcliffe to Haldane, 24 February 1912, Roberts MSS, R62/58. Roberts showed the whole correspondence (which he had been given by Northcliffe) to Henry Wilson who was always delighted to hear anything to Repington's disadvantage. See Wilson diary, 4 March 1912, Wilson MSS, 73/1/27.
2 For comments on Repington, see for example, Commons Questions, 27 February 1912, *Hansard*, v:34:1167–71; Army Estimate Debates, 6 and 12 March 1912, *ibid.*, v:35:406–7, 415, 455–6 and 990.
3 Repington to Haldane, 27 November 1912, Haldane MSS, 5909, ff. 272–3.
4 See Saunders to Maxse, 16 May 1912, Maxse MSS, 466, ff. 76–8. 'I believe that Grey and the Foreign Office are well armed against Marschall's methods. Crowe knows his ways thoroughly.... He is very pleasant to talk to, but he resorts to sudden and violent bluff after the manner of a special pleader which he has never shaken off.... If his bluff is coolly faced and he is pinned to his words he collapses. But journalists are never allowed to see this side of his tactics and they often go on representing him as most conciliatory when behind the scenes he is raging and bluffing for all his worth. It was to enlighten the journalists and not the FO that I wrote. But Maxwell (*Daily Mail*) and others who haven't the brains of a rabbit and want their daily snippet of news besides the *prestige*(!) of knowing a live Ambassador, will continue to prophesy false things.'
   The other cause of concern about Marschall's appointment was the widespread fear that the Triple Entente was very insecure. There was a desperate desire that the Germans would accept it as a permanent factor that added stability to the European diplomatic scene. The Port Baltic meeting of the Tsar and Kaiser in July was consequently presented by Mackenzie of *The Times*'s Berlin office as German recognition of the Triple Entente's virility and that the equilibrium between Entente and Triple Alliance was now recognised in Berlin as the best security and guarantee of future European peace. See also the emphasis placed on this in the summary of the year's events in foreign policy, *The Times*, 31 December 1912.
   The sudden, unexpected but convenient death of Marschall in September

allowed *The Times* to give the Ambassador credit for the 'recognition' by Germany of the 'value' of the Triple Entente. Marschall's death converted him from a potential danger to the friend of the Triple Entente. See *The Times*, 25 September 1912.

5   The friendship between the two men was soon established after Dawson's return to Printing House Square, and handsomely acknowledged by Repington when Dawson succeeded Buckle as editor. 'It is a very pleasant change to have an editor who takes an interest in army matters . . . your criticisms have been most valuable. . . . It is a very pleasant change for me to work in close cooperation with my editor and I'm sure that by pulling together we can more than double the effect of individual effort.' See Repington to Robinson (Dawson), 22 January and 25 February 1913, Times Archive.

6   Repington to Dawson, 7 August 1912, Times Archive.

7   See L. S. Amery, *My Political Life* (London, 1953), vol. I, pp. 407–12. Amery argued that it was a vital British interest that she should send an expeditionary force adequate to resist any German march through Belgium to crush the French left wing. See *Hansard*, v:40;1341–2. Lee argued that there was 'a total divorce between military expenditure and national strategic requirements', to which Seely responded that it would be wrong for him to tell the House what the BEF would do in the event of war. It was enough for them to know 'it is absolutely ready to go on expedition and I am persuaded that wherever it goes it will fight well'. *Hansard*, v:69:1107 and 1289.

8   See Wilson's diary, 7, 11 and 12 January 1912, Wilson MSS, 73/1/27.

9   My emphasis. Roberts to Churchill, 21 and 24 January 1912; Churchill to Roberts, 23 January 1912. The letters are quoted in full in D. James, *Lord Roberts* (London, 1954), pp. 451–6.

10 Not only Churchill, but also Lloyd George admitted the need for conscription, but added that it was a proposal suitable only for a National party programme, or 'could only be done with the agreement of the other side', i.e. the Tories, exactly the point that Repington made frequently. See, *inter alia*, Wilson's diary, 5 November 1912; Lord Riddell, *More Pages from my Diary* (London, 1934), pp. 130–1 and 140.

11 Almeric Fitzroy, *Memoirs* (London, 1927), vol. I, p. 399.

12 See, for an earlier example, B. Drake and M. I. Cole (eds), *Our Partnership* (London, 1948), p. 380.

13 Lee to Bonar Law, 21 January 1912, Bonar Law MSS. Lloyd George told Henry Wilson that it had been Balfour's opposition to conscription that had been crucial to its rejection when 'proposed by the Radicals at the Round Table Conference after the King's death'. Wilson's diary, 5 November 1912.

14 Speech reported, *The Times*, 13 January 1912.

15 See Haldane to Mother, 1 February 1912, Haldane MSS, 5987, ff. 41–2; Maurice, *Haldane 1856–1915* (London, 1937), vol. I, pp. 290 and 320–1.

16 *Nation*, 27 January 1912. The article was entitled, 'The testing of Sir Edward Grey' which interestingly reveals the different position adopted towards Haldane's relationship with Grey, compared with the attitude of Tories like Maxse.

17 See *Nation*, 14 October, 25 November and 30 December 1911.

18 W. Fox to L. Courtney, 9 January 1912, Courtney Collection, vol. X.

19 Repington to Buckle, 8 February 1912, Times Archive.

20 M. V. Brett (ed.) *The Journals and Letters of Viscount Esher* (London, 1934–8), vol. III, pp. 79–80.

21 Nicolson to Bertie, 8 February 1912, FO 800/171. Goschen described Nicolson as being 'in despair'. Nicolson, like Goschen, was 'sick' at the idea of negotiations

between the two governments being opened by the two financiers, Cassel and Ballin. Goschen, backed by Grey, suggested Cassel and Ballin need not be further involved. It was Haldane who wished to retain their services. Goschen hinted in his diary that a covert arrangement might be in the process of construction as between the French government and German financiers the previous year in Morocco. See Goschen's diary, 5 February 1912, in, C. H. D. Howard (ed.), pp. 259–60.

22 See *British Documents on the Origins of the War, 1898–1914* (London, 1927) (hereafter referred to as *BD*), vol. VI, P. 750; Z Steiner, *The Foreign Office and Foreign Policy*, p. 127.

23 Quoted in S. Koss, *Sir John Brunner: Radical Plutocrat* (Cambridge, 1970), pp. 252–3.

24 Reported in *Daily Mail*, 4 August 1911.

25 Maxse to Bonar Law, 20 May 1912, Bonar Law MSS, 26/3/32. Of course there was a divide on policy in the Liberal camp, boldly and frequently advertised in the Radical press campaign against Grey. There was, however, no good reason for Maxse to suppose that there was any difference between Haldane and Grey.

There was a divide on policy in the Tory camp, between the 'Europeanists' who extolled Balance of Power ideas, and that section of the 'imperialists' who laid greatest stress upon imperial unity. The problem was to be highlighted in the press when in May 1911, Ned Grigg wrote in *The Times*, 'A single foreign policy cannot be permanently reconciled with five separate systems of commercial treaties and five separate systems of defence.' This, of course, raised not only strategic but economic concerns over the Tory party's commitment to food taxes and the full diet of tariff reform. Repington when considering the relationship between imperial and European defence problems demanded 'common strategic control'. This would never be realised so long as Unionists remained divided about the *immediacy* of the threat posed by Germany. Grigg, and those who thought like him, as they believed that Germany posed no immediate threat, sought the replacement of European guarantees and commitments to France and Russia by an *extra* European imperial system of defence commitments between Britain and her dominions – 'giving the Dominions the kind of voice on foreign policy and defence they are presently denied. . . . The Dominions cannot long be expected to accept a system of defence and foreign policy in which they have no voice, and on our side we want their partnership far more than their support.' *The Times*, 25 June 1912. On this problem, see *History of the Times* (London, 1947) (hereafter referred to as *HoT*), vol. IV, part I, pp. 1–34. 'The New Imperialism', where it is discussed fully in relation to tensions within Printing House Square.

26 *Daily Mail*, 10 February 1912.

27 See A. Chamberlain, *Politics from Inside* (London, 1936), pp. 420 and 422.

28 At the best, this perverse interpretation might be seen as a total misrepresentation of Asquith's intention in recommending the award for Grey as a snub for Grey's Liberal critics and an assertion that the government would continue in its policy of attachment to ententes and Balance of Power notions. See K. G. Robbins, *Sir Edward Grey* (London, 1971), p. 255.

29 Haldane to Mother, 15 February, 3 and 13 March 1912, Haldane MSS, 5987, ff. 60, 79, 100–1 and 110.

30 Maxse to Tyrrell, 8 March 1912, FO 800/109.

31 For editorial comment on Haldane's speech, see *Daily Mail*, 29 June 1912, and on Balfour's article, 24 and 27 May 1912.

32 See, for example, Midleton, *Records and Reactions* (London, 1939), p. 284, where

the author advances this as a reason why the Unionists opposed Haldane's membership of the War Cabinet.

33   Northcliffe to Maxse, 15 May 1912, Maxse MSS, 468, f. 334.

34   The measure of Percy's vitriolic comment can be judged from Wilson's diary entry for Sunday, 14 July 1912. 'Lord Percy came for a couple of hours and we discussed many things, and *I got him to change substantially a too violent article he had written against Haldane* for next month's National' (my emphasis).

35   Willoughby de Broke to Maxse, 11 June 1912, Maxse MSS, 466, ff. 92–4.

36   Garvin to Bonar Law, 13 and 15 March 1912, Bonar Law MSS, 25/3/28–33. Five days before the *Pall Mall Gazette* leader of 31 May, Roberts had written to Garvin complaining of insufficient support for his campaign from the press generally and Garvin in particular. See Roberts to Garvin, 26 May 1912, Garvin MSS.

37   *Pall Mall Gazette*, 31 May 1912.

38   See Roberts to Garvin, 18 June 1912 (copy) Roberts 7101/23/125/2/p. 65.

39   *Hansard*, v:35:1549ff.

40   *The Times*, 19 March 1912.

41   Fisher to Garvin, 9 January 1912, Garvin MSS. For source, see, Bacon, *Lord Fisher* (London, 1929), vol. II, p. 143.

42   Arthur Marder, *From the Dreadnought to Scapa Flow: the Royal Navy in the Fisher Era, 1904–1919* (5 vols), vol. 1, *The Road to War, 1904–1914* (Oxford, 1961), p. 264.

43   Fisher to Garvin, 3 November 1911, Garvin MSS.

44   *Ibid.*

45   Fisher to Garvin, 9 January 1912, *ibid.*

The 'Islanders' was a society created by Esher in March 1909. He was convinced that it was the most effective way of securing a big navy. Its policy is neatly summed up in a letter from Esher to Strachey, 9 February 1912, S/6/1/8. 'There is one *safe* policy and one only. Two ships or keels to every one German. *That* is the only safeguard of peace – and of an individual Empire. It may be expensive but as it is *vital*, expense cannot be seriously taken into account.'

Gerard Fiennes was assistant editor of the *Pall Mall Gazette;* Alan Burgoyne was founder and editor of the *Navy League Annual.* When Stead died in the *Titanic* disaster, Fisher recognised that he had lost one of his most delightful, idiosyncratic yet powerful press allies. He wrote a number of letters to friends, but none better than that to Garvin, 20 April 1912, Garvin MSS.

> And what a loss is dear old Stead! A single-minded, God-
> fearing pricker of bubble reputations and ruthless exploder
> of gas-bags! . . . He was *the fust man* who in Berlin said to the
> Great Man, 'Don't you worry. Our relations will always be
> cordial! Whenever you build one Dreadnought, we will build
> *two!*' Yes! He was the *first* 'Wild Man' in Beresford's list
> who proclaimed the doctrine of 'Two Keels to One!' Let us
> feel thankful, my good friend, that his dear spirit (*now
> assuredly happy*) delights in the thought that we his friends on
> earth won't ever forget all his splendid endeavours.

46   A. J. Marder (ed.) *Fear God and Dread Nought* (London, 1952–9), vol. II, p. 437.

47   See *Hansard*, v:41:837–64. His argument that 'the direct cause' of his seeking supplementary estimates was 'to be found in the New Germany Navy Law' was clever but inaccurate. In fact, the German Defence Bill (*Wehrvorlagen*) gave most

money to the Germany army and the construction increases for the imperial navy were one extra Dreadnought for 1913 and 1916, and one at an unspecified date. Because the Novelle was much *better* than had been anticipated the British press handled its passage through the Reichstag in April lightly.

48　A. J. Marder (ed.), *op. cit.*, vol. II, p. 469.

49　See for example *Manchester Guardian*, 27 May 1912.

50　Henry Wilson's diary, 6 May 1912, Wilson MSS, 73/1/27.

51　See the account of Nicolson's conversation in A. Chamberlain, *op. cit.*, pp. 485–6.

52　Wilson's diary, 29, 30 and 31 May 1912. Some part of the confusion at Printing House Square, other than differences of opinion, is explained by a letter of Lovat Fraser to Garvin, 29 September 1912, Garvin MSS. However, it must be remembered that Fraser was at odds with Dawson who did not like him writing for Garvin.

> The Board has been packed with purely administrative people.
> They want to sweat the writing men. The 'Times' will never
> be saved by administration, only they won't see that; and Lord
> N, who is about to take his coat off and spend the autumn and
> winter in the 'Times' office, still clings to the idea that writing is
> a minor matter. As you know, writing and policy are the first
> secrets of the salvation of the 'Times', of all papers. Hardly any
> of those who are left have any notion of policy, and not one of
> the senior men can write at all, except Grigg, who is being treated
> very much as I am. Dawson's capacity is purely executive; he
> knows his own weakness but is very much fettered.

53　See Esher to Balfour, 30 May 1912, Balfour Ad MSS 49719, ff. 217–18, and memorandum (similar to that sent to the king and quoted in Marder, *op. cit.*, pp. 290–1), ff. 219–23.

54　See Beresford to Maxse, 10 and 22 June 1912, Maxse MSS, 466, ff. 87 and 104–5.

55　See Grey's exchange with Balfour in June. 'The Mediterranean position will oblige this or any Government to consider our relations with France very carefully.' Grey to Balfour, 16 June 1912; Balfour to Grey, 12 June 1912, 'Memorandum on Anglo-French relations', Balfour Ad MSS 49731, ff. 1–6, 12. Grey's disposition, as evidenced by his attitude to Cambon's embarrassing requests in 1911 and 1912, was never to ask searching questions about the 'exact' nature of the entente relationships.

56　M. V. Brett (ed.), *op. cit.*, vol. III, p. 100.

57　Churchill asked only for an extra million pounds. There had been a revenue surplus of approximately six and a half million in the budget from the previous year and the Chancellor had held this over for 'possible contingencies'. He had specifically stated that the main contingent factor was 'that the existing programmes of other naval Powers will not be increased'. Clearly the Novelle changed the position, though see no. 47, pp. 446–7, *supra*. What the economists had really feared was that Churchill would ask for most or all the six and a half million. The navalists were very angry as they assumed Churchill would ask for all the six and a half million. The implausible assumption was that Lloyd George would use the balance 'for the purpose of trying to bribe the middle class by remission of income tax next year'. Churchill had earlier told all and sundry that if he did not get all the surplus he would resign. See H. W. Wilson to Maxse, 15 April 1912, Maxse MSS, 466, f. 64.

58 Fisher to Bonar Law, 27 July 1912, Law MSS, 26/5/42.

59 See *Daily News*, 24 July 1912; *Nation*, 27 July 1912.

60 On this campaign and its failure, see A. J. A. Morris, *Radicalism Against War 1906–14* (London, 1972), pp. 327ff.

61 For quotations from the navalist press, see A. J. Marder, *op. cit.*, p. 299. The confusion was sometimes deliberate. For example, a leading article in the *Daily Mail*, 4 January 1910, contained a diagram suggesting that under the Liberal government the British had built sixteen Dreadnoughts, and the Germans in the same period seventeen. Vincent Baddley from the Admiralty pointed out to Asquith that this was 'most misleading as it is not explained that the German figures include a year's programme in advance'. Asquith MSS, vol. 24, ff. 1–2.

62 Grigg to Garvin, 15 December 1912, Garvin MSS.

63 Quoted in R. Mackay, *Fisher of Kilverstone* (Oxford, 1973), p. 438.

64 Beresford to Blumenfeld, 31 July 1912, Blumenfeld MSS, BERE 17. Fisher, in fact, lost money by accepting the chairmanship. He sold all his Shell Oil shares 'at great prospective loss as soon as the terms of his appointment were agreed'. Mackay *op. cit.*, p. 438.

65 Churchill to Garvin, 8 August 1912, Garvin MSS.

66 Churchill to Garvin, 10 August 1912, *ibid.*

67 Roberts to Garvin, 22 September 1912, *ibid.*

68 Roberts to Garvin, 1 November 1912, *ibid.*

69 Roberts to Garvin, 4 November 1912, *ibid.*

70 Reported in *The Times*, 23 October 1912.

71 *Nation*, 24 October 1912.

72 *Manchester Guardian*, 28 October 1912; *Daily News* 30 October 1912.

73 *Evening Standard*, 30 October 1912.

74 Bromley Davenport to Gwynne, 29 October 1912, *Morning Post*, letters, 30 October 1912.

75 Roberts to Maxse, 19 July 1912, Maxse MSS, 466, f. 125.

76 Roberts to Garvin, 1 December 1912, Garvin MSS.

77 *Daily Mail*, 28 November 1912.

78 For Blumenfeld's recruitment by Roberts, see Roberts to Blumenfeld, 22 September 1912, reproduced in R. D. Blumenfeld's *All in a Lifetime* (London, 1931), p. 146.

79 Wilson's diary, 21 November and 10 December 1912, Wilson 73/1/27.

80 See Strachey to Gwynne, 8 November 1912, S/7/9/5; Roberts to Strachey, 15 November 1912; Strachey to Roberts, 13 November 1912, S/12/3/52.

81 See Strachey to Roberts, 28 November 1912, S/12/3/53.

82 F. S. Oliver to Dawson, 29 November 1912, Milner Dep. 13, ff. 21–5.

83 Repington to Dawson, 7 December 1912, Times Archive.

84 Repington to Haldane, 27 November 1912, Haldane MSS, 5909, ff. 272–3. The same day Repington sent a detailed, four foolscap-page note to his editor dealing with these same points in great detail: Times Archive.

85 Haldane to Spender, 28 November 1912, Spender Ad MSS 46390, f. 174.

86 Haldane to Mother, 29 November 1912, Haldane MSS, 5988, f. 209.

87 Dawson to Repington, 10 December 1912, Times Archive. This argument of Dawson's was the stock 'non military' point in the case of many conscriptionists – stressing the 'moral' virtues of national service. In effect, therefore, Repington took issue with his editor on the military arguments.

88 Repington to Dawson, 11 December 1912, Times Archive.
89 Dawson to Repington, 11 December 1912, *ibid.*
90 Northcliffe was never reluctant to conduct a campaign against another Tory newspaper. There had been, for example, a violent exchange with the *Morning Post* in March. See Lady Bathurst to Gwynne, 8 and 12 March 1912, Gwynne MSS 15. Gwynne at the same time was quarrelling with Max Aitken to whom he wrote on 21 March 1912, 'With your permission we will bury the hatchet. . . . My excuse must be zeal for the *Morning Post.* I have to fight the monopoly of the *Times* every day of my life and my letter to you was written in sorrow and in anger that I should have to say to you "et tu Brute".' Gwynne MSS 14.
91 *Nation*, 28 December 1912.
92 The *Round Table*, a quarterly edited by Philip Kerr, first appeared in 1910. It promoted imperialist ideas and because it was closely associated in its foundation with Milner and his 'Kindergarten', the original Kindergarten members were often called,. after 1910, 'Round Tablers'. Amery became detached from the group because of his greater interest in tariff reform.
93 L. S. Amery to H. A. Gwynne, 3 January 1913, Gwynne MSS 14.
94 The whole story is told from Garvin's point of view in A. M. Gollin, *The Observer and J. L. Garvin* (London, 1960), pp. 366–85.
95 Dawson to Chirol, 9 January 1913, Times Archive.
96 Not only Repington's influence but also Grigg's was increased by Garvin's intemperate criticisms. Throughout the year Grigg had been 'much agitated' and had frequently cautioned Dawson 'about the movement in the "PMG" for alliance with France'. See Dawson's diary, 29 May 1912, MS Dawson 18, f. 79.
97 Comments from several German newspapers translated in Twells Brex, *Scaremongerings from the 'Daily Mail', 1896–1914* (London, 1914), p. 122.
98 Steed to Dawson, 19 October 1912, Times Archive. On Saunders relations with Tardieu, see *HoT*, vol. IV, part I, pp. 78ff.
99 Dawson to Steed, 14 October 1912, Times Archive. For the British Foreign Office view, see *BD*, vol. IX, part II, pp. 1–474.
100 Lovat Fraser to Garvin, 30 October 1912, Garvin MSS.
101 War correspondents experienced grave difficulties in getting accurate information about military events and relaying it to London. The Turkish armies were made to appear to be worse than actually was the case. See *HoT*, vol. IV, part I, p. 77; H. Wagner, *With the Victorious Bulgarians* (London, 1913); Lionel James, *With the Conquered Turk* (London, 1913).
102 Dawson to Steed, 5 November 1912, Times Archive.
103 Dawson to Steed, 6 November 1912, *ibid.*
104 Dawson to Steed, 16 December 1912, *ibid.* It is fair to note that Dawson's instructions shared the general temper and spirit of the instructions received in increasing numbers at Printing House Square from Northcliffe.
105 *The Times*, 9 November 1912.
106 Reported in *The Times*, 13 November 1912.
107 See Dawson to Steed, 16 December 1912, Times Archive.
108 Mackenzie to Dawson, 13 January 1913, *ibid.*
109 See Steed to Dawson, 5 January 1913, *ibid.*
110 Dawson to Steed, 26 November 1912, *ibid.*
111 *The Times*, 13 February 1912.
112 Quoted in *HoT*, vol. IV, part I, p. 101.
113 Northcliffe to Dawson, 1 March 1913 (copy), Times Archive.

Chapter 21: Military matters: Repington fights real and imagined foes

1 Dawson to Northcliffe, 2 March 1913 (copy), Times Archive.

2 The speeches were to be written for Roberts by the ailing Professor Cramb. As the appeal was directed to the Liberal and Labour parties, Roberts could not be supported by his usual stalwarts, like Milner, who were too closely identified with the Tories.

3 Diary, 21 January 1913, MS Dawson 19, f. 15. Roberts did speak in the Lords' debate to the effect that the government had tried everything but compulsion to solve the military problem, and everything else had failed. Roberts's apparent 'reasonableness' might well be explained by General Wilson's absence in France because it was the DMO who was most dedicated to smashing the Territorial 'farce'.

4 Repington to Dawson, 22 January 1913, Times Archive. Repington's concern for Dawson's good opinion and his respect for the editor's views on military matters was quite genuine. See his remarks to Esher in Esher's memorandum, 14 February 1913, cited below.

5 Repington to Dawson, 1 February 1913, Times Archive.

6 Esher, memorandum of a conversation with Repington, dated 14 February, although the conversation must have taken place at the latest on 6 February. It was sent to Asquith. Part of this document is printed in M. V. Brett (ed.), *The Journals and Letters of Viscount Esher* (London, 1934–8), vol. III, pp. 118–21; the full text in Asquith MSS, 24, ff. 116–21.

7 See S. R. Williamson Jnr, *The Politics of Grand Strategy* (Cambridge, Mass., 1969), p. 306. H. R. Moon, 'The Invasion of the United Kingdom, 1888–1914', unpublished PhD, London, 1970, p. 433, argues for Churchill on the basis of the 1912 manoeuvres.

8 See and cf. 'Master mariner' in *Contemporary Review*, January 1912, and Col. Chas Callwell in *National Review*, April 1912.

9 Notes, 17 October 1912, quoted in A. J. Marder, *From the Dreadnought to Scapa Flow: the Royal Navy in the Fisher Era, 1904–1919* (5 vols), vol. 1, *The Road to War, 1904–1914* (Oxford, 1961), pp. 352–3.

10 See Wilson's diary, 9 and 14 February 1913; C. E. Callwell, *Sir Henry Wilson: His Life and Diaries* (London, 1927), vol. I, p. 122.

11 Repington to Seely, 11 February 1913, Seely MSS, S 20/f.153; *The Times*, 12 February 1913.

12 On the 'Suicide Club's' campaign, see A. J. A. Morris *Radicalism Against War, 1906–1914* (London, 1972), pp. 333–47.

13 Dawson was in a better position to judge Lichnowsky's words than the Radicals. See Dawson to Aunts, 12 January 1913, Dawson MS, 57, ff. 69–72. 'The German Ambassador is full of gloom about the prospects of peace.... I've had a good deal of talk with him and think he's thoroughly nervous and overworked already.'

14 Dawson to Saunders, 21 February 1913, Times Archive.

15 The French government took a particular interest in Roberts's activities though the military attaché in London, de la Panouse doubted that he would ever open 'les yeux à l'opinion anglaise sur la nécessité d'adopter le service universel'. Panouse to the Minister of War, 15 March 1913, French Military Archives, Box no. 7 N 1228: Attachés Militaires Grande Bretagne 1913–14.

16 Northcliffe to Dawson, 6 March 1913, Times Archive. He also wrote on the same subject to, among others, Strachey, Maxse and Esher. Northcliffe's interest in this subject was reflected in a series of articles in the *Daily Mail*, 17 and 25 February, 31 March, 1, 3 and 10 April 1913.

17   See Midleton, *Records and Reactions, 1856–1939* (London, 1939), pp. 280–3.
18   See particularly Repington's articles on 5 and 13 May 1913.
19   *National Review*, June 1913. Moon suggests (*op. cit.*, p. 449) that the author, 'Navalis', was Repington. It might have been H. W. Wilson using material provided by Repington.

Maxse and his group of friends shared a conviction with critics of the extreme left that there was a web of corruption controlling British public and political life. Although the main target of the right-wing critics was the Liberal party, they did not entirely exclude members of their own party. Balfour was particularly suspect on this as on other counts. Their conspiracy theory amounted to the conviction that Britain's future survival as a Great Power was being eroded by the corrupting influence of cosmopolitan financiers – the plutocrats. It happened that financial scandals were a feature of political life in most West European countries in the decades before 1914. The uncertainties promoted by novel and rapidly changing circumstances could lead even a serious scholar of political behaviour like Ostrogorski to conclude that democracy could be equated with plutocracy.

There is much interesting material on the envy promoted by the newly and massively rich Edwardians in Jamie Camplin's fascinating and entertaining study, *The Rise of the Plutocrats* (London, 1978).

20   See Repington to Dawson, 13 April 1913, Times Archive. 'He cannot tell how things will go, but adds that we have the brains of the committee on our side and hopes for the best.'
21   Repington to Dawson, 1 April 1913, Times Archive.
22   See Wilson's diary, 21 and 23 February, 4 March, 13, 14 April 1914.
23   *Ibid.*, 5 August and 9 December 1913.
24   The earliest example I found of Law admitting his personal conversion to national service was in Wilson's diary, 26 October 1912. However, he changed his reasons for supporting compulsion depending upon his audience. Thus, to Repington he said he owed his conversion to the arguments in the memorandum submitted to the invasion inquiry on air power.
25   Repington to Dawson, 13 April 1913, Times Archive.
26   See Wilson's diary, 10 April 1913. For a short period after this meeting, references to Repington in the diaries are marginally less poisonous.
27   Rose died the week following the Bill's second reading! The farce that compulsion was not a party political issue was clung to in the Commons with an extraordinary tenacity. At Question Time on 16 April 1913, Rowland Hunt suggested to the Prime Minister that the subject ought to be non-party, to which Asquith replied ingenuously that as far as he knew it was and he trusted it would not become one! Hunt asked the same question twice in 1912 on 5 March and 21 November, twice in 1913, on 16 April and 30 July, and once in 1914, on 15 July.
28   See Repington to Dawson, 13 April 1913, *supra*; *The Times*, 14 April 1913.
29   See Wilson's diary, 7 April 1913; C. E. Callwell, *op. cit.*, vol. I, p. 125. For a more balanced view than Wilson's on the opinion of the General Staff concerning compulsion, see Ewart's diary, 23 January 1913. 'There is no large body of opinion in the Army in favour of Compulsory Service if limited to Home Defence ... plenty of "whole-Hoggers" who would like to see out and out conscription for general service in war.'
30   CAB 16/28A, Appendix V.
31   Esher to Asquith, 25 June 1913 (copy), Balfour Ad MSS 49719, ff. 244–5.
32   There was considerable debate whether Roberts and Repington alone should attend. Asquith decided all four could be present.

33   Repington to Dawson, 6 July 1913, Times Archive.
34   Repington to Dawson, 17 July 1913, *ibid.*
35   CAB 16/28A, Appendix VI.
36   See Moon, *op. cit.,* pp. 447–8.
37   See Percy to Maxse, 7 December 1912, Maxse MSS, 466, f. 229. Seely had first used the argument to counter claims by Territorial Officers themselves seeking compulsion for Home Defence, encouraged specifically by a speech made by Roberts at Holborn, and printed with the enthusiastic cooperation of the *Daily Mail.* There is an undated letter of Percy's from this period that suggests the whole plan was Henry Wilson's. See Percy to Maxse, n.d. Maxse MSS, 468, f. 479.
38   Percy to Maxse, 22 May 1913, *ibid.,* f. 337.
39   Percy to Maxse, 16 March 1913, *ibid.,* f. 310. The Maxse group entertained the hope for a few months before mid-summer 1913, that a general election would soon be called.
40   Roberts to Garvin, 25 May 1913, Garvin MSS.
41   Maxse to Northcliffe, 10 June 1913, Northcliffe Dep. 4890/XXIII.
42   *Daily Mail,* 31 March 1913.
43   *Ibid.,* 26 April 1913.
44   *Ibid.,* 22 April 1913.
45   *The Times,* 9 July 1913.
46   For Churchill's complaint, see Minutes of 10th Meeting of Inquiry, CAB 16/28A, p. 89. The *Daily Mail* obviously improved its source of information for the 1913 manoeuvres as it was able to provide substantially accurate accounts during their course. See, for example, 'The enemy ashore', *Daily Mail,* 25 July 1913. The figures the *Mail* quoted for the 1912 manoeuvres, which were approximately twice the actual numbers landed, were also quoted by Repington in his September articles, supposedly written by von Donner und Blitzen.
47   There is a large file of correspondence between Bridgeman and Sandars in the Sandars MSS, for this period which, *inter alia,* indicates the *Morning Post* report on Bridgeman's 'health' was no accident. Sandars had many contacts with the Tory press, and it would have been easy for him to leak information to them.
48   Esher noted that when Asquith told Lloyd George that he wanted Battenberg, the Chancellor was 'horrified at the idea of a German holding the supreme place. Asquith says LG is an excellent foolometer and that the public would take the same view.' M. V. Brett (ed.), *op. cit.,* vol. III, p. 61. Certainly this was the view held by Garvin, Gwynne and Maxse.
49   See R. S. Churchill, *W. S. Churchill – Young Statesman* (London, 1967), vol. II, pp. 432–41; A. J. Marder, *op. cit.,* pp. 258–9.
50   Bridgeman to Sandars, 28 July 1913, Sandars MSS, 765, ff. 131–3.
51   Memorandum by Sandars after conversation with Bridgeman, 29 July 1913, *ibid.,* ff. 134–5.
52   *The Times,* 2 and 8 September 1913.
53   See Lord Sydenham, *My Working Life,* pp. 299–300.
54   Churchill to Asquith, 30 August 1913, quoted in Moon, *op. cit.,* pp. 458–9.
55   CAB 16/28A, p. 315.
56   Ian Hamilton to Seely, 15 September 1913, Seely MSS, S18/ff. 60–7.
57   *Hansard,* Lords, v:14:191.
58   See Williamson, *op. cit.,* pp. 310–11.
59   See *Hansard* for 25 February, 4, 11 and 17 March, 27 April, 11 and 29 June and 27 July 1914.

60   Percy to Maxse, 26 November 1913, Maxse MSS, 468, f. 452.

61   See point 1 of Esher's note of his conversation with Repington, 14 February 1913, *ante*. Confirmation of this intention is clear from Dawson to Repington, 24 July 1913, Times Archive: 'We have tried to shepherd this Government into adopting the principle of compulsory training.'

62   Repington to Dawson, 11 December 1912, Times Archive.

63   For details of this group, its campaign and publications, see Denis Hayes, *Conscription Conflict* (London, 1949), pp. 136ff.

64   Percy to Maxse, 17 December 1913, Maxse MSS, 468, f. 465.

65   Diary entry, 29 July 1913, Wilson MSS, 73/1/27.

66   When National Service was introduced in Australia and New Zealand, a leading article in the *Daily Mail* (24 September 1912) asked, as the Australians and New Zealanders had accepted national service 'because their statesmen honestly told them it was essential for their security', how could it be argued that 'Britain's need is less'? See also, *Daily Mail*, 28 February 1914. 'That duty [conscription], loyally accepted by two of our daughter nations, is even more imperative for us, because we lie nearer the seat of danger.' Again, the conscription argument was attached to the issue of invasion.

67   Amery to Law, 1 September 1913, Law MSS, 30/2/2.

68   Roberts to Garvin, 25 November 1913, Garvin MSS.

69   D. Hayes, *op. cit.*, p. 134.

70   The £400 limit was the same as that adopted by Parliament for the payment of MPs. It had been agreed on that occasion that 'nobody can be a gentleman on less than £400 per annum'. The education clause covered public schools and universities.

71   The roots of the idea in the nineteenth century can clearly be discerned in Disraeli's romantic notions of a Young England, spelled out most attractively in his three-volume novel, *Coningsby or the New Generation* (1844). Carlyle was another with his head buried in the sands of a hopelessly romanticised past. But in the 'poetry' of Lord John Manners, Disraeli's friend, we find the 'purest' expression of these sentiments.

> Each knew his place – king, peasant, peer or priest,
> The greatest owned connexion with the least;
>
> Let wealth and commerce, laws and learning die,
> But leave us still our old nobility.
> *England's Trust* (1850)

72   De Broke to Blumenfeld, 2 March 1914, Blumenfeld MSS, WIL 2.

73   Haldane to de Broke, 3 March 1914, de Broke MSS, WB/9/5.

74   Sydenham to de Broke, 2 March 1914, *ibid.*, WB/9/4.

75   Walter Runciman to C. P. Trevelyan, 4 January 1914, C. P. Trevelyan MSS, CPT 17. For the problems Trevelyan experienced in writing and publishing his pamphlet, see A. J. A. Morris, *Trevelyan, Portrait of a Radical* (Belfast, 1977), pp. 112–13.

76   C. P. Trevelyan, *Democracy and Compulsory Service* (London, 1913), p. 28.

77   See *Standard*, 15 March 1914; W. D. Sanderson to de Broke, 16 March 1914, de Broke MSS, WB/9/18.

78   *The Times*, 19 to 22 August 1913.

79   The British Radical press, while never approving the action at Zabern and the subsequent trial, nevertheless in its 1914 campaign for disarmament 'explained' German militarism as the natural consequence of pressure by Russia and the

revanchist spirit in France that would not accept the loss of Alsace-Lorraine. See, for example, *Nation*, 21 March 1914.

80 See Wile to H. G. Price, 6 December 1913, Northcliffe Dep. 4890/LV. The best and most recent account of the Zabern Incident is in David Schoenbaum, *Zabern 1913: Consensus Politics in Imperial Germany* (London, 1982). For Schoenbaum's estimate of Wile, see pp. 171–2.

81 See Steed's own account in *Through Thirty Years* (London, 1924), vol. I, pp. 381ff.

82 *The Times*, 12 January 1914.

83 See Northcliffe to Steed, 22 January 1914; Steed to Northcliffe 1 February 1914, Northcliffe Dep. 4890/XCIV.

Chapter 22: Over the brink

1 Quoted in R. Pound and G. Harmsworth, *Northcliffe* (London, 1959), p. 448.

2 See T. Clarke, *My Northcliffe Diary* (London, 1931), p. 50. As Clarke noted, 'The *Mail* was sixteen years old, a well-established money-maker, with no rival to be afraid of. No Beaverbrook had yet appeared on the horizon to stiffen the challenge of the *Daily Express*. Among us in the *Mail* office there was a feeling of ascendancy over all the other papers.... Any qualms about being considered vulgar upstarts of material success were allayed by the fact that respectability was also ours, now that *The Times* was of the family.' For the influence of *The Times* on the *Mail*, see Clarke's story on p. 51.

3 Unless otherwise ascribed, quotations in this paragraph are taken from *History of the Times* (London, 1947) (hereafter referred to as *HoT*), vol. IV, part 1, pp. 120–41.

4 T. Clarke, *op. cit.*, p. 52.

5 Diary, 19–21 January 1914, MS Dawson 20, ff. 10–11.

6 George Saunders retired on 31 March 1914 at the age of 60. He had long wanted to retire from journalism. Braham, however, had been goaded into leaving *The Times* in January by Northcliffe who had said to him, 'I don't like Jews in high places.' Braham left for Australia and did not return until 1928 when Dawson was more than happy to resecure his services as a leader writer.

7 Dawson to John Walter, 29 January 1914, MS Dawson 64, ff. 1–4.

8 Quoted in Pound and Harmsworth, *op. cit.*, p. 450.

9 Northcliffe to Walter, 21 February 1914, Times Archive.

10 D. C. Watt, 'The British reactions to the assassination at Sarajevo', in *European Studies Review*, 1971, vol. I, no. 3, p. 236.

11 In particular, Steed distrusted Austrian Jews as he thought they were disposed to Pan-Germanism. The prejudice of proprietor and journalist was to be particularly important in the last crisis before the outbreak of war in their response to the Rothschilds. See below.

12 Wile to Northcliffe, 14 March 1914, Northcliffe Dep. 4890/LV.

13 See Clarke, *op. cit.*, pp. 53–4.

14 'Modern warfare', *Daily Mail*, 8, 9 and 10 April 1913.

15 On Wells's ideas about warfare, see his *Experiments in Autobiography* (London, 1934), vol. II, pp. 677–93.

16 From 1913 onwards there was growing official concern about the influence of the submarine on naval warfare and defensive and offensive strategy. Fisher, although the father of the Dreadnought, eagerly examined the possibilities inherent in this new weapon. The best, most complete account on this subject is in R. Mackay, *Fisher of Kilverstone* (Oxford, 1973), pp. 444ff.

17 Both Dawson and Northcliffe had been against the securing of a controlling interest (for £2 million) in the Anglo-Persian Oil Company. Commenting on Dawson's editorials in June 1914, Repington wrote, 'they have been brilliant but I ought to tell you that I am in favour of the Agreement which seems to me necessary ... the arguments in favour outweigh altogether the objections to it.' Repington to Dawson, 18 June 1914, Times Archive. On oil supply, see A. J. Marder, *From the Dreadnought to Scapa Flow: the Royal Navy in the Fisher Era, 1904–1919* (5 vols), vol. 1, *The Road to War, 1904–1914* (Oxford, 1961), pp. 269–71; *Past and Present*, April 1968, no. 39, pp. 139–68.

18 *The Times*, 27 March 1913.

19 Quoted and translated in T. Brex, *Scaremongerings from the 'Daily Mail', 1896–1914* (London, 1914), p. 129.

20 See *British Documents on the Origins of the War, 1898–1914* (London, 1927)(hereafter referred to as *BD*), vol. X, part II, p. 721.

21 T. Brex, *op. cit.*, p. 136.

22 See *BD*. vol. X, part II, pp. 734–8.

23 *Labour Leader*, 27 November 1913.

24 M. V. Brett (ed.), *The Journals and Letters of Viscount Esher* (London, 1934–8), vol. III, p. 142.

25 *Pall Mall Gazette*, 27 March 1913.

26 Maxse's *National Review* was the exception.

27 On this Radical reductionist campaign, see S. E. Koss, *Sir John Brunner, Radical Plutocrat* (Cambridge, 1970), pp. 262–4; and A. J. A. Morris, *Radicalism Against War, 1904–14* (London, 1972), pp. 333–47.

28 See, for example, the exchange of letters between Walter Runciman and Trevelyan in A. J. A. Morris, *C. P. Trevelyan: Portrait of a Radical* (Belfast, 1977), pp. 114–15; M. V. Brett (ed.), *op. cit.*, vol. III, p. 151.

29 In the autumn of 1913, in speeches at Bedford, Swindon and Middlesbrough, Lloyd George had unfolded his land programme which coincided with the publication of the Land Inquiry Committee Report. A fixed legal wage for agricultural workers was proposed and the setting up of a Ministry of Land to complete the revision of the land survey started by the 1909 budget. Land Taxation was a measure much favoured by a significant proportion of Liberal MPs. However, there was a divide in the party on this subject and a further divide between those who placed priority upon urban rather than rural taxation. The Land Values Taxation scheme was overtaken by the war.

30 Balfour to Selborne, 7 January 1914, Selborne MSS, I, ff. 144–6.

31 See *The Times*, 4 and 7 January 1914.

32 T. Wilson (ed.), *The Political Diaries of C. P. Scott, 1911–1928* (London, 1970), p. 80.

33 W. S. Churchill, *The World Crisis, 1911–1918* (abridged and revised single volume edition, London, 1931), pp. 102–3.

34 See Morley's comments quoted in Scott's diary in T. Wilson (ed.), *op. cit.*, p. 74.

35 *Concord*, April 1914, p. 3. *Concord* in the same article referred to 'the difficulties of our friends in the House of Commons'. The Radical reductionists regretted the money spent on armaments that they thought would better have been spent on a programme of much needed social reforms. They agreed with Snowden's attack on the armaments lobby (see, *Hansard*, v:59:1896ff.) but they could not press their differences to a successful vote. On the two occasions the House divided, 2 and 23 March 1914, the largest number in the reductionist lobby was 35. The fact was there was nothing they could do. If they brought down the

government it could only be replaced by a Tory administration that would spend more on armaments. This was well recognised by C. P. Scott and probably accounts for the *Manchester Guardian*'s grudging acceptance of Churchill's estimates. See T. Wilson (ed.), *op. cit.*, p. 77. The most convenient excuse with which to hide their impotence was to claim they had acceded because of the Ulster troubles – but no one was convinced by this argument.

36 *Daily News*, 19 March 1914.

37 In December 1912, the Canadian Parliament had laid before it an emergency Naval Bill authorising the expenditure of £7 million on three super-Dreadnoughts to be placed at the disposal of the imperial government. The measure had been agreed between R. L. Borden, the Canadian Tory party's leader, and Churchill at an earlier meeting in August. However, the Canadian Liberal party under W. Laurier argued that it was for the Canadian Parliament to determine the action taken by any Canadian ship and the Bill was rejected by the Canadian Senate in May 1913. The decision caused great distress among the imperialist group at Printing House Square. See Willison to Grigg, 6 May 1913, Times Archive. *The Times* claimed that Churchill had calculated as though the three Canadian Dreadnoughts would be available, and more, that he used them twice in his calculations, for service in the Mediterranean and in the North Sea.

38 Dawson to Repington, 27 February 1914, Times Archive.

39 Diary, 24 and 25 March 1914, MS Dawson 20, ff. 42–3.

40 See Dawson to Repington, 4 March 1914, Times Archive.

41 Repington to Dawson, 18 June 1914, *ibid.*

42 *The Times*, 8 April 1914.

43 See H. W. Steed, *Through Thirty Years* (London, 1924), vol. I, p. 391. Steed's account of the Lavisse letter is followed in *HoT*, vol. IV, part I, pp. 167–70. I have not been able to trace any proof that Steed did in fact contact the Foreign Office, but it seems likely, because of Poincaré's involvement and the fact that other factual statements by Steed in this section can be confirmed, that he is stating what actually happened.

44 *Daily News*, 23 April 1914. See also *The Times*, same date.

45 *New Age*, 30 April 1914, p. 806.

46 *Manchester Guardian*, 23 April 1914.

47 In *Twenty Five Years* (London, 1925), vol. I, pp. 285–7, Grey asked himself, 'What was the motive of the French Government?' He concluded that the French 'simply desired to reassure Russia and keep her loyal'. Grey makes himself out to be a credulous simpleton. He could not fail to recognise the political implication of the conversations.

48 Isvolsky expressed his amazement; Sazonov was delighted with the conversations' 'great importance . . . from a general political point of view'. Benckendorff, in his report to St Petersburg, summed up the position. 'I doubt whether any better guarantee for joint military operations in the event of war could be found than the spirit of this Entente, as it now reveals itself, strengthened by the existing military agreements.' See H. Lutz, *Lord Grey and the World War* (London, 1928), pp. 180–1.

49 The Cabinet approved of the talks on 12 May, as covered by the Grey Cambon exchange of November 1912. Grey, at a meeting with Cambon and Benckendorff, handed over a copy of this letter. (See *BD*, vol. X, part II, p. 541). Grey talked of strategy, but the least gifted strategist would have recognised the value of the talks did not relate to naval strategic dispositions. In any event, the British naval attaché's reports had made clear earlier that the Russian Baltic fleet was a negligible

force. See A. J. Marder, *op. cit.*, pp. 309–10. The story of Wolff's involvement is told in O. J. Hale, *Publicity and Diplomacy* (New York, 1940), pp. 442–3.

50 *Manchester Guardian*, 12 June 1914. For Grey's answers to Byles and King, see, *Hansard*, v:63:457–8.

51 *Nation*, 30 May and 20 June 1914.

52 *The Times* and *Westminster Gazette*, 13 June 1914.

53 The *John Bull* article asserted that the murder had been planned and carried out by the Serbian Secret Service whose bureau was in their London legation. On 11 July, *John Bull* published a facsimile of a document, purporting to be on Serbian legation notepaper, with a plan of the assassination. The accompanying article said that 'Serbia ought to be wiped out'. Boschkovitch, the Serbian minister, was advised by Arthur Nicolson that there was no good ground for a libel action against the journal and that the government could not suppress the journal. The editor, Bottomley, then more concerned about his racing activities in Belgium, exercised no control over articles criticising the Serbs that continued to appear in *John Bull* long after the rest of the British press had changed its tune and was attacking Austria. An article claiming the Austrian ultimatum was inspired by their original article of 11 July, actually appeared after war had been declared, headlined, 'To hell with Serbia'. See *John Bull*, 4, 11 July and 8 August 1914; Julian Symonds, *Horatio Bottomley* (London, 1955), p. 162; *BD*, vol. XI, p. 38.

54 In strange alliance, Tory *Morning Post* and Labour *Daily Citizen* expressed distrust of Austria.

55 Press attitudes in these last few weeks before the outbreak of war are examined in a number of books including J. F. Scott, *Five Weeks* (London, 1927); Theodor Wolff, *The Eve of 1914* (London, 1935); Emil Ludwig, *July 1914* (London, 1929); O. J. Hale, *op. cit.*, ch. X. Steed gives his own egocentric but substantially accurate account in chs X and XI of his *Through Thirty Years*. The most recent and best account of the period from 28 June to 1 August 1914 is in D. C. Watt's article, *loc. cit.*

56 See *BD*, vol. XI, p. 46.

57 H. W. Steed, *op. cit.*, vol. I, p. 394.

58 Steed gives interesting first-hand accounts of both the Agram and Friedjung trials, *op. cit.*, vol. I, pp. 306–16. The Austro-Hungarian Foreign Office was fully implicated in a series of forgeries, designed to encompass the deaths of leading members of the Serbo-Croat Coalition. Fifty-three innocent Serbs would have been executed on false evidence had war between Austria and Serbia broken out in the spring of 1909.

59 D. C. Watt's translation from the documents, *op. cit.*, p. 241, fns 33 and 37.

60 Based upon Mensdorff to Berchtold, 17 July 1914, translated in *HoT*, vol. IV, part I, p. 185.

61 There is a confused account of this episode in Spender's *Life, Journalism and Politics* (London, 1927), vol. II, pp. 8–10, and a draft made in August 1914 in his private papers, Spender Ad MSS 46392. Like Watt, *op. cit.*, p. 243, I have followed the latter.

62 *The Times*, 16 July 1914.

63 Mensdorff thought the article had been written by Steed.

64 For press and diplomatic reaction to the two articles, see *BD*, vol. XI, pp. 46, 47, 60 and 108.

65 Perhaps because the *Daily Telegraph* was known for its pro-German bias, in the same way that the support given Austria generally before and after the ultimatum by the Liberal Radical press was also ignored. It might simply be a reflection of

what, in diplomatic circles, were considered 'official' newspapers, close to or 'inspired' by government thinking.

A long report from Vienna by Dillon published in the *Daily Telegraph* on 27 July was noted by Arthur Nicolson in a minute. 'Dr Dillon is an intimate friend of Count Berchtold and he is evidently stating the Austrian case with a naked simplicity which is notable.' See *BD*, vol. XI, p. 123.

66 Franckenstein again called on Spender providing the editor with the same dossier of material from the Serbian press earlier given to Lansdowne. Spender was not impressed. After the issue of Austria's ultimatum he concluded the approaches to him were evidence of complicity between high officers of state in Germany and Austria who knew and were preparing for what was coming, but he excluded Mensdorff and Lichnowsky as innocent. See Spender, *op. cit.*, vol. II, pp. 11–12.

67 I have generally followed Steed's own account of these events in his *Through Thirty Years*, vol. I, pp. 404ff. The inconsistencies between Steed's account and Mensdorff's reports to Berchtold, published in the *Austrian Documents*, are dealt with and resolved in Steed's favour in *HoT*, vol. IV, part I, p. 187, fn. 1, and *ibid.*, vol. IV, part II, appendix II, pp. 1063–4.

68 Steed's book, *The Hapsburg Monarchy* (London, 1913), which *inter alia*, had pointed out that Serbian successes in arms had weakened Austria and inevitably thrust Austria, Hungary and Germany together in the face of a common Slavonic problem, had been banned in Vienna in April 1914 and existing copies confiscated by the police. Steed had never cultivated Mensdorff and it was most unlikely that the Emperor's representative in London would invite to luncheon the author of a book condemned as 'an insult to Francis Joseph'.

69 See their notes to de Bunsen's telegram to Grey, *BD*, vol. XI, p. 59. On narrow strategic grounds, Crowe and Nicolson were correct. The rumour de Bunsen sent was that the Austrians were preparing to secure Mount Lovchen which dominated Montenegro thus preventing cooperation between Montenegro and Serbia. Such rumours had been current for two months. Italy, however, would not have allowed such a move because it threatened her position in the Adriatic. The Germans would not have allowed the Austrians to offend Italy. See Count de Salis despatch to Grey, 26 July 1914, *ibid.*, vol. XI, p. 337.

70 The attitude adopted by Gwynne and Garvin is particularly difficult to understand. It might have been that the Irish problem dominated their thinking to such an extent that they temporarily misjudged the significance of European events. Lichnowsky in a letter to Bethmann on April 20 had noted the 'remarkable moderation' of Garvin's comments in the *Observer*. See E. T. C. Dugdale, *German Diplomatic Documents* (reprint, New York, 1969), vol. IV, p. 362.

For the way in which the Germans employed selective quotation from the British press to impress the Russians that Britain would remain neutral, see Buchanan to Grey, 25 and 26 July 1914, *BD*, vol. XI, pp. 99 and 106–7.

71 See D. C. Watt, *op. cit.*, p. 246.

72 For example, Lloyd George told C. P. Scott on 27 July that opinion in *The Times* was ahead of that of Grey's officials at the Foreign Office whose anti-Germanism was notorious in Radical circles. See J. L. Hammond, *C. P. Scott of the Manchester Guardian* (London, 1934), p. 177.

73 Kate Courtney's diary, 30 July 1914, Courtney MSS.

74 Courtney to A. G. Gardiner, 30 July 1914, A. G. Gardiner MSS.

75 J. A. Spender, *Life, Journalism and Politics*, vol. II, p. 12.

76 *Daily Chronicle*, 1 August 1914.

77 C. P. Trevelyan, *Memorandum on Beginning of War*, p. 1. See also similar comments

in the diaries of John Burns (2 August 1914, Ad MSS 46336) and Richard Holt, (2 August 1914, Holt MSS). A variation on this conspiracy theme was that propounded by G. O. Trevelyan: the Tories had struck a bargain over Ireland with the government, the price being the government's abandonment of neutrality. See Trevelyan to Mother, 2 August 1914, C. P. Trevelyan MSS, CPT Ex 69.

78 *Manchester Guardian*, 4 August 1914.
79 O. J. Hale *op. cit.*, p. 463.
80 *Manchester Guardian*, 1 August 1914. For a detailed account of reaction by the Radical press during these crucial days, see A. J. A. Morris, *Radicalism Against War*, pp. 405ff.
81 Fitzmaurice to Spender, 31 July 1914, Spender Ad MSS 46392, ff. 159–60.
82 Quoted from H. W. Steed, *Through Thirty Years* (London, 1924), vol. II, p. 7. There are a number of accounts of these events, and a degree of confusion over the exact dates and also the importance attached to certain actions by individuals. These last can be explained by the anxiety of authors to suggest the importance of the part they played, and, their ignorance of other important factors. The differences in dating are minor and probably reflect the writing up of events at a later date. For Wilson and Maxse, see C. E. Callwell, *Sir Henry Wilson: His Life and Diaries* (London, 1927), vol. I, pp. 153ff. For a senior Tory politician's account, see A. Chamberlain, *Down the Years*, (London, 1935), ch. VI.

The weekend habit died hard. Most Liberal ministers were out of London the previous weekend – the Foreign Secretary fishing in Hampshire. As late as 31 July, Asquith and Lloyd George confirmed arrangements to spend 1 and 2 August away from London. The action of leading Tories is therefore quite understandable.

83 Bonar Law to Asquith, 2 August 1914, Bonar Law MSS 37/4/1. The omission of any mention of Belgium compares strangely with its frequent citation in the Tory press. Consternation had been caused at the Foreign Office by a report in the *Evening Standard*, 31 July 1914, claiming on the authorisation of both Asquith and Grey that Britain would come to the assistance of Holland or Belgium if the neutrality of either was infringed by Germany. Eyre Crowe informed the Netherland's government that the alleged authorisation was a myth. See *BD*, vol. XI, p. 269.
84 Dawson's diary, 31 July 1914, Dawson MS 20, f. 112.
85 Quoted in E. Wrench, *Geoffrey Dawson and Our Times*, (London, 1955), p. 104.
86 Northcliffe to Repington, 31 July 1914, Northcliffe Dep. 4890/CI.
87 Steed, *op. cit.*, vol. II, p. 9.
88 *Manchester Guardian*, 2 August 1914.
89 H. W. Steed, *op. cit.*, vol. II, p. 11. There was no leading article in the next day's 'special' edition.
90 *Ibid.*, p. 12.
91 Dawson, 'Notes of some critical Sundays', MS Dawson 64, ff. 68–74.
92 Gwynne to Tyrrell, 1 August 1914, Gwynne MSS 24.
93 For the details of this letter and Ballin's status as an agent of Germany, see Steed, *op. cit.*, vol. II, pp. 16–25; *HoT*, vol. IV, part I, p. 213; part II, pp. 1064–5.
94 Text of instructions quoted in *HoT*, vol. IV, part I, pp. 213–14.
95 See Dawson's Notes, *ante*.
96 Dawson's diary, 3 August 1914, MS Dawson 20, f. 113.
97 Dawson's diary, 4 August 1914, *ibid.*, f. 114.

Epilogue: Account rendered: the rewards of excess

1 Quoted in Howard Weinroth, 'Norman Angell and The Great Illusion', in *Historical Journal*, 1974, vol. XVII, no. 3, p. 573.
2 Bertrand Russell, 'Some psychological difficulties', in Julian Bell (ed.), *We Did Not Fight* (London, 1935), p. 329.
3 F. S. Oliver to Milner, 5 August 1914, Milner MSS, Dep. 349, ff. 216–17.
4 Herbert Praed to Bonar Law, 5 June 1912, Law MSS 26/4/9. Astor had to wait for his peerage. The next year's list was already fully subscribed.
5 H. A. Gwynne to Asquith, 23 October 1914 (copy), Gwynne MSS 14.
6 This letter was quoted in part by Steed in a memorandum dated 29 November 1908, Times Archive.
7 Lady Bathurst to Gwynne, 8 March 1912 (?), Gwynne MSS 15.
8 Chirol to Strachey, 19 April 1906, Strachey Papers, S/4/9/8.
9 Moberly Bell to Strachey, 1 June 1904, *ibid.*, S2/9/10.
10 M. Ostrogorski, *Democracy and the Organisation of Political Parties* (London, 1901), vol. I, p. 410.
11 See Grey's 'Some thoughts on public life', in *Fallodon Papers* (London, 1926), pp. 87–111, particularly pp. 100–1.
12 Arnold White to Mrs Adair, 11 April 1914, Blumenfeld MSS, WHI/7. White's claim concerning the disinterest of the party mandarins was less than fair to the Chief Whip. See Chapter XVI, *ante.*
13 See *World*, 21 June 1910; M. V. Brett (ed.) *The Journals and Letters of Viscount Esher* (London, 1934–8), vol. III, p. 121. Esher's taste for journalism was acquired when he formed a close relationship with W. T. Stead in 1883. He was involved in and impressed by the *Pall Mall Gazette*'s campaign in 1884 to send General Gordon to Khartoum to which the government had reluctantly to agree because of public enthusiasm for the idea.
14 Rosebery to Strachey, 24 February 1905 (copy), Rosebery MSS, 10170, ff. 16–17.
15 See Strachey to Rosebery, 21 November 1910, *ibid.*, 10122, ff. 314–15.
16 Strachey to Carson, 21 November 1914, Carson MSS, D1507/1914/36.
17 This first meeting was on 29 October 1901, M. V. Brett (ed.), *op. cit.*, vol. I, p. 311.
18 Strachey to Newton, 18 July 1911, (copy), S/11/1/5.
19 An interesting comparison is with Lady Bathurst. See her letters to H. A. Gwynne, 12 March, 15 July and 21 November 1912, Gwynne MSS 15. Gwynne accepted with good grace Lady Bathurst's interference with the *Morning Post*, although he did not take proprietorial interference lightly as is clear from his letter to Balfour after leaving the *Standard*, 6 May 1911, Balfour Ad MSS 49797, ff. 113–14. Apparently Gwynne did not resent Sandars interfering with his editorial prerogative. See Knollys to Sandars, 14 and 17 June 1910, *ibid.*, 49686, ff. 38–9.
20 The Radicals were following a pattern that had been established as early as 1907. Examples are quoted in Caroline Playne, *The Pre-War Mind in Britain* (London, 1928), pp. 116–17.
21 Marlowe to Northcliffe, 26 May 1907, Northcliffe Dep. 4890/XLVI.
22 H. W. Wilson to Maxse, 22 July 1911, Maxse MSS, 463, f. 110.
23 Ian Hamilton to Strachey, 4 September 1909, S/8/5/1.
24 Clarke to Chirol, 4 April 1905, Sydenham Ad MSS 50832, ff. 15–19.
25 See Zara Steiner, *The Foreign Office and Foreign Policy, 1898–1914* (Cambridge, 1969), p. 186, fn. 1.
26 Steed accepted the arrangement that had been made by Lavino when he was *The Times*'s Vienna correspondent. Lavino counted its greatest advantage was that the

Daily Telegraph correspondent also used the *Tageblatt* and Lavino therefore knew in advance what information he was sending back to London.

27 Steed to Moberly Bell, 19 October 1908, Times Archive.
28 Steed to Moberly Bell, 16 July 1908, *ibid.*
29 Steiner, *op. cit.*, p. 188.
30 New arrangements had been introduced in House of Commons procedure in 1906 with the intention of making it easier to question the Foreign Secretary. They were a failure. See *Hansard*, iv:152:340–1 and 802–4. See also J. A. Spender, *The Public Life*, vol. II, p. 40. On the limitations of questions in the House on foreign policy questions, see F. Gosses (trans. E. C. Van der Gaaf), *The Management of British Foreign Policy before the First World War* (Amsterdam, 1948).
31 The trouble with Blue Books was that they were carefully edited and were published more with an eye to possible foreign responses than to inform domestic critics. On this subject, see Steiner, *op. cit.*, pp. 194–6; Temperley and Penson, 'British secret diplomacy from Canning to Grey', in *Cambridge Historical Journal* 1938, vol. VI, pp. 1–32.
32 See *British Documents on the Origins of the War, 1898–1914* (London, 1927), (hereafter referred to as *BD*), vol. XI, p. 157.
33 *Ibid.*, pp. 99 and 106–7.
34 H. R. Moon, 'The invasion of the United Kingdom, 1888–1914', unpublished PhD, London, 1970, p. 652.
35 In 1908 and 1913 just as in previous scares in 1900 and 1888.
36 Northcliffe to Repington, 20 August 1913 (copy), and Repington to Northcliffe, 22 August 1913, Northcliffe Dep. 4890/CI.
37 See F. Hirst, *The Six Panics and Other Essays* (London, 1913), *passim*.
38 See *BD*, vol. VII, p. 132; M. V. Brett (ed.), *op. cit.*, vol. II, p. 355; A. J. Marder (ed.), *Fear God and Dread Nought* (London, 1952–9), vol. II, pp. 204–6.
39 Zara Steiner, 'Views of war', in *Moirae*, 1980, vol. V, p. 30.
40 *Pace*, the 'King and Country' debate in the Oxford Union in 1933 (see the article by M. Ceadel in *Historical Journal*, 1979, vol. 22, no. 2, pp. 397–422), Oxford University tended to take a more 'hawkish' view than did Cambridge. Bertie Russell and Browne were two leading Radical and pacifist dons at Cambridge. The history faculty at Oxford quickly rushed into print in August 1914 and thereafter throughout the war, with a series of patriotic *Reports*. Professor Cramb was a don at London University which, like other British universities, tends to live in the shadow of Oxbridge. Perhaps in this context it is just worth mentioning that the present Regius Professors at both ancient universities (one of whom is a distinguished military historian), are originally London University men.
41 Quoted in J. A. Terraine, 'The inferno: 1914–18', in Theo Barker (ed.), *The Long March of Everyman* (London, 1975), p. 169.
42 John Morley, *Recollections* (London, 1917), vol. II, pp. 172 and 175.
43 *Nation*, 9 June 1912.
44 See the editor's 'Introduction' to A. J. A. Morris (ed.), *Edwardian Radicalism 1900–1914* (London, 1974), p. 9.
45 See my review of D. Ayerst's *Guardian: Biography of a Newspaper*, in *Political Quarterly*, vol. 42, no. 4, pp. 458–9.
46 See A. J. Mayer, 'Internal crisis and war since 1870', in C. L. Bertrand (ed.), *Revolutionary Situations in Europe* (Montreal, 1977), *passim*.
47 Geoffrey Searle, 'The revolt from the right in Edwardian England', in Kennedy and Nicholls (eds), *Nationalist and Racialist Movements in Britain and Germany before 1914* (London, 1981), p. 35. All the essays in this book are extremely useful, but

Searle's essay brilliantly and, in my opinion, accurately summarises almost all the weakness of the British pre-war Radical Right.

48 See Dilwyn Porter, 'Pearson and the Tariff Reform League', in *Moirae*, vol. V, pp. 111–12. On the Birmingham 'tradition' of aggressive politicking, see P. C. Griffiths, 'Popular disturbance and historical change: the Aston riots of 1884', in *Moirae*, vol. I, pp. 36–43. See also the same author's, 'The origins and the development of the National Liberal Federation', unpublished BLitt, Oxford, 1973.

49 See, for example, A. J. A. Morris, *C. P. Trevelyan: Portrait of a Radical* (Belfast, 1977), p. 40.

50 See Richard Price, *An Imperial War and the British Working Class* (London, 1972), pp. 157–8.

51 See *Portrait of a Radical, op. cit.*, pp. 125–34.

52 See S. E. Koss, *Lord Haldane: Scapegoat for Liberalism* (New York, 1969), pp. 124–218.

Select bibliography

I Unpublished sources

A. Private papers

Sir J. C. Ardagh Papers, Public Record Office, Kew.
H. O. Arnold Forster Papers, British Library.
H. H. Asquith Papers, Bodleian Library.
W. W. Astor Papers (miscellaneous), Library of Congress, Washington.
A. J. Balfour Papers, British Library.
C. F. Moberly Bell Papers, Times Archive.
Sir F. L. Bertie Papers, Public Record Office, Kew.
Sir R. Blennerhassett Papers, Cambridge University Library.
R. D. Blumenfeld Papers, House of Lords Record Office.
A. Bonar Law Papers, House of Lords Record Office.
Sir C. A. G. Bridge Papers, National Maritime Museum, Greenwich.
G. E. Buckle Papers, Times Archive.
J. Burns Diary, British Library.
Sir Henry Campbell-Bannerman Papers, British Library.
Sir E. H. Carson Papers, Northern Ireland Public Record Office, Belfast.
Austen Chamberlain Papers, Birmingham University Library.
Joseph Chamberlain Papers, Birmingham University Library.
Sir V. Chirol Papers, Times Archive.
L. Cope-Cornford Papers, National Maritime Museum, Greenwich.
Kate and Leonard Courtney Papers, British Library of Economic and Political Science, London.
Lord Crewe (R. O. A. Crewe-Milnes, Baron Houghton) Papers, Cambridge University Library.
E. Crowe Papers, Public Record Office, Kew.
L. Curtis Papers, Bodleian Library.
Lord Curzon Papers, Public Record Office, Kew.
Geoffrey Dawson (Robinson) Papers, Bodleian Library; Times Archive.
J. E. Edmonds Papers, Military Archives, King's College, London.
Lord Esher Papers, Churchill College, Cambridge.
J. S. Ewart Papers, Scottish Record Office, Edinburgh.
A. G. Gardiner Papers, British Library of Economic and Political Science, London.
J. L. Garvin Papers, Humanities Center, University of Texas, Austin.
D. Lloyd George Papers, House of Lords Record Office.
G. J. Goschen Papers, Bodleian Library.
Sir Edward Grey Papers, Public Record Office, Kew.
E. W. M. Grigg Papers, Bodleian Library.

H. A. Gwynne Papers, Bodleian Library.
Lord Haldane (R. B. Haldane) Papers, National Library of Scotland.
Sir I. S. M. Hamilton Papers, Military Archives, King's College, London.
Lord Hardinge of Penshurst (Charles Hardinge) Papers, Cambridge University Library;
    Public Record Office, Kew.
Sir M. Hankey Papers, Churchill College, Cambridge.
Richard Holt Diary, Liverpool Public Library.
Sir Archibald Hurd Papers, Churchill College, Cambridge.
Sir J. R. Jellicoe Papers, British Library.
Lord Kitchener Papers, Public Record Office, Kew.
Lord Lansdowne Papers, Public Record Office, Kew.
Sir F. Lascelles Papers, Public Record Office, Kew.
A. T. Mahan Papers, Library of Congress, Washington.
R. Marker (Kitchener-Marker) Papers, British Library.
Ivor Maxse Papers, Imperial War Museum, London.
L. J. Maxse Papers, West Sussex Record Office, Chichester.
R. McKenna Papers, Churchill College, Cambridge.
Lord Midleton (St John Brodrick) Papers, Public Record Office, Kew; British Library.
Lord Milner Papers, Bodleian Library.
H. W. Nevinson's Diary, Bodleian Library.
Sir A. Nicolson Papers, Public Record Office, Kew.
Sir G. H. U. Noel Papers, National Maritime Museum, Greenwich.
Lord Northcliffe (A. Harmsworth) Papers, British Library.
A. A. W. H. Ponsonby Papers, Bodleian Library.
C. à Court Repington Papers, Times Archive.
Lord Roberts Papers, Army Museums Ogilby Trust; Public Record Office, Kew.
Lord Rosebery Papers, National Library of Scotland, Edinburgh.
W. Runciman Papers, Newcastle-upon-Tyne University Library.
J. J. Sandars Papers, Bodleian Library.
Lord Sanderson (Sir T. H. Sanderson) Papers, Public Record Office, Kew.
George Saunders Papers, Churchill College, Cambridge; Times Archive.
J. E. B. Seely Papers, Nuffield College, Oxford.
Lord Selborne Papers, Bodleian Library.
E. J. W. Slade Diary, National Maritime Museum, Greenwich.
J. A. Spender Papers, British Library.
Sir C. Spring-Rice Papers, Churchill College, Cambridge; Public Record Office, Kew.
H. W. Steed Papers, Times Archive.
J. St Loe Strachey Papers, House of Lords Records Office.
Lord Sydenham of Combe (George Clarke) Papers, British Library.
J. R. Thursfield Papers, National Maritime Museum, Greenwich; Times Archive.
C. P. Trevelyan Papers, Newcastle-upon-Tyne, University Library.
Lord Tweedmouth Papers, Naval Library, Ministry of Defence, London.
Sir F. H. Villiers Papers, Public Record Office, Kew.
Sir D. M. Wallace Papers, Cambridge University Library; Times Archive.
Arnold White Papers, National Maritime Museum, Greenwich.
E. V. Wile Papers, Library of Congress, Washington.
Spenser Wilkinson Papers, Army Museums Ogilby Trust.
Willoughby de Broke Papers, House of Lords Record Office.
Sir Henry Wilson Papers, Imperial War Museum, London.

B. Other papers

Courtesy of Geoffrey Pocock, transcript of Roger Pocock's Pocket Diary for the pre-war period.

Courtesy of Keith Jeffery, transcripts of French Military Attachés' Reports from the French Military Archives.

National Peace Council, London, memoranda and minutes of meetings up to August 1914.

Times Archive, material listed under subject indices and not listed above under Private Papers.

Bodleian Library, *Round Table* Papers and Conservative Party Papers before 1914.

Public Record Office, Kew, various Cabinet, War Office, Foreign Office and Admiralty Papers as given in detail in source notes. On the subject of Press secrecy: CAB 17/91; 16/8; 3/2/1 47A; 4/4/2 167 and 168B; WO 32/6466 and 7137–41; ADM 1/8030; 116/4082; FO 881/9945.

2 Printed sources

A. Books

Aberdeen, Ishbel (ed.), *Edward Majoribanks Lord Tweedmouth*, London, 1909.

Albertini, L., *Origins of the 1914 War*, Oxford, 1952–7.

Amery, L. S., *My Political Life*, London, 1953.

Anderson, E. N., *The First Moroccan Crisis, 1904–06*, Chicago, 1930.

Anderson, P. H., *The Background of Anti-English Feeling in Germany, 1890–1902*, Washington, 1939.

Angell, N., *Europe's Optical Illusion*, London, 1909.

Angell, N., *The Public Mind*, London, 1927.

Angell, N., *After All*, London, 1951.

Anonymous, *History of The Times*, vol. III and vol. IV, part 1, London, 1947–52.

Arnold-Forster, H. O., *Military Needs and Military Policy*, London, 1908.

Arnold-Forster, Mary, *Memoir of H. O. Arnold-Forster*, London, 1910.

Arthur G., (ed.), *Letters of Lord and Lady Wolseley*, London, 1922.

Asquith, H. H., *Memories and Reflections 1852–1927*, London, 1928.

Asquith, H. H., *Fifty Years of Parliament*, London, 1926.

Asquith, H. H., *The Genesis of the War*, London, 1923.

Asquith, Margot, *Autobiography*, London, 1920.

Ayerst, David, *Biography of a Newspaper*, London, 1971.

Bacon, R., *Lord Fisher*, London, 1929.

Baden-Powell, R., *My Adventures as a Spy*, London, 1915.

Balfour, M., *The Kaiser and his Times*, London, 1964.

Bassett, A. T., *Life of John Edward Ellis*, London, 1914.

Beckett, I. and Gooch, J. (eds), *Politicians and Defence*, Manchester, 1981.

Bell, E. H. C. Moberly, *Life and Letters of C. F. Moberly Bell*, London, 1927.

Belloc, H., *The Free Press*, London, 1918.

Belloc, H., *The House of Commons and Monarchy*, London, 1920.

Belloc and Chesterton, C., *The Party System*, London, 1910.

Bennett, G., *Charlie B*, London, 1968.

Beresford, C., *Memoirs*, London, 1914.

Beresford, C., *The Betrayal*, London, 1912.

Berghahn, V. R., *Germany and the Approach of War in 1914*, London, 1973.

von Bernstorff, *Memoirs*, London, 1936.
Birkenhead, *Rudyard Kipling*, New York, 1978.
Blake, R., *The Unknown Prime Minister*, London, 1955.
Blatchford, R., *My Eighty Years*, London, 1931.
Blewett, N., *The Press, the Parties and the People: The General Elections of 1910*, London, 1972.
Blumenfeld, R. D., *R.D.B.'s Diary*, London, 1930.
Blumenfeld, R. D., *All in a Lifetime*, London, 1931.
Blumenfeld, R. D., *The Press in my Time*, London, 1933.
Blunt, W. S., *My Diaries*, single volume edition, London, 1931.
Brailsford, H. N., *The War of Steel and Gold*, London, 1914.
Brendon, P., *Eminent Edwardians*, London, 1979.
Brett, M. V. (ed.), *Journals and Letters of Viscount Esher*, London, 1934–8.
Brex, T., *Scaremongerings from the 'Daily Mail', 1896–1914*, London, 1914.
Browne, E. C., *National Service*, Glasgow, 1904.
Bruce, H. J., *Silken Dalliance*, London, 1947.
von Bülow, *Memoirs*, London, 1931–2.
Bundock, C. J., *The National Union of Journalists*, Oxford, 1957.
de Bunsen, V., *Charles Roden Buxton*, London, 1948.
Burnham *Peterborough Court*, London, 1958.
Buxton, C. R., *Turkey in Revolution*, London, 1909.
Callwell, C., *Sir Henry Wilson: His Life and Diaries*, London, 1927.
Camplin, J., *The Rise of the Plutocrats*, London, 1978.
Camrose, *British Newspapers and their Controllers*, London, 1947.
Carroll, E. M., *French Public Opinion and Foreign Affairs*, New York, 1931.
Carroll, E. M., *Germany and the Great Powers, 1886–1914*, New York, 1938.
Ceadel, M., *Pacifism in Britain, 1914–1945*, Oxford, 1980.
Cecil, Lady Gwendoline, *Life of Salisbury*, London, 1921–32.
Chamberlain, A., *Politics from Inside*, London, 1936.
Chamberlain, A., *Down the Years*, London, 1935.
Chatfield, Lord, *The Navy and Defence*, London, 1942.
Chirol, V., *Fifty Years in a Changing World*, London, 1927.
Churchill, R. P., *The Anglo-Russian Convention*, New York, 1939.
Churchill, R. S., *W. S. Churchill – Young Statesman*, London, 1967.
Churchill, R. S., *Companion Volume* III, 3 Parts, London, 1969.
Churchill W. S., *The World Crisis* (abridged and revised edn.), London 1932.
Clark, A. (ed.), *Viscount Lee of Fareham: A Good Innings*, London, 1974.
Clarke, G. S. and Thursfield, J., *The Navy and the Nation*, London, 1897.
Clarke, I. F., *Voices Prophesying War*, London, 1966.
Clarke, T., *Northcliffe in History*, London, 1950.
Cline, C. A., *E. D. Morel*, Belfast, 1980.
Conwell-Evans, T. P., *Foreign Policy from a Back-Bench, 1904–1918*, Oxford, 1932.
Cook, E. T., *Delane of The Times*, London, 1915.
Courtney, Mrs, *The Making of an Editor: W. L. Courtney, 1850–1928*, London, 1930.
Cudlipp, H., *Publish and be damned!*, London, 1953.
Dark, S., *The Life of Sir Arthur Pearson*, London, n.d.
David, E. (ed.), *Inside Asquith's Cabinet: Diaries of Charles Hobhouse*, London, 1977.
Drake, B. and Cole, M. (eds), *Our Partnership*, London, 1948.
Dugdale, B., *Arthur James Balfour*, London, 1936.
Dunlop, J. K., *The Development of the British Army, 1899–1914*, London, 1938.
Elton, *Life of Ramsay MacDonald*, London, 1939.

Escott, T. H. S., *Masters of English Journalism*, London, 1911.

Farrer, J. A., *England under Edward VII*, London, 1913.

Farrer, J. A., *Invasion and Conscription*, London, 1909.

Fisher, *Memories and Records*, New York, 1920.

Fitzroy, Almeric, *Memoirs*, London, 1927.

Fraser, Peter, *Lord Esher, a Political Biography*, London, 1973.

Fry, A., *A Memoir of Sir Edward Fry*, Oxford, 1921.

Fyfe, Hamilton, *The Making of an Optimist*, London, 1921.

Fyfe, Hamilton, *Northcliffe: An Intimate Biography*, London, 1930.

Fyfe, Hamilton, *Sixty Years of Fleet Street*, London, 1949.

Gardiner, A. G., *The War Lords*, London, 1915.

Gardiner, A. G., *Life of George Cadbury*, London, 1923.

Garvin, J. L., *Life of Joseph Chamberlain*, London, 1932–4.

Garvin, K., *J. L. Garvin: A Memoir*, London, 1948.

George, David Lloyd, *War Memoirs*, London, 1934.

Gibbs, P., *Adventures in Journalism*, London, 1923.

Gibbs, P., *Crowded Company*, London, 1946.

Gibbs, P., *The Pageant of the Years*, London, 1946.

Gollin, A. M., *The Observer and J. L. Garvin*, London, 1960.

Gollin, A. M., *Balfour's Burden: Arthur Balfour and Imperial Preference*, London, 1965.

Gooch, G. P., *Life of Lord Courtney*, London, 1920.

Gooch, G. P., *Before the War*, reprint edition, New York, 1967.

Gooch, J., *The Prospect of War*, London, 1981.

Graham, G. S., *The Politics of Naval Supremacy*, Cambridge, 1965.

Grenville, J. A. S., *Lord Salisbury and Foreign Policy*, London, 1969.

Grey, Edward, *Twenty Five Years*, London, 1925.

Grey, Edward, *Fallodon Papers*, London, 1926.

Grigg, J. P., *Lloyd George, The People's Champion: 1902–1911*, London, 1978.

Gwynn, S. (ed.), *The Letters and Friendships of Sir Cecil Spring Rice*, London, 1929.

Haldane, R. B., *Richard Burdon Haldane: An Autobiography*, London, 1929.

Haldane, R. B., *Before the War*, London, 1920.

Hale, O. J., *Germany and the Diplomatic Revolution*, Philadelphia, 1931.

Hale, O. J., *Publicity and Diplomacy*, New York, 1940.

Halévy, E. *Imperialism and the Rise of Labour, 1895–1905*, paperback edition, London, 1961.

Halévy, E., *The Rule of Democracy, 1905–1914*, paperback edition, London, 1961.

Hamer, W. S., *The British Army*, Oxford, 1970.

Hamilton, I., *Compulsory Service*, London, 1910.

Hammerton, J., *Books and Myself*, London, n.d.

Hammond, J. L., *C. P. Scott*, London, 1934.

Hankey, M., *The Supreme Command, 1914–18*, London, 1961.

Hardinge of Penshurst, *Old Diplomacy*, London, 1947.

Harris, W., *J. A. Spender*, London, 1936.

Hayes, D., *Conscription Conflict*, London, 1949.

Headlam, C. (ed.), *The Milner Papers*, London, 1933.

Herwig, H. H., *Luxury Fleet: The Imperial German Navy, 1888–1918*, London, 1980.

Higginbottom, F. J., *The Vivid Life*, London, 1934.

Hindle, W., *The Morning Post, 1772–1937*, London, 1937.

Hinsley, F. H. (ed.), *British Foreign Policy under Sir Edward Grey*, Cambridge, 1977.

Hirst, Francis, *Commerce and Property in Naval Warfare*, London, 1906.

Hirst, Francis, *The Six Panics*, London, 1913.

Howard, C. H. D., *Splendid Isolation*, London, 1967.
Howard, C. H. D. (ed.), *The Diary of Edward Goschen, 1900–1914*, London, 1980.
Howard, Michael, *Studies in War and Peace*, London, 1971.
Hughes, R., *First Sea Lord*, London, 1969.
Hurd, Archibald, *Who Goes There?*, London, 1941.
Hynes, Samuel, *The Edwardian Turn of Mind*, Princeton, 1968.
Ingram, K., *Fifty Years of the National Peace Council*, London, 1958.
James, D., *Lord Roberts*, London, 1954.
James, L., *With the Conquered Turk*, London, 1913.
James, R. R., *Rosebery*, London, 1964.
James, R. R., *The British Revolution*, paperback edition, London, 1978.
Johnson, F. A., *Defence by Committee*, Oxford, 1960.
Jones, Kennedy, *Fleet Street and Downing Street*, London, 1920.
Jones, Tom, *Lloyd George*, London, 1951.
Jordan, G. (ed.), *Naval Warfare in the Twentieth Century*, London, 1977.
Kennedy, P., *The Rise and Fall of British Naval Mastery*, London, 1976.
Kennedy, P., *The Rise of the Anglo-German Antagonism, 1860–1914*, London, 1980.
Kennedy, P. (ed.), *The War Plans of the Great Powers, 1880–1914*, London, 1979.
Kennedy, P. and Nicholls, A. (eds), *Nationalist and Racialist Movements in Britain and Germany before 1914*, London, 1981.
Kerr, Admiral, *Prince Louis of Battenberg*, London, 1934.
King, C. T., *The Asquith Parliament*, London, 1910.
Kitchin, F. H. *Moberly Bell and his Times*, London, 1925.
Koch, H. W. (ed.), *The Origins of the First World War: Great Power Rivalry and German War Aims*, London, 1972.
Koss, S. E., *Lord Haldane: Scapegoat for Liberalism*, New York, 1969.
Koss, S. E., *Sir John Brunner, Radical Plutocrat*, Cambridge, 1970.
Koss, S. E., *Fleet Street Radical: A. G. Gardiner and the 'Daily News'*, London, 1973.
Koss, S. E., *Asquith*, London, 1976.
Koss, S. E. , *The Rise and Fall of the Political Press in Britain: The Nineteenth Century*, London, 1981.
Labour Research Department *The Press*, London, 1922.
Lee, A. J., *The Origins of the Popular Press, 1855–1914*, London, 1976.
Lee, Sidney, *King Edward VII*, London, 1927.
Le Queux, W., *Things I Know*, London, 1923.
Lindley, F., *Lord Lovat, 1871–1933*, London, 1935.
Lucas, R., *Lord Glenesk and the 'Morning Post'*, London, 1910.
Lucy, Henry, *The Diary of a Journalist*, London, 1920.
Ludwig, Emil, *July 1914*, London, 1929.
Lutz, Hermann (trans. E. W. Dickes), *Lord Grey and the World War*, London, 1928.
Luvaas, Jay, *The Education of an Army*, London, 1965.
Mackay, R., *Fisher of Kilverstone*, Oxford, 1973.
Magnus, P., *King Edward the Seventh*, London, 1964.
Mansfield, F. J., *Gentlemen, the Press!* London, 1943.
Marder, A. J. *British Naval Policy*, London, 1941.
Marder, A. J., *Portrait of an Admiral*, London, 1952.
Marder, A. J., *The Road to War, 1904–1914*, Oxford, 1961.
Marder, A. J. (ed.), *Fear God and Dread Nought*, London, 1952–9.
Masterman, Lucy, *C. F. G. Masterman*, London, 1939.
Matthew, H. C. G., *The Liberal Imperialists*, Oxford, 1973.
Maurice, F., *Haldane, 1856–1915*, London, 1937.

Maxse, L. J., *Germany on the Brain*, London, 1915.
Mckail, J. W. and Wyndham, G. (eds), *Life and Letters of George Wyndham*, London, 1926.
McKenzie, F. A., *The Mystery of the 'Daily Mail', 1896–1921*, London, 1921.
Midleton, *Records and Reactions, 1856–1939*, London, 1939.
Moberley Bell, E. H. C., *Life and Letters of C. F. Moberly Bell*, London, 1927.
Monger, G. W., *The End of Isolation*, London, 1963.
Morris, A. J. A., *Radicalism Against War, 1906–1914*, London, 1972.
Morris, A. J. A., *C. P. Trevelyan: Portrait of a Radical*, Belfast, 1977.
Morris, A. J. A. (ed.), *Edwardian Radicalism, 1900–1914*, London, 1974.
Murray, B. K., *The People's Budget 1909–10*, Oxford, 1980.
Naylor, L. E., *The Irrepressible Victorian*, London, 1965.
Nevinson, H. W., *Fire of Life*, London, 1935.
Newton, *Lord Lansdowne*, London, 1929.
Newton, *Retrospection*, London, 1941.
Nicolai, W., *The German Secret Service*, London, 1924.
Nicolson, H., *Lord Carnock*, London, 1930.
Noel-Baker, P., *The Private Manufacture of Armaments*, London, 1936.
O'Brien, T. H., *Milner*, London, 1979.
Oliver, F. S., *Ordeal by Battle*, London, 1915.
D'Ombrain, N., *War Machinery and High Policy*, Oxford, 1973.
Ostrogorski, M., *Democracy and the Organisation of Political Parties*, London, 1902.
Owen, F., *Tempestuous Journey*, London, 1954.
Padfield, P., *The Great Naval Race*, London, 1974.
Pemberton, Max, *Northcliffe: A Memoir*, London, n.d.
Playne, Caroline, *The Pre-War Mind in Britain*, London, 1928.
Pocock, R., *Chorus to Adventurers*, London, 1931.
Pocock, R. (ed.), *Frontiersman's Pocket Book*, London, 1909.
Ponsonby, A., *Democracy and Diplomacy*, London, 1915.
Ponsonby, A., *Falsehood in War-Time*, London, 1928.
Pope, W. M., *Twenty Shillings in the Pound*, London, 1948.
Porter, B., *Critics of Empire*, New York, 1968.
Pound, R. and Harmsworth, G., *Northcliffe*, London, 1959.
Price, R., *An Imperial War and the British Working Class*, London, 1972.
Pudeston, W. D., *Mahan*, London, 1939.
Ramsden, J., *The Age of Balfour and Baldwin 1902–1940*, London, 1978.
Rathcreedan, *Memories of a Long Life*, London, 1931.
Repington, C. A., *Imperial Strategy*, London, 1906.
Repington, C. A., *Essays and Criticisms*, London, 1911.
Repington, C. A., *Vestigia*, London, 1919.
Repington, C. A., *The First World War, 1914–18*, London, 1920.
Repington, Mary, *Thanks for the Memory*, London, 1938.
Rich, N., *Friedrich von Holstein*, Cambridge, 1965.
Rich, N. and Fisher, M. H. (eds), *The Holstein Papers*, Cambridge, 1957.
Riddell, *More Pages from my Diary, 1908–14*, London, 1934.
Robbins, K. G., *Sir Edward Grey*, London, 1971.
Robbins, K. G., *The Abolition of War*, Cardiff, 1976.
Roberts, Lord, *et al.*, *Fallacies and Facts*, London, 1911.
Ronaldshay, *The Life of Lord Curzon*, London, 1928.
Roskill, Stephen, *Man of Secrets*, London, 1970.
Roskill, Stephen, *Earl Beatty*, London, 1980.

Ryan, A. P., *Lord Northcliffe*, London, 1953.
Saunders, G., *The Last of the Huns*, London, 1915.
Scally, R. J., *The Origins of the Lloyd George Coalition*, Princeton, 1975.
Shee, G. F., *The Briton's First Duty*, London, 1901.
Schoenbaum, D., *Zabern 1913*, London, 1982.
Schurman, D. M., *The Education of a Navy*, London, 1965.
Scott, J. W. Robertson, *Life and Death of a Newspaper*, London, 1952.
Searle, G. R., *The Quest for National Efficiency*, Oxford, 1971.
Seely, J. E. B., *Adventure*, London, 1930.
Semmel, B., *Imperialism and Social Reform*, London, 1960.
Shanks, E., *Rudyard Kipling*, New York, 1970.
Sladen, N. S. B., *The Real LeQueux*, London, 1938.
Smith, Janet Adam, *John Buchan: A Biography*, London, 1965.
Soames, Jane, *The English Press*, London, 1936.
Spender, J. A., *Life, Journalism and Politics*, London, 1927.
Spender, J. A., *The Public Life*, London, 1925.
Spender, J. A., *Men and Things*, London, 1937.
Spinner, T. J., Jnr, *George Joachim Goschen*, Cambridge, 1973.
Stansky, P., *Ambitions and Strategies*, Oxford, 1964.
Steed, H. W., *Through Thirty Years*, London, 1924.
Steed, H. W., *The Press*, London, 1938.
Steinberg, J., *Yesterday's Deterrent*, London, 1965.
Steiner, Zara, *The Foreign Office and Foreign Policy, 1898–1914*, Cambridge, 1969.
Steiner, Zara, *Britain and the Origins of the First World War*, London, 1977.
Steinhauer, G. and Felstead, B. T., *The Kaiser's Master Spy*, London, 1930.
Strachey, Amy, *St. Loe Strachey: His Life and his Paper*, London, 1930.
Strachey, J. St Loe, *The Adventure of Living*, London, 1922.
Swartz, M., *The Union of Democratic Control*, Oxford, 1971.
Swinnerton, F. (ed.), *The Journals of Arnold Bennett*, London, 1954.
Sydenham of Combe, *My Working Life*, London, 1927.
Symons, Julian, *Horatio Bottomley*, London, 1955.
Taylor, A. J. P., *The Struggle for Mastery in Europe, 1848–1918*, Oxford, 1954.
Taylor, A. J. P., *Beaverbrook*, London, 1972.
Taylor, C. C., *The Life of Admiral Mahan*, London, 1920.
Taylor, H. A., *Robert Donald*, London, 1935.
Thomas, W. B., *The Story of the 'Spectator', 1828–1928*, London, 1928.
Trevelyan, G. M., *Grey of Fallodon*, London, 1936.
Tuchman, B. W., *The Proud Tower*, London, 1966.
Tyler, J. E., *The British Army and the Continent, 1904–14*, London, 1938.
Ullswater, *A Speaker's Commentaries*, London, 1925.
Wagner, H., *With the Victorious Bulgarians*, London, 1913.
Wallace, L. P. and Askew, W. C. (eds), *Power, Public Opinion and Diplomacy*, North Carolina, 1959.
Wemyss, Lady, *The Life and Letters of Lord Wester Wemyss*, London, 1935.
Whyte, F., *Life of W. T. Stead*, London, 1925.
Wile, F. V., *Our German Cousins*, London, 1910.
Wilkinson, Spenser, *Thirty Five Years*, London, 1933.
Williamson, S. R., Jnr, *The Politics of Grand Strategy*, Cambridge, Mass., 1969.
Willoughby de Broke, *The Passing Years*, London, 1924.
Wilson, J., *CB: A Life of Sir Henry Campbell-Bannerman*, London, 1973.
Wilson, T. (ed.), *The Political Diaries of C. P. Scott, 1911–1928*, London, 1970.

Winter, J. M., *Socialism and the Challenge of War*, London, 1974.
Winterton, *Pre-War*, London, 1932.
Wrench, E., *Uphill*, London, 1934.
Wrench, E., *Struggle, 1914–20*, London, 1935.
Wrench, E., *Geoffrey Dawson and Our Times*, London, 1955.
Young, K., *Arthur James Balfour*, London, 1963.
Zebel, S. H., *Balfour: A Political Biography*, Cambridge, 1973.

B. Collected documents

Gooch, G. P. and Temperley, H., *British Documents on the Origins of the War, 1898–1914*, London, 1926–38.
Lepsius, J., Mendelssohn-Bartholdy, A. and Thimme, F., *Die Grosse Politik der Europäischen Kabinette, 1871–1914*, Berlin, 1922–7.
Dugdale, E. T. S., *German Diplomatic Documents, 1871–1914*, reprint edition, London, 1969.
Documents Diplomatiques Français, 1871–1914, Paris, 1930–53.
Hansard, Parliamentary Debates, fourth and fifth series, 1896–1914.

C. Articles, essays and theses

Allison, M. J., 'The national service issue, 1899–1914', London PhD, 1975.
Andrew, C. M., 'The mobilization of British Intelligence for the two world wars', in N. F. Driesziger (ed.), *Mobilization for Total War*, Ontario, 1981.
Beckett, I. W. F., 'The English Rifle Volunteer Movement, 1859–1908', London PhD, 1975.
French, D., 'Spy Fever in Britain, 1900–15', in *Historical Journal*, vol. XXI, 1978.
Green, David, 'The Stratford by-election, May 1909: National defence and party politics', in *Moirae*, vol. V, 1980, pp. 92–110.
Hibbert, L., 'The role of military and naval attachés in the British and German services, 1871–1914', Cambridge PhD, 1954.
Howard, Michael, 'Empire, race and war in pre-1914 Britain', in Lloyd Jones, Pearl and Worden (eds), *History and Imagination*, London, 1981.
Jordan, G. H. S., 'The politics of conscription in Great Britain, 1905–16', University of California, Irvine, PhD, 1974.
Moon, H. R., 'The Invasion of the United Kingdom, 1888–1914', London, PhD, 1970.
Morris, A. J. A., 'Leo Maxse and the German peril', in *Moirae*, vol. IV, 1979, pp. 8–31.
Morris, A. J. A. , 'And is the Kaiser coming for tea?' in *Moirae*, vol. V, 1980, pp. 33–91.
Morris, A. J. A., 'A not so silent service', in *Moirae*, vol. VI, 1981, pp. 42–81.
Morris, A. J. Ll., 'George Saunders: a case study in diplomacy and publicity', in *Moirae*, vol. VI, 1981, pp. 16–41.
Palmer, Alistair, 'The origins of the D Notice Committee', an unpublished essay, 1980.
Pocock, Geoffrey, 'The road for the rest', unpublished biography of Roger Pocock, 1978.
Porter, Dilwyn, 'Joseph Chamberlain and the origin of the tariff reform movement', in *Moirae*, vol. III, 1978, pp. 1–10.
Porter, Dilwyn, 'Pearson and the Tariff Reform League', in *Moirae*, vol. V, 1980, pp. 111–121.
Porter, Dilwyn, '"Fiscalitis": a suitable case for treatment', in *Moirae*, vol. VI, 1981, pp. 104–8.
Pryce, D. G., 'The military spirit and the doctrine of the offensive in Britain, 1901–14', London MA, 1973.

Ramsden, J. A., 'The organisation of the Conservative and Unionist Party in Britain, 1910–30', Oxford DPhil, 1975.

Robbins, K. G., 'Britain in the summer of 1914', in *Moirae*, vol. VI, 1981, pp. 82–94.

Ropp, T., 'Conscription in Great Britain, 1900–14: a failure in civil-military communications?', in *Military Affairs*, vol. 20, 1956, pp. 71–76.

Ryan, W. M., 'Repington: a study in the interaction of personality, the press and power', University of Cincinnati PhD, 1976.

Steinberg, J., 'The Copenhagen complex', in *Journal of Contemporary History*, vol. I, 1966, no. 3, pp. 23–46.

Steinberg, J., 'The Kaiser's navy and German society', in *Past and Present*, July 1964, no. 28, pp. 102–10.

Steiner, Zara, 'Views of War', in *Moirae*, vol. V, 1980, pp. 14–32.

Stapleton, Laetitia, 'Lt. Col. Charles á Court Repington CMG', in *Army Quarterly*, vol. 105, no. 2.

Wank, S., 'Varieties of political despair', in S. J. Winters and J. Held (eds), *Intellectual and Social Developments in the Habsburg Empire from Maria Teresa to World War I*, New York, 1975.

Watt, D. C., 'The British reaction to the assassination at Sarajevo', in *European Studies Review*, vol. I, 1971, no. 3, pp. 233–47.

Weinroth, H., 'The British Radicals and the balance of power, 1902–14', in *Historical Journal*, vol. XIII, 1970, pp. 653–82.

Weinroth, H., 'Norman Angell and "The Great Illusion" ', in *Historical Journal*, 1974, vol. XVII, no. 3, pp. 551–74.

Yule, Peter, 'The tariff reform movement and Germany, 1900–1914', in *Moirae*, vol. VII, 1982, pp. 1–17.

D. Miscellaneous

Annual Register, 1896–1914.

Butler, D. and Freeman, J., *British Political Facts*, second edition, London, 1968.

Dictionary of National Biography, Twentieth Century, 1900–50.

Stenton, M. and Lees, S., *Who's Who of British Members of Parliament*, vol. II, Hassocks, Sussex, 1978.

Pelling, H., *Social Geography of British Elections, 1885–1910*, New York, 1967.

Vincent J. and Stenton, M. (eds), *McCalmont's Parliamentary Poll Book, 1832–1918*, Brighton, 1971.

Peace Year Book, 1910–14

Reformers' Year Book

Whitaker's Almanack

Who was Who

Who's Who

Newspapers and journals referred to, cited or quoted in the text are listed separately in the subject index.

Biographical index

Aehrenthal, Alois Lex, Count von. Austro-Hungarian Foreign Minister (1906–11), 251, 258, 262–3

Aitken, Max. Canadian millionaire, political 'fixer', 270, 274

Amery, Leopold Charles Maurice Stennett. Journalist, *The Times* editorial staff, military authority, from 1911 Unionist M.P., 35, 62, 242, 244, 271, 308, 324, 339, 449

Andrássy, Julius, Count. Hungarian Minister of the Interior, 261

Angell, Norman (Ralph Lane). Manager of *Continental Daily Mail*, author of *The Great Illusion*, 266, 363

Ardagh, Sir John Charles. Major General, DMO & I (1896–1901), 90, 92

Armstrong, Sir George Elliot. Former Lieutenant RN, bitter opponent of Fisher, editor of *Globe*, part proprietor of *People*, 192–3

Appleyard, R. Journalist, supporter of Fisher, 181

Arnold-Forster, Hugh Oakeley. Unionist M.P., Secretary of Admiralty (1900–3), Secretary of State for War (1903–5), 91, 93–4, 107, 109–13, 117, 127, 129, 137, 165, 169, 218, 224–7, 230, 232, 426

Asquith, Herbert Henry. Liberal Imperialist M.P., Chancellor of the Exchequer (1905–8), from 1908, Prime Minister, 38, 70, 138, 142–4, 146, 163, 166, 171–2, 175–9, 183, 191–2, 194, 197, 221, 226, 255–7, 263, 278, 289–92, 302–3, 310–11, 313–14, 322, 326, 332–3, 337–8, 349, 351, 353, 358–9, 361, 365, 371, 380, 383, 386, 416, 459

Asquith, Emma Alice Margaret 'Margot' (née Tennant). Loquacious wife of Liberal Prime Minister, 38, 70, 191, 211, 417

Aston, George Grey. Brigadier General, friend of Repington, 137

Astor, Waldorf. From 1910 Unionist M.P. for Plymouth, conscriptionist, 428

Astor, William Waldorf. Owner of *Pall Mall Gazette*, and after 1910, the *Observer*, 275, 324, 365

Austin, Alfred. Leader writer for *Standard*, Imperialist, friend of Salisbury, arguably worst ever poet laureate, 16, 22, 37, 373, 388

Bacon, Reginald Hugh Spencer. Rear Admiral, close friend and later biographer of Fisher, 128, 193

Baden-Powell, Sir Robert Stephenson Smyth. Lieutenant General, 'hero' of Mafeking, credulous spy-hunter, founder of Boy Scout movement, 156–7, 237

Baker, Sir John. Liberal M.P. for Portsmouth, succeeded on death in 1909 by Lord Charles Beresford, 211

Baldwin, Stanley. From 1908, Unionist M.P., cousin of Rudyard Kipling, 243

Balfour, Arthur James. Unionist politician, nephew of Salisbury, Prime Minister (1902–5), Tory leader until 1911, founder of the Committee of Imperial Defence (CID), considered by some a defence 'expert', 30–1, 53, 55, 57, 62–6, 68–9, 103–6, 109, 112, 117–21, 127, 129, 132–3, 136–7, 140, 144, 146–7, 149–50, 163, 171, 178, 185–7, 191–2, 197, 204–7, 209–12, 215–16, 218, 221–2, 226, 229, 235–9, 245–8, 256, 267–8, 274, 282, 294, 303, 309, 313, 318, 332, 350, 359, 362, 365, 370, 373, 377, 381, 394, 397, 429, 444, 460

Ballard, George Alexander. Captain RN, Director of Admiralty Operations, Chairman of War Plans Committee (1906–7), 278

Ballin, Albert. German businessman, shipowner, friend of Kaiser William, 66, 310, 361, 376, 397, 445

Barclay, Sir Thomas. Liberal M.P., journalist, author, supported improved Anglo-German relations, founder of International Brotherhood Alliance (FIG), 77

Subject index